MASTER THE™

HiSET® EXAM

PETERSON'S®

About Peterson's®

Peterson's®, a Nelnet company, has been your trusted educational publisher for over 50 years. It's a milestone we're quite proud of, as we continue to offer the most accurate, dependable, high-quality educational content in the field, providing you with everything you need to succeed. No matter where you are on your academic or professional path, you can rely on Peterson's for its books, online information, expert test-prep tools, the most up-to-date education exploration data, and the highest quality career success resources—everything you need to achieve your education goals. For our complete line of products, visit **www.petersons.com**.

For more information, contact Peterson's, 3 Columbia Circle, Albany, NY 12203-5158; 800-338-3282 Ext. 54229; or visit us online at **www.petersons.com**.

ISBN: 978-0-7689-4187-6

Printed in the United States of America

10 9 8 7 6 5 4 3 2 1   20 19 18

Second Edition

Petersonspublishing.com/publishingupdates

Check out our website at www.petersonspublishing.com/publishingupdates to see if there is any new information regarding the test and any revisions or corrections to the content of this book. We've made sure the information in this book is accurate and up-to-date; however, the test format or content may have changed since the time of publication.

Contents

Contents

Contents

Before You Begin

You've decided to get your high school diploma by preparing to take the HiSET® exam. This is a great step! By now, you know that a high school diploma is a very important document to possess. Once you have your high school credential, you will be able to take advantage of training and educational opportunities beyond the high school level and increase your earning potential.

You want to do your best on the HiSET® exam, and that's why you purchased this book. Used correctly, this guide will show you what to expect while giving you the most effective practice with subjects you can expect to see on the actual exam. Peterson's *Master the™ HiSET® Exam* provides you with the necessary tools to make the most of the study time you have, including:

- **Part I** is an introduction to the HiSET® exam. You'll find out about the structure of the entire exam, what each subtest of the exam covers, how you sign up and where you can take the exam, and what you need to do to get ready for test day.

- **Parts II–VI** review the subject matter for each subtest of the HiSET® exam (Language Arts—Reading, Language Arts—Writing, Mathematics, Science, and Social Studies) and offer you powerful strategies for attacking every question type you'll encounter in the actual exam.

- **Part VII** consists of two full-length Practice Tests, with answer explanations for each question. Each test contains a similar number and mix of question types you'll encounter on the actual exam. To accurately measure your performance on these Practice Tests, be sure to adhere strictly to the stated time limits for each section.

THE REVIEW SECTIONS

The Language Arts sections provide an opportunity to improve your language skills, which are necessary for good performance in reading, writing, and all other academic areas. The reading selections consist of a wide range of reading matter, from nonfiction to a scene from a novel to business memos and e-mails. Writing questions will examine usage, organization, and mechanics skills in a variety of situations.

The Mathematics section provides user-friendly explanations of math processes in recognition of the particular difficulty that many students have in this area. The review, examples, and answer explanations will help you better comprehend the difficult concepts in the tested areas of numbers and number operations; geometry; data analysis, probability, and statistics; and algebraic concepts.

The Science section reviews those subjects that will appear on the actual HiSET® Science subtest: life science, physical science, and earth science. The review will help you with your ability to recall and understand information, draw inferences and conclusions, evaluate data, and apply concepts and ideas to other situations.

The Social Studies review covers history, civics and government, economics, and geography. The review will help you sharpen your comprehension, analysis, evaluation, and application skills for the actual exam.

THE PRACTICE TESTS

When you have completed your reviews, take the Practice Tests under simulated test conditions to further sharpen your skills. Find a quiet place where you won't be distracted or interrupted, set a timer for the required time, and work through each test as though it were test day.

SPECIAL STUDY FEATURES

Overview

Each chapter begins with a bulleted overview listing the topics that will be covered in the chapter. You know immediately where to look for a topic that you need to work on.

Bonus Information

As you work your way through the book, check the margins to find bonus information and advice. You'll find the following kinds of information:

Note

Notes highlight need-to-know information about the HiSET® exam, whether it's details about applying and scoring or the structure of a question type.

Tip

Tips provide valuable strategies and insider information to help you score your best on your exam.

Alert!

Alerts do just what they say—alert you to common pitfalls and misconceptions you might face or hear regarding these exams.

Summing It Up

Each review chapter ends with a point-by-point summary that captures the most important items. The summaries are a convenient way to review the content of the chapters.

YOU'RE WELL ON YOUR WAY TO SUCCESS

Remember that knowledge is power. By using Peterson's *Master the™ HiSET® Exam*, you will prepare with the most comprehensive test-preparation guide available. We look forward to helping you receive your high school equivalence credential. Good luck!

GIVE US YOUR FEEDBACK

Peterson's publishes a full line of resources to help guide you. Peterson's publications can be found at high school guidance offices, college libraries and career centers, your local bookstore or library, and online at www.petersonsbooks.com.

We welcome any comments or suggestions you may have about this publication.

Peterson's, a Nelnet Company
3 Columbia Circle
Suite 205
Albany, NY 12203-5158
E-mail: custsvc@petersons.com

PART I

INTRODUCTION

All About the HiSET® Exam

chapter 1

OVERVIEW

- **Get Ready for HiSET® Exam Success!**
- **The HiSET® Exam: Test Sections**
- **The HISET® Exam: Key Information**
- **Are You Ready to Move Forward?**

GET READY FOR HISET® EXAM SUCCESS!

Are you looking to earn your high school equivalency credential, demonstrate your academic and job readiness, and create new opportunities for education and career advancement? If so, then taking the HiSET® exam just might be the perfect decision. If you're wondering if the HiSET® exam is the right move for you, then keep reading!

If you're just getting started on your journey to HiSET® exam success, earning your high school equivalency credential might seem like a real challenge. But you shouldn't worry—you've already made a great first step by getting this book!

Master the™ HiSET® Exam provides all the information you'll need along your journey—a complete overview of the HiSET® exam, including what you'll need to know for test day, how to register, what the exam will cost, and what to expect on each of the five subtests; expert test advice and proven strategies for achieving great scores; and plenty of practice and review to get you ready for success!

We suggest that you work your way slowly and carefully through this entire book, spending extra time on your weakest areas. It's our hope that by the time you reach the end, you'll be ready for the next big step in your journey toward success—conquering the official HiSET® exam. We wish you the very best of luck with your preparation and on test day!

THE HISET® EXAM: TEST SECTIONS

The HiSET® exam is designed to test your high school level knowledge in the following five core subject area subtests:

- Language Arts—Reading
- Language Arts—Writing
- Mathematics

- Science
- Social Studies

Getting a passing score on all five HiSET® exam subtests indicates that your academic skills are at an appropriate high school level, making you eligible to receive your high school equivalency credential—and opening fantastic new pathways to a more rewarding career, a college education, and a life full of amazing new options. Let's take a closer look at each test section, so you'll know exactly what to expect.

Language Arts—Reading

The HiSET® Language Arts—Reading subtest is designed to measure your ability to understand and analyze a wide array of informational and literary written passages and reading materials.

NOTE

For the most up-to-date information regarding the HiSET® exam, visit the official ETS website: http://hiset.ets.org/.

HiSET® Language Arts—Reading Subtest Snapshot

- **Number of questions:** 40 multiple-choice questions
- **Test time:** 65 minutes
- **Key test areas:** evaluation and analysis of literary and informational texts

---

The multiple-choice questions you'll see on the subtest can include analysis of passages spanning a variety of genres and formats, including essays, memoirs, biographies, poetry, and editorials (ranging from 400 to 600 words). Key areas tested on the HiSET® Language Arts—Reading subtest include:

- **Comprehension:** understanding key words and phrases and determining meaning, purpose, and impact

- **Analysis:** determining themes, topics, and main ideas; identifying purpose and viewpoint; analyzing text interpretations; and recognizing style, mood, facts vs. opinions, observations, conclusions, assumptions, and tone

- **Synthesis and Generalization:** making predictions, conclusions, and generalizations; analyzing source information; and comparing and contrasting texts

- **Inference and Interpretation:** interpreting language in texts, applying information, drawing conclusions and meanings, making key inferences, and inferring motives

Language Arts—Writing

The HiSET® Language Arts—Writing subtest is designed to measure your ability to create and recognize appropriate and effective written material. There are two parts to this subtest: Part 1 is a multiple-choice exam that tests your ability to recognize and fix errors in writing, and Part 2 tests your ability to create a piece of writing based on a given prompt.

HiSET® Language Arts—Writing Subtest Snapshot

- **Number of questions**
  - **Part 1:** 50 multiple-choice questions
  - **Part 2:** 1 essay question

- **Test time**
  - **Parts 1 and 2:** 120 minutes; you can move between Parts 1 and 2 during the exam.

- **Key test areas**
  - **Part 1:** language facility, organization of ideas, and writing conventions
  - **Part 2:** organization of ideas, development of ideas, writing conventions, and language facility

---

On Part 1 of the subtest, you'll be given a series of written passage drafts, with each passage presented in two versions. One version will be a straightforward presentation of the text; the second version will be in an expanded format, with various pieces of text underlined, corresponding to an associated set of multiple-choice questions. The multiple-choice questions you'll see on the exam can include recognizing and fixing issues involving clarity, organization, diction, usage, structure, and language mechanics. The written passages can come in a variety of formats, including reports, news articles, essays, letters, and excerpts.

On Part 2 of the subtest, you'll be given two passages that express differing opinions on an issue of importance. You will be asked to write an essay in which you explain your own opinion on the same issue. Your essay will be scored based on your ability to develop carefully constructed, compelling ideas that demonstrate your proficiency in grammar, language facility, and standard writing conventions.

Key areas tested on Part 1 of the HiSET® Language Arts—Writing subtest include:

- **Writing Conventions:** demonstrate understanding of appropriate grammar, spelling, punctuation, capitalization, and idiomatic usage and correct verb, modifier, and pronoun forms

- **Language Facility:** demonstrate understanding of appropriate verb tense consistency, effective sentence structuring and combining, coordination and subordination, modifier placement, and parallelism

- **Organization of Ideas:** demonstrate understanding of appropriate content relevance, sentence and paragraph structure and placement, and word choice

Key areas tested on Part 2 of the HiSET® Language Arts—Writing subtest include:

- **Writing Conventions:** demonstrate knowledge of appropriate grammar, mechanics, and usage

- **Language Facility:** demonstrate the ability to use appropriate sentence structure, tone, voice, expression, and word choice

- **Development of Ideas:** demonstrate the ability to present and explain central and supporting ideas

- **Organization of Ideas:** demonstrate the ability to present key parts of a piece of writing in a logical and organized manner, including introduction, transitions, and conclusion

Mathematics

The HiSET® Mathematics subtest is designed to measure your ability to answer quantitative questions using your reasoning and mathematical skills. The multiple choice questions you'll see on test day will include a mix of practical, real-world problem solving and abstract math concepts. Good news—you have the option to use a calculator on test day if you'd like! You can not bring your own calculator on test day, but there will be calculators available at the testing center if you request one. Please be sure to refer to the policies for calculator usage in the state that you'll be using them. The subtest includes a formula sheet that will help you calculate the area, volume, and perimeter or circumference. It also includes a conversion chart for common measurements, like foot to inches, gallon to quarts, and pound to ounces. However, there are some formulas that will not be on the formula sheet provided. These include the quadratic formula, distance formula, and the Pythagorean theorem.

HiSET® Mathematics Subtest Snapshot

- **Number of questions:** 50 multiple-choice questions
- **Test time:** 90 minutes
- **Key test areas:** algebra; data analysis, probability, and statistics; numbers and operations; and measurement and geometry

---

You'll encounter a wide variety of math questions on the exam, including word problems and questions that ask you to review and analyze graphs, charts, tables, pictures, and diagrams. Key areas tested on the HiSET® Mathematics exam include:

- **Algebra:** solving algebraic equations, simplifying algebraic expressions, and understanding variables and algebraic symbols, linear functions and nonlinear functional relations, and inequalities

- **Data Analysis, Probability, and Statistics:** understanding relationships among presented data and events, data collection concepts, counting principles, distribution patterns and analysis, variability, and measures of central tendency

- **Numbers and Operations:** exponents, radicals, ratios, absolute value, vectors, matrices, proportions, percentages, operations properties, real numbers, estimation, computation

- **Geometry and Measurement:** properties of geometric shapes, including volume, area, length, perimeter, angles, and line and triangle theorems

Science

The HiSET® Science subtest is designed to measure your ability to understand and apply scientific principles, knowledge, and inquiry, as well as to analyze scientific information. The multiple-choice questions you'll see on the exam will be based on reported science investigations from journal sources, which can include data presented in charts, tables, and graphs.

HiSET® Science Subtest Snapshot

- **Number of questions:** 50 multiple-choice questions
- **Test time:** 80 minutes
- **Key test areas:** Earth science, life science, and physical science

---

You'll encounter a wide variety of science questions on the exam, which may ask you to identify and evaluate research questions, designs, and procedures and analyze scientific conclusions in chemistry, botany, physics, astronomy, health, and zoology. Key areas tested on the HiSET® Science subtest include:

- **Earth Science:** planetary movements and properties of planetary materials and geologic structures

- **Life Science:** understanding and evaluating biological concepts involving living organisms, including functioning, life cycles, environments, interdependencies, and relationships

- **Physical Science:** analyzing and understanding observable physical properties, including shape, weight, size, temperature, color, and motion, as well as scientific principles involving magnetism, heat, light, and electricity

Social Studies

The HiSET® Social Studies subtest is designed to measure your ability to understand and analyze social studies information, procedures, and methods; draw conclusions; judge source and inference reliability; and recognize opinion vs. fact. The multiple-choice questions you'll see on the exam can include analysis of a variety of primary documents, including tables, charts, maps, graphs, reading passages, timelines, posters, and cartoons.

HiSET® Social Studies Subtest Snapshot

- **Number of questions:** 50 multiple-choice questions
- **Test time:** 70 minutes
- **Key test areas:** geography, civics, government, history, and economics

---

You'll encounter a wide variety of social studies questions on the exam, asking you to evaluate and analyze information in economics, anthropology, sociology, political science, psychology, and geography. Key areas tested on the HiSET® Social Studies subtest include the following:

- **Geography:** analyzing human and physical geography, including related economic, political, and social factors and visual and technological tools

- **Civics/Government:** understanding the roles and contexts of citizenship, including individual rights and responsibilities, authority, and power structures and analyzing existing government structures

- **Economics:** understanding the effects of economic conditions on society and government over time—both within and across economies—and the effects of technology, supply, and demand

- **History:** understanding the interplay of historical events and their political, economic, and cultural impact on the past, present, and future

THE HISET® EXAM: KEY INFORMATION

Here's an overview of common questions regarding the HiSET® exam and what you need to know between now and test day, including how to apply, what you'll need, information to determine if the HiSET® exam is right for you, and more. See, we've got you covered!

Which States Offer the HiSET® Exam?

The following states currently offer the HiSET® exam:

California (Long Beach School for Adults, Los Angeles Unified School District, Chula Vista Adult School)	Illinois	Missouri
	Iowa	Montana
	Louisiana	Nevada
	Maine	New Hampshire
	Massachusetts	New Jersey
Colorado	Michigan	New Mexico
Hawaii	Mississippi	North Carolina

Oklahoma	Tennessee	Wyoming
Pennsylvania	Texas	

The following U.S. Territories currently offer the HiSET® exam:

American Samoa	Marshall Islands	Palau
Guam	Northern Mariana Islands	

Am I Eligible to Take the HiSET® Exam?

If your state currently accepts the HiSET® exam and you are not currently enrolled in high school, and you haven't graduated from high school, you may be eligible. You should check the eligibility requirements in your state by visiting the official HiSET® exam website: http://hiset.ets.org/requirements/.

How Do I Sign Up for the HiSET® Exam?

Once you determine that the HiSET® exam is offered in your state and that you meet the eligibility requirements, it is recommended that you create an online account through the HiSET® exam Information and Registration Portal (https://ereg.ets.org/ereg-web/public/signin/HSE). After creating your account, you can log in, register, and pay for a test; view your appointment confirmation and scores; reschedule or cancel a test if needed; and more (features vary by state). You can also register to take the exam at a test center that's convenient for you by calling ETS customer service. Visit the official HiSET® exam website to learn more about individual state requirements for account setup and registration.

What Options Are Available for Taking the HiSET® Exam?

The HiSET® exam is offered in English or Spanish and can be taken as a paper-based test or on a computer—the choice is yours. You also have the option to take all five subtests in one day or across multiple days, whichever setup is most convenient for you.

Where Can I Take the HiSET® Exam?

There are test centers located throughout each state that offer the HiSET® exam. You can schedule an appointment to take the HiSET® exam at a test center that's convenient for you. Visit the HiSET® exam website to see available test centers in your area.

How Much Does the Test Cost?

Each of the five HiSET® exam subtests costs $10. Payment is required when you schedule the exam, and there may be state-specific fees included as well. Check the official HiSET® exam website to learn more about payment options and policies.

What Should I Bring—and Not Bring—on Test Day?

You should arrive at your test center on test day with plenty of time to spare, along with the following:

- A printed copy of your appointment confirmation (optional but recommended)
- Valid identification that meets your state requirements (for requirements go online to http://hiset.ets.org/requirements)
- Comfortable, layered clothing that can be removed or put on based on the room temperature
- If applicable, a method of payment for your test center administration fee

Visit the official HiSET® exam website for possible additional state requirements.

The following items should *not* be brought to the test center:

- Calculators
- Mechanical pens
- Pencils and erasers
- Headphones
- Watches with alarms or calculators
- Rulers
- Dictionaries
- Paper or digital translation devices
- Cell phones
- Electronic tablets
- Food and drinks
- Books and papers
- Recording, listening, or photographic devices
- Highlighters
- Test aids that have not been approved of in advance. If you require specific accommodations due to a disability or health condition, they must be requested in advance. Visit the official HiSET® exam website for more information.

How Is the HiSET® Exam Scored?

After taking the exam, you'll receive an official HiSET® Comprehensive Score Report, which includes a detailed breakdown of your score(s) on each of the five exam subtests. In order to achieve a passing score, you'll need to meet the following criteria:

- A total scaled score of at least 45 out of 100 on all five subtests on the HiSET® exam
- A minimum score of 8 out of 20 on each subtest
- A minimum score of 2 out of 6 for the essay test

Please note that your state may have specific requirements for earning a passing score. The official ETS HiSET® exam website includes information regarding state-specific requirements.

When Will I Receive My Scores?

After taking the official HiSET® exam, you'll receive your scores for the multiple-choice tests you have taken within three to five business days. You'll receive your scores for the essay test within six to ten business days.

Are Special Accommodations Available for Test-Takers?

There are accommodations available for certain special needs, including assistive technology, time and room accommodations, and more. If you think you might need a specific accommodation, contact ETS before scheduling a test appointment. The process can take six weeks or more, so make sure to factor in the approval time when scheduling your exam.

ARE YOU READY TO MOVE FORWARD?

If you've reviewed the information in this chapter carefully, then congratulations—you now have a solid understanding of what the HiSET® exam is all about and what you can expect on test day. You're already a step ahead of the competition!

You're now ready to move forward in *Master the HiSET® Exam*. The chapters in this book provide an in-depth look at all five subtests on the exam, with thorough practice and careful review for every concept and topic tested. Along the way, you'll also get advice and strategies for getting your best possible scores—so make sure you pay close attention!

We wish you the very best of luck on your journey to HiSET® exam success—but you have more than luck on your side. With *Master the HiSET® Exam,* you're equipped with the practical preparation tools you need to achieve your goals. Along the way, it might get difficult and you might get frustrated, but don't forget—we're right alongside you!

PART II

LANGUAGE ARTS—
READING

Comprehension

OVERVIEW

- Understand and recognize repetition
- Use context to define words and phrases
- Notice how word choice affects mood and tone
- Summing It Up

The HiSET® Language Arts—Reading subtest requires you to read an assortment of passages and answer a series of multiple-choice questions relating to each passage. Both passages and questions are varied, testing your comprehension, inference and interpretation, analysis, and synthesis and generalization skills with both informational and literary passages. These next three chapters explain each question type that will appear on the HiSET® and include a brief sample passage and one or two sample questions for each concept.

The Language Arts—Reading subtest comprehension questions test how well you understand essential information in a reading passage. These question types will ask you to recall details, define words and phrases, and analyze what these words and phrases mean within the context of the passage.

Passages on the HiSET® are considerably longer than the paragraphs in this chapter and begin with an introduction that should help orient you since the passages are often excerpted from larger works. Absorbing the information necessary to answer the questions requires active reading. This means you should not simply read a passage from start to finish before tackling the questions; you should approach the reading material more fully engaged. Skim through it quickly to get an idea of its important details and ideas before reading it more thoroughly. Think about what the passage's main idea might be. How is it organized?

As you read the passage word for word, take notice of key words that might help you evaluate the author's attitude about the topic, draw conclusions about the text, make predictions about what might happen next, analyze its tone or mood, or help you define unfamiliar vocabulary words. These are just a few of the tasks you will have to accomplish when you move on to the questions.

UNDERSTAND AND RECOGNIZE REPETITION

Sometimes, a HiSET® passage will contain restated, or repeated, information. An author might restate facts, important words, or certain phrasing to emphasize their importance or to refresh the reader's memory. Your ability to recognize such restatements and how they affect the author's message is a key indicator of how well you've comprehended a passage. Be aware of when an author uses repetition—this writing device usually means he or she wants you to come away from reading a portion of writing with this repeated bit in mind.

Let's look at a sample HiSET® question that asks you to identify an example of restated information. Read the following excerpt from *The Mysterious Stranger* by Mark Twain. Then answer the question that follows.

> It was in 1590—winter. Austria was far away from the world, and asleep; it was still the Middle Ages in Austria, and promised to remain so forever. Some even set it away back centuries upon centuries and said that by the mental and spiritual clock it was still the Age of Belief in Austria. But they meant it as a compliment,
> 5 not a slur, and it was so taken, and we were all proud of it. I remember it well, although I was only a boy; and I remember, too, the pleasure it gave me.
> Yes, Austria was far from the world, and asleep, and our village was in the middle of that sleep, being in the middle of Austria. It drowsed in peace in the deep privacy of a hilly and woodsy solitude where news from the world hardly
> 10 ever came to disturb its dreams, and was infinitely content. At its front flowed the tranquil river, its surface painted with cloud-forms and the reflections of drifting arks and stone-boats; behind it rose the woody steeps to the base of the lofty precipice; from the top of the precipice frowned a vast castle, its long stretch of towers and bastions mailed in vines; beyond the river, a league to the left,
> 15 was a tumbled expanse of forest-clothed hills cloven by winding gorges where the sun never penetrated; and to the right a precipice overlooked the river, and between it and the hills just spoken of lay a far-reaching plain dotted with little homesteads nested among orchards and shade trees.

1. Which of the following lines restates information from earlier in the passage?
   (A) Some even set it away back centuries upon centuries and said that by the mental and spiritual clock it was still the Age of Belief in Austria.
   (B) I remember it well, although I was only a boy; and I remember, too, the pleasure it gave me.
   (C) Yes, Austria was far from the world, and asleep, and our village was in the middle of that sleep, being in the middle of Austria.
   (D) It drowsed in peace in the deep privacy of a hilly and woodsy solitude where news from the world hardly ever came to disturb its dreams, and was infinitely content.

The correct answer is (C). It repeats the excerpt's second sentence—"Austria was far away from the world, and asleep; it was still the Middle Ages in Austria, and promised to remain so forever"—nearly word for word in order to emphasize the isolated nature of Austria.

USE CONTEXT TO DEFINE WORDS AND PHRASES

When you are faced with a reading passage on the HiSET®, you might not understand every vocabulary word or literary description you see. But that doesn't mean you can't figure out the message the author is trying to express! Understanding *how* unfamiliar words and phrases are used in a passage will help you to comprehend the passage as a whole.

Analyzing the **context** in which such words and phrases are used will help you to define them on the HiSET®. For example, you may be unfamiliar with the word "churlish," but reading it in the middle of a sentence such as, "The churlish man yelled at the waiter," will help you to deduce that "churlish" means "rude," since yelling at a waiter is something a rude person might do.

When you read passages and come across something unfamiliar, pay attention to what is around the word or phrase. What is the mood of the people involved? What are the characters doing in the moment? What is the atmosphere, and what word would you use to describe it? Then compare your descriptions to the answer choices to find one that matches most closely.

Let's look at some sample questions that test this HiSET® concept. Read the following excerpt from *The Island of Dr. Moreau* by H.G. Wells. Then answer the questions that follow.

> THAT night land was sighted after sundown, and the schooner hove to. Montgomery <u>intimated</u> that was his destination. It was too far to see any details; it seemed to me then simply a low-lying patch of dim blue in the uncertain blue-grey sea. An almost vertical streak of smoke went up from it into the sky. The captain
> 5 was not on deck when it was sighted. After he had <u>vented his wrath</u> on me he had staggered below, and I understand he went to sleep on the floor of his own cabin. The mate practically assumed the command. He was the gaunt, taciturn individual we had seen at the wheel. Apparently he was in an evil temper with Montgomery. He took not the slightest notice of either of us. We dined with him
> 10 in a sulky silence, after a few ineffectual efforts on my part to talk. It struck me too that the men regarded my companion and his animals in a singularly unfriendly manner. I found Montgomery very reticent about his purpose with these creatures, and about his destination; and though I was sensible of a growing curiosity as to both, I did not press him.

2. What does "intimated" (line 2) mean?
   (A) Implied
   (B) Asked
   (C) Created
   (D) Wrote

The correct answer is (A). This question can be answered by studying how the word in question is used in the context of the passage. Try substituting each answer choice for "intimated" in the passage. You should find that choice (A) "implied" is the only choice that makes sense in context.

3. What does "vented his wrath" (line 5) mean?
   (A) Showed his joy
   (B) Offered his apologies
   (C) Performed his routine
   (D) Expressed his anger

The correct answer is (D). "Expressed his anger" is the phrase that makes the most sense in place of "vented his wrath," since the characters in the passage all seem to be in very unpleasant moods.

TIP

On tricky vocabulary questions, replace the unknown word with a word of your own, without looking at the answer choices. Then, compare your answer with the four choices to see if one matches up.

NOTICE HOW WORD CHOICE AFFECTS MOOD AND TONE

As a careful reader, you must be aware of the specific words a writer uses to convey a story, informative speech, poem, or any other passage of writing. Writers choose their words very carefully in order to create a certain tone that is as important to a passage's meaning as the information it presents.

For example, the biographer of someone like Dr. Martin Luther King, Jr., might use words such as "inspirational," "strong," or "compassionate" to indicate that he was an extraordinary leader. An author of a spooky story may use words such as "gloomy" or "foreboding" to set the necessary mood. On the HiSET®, you will see questions that ask you to identify how and why the author chooses certain words to create meaning or set the tone of a passage.

Read the following excerpt from *Moby Dick* by Herman Melville. Then answer the sample questions about language and tone that follow.

> <u>Thundering</u> with the butts of three clubbed handspikes on the forecastle deck, Daggoo roused the sleepers with such judgment claps that they seemed to exhale from the scuttle, so instantaneously did they appear with their clothes in their hands.
>
> 5   "What d'ye see?" cried Ahab, flattening his face to the sky.
> "Nothing, nothing sir!" was the sound hailing down in reply.
> "T'gallant sails!- stunsails! alow and aloft, and on both sides!"
> All sail being set, he now cast loose the life-line, reserved for swaying him to the main royal-mast head; and in a few moments they were hoisting him
> 10 thither, when, while but two thirds of the way aloft, and while peering ahead through the horizontal vacancy between the main-top-sail and top-gallant-sail, he raised <u>a gull-like cry</u> in the air. "There she blows!- there she blows! A hump like a snow-hill! It is Moby Dick!"

4. The author's use of the word "Thundering" (line 1) helps establish a tone that is

   (A) comical.

   (B) serene.

   (C) exciting.

   (D) educational.

The correct answer is (C). A "thundering" sound is so loud it makes one's heart race, so the author's use of it in the passage sets an exciting tone. It certainly does not set a tone that is comical or educational, so choices (A) and (D) can be eliminated, and serene, choice (B), is the opposite of exciting.

5. When the author writes that Ahab made "a gull-like cry" (line 12), he indicates that Ahab was
   (A) miserable.
   (B) agitated.
   (C) bored.
   (D) careful.

The correct answer is (B). A "gull-like cry" is high-pitched, which suggests an agitated state. If you do not know the meaning of "agitated," you can still deduce choice (B) is the correct answer by eliminating the other choices, none of which suggest the disposition of someone who is raising a "gull-like cry."

SUMMING IT UP

- Authors will often repeat information within a passage to emphasize its importance. Notice when information is restated as you are reading, and make a note of why the author makes this choice—usually, this information will come up in a question on the HiSET®.

- It is common to come across unfamiliar vocabulary on the HiSET®. Read around the word or phrase you don't recognize to get a sense of what is going on in the paragraph. Restate what you think is the definition in your own words, then look for an answer choice that matches as closely as possible.

- Words are not only in a passage to tell a story or explain a point of view—they also are used to set a specific tone. As you read a passage on the HiSET®, notice how an author uses certain vocabulary, punctuation, and phrases to give it meaning and set a mood.

Inference, Interpretation, and Synthesis

OVERVIEW

- **Learn to read between the lines**
- **Infer the traits, feelings, and motives of characters**
- **Apply information**
- **Interpret nonliteral language**
- **Synthesize information across multiple sources**
- **Summing It Up**

Some Reading questions on the HiSET® require you to draw conclusions to find the correct answers. These answers are not explicit in the passage, so you will need to use your reasoning skills to read deeper into the meaning of the passage to find the answers that make the most sense. These questions test your skills of **inference** and interpretation.

LEARN TO READ BETWEEN THE LINES

You will need to draw on information both presented in the passage and from your own life experiences to answer certain questions on the HiSET®. You might have to make an assumption about a character's personality based only on his or her behavior presented in a small excerpt. You might have to use clues and details the writer provides when describing a place's physical characteristics to determine its weather or its inhabitants. Essentially, you will have to make an educated guess, drawing from only the words on the page, to answer questions beyond the scope of the words themselves. As you read passages on the HiSET®, keep this in mind and not only take note of *what* the author is describing, but also *why* he or she is describing it in a certain way.

Let's take a look at some examples of the types of inference questions you might see on the exam. Read the following excerpt from *Our Mutual Friend* by Charles Dickens and answer the sample questions that follow.

In these times of ours, though concerning the exact year there is no need to be precise, a boat of dirty and disreputable appearance, with two figures in it, floated on the Thames, between Southwark bridge which is of iron, and London Bridge which is of stone, as an autumn evening was closing in.

5 The figures in this boat were those of a strong man with ragged grizzled hair and a sun-browned face, and a dark girl of nineteen or twenty, sufficiently like him to be recognizable as his daughter. The girl rowed, pulling a pair of sculls very easily; the man, with the rudder-lines slack in his hands, and his hands loose in his waistband, kept an eager look out. He had no net, hook, or

10 line, and he could not be a fisherman; his boat had no cushion for a sitter, no paint, no inscription, no appliance beyond a rusty boathook and a coil of rope,

and he could not be a waterman; his boat was too crazy and too small to take in cargo for delivery, and he could not be a lighterman or river-carrier; there was no clue to what he looked for, but he looked for something, with a most intent and
15 searching gaze. The tide, which had turned an hour before, was running down, and his eyes watched every little race and eddy in its broad sweep, as the boat made slight head-way against it, or drove stern foremost before it, according as he directed his daughter by a movement of his head. She watched his face as earnestly as he watched the river. But, in the intensity of her look there was a
20 touch of dread or horror.

1. Based on details in the passage, the reader can infer that the boat
   (A) belongs to the girl.
   (B) was used in a crime.
   (C) is extremely old.
   (D) can barely stay afloat.

The correct answer is (C). The boat in which the two people sail is "dirty and disreputable" and has "no cushion for a sitter, no paint, no inscription, no appliance beyond a rusty boathook and a coil of rope." Based on its rough condition, the reader can conclude it is very old, so choice (C) is the best answer.

The passage does not expressly state something as direct as, "The boat the duo sailed in was very old." Instead, it asks the reader to infer this from a detailed physical description of the boat and of the girl's reaction to their journey. Authors not only use descriptive words to add interest to a story; they are also there to give important information.

Let's take a look at another question.

2. Based on details in paragraph 2, the girl and man most likely
   (A) perform this activity regularly.
   (B) are searching for a person.
   (C) are not actually father and daughter.
   (D) wish their boat had a larger crew.

The correct answer is (A). The man and girl in the boat perform their errand without speaking, the man communicating to his daughter with just "a movement of his head." Based on such information, you can infer that they have done the activity they perform often enough to have their routine so well-memorized they do not even have to speak.

As you can see from this question, when reading a passage, you must be mindful of the smallest details because they can help you draw conclusions and deduce meanings about the text. Look for clues about characters, plot, and the author's intentions so you can answer questions that require you to draw conclusions that are not explicitly stated in the passage. Notice if the author takes the time to describe something in detail—someone's personality, the way a place looks, the smell of a room, the vocabulary and slang of someone's speech, for example.

> **TIP**
>
> Take note of why and how an author takes the time to describe someone or something—there is likely to be a HiSET® question asking about the subject of the description. unfamiliar.

Read the excerpt from *The Lost World* by Sir Arthur Conan Doyle. Then answer the sample questions that follow.

> I stood like a man paralyzed, still staring at the ground which I had traversed. Then suddenly I saw it. There was movement among the bushes at the far end of the clearing which I had just traversed. A great dark shadow disengaged itself and hopped out into the clear moonlight. I say "hopped" advisedly, for the beast
> 5 moved like a kangaroo, springing along in an erect position upon its powerful hind legs, while its front ones were held bent in front of it. It was of enormous size and power, like an erect elephant, but its movements, in spite of its bulk, were exceedingly alert. For a moment, as I saw its shape, I hoped that it was an iguanodon, which I knew to be harmless, but, ignorant as I was, I soon saw
> 10 that this was a very different creature. Instead of the gentle, deer-shaped head of the great three-toed leaf-eater, this beast had a broad, squat, toad-like face like that which had alarmed us in our camp. His ferocious cry and the horrible energy of his pursuit both assured me that this was surely one of the great flesh-eating dinosaurs, the most terrible beasts which have ever walked this earth. As
> 15 the huge brute loped along it dropped forward upon its fore-paws and brought its nose to the ground every twenty yards or so. It was smelling out my trail. Sometimes, for an instant, it was at fault. Then it would catch it up again and come bounding swiftly along the path I had taken.

3. Based on this passage, the reader can conclude that the narrator is
   (A) shocked to see a dinosaur.
   (B) a prehistoric man.
   (C) ignorant of dinosaurs.
   (D) used to seeing dinosaurs.

The correct answer is (D). The narrator is too articulate and aware of modern names for dinosaurs to be a prehistoric man or to be ignorant of dinosaurs. He says he was expecting the creature to be an iguanodon, which is a kind of dinosaur, so he clearly is not shocked to see dinosaurs.

4. Based on this passage, the reader can conclude the dinosaur is
   (A) friendly.
   (B) baffled.
   (C) frightened.
   (D) hungry.

The correct answer is (D). As for the dinosaur, it is a flesh-eater and sniffing the narrator's trail. Based on such information, you can conclude this dinosaur is hungry and hunting the narrator.

Make Predictions

On the HiSET®, you will not only have to draw conclusions about what is happening in a reading passage but you will also have to draw conclusions about what will happen *after* the excerpt ends. After you finish a passage, especially a literary passage that tells a story, use clues, details, and patterns in the passage to make predictions about what will happen next. Take a look at the following excerpt from *Wuthering Heights* by

TIP

Description is an author's way of giving you insight into a world without making overly obvious statements.

Emily Brontë and the sample question that follows for an example of how the HiSET®
tests this skill.

> I have just returned from a visit to my landlord—the solitary neighbour that I
> shall be troubled with. This is certainly a beautiful country! In all England, I
> do not believe that I could have fixed on a situation so completely removed from
> the stir of society. A perfect misanthropist's heaven: and Mr. Heathcliff and I
> 5 are such a suitable pair to divide the desolation between us. A capital fellow! He
> little imagined how my heart warmed towards him when I beheld his black eyes
> withdraw so suspiciously under their brows, as I rode up, and when his fingers
> sheltered themselves, with a jealous resolution, still further in his waistcoat, as
> I announced my name.
> 10   'Mr. Heathcliff?' I said.
> A nod was the answer.
> 'Mr. Lockwood, your new tenant, sir. I do myself the honour of calling as soon
> as possible after my arrival, to express the hope that I have not inconvenienced
> you by my perseverance in soliciting the occupation of Thrushcross Grange: I
> 15 heard yesterday you had had some thoughts—'
> 'Thrushcross Grange is my own, sir,' he interrupted, wincing. 'I should not
> allow any one to inconvenience me, if I could hinder it—walk in!'

5. What will most likely happen next?
   (A) Mr. Lockwood and Mr. Heathcliff will have a terrible argument.
   (B) Mr. Heathcliff will tell Mr. Lockwood about his childhood.
   (C) Mr. Lockwood will admit he is actually an old friend of Mr. Heathcliff's.
   (D) Mr. Lockwood will have some trouble getting to know Mr. Heathcliff.

The correct answer is (D). Predictions can only be made based on information actually
in the passage. Therefore, the answer to this question can be selected using the process
of elimination. Is there any evidence that Mr. Lockwood and Mr. Heathcliff are about to
have a terrible argument? Perhaps Mr. Heathcliff is not being very friendly, but there
is no reason to believe he is getting ready to argue, so you can eliminate choice (A).
Since Mr. Heathcliff does not seem very talkative, it is unlikely he is about to divulge
personal information about his childhood, which means you can rule out choice (B).
There is no reason to believe the two men have ever met before, which makes it unlikely
they are old friends, choice (C). So what do we know from the passage? We know that
Mr. Heathcliff is a bit rude and standoffish. We know that Mr. Lockwood is comparatively friendly and talkative. Therefore, it is reasonable to predict that Mr. Lockwood
will try to get to know Mr. Heathcliff better but will have some trouble accomplishing
that. Therefore, the best answer is choice (D).

INFER THE TRAITS, FEELINGS, AND MOTIVES OF CHARACTERS

Sometimes you will have to make deeper inferences about the person who is narrating
the story, poem, or informational passage on the HiSET®. Using clues in the text, you
will make assumptions about someone's personality and behavioral traits, how that
person feels, and what motivates him or her act in a certain way. Making inferences

about a character or narrator's traits, feelings, and motives will help you derive a richer understanding of the text. Ask yourself *who* is speaking and *how* he or she is presenting the story to you, the reader, as you make your way through a passage. Asking yourself these questions as you read will help clarify what is going on inside a narrator's head.

Read the excerpt from "The Raven" by Edgar Allen Poe. Then answer the sample questions that follow.

> Once upon a midnight dreary, while I pondered, weak and weary,
> Over many a quaint and curious volume of forgotten lore,
> While I nodded, nearly napping, suddenly there came a tapping,
> As of some one gently rapping, rapping at my chamber door.
> 5 "'T is some visiter," I muttered, "tapping at my chamber door—
>
> Only this, and nothing more."
> Ah, distinctly I remember it was in the bleak December,
> And each separate dying ember wrought its ghost upon the floor.
> Eagerly I wished the morrow:—vainly I had sought to borrow
> 10 From my books surcease of sorrow—sorrow for the lost Lenore—
> For the rare and radiant maiden whom the angels name Lenore—
> Nameless here for evermore.

6. Based on details in the poem, which of the following best describes the narrator?
   (A) Melancholy
   (B) Bored
   (C) Contented
   (D) Generous

The correct answer is (A). The narrator drops clues that will help you answer this question when describing the night as "dreary," his feelings as "weak and weary," and the month as "bleak." His gloomy choice of words indicates that his state of mind is very melancholy.

7. Based on details in the poem, the reader can conclude the narrator
   (A) is very popular.
   (B) misses someone.
   (C) has trouble sleeping.
   (D) believes in ghosts.

The correct answer is (B). His lamentations for "the lost Lenore" in the second stanza should help you infer that he misses her.

It would be more direct if Poe had said something as simple as, "I am very melancholy because I miss Lenore," but it certainly would not be as poetic! Instead, he lets his language and tone set the mood and make it easy to infer how he is feeling.

APPLY INFORMATION

Passages on the HiSET® can also be historical or informational. Some questions on the exam will test your ability to figure out the best practical application for information in a passage. To prepare yourself to answer questions like this, you should ask yourself *why* an author is telling his or her story or information as you read it.

A piece of writing may be entertaining, educational, or informative, but it also may be put to more practical use. The purpose of a passage may be to help support an argument or encourage someone to do something constructive. A piece of writing may also serve as valuable research when writing an essay, or even as a fictional response to events going on in the world. Is a passage motivating? Discouraging? Entertaining? As a reader, think about what emotions the author is trying to stir within an audience.

Read the following excerpt from *On War* by General Carl von Clausewitz, and answer the question that follows.

> According to the notion we have formed of tactics and strategy, it follows, as a matter of course, that if the nature of the former is changed, that change must have an influence on the latter. If tactical facts in one case are entirely different from those in another, then the strategic, must be so also, if they are to continue
> 5 consistent and reasonable. It is therefore important to characterise a general action in its modern form before we advance with the study of its employment in strategy.
> What do we do now usually in a great battle? We place ourselves quietly in great masses arranged contiguous to and behind one another. We deploy rela-
> 10 tively only a small portion of the whole, and let it wring itself out in a fire-combat which lasts for several hours, only interrupted now and again, and removed hither and thither by separate small shocks from charges with the bayonet and cavalry attacks. When this line has gradually exhausted part of its warlike ardour in this manner and there remains nothing more than the cinders, it is
> 15 withdrawn and replaced by another.

8. Information in this passage would be most useful for
   (A) encouraging someone to join the military.
   (B) understanding why nations go to war.
   (C) plotting a battle strategy.
   (D) winning a game of chess.

The correct answer is (C). This passage includes tactics for winning a battle. The most practical use for such a passage is to use its relevant information to plot a battle strategy.

INTERPRET NONLITERAL LANGUAGE

Writers usually intend the words they choose to mean exactly what they seem to mean. This is **literal** language. However, writers also use words in ways that veer from their precise meanings for descriptive and artistic reasons. This is **nonliteral**, or **figurative**, language. There are many kinds of figurative language, including:

- **Simile:** a comparison that uses connective words such as "like", "as", and "than" to link the things being compared (ex: "She is as smart as a fox")

- **Metaphor:** a comparison without any connective words (ex: "The villain's heart is a block of ice")

- **Personification:** a phrase ascribing human traits and abilities to inanimate objects (ex: "The sun smiled down at me")

- **Hyperbole:** exaggeration (ex: "That cake is bigger than a house")

- **Idiom:** a common expression or cliché (ex: "A penny for your thoughts")

Take note when you see such language in a passage, and take the time to translate the nonliteral language into your own words. You will have to interpret the meaning of nonliteral language on the HiSET® in order to dig deeper into a passage's tone and meaning. Read the excerpt from *White Fang* by Jack London to see some examples in action. Then answer the sample questions that follow.

> Dark spruce forest frowned on either side the frozen waterway. The trees had been stripped by a recent wind of their white covering of frost, and they seemed to lean towards each other, black and ominous, in the fading light. A vast silence reigned over the land. The land itself was a desolation, lifeless, without
> 5 movement, so lone and cold that the spirit of it was not even that of sadness. There was a hint in it of laughter, but of a laughter more terrible than any sadness—a laughter that was mirthless as the smile of the sphinx, a laughter cold as the frost and partaking of the grimness of infallibility. It was the masterful and incommunicable wisdom of eternity laughing at the futility of life and
> 10 the effort of life. It was the Wild, the savage, frozen-hearted Northland Wild.

9. Read the following sentence (lines 3–4) from the passage:

   A vast silence reigned over the land.

   This means

   (A) a king ruled the area.

   (B) the animals had been tamed.

   (C) snow had begun falling.

   (D) the area was quiet.

The correct answer is (D). Silence is not a human being, so it is not capable of actually reigning over the land as a king might. The nonliteral sentence in this question is an example of personification, and it means that the area was quiet.

The preceding line, "Dark spruce forest frowned on either side the frozen waterway," is another example of nonliteral language. Does a forest really frown? No, of course not. But this instance of personification sets the tone for the passage right at its start—the forest is gloomy, moody, and sad.

Let's take a look at another question asking about nonliteral language.

10. The phrase "a laughter that was mirthless as the smile of the sphinx (line 7)" refers to something that

    (A) does not actually exist.

    (B) seems joyful but is not.

    (C) causes great sorrow.

    (D) is from ancient history.

The correct answer is (B). The phrase in the question compares the smile of the sphinx, a stoic mythological creature, to mirthless laughter. Both laughter and a smile indicate joyfulness, but the sphinx and the word "mirthless" indicate a lack of joy.

When the HiSET® asks about the meaning of a phrase, always look at its surrounding language to give you more clues. The passage presented paints a picture of cold and loneliness in almost every sentence. Therefore, most sentences and phrases will stay within this general tone. Understanding a phrase's place within a larger passage will make interpreting it easier.

SYNTHESIZE INFORMATION ACROSS MULTIPLE SOURCES

Some HiSET® questions ask you to analyze a work of writing in comparison to the one presented to you, in order to think beyond the specific information in the main passage. For these questions, you will be presented with a sentence or short paragraph that is unrelated to the passage. Then, you must use your understanding of the main passage *and* the new text to answer the question.

Let's look at an example. Read the excerpt from Preface from *History of the Decline and Fall of the Roman Empire* by Edward Gibbon. Then answer the sample question that follows.

> The great work of Gibbon is indispensable to the student of history. The literature of Europe offers no substitute for "The Decline and Fall of the Roman Empire." It has obtained undisputed possession, as rightful occupant, of the vast period which it comprehends. However some subjects, which it embraces,
> 5 may have undergone more complete investigation, on the general view of the whole period, this history is the sole undisputed authority to which all defer, and from which few appeal to the original writers, or to more modern compilers. The inherent interest of the subject, the inexhaustible labor employed upon it; the immense condensation of matter; the luminous arrangement; the general
> 10 accuracy; the style, which, however monotonous from its uniform stateliness, and sometimes wearisome from its elaborate art, is throughout vigorous, animated, often picturesque always commands attention, always conveys its meaning with emphatic energy, describes with singular breadth and fidelity, and generalizes with unrivalled felicity of expression; all these high qualifications have secured,
> 15 and seem likely to secure, its permanent place in historic literature.

11. Read the following paragraph.

    Stylistically, Gibbon's work is without peer, relaying Roman history with the fluidity and lyrical rhythm of great literature. His "facts," however, are often way off base, as his emphasis on the role the Empire's lethargy regarding current affairs played in its downfall is almost absurdly overstated considering the lack of evidence to support such a claim.

    How does this paragraph differ from the main passage?

    (A) It is critical of Gibbon's ability to present his information successfully.

    (B) It does not view Gibbon as the sole authority on the Roman Empire.

    (C) It is very complimentary of Gibbon's unique style of writing.

    (D) It contends that Gibbons did not perform any research to support his writing.

The correct answer is (B). A careful reading of both the main passage and the paragraph unique to this question is necessary for answering it. Although the paragraph is critical of Gibbon, it is hardly critical of his ability to present his information, even praising his style as "without peer," so you can eliminate choice (A). You can eliminate choice (C), as well, because the writer of the main passage compliments his style, as well, stating that it is "vigorous, animated, often picturesque" and "always commands attention." Choice (D) is not the best answer, because although the writer of the passage is critical of Gibbon's conclusions, she never suggests he performed no research to support it. She simply points out that there are problems with his "facts," which should lead you to conclude that the paragraph's writer does not believe Gibbon should be considered "the sole authority on the Roman Empire" as the writer of the paragraph does when he writes that Gibbon's book "is the sole undisputed authority to which all defer." Therefore, the best answer is choice (B).

SUMMING IT UP

- HiSET® Reading questions often call upon you to **infer** meaning from the passage—that is, to make an assumption about characters or other subjects of a passage that are not plainly spelled out. Pay attention to how and why an author describes people, places, and things. What is he or she saying about a subject?

- Notice if the author takes the time to describe something in detail—someone's personality, the way a place looks, the smell of a room, the vocabulary and slang of someone's speech, for example.

- After you finish a passage, make a prediction about what is likely to happen next.

- Ask yourself *who* is speaking and *how* he or she is presenting the story to you, the reader, as you make your way through a passage—this will help you gain a better understanding of a narrator's tone, mood, and state of mind.

- When you come across an informative passage, ask yourself *why* an author is telling his or her story or information as you read it.

- Pay attention to **nonliteral** language in HiSET® passages, and take the time to translate it into your own words to interpret exactly what the author is saying.

- Treat smaller passages found within HiSET® questions as you would larger passages—infer the author's message and compare it to the message of the main passage at hand.

Analysis

chapter 4

OVERVIEW

- Analyze multiple interpretations of a text
- Determine the main idea, topic, or theme
- Identify opinions, facts, assumptions, observations, and conclusions
- Recognize aspects of an author's style, structure, mood, or tone
- Summing It Up

Authors may intend their writing to simply share useful information or tell an entertaining story. However, even within the most straightforward passage, an author uses language in complex ways to convey deeper meanings. The questions on the HiSET® Language Arts—Reading subtest ask you to analyze reading passages and uncover their main ideas, themes, purposes, and viewpoints. You will also be expected to understand how authors convey their messages by using particular writing styles and techniques.

ANALYZE MULTIPLE INTERPRETATIONS OF A TEXT

Writers often use language in abstract ways to set a mood or convey a message indirectly. Such works will require you to read deeply in order to interpret an author's meaning. This can be tricky, because different readers may have different interpretations of a single piece of writing. For example, one person may read a poem and conclude it is simply about a bird. Another may read the same poem and interpret it as a symbolic expression of the poet's happiness or love of nature.

On the HiSET®, you will sometimes be asked to analyze multiple interpretations of passages and poems. This might involve finding evidence to support one interpretation or using someone else's differing interpretation to develop a conclusion you might not have considered.

Let's take a look at what this type of question will look like on the exam. Read the excerpt from "Envy and Avarice" by Victor Hugo and answer the sample questions that follow.

> Envy and Avarice, one summer day,
> Sauntering abroad
> In quest of the abode
> Of some poor wretch or fool who lived that way—
> 5 You—or myself, perhaps—I cannot say—
> Along the road, scarce heeding where it tended,

31

Their way in sullen, sulky silence wended;
For, though twin sisters, these two charming creatures,
Rivals in hideousness of form and features,
10 Wasted no love between them as they went.
Pale Avarice,
With gloating eyes,
And back and shoulders almost double bent,
Was hugging close that fatal box
15 For which she's ever on the watch
Some glance to catch
Suspiciously directed to its locks;
And Envy, too, no doubt with silent winking
At her green, greedy orbs, no single minute
20 Withdrawn from it, was hard a-thinking
Of all the shining dollars in it.

1. What line from the poem supports the analysis that the poet has contempt for his topic?

    (A) Along the road, scarce heeding where it tended.

    (B) For, though twin sisters, these two charming creatures.

    (C) Rivals in hideousness of form and features.

    (D) And Envy, too, no doubt with silent winking.

The correct answer is (C). "Rivals in hideousness of form and features" refers to Envy and Avarice, who are personifications of those negative emotions. By referring to those characters as "hideous," the poet expresses his contempt, or utter dislike, for the emotions they represent.

You might not have initially thought the author disliked his topic when you read the passage. However, after you read a question like this (one that asks about personality, or mood, or something else intangible) you will need to go back and find evidence for an interpretation—even if you do not agree with it!

2. Which of the following best supports the theory that the poet believes money has destructive powers?

    (A) He refers to the box containing money as "fatal."

    (B) He refers to Envy's eyes as "green" and "greedy."

    (C) He states that Envy thinks about the money "hard."

    (D) He states that people look at the money box "suspiciously."

The correct answer is (A). The word "fatal" refers to that which causes death or destruction.

DETERMINE THE MAIN IDEA, TOPIC, OR THEME

The HiSET® includes questions that test your ability to identify the overall purpose or meaning of both a passage as a whole and of specific paragraphs or sections within the passage. Such questions may ask you to identify the **main idea** (the overall purpose of the passage or paragraph), the **topic** (the subject of the passage or a paragraph), or **theme** (the unifying thought behind the passage or paragraph).

As you read a passage on the exam in preparation to answer a set of questions, ask yourself after every paragraph, "What is the purpose of this paragraph and why is it a part of this passage?" After you finish the passage and before you start to answer the questions, ask yourself, "What is the purpose of this passage? Why did the author write this?"

Read the excerpt from *My Ántonia* by Willa Cather. Then answer the sample questions that follow.

> Jake and Otto served us to the last. They moved us into town, put down the carpets in our new house, made shelves and cupboards for grandmother's kitchen, and seemed loath to leave us. But at last they went, without warning. Those two fellows had been faithful to us through sun and storm, had given us things
> 5 that cannot be bought in any market in the world. With me they had been like older brothers; had restrained their speech and manners out of care for me, and given me so much good comradeship. Now they got on the westbound train one morning, in their Sunday clothes, with their oilcloth valises—and I never saw them again. Months afterward we got a card from Otto, saying that Jake had
> 10 been down with mountain fever, but now they were both working in the Yankee Girl Mine, and were doing well. I wrote to them at that address, but my letter was returned to me, 'Unclaimed.' After that we never heard from them.

3. This passage is mainly about
   (A) traveling on trains.
   (B) parting with close associates.
   (C) saying goodbye to brothers.
   (D) working in mines.

The correct answer is (B). This question requires you to identify the topic of this passage, which is the narrator parting ways with two men who "had been like older brothers." Keep in mind that they are not actually brothers, which is why choice (C) is not the best answer.

4. A theme of this passage is
   (A) the value of complete faithfulness.
   (B) the strong bonds between people.
   (C) the importance of doing good work.
   (D) the fleeting nature of relationships.

The correct answer is (B). That theme of a bond that is so close it makes the characters feel like family should help you conclude that choice (B) is the best answer. Other answer choices refer to things mentioned in the passage (faithfulness, doing good work) that are not integral enough to it to be considered important themes.

Identify the Author's or Speaker's Purpose or Viewpoint

The HiSET® will often ask you to identify the author's purpose or viewpoint. **Purpose** is her or his reason for writing a particular piece. His or her **viewpoint** is the opinion

ALERT!

Be sure not to mistake the individual details of a passage or paragraph for the larger ideas, topics, and themes these questions require you to identify.

or perspective expressed *about* the topic of the piece. An author rarely states a viewpoint explicitly, but it can be detected by examining the words chosen to express an opinion. Is he enthusiastic? Angry? Encouraging? Doubtful? What mood do you infer as you read through the passage?

Read the excerpt from President Woodrow Wilson's 1919 address about the League of Nations and answer the sample questions that follow.

It gives me pleasure to add to this formal reading of the result of our labors that the character of the discussion, which occurred at the sittings of the commission was not only of the most constructive but of the most encouraging sort. It was obvious throughout our discussions that, although there were subjects upon
5 which there were individual differences of judgment with regard to the method by which our objects should be obtained, there was practically at no point any serious differences of opinion or motive as to the objects which we were seeking.

Indeed, while these debates were not made the opportunity for the expression of enthusiasm and sentiments, I think the other members of the commission will
10 agree with me that there was an undertone of high respect and of enthusiasm for the thing we were trying to do which was heartening throughout everything.

5. The author wrote this passage to

   (A) explain the purpose of the League of Nations.

   (B) describe the creation of the League of Nations.

   (C) prove the League of Nations is necessary.

   (D) show how the League of Nations serves people.

The correct answer is (B). This question asks you to identify the author's purpose for writing this passage. Process of elimination is one way to find the correct answer, since the author does not explain the League of Nation's purpose, try to prove anything about it, or say anything about how it serves the American people. He does, however, describe the process of its creation.

6. The author of this passage seems to believe

   (A) the debates that led to the League of Nations were unnecessarily bitter.

   (B) everyone involved in creating the League of Nations was constructive.

   (C) the creation of the League of Nations was a positive experience.

   (D) the League of Nations is the most important organization in the country.

The correct answer is (C). Since he describes that creation in positive terms, lauding his co-creators for being respectful and enthusiastic, you can conclude the correct answer to this question is choice (C), which captures the author's viewpoint about the League's creation.

IDENTIFY OPINIONS, FACTS, ASSUMPTIONS, OBSERVATIONS, AND CONCLUSIONS

An important part of becoming a better reader is the ability to read critically.

Sometimes, a writer is not necessarily imparting facts, but rather presenting his or her own opinions or assumptions. General observations, especially ones that *cannot* be

ALERT!

With purpose and viewpoint questions, pay attention to the passage as a whole. Incorrect answers might include viewpoints from individual paragraphs, but the question is likely asking you to analyze the entire passage.

ALERT!

Do not always take a writer's statements at face value! Just because they are in a passage, and sound official, does not mean they are factual.

proven by evidence, are often what the author thinks or feels, and not what is probably true. Ask yourself—can I prove this statement with facts and evidence? If not, the author is inserting his or her own feelings and point of view.

Read the following excerpt from *The Frontier in American History* by Frederick Jackson Turner. Then answer the sample questions that follow.

It is a wonderful chapter, this final rush of American energy upon the remaining wilderness. Even the bare statistics become eloquent of a new era. They no longer derive their significance from the exhibit of vast proportions of the public domain transferred to agriculture, of wildernesses equal to European nations changed
5 decade after decade into the farm area of the United States. It is true there was added to the farms of the nation between 1870 and 1880 a territory equal to that of France, and between 1880 and 1900 a territory equal to the European area of France, Germany, England, and Wales combined. The records of 1910 are not yet available, but whatever they reveal they will not be so full of meaning as
10 the figures which tell of upleaping wealth and organization and concentration of industrial power in the East in the last decade. As the final provinces of the Western empire have been subdued to the purposes of civilization and have yielded their spoils, as the spheres of operation of the great industrial corporations have extended, with the extension of American settlement, production and
15 wealth have increased beyond all precedent.
    The total deposits in all national banks have more than trebled in the present decade; the money in circulation has doubled since 1890. The flood of gold makes it difficult to gauge the full meaning of the incredible increase in values, for in the decade ending with 1909 over 41,600,000 ounces of gold were mined in the
20 United States alone. Over four million ounces have been produced every year since 1905, whereas between 1880 and 1894 no year showed a production of two million ounces. As a result of this swelling stream of gold and instruments of credit, aided by a variety of other causes, prices have risen until their height has become one of the most marked features and influential factors in American life,
25 producing social readjustments and contributing effectively to party revolutions.

7. Which of the following is an assumption in the first paragraph?

(A) It is a wonderful chapter, this final rush of American energy upon the remaining wilderness.

(B) It is true there was added to the farms of the nation between 1870 and 1880 a territory equal to that of France, and between 1880 and 1900 a territory equal to the European area of France, Germany, England, and Wales combined.

(C) The records of 1910 are not yet available, but whatever they reveal they will not be so full of meaning as the figures which tell of upleaping wealth and organization and concentration of industrial power in the East in the last decade.

(D) As the final provinces of the Western empire have been subdued to the purposes of civilization and have yielded their spoils, as the spheres of operation of the great industrial corporations have extended, with the extension of American settlement, production and wealth have increased beyond all precedent.

The correct answer is (C). There is an important clue to help you answer this question: when the writer states that something has not happened yet, but he is going to draw a conclusion about it anyway, he is making an assumption. This is what he does in answer choice (C).

8. Which of the following is an observation in the second paragraph?
    (A) The total deposits in all national banks have more than trebled in the present decade …
    (B) … the money in circulation has doubled since 1890.
    (C) The flood of gold makes it difficult to gauge the full meaning of the incredible increase in values …
    (D) …in the decade ending with 1909 over 41,600,000 ounces of gold were mined in the United States alone.

The correct answer is (C). You can figure out the answer to this question by eliminating the answer choices that present nothing but hard facts. Doing so leaves choice (C), which is an observation about factors that make reaching a conclusion difficult.

RECOGNIZE ASPECTS OF AN AUTHOR'S STYLE, STRUCTURE, MOOD, OR TONE

How a writer tells a story or imparts information can be just as important as the story or information itself. The style, structure, mood, and tone of a piece can affect its meaning or simply make it more interesting to read. Here are definitions and examples of some literary elements you will see in HiSET® passages:

- **Style:** the basic way the author chooses to write or the voice she or he uses. A piece can have a style that is conversational or informal, business-like or formal, educational or authoritative, etc.

- **Structure:** how the piece is organized. Different kinds of structures include cause and effect, compare and contrast, chronological order, sequential order, and division into categories.

- **Mood:** the atmosphere of a piece and the emotions it makes the reader feel. There are a large variety of moods: cheerful, excited, melancholic, frightening, welcoming, peaceful, suspenseful, etc.

- **Tone:** how the author feels about the subject of a piece. Descriptions of tone include admiring, commanding, humorous, angry, nostalgic, mocking, romantic, scholarly, scornful, tender, serious, etc.

The HiSET® requires you to identify the style, structure, mood, and/or tone of various reading passages. For example, read the excerpt from *Manners, Custom and Dress During the Middle Ages and During the Renaissance Period* by Paul Lacroix. Then answer the sample questions that follow.

Under the two Philips, his successors, this magnificence increased, and descended to the great vassals, who were soon imitated by the knights "bannerets." There

seemed to be a danger of luxury becoming so great, and so general in all classes of feudal society, that in 1294 an order of the King was issued, regulating in
5 the minutest details the expenses of each person according to his rank in the State, or the fortune which he could prove. But this law had the fate of all such enactments, and was either easily evaded, or was only partially enforced, and that with great difficulty. Another futile attempt to put it in practice was made in 1306, when the splendour of dress, of equipages, and of table had become still
10 greater and more ruinous, and had descended progressively to the bourgeois and merchants...

    After the death of the pious Jeanne de Navarre, to whom perhaps we must attribute the wise measures of her husband, Philip le Bel, the expenses of the royal household materially increased, especially on the occasions of the mar-
15 riages of the three young sons of the King, from 1305 to 1307. Gold, diamonds, pearls, and precious stones were employed profusely, both for the King's garments and for those of the members of the royal family. The accounts of 1307 mention considerable sums paid for carpets, counterpanes, robes, worked linen, &c. A chariot of state, ornamented and covered with paintings, and gilded like
20 the back of an altar, is also mentioned, and must have been a great change to the heavy vehicles used for travelling in those days.

9. Which of the following describes the structure of this passage?

    (A) Cause and effect

    (B) Chronological order

    (C) Compare and contrast

    (D) Sequential order

The correct answer is (B). A key to answering this question is the author's references to years: 1294, then 1306, and then 1307. The fact that the numbers increase over the course of the passage indicates it was written in chronological order, which is the order in which the events described occurred.

10. Which of the following best describes the tone of this passage?

    (A) Straightforward

    (B) Approving

    (C) Indignant

    (D) Poignant

The correct answer is (A). This requires a closer reading, and though the writer seems to make the occasional judgment by using words such as "splendour," "ruinous," and "wise," his attitude about his topic cannot really be detected by the words he uses. His overall lack of judgment results in a straightforward tone.

Literary and Argumentative Techniques

Sometimes, a writer creates a piece to manipulate readers into feeling, thinking, or gathering information in a certain way. This is especially true of fiction writers, who use various **literary techniques** to accomplish such manipulation. The following table gives you some examples of literary techniques you will see on the HiSET®:

Pathos	A scene that stirs the reader's feelings.
Repetition	A word, line, or idea repeated for emphasis.
Flash Forward	An interlude that moves ahead in the narrative.
Flashback	An interlude that moves backward in the narrative.
Foreshadowing	A hint of an event to come later in the narrative.
Prologue	An introductory passage distinct from the narrative that follows.
First Person Narrative	A story told from the point of view of a character in it.
Third Person Narrative	A story told from the point of view of a narrator who is not involved in the story.

Writers of persuasive essays, like newspaper editorials or impassioned speeches, use **argumentative techniques** to effectively make their point. HiSET® questions might ask you whether an author is using one of the following methods to persuade or will ask you to identify which specific technique is being used.

Proposition and Support	An idea or belief followed by details that support it.
Evidence	Information presented to support an argument.
Opposing Viewpoints	An opinion that counters a general viewpoint.
Counterarguments	A statement that refutes someone else's opinion.
Emotional Appeal	Words intended to stir the reader's feelings.
Logical Appeal	Statements intended to appeal to the reader's intellect.
Generalization	Broad statements about ideas, people, beliefs, organizations, and events.

Read the excerpt from *Black Beauty* by Anna Sewell. Then answer the sample questions that follow.

Before I was two years old a circumstance happened which I have never forgotten. It was early in the spring; there had been a little frost in the night, and a light mist still hung over the woods and meadows. I and the other colts were feeding at the lower part of the field when we heard, quite in the distance, what sounded
5 like the cry of dogs. The oldest of the colts raised his head, pricked his ears, and said, "There are the hounds!" and immediately cantered off, followed by the rest of us to the upper part of the field, where we could look over the hedge and see several fields beyond. My mother and an old riding horse of our master's were also standing near, and seemed to know all about it.
10   "They have found a hare," said my mother, "and if they come this way we shall see the hunt."

11. Which of the following literary devices does the author use in this passage?
   (A) Prologue
   (B) Framing device
   (C) Flash forward
   (D) Flashback

The correct answer is (D). A flashback is when the author breaks from the present to describe something that happened in the past. In the passage, the author writes "Before I was two years old" to let the reader know the action that follows took place in the past.

12. Which literary device does the author use to tell this story?
   (A) First person narrative
   (B) Third person narrative
   (C) Extended metaphor
   (D) Repetition

The correct answer is (A). This is a more general question about how the author tells the story, and her use of the personal pronouns "I" and "my" lets us know that she is telling the story from the first person point of view.

SUMMING IT UP

- Different readers may have different interpretations of a passage. When reading a passage, open yourself up to what different people may read into a piece of writing. You might be asked to find evidence to support your own interpretation or to back up an interpretation you might not first agree with.

- Always be aware of the **main idea** of a HiSET® passage, as well as how each individual paragraph fits into this main idea. Ask yourself, "What is the purpose of each paragraph and why is it a part of this passage?" "What is the purpose of this passage and why did the author write this?"

- You should be able to identify when a writer is presenting opinions and when he or she is presenting facts. Can the statement be backed up by hard evidence? Only then is a statement definitely a fact. Do not always take an author's statements at face value.

- HiSET® Reading questions will ask not only about the actual words on the page, but also about *how* a passage is written. Be aware of the language an author uses and how this sets the tone of a piece. Also be aware of how he or she structures a piece. Is it in chronological order? Does it set up a problem and then fix it?

PART III
LANGUAGE ARTS—WRITING

Organization of Ideas

chapter 5

OVERVIEW

- Create and recognize strong opening, transitional, and closing sentences
- Evaluate the relevance of context
- Recognize logical transitions and related words and phrases
- Summing It Up

The HiSET® Language Arts—Writing subtest evaluates your ability to write and revise written work to make it clear and correct. Questions in the multiple-choice section of the test will ask you to identify and fix mistakes in organization, grammar, punctuation, and spelling. There are 50 questions on the multiple-choice part of the Language Arts—Writing subtest, and you will have a combined total of 120 minutes to complete both the multiple-choice and essay sections of the test (we'll cover the essay section in chapter 8)..

On the test, you will be given four passages. Each is a selection from a draft of a piece of writing. Each passage is printed twice: first in a box, printed normally, and then spread out with underlined portions numbered for each question. The passages represent kinds of writing that high school students are asked to read or write in school and in their lives, such as newspaper articles, essays, letters, blog posts, and reports.

Some of the questions on the Language Arts—Writing subtest are about fixing mistakes—choosing the correct answer or eliminating the wrong ones—but you will also be asked to identify the best revision out of the options, assessing how ideas are put together for the clearest and most accurate writing. This chapter will review the principles of organization that make writing clear, logical, and smooth.

CREATE AND RECOGNIZE STRONG OPENING, TRANSITIONAL, AND CLOSING SENTENCES

The passages on the HiSET® Language Arts—Writing subtest will consist of two or more paragraphs. In general, a paragraph will contain the discussion or explanation of one main idea. For example, there may be a claim and the evidence that supports it or a general statement with a few specific examples. A paragraph break indicates the move to a new idea.

Within a paragraph, the order of sentences can help you understand information and see how ideas connect.

Opening Sentences

The opening sentence establishes the main idea of a paragraph. This is also sometimes called a **topic sentence.** Let's take a look at a sample paragraph.

> **There are many benefits to creating a personal budget.** Tracking your spending can help you become more aware of where your money is going. Recording income helps you know exactly how much money you have available to spend. Projecting future income and expenses helps you plan for the future. Being aware of your spending and thinking about your financial future make you more able to adapt to change and to make informed decisions about your money. When you take the mystery and sense of randomness out of your finances, you will feel less stressed. Remember, you are in control of your finances; don't let them control you.

The opening sentence tells you what to expect from the paragraph: a list or discussion of some of the many benefits to creating a personal budget. Try writing an opening sentence for the following paragraph.

> _____. In ancient times, eclipses were thought to be messages from the gods. In ancient China, astrologers interpreted eclipses as prophesies for the emperor's future. The Babylonians believed an eclipse was a bad omen for the king. In Europe in the 1600s, astronomers published the mathematical work that predicted eclipses in part to ease public superstition about these events.

> _____

> _____

This paragraph is about superstitions and beliefs about eclipses through history. An appropriate opening sentence could be something like:

> *Many cultures throughout history have had superstitious beliefs about eclipses.*

This opening sentence gives the main idea of the paragraph. The subsequent sentences give specific examples that support this idea and show how it is true.

Closing Sentences

The end of a paragraph is also important for you to notice and comprehend as a reader. A closing sentence can help you understand the detailed information you've just read, or it can explain the implications of information. Just as an essay has an introduction and a conclusion, so can a paragraph:

> There are many benefits to creating a personal budget. Tracking your spending can help you become more aware of where your money is going. Recording income helps you know exactly how much money you have available to spend. Projecting future income and expenses helps you plan for the future. Being aware of your spending and thinking about your financial future make you more able to adapt to change and to make informed decisions about your money. When you take the

mystery and sense of randomness out of your finances, you will feel less stressed. **Remember, you are in control of your finances; don't let them control you.**

In this paragraph, the opening sentence introduces the main idea. The sentences that follow list the detailed information that was promised in the opening. The closing sentence restates and reframes the main idea, emphasizing that the actions described in this paragraph add up to a sense of personal control over one's budget. There is a take-away message of empowerment—the reader is told how to understand the *meaning* of the preceding information.

Transitional Sentences

Opening and closing sentences can also function, alone or together, as transitions between paragraphs. Let's look back at our paragraph about eclipses:

Many cultures throughout history have had superstitious beliefs about eclipses. In ancient times, eclipses were thought to be messages from the gods. In ancient China, astrologers interpreted eclipses as prophesies for the emperor's future. The Babylonians believed an eclipse was a bad omen for the king. In Europe in the 1600s, astronomers published the mathematical work that predicted eclipses in part to ease public superstition about these events.

Opening sentences that refer to the prior paragraph help a reader transition between ideas. The next paragraph in this article could begin:

While many ancient cultures were superstitious about eclipses, others used surprisingly sophisticated mathematics to understand the reality of this phenomenon.

That opening shows the relationship between the preceding paragraph—on superstitious beliefs—and the next one.

Closing sentences can also propel the reader into the next paragraph. Here's another way to end the paragraph on personal budgets:

There are many benefits to creating a personal budget. Tracking your spending can help you become more aware of where your money is going. Recording income helps you know exactly how much money you have available to spend. Projecting future income and expenses helps you plan for the future. Being aware of your spending and thinking about your financial future make you more able to adapt to change and to make informed decisions about your money. When you take the mystery and sense of randomness out of your finances, you will feel less stressed. **With your sights set on these goals, you're ready to begin.**

This closing sentence reiterates the importance of the preceding paragraph and sends the reader forward with a question: *Where do I begin?* You can expect that the next paragraph will help the reader understand how to get started with a budget.

On the HiSET® Writing test, you can use these principles to figure out where new paragraphs should start and to put sentences in order. Let's look at some practice questions that mirror those you will see on test day.

[1] I consider myself lucky to have grown up learning how to clean. [2] Of course, I didn't feel lucky at the time. [3] Chores were never what I wanted to be doing. [4] But once I grew up and began living on my own, I realized how valuable these chores had been: I knew how to take care of my home. [5] I felt so self-sufficient. [6] I've realized, though, that many people aren't raised with these skills. [7] Some people grow up without being asked to help with housework. [8] Others are raised by wealthy parents who hire house-cleaners—children definitely don't pitch in, then! [9] So while these people's childhoods were free from chores, they realize in adulthood that they're lacking crucial life-skills.

1. The writer of this article is considering splitting this paragraph into two paragraphs. Which sentence should start a new paragraph?
   (A) 3
   (B) 4
   (C) 5
   (D) 6

The correct answer is (D). This sentence begins the shift from the writer's own experience to a description of the contrasting experience of other people.

2. Which of the following would be an effective addition to the end of the passage?
   (A) While there are many ways to get their homes clean, I believe they're missing out on valuable rewards if they aren't able to do this themselves.
   (B) Life-skills come in many varieties, including abilities to cook, balance one's budget, and navigate without driving directions.
   (C) Not all life-skills are crucial.
   (D) A childhood free from chores leaves room for many fun activities, which gives children the space to develop interests that may last them their whole lives.

The correct answer is (A). This sentence concludes this paragraph, expressing the implications and importance of the preceding information.

EVALUATE THE RELEVANCE OF CONTEXT

The HiSET® Language Arts—Writing subtest will ask you to use **context,** or the meaning of a word or phrase in relation to the words and phrases around it, to make editing decisions about what to keep, what to cut, and what to change.

Some context will come from within the passage. This includes not only your sense of the main purpose of the passage as a whole, but also the specific paragraph you're examining. Keep in mind what the specific paragraph is trying to say, and then use that context to evaluate whether a sentence fits. Let's look at a sample:

Your local farmers' market offers more than just vegetables. Some farmers sell eggs or dairy products. Local vendors also sell their wares: baked goods, flowers, and even local beer. Dried and fresh flowers are wonderful additions to your decor year-round. Even in winter, when produce may be scarce, don't forget about the bounty available at your farmers' market.

Think about this paragraph as a whole—what is its purpose? This paragraph is explaining that, even in winter, a farmers' market has many offerings. Did you notice a sentence that didn't contribute to that? Let's break it up sentence-by-sentence to make it easier to read:

1. Your local farmers' market offers more than just vegetables.
2. Some farmers sell eggs or dairy products.
3. Local vendors also sell their wares: baked goods, flowers, and even local beer.
4. Dried and fresh flowers are wonderful additions to your decor year-round.
5. Even in winter, when produce may be scarce, don't forget about the bounty available at your farmers' market.

Although sentence 4 follows from what came before—it's about flowers—and shares the concerns about the current season seen in the sentence that follows, sentence 4 isn't about the farmers' market. It's about flowers. It doesn't match up with the context of the paragraph.

Another useful source of contextual information that shouldn't be overlooked is the context of passages as a whole. Each passage on the HiSET® Writing test will be prefaced by instructions. Part of the instructions will be the same, with only minor changes, every time: "Read quickly through the draft in the box below. Then go to the spread-out version and consider the suggestions for revision." However, there is also important information in the instructions:

"Read quickly through the draft *of a feature article* below."

"After attending a school board meeting, *a blogger wrote the following article*."

"Read quickly through the draft *of an office memo*."

These instructions, along with the passage itself, give you important context for the draft you're revising. Is it an office memo? A blog post? A newspaper article? A scientific report? Different styles of writing have different criteria for important and relevant information.

Consider the following draft of an office memo:

Jeanne Clark has been a vital member of our team for six years, and we are sad to see her go. However, we are grateful for everything Jeanne has brought to her colleagues and to this company. Her contributions toward landing the Greenfield account were especially valuable. Additionally, Jeanne's son recently started college. Please join us in the kitchen at 3 p.m. to wish Jeanne well and thank her for all of her hard work. Cake will be served.

What is relevant to the audience of the memo? The audience is Jeanne's coworkers—they need the information about the 3 p.m. send-off, and the promise of cake will help them decide whether or not to attend. On the other hand, Jeanne's family life isn't relevant to the context. This is a professional memo, and its concerns are the office and Jeanne's professional track record. The sentence about her son starting college may be true and grammatically correct, but context tells us that it doesn't belong.

Here's a question to practice applying these concepts, as you'll be asked to on test day:

After attending a local press conference, a blogger wrote the following draft of an article:

Yesterday afternoon, Mayor Ringerud spoke to reporters about the cancellation of the Main Street Business District plan. She began with a prepared statement, which covered the history of the plan, the city council's initial enthusiasm, and the subsequent public protests. Councilwoman Mendez, who is serving her second term, stood behind the mayor as she spoke.

3. Which of the following would be most relevant to include here?
   (A) (No change; best as written)
   (B) Who is running for reelection
   (C) Councilwoman Mendez had been the plan's most outspoken advocate
   (D) Who will be speaking at Thompson Community College next week

The correct answer is (C). This choice explains Councilwoman Mendez's relationship to the Business District plan, which is the subject of the mayor's press conference and of the passage.

RECOGNIZE LOGICAL TRANSITIONS AND RELATED WORDS AND PHRASES

Transitional words and phrases help you move from one idea to the next. They help readers understand how ideas are related and they create a sense of flow between paragraphs in a passage. Appropriate transitions reflect the relationships between facts. For example, here are two sentences:

John wanted to eat a healthy meal. He went to Café Blanche for dinner.

These sentences give us some facts, but the relationship between John's goal and his restaurant choice isn't clear. Now look at how much more information we can get with transitions:

John wanted to eat a healthy meal. Therefore, he went to Café Blanche for dinner.

or

John wanted to eat a healthy meal. However, he went to Café Blanche for dinner.

Transitions have a strong impact on the meaning of a passage. When the relationship between two ideas is clear from the sentences themselves, make sure that transitions match this relationship, instead of clashing with it.

John wanted to eat a healthy meal. However, he chose a big salad.

Normally we'd think that a big salad is a healthy meal! This "however" clashes with that meaning. A good correction would be:

John wanted to eat a healthy meal. Therefore, he chose a big salad.

If you don't have the option to change the transition word, you may be able to change the surrounding sentences to match. If your option is to change "a big salad," you could choose:

John wanted to eat a healthy meal. However, he chose a giant slice of cake.

Transitions can also help readers follow sequences of ideas or events. Listing transitions such as "first," "second," and "finally" help readers see when ideas are connected in a list. Transitions can also illuminate the chronology of events:

Before eating cake, John ate a salad. Then he went for a walk. Later, he felt good about his choices.

Here are some common transition words and their uses:

Cause and Effect	Contrast	Similarity/Addition	Chronology
Therefore	However	Additionally	First
Thus	Although	Furthermore	Second
Consequently	Instead	In addition	Finally
As a result	On the other hand	Indeed	Later
			Before
			Next

Let's put these ideas into practice with a few test-style questions.

Directions: The following questions offer options for improvement for each under-lined part. Select the answer choice for each that best improves the written passage.

While it may seem that daycare is very similar to babysitting, only scaled up, it is actually a complex business operation. <u>Furthermore</u>, there are legal
1
and regulatory concerns. Once you are caring for more than three children for more than three hours, you must obtain a license from the state. <u>As a result</u>, this
2
should not be daunting. There are state administrators to help you with the process, and once you've filed your registration the license is good for seven years.

1. **(A)** (no change)
   (B) Then
   (C) Next
   (D) As a result

The correct answer is (A). "Furthermore" indicates a point that is in line with the preceding idea and adds to it with a new consideration.

2. **(A)** (no change)
   (B) However
   (C) By the way
   (D) Finally

The correct answer is (B). "However" indicates a contrasting idea—the prior sentence was about the challenges to opening a daycare business; this transition leads into urging the reader not to be intimidated by these challenges.

SUMMING IT UP

- A strong paragraph will contain the discussion or explanation of one main idea. A paragraph's opening sentence introduces this main idea, and its closing sentence helps summarize the information within the body of the paragraph. Transitional sentences smooth the connections between paragraphs.

- **Context** is the meaning of a portion of a passage in relation to the words and phrases around it. On the HiSET®, you will be asked to decide whether or not a sentence is relevant to the passage. Review the paragraph around it—while also keeping in mind the goal and purpose of the passage as a whole—to determine if the sentence should remain or go.

- Transitional words and phrases can both make a paragraph easier to read and change the meaning of a passage if they are used incorrectly. Recognize in a passage when transitional words are used between facts to tell how two concepts are related to one another.

Writing Conventions

chapter 6

OVERVIEW

- Verbs
- Pronoun forms
- Modifiers, comparatives, and superlatives
- Maintain grammatical agreement
- Recognize idiomatic usage
- Recognize and use correct capitalization, punctuation, and spelling
- Summing It Up

You can think of conventions as the ground rules to which writers and readers agree regarding grammar, mechanics, and sentence construction. Writers follow these rules so that their work is clear and accessible to readers. We'll use some grammatical terminology here only to be able to name what we're talking about, but the HiSET® Language Arts—Writing subtest won't ask you to know the names of verb tenses or grammatical forms. Instead, the test will ask you to use your understanding of writing conventions to revise writing into its clearest and best form. In this chapter, we'll cover the writing conventions the HiSET® will test you on and some of the ways those rules will appear on the test.

VERBS

Verbs tell you what is happening in a sentence:

Gina **walked.**

Jorge **ran.**

Diana **stood** still.

But they also give information about *when* an action occurs:

Jorge **runs.**

Jorge **ran.**

Jorge **will run.**

HiSET® writing questions won't ask you to know the names of verb forms, but some will ask you to know the correct forms for different situations.

Basic Verb Tenses

Tense Name	Examples	Use
Simple Present	I *walk*. Tanner *hopes*. We *wait*.	Actions happening now
Present Participle	The water *is running*. Diana and Amber *are jogging*.	Ongoing actions
Present Perfect	Jessie *has taken* many classes. I *have lived* here since 1991.	Actions that took place at an undefined point in the past; actions that started in the past and continue into the present
Simple Past	We *watched*. The leaves *fell*.	Completed past actions
Past Perfect	I *had wanted* to be a doctor until I watched a surgery.	Actions that took place in the past before another past action

The **future tense** is formed with the helping verb "will." **Helping verbs** carry information about tense, intention, and ability. Consider how these sentences are different:

Natalia **will run** for mayor.

Natalia **may run** for mayor.

Natalia **could have run** for mayor.

In the first sentence, Natalia's future candidacy is planned, or intended. In the second sentence, Natalia is able to run for mayor, but it's unknown whether she plans to. The third sentence conveys that, in the past, Natalia was able to run for mayor, but she did not.

"Will" is a helping verb that conveys future actions—"It will be my birthday tomorrow"—and intentions—"I will go out to dinner tomorrow night." Here are some helping verbs that convey other useful meanings:

Present/Past	Meaning	Example
will/would	intention	Dan said he would help me move the furniture.
can/could	ability	Elizabeth can handle the report by herself.
might/might have	possibility	I might have forgotten my keys at home.
should/should have	recommendation	You should have reminded me about my keys!
have to/had to	necessity	I had to call a locksmith last week.

The Subjunctive Mood

Although it looks like a new conjugation form, the **subjunctive** mood actually conveys information about intention, much like helping verbs do. Use the subjunctive to indicate that something is hoped for or that it is wished for but not true. In the subjunctive mood, use *were* in place of was:

> If Dennis **were** taller, those pants would fit him perfectly.

> If only salt water **were** potable, then droughts would be no problem.

Some verbs are notoriously tricky. These pairs are closely related, but they have distinct uses:

> lie vs. lay

> sit vs. set

> rise vs. raise

In each pair, the first verb is something that a subject does *for itself*—an **intransitive** verb—while the second is something that the subject does *to an object*—a **transitive** verb. You don't have to remember what these kinds of verbs are called, but you do need to remember how to use them:

> Before I **lie** down in my bed, I will **lay** down my pen, or else I'll get ink on my pillow.

> Let's **sit** down on these chairs, and **set** our cups on the table.

> When the sun **rises,** you should **raise** the curtains to let in the light.

Not only are these verbs tricky to keep straight, but they are also tricky to conjugate. Here's a guide, followed by some examples of the verbs in action:

Present	Past	Past Participle (use with *have*, *has*, *had*)
lie	lay	lain
lay	laid	laid
sit	sat	sat
set	set	set
rise	rose	risen
raise	raised	raised

I'm going to **lie** down in bed.

Kesha couldn't remember where she had **laid** down her map.

Margaret **sat** next to David.

Arthur **set** his cup down.

Dean wished he had **risen** earlier in the morning.

Calvin always **raised** his hand in class.

TIP

The *if* is a big clue that the subjunctive mood is called for, as is the implied negation of the wish. Salt water isn't actually potable, and Dennis is too short for those pants.

PRONOUN FORMS

Writing would be very awkward without pronouns. Here's an example of a writing sample that does *not* use this grammatical tool:

> Marissa told Steve that Marissa wanted Steve to check the mail because although Marissa and Steve were waiting for a letter, Marissa knew that Steve was forgetful, and Marissa worried Steve wouldn't remember the letter.

Pronouns are words that stand in for nouns:

> Marissa told Steve that she wanted **him** to check the mail because although **they** were expecting a letter, **she** knew that **he** was forgetful, and **she** worried **he** wouldn't remember **it**.

Both of those sentences are long, but the one that uses pronouns reads much more smoothly! Yet notice how the effective use of pronouns assumes that the reader has some necessary context—Marissa, Steve, and the letter are all named before they are referred to by pronouns. Proper pronoun use requires careful awareness of all of the information that pronouns convey.

Personal pronouns refer to people or things. The trickiest aspect of choosing the correct personal pronoun is differentiating between *subject* and *object*.

Subject	Object
I	me
you	you
he	him
she	her
it	it
we	us
they	them

The subject is the character doing the action; the object is the entity acted upon:

> He talked to me. (**He** is the subject; **me** is the object.)

> She gave the presentation to them. (**She** is the subject; **them** is the object.)

> You can join us here. (**You** is the subject; **us** is the object.)

Remember that even when there is more than one person receiving an action, the object is still the object:

> David gave the books to Raina and **me**.

> **She** and Marcos took the books to the library.

In the first sentence, David is the subject—he's doing the giving—and the phrase "Raina and me" is the object. In the second sentence, "she" and "Marcos" are both doing the taking—they, combined, are the subject.

Also keep in mind that in comparisons that use "than," you should always use the *subject* pronouns:

Claudia is taller than **I**.

"I" is not the object here. There's an implied verb following it: Claudia is taller than I *[am]*.

Serena can do as many pushups as **he**.

Serena can do as many pushups as he *[can]*.

Pronouns that don't refer to specific people or things are called **indefinite pronouns**. Some indefinite pronouns are either always singular or always plural.

Singular:

anyone, anybody, everyone, everybody, no one, nobody, someone, somebody, either, neither, each, one

Nobody is going to like that proposal

Each of the puppies was friendly.

Either book is a great gift.

Plural:

both, few, many, several

Both of those books are great gifts.

Both books are great gifts.

Other indefinite pronouns are singular or plural depending on what they refer to: all, any, most, none, or some.

Some of the water is contaminated.

Some of the samples are contaminated.

All of my ideas are fantastic.

All of my mind is focused.

Who, whom, what, that, and which are also pronouns. Who and whom refer to people. Use who for *subjects* and whom for *objects*:

Subject: *Who* do you think wants to drive?

Object: *Whom* are you looking for?

To ask questions about things that are not people, use "what" for both subjects and objects:

Subject: *What* is making that noise?

Object: *What* are you looking for?

Choosing between "that" and "which" can be difficult. Use "which" in clauses that are *not* crucial to the sentence—they're usually set off by commas:

The legislation, which was introduced last week, is up for a vote.

Otherwise, use "that":

The car that I wanted to buy was not available.

The TV show that I love got canceled.

To refer to a person, though, always use "who":

The waitress who was serving us disappeared before we got our check.

The waiter, who reminded me of my brother, was very friendly.

MODIFIERS, COMPARATIVES, AND SUPERLATIVES

Modifiers can be words (adjectives or adverbs) or phrases:

I bought a **blue** car.

I **hurriedly** bought a car.

I'm looking for a dress in **light pink.**

"Blue" is an adjective; it modifies "car."

"Hurriedly" is an adverb; it modifies "bought."

"Light" is an adverb; it modifies "pink." "Pink" is an adjective; it modifies "dress."

Make sure that you use adjectives to modify nouns and adverbs to modify verbs.

Incorrect: Jim runs fast.

Correct: Jim runs **quickly.**

The **comparative** form, often ending in *-er*, differentiates between two things or people: taller, smarter, shorter, faster, better. You can also use "more" or "less."

Danika's proposal is the **longer** of the two.

This recipe calls for **more** sugar than the other one.

The **superlative** form allows you to compare more than two things. These adjectives often end with *-est*: tallest, smartest, shortest, fastest, best. Instead of "more" or "less," here, use "most" or "least."

Don't necessarily buy the **cheapest** car you see.

We couldn't hire the **least** experienced applicant, no matter how friendly he was.

This is the **best** day of my life. (Assuming you've been alive for more than two days.)

Make sure that if you're using a comparative or superlative modifier, you don't also use more/less or most/least.

Incorrect: She has the most prettiest voice I've ever heard.

Correct: She has the **prettiest** voice I've ever heard.

Also correct: She has the **most mellifluous** voice I've ever heard.

Fewer vs. Less

"Fewer" concerns the number of items. "Less" has to do with amounts of uncountable things:

Shannon moved so her commute would require **fewer** transfers.

Abdul wanted to spend **less** time on the train.

For example, hours are countable, but the concept of "time" is measured as an amount:

Incorrect: They both wanted to spend **less** hours in transit.

Correct: They both wanted to spend **fewer** hours in transit.

Also correct: They both wanted to spend **less** time in transit.

Bad vs. Badly, Good vs. Well vs. Well

"Bad" is an adjective and "badly" is an adverb:

He's not a **bad** dog, he's just been treated **badly.**

"Well" is the adverb form of "good":

Marina had a **good** feeling about the job because she interviewed **well.**

However, "well" also has a function as an adjective, meaning healthy:

Clark went back to work once he was **well.**

Verb, pronoun, and modifier forms are an important foundation to your work on the HiSET® Writing test. Here's how these concepts may appear on the test:

TIP

Double comparisons don't add emphasis. They add redundancy.

Directions: The following two questions offer options for improvement for each underlined part. Select the answer choice for each that best improves the written passage.

The Apollo program consisted of eleven crewed missions, <u>six of whom landed</u>
1
on the moon. In previous space flights, astronauts <u>were orbiting</u> the Earth, but
2
in the Apollo program, 12 astronauts actually walked on the moon.

1. **(A)** (no change)
   (B) six of which landed
   (C) six of whom have landed
   (D) six of which have landed

The correct answer is (B). The pronoun in this selection refers to the missions, an inanimate entity, so it should be *which*. "Landed" is correct because the actions occurred in the past and are not ongoing.

2. **(A)** (no change)
   (B) was orbiting
   (C) they orbited
   (D) had orbited

The correct answer is (D). The action referred to happened in the past, prior to another past event (the Apollo program).

MAINTAIN GRAMMATICAL AGREEMENT

Grammar reflects meaning, and in order for meaning to be communicated, it has to be clear in a sentence. One way we make meaning clear is through agreement—ensuring that the elements of a sentence match up.

Subject/Verb Agreement

If the subject is singular, the verb must be singular. If the subject is plural, the verb must be plural.

Incorrect: Akeelah and I was walking to work.

Correct: Akeelah and I **were** walking to work.

"And" creates a plural subject. If two single subjects are joined by "or," the resulting compound subject is singular:

Correct: Either Danny or Sean **wants** to come to dinner.

Although Danny and Sean are both named, only one of them wants to come to dinner. But what if the components of the joined subject are plural?

Either the girls or the boys **were** responsible.

If one half of a compound subject is plural and the other half is singular, the verb should agree with the subject that's closest:

Either Victoria or the boys **were** responsible.

Either the boys or Victoria **was** responsible.

This gets trickier when clauses complicate our understanding of who exactly the subject is:

Incorrect: One of the job candidates are coming in for a second interview.

Although the plural word "candidates" comes right before the verb, it isn't actually the subject. "Of the job candidates" is a prepositional phrase. It's modifying "one." And who is coming? *One* is coming. One of what? One *of the job candidates*.

Correct: One of the job candidates **is** coming in for a second interview.

When the verb of a sentence comes before the subject—an inverted sentence—subject-verb agreement can be harder to correct instinctively. Make sure you identify the subject and then check if the verb agrees:

Incorrect: There's many reasons she might have turned down the job.

Correct: There **are** many reasons she might have turned down the job.

This example is particularly tricky because the verb is hidden in a contraction: "there's" instead of "there is." The contraction itself isn't incorrect, but it obscures the verb from our ears and eyes.

Pronoun/Antecedent Agreement

Pronouns need to match their antecedents—the words they replace—for grammatical correctness and so that readers understand what's going on. If a pronoun doesn't agree with its antecedent, readers may not understand what noun the pronoun is standing in for.

Incorrect: Kerry and Adella were late for her visit.

Correct: Kerry and Adella were late for **their** visit.

Remember that collective nouns like team or family are still singular:

Incorrect: The team were thrilled to win the game.

Correct: The team **was** thrilled to win the game.

Incorrect: The band play here every Tuesday.

Correct: The band **plays** here every Tuesday.

This gets more challenging with indefinite pronouns:

Incorrect: Each of the puppies wagged their tail.

"Each" is a singular indefinite pronoun, and it is the subject of this sentence. ("Of the puppies" is a prepositional phrase.) Since "each" is singular, the possessive pronoun that goes with tail needs to be singular.

Correct: Each of the puppies wagged **its** tail.

Also make sure that pronouns aren't a slippery slope to switching subjects as a sentence goes along:

If one wants to do well on the test, **he** should make sure to study.

"One" and "he" are both singular pronouns, but they're different and have different meanings. Be consistent with your pronoun choices.

Incorrect: Everyone has to keep an eye on their bags.

Correct: Everyone has to keep an eye on **his or her** bag.

"Everyone" is a singular pronoun. You can't switch to a plural possessive later on just to avoid gendered words. Even though "his or her" is wordy, it's the grammatically correct choice.

Let's put this understanding of agreement into practice as you'll see it on the day of the test:

Directions: The following questions offer options for improvement for each underlined part. Select the answer choice for each that best improves the written passage.

In the interest of cutting costs, we have

decided to eliminate the free coffee and

tea service from the office kitchen.

Many of you have told us that they
                              3

rarely take advantage of the office
3

coffee. There's so many great coffee
                        4

shops near the office, and we hope you'll
4

take advantage of them.

3. **(A)** (no change)
   (B) Many employees have told us that you rarely take advantage
   (C) Many of you have told us that you rarely take advantage
   (D) Many of you has told us that rarely taking advantage

The correct answer is (C). The pronouns in the original sentence, "you" and "they," do not agree. Only choice (C) corrects this issue without introducing additional errors.

4. **(A)** (no change)
   (B) There's so many great coffee shop
   (C) There are so many great coffee shop
   (D) There are so many great coffee shops

The correct answer is (D). "Shops" is plural, so the verb, "there are," needs to agree. Be careful to read each of the answer choices before making your selection. If you picked choice (C), you may have missed that the word "shop" appeared instead of "shops".

RECOGNIZE IDIOMATIC USAGE

Some writing conventions are just that: conventions. They don't follow set rules, but rather are just customs of English writing.

Many words have standard prepositions that go with them:

Incorrect: Tyrone is anxious of his test tomorrow.

Correct: Tyrone is anxious **about** his test tomorrow.

Familiarize yourself with these prepositional idioms so that you can recognize mistakes on test day.

a critic of	fond of
according to	grateful for (something)
afraid of	grateful to (someone)
agreed to	impressed with
anxious about	in a world where
apologize for (something)	inconsistent with
apologize to (someone)	interested in
attributed to	listening to
blame on	necessary to
capable of	planning to
complain about	popular with
conform to	protested against
congratulate on	provide for
consist of	regarded as
disintegrates into	suspicious of
evolved from	with regard to
far from	

Here are two questions you might see on HiSET® that ask you to recognize idiomatic usage:

Directions: The following questions offer options for improvement for each underlined part. Select the answer choice for each that best improves the written passage.

When I was growing up, my mother always seemed anxious <u>with</u> how I **5** would fit into the world. I attribute this to her own social discomfort. In a world where women were so often expected to be pleasant and polite, my mother was never regarded <u>as</u> proper. However, I'm **6** grateful to her for teaching me to be my own person, capable of living according to my own inner compass.

5. **(A)** (no change)
   (B) about
   (C) from
   (D) of

The correct answer is (B). "About" is the correct preposition for "anxious."

6. **(A)** (no change)
   (B) to
   (C) like
   (D) to be

The correct answer is (A). "Regarded as" is the correct idiomatic phrase.

RECOGNIZE AND USE CORRECT CAPITALIZATION, PUNCTUATION, AND SPELLING

Capitalization

There are three cases for capitalization:

1. the start of a sentence
2. a proper noun
3. the pronoun "I"

When you quote a sentence within a sentence, still capitalize:

She asked, "What time will you be home?"

Quotations aren't capitalized if they aren't full sentences, though:

She asked what he thought the "best practices" were for the industry.

The same applies for sentences and non-sentences in parentheses:

Marianne was fired for failing to complete projects (including one that lost the company a major account).

Marianne was fired for failing to complete projects. (One such failure lost the company a major account.)

Capitalize proper nouns, names, days of the week, months, countries, nationalities, religions, and publications:

Jenna, a Canadian author, wrote *Into the Darkness* last May. The novel, about a Jewish professor, will be published on Tuesday.

Capitalize titles, but not jobs:

President Ronald Reagan served as *president* for two terms.

Capitalize regions, but not directions:

She is from the Midwest.

Drive west for 20 miles.

Punctuation

Punctuation marks give readers crucial information about meaning.

Christian loves cooking, his dog, and spending time with his family.

Christian loves cooking his dog and spending time with his family.

That one comma makes a big difference!

TIP

If the title comes before a name, capitalize it. If not, then don't.

Here's a quick rundown of the most important punctuation marks:

Action	Punctuation
End a sentence	period (.)
Separate items in a list	comma (,) but if any list items have commas in them, use a semicolon (;)
Separate a modifying clause	comma (,) (Jerry, who lives upstairs, listens to a lot of salsa music.)
Introduce a list	colon (:)
Connect two independent clauses	semicolon (;) (One of the boys was crying; the other boy just looked on.) comma (,) with a conjunction (Jenny left the report on my desk, but she never proofread it.)
Indicate possession	apostrophe (')
Indicate a conjunction	apostrophe (') (It is → It's)

Apostrophes can be especially tricky, as their presence changes the meaning of a word:

It's vs. Its

Jennifer's vs. Jennifers

Possessive vs. Plural

Remember that a plural noun has an s on the end but no apostrophe. An apostrophe signals a possessive.

Jennifer's flowers are lovely.

To indicate the possessive form of a plural noun, put the apostrophe after the s:

Jennifer's flowers' stems are very strong.

Apostrophes also form contractions:

They are → They're

It is → It's

Who is → Who's

Spelling

The most important spelling mistakes are those than can impede a reader's understanding. In some cases, one small mistake can turn a word into an entirely different word with an entirely different meaning:

Ellie's favorite time is *mourning*.

Ellie's favorite time is *morning*.

Unless Ellie enjoys grief, the first sentence has a mistake. Familiarize yourself with common homonyms—different words that sound the same—so you can catch these mistakes on test day.

Accept	receive
Except	other than (preposition); exclude (verb)
Affect	influence (verb)
Effect	result or impact (noun)
All ready	fully prepared
Already	previously
Buy	purchase (verb)
By	near or through (preposition)
Every day	each day
Everyday	usually or generally
Hear	perceive sound (listen)
Here	in this place (adverb)
May be	might be
Maybe	perhaps
Morning	the first part of the day
Mourning	grieving
Passed	went by (verb, past tense)
Past	beyond or the time period that has already occurred
Than	(indicates comparison)
Then	(indicates sequence)
Their	(possessive pronoun for *they*)
There	(indicates location)
To	in the direction of (preposition)
Too	also (adverb)
Two	number

Now that we've gone over the rules for capitalization, punctuation, and spelling, here are a few questions to give you a sense of how these topics may come up on test day:

Directions: The following questions offer options for improvement for each underlined part. Select the answer choice for each that best improves the written passage.

When you enter the museum, the first thing you see is a grand staircase. <u>Some</u>
7
<u>think this staircase is ostentatious. I</u>
7
<u>think it's beautiful.</u> By the time you
7
arrive, <u>the museum is all ready busy</u>
8
and full of visitors. To the left and right, patrons buy their tickets.

7. How could you combine these sentences?
   (A) (They should not be combined.)
   (B) Some think this staircase is ostentatious, I think it's beautiful.
   (C) Some think this staircase is ostentatious; I think it's beautiful.
   (D) Some think this staircase is ostentatious; but I think it's beautiful.

The correct answer is (C). You can use a semicolon to join two independent clauses when their ideas are related. You can only use a comma to join independent clauses when a conjunction is also used.

8. **(A)** (No change)
   (B) the museum is already busy
   (C) the Museum is already busy
   (D) the museum is all ready busy

The correct answer is (B). "Museum" should only be capitalized when it appears in a name. "All ready" means prepared; "Already" means previously.

SUMMING IT UP

- **Verbs** tell you both what is happening in a sentence and when the action took place—consider the difference between *he runs* and *he ran* or *he will run* and *he has run*. **Helping verbs** carry information about tense, intention, and ability—some examples are will/would, can/could, might/might have, should/should have, and have to/had to. Use the **subjunctive** to indicate that something is hoped or wished for but not true—*If I were student council president, things would be different.*

- **Pronouns** are words that stand in for nouns to make sentences more concise and smooth. Subject pronouns (I, you, he, she, it, we, they) take the place of subjects that perform the action in a sentence; object pronouns (me, you, him, her, it, us, them) take the place of the entity in the sentence being acted upon.

- "That" and "which" are also pronouns. Use "which" in clauses that are *not* crucial to the sentence (a clause usually set apart by commas)—otherwise, use "that."

- Use **modifiers** to describe things—adjectives describe nouns and adverbs describe verbs. The **comparative** form (often ending in -*er*,) differentiates between two things or people; the **superlative** form (often ending in -*est*) compares more than two things.

- If the subject is singular, the verb must be singular. If the subject is plural, the verb must be plural—Belle *wants* to come to dinner, Belle and Joel *want* to come to dinner. Collective nouns (like team or family) are singular—The Silversteins *want* to eat pizza for dinner.

- Always capitalize the start of a sentence, a proper noun, the pronoun "I," days of the week, months, countries, nationalities, religions, and publications.

- Beware of apostrophe placement—a misplaced apostrophe can change the meaning of a word. For example: "it's" means *it is*, and is a contraction, while "its" is a possessive and shows ownership. A plural noun has an *s* on the end but no apostrophe. An apostrophe signals a possessive.

Language Facility

chapter 7

OVERVIEW

- Coordination and subordination
- Parallelism
- Modifier replacement
- Maintaining consistent verb tense
- Effective sentence combining
- Summing It Up

When you write, you make decisions about how to convey meaning through language. Chapter 6 covered the rules and conventions that make writing correct so that any reader can understand it. This chapter will go over the choices the HiSET® Language Arts—Writing subtest will ask you to make when using Standard Written English to convey a specific meaning.

COORDINATION AND SUBORDINATION

When the ideas of two sentences are closely related, you may want to combine them into one sentence to convey the relationship between these ideas. Coordination and subordination are two ways of combining sentences.

Coordinating conjunctions are the glue between the two clauses. The most common conjunctions are: and, but, for, or, nor, so, yet.

Use coordination when the two clauses that will make up your new sentence are of equal relationship. You can see here that the order of the clauses doesn't change the meaning of the new sentence:

I like to run. I like to dance.	I like to run and to dance. *or* I like to dance and to run.
Shelly liked children. Shelly didn't want a baby.	Shelly liked children, yet she didn't want a baby. *or* Shelly didn't want a baby, yet she liked children.

Use a comma before the coordinating conjunction if both clauses are independent—if each has a subject and verb. If you omit a verb for concision when you combine sentences, don't use a comma.

Two independent clauses: Mark looked at new TVs, but he didn't buy one.

Not two independent clauses: Mark looked at new TVs but didn't buy one.

Subordinating conjunctions allow you to combine two clauses in which one clause is *dependent*—it relies on the other clause for meaning.

Two independent clauses:

I ran to the store.

It was raining.

Subordination combines the clauses into one sentence and shows the relationship between the two ideas:

I ran to the store **because** it was raining.

Unlike in coordination, in subordination the meaning completely changes when you flip the order:

It was raining **because** I ran to the store.

Unless you are a wizard, that doesn't make sense!

Subordinating conjunctions include: after, although, as, as if, because, before, even if, even though, if, if only, rather than, since, that, though, unless, until, when, where, whereas, wherever, whether, which, and while.

You can also put the subordinate clause at the beginning of a sentence, followed by a comma:

Because it was raining, I ran to the store.

Here are a few more examples:

Alana decided to go for a walk because it was a beautiful day.
Because it was a beautiful day, Alana decided to go for a walk.

Meg is going to dance until the party is over.
Until the party is over, Meg is going to dance.

Bill takes pictures wherever he goes.
Wherever he goes, Bill takes pictures.

PARALLELISM

When words are grouped together in pairs or a list, make sure they are the same tense and part of speech:

Incorrect: Tanner likes running, dancing, and to ski.

Correct: Tanner likes **running**, **dancing**, and **skiing**.

Also correct: Tanner likes t**o run**, **dance**, and **ski**.

In the incorrect version, two of the list items are gerunds (*running* and *dancing*), but the third is in the infinitive (*to ski*).

Parallelism is important not only in lists, but also in sentences built on the "not only"/"but also" framework. If you have a "not only," you always need a "but also."

Incorrect: Miranda was not only a great singer but also danced well.

"A great singer" is an adjective and a noun; "danced well" is a verb and adverb. There is no parallelism here.

Correction: Miranda was not only **a great singer** but also **a lovely dancer.**

Also correct: Miranda not only **sang well,** but she also **danced beautifully.**

The important rule in parallel constructions is that all of the parallel items in a sentence match in format.

MODIFIER PLACEMENT

Modifiers should be placed as close to the words they are modifying as possible.

Have you ever seen a sign like this?

Please only throw recyclables into this bin.

Although you can infer the sign's meaning, this sentence's grammar implies that "only" modifies "throw," meaning that you should not just *put* recyclables into the bin, you need to *throw* them in.

What if the sign read like this?

Please throw recyclables only into this bin.

In this case, "only" could also be modifying "into this bin," meaning that the *only* place you should be throwing recyclables is into that specific bin. While that's probably true (you should not just throw your recyclables onto the floor or into a random garbage can), if the sign actually wants you to throw *nothing but* recyclables into the bin, it should say:

Please throw only recyclables into this bin.

"Only" is next to "recyclables," and so that's what it modifies. "Only recyclables" is what you should throw into the bin.

> **TIP**
>
> If you're listing verbs in the infinitive, make sure you're consistent with the "to": Tanner likes to run, to dance, and to ski. Tanner likes to run, dance, and ski. Both correct!

Placement is also important with modifying phrases. If a modifying phrase isn't adjacent to what it modifies, its meaning becomes muddled:

Sleeping soundly, Maria patted the baby's head.

The baby's the one sleeping, but the modifying phrase, "sleeping soundly," is adjacent to "Maria." Unless Maria's sleepwalking, the sentence should be corrected:

Maria patted the soundly sleeping baby's head.

That's a little wordy. Try saying "soundly sleeping baby" five times fast. In a case where simple rearrangement doesn't give you an elegant sentence, you may need to rephrase the sentence:

As the baby slept soundly, Maria patted his head.

Incorrect: Flying soundlessly, I watched the birds in the sky.

Correct: I watched the birds flying soundlessly in the sky.

Lastly, make sure that the noun being modified is present in the sentence:

Incorrect: While getting ready in the morning, my dog waits to be taken for a walk.

Correct: While I get ready in the morning, my dog waits to be taken for a walk.

Also correct: My dog waits to be taken for a walk while I get ready in the morning.

Here are some questions that will let you practice your understanding of subordination/coordination, parallelism, and modifier placement in test-style questions:

Directions: The following two questions offer options for improvement for each underlined part. Select the answer choice for each that best improves the written passage.

Ever since the Mason Street bike lane was proposed last March, debate on the topic has been vigorous. Mayor Greenspan has stayed out of the fray, but members of the town council have shown no such restraint. Councilwoman Viajes has been <u>meeting with bike</u> **1** <u>lane proponents, advocating for bike</u> **1** <u>lane infrastructure, and even</u> **1** <u>participated in a bike lane counter-</u> **1** <u>protest.</u> This is unacceptable. <u>Only</u> **1** **2** <u>elected officials should express their</u> **2** <u>opinions through their votes.</u> **2**

1. **(A)** (No change)
   (B) meeting with bike lane proponents, advocating for bike lane infrastructure, and even participating in a bike lane counter-protest.
   (C) met with bike lane proponents, advocating for bike lane infrastructure, and even participating in a bike lane counter-protest.
   (D) met with bike lane proponents, advocating for bike lane infrastructure, and even participated in a bike lane counter-protest.

The correct answer is (B). Only in this answer choice are the three verbs in the list (meeting, advocating, and participating) conjugated the same.

2. Before what word should "only" be placed?
   (A) (No change)
   (B) should
   (C) express
   (D) through

The correct answer is (D). Place modifiers as close as possible to the words they modify.

MAINTAINING CONSISTENT VERB TENSE

In complex sentences and stories, verb tense is crucial to the reader's understanding. Even correctly conjugated verbs can be wrong if they don't add up to a clear and correct narrative in context.

First of all, make sure that tense is consistent: if a story starts out in present tense, it should stay there. Mixing tenses will confuse your reader. Sometimes you won't have context that tells you whether something should be in past tense or present tense—always remember, the important thing then is to make your tense consistent.

> **Incorrect:** When Jake studies for tests, he got better grades.
>
> **Correct:** When Jake **studies** for tests, he **gets** better grades.
>
> **Also correct:** When Jake **studied** for tests, he **got** better grades.

The two correct sentences have different meanings. On the HiSET®, you might use context to decide whether past or present is appropriate, or the answer choices might only allow you to alter one of the verbs. In the second case, use the unalterable verb as your guide, and change what you can change to match it.

Here's an example of how the HiSET® Writing test may ask you to use these skills:

> **Directions:** The following two questions offer options for improvement for each underlined part. Select the answer choice for each that best improves the written passage.

Mariah <u>wants</u> to be a nurse until she
3

volunteered in an ER. From that experience, she learned that nursing

<u>isn't</u> for her, so she decided to study to
4

be a teacher instead.

3. **(A)** (No change)
   (B) wanted
   (C) will want
   (D) had wanted

The correct answer is (D). "Had wanted" indicates a past experience that ended after another past event. "Until" is a clue here—the first action happened for a while *until* the second action stopped or interrupted it.

4. **(A)** (No change)
   (B) wasn't
   (C) weren't
   (D) won't be

The correct answer is (A). Based on context, Mariah believes, in the present moment, that nursing is not the right career path for her.

EFFECTIVE SENTENCE COMBINING

The HiSET® Writing test will often ask you to combine sentences. You'll have to evaluate whether two sentences should be combined and determine the best way to do so.

A complete sentence has a subject and predicate. The **subject** is the entity performing the action of a sentence; the **predicate** is what the subject does.

The simplest subject/predicate pair is a subject and a verb:

Kanitha ran.

I hope.

Snow falls.

Subjects can be compound:

Naomi and Jack took a walk.

As can predicates:

Kathryn **went to the mall** and **bought three new dresses**.

In each sentence, though, there is one subject—the entity completing the action. (The two people in a compound subject complete the action together.) There may be multiple verbs in the predicate, but they are the actions taken by the subject or, in the case of nouns ("mall" and "dresses"), they are the objects of actions.

Before we continue to learn about building more complex sentences, let's look at what's *not* a sentence: a fragment. A **sentence fragment** lacks either a subject or predicate. It is an incomplete sentence and needs to be revised or combined with another sentence in order to be correct.

Some fragments are missing their subjects:

Leaving her coworkers scrambling to cover for her.

Ask yourself, Who is doing the action in this sentence? Who is leaving her coworkers? It's not stated in that fragment, so the fragment cannot stand alone.

Other fragments have no main verbs:

An excellent charity to consider for your donation.

What is an excellent charity? This fragment describes a thing, but there is no action. If you find a fragment, it needs to be revised into a complete sentence or connected to another sentence.

Dependent clauses, which were discussed earlier in this chapter, also need to be combined with another sentence. They are not complete ideas and cannot stand alone. The signal of a lonely dependent clause is a subordinating conjunction. If that conjunction isn't connecting two clauses, then you have a fragment:

Incorrect: Because the weather was bad.

Correct: We went to the movies because the weather was bad.

Also correct: Because the weather was bad, we went to the movies.

A sentence can start with a subordinating conjunction, but only if there are still two clauses.

Incorrect: Whenever you feel like leaving.

Correct: I'm happy to go whenever you feel like leaving.

Combining Sentences

When you encounter a fragment, you'll need to edit it to make it part of a complete sentence. However there are also cases where two complete, grammatically correct sentences should be combined in order to more clearly communicate their ideas. Transitions can clarify the relationships between ideas, which helps writing flow better:

Not great: William was a great employee. His raises didn't reflect this.

Much better: William was a great employee, but his raises didn't reflect this.

You can also use a semicolon to indicate that two independent clauses are closely related:

I am excited to work at MainCorp; I intend to stay there for many years.

Here's a test-style question that asks you to make decisions about combining sentences:

Directions: The following question offers options for improvement for the underlined part. Select the answer choice for each that best improves the written passage.

Until the birth of the American rail

system, timekeeping was a local

concern. Each city or town set its own

time by the rising and setting of the sun.

Travel between towns was so slow. This
5

never became a problem. The need for
5

consistent train schedules eventually

led to the establishment of time zones.

5. What is the best way to combine these sentences?
   - **(A)** (They should not be combined.)
   - **(B)** Travel between towns was so slow that this never became a problem.
   - **(C)** Travel between towns was so slow, however this never became a problem.
   - **(D)** Travel between towns was so slow, and this never became a problem.

The correct answer is (B). This choice correctly reflects the cause-and-effect relationship between slow travel and the lack of a problem.

SUMMING IT UP

- **Coordination** and **subordination** are two ways of combining sentences. Use coordinating conjunctions—and, but, for, or, nor, so, yet—when the two clauses that will make up your new sentence are of equal relationship. Subordinating conjunctions—after, although, as, as if, because, before, even if, even though, if, if only, rather than, since, that, though, unless, until, when, where, whereas, wherever, whether, which, and while—allow you to combine two clauses in which one clause is *dependent*, meaning it relies on the other clause for meaning.

- Always practice **parallelism** within sentences—when words are grouped together in pairs or a list, make sure they are all the same tense and part of speech. Do not switch formats in the middle of the sentence.

- Modifiers and modifying phrases should be directly next to the words they are describing. If a modifier is in a different part of the sentence, its meaning is unclear and it could be linked to an unrelated word.

- Consistent verb tense is important within a passage—if a story starts out in present tense, it should stay there. Even if you're not sure of the timing of a passage, always aim to keep tenses consistent.

- When you combine sentences, make sure they are complete and have a subject and predicate. The subject performs the action of a sentence and the **predicate** is what the subject does. A **sentence fragment** lacks either a subject *or* predicate.

Constructing an Essay

chapter 8

OVERVIEW

- What is tested on the HiSET® essay sub-test?
- Developing a strong HiSET® essay
- Developing a central claim or thesis
- Demonstrating strong writing conventions
- Effectively organizing your ideas
- Demonstrating excellent language facility
- Additional practice
- Summing It Up

WHAT IS TESTED ON THE HISET® ESSAY SUB-TEST?

The essay portion of the HiSET® exam provides you with the opportunity to demonstrate your ability to craft an effective written response to a specific issue. You'll encounter two pieces of writing on a specific subject; each piece will reflect a viewpoint on the subject and include various pieces of evidence to support the claims being made—expect the viewpoints in the two pieces to be in opposition to each other on some level.

You will then be asked to develop an essay that reflects your own position on the issue at hand, addresses the claims made in the two passages provided, and acknowledges and discusses points of view and ideas that may oppose your own.

Remember, you'll have a combined total of 120 minutes on test day to complete the entire Language Arts-Writing subtest—which includes both the 50-question multiple-choice section and the essay question. You'll have to work efficiently in order to make the most of your time on test day, which is why advance preparation is key!

The prompt and evidence-based passages that you'll encounter on test day can be based on a wide array of subjects, so your goal between now and test day should not be to become a master in as many subjects as possible—instead, you should focus on building and strengthening your ability to do the following:

- Develop a central position or claim that reflects your point of view on the subject covered in the essay prompt.

- Analyze and synthesize the information in the two evidence-based texts provided, noting the strengths and weaknesses of each one, to bolster your position.

- Organize your ideas effectively in your writing, to best serve the central claim of your essay

- Demonstrate a thorough understanding of the core tenets of English-language writing conventions.

In order to receive a passing score on the HiSET® exam, you'll need to get a minimum score of 2 out of 6. However, if you're setting your sights a bit higher and want to receive a top score on test day, you're going to have to craft an exemplary written response to the issue provided that effectively addresses all of the core content categories covered on the exam (we'll look closer at each of these in this chapter):

- Development of a Central Claim or Thesis

- Writing Conventions

- Organization of Ideas

- Language Facility

DEVELOPING A STRONG HISET® ESSAY

Let's take a look at an example that illustrates how these four core content categories are factored into your test day score, and why they are so essential for crafting a strong essay. Suppose you encounter the following prompt on test day:

Directions: This is a test of your writing skills. Your response will be scored based on:

- Development of a central position through explanation of supporting reasons and examples from passages and personal experience

- Language use, including varied word choice, varied sentence constructions, and appropriate voice

- Clarity and correctness of writing conventions

- Clear organization of ideas, including an introduction and conclusion, logical paragraphs, and effective transitions

Below you will find two passages in which the authors put forth differing perspectives on an issue of importance. Read both passages carefully, noting the strengths and weaknesses of each discussion. Then, you will write an essay in which you explain your own opinion on the issue.

You're delivering a presentation to your political science class on the idea of using the Internet to allow individuals to vote for the next president of the United States. While researching the subject, you came across the following excerpts.

Making the Most of Available Technology for Voting

1 Simply put, the Internet has revolutionized the way we live in a variety of fundamental ways. From keeping in touch with friends and family to buying the things we need and more, the potential that the Internet seems to possess for making our lives easier seems nearly limitless. We trust the Internet to handle a wide range of sensitive and personal tasks, including banking and making purchases both large and small, so why not allow individuals to vote using the Internet?

2 The United States has long wrestled with the question of why voter turnout for major elections—including the election for president of the United States—is so low. The Institute for Voter Turnout had recently released a policy assessment designed to address the issue of voter engagement. Among the key areas covered in the assessment is to make voting easier and less time- and labor-intensive. The assessment goes on to claim that individuals today are busier than ever before and deal with a wide variety of distractions and time drains—all of which means that efforts to engage individuals in a new process in their lives requires making it as easy and effortless as possible. At the conclusion of the assessment, the Institute for Voter Turnout asks key policy makers the following: "In a world where personal banking and stock trading exists at our fingertips, why shouldn't voting?"

3 A 2017 research survey was recently administered and published that indicated that adults of legal voting age were open to the idea of utilizing an online voting system, provided it was secure. A majority of those asked responded that if they were given a secure method of voting in major national elections online, they would take advantage of it, and be more likely to vote. Those who responded in the affirmative regarding implementing online voting also indicated that they think online voting would help stimulate and increase voter turnout overall, with the majority of responders claiming that "online voting would likely greatly enhance voter turnout."

4 Today, we trust the Internet to handle a wide array of highly sensitive and personal tasks. Why shouldn't we help level the playing field when it comes to voting for the president of the United States, and make it easier for all eligible adults to cast their votes?

Internet Voting: A Dangerous Path

1 The idea of making it easier for every single eligible adult in the United States to vote for the president is certainly a compelling one. After all, what form of truly representative democracy better approaches this ideal than a governing body that more fully reflects the will and choice of the voting populace? However, some ideas—like Internet voting—pose just as many risks as potential rewards, and are simply not ready for realistic implementation.

2 The Center for Voting Advocacy has recently released results of an opinion survey regarding the issue of Internet voting safety and security. This comprehensive survey captured representative opinions of voting-eligible individuals from all 50 states, across a wide cross-section of demographic categories. The study found that 64% of voting-eligible adults do not feel like Internet voting is safe enough right now for actual implementation. According to these individuals, the most popular reason why

they feel we are not ready for Internet voting is that they're afraid that "Internet voting is not safe from potential hackers." A few talented yet nefarious hackers can wreak havoc on our electoral system, and completely undermine its integrity.

3 Dr. Morton Pembroke, social psychologist and leading expert in the area of group dynamics, has studied this issue extensively and has recently published his findings. According to Dr. Pembroke, inviting the potential risk of fraud from hackers into our electoral system—one of America's most sacred and important institutions and individual forms of responsibility—would have no less effect than "a complete potential erosion of one of the key civic pillars in the United States." Furthermore, Dr. Pembroke provides the following warning: "Individual faith in government and entrenched systems of governmental power is already at an all-time low. We would be well advised as a nation not to allow anything to cause further erosion. Unless Internet voting can be guaranteed to be completely secure—and I'm not sure that that will ever be possible—it should not be seriously considered for use."

4 Prevailing popular opinion and the opinions of experts in the field should not only be taken into consideration, they should be wisely heeded in an effort to avoid allowing chaos and potential corruption into our most sacrosanct of institutions. New ideas, even potentially good ones, sink or swim by the risks they pose; Internet voting is simply too mush of a risk to implement at present.

Write an essay in which you explain your own position on the issue of whether or not the United States should allow Internet voting for presidential elections.

Be sure to use evidence from the passages provided as well as specific reasons and examples from your own experience and knowledge to support your position. Remember, every position exists within the context of a larger discussion of the issue, so your essay should, at minimum, acknowledge alternate and/or opposing ideas. When you have finished your essay, review your writing to check for correct spelling, punctuation, and grammar.

Okay, so now you know the task you're facing—you need to develop an essay that showcases your point of view on Internet voting for presidential elections. Where should you begin?

The best place to get started is to know exactly what the official essay readers will be looking for on test day when they read and evaluate your essay. Use the following checklist to make sure you're appropriately addressing each of the four main content categories that your writing will be graded on.

Development of a Central Claim or Thesis	Writing Conventions	Organization of Ideas	Language Facility
Does your essay present an effective and clearly discernible central point of view regarding the issue at hand?	Does your essay showcase proper English-language grammar?	Does your essay have a clear and introduction and conclusion, as well as body paragraphs?	Do you use varied and compelling vocabulary and make precise and sophisticated word choices?
Does your essay present ideas and evidence that support your claim?	Does your writing reflect a strong understanding of usage and mechanics?	Are your ideas presented in a logical order?	Are there a variety of engaging sentence structures?
Does your essay acknowledge and address opposing points of view?		Do you use transitions to effectively connect your ideas?	Does your writing strongly express your unique individual voice?
		Do you use paragraphs to properly organize your ideas?	

These are the questions you should ask yourself when you're developing your essay and evaluating its effectiveness.

We'll return to our sample essay prompt at the end of the chapter, where you'll have the opportunity to develop your own sample essay. But first, let's take a closer look at how to develop, organize, and express your ideas within the context of these core context areas—for great essay results!

DEVELOPING A CENTRAL CLAIM OR THESIS

When you're presented with the task of developing a piece of writing that reflects your point of view on a specific issue, you should always make your point of view as clear and as confident as possible. That may sound obvious, but you'd be surprised by how many people fail to do so when facing test pressure and a ticking clock on exam day.

The heart of your essay is your thesis, your central claim on the issue at hand. An essential element of completing the HiSET® exam is making sure your thesis responds to the prompt. A strong thesis not only stays on-topic, but it also takes a clear stance. After all, you'll be spending your whole essay proving and supporting the claim you make in your thesis. An off-topic essay will be severely penalized.

Let's look at an example. On test day, you might be asked to write an essay that states your opinion on whether or not a city should regulate nighttime entertainment in an effort to control noise pollution. You'll encounter two passages that take opposing viewpoints on this issue, with evidence that support both sides.

At the early planning stages of your essay response, you should craft your essay's central claim. Which of the following seems like a more effective claim to base your essay upon?

> **Claim #1:** Noise doesn't bother me at night, so I think it's ok for things to be noisy.
>
> **Claim #2:** I don't think cities should regulate nighttime entertainment in an effort to control noise pollution—prohibiting activities because they are noisy would too broadly harm vital elements of a city's cultural life and economy.

Claim #1 takes a very narrow and personal stance—just because you're okay with noise, does that make it a sound citywide policy? What about other factors beyond your personal preference? This is not a very solid foundation upon which to build an essay.

Claim #2 is a much better choice. It directly addresses the issue and presents a confident opinion, and also includes a firm rationale for the claim (the negative impact on a city's cultural life and economy).

Supporting Ideas

Now that you have a central claim, you can begin developing your essay. In order to convince your reader that your thesis is correct, you'll need strong supporting ideas. Your thesis summarizes your argument; your supporting ideas explain *why* your thesis is compelling.

A good approach at this stage would be to create a list of ideas that support your central claim. Take a few moments to brainstorm. Here are a few examples:

Central Claim: I don't think cities should regulate nighttime entertainment in an effort to control noise pollution—prohibiting activities because they are noisy would too broadly harm vital elements of a city's cultural life and economy.

Supporting Ideas:

- Urban nightlife is a major reason why people are attracted to cities, and contributes to a rich and varied culture.

- Nightlife helps to bolster and stimulate tourism and city economies.

Ideas like these should be incorporated into your writing in a logical and organized way (more on organization later). Remember, it's *essential* to provide concrete evidence to support your essay's central claim. Supporting ideas will help you structure the body paragraphs of your essay.

Evidence

Supporting ideas explain why your thesis is compelling, but you still need evidence and explanations to prove that your supporting ideas are strong. Each supporting idea must be backed up by evidence or examples in order for your essay to be truly effective.

Make sure you utilize the information in the passages in support of your perspective. Perhaps one of the two passages provided includes a survey that asks individuals if they are bothered by nighttime noise pollution in cities, and the results indicate that the vast majority of respondents are not—this may be something worth including in your essay.

Perhaps you have some personal experience with the issue at hand that supports your central position—if so, it may be a good idea to include such information. This can often be a powerful and poignant way to strengthen your argument.

Here's an example.

Supporting idea: Nightlife helps to bolster and stimulate tourism and city economies

Evidence:

- The recent rock concert at my city's midtown convention center drew a record attendance and attracted tourists from all over the world.

- The convention center that hosts nightly concerts is a major source of employment in my city.

Don't forget to bolster your essay's supporting ideas with sound evidence—the official essay readers on test day will be looking to make sure you do just that, and your score will reflect how well you do this.

Addressing Counterarguments

Remember, a high-scoring essay will also directly address possible counterarguments to your claim; therefore, it would be a good idea to create a list of counterarguments and defenses. For example:

- Counterargument: Loud noises from nightlife keep people awake at night.

- Defense: Other nighttime city noises, like traffic, will still remain and keep people awake at night, so cracking down on nighttime activities will not make cities completely quiet

- Remember the keys to developing an essay that presents and supports a strong central claim:

- It will include a clear and easily discernible primary point of view that directly relates to the issue at hand.

- It will include relevant ideas that firmly support your central claim.

- It will address possible counterarguments in a way that further strengthens your position.

Demonstrating Strong Writing Conventions

When developing your HiSET® essay, *how* you deliver your thoughts is just as important as what you have to say. This means that your writing has to reflect a strong understanding of the fundamentals of English-language writing conventions, including grammar, usage, and mechanics. Nothing takes the credibility away from a strong message than it being poorly written and full of errors.

We'll cover the fundamentals of strong writing conventions here; use this information, along with what you already know about the rules for good writing, and you'll be in great shape on test day.

Clauses

Just as you can't have a sentence without a subject and verb that express a complete thought, you can't have a sentence without clauses.

We'll let you in on a little secret: a subject and verb that express a complete thought is a clause. It's an independent clause, because it can stand on its own.

- **Independent clause:** *The vase falls.*

A clause that *can't* stand on its own, because it *does not* have its own subject and verb, is a **dependent** or **subordinate** clause.

- **Subordinate clause:** *from the table*

A subordinate clause *needs* to be paired with an independent clause to be part of a complete sentence, like this:

> *The vase falls from the table.*

Conjunctions

You may have noticed the important role that **conjunctions** play in various sentence structures. They are the words that connect clauses and phrases in sentences, and help writers clearly and effectively communicate sentences with multiple thoughts and ideas.

When a conjunction joins independent clauses of equal importance, it is known as a **coordinating conjunction.**

For example:

> *The brownies were fantastic but the cake was burnt.*

In this compound sentence, but is the coordinating conjunction. If you divide the sentence before and after the coordinating conjunction, you will still have two independent clauses of equal importance:

For example:

> *The brownies were fantastic.*
> *The cake was burnt.*

If a conjunction joins a subordinate clause to an independent clause, it is known as a **subordinating conjunction.**

The vacation that I didn't want to take was actually amazing.

In this sentence, the subordinate clause is that *I didn't want to take*, which is not a complete sentence on its own. The subordinating conjunction is *that*.

Fragments and Run-ons

Two of the most common sentence structure errors are **fragments** and **run-ons**. Make sure your writing is free of both of these errors—they can really hurt your essay score.

A **fragment** is a piece of a sentence, and is not complete on its own.

For example:

Racing through the woods.

Who or what was racing through the woods? We'll never know until we fix this sentence fragment. This sentence needs a subject, as follows:

The hungry squirrel was racing through the woods.

Mystery solved! The subject-verb pair *The hungry squirrel was* rescued this sentence from the confusing fragment heap.

Run-on sentences are the opposite of fragments, but they are just as incorrect. They are full of words, but their lack of coherent structure keeps them from expressing ideas clearly.

For example:

The hungry squirrel was racing through the woods, the warm spring afternoon.

This run-on sentence needs a preposition to join its first and second parts (that comma splice does not do the job on its own):

The hungry squirrel was racing through the woods during the warm spring afternoon.

Now it's a clearly expressed thought!

Modifiers

Modifiers such as **adjectives** and **adverbs**, and descriptive phrases and clauses need to be placed correctly in sentences. Otherwise, you can end up with some *very* bewildering thoughts.

Two common modifier issues that you can expect to encounter on the HiSET® are **misplaced modifiers** and **dangling modifiers**. Let's examine them more closely.

A **misplaced modifier** creates confusion because it's not placed next to the word it's supposed to modify.

For example:

Alice walked across the room because she didn't want to disturb her baby sister resting in the room below hers carefully.

In this sentence, the modifier *carefully* is not where it should be. In fact, its placement makes it seem as though *her baby sister* was resting carefully. How do you rest carefully? You have to be conscious and careful about where information is placed in sentences.

The adverb *carefully* would be put to better use modifying *walked*:

> *Alice walked carefully across the room because she didn't want to disturb her baby sister resting in the room below hers.*

Excellent! In this sentence, the modifier *carefully* is no longer misplaced.

Dangling modifiers are often more confusing than misplaced ones. They don't modify anything at all. Take a look at this sentence:

> *Excited about the trip, slept poorly last night.*

The modifier in this sentence is *Excited about the trip*. But there's a problem: we don't know exactly *who* was excited about the trip. This sentence's lack of a subject leaves the modifier dangling without anything to modify. A subject needs to be added to give the modifier something to do, as follows:

> *Excited about the trip, Frankie slept poorly last night.*

The addition of the subject *Frankie* gives the phrase *excited about the trip* something to modify.

Parallel Structure

Sentences with correct **parallel structure** have all of their parts moving cohesively and in the same tense and direction. You can't place a word or phrase that's going backward into the past alongside one that's moving into the future in the same group, for example. **Parallel structure** crumbles when groups of words combine different types of phrases, clauses, and parts of speech.

For example:

> *On Friday afternoon I will finish my homework, mow the lawn, and went to the movies.*

This sentence begins by describing things that are going to happen in the future—*On Friday afternoon* be precise. Everything is smooth until that final phrase: *went to the movies*. It's written in the *past tense*, which violates the parallel structure of a sentence that is otherwise written in the *future tense*. Let's take a look at a revised version of the sentence:

> *On Friday afternoon I will finish my homework, mow the lawn, and go to the movies.*

This version corrects the parallel structure by putting the phrase *went to the movies* into the future tense (*go to the movies*), where it belongs.

End-of-Sentence Punctuation

Every sentence must eventually come to an end, which means that the one form of punctuation you will always see in every complete sentence is end-of-sentence punctuation.

These are probably the very first punctuation marks you learned about:

- **The period (.):** Good for ending most declarative sentences.
- **The exclamation point (!):** Used for ending exclamations, which indicate extreme excitement.
- **The question mark (?):** Absolutely necessary for ending questions.

Commas

Let's continue with one of the most common forms of punctuation—and one that's commonly misused.

Some writers overuse **commas**, and using them without rhyme or reason can make your sentences awkward or confusing.

Here's an example of a sentence with way too many commas:

After, Jacob finished the final, exam he breathed, a huge sigh of relief stretched, his arms and smiled.

It's quite a mouthful, and it's a bit difficult to figure out what's happening. Let's take a look at the corrected version:

After Jacob finished the final exam he breathed a huge sigh of relief, stretched his arms, and smiled.

This version is much easier to follow!

Quotations

When quoting a complete phrase that someone said, **quotation marks** are needed and one or more commas are required to separate it from the rest of the sentence. See how the commas are used in these examples:

Bella declared, "That song was the best one I've heard all summer."

"That song was the best one I've heard all summer," Bella declared.

"That song," Bella declared, "was the best one I've heard all summer."

However, if that quotation includes end-of-sentence punctuation, a comma is not needed at the end of it.

For example:

"That song was the best one I've heard all summer!," Bella declared. (**Wrong!**)

"That song was the best one I've heard all summer!" Bella declared. (**Right!**)

Apostrophes and Possession

Apostrophes are most often used to indicate that a word is a contraction, or to show possession in a sentence.

The correct use of apostrophes in **contractions** mostly depends on placing the apostrophe in the right place within a word:

Ca'nt (**wrong!**)

Can't (**right!**)

You'll also need to recognize when a word that looks like a contraction is not a contraction:

it's (a contraction of *it is*)

its (the possessive form of *it*)

Using apostrophes in possessive words is a little trickier. For the most part, the apostrophe will be placed before the letter -*s*.

For example:

Diane's purse

However, if the possessive word ends with an *s*, the apostrophe belongs after the -*s*.

For example:

the cactus' needles

This rule is different when a specifically named person is doing the possessing. For people whose names end in *s*, an apostrophe and an extra *s* is required.

For example:

Cyrus's new skateboard

When more than one noun is doing the possessing, only the last noun in the pair or list needs an apostrophe.

For example:

Dorian and Ella's sleepover party

Colons

Colons are typically used to introduce a list or series of examples:

Jeremy bought everything he needed for his upcoming backpacking trip: a canteen, hiking boots, a sleeping bag, and a tent.

Colons are also used to offset and emphasize an example:

My favorite novel offers a powerful lesson: revenge is often unexpected.

They can also be placed after a salutation in a letter:

To whom it may concern:

And can be used to separate a title from a subtitle in a piece of work like a book or movie:

Space Voyager: The Sequel

However, colons should *not* be used to separate objects and verbs, or prepositions and objects:

Incorrect: *This new game is: boring.*

Incorrect: *Many ingredients taste great on pizza: pepperoni, mushroom, olives, and many others.*

Semicolons

Semicolons can be used in place of conjunctions in compound sentences, joining the independent clauses just as *and, or, but,* or *because* would:

For example:

I was terrified over the scary movie; I barely slept at all last night.

As previously mentioned, semicolons are also used in complex lists that contain items with commas, to keep all those commas from becoming confusing.

For example:

This anniversary cake only contains the tastiest ingredients: chocolate, which I bought at the gourmet store; raspberries, which I grew in my yard; and fresh vanilla, which I got from the best market in town.

Parentheses

Sometimes, a few extra details are needed to make a sentence as informative as it can be— but those details aren't always easy to cram into the natural flow of the sentence. In such cases, parentheses are in order. **Parentheses** are often used to enclose additional examples that tend to be a little less relevant to a sentence than the ones you'd place between dashes.

For example:

My coworker Doug Lane (who is retiring at the end of the year) is delivering a major presentation to the senior staff this afternoon.

Nouns

The subject of any sentence is always a **noun**: the **person**, **place**, or **thing** performing the action that the sentence describes.

The nice thing about nouns is that they really only have two general forms: singular and plural.

- The **singular** form is the most basic: *goose, bird, otter, lampshade, mango,* and *mushroom*—these are all nouns in their most basic singular form.

- Making a singular noun **plural** is often as simple as adding the letter s to the end (for example: *cat–cats*). Plural nouns only get tricky when they are *irregular*— hard-and-fast rules for creating irregular plural nouns are often tough to apply to a language as complicated as English. We can't simply say that you're *always* safe adding *-es* to the end of all nouns that end in *-o* to make them plural. For example, the plural of *avocado* is *avocados.*

Subject/Verb Agreement

Every complete sentence has a **subject** and a **verb**.

- The subject is the noun doing the action.

- The verb is the action that the subject is doing.

Simple, right? Actually, it can be—a sentence with just a subject and a verb can be really simple.

For example:

> *The wolf howls.*

That sentence only has three words, but it's still a complete sentence because it has a subject and a verb. Just as importantly, the subject and verb agree: the singular subject *wolf* agrees with the singular verb *howls*. (That's right: the verb is singular even though it ends with the letter *-s*.)

Determining whether or not subjects and verbs are in agreement can get a little more complicated in sentences with compound subjects.

For example:

> *The wolf and the coyote howl.*

Neither *wolf* nor *coyote* ends with an *s*, so they may not look plural, but they work together as a compound subject when joined with a conjunction (*and*). This means that they require a plural verb and, as you may have guessed, the plural verb does not end in an extra *-s*.

However, if the conjunction were *or* or *nor*, a singular verb would be required.

For example:

> *Neither the wolf nor the coyote howls.*

Once again, the compound subject and verb are in agreement.

Pronouns

Selecting appropriate pronouns, given the context of the sentences they will appear in, is another challenge you should be prepared to face on the exam.

Perspective will be a factor when figuring out the best way to use pronouns on test day. Let's look at a few essential rules:

- A **first person pronoun** (*I, me, we, us*) is necessary when a writer is referring to her or himself.

- A **second person pronoun** (*you*) is needed when the writer is addressing the reader.

- When the pronoun refers to a third person who is neither writing nor reading the passage, a **third person pronoun** (*she, he, her, him, they, them*) is needed.

Choosing the right pronoun can be tricky in sentences that pair them with nouns. Which of the following examples is correct?

Wesley and I went to the movies.

Wesley and me went to the movies.

In such cases, try removing the noun and saying the sentence with just the pronoun: *I went to the movies* (right!); *me went to the movie* (wrong!). Chances are, the wrong pronoun will now seem more obvious.

Verb Tense

Verbs are words that refer to action, and their **tense** indicates *when* that action happened. Past, present, and future are the most common tenses:

- Did the action already happen? If so, then the verb is in the **past tense**.

- Are you still waiting for the action to happen? If so, then the verb is in the **future tense**.

- **Present tense** indicates an action that is happening now.

Adjectives and Adverbs

As we've already established, the only *completely essential* elements of a sentence are its subject and verb.

For example:

The jaguar prowls.

Once again, this is a complete sentence. But is it a particularly *interesting* sentence? Writing a sentence with nothing but a subject and a verb is like making soup with nothing but water and tomatoes. Where are the other flavors, the words that give a sentence some unique and memorable character?

In a sentence, **adjectives** (words that describe nouns) and **adverbs** (words that describe verbs) add some extra sentence flavor. Think of them as the spices of a sentence.

Let's add some spice to our previous example:

The stealthy jaguar prowls silently in the tall grass.

Now there's a sentence that paints a more vivid picture! The adjective *stealthy* shows us that the jaguar may be tracking prey. The adverb *silently* shows us that the jaguar is likely a careful predator. It's certainly a more engaging sentence now.

We know there's *a lot* to know regarding writing conventions—but the more prepared you are, the more confident and ready you'll be when you're face-to-face with the essay prompt and begin writing on test day!

EFFECTIVELY ORGANIZING YOUR IDEAS

Just as important as the components of your argument—your strong central claim, supporting ideas, and evidence—is the organization of those components. Just like stories, essays have a clear beginning (introduction), middle (body paragraphs), and end (conclusion).

For the HiSET® exam, your introduction and conclusion should each be one paragraph long. Your body should be around three paragraphs, with a rough goal of having one strong supporting idea or counterargument per paragraph, along with relevant contextual evidence that strengthens your central claim.

Following this standard structure makes your essay accessible for your readers (who, in this case, are grading your test) and eliminates any time-consuming structural decision-making on test day. Less time spent making decisions means more time for brainstorming, writing, and proofreading.

In addition to following the rules of standard essay structure, you want to make sure your ideas are presented in a logical order. For example, if you have a supporting idea that builds off of another one, make sure to put them in the correct order. You also don't want to introduce any new ideas within your essay's conclusion.

When crafting your essay, you also want to make sure that your ideas transition effectively. Having awkward, abrupt, or confusing idea shifts in your writing can weaken your argument and cost you points on test day. Make sure your ideas flow smoothly and logically—both within and between your paragraphs.

Introduction

The introduction of your essay is your opportunity to make a strong and lasting impression on the essay readers.

Use your essay opening to grab the reader's attention, confidently introduce your perspective and central claim regarding the issue at hand, and explain why you think it's an important issue worth exploration.

A strong essay introduction can really keep readers interested in what you have to say. A weak introduction can be a challenge to overcome and can make it difficult for you to keep readers engaged.

Consider the following tools for starting your essay:

- A memorable and relevant quote

- A powerful emotional connection between you and the central issue of the essay prompt that explains why it's important to you

- An interesting question posed to your readers

Make every opportunity to introduce the central idea or thesis of your essay *as early as possible*. With limited time to craft your essay on test day, you should make readers aware of your main idea quickly, and allow yourself ample time to develop adequate and convincing support in the body of your essay.

A good tip for crafting the central claim of your essay is to rework the essay prompt, which will clearly indicate the issue at the heart of the essay task, working in your own thoughts on the subject.

Body

The body of your HiSET® essay should consist of around three paragraphs—one for each of your supporting ideas, with evidence and examples for each in its appropriate paragraph. A good approach is to open each paragraph with its main idea—like a mini-thesis for that paragraph—and then go on to explain and describe the examples that show the reasoning behind your ideas. Make sure you take advantage of relevant support from the passages provided on test day to strengthen and support your essay.

As you put paragraphs together, use effective transitions to help show your reader the connections between your ideas. Especially in the body of your essay, transitions between paragraphs give your writing a sense of flow, so that it doesn't feel like a list. Sequence words like *first*, *second*, and *last* can be useful, as well as transitions that signal continuation, like *first of all*, *furthermore*, and *additionally*, since all of your body paragraphs contribute to the same idea.

Don't forget to address opposing viewpoints in your essay, using relevant information from the two passages provided. A great argument always addresses and defends itself against counterarguments, and doing so in your HiSET® essay will only strengthen your written piece.

Conclusion

Just as important as a strong introduction is ending your essay with an unforgettable conclusion. Remember, you want to leave a positive and lasting impression in the minds of official HiSET® essay readers.

Your conclusion wraps up your argument and leaves the reader with a strong last impression. You also want to leave your reader feeling convinced that your viewpoint is a valid one, with the sense that they've read a compelling and cohesive argument. The conclusion is where you reinforce that takeaway.

Aside from restating your main idea, how can you make sure your conclusion is strong and effective? Make sure the conclusion of your essay does the following:

- Neatly ties up the ideas you've provided throughout your essay
- Reasserts the importance and value of your central position on the topic
- Includes relevant and insightful ideas for further exploration

Consider using the strategies mentioned earlier for creating a powerful introduction when developing your essay's conclusion: a memorable and relevant quote, an emotional personal connection or call to action that demonstrates your passion toward the main issue, or a provocative question can help you conclude on a high note.

DEMONSTRATING EXCELLENT LANGUAGE FACILITY

Beyond following the rules of grammar, usage, and mechanics, you can—and should—make key stylistic choices in how you express yourself in your writing, to make your essay more than correct—to make it engaging and really stand out.

Effectively communicating your ideas to readers in a compelling and sophisticated way requires demonstrating excellent language facility. This means asking yourself the following questions when evaluating your writing:

- Do you use a variety of engaging sentence structures?

- Do you use varied and compelling vocabulary and make precise and sophisticated word choices?

- Does your writing strongly express your unique individual voice?

Let's take a closer look at how to best utilize language facility to make your HiSET® essay shine!

Sentence Structure

Effective writing doesn't necessarily consist of lots of complicated or sophisticated sentences. Writing feels interesting when sentences are *varied*. Too much repetition of sentence structure—whether simple or complex—can feel repetitive and doesn't show much skill.

Be sure to vary your sentence structures in your HiSET® essay to keep your reader engaged. There are four different basic sentence structures:

- A **simple sentence** has only one independent clause:

    The faucet drips.

    The ceiling leaks.

- A **compound sentence** has two independent clauses that are typically joined in one of two ways:

1. With a **conjunction** (for example *if*, *and*, and *but*) to connect the clauses:

    The faucet drips and the ceiling leaks.

2. With a **semicolon**:

    The faucet drips; the ceiling leaks.

- A **complex sentence** has at least two independent clauses and one subordinate clause:

The faucet drips in the tub and the ceiling leaks.

- A **compound-complex sentence** has at least two independent clauses and at least two subordinate clauses:

    The faucet drips in the tub and the ceiling leaks on the floor.

    The faucet drips in the tub; the ceiling leaks on the floor.

Word Choices

The HiSET® essay is your chance to show that you have a strong vocabulary at your disposal. The right choice of words ensures that your ideas come through precisely as you mean them. Remember, when your word choices are exact and interesting, your sentences really pack an effective punch!

Whenever possible, try and avoid vague words, and replace them with more specific choices. Here's an example:

There was a loud noise.

What kind of noise was there? Look how much more information we can get from one word:

There was a loud *crash*.

There was a loud *bang*.

There was a loud *crack*.

There was a loud *thud*.

Here's another example. Instead of "My foot hurt," what about:

My foot *throbbed*.

My foot *burned*.

My foot *ached*.

Here you have three specific words with very different meanings.

Another signal for an opportunity to improve word choice is "very." Almost any time you use "very," you could be using a more interesting and more precise word:

The sand was *very hot*.

The sand was *scorching*.

I was very *tired*.

I was *exhausted*.

The room was *very quiet*.

The room was *hushed*.

The tree was *very old*.

The tree was *ancient*.

Swapping "very + adjective" for one precise adjective also makes your writing less wordy and more direct.

Expressing Your Unique Voice

When the official essay readers are reviewing your HiSET® essay, they're going to be checking to see if your essay has a unique voice—this means that it expresses who you are as a person, and what you believe in and stand for.

This is an important point—when you're deciding what point of view to take on the issue provided in the essay prompt, your best bet is *always* to be honest, instead of trying to respond in a way you think the essay readers will agree with or appreciate. Why? Because when you're being honest in your writing, your passion, beliefs, and voice are much more likely to shine through.

The essay readers will also be looking to see if your writing has a discernible and appropriate style and tone. What does this mean?

Whenever you're writing something, you should think about the audience, which will help guide the appropriate style and tone to use. For example, you shouldn't be using the same formal style and tone in a professional letter or technical academic journal article as you would in a casual email or friendly letter. For the HiSET® exam, you should seek to utilize the sort of confident tone typically used for a school-related project, not too casual or relaxed, and free from slang or exaggerated (and confusing!) abbreviations. Use the model essay in the practice section at the end of this chapter as a guide.

Here's the bottom line: When you're writing your HiSET® essay, following the rules of good essay construction, organization, and style will help ensure that your thoughts and ideas are being effectively communicated.

Additional Practice

Now it's your turn! Let's revisit our sample prompt from earlier in the chapter, take everything we've covered in this chapter, and develop an essay response.

After you finish, take a look at the given sample Score 6 essay as a model for what an ideal response might look like.

Directions: This is a test of your writing skills. Your response will be scored based on:

- Development of a central position through explanation of supporting reasons and examples from passages and personal experience

- Language use, including varied word choice, varied sentence constructions, and appropriate voice

- Clarity and correctness of writing conventions

- Clear organization of ideas, including an introduction and conclusion, logical paragraphs, and effective transitions

Below you will find two passages in which the authors put forth differing perspectives on an issue of importance. Read both passages carefully, noting the strengths and weaknesses of each discussion. Then, you will write an essay in which you explain your own opinion on the issue.

You're delivering a presentation to your political science class on the idea of using the Internet to allow individuals to vote for the next President of the United States. While researching the subject, you came across the following excerpts.

Making the Most of Available Technology for Voting

1 Simply put, the Internet has revolutionized the way we live in a variety of fundamental ways. From keeping in touch with friends and family to buying the things we need and more, the potential that the Internet seems to possess for making our lives easier seems nearly limitless. We trust the Internet to handle a wide range of sensitive and personal tasks, including banking and making purchases both large and small, so why not allow individuals to vote using the Internet?

2 The United States has long wrestled with the question of why voter turnout for major elections—including the election for president of the United States—is so low. The Institute for Voter Turnout had recently released a policy assessment designed to address the issue of voter engagement. Among the key areas covered in the assessment is to make voting easier and less time- and labor-intensive. The assessment goes on to claim that individuals today are busier than ever before and deal with a wide variety of distractions and time drains—all of which means that efforts to engage individuals in a new process in their lives requires making it as easy and effortless as possible. At the conclusion of the assessment, the Institute

for Voter Turnout asks key policy makers the following: "In a world where personal banking and stock trading exists at our fingertips, why shouldn't voting?"

3 A 2017 research survey was recently administered and published that indicated that adults of legal voting age were open to the idea of utilizing an online voting system, provided it was secure. A majority of those asked responded that if they were given a secure method of voting in major national elections online, they would take advantage of it, and be more likely to vote. Those who responded in the affirmative regarding implementing online voting also indicated that they think online voting would help stimulate and increase voter turnout overall, with the majority of responders claiming that "online voting would likely greatly enhance voter turnout."

4 Today, we trust the Internet to handle a wide array of highly sensitive and personal tasks. Why shouldn't we help level the playing field when it comes to voting for the president of the United States, and make it easier for all eligible adults to cast their votes?

Internet Voting: A Dangerous Path

1 The idea of making it easier for every single eligible adult in the United States to vote for the president is certainly a compelling one. After all, what form of truly representative democracy better approaches this ideal than a governing body that more fully reflects the will and choice of the voting populace? However, some ideas—like Internet voting—pose just as many risks as potential rewards, and are simply not ready for realistic implementation.

2 The Center for Voting Advocacy has recently released results of an opinion survey regarding the issue of Internet voting safety and security. This comprehensive survey captured representative opinions of voting-eligible individuals from all 50 states, across a wide cross-section of demographic categories. The study found that 64% of voting-eligible adults do not feel like Internet voting is safe enough right now for actual implementation. According to these individuals, the most popular reason why they feel we are not ready for Internet voting is that they're afraid that "Internet voting is not safe from potential hackers." A few talented yet nefarious hackers can wreak havoc on our electoral system, and completely undermine its integrity.

3 Dr. Morton Pembroke, social psychologist and leading expert in the area of group dynamics, has studied this issue extensively and has recently published his findings. According to Dr. Pembroke, inviting the potential risk of fraud from hackers into our electoral system—one of America's most sacred and important institutions and individual forms of responsibility—would have no less effect than "a complete potential erosion of one of the key civic pillars in the United States." Furthermore, Dr. Pembroke provides the following warning: "Individual faith in government and entrenched systems of governmental power is already at an all-time low. We would be well advised as a nation not to allow anything to cause further erosion. Unless Internet voting can be guaranteed to be completely secure—and I'm not sure that that will ever be possible—it should not be seriously considered for use."

4 Prevailing popular opinion and the opinions of experts in the field should not only be taken into consideration, they should be wisely heeded in an effort to avoid allowing chaos and potential corruption into our most sacrosanct of institutions. New ideas, even potentially good ones, sink or swim by the risks they pose; Internet voting is simply too much of a risk to implement at present.

Write an essay in which you explain your own position on the issue of whether or not the United States should allow Internet voting for presidential elections.

Be sure to use evidence from the passages provided as well as specific reasons and examples from your own experience and knowledge to support your position. Remember, every position exists within the context of a larger discussion of the issue, so your essay should, at minimum, acknowledge alternate and/or opposing ideas. When you have finished your essay, review your writing to check for correct spelling, punctuation, and grammar.

_____

_____

_____

_____

_____

_____

_____

_____

_____

_____

_____

_____

_____

_____

Sample Score 6 Essay

Of course your essay will vary from this one, but use it as a guide for evaluating your own work. If possible, find someone with excellent writing skills—a parent, peer, or teacher perhaps—and ask them to read and evaluate your essay and provide you with helpful feedback.

Sample Essay (Score 6):

In a free and democratic country, there is no more important civic responsibility than casting one's vote for who is elected to lead the nation forward as its president. Unfortunately, in the United States, the process isn't equal for everyone. Yes, every adult of legal age and eligibility has the opportunity to cast a vote every four years in their state of legal residence—however, one's life circumstances can greatly impact how easy and realistic it is to go to his or her designated polling center and actually vote. An Internet-enabled presidential election system that takes full advantage of the technological advances that the United States has witnessed in recent decades will help make voting easier and fairer for everyone. It will also help address the problem of low voter engagement and turnout.

The reasons why people may have difficulty voting under our current system are many and varied. Some people have overwhelmingly busy lives that include work conflicts and family obligations. Why shouldn't our modern, technologically advanced nation take advantage of the ease and convenience of the Internet to make voting easier for these people, especially if there's popular support for doing so, based on the 2017 policy assessment and survey performed by the Institute for Voter Turnout?

Furthermore, some individuals have mobility limitations and limited or no access to feasible transportation, which may make getting to their designated polling centers extremely difficult. Rather than having their voices go unheard when it's time to select our next president, shouldn't we take every available opportunity to make voting easy and quick for everyone?

Some people may argue that the Internet is far from a completely safe and secure environment, which may pose a threat to the integrity of our electoral process. However, we trust the Internet for a variety of personal and highly sensitive tasks, like banking and shopping. If we can trust the Internet with our life savings and credit card information, why can't an advanced, technologically progressive country like the United States build a secure online voting system that we can trust?

The United States was built upon a foundation of equality, reason, and justice for all of its citizens. Fears of security regarding Internet voting aside, isn't having people who find it difficult to get out to vote feeling disconnected and forgotten by the very elected representatives who pledge to support them the greatest danger of all? What greater threat is there to a free democracy than a disengaged and disenfranchised populace?

The makers of the HiSET® exam recognize how important good writing skills are—both in the classroom and in the world of work—and the test is designed to make sure your skills are in good shape. Be sure to use all of the information in this chapter to build your writing skills, and to get confident and prepared for test day!

SUMMING IT UP

- The essay portion of the HiSET® exam provides you with the opportunity to demonstrate your ability to craft an effective written response to a specific issue.

- The prompt issue and evidence-based passages that you'll encounter on test day can be based on a wide array of subjects, so your goal between now and test day should *not* be to become a master in as many subjects as possible—instead, you should focus on building and strengthening your ability to:

  ○ Develop a central position or claim that reflects your point of view on the subject covered in the essay prompt.

  ○ Analyze and synthesize the information in the two evidence-based texts provided, noting the strengths and weaknesses of each one, to bolster your position.

  ○ Organize your ideas effectively in your writing, to best serve the central claim of your essay.

  ○ Demonstrate a thorough understanding of the core tenets of English-language writing conventions.

- In order to receive a passing score on the HiSET® exam, you'll need to get a minimum score of 2 out of 6.

- The core content categories covered on the exam are as follows:

  ○ **Development of a Central Claim or Thesis**

    □ Does your essay present an effective and clearly discernible central point of view regarding the issue at hand?

    □ Does your essay present ideas and evidence that support your claim?

    □ Does your essay acknowledge and address opposing points of view?

  ○ **Writing Conventions**

    □ Does your essay showcase proper English-language grammar?

    □ Does your writing reflect a strong understanding of usage and mechanics?

    □ Organization of Ideas

    □ Does your essay have a clear and introduction and conclusion, as well as body paragraphs?

    □ Are your ideas presented in a logical order?

    □ Do you use transitions to effectively connect your ideas?

    □ Do you use paragraphs to properly organize your ideas?

  ○ **Language Facility**

    □ Do you use varied and compelling vocabulary and make precise and sophisticated word choices?

    □ Are there a variety of engaging sentence structures?

    □ Does your writing strongly express your unique individual voice?

- Use specific words to get your point clearly across. For example, instead of, "There was a loud noise," you could write "There was a loud crash," for a more interesting and specific image.

- Although you don't need to be excessively formal in your essay, you shouldn't be too casual, either (For example, don't write something like "I gotta believe …."—write "I have to believe ….").

- Your introduction introduces the topic of your essay, hooks the reader's attention, and states your thesis. Your conclusion wraps up your argument, leaving the reader with a strong final impression. Your body should consist of three paragraphs—one for each of your three supporting ideas, with evidence and examples for each in its paragraph. Open each paragraph with its main idea, and then go on to explain and describe the examples that show the reasoning behind your ideas.

- Vary your sentence structure to keep your essay interesting and the reader engaged. Switch around your sentence length, and include simple, compound, and complex sentences in each paragraph. After you finish your essay, read through it again, note places that can use more sentence variety, and edit accordingly.

PART IV

MATHEMATICS

Numbers and Operations on Numbers

chapter 9

OVERVIEW

- **Properties of real numbers**
- **Absolute value and ordering**
- **Exponents and exponent rules**
- **Radicals**
- **Estimation with real numbers**
- **Ratios and proportions**
- **Percents**
- **Vectors and matrices**
- **Summing It Up**

The HiSET® Mathematics subtest uses multiple-choice questions to test your knowledge in four distinct categories: Numbers and Operations on Numbers; Measurement and Geometry; Data Analysis, Probability, and Statistics; and Algebraic Concepts. This section of the book reviews the main topics in each of these categories by gathering useful formulas and illustrations, highlighting common errors, and working through sample test questions for each topic. Working carefully through this material will help you master the topics most commonly assessed on the HiSET® exam.

The basics of arithmetic are built into your everyday life. In fact, you likely perform numerous computations (such as calculating tips, sale discounts, or recipe modifications) each day without really thinking about the number properties behind your calculations. This chapter will review number basics that are behind all mathematics. You will need to master these skills and rules in order to answer all levels of math questions on the HiSET® exam.

PROPERTIES OF REAL NUMBERS

You learned about the real number system in stages throughout elementary school, starting with the **natural numbers.** The natural numbers are also known as the "counting numbers"—1, 2, 3, 4, and so on. When two or more natural numbers are multiplied, the result is called a **product,** and each number being multiplied is a **factor**. We also say that a natural number is a multiple of each of its factors. For instance, in the expression $2 \times 3 \times 7 = 42$, 42 is the product and 2, 3, and 7 are factors of 42. We say 42 is a **multiple** of 2, 3, and 7.

A natural number other than 1 is **prime** if it can only be written as a product of itself and 1; otherwise, a number is called **composite.** For instance, 3, 11, 29, and 71 are all prime, but 24 is composite because $24 = 4 \times 6$.

Every composite number can be written as a product of only prime numbers called the **prime factorization** of the number. For instance, $90 = 2 \times 3 \times 3 \times 5$. This product can be written more succinctly as $90 = 2 \times 3^2 \times 5$, where we have used an **exponent** on 3. This shorthand notation works for any natural number that occurs any number of times. We will discuss exponents later on in the chapter.

The following divisibility rules are useful when determining the factors of a natural number:

> **TIP**
>
> For instance, 1,245 is divisible by 3 because the digit sum $(1 + 2 + 4 + 5 = 12)$ is divisible by 3.

Natural Number	A Natural Number n Is Divisible by the Number in the Left Column, If ...
2	The number n ends in 0, 2, 4, 6, or 8.
3	The digit sum* of n is divisible by 3.
4	The last two numbers of n, taken as a number in and of itself, is divisible by 4.
5	The number n ends in 0 or 5.
6	The number n is divisible by both 2 and 3.
9	The digit sum of n is divisible by 9.
10	The number n ends in 0.

The digit sum is the sum of all digits in the numeral n.

The **greatest common factor (GCF)** of two natural numbers x and y is the *largest* natural number that is a factor of both x and y, while the **least common multiple (LCM)** of x and y is the *smallest* natural number that is a multiple of both x and y. For instance, the GCF of 18 and 24 is 6, while the LCM is 72.

1. Which of the following statements is FALSE?

   (A) The greatest common factor of 5 and 20 is 5.

   (B) 100 is a multiple of 5.

   (C) 40 divides 120.

   (D) The least common multiple of 10 and 20 is 40.

   (E) 5 is a factor or 125.

The correct answer is (D). Knowing the terminology and being able to distinguish the different terms is an important skill to master. While it is true that 40 is a multiple of both 10 and 20, it is not the *least* common multiple; 20 is the least common multiple.

Integers

The set of integers is comprised of the natural numbers, their negatives, and 0. We write this as the set $\{..., -3, -2, -1, 0, 1, 2, 3, ...\}$. Arithmetic involving integers is the same as for natural numbers, but you must be careful with negative signs. The following rules and terminology are useful when working with integers:

1.	$-(-a) = a$, for any integer a.
2.	$a - (-b) = a + b$, for any integers a, b.
3.	An integer is *even* if it is a multiple of 2.
4.	An integer is *odd* if it is not a multiple of 2.
5.	Sums of positive integers are positive.
6.	Sums of negative integers are negative.
7.	A product of two negative integers is positive.
8.	A product of one positive and one negative integer is negative.

A **rational number** is a quotient of two integers, denoted by $\frac{a}{b}$, where $b \neq 0$.

The top number is called the **numerator,** and the bottom number is called the **denominator.** Such a fraction is simplified, or in reduced form, if a and b do not share common factors. If $a \neq 0$, the **reciprocal** of $\frac{a}{b}$ can be computed by flipping the fraction over to get $\frac{b}{a}$.

The following table features the rules of fractional arithmetic:

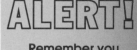

ALERT!

Remember you cannot divide by 0!

Arithmetic Operation	Rule (in Symbols)	Interpretation
1. Sum/Difference (same denominator)	$\frac{a}{b} \pm \frac{c}{b} = \frac{a \pm c}{b}$	When fractions have the same denominator, just add/subtract the numerators.
2. Sum/Difference (different denominators)	$\frac{a}{b} \pm \frac{c}{d} = \frac{ad \pm cb}{bd}$	When fractions have different denominators, first get a common denominator. Apply it to the fractions, and then add the numerators.
3. Multiply by −1	$-\frac{a}{b} = \frac{-a}{b} = \frac{a}{-b}$	When multiplying a fraction by −1, you can multiply either the numerator or denominator by −1, but NOT both.
4. Product	$\frac{a}{b} \times \frac{c}{d} = \frac{ac}{bd}$	When multiplying two fractions, you can simply multiply their numerators and their denominators.
5. Quotient	$\frac{a}{b} \div \frac{c}{d} = \frac{a}{b} \times \frac{d}{c} = \frac{ad}{bc}$ $\frac{\frac{a}{b}}{\frac{c}{d}}$ means $\frac{a}{b} \div \frac{c}{d}$	When dividing two fractions, convert to a multiplication problem.

When performing
arithmetic
operations involving
fractions, simplifying
all fractions *first*
will lead to smaller
numbers that are
easier to work with.

The following are some common errors when working with fractions:

Statement	Interpretation	Example
$\dfrac{a}{b} + \dfrac{c}{d} \neq \dfrac{a+c}{b+d}$	When adding fractions, you do not simply add the numerators and denominators. You must first get a common denominator.	$\dfrac{1}{2} + \dfrac{1}{2} \neq \dfrac{1+1}{2+2}$ $= 1 \qquad \dfrac{2}{4} = \dfrac{1}{2}$
$\dfrac{a}{b+c} \neq \dfrac{a}{b} + \dfrac{a}{c}$	You cannot pull a fraction apart as a sum of two fractions when the sum occurs in the denominator.	$\dfrac{1}{2+2} \neq \dfrac{1}{2} + \dfrac{1}{2}$ $= \dfrac{1}{4} \qquad = 1$
$\dfrac{a}{a+b} \neq \dfrac{\cancel{a}}{\cancel{a}+b}$	You cannot cancel *terms* in the numerator and denominator. You can only cancel *factors*.	$\dfrac{4}{4+8} \neq \dfrac{\cancel{4}}{\cancel{4}+8}$ $= \dfrac{1}{3} \qquad = \dfrac{1}{8}$

Decimal Operations

All rational numbers can be converted into decimals by dividing their numerators by their denominators. The arithmetic of decimals is the same as the arithmetic of natural numbers, with the one additional task of correctly positioning the decimal point. The following are some rules of thumb to apply when working with decimals:

- When *adding or subtracting decimals*, line up the decimal points and add or subtract as you would natural numbers, keeping the decimal point in the same position.

- When *multiplying* decimals, multiply the numbers as you would natural numbers, and to determine the position of the decimal point, count the number of digits present after the decimal point in all numbers being multiplied and move that many steps from the right of the product and put the decimal point.

Any decimal that neither repeats nor terminates is said to be **irrational.** Some common irrational numbers are $\sqrt{2}$, π, and e.

Property Names

The following properties apply for *all* real numbers a, b, and c:

Property Name	Rule (in Symbols)	Interpretation
Commutative	$a + b = b + a$ $a \times b = b \times a$	The order in which real numbers are added or multiplied is not relevant.
Associative	$(a + b) + c = a + (b + c)$ $(a \times b) \times c = a \times (b \times c)$	The manner in which terms of a sum or a product comprised of more than two terms are grouped is not relevant.

Distributive	$a \times (b + c) = a \times b + a \times c$	To multiply a sum by a real number, multiply each term of the sum by the number and add the results.
FOIL	$(a + b) \times (c + d) = a \times c + a \times d + b \times c + b \times d$	This follows from using the distributive property twice. The acronym FOIL means "First, Outer, Inner, Last", and signifies all combinations of terms to be multiplied.
Zero Factor Property	If $a \times b = 0$, then either $a = 0$ or $b = 0$, or both	If a product of real numbers is zero, then at least one of the factors must be zero.

Often, you need to simplify an arithmetic expression involving all types of numbers and operations. In order to do so, you must use the following rules that tell us the **order of operations**:

- **Step 1:** Simplify all expressions contained within parentheses.

- **Step 2:** Simplify all expressions involving exponents.

- **Step 3:** Perform all multiplication and division as it arises from left to right.

- **Step 4:** Perform all addition and subtraction as it arises from left to right.

- If there are multiple groupings, apply the same steps *within* each grouping.

2. Simplify the following: $\frac{1}{2} - \frac{3}{5}\left(\frac{1}{6} - \frac{2}{3}\right)$

   (A) $\frac{1}{20}$

   (B) $\frac{4}{5}$

   (C) $\frac{1}{5}$

   (D) $\frac{1}{10}$

   (E) $-\frac{1}{5}$

The correct answer is choice (B). Applying the order of operations, we simplify the quantity within the parentheses first by getting a common denominator, namely 6. We then multiply that result by the fraction in front of the parentheses, keeping in mind that the product of two negative rational numbers is positive. Finally, we simplify the resulting sum and simplify:

$$\frac{1}{2} - \frac{3}{5}\left(\frac{1}{6} - \frac{2}{3}\right) = \frac{1}{2} - \frac{3}{5}\left(\frac{1}{6} - \frac{4}{6}\right) = \frac{1}{2} - \frac{3}{5}\left(-\frac{3}{6}\right) = \frac{1}{2} + \frac{3}{5} \times \frac{3}{6} = \frac{1}{2} + \frac{3}{10} = \frac{5}{10} + \frac{3}{10} = \frac{8}{10} = \frac{4}{5}$$

ABSOLUTE VALUE AND ORDERING

The **real number line** is a convenient way of gauging the relative position of real numbers with respect to 0. Notice that the integers 5 and –5 are both 5 units away from 0, even though they occur on either side of 0.

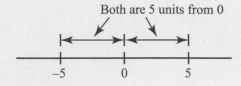

Both are 5 units from 0

For any real number a, the **absolute value** of a, denoted $|a|$, measures the distance between a and 0. Since distance is a non-negative quantity, this definition works for integers, rational numbers, and irrational numbers alike. For instance, $|6| = 6$ and $|-6| = 6$. Often, we are interested in computing the *distance* between two real numbers p and q. This is interpreted as the length of the segment on the number line joining p and q, and is computed as $|p - q|$.

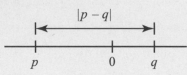

The following are some useful properties of absolute value:

Property (in symbols)	Property (in words)
1. $|a| = b$, whenever $a = b$ or $-a = b$	The real numbers b and $-b$ are both $|b|$ units from the origin.
2. $|a \times b| = |a| \times |b|$	The absolute value of a product is the product of the absolute values.
3. $\left|\dfrac{a}{b}\right| = \dfrac{|a|}{|b|}$, whenever $b \neq 0$	The absolute value of a quotient is the quotient of the absolute values.
4. In general, $|a + b| \neq |a| + |b|$	In general, the absolute value of a sum does not equal the sum of the absolute values.

3. Simplify the following expression: $|-3 - 5^2|$
   - **(A)** 7
   - **(B)** 13
   - **(C)** 22
   - **(D)** 28
   - **(E)** 64

The correct answer is (D). Don't forget about the order of operations! Here, we first evaluate the term with the exponent, then simplify the resulting expression, and finally take the absolute value:

$$|-3 - 5^2| = |-3 - 25| = |-28| = 28$$

Ordering

What does it mean for a real number p to be *less than* another real number q, written $p < q$? Pictorially, q would lie further to the right along the real number line than p, as shown below:

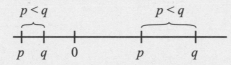

We also say that q is *greater than* p: $2 \leq 3.112$, $\pi \geq 3.11$

The following are some important properties involving inequalities of real numbers:

Rule (in symbols)	Rule (in words)
1. If $0 < a < b$, then $\frac{1}{b} < \frac{1}{a}$.	If a and b are both positive and a is less than b, then the reverse inequality is true of the reciprocals of a and b.
2. If $a > 1$, then $a^2 > a$.	If a real number is greater than 1, then it is less than its square. (Said differently, squaring a number greater than 1 results in a larger number.)
3. If $0 < a < 1$, then $a^2 < a$.	If a real number is between 0 and 1, then it is greater than its square. (Said differently, squaring a number between 0 and 1 results in a smaller number.)
4. If $0 < a < b$, then $-b < -a < 0$.	If a and b are both positive and a is less than b, then the reverse inequality is true of the negatives of a and b.
5. If $a < b$ and $c < d$, then $a + c < b + d$.	You can add the left sides and right sides of inequalities involving the same sign, and the sums satisfy the same inequality.

4. Fill in the blank with the correct value: $-\left(\dfrac{1}{5}\right)^2 \geq$ _____.

    (A) $-\dfrac{1}{5}$

    (B) $-\dfrac{1}{125}$

    (C) $\dfrac{1}{25}$

    (D) $\dfrac{1}{10}$

    (E) $\dfrac{1}{5}$

The correct answer is (A). The most direct way to answer this question is to simplify the quantity and compare it to each of the given values. Using the order of operations, we see that $-\left(\dfrac{1}{5}\right)^2 = -\dfrac{1}{25}$. This value is further to the right on the number line than $-\dfrac{1}{5}$.

EXPONENTS AND EXPONENT RULES

When b and n are natural numbers, we define b^n (read "b to the power n") to mean $\underbrace{b \times \ldots \times b}_{n\ \text{times}}$. Here, b is called the **base** and n is the **exponent.**

The following properties apply for all real number exponents. They are useful especially when solving various algebra problems, a task we undertake in chapter 12. For the following, assume that the bases a and b are greater than 1, and that the exponents n and m are real numbers.

Exponent Rule (in symbols)	Interpretation
1. $a^0 = 1$	The result of raising any nonzero real number to the zero power is 1.
2. $a^{-n} = \dfrac{1}{a^n}$, $\quad a^n = \dfrac{1}{a^{-n}}$	A term in the numerator that is raised to a negative exponent is equivalent to a term in the denominator with the same base, but positive exponent, and vice versa.
3. $a^n \times a^m = a^{n+m}$	When multiplying terms with the same base raised to powers, you add the powers.
4. $\dfrac{a^n}{a^m} = a^{n-m}$	When dividing terms with the same base raised to powers, you subtract the powers.
5. $\left(a^n\right)^m = a^{n \cdot m}$	When raising a term that is already raised to a power to another power, you multiply the powers.

6. $(a \times b)^n = a^n \times b^n$	When raising a product to a power, apply the power to each term and multiply the results.
7. $\left(\dfrac{a}{b}\right)^n = \dfrac{a^n}{b^n}$	When raising a quotient to a power, apply the power to each term and divide the results.
8. If $a = b$, then $a^n = b^n$, for any exponent n.	If two real numbers are equal, then their powers are also equal.
9. If $0 < a < b$, then $a^n < b^n$, for any positive exponent n.	If a is less than b, then you can raise both sides of the inequality to a positive power without having to reverse the sign.

It is very common to not only apply the exponent rules incorrectly, but also to mistakenly apply rules that do not even exist! The following are some common errors that arise when working with exponents:

Statement	Interpretation	Example
$(a + b)^n \neq a^n + b^n$	The power of a sum is not equal to the sum of the powers.	$(2 + 3)^3 \neq 2^3 + 3^3$
$a^n \times b^m \neq (a \times b)^{n+m}$	You cannot write the product of terms with different bases raised to different powers as a single product raised to a power.	$3^2 \times 5^3 \neq (3 \times 5)^{2+3}$
$\dfrac{a^n}{b^m} \neq \left(\dfrac{a}{b}\right)^{n-m}$	You cannot write the quotient of terms with different bases raised to different powers as a single quotient raised to a power.	$\dfrac{3^2}{5^3} \neq \left(\dfrac{3}{5}\right)^{2-3}$
$-a^2 \neq (-a)^2$	If the negative sign is *outside* the parentheses of a quantity being squared, then the square does not apply to it.	$(-5)^2 = (-5)(-5) = 25$ $-5^2 = (-1)(5)(5) = -25$

5. Which of the following is equivalent to $\dfrac{3^{-2} \times 2^3}{3^2 \times 2^{-1}}$?

  (A) $\left(\dfrac{3}{2}\right)^4$

  (B) $\left(\dfrac{2}{3}\right)^4$

  (C) 1

  (D) 4

  (E) $\dfrac{4}{9}$

The correct answer is (B). You must apply the exponent rules as follows:

$$\frac{3^{-2} \cdot 2^3}{3^2 \cdot 2^{-1}} = \frac{2^1 \cdot 2^3}{3^2 \cdot 3^2} \quad \text{(by Property 2)}$$

$$= \frac{2^{1+3}}{3^{2+2}} \quad \text{(by Property 3)}$$

$$= \frac{2^4}{3^4}$$

$$= \left(\frac{2}{3}\right)^4 \quad \text{(by Property 7)}$$

6. Which of the following statements is FALSE?

(A) $(2 \cdot a)^3 = \dfrac{8}{a^{-3}}$

(B) $\left(3^2\right)^5 = 3^{10}$

(C) $\left(\dfrac{3}{5}\right)^{-2} = \dfrac{25}{9}$

(D) $\left(\dfrac{2^{-2}}{3^{-2}}\right)^{-2} = \dfrac{3^4}{2^4}$

(E) $-(-3)^2 = -9$

The correct answer is (D). This problem again requires that you correctly apply various exponent rules and to identify when they have been used inappropriately. Observe the operations for choice (D):

$$\left(\frac{2^{-2}}{3^{-2}}\right)^{-2} = \frac{\left(2^{-2}\right)^{-2}}{\left(3^{-2}\right)^{-2}} = \frac{2^4}{3^4} \neq \frac{3^4}{2^4}.$$

RADICALS

You likely have memorized in your math studies that $\sqrt{49} = 7$ and $\sqrt{81} = 9$. But do you know why, and what the radical symbol really means? The definition of a **square root** of a non-negative real number a is another number b whose square is a—that is $b^2 = a$. In such case, we write $\sqrt{a} = b$.

Note that $(-7)^2 = 49$ and $(-9)^2 = 81$, so -7 and -9 are also square roots of 49 and 81, respectively. When the square root symbol $\sqrt{}$ is used, it is understood to mean the *positive* (or *principal*) root. Square roots of negative numbers are not *real* numbers, but rather they are *imaginary*—we will study this topic later in the chapter.

A **cube root** of a real number a is another number b whose cube is a, that is $b^3 = a$. In such case, we write $\sqrt[3]{a} = b$. For instance, $\sqrt[3]{64} = 4$ and $\sqrt[3]{-125} = -5$. General n^{th}

roots can be defined in a similar way for any natural number n. We collectively refer to roots of any kind as **radicals.**

We can also describe radicals using fractional exponents. For instance, raising both sides of the equation $b^2 = a$ to the $\frac{1}{2}$ power yields $\underbrace{\left(b^2\right)^{\frac{1}{2}}}_{=b} = \underbrace{a^{\frac{1}{2}}}_{=\sqrt{a}}$. So, $\sqrt{a}$ can be expressed as $a^{\frac{1}{2}}$.

The following chart goes into more detail about useful properties of radicals, as consequences of the exponent rules:

Radical Rule (in symbols)	Interpretation
1. $\left(\sqrt[n]{a}\right)^n = a$, for any natural number n. Specifically, $\left(\sqrt{a}\right)^2 = a$.	Raising an nth root to the nth power gives back the original radicand.
2. $\sqrt{a^2} = \lvert a \rvert$	Since the square root symbol means the *principal* root and a could technically be negative, we must take the absolute value of a to get $\sqrt{a^2}$.
3. $\sqrt{a \cdot b} = \sqrt{a} \cdot \sqrt{b}$, whenever $a \geq 0$ and $b \geq 0$.	Square root of a product is the product of the square roots. (This extends to all nth roots and when n is odd, the restriction on the sign of a and b is dropped.)
4. $\sqrt{\dfrac{a}{b}} = \dfrac{\sqrt{a}}{\sqrt{b}}$, whenever $a \geq 0$ and $b > 0$.	Square root of a quotient is the quotient of the square roots. (This extends to all nth roots and when n is odd, the restriction on the sign of a and b is dropped.)
5. $\dfrac{1}{\sqrt{a}} = \dfrac{1}{\sqrt{a}} \cdot \dfrac{\sqrt{a}}{\sqrt{a}} = \dfrac{\sqrt{a}}{a}$, whenever $a > 0$.	You can clear a square root from the denominator of a fraction by multiplying top and bottom by it. (This is often called "multiplying by the *conjugate*" or "*rationalizing* the denominator.")
6. If $a = b$ and a and b are non-negative, then $\sqrt{a} = \sqrt{b}$.	If two non-negative real numbers are equal, then their square roots are also equal.
7. If $0 < a < b$, then $\sqrt{a} < \sqrt{b}$.	If a is less than b, then you can take the square root on both sides of the inequality without having to reverse the sign.

TIP

Remember, $\sqrt[3]{a} = a^{\frac{1}{3}}$ and more generally, $\sqrt[n]{a} = a^{\frac{1}{n}}$.

The properties in this table can be used to simplify radicals. For instance:

$$\sqrt{48} = \sqrt{3 \cdot 16} = \sqrt{3} \cdot \sqrt{16} = \sqrt{3} \cdot 4 = 4\sqrt{3}$$

The following are some common errors with examples that arise when working with radicals:

Statement	Interpretation	Example
$\sqrt{a+b} \neq \sqrt{a} + \sqrt{b}$	The square root of a sum is not the sum of the square roots. (This fact is true for all n^{th} roots.)	$\underbrace{\sqrt{16+9}}_{=\sqrt{25}\,=\,5} \neq \sqrt{16} + \sqrt{9}$
$\sqrt{a^2 + b^2} \neq a + b$	This is a special case of the one above.	$\underbrace{\sqrt{4^2 + 3^2}}_{=\sqrt{25}\,=\,5} \neq 4 + 3$

How do you *add* radical expressions? Well, it depends. If the terms of the sum have the same radical parts, we can just add the coefficients:

$$4\sqrt{3} + 8\sqrt{3} = (4+8)\sqrt{3} = 12\sqrt{3}$$

However, terms that have different radical parts cannot be combined:

$$3\sqrt{3} + 2\sqrt{7} - 9\sqrt{3} = (3-9)\sqrt{3} + 2\sqrt{7} = -6\sqrt{3} + 2\sqrt{7}$$

7. Which of the following is equivalent to $\dfrac{36\sqrt{5}}{18\sqrt{30}}$?

   (A) $\dfrac{4}{\sqrt{6}}$

   (B) $3\sqrt{6}$

   (C) $\dfrac{1}{3}$

   (D) $\sqrt{\dfrac{1}{3}}$

   (E) $\dfrac{\sqrt{6}}{3}$

The correct answer is (E). We must use the properties of radicals, together with how fractions are multiplied, to simplify this expression:

$$\frac{36\sqrt{5}}{18\sqrt{30}} = \frac{18 \cdot 2\sqrt{5}}{18\sqrt{5 \cdot 6}} = \frac{2\sqrt{5}}{\sqrt{5} \cdot \sqrt{6}} = \frac{2}{\sqrt{6}}$$

Finally, we rationalize the denominator by multiplying the numerator and denominator by $\sqrt{6}$:

$$\underbrace{\frac{36\sqrt{5}}{18\sqrt{30}} = \frac{2}{\sqrt{6}}}_{\text{From above}} = \underbrace{\frac{2}{\sqrt{6}} \cdot \frac{\sqrt{6}}{\sqrt{6}}}_{\substack{\text{Rationalizing the}\\\text{denominator}}} = \frac{2\sqrt{6}}{6} = \frac{\sqrt{6}}{3}$$

8. Which of the following is equal to the expression $\left(\sqrt{2} - \sqrt{27}\right)^2$?
   - **(A)** −25
   - **(B)** 25
   - **(C)** $23\sqrt{6}$
   - **(D)** $29 - 6\sqrt{6}$
   - **(E)** $29 + 6\sqrt{6}$

The correct answer is (D). This problem requires us to use the distributive property, as well as some properties of how to simplify radicals. We first apply the FOIL technique and then simplify the various products:

$$\left(\sqrt{2} - \sqrt{27}\right)^2 = \left(\sqrt{2} - \sqrt{27}\right) \cdot \left(\sqrt{2} - \sqrt{27}\right)$$
$$= \left(\sqrt{2} \cdot \sqrt{2}\right) - \left(\sqrt{2} \cdot \sqrt{27}\right) - \left(\sqrt{27} \cdot \sqrt{2}\right) + \left(\sqrt{27} \cdot \sqrt{27}\right)$$
$$= 2 - \left(\sqrt{2} \cdot 3\sqrt{3}\right) - \left(3\sqrt{3} \cdot \sqrt{2}\right) + 27$$
$$= 2 - 6\sqrt{2} \cdot \sqrt{3} + 27$$
$$= 29 - 6\sqrt{6}$$

ESTIMATION WITH REAL NUMBERS

On some HiSET® Mathematics questions, you will see computations that feature numbers so large that working with them directly is difficult. This is also true with expressions that involve irrational numbers.

A common technique when estimating is to round large numbers to the nearest *thousand, ten thousand,* etc. For example, suppose you want to round a whole number to the nearest thousand. Look at the digit to the immediate right, which in this case is the hundreds place. If that digit is 5 or greater, increase the digit in the thousands place by one, and replace all digits to its right by zeros; if the digit is 4 or less, keep the thousands place as is and replace all digits to its right by zeros. For example, 343,783 rounded to the nearest thousand is 344,000, while 214,332,499 rounded to the nearest thousand is 214,332,000. The same technique works when rounding any real number expressed as a decimal to any place desired.

Estimating roots, such as $\sqrt{31}$ and $\sqrt[3]{4}$, can be tricky. Sometimes, providing a single estimate is not easily done, but providing a *range* of values is doable and useful. For instance, we cannot compute $\sqrt{31}$ directly very easily, but we can determine numbers whose square roots are easily computed on either side of 31, namely 25 < 31 < 36. Then, we know that $\underset{=\,5}{\sqrt{25}} < \sqrt{31} < \underset{=\,6}{\sqrt{36}}$, so that $5 < \sqrt{31} < 6$. The same trick works for estimating cube roots, except in that case you want to find two numbers for which the *cube* root, not *square* root, is easily computed.

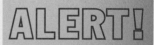

ALERT!

Don't waste time with complicated numbers! In order to answer a question as quickly as possible, you should resort to smart approximation.

Other irrational numbers, such as π and e, enter into HiSET® computations. Common approximations for these are $\pi \approx 3.14$ and $e \approx 2.718$.

9. Which of the following is an appropriate range for the sum $\sqrt{45} + \sqrt[3]{29}$?
   (A) Between 7 and 9
   (B) Between 9 and 11
   (C) Between 11 and 13
   (D) Between 12 and 16
   (E) Between 20 and 30

The correct answer is (B). The idea is to determine a range for each of the roots separately, as shown above, and then add the lower and upper bounds to get the range for the sum:

$$\sqrt{36} < \sqrt{45} < \sqrt{49}, \text{ so that } 6 < \sqrt{45} < 7,$$
$$\sqrt[3]{27} < \sqrt[3]{29} < \sqrt[3]{64}, \text{ so that } 3 < \sqrt[3]{29} < 4.$$

So, adding the left and right endpoints, respectively, yields the range $9 < \sqrt{45} + \sqrt[3]{29} < 11$. This means that the range is between 9 and 11.

10. Rounding the quantity $10{,}006.93 \times 0.2$ to the nearest tenth yields which of the following?
    (A) 2,001.40
    (B) 2,001.00
    (C) 2,000.00
    (D) 2,000.39
    (E) 2,000.386

The correct answer is (A). First, compute the given product to get $10{,}006.93 \times 0.2 = 2{,}001.386$. Now, the digit in the tenths place is 3 and the digit to its immediate right is 8, which is larger than 5. So, rounding the decimal to the nearest tenth yields 2,001.4.

RATIOS AND PROPORTIONS

A **ratio** is a comparison of one positive quantity x to another positive quantity y expressed as a fraction $\frac{x}{y}$, or sometimes using the notation $x:y$ (read "x to y"). It is often convenient to think of this as in words as "for every x of one type, there are y of the second type." For example, if there are 2 girls to every 1 boy in a class, we say that the ratio of girls to boys is 2:1, or 2 to 1, and write the fraction $\frac{2}{1}$. Likewise, if there are 4 dogs for every 3 cats in a kennel, we say that the ratio of dogs to cats is 4:3, or 4 to 3, and write the fraction $\frac{4}{3}$.

The order in which a ratio is expressed is important because of its representation as a fraction. Consider the "dogs to cats" example in the above paragraph. We could alternatively describe the ratio as 3 cats for every 4 dogs, and say the ratio of cats to dogs is 3:4 and write the fraction $\frac{3}{4}$. This conveys the same information. However, since $\frac{3}{4} \neq \frac{4}{3}$, the two ratios are not *equal*. So, keep in mind that order matters when writing down a ratio $a:b$.

Ratios can often be simplified in the same manner as fractions. For instance, the ratio describing the scenario "there are 5 dead batteries for every 20 working batteries" is $\frac{5}{20}$, which is equivalent to $\frac{1}{4}$. This simplified fraction can be used to express the scenario equivalently as "there is 1 dead battery for every 4 batteries."

11. Consider the scenario "for every 4 country songs, there are 6 pop songs on Alex's MP3 player." Which of the following is NOT an accurate depiction of the ratio of country songs to pop songs?

    (A) 2:3

    (B) $\frac{12}{8}$

    (C) $\frac{10}{15}$

    (D) $\frac{4}{6}$

    (E) 24 to 36

The correct answer is choice (B). This problem assesses the various ways in which to equivalently express a given ratio. The only one among the choices that is incorrect is choice (B) because the numerator and denominator should be interchanged. As written, this is a ratio for pop songs to country songs.

A **proportion** is an equation relating two ratios. In symbols, a proportion is expressed by setting two fractions equal to each other, say $\frac{a}{b} = \frac{c}{d}$. This is often read as "a is to b as c is to d." Proportions are often formulated when one ratio is known and one of the two quantities in an equivalent ratio is unknown.

Here is an example:

> Suppose it is known that there are 3 soccer balls for every 5 footballs in the storage locker room. If the last count was 40 footballs, how many soccer balls are in the storage room?

To solve this problem, let s denote the number of soccer balls in the storage room. We set up the proportion $\frac{3}{5} = \frac{s}{40}$. To solve for s, we cross-multiply to get $3(40) = 5s$, or $120 = 5s$. Dividing both sides by 5 then yields $s = 24$. So, there are 24 soccer balls in the storage room.

NOTE

You will be asked to solve proportions within many different types of HiSET® Mathematics problems, including similar triangles and changing units of measure.

12. A marine biologist wants to estimate the population of minnows in a lake. He catches 400 minnows, marks them with fluorescent paint, and returns them to the lake. The next day, he catches 600 minnows and discovers that 75 of them are marked. Which of the following is the size of the minnow population?

(A) 150
(B) 300
(C) 600
(D) 3,200
(E) 24,000

The correct answer is (D). We set up a proportion to find the total number m of minnows in the lake. Assuming that the marked minnows disperse throughout the lake in the same manner as those unmarked, it makes sense to set up the proportion, "75 marked minnows is to 600 caught as 400 marked minnows is to the total minnow population m." We express this in fractional form as $\frac{75}{600} = \frac{400}{m}$. To solve for m, we cross-multiply to get $75m = 400(600)$, so that $m = 3{,}200$.

PERCENTS

The word **percent** means per hundred. A percent is used to express the number of *parts* of a *whole*. For instance, 25 percent means "25 parts of 100," which can be expressed as the fraction $\frac{25}{100}$ or as the decimal 0.25. It is also denoted as 25%. All three representations are equivalent. (Note that to go from decimal form to percent form, you simply move the decimal point two units to the right and affix the % sign; to convert in the opposite manner, move the decimal point two units to the left, insert a decimal point and drop the % sign.)

The following are some common question types you will see on the HiSET® Mathematics subtest that ask you to work with percents:

Problem Type	Method Used to Solve the Problem	Example
What percent of x is y?	Divide y by x, then convert the decimal to a %.	**Q:** What percent of 200 is 40? **A:** $\frac{40}{200} = \frac{1}{5} = 0.20 = 20\%$
Compute $x\%$ of y.	Convert $x\%$ to a decimal and multiply by y.	**Q:** Compute 43% of 6. **A:** $0.43(6) = 2.58$
x is $y\%$ of what number z?	Convert $y\%$ to a decimal, multiply it by z, and set equal to x. Solve for z.	**Q:** 24 is 40% of what number z? **A:** Solve $0.40z = 24$ for z to get $z = 60$.

13. One-fourth of the rainforest's population is monkeys and one-fifth of the rest is reptiles. What percent of the rainforest's population is reptiles?

   (A) 6%

   (B) 20%

   (C) 33%

   (D) 50%

   (E) 75%

The correct answer is (A). Let p denote the rainforest's population. Since one-fourth of it is monkeys, three-fourths is NOT monkeys. We are told that one-fifth of *this* amount is reptiles. In symbols, the reptile population is $\frac{1}{5}\left(\frac{3}{4}p\right) = \frac{3}{20}p = 0.06p$. So, 6% of the rainforest's population is monkeys.

Other common applications involving percents are computing tips and discounts. Consider the following sample problem.

14. A department store marked down all of its winter snow apparel by 35%. The following week the remaining items were marked down again 20% off the sale price. When Kendra bought two hats and a pair of gloves, she presented a coupon that gave her an additional 15% off. What percent of the original price did Kendra save?

   (A) 44.2%

   (B) 52%

   (C) 55.8%

   (D) 65%

   (E) 70%

The correct answer is (C). Let p be the original price of the items Kendra purchased. We don't care about the exact value of p, but rather what percent of it Kendra ends up paying. The price during the first week of the sale is $p - 0.35p = 0.65p$. The price of these items the next week, prior to the coupon, is $0.65p - 0.20(0.65p) = 0.65p - 0.13p = 0.52p$. (The important point here is that subsequent discounts are applied to the most recent price each time!) Finally, applying the 15% coupon yields the price $0.52p - 0.15(0.52p)$ $= 0.52p - 0.078p = 0.442p$. So, Kendra paid 44.2% of the original price. So, she saved 55.8% of the original price.

VECTORS AND MATRICES

A **vector** in the plane is often depicted as an arrow and labeled using a boldface letter, like **v**. If the tail of the vector **v** is at the origin, then **v** can be expressed using the point in the plane at which the arrowhead lands, say $\langle v_1, v_2 \rangle$. Here, v_1 and v_2 are called the *components of* **v**. We can characterize a vector in terms of its length (distance from origin to head) and its direction (angle from positive x-axis to the directed line segment).

TIP

If **u** is a vector in the plane whose tail has coordinates $A(a_1, a_2)$ and whose head has coordinates $B(b_1, b_2)$, **u** = $\langle b_1 - a_1, b_2 - a_2 \rangle$.

If we were to alter either of these two measurements, the head of the arrow would end at a different point P, and therefore would not give rise to the same vector.

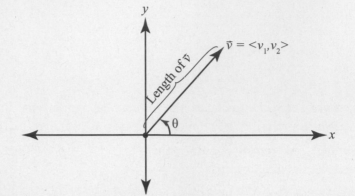

The following are some basic concepts that arise when working with vectors:

Term/Operation	Algebraic Definition	Geometric Interpretation
u is *equivalent* to **v** (Denoted: **u = v**)	$u_1 = v_1, \; u_2 = v_2$ *Corresponding components are equal.*	**u** and **v** have the same magnitude and direction.
Length (or *magnitude*) of **u** (Denoted: $\|\mathbf{u}\|$)	$\|\mathbf{u}\| = \sqrt{u_1^2 + u_2^2}$	Distance from tail to head.
Addition: **u + v**	$\mathbf{u} + \mathbf{v} = \underbrace{\langle u_1 + v_1, \; u_2 + v_2 \rangle}_{\text{Add componentwise}}$	Vector emanating from tail of **u** to head of **v**.
Zero Vector: **0**	The vector **0** that satisfies **u + 0 = u**, for all vectors **u**. That is, $\mathbf{0} = \langle 0, 0 \rangle$	A point at the origin.
Scalar Multiplication: $c\mathbf{u}$ where c is a real number	$c\mathbf{u} = \langle c\,u_1, \; c\,u_2 \rangle$	If $c > 0$, then $c\mathbf{u}$ is the vector in the direction of **u** with length $c\|\mathbf{u}\|$. If $c < 0$, then $c\mathbf{u}$ is the vector in the direction of **u** with length $c\|\mathbf{u}\|$. If $c = 0$, then $c\mathbf{u}$ is the zero vector.
Subtraction: **u − v**	$\mathbf{u} - \mathbf{v} = \underbrace{\langle u_1 - v_1, \; u_2 - v_2 \rangle}_{\text{Subtract componentwise}}$	The vector emanating from the head of **v** to the head of **u**.

15. Let $\mathbf{u} = \langle -1, 4 \rangle$ and $\mathbf{v} = \langle -2, -1 \rangle$. Which of the following is equivalent to $-2\mathbf{u} + 3\mathbf{v}$?

    (A) $\langle -4, -11 \rangle$

    (B) $\langle -3, 3 \rangle$

    (C) $\langle 8, -5 \rangle$

    (D) $\langle 1, 5 \rangle$

    (E) $\langle -4, 3 \rangle$

The correct answer is (A). We use the definition of scalar multiplication and then addition to simplify this sum:

$$-2\mathbf{u} + 3\mathbf{v} = -2\langle -1, 4 \rangle + 3\langle -2, -1 \rangle = \langle 2, -8 \rangle + \langle -6, -3 \rangle = \langle 2 - 6, -8 - 3 \rangle = \langle -4, -11 \rangle$$

A **matrix** is an array of real numbers. If a matrix **A** has r rows and c columns, we say **A** is an $r \times c$ (read "r by c") matrix. A matrix is written by listing all of its entries in an array, enclosed by brackets. Some examples are

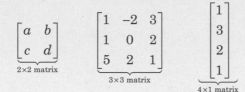

$$\begin{bmatrix} a & b \\ c & d \end{bmatrix}$$
2×2 matrix

$$\begin{bmatrix} 1 & -2 & 3 \\ 1 & 0 & 2 \\ 5 & 2 & 1 \end{bmatrix}$$
3×3 matrix

$$\begin{bmatrix} 1 \\ 3 \\ 2 \\ 1 \end{bmatrix}$$
4×1 matrix

We can perform the same arithmetic operations on matrices as on vectors, the punch line being that these operations are performed "componentwise." The following is a list of some basic operations on 2×2 matrices (all letters stand for real numbers):

Term/Operation	Definition
Equality: $\begin{bmatrix} a & b \\ c & d \end{bmatrix} = \begin{bmatrix} e & f \\ g & h \end{bmatrix}$	$\begin{bmatrix} a & b \\ c & d \end{bmatrix} = \begin{bmatrix} e & f \\ g & h \end{bmatrix}$ whenever $\underbrace{a = e,\ b = f,\ c = g,\ d = h}_{\text{corresponding entries are equal}}$
Sum: $\begin{bmatrix} a & b \\ c & d \end{bmatrix} + \begin{bmatrix} e & f \\ g & h \end{bmatrix}$	$\begin{bmatrix} a & b \\ c & d \end{bmatrix} + \begin{bmatrix} e & f \\ g & h \end{bmatrix} = \begin{bmatrix} a+e & b+f \\ c+g & d+h \end{bmatrix}$ In words, add corresponding entries to get the sum.
Difference: $\begin{bmatrix} a & b \\ c & d \end{bmatrix} - \begin{bmatrix} e & f \\ g & h \end{bmatrix}$	$\begin{bmatrix} a & b \\ c & d \end{bmatrix} - \begin{bmatrix} e & f \\ g & h \end{bmatrix} = \begin{bmatrix} a-e & b-f \\ c-g & d-h \end{bmatrix}$ In words, subtract corresponding entries to get the difference.
Scalar Multiplication: $k\begin{bmatrix} a & b \\ c & d \end{bmatrix}$	$k\begin{bmatrix} a & b \\ c & d \end{bmatrix} = \begin{bmatrix} ka & kb \\ kc & kd \end{bmatrix}$ In words, multiply all entries by the constant k.
Product: $\begin{bmatrix} a & b \\ c & d \end{bmatrix} \cdot \begin{bmatrix} e & f \\ g & h \end{bmatrix}$	$\begin{bmatrix} a & b \\ c & d \end{bmatrix} \cdot \begin{bmatrix} e & f \\ g & h \end{bmatrix} = \begin{bmatrix} ae+bg & af+bh \\ ce+dg & cf+dh \end{bmatrix}$ In words, multiply corresponding entries in row 1 and column 1, and add the results to get the entry in 1st row and 1st column. Do the same for all other entries.
Determinant: $\det\begin{bmatrix} a & b \\ c & d \end{bmatrix}$	$\det\begin{bmatrix} a & b \\ c & d \end{bmatrix} = ad - bc$
Inverse: $\begin{bmatrix} a & b \\ c & d \end{bmatrix}^{-1}$	This is the matrix for which $\begin{bmatrix} a & b \\ c & d \end{bmatrix}^{-1} \cdot \begin{bmatrix} a & b \\ c & d \end{bmatrix} = \begin{bmatrix} a & b \\ c & d \end{bmatrix} \cdot \begin{bmatrix} a & b \\ c & d \end{bmatrix}^{-1} = \underbrace{\begin{bmatrix} 1 & 0 \\ 0 & 1 \end{bmatrix}}_{\text{Identity Matrix}}.$ The inverse exists whenever $\det\begin{bmatrix} a & b \\ c & d \end{bmatrix} \neq 0$. In such case, $\begin{bmatrix} a & b \\ c & d \end{bmatrix}^{-1} = \frac{1}{ad-bc}\begin{bmatrix} d & -b \\ -c & a \end{bmatrix}.$

16. Determine the value of x that makes the following equation true:

$$2\begin{bmatrix} x & -1 \\ 1 & 2 \end{bmatrix} - \begin{bmatrix} -3 & 1 \\ 0 & -1 \end{bmatrix} = \begin{bmatrix} 7 & -3 \\ 2 & 5 \end{bmatrix}$$

(A) -1

(B) 0

(C) 1

(D) 2

(E) 3

The correct answer is (D). We simplify the left side of the equation using the rules for multiplying a matrix by a scalar and subtracting matrices. Then, we equate corresponding entries to get an equation to solve for x:

$$2\begin{bmatrix} x & -1 \\ 1 & 2 \end{bmatrix} - \begin{bmatrix} -3 & 1 \\ 0 & -1 \end{bmatrix} = \begin{bmatrix} 7 & -3 \\ 2 & 5 \end{bmatrix}$$

$$\begin{bmatrix} 2x & -2 \\ 2 & 4 \end{bmatrix} - \begin{bmatrix} -3 & 1 \\ 0 & -1 \end{bmatrix} = \begin{bmatrix} 7 & -3 \\ 2 & 5 \end{bmatrix}$$

$$\begin{bmatrix} 2x+3 & -2-1 \\ 2-0 & 4+1 \end{bmatrix} = \begin{bmatrix} 7 & -3 \\ 2 & 5 \end{bmatrix}$$

$$\begin{bmatrix} 2x+3 & -3 \\ 2 & 5 \end{bmatrix} = \begin{bmatrix} 7 & -3 \\ 2 & 5 \end{bmatrix}$$

Since two matrices are equal only when their corresponding entries are the same, we must have $2x + 3 = 7$. Solving this equation yields $x = 2$.

SUMMING IT UP

- A **product** is the result of multiplying two or more **factors**. A prime number can only be divided by 1 and itself, and every number has a **prime factorization**, which breaks it down into only its prime factors.

- The **greatest common factor** of two numbers is the *largest* natural number that is a factor of both, while the **least common multiple** of two numbers is the *smallest* natural number that is a multiple of both.

- In order to simplify expressions, you must follow the **order of operations**: simplify all expressions contained within parentheses, then simplify all expressions involving exponents, then perform all multiplication and division as it arises from left to right, then perform all addition and subtraction as it arises from left to right.

- The **absolute value** of any real number a (denoted $|a|$) measures the distance between a and 0. Distance is always a positive value.

- If b and n are natural numbers, then $b^n = \underbrace{b \times \ldots \times b}_{n \text{ times}}$.

- A **square root** of a non-negative real number a is another number b whose square is a—that is $b^2 = a$. A **cube root** of a real number a is another number b whose cube is a, that is $b^3 = a$.

- To round a number, look at the digit to the immediate right of the digit that you want to round. If that right digit is 5 or greater, increase the previous digit by one, and replace all digits to its right by zeros; if the digit is 4 or less, keep the previous digit as-is, and replace all digits to its right by zeros.

- Providing a single estimate for a root is difficult, so instead figure out a *range* of values for the root.

- A **ratio** is a comparison of one positive quantity x to another positive quantity y expressed as a fraction $\frac{x}{y}$, or sometimes using the notation $x{:}y$ (read "x to y"). The order in which a ratio is expressed is important because of its representation as a fraction. A **proportion** is an equation relating two ratios.

- The word **percent** means per hundred, and a percent is used to express the number of *parts* of a *whole*. To go from decimal form to percent form, move the decimal point two units to the right and affix the % sign; to convert from a percent to a decimal, move the decimal point two units to the left, insert a decimal point and drop the % sign.

- If the tail of the vector **v** is at the origin, then **v** can be expressed using the point in the plane at which the arrowhead lands $\langle v_1, v_2 \rangle$. Characterize a vector in terms of its length (distance from origin to head) and its direction (angle from positive x-axis to the line segment).

• A **matrix** is an array of real numbers. Some examples are

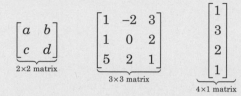

Measurement and Geometry

OVERVIEW

- **Units of Measurement**
- **Angles**
- **Triangles**
- **Quadrilaterals, Polygons, and Circles**
- **Solids**
- **Perimeter**
- **Area**
- **Surface Area**
- **Volume**
- **Density**
- **Summing It Up**

Measurement and geometry questions comprise about one-fifth of the questions on the HiSET® Mathematics subtest. More so than other branches of math, these topics require you to be familiar with specific formulas, terminology, and rules in order to understand figures presented to you and to solve problems. This chapter focuses on reviewing the main definitions and formulas, along with their applications, of the high school measurement and geometry you will see covered on the exam.

UNITS OF MEASUREMENT

Different units of measurement are associated with different types of quantities, such as time, length, speed, liquid measures, area, etc. Knowing how to convert from one type to another is important when you are asked to solve problems where similar quantities are expressed using different units. Below are some common units of measure expressed in equivalent ways:

Type of Quantity Being Measured	Units of Measure and Their Conversions
Length	1 foot = 12 inches 1 mile = 1,760 yards = 5,280 feet 1 yard = 3 feet = 36 inches
Time	1 minute = 60 seconds 1 day = 24 hours 1 hour = 60 minutes = 3,600 seconds

Type of Quantity Being Measured	Units of Measure and Their Conversions
Area	1 square foot = 12^2 square inches 1 square yard = 3^2 square feet *Note:* ft.^{2} means square feet 1 square mile = $5,280^2$ square feet
Volume	1 cubic foot = 12^3 cubic inches 1 cubic yard = 3^3 cubic feet *Note:* ft.^{3} means cubic feet
Liquid Measure	1 gallon = 4 quarts = 8 pints = 16 cups 1 quart = 2 pints = 4 cups 1 pint = 2 cups
Weight	1 pound = 16 ounces 1 ton = 2,000 pounds

If converting from a smaller unit of measure to a larger one, you divide by the conversion factor, whereas if you are converting from a larger unit of measure to a smaller one, you multiply by the conversion factor. Let's see what this look like as a HiSET® question.

1. Alex ran 6,160 yards total at baseball practice. What is this distance measured in feet?

   (A) 3.5

   (B) 2,053.3

   (C) 12,320

   (D) 18,480

   (E) 73,920

The correct answer is (D). Since there are 3 feet in 1 yard and we are converting from a larger unit of measure to a smaller one, we multiply 6,160 by 3 to get 18,480.

Unit conversions are also used to determine the **unit price** of an item. For instance, if a 1-gallon barrel of paint costs $28.50, what is the cost per pint? To answer such a question, we simply determine the number of pints in a gallon, which is 8, and divide the price by 8 to get $3.5625, or approximately $3.56 per pint.

Technically, converting units involves using a ratio. In the first sample question, converting the units was simply a matter of multiplying by a single number, so formally using a ratio would not be necessary. However, when more than one unit of measure is involved, it is convenient to use ratios to see the units cancel. This next sample problem illustrates how ratios can be useful.

2. Dick's new car can reach the speed of 75 miles per hour in about 6 seconds. What is this speed in feet per minute?

   (A) $\dfrac{75 \times 60}{5,280}$ feet per minute

   (B) $\dfrac{75 \times 3,600}{5,280}$ feet per minute

   (C) $\dfrac{75 \times 5,280}{60}$ feet per minute

(D) $\dfrac{75 \times 5,280}{3,600}$ feet per minute

(E) $\dfrac{75 \times 3,600}{5,280}$ feet per minute

The correct answer is (C). This time, we use ratios to help us visualize the cancellation of units. Since there are 5,280 feet in 1 mile and 60 minutes in 1 hour, we have:

$$\frac{75 \ \cancel{\text{miles}}}{1 \ \cancel{\text{hour}}} \times \frac{1 \ \cancel{\text{hour}}}{60 \ \text{minutes}} \times \frac{5,280 \ \text{feet}}{1 \ \cancel{\text{mile}}} = \frac{75 \times 5,280}{60} \ \text{feet per minute}$$

ANGLES

Angles are classified according to their "size" or **measure**, which is provided using the unit **degrees**. The notation $\mathrm{m}(\angle A)$ is used to denote the measure of angle (A). The following table reviews basic angle terminology:

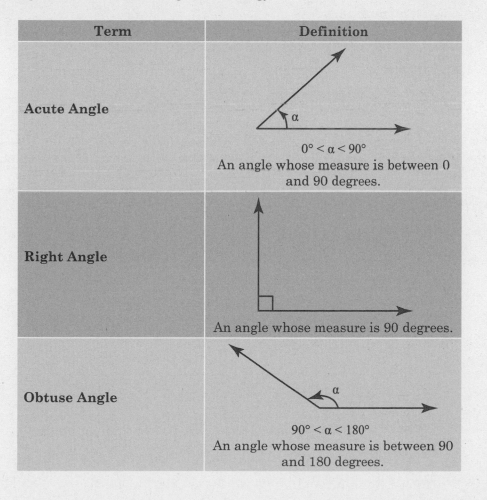

Term	Definition
Acute Angle	$0° < \alpha < 90°$ An angle whose measure is between 0 and 90 degrees.
Right Angle	An angle whose measure is 90 degrees.
Obtuse Angle	$90° < \alpha < 180°$ An angle whose measure is between 90 and 180 degrees.

Term	Definition
Straight Angle	180° 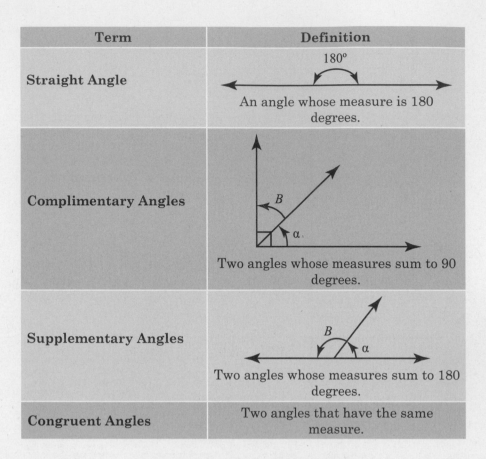 An angle whose measure is 180 degrees.
Complimentary Angles	Two angles whose measures sum to 90 degrees.
Supplementary Angles	Two angles whose measures sum to 180 degrees.
Congruent Angles	Two angles that have the same measure.

Other pairs of angles are important as well. Consider the following diagram. Then look at the table below, which defines all the numbered angles in relation to one another.

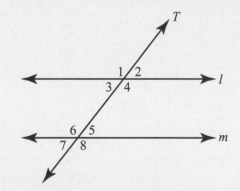

Term	Examples from Diagram
Vertical Angles	$\angle 1$ and $\angle 4$, $\angle 6$ and $\angle 8$
Adjacent Angles	$\angle 1$ and $\angle 3$, $\angle 7$ and $\angle 8$
Corresponding Angles	$\angle 1$ and $\angle 6$, $\angle 3$ and $\angle 7$
Alternate Interior Angles	$\angle 4$ and $\angle 6$, $\angle 3$ and $\angle 5$

3. Which of the following statements is FALSE?

(A) Corresponding angles are congruent when formed by two parallel lines cut by a transversal.

(B) Alternate interior angles can be congruent.

(C) Vertical angles are congruent.

(D) Adjacent angles can be supplementary.

(E) Corresponding angles must be supplementary.

The correct answer is (E). This problem requires you to understand the relationships between different types of angles. Of them, the statement in choice (E) is false. For instance, assuming the two lines l and m are parallel, if $\angle 2$ is acute, then its corresponding angle $\angle 5$ is acute and so, the sum of their measures cannot be 180 degrees.

4. Consider the following diagram:

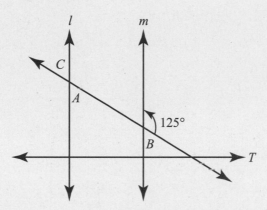

Assuming that lines l and m are parallel, which of the following are the measures of $\angle A$ and $\angle C$?

(A) m($\angle A$) = 55° , m($\angle C$) = 55°

(B) m($\angle A$) = 55° , m($\angle C$) = 125°

(C) m($\angle A$) = 65° , m($\angle C$) = 115°

(D) m($\angle A$) = 45° , m($\angle C$) = 45°

(E) m($\angle A$) = 125° , m($\angle C$) = 125°

The correct answer is (A). We must use knowledge about the relationships between various pairs of angles when the lines forming them are parallel. First, m($\angle B$) + 125° = 180° , so that m($\angle B$) = 55° , because those two angles together form a straight angle. Next, $\angle A$ and $\angle B$ are corresponding angles. Since l and m are parallel, they have the same measure. So, m($\angle A$) = 55° . Finally, since $\angle A$ and $\angle C$ are vertical angles, they are congruent. So, m($\angle C$) = 55° .

TRIANGLES

HiSET® Mathematics questions will ask you questions that directly involve triangles. But you will also find triangles hidden within other geometry problems—they arise when solving many different types of applied problems. Knowing the rules and terminology of triangles is vital to mastering geometry questions on the exam.

Triangles are classified using their angles and sides, as follows:

Type	Defining Characteristic	Illustration
Acute	All three angles are acute.	
Right	One of the angles is a right angle. (The other two, therefore, must be acute.)	
Obtuse	One of the angles is obtuse. (The other two, therefore, must be acute.)	
Scalene	All three sides have different lengths.	

Type	Defining Characteristic	Illustration
Isosceles	At least two sides have the same length; that is, at least two sides are *congruent*.	
Equilateral	All three sides have the same length; that is, all three sides are *congruent*.	

Two important rules that all triangles obey are the **Triangle Sum Rule** and **Triangle Inequality**. The Triangle Sum Rule says that the sum of the measures of the three angles in any triangle must be 180°, and the Triangle Inequality says that the sum of the lengths of any two sides of a triangle must be strictly larger than the length of the third side. It is impossible to construct a triangle that does not satisfy *both* of these conditions.

The sides of right triangles are particularly interesting because their lengths are related by the **Pythagorean theorem.** For the right triangle shown below, the sides with lengths a and b are called *legs* and the side opposite the right angle is the **hypotenuse**; the hypotenuse is the longest side of a right triangle. The Pythagorean theorem says that $a^2 + b^2 = c^2$.

The Pythagorean theorem ONLY works for right triangles!

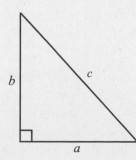

There are two triangles whose angles are such that we can represent the lengths of all sides using nice relationships—they are called $30 - 60 - 90$ and $45 - 45 - 90$ triangles, where the numbers stand for the angle measures. The following are the lengths of the sides of such triangles:

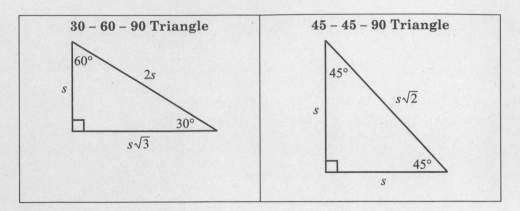

| 30 – 60 – 90 Triangle | 45 – 45 – 90 Triangle |

5. Which of the following triples can be the sides of a right triangle?

(A) 1, 3, 3

(B) 5, 12, 13

(C) 6, 7, 14

(D) 5, 5, 9

(E) 3, 6, 7

The correct answer is (B). The sides of a right triangle must satisfy the Pythagorean theorem. The only triple that does so is the one in choice B because $5^2 + 12^2 = 13^2$.

Consider two triangles $\triangle ABC$ and $\triangle DEF$, shown below:

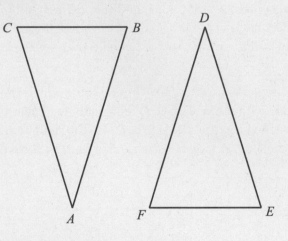

We say $\triangle ABC$ and $\triangle DEF$ are **congruent** if all three corresponding pairs of angles are congruent AND all three corresponding sides are congruent. We identify **corresponding** sides of two triangles using the order in which their vertices (i.e., points where two sides meet) are written. Here, vertex A corresponds to vertex D, B to E, and C to F. An important consequence of congruence is that congruent triangles have the same perimeter and area. (These are discussed later in the chapter.)

Even if two triangles $\triangle ABC$ and $\triangle DEF$ are not congruent, they can still be proportional to each other in the sense that the ratios of the three pairs of corresponding sides are the same; that is, $\dfrac{AB}{DE} = \dfrac{BC}{EF} = \dfrac{AC}{DF} = k$, where k is a positive number. In such case, we say $\triangle ABC$ and $\triangle DEF$ are **similar.** Note that if two triangles are congruent, then this common ratio $k = 1$.

Corresponding angles in two similar triangles must be congruent. A common method for showing two triangles are similar is by showing they share two pairs of congruent angles. Take a look at the following sample problem.

6. Consider the following diagram, where it is assumed that AB is parallel to CD:

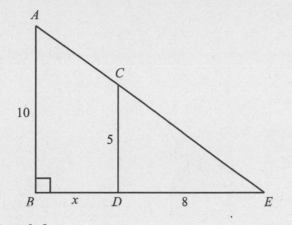

What is the value of x?

(A) 4

(B) 6

(C) 8

(D) 10

(E) 16

The correct answer is (C). Since AB is parallel to CD, we know that $\angle A$ is congruent to $\angle C$ since they are corresponding angles. For the same reason, we know that $\angle B$ and $\angle D$ are both right angles. Therefore, $\triangle ABE$ is similar to $\triangle CDE$. As such, corresponding sides are in the same proportion. Applying this yields the equation $\frac{AB}{CD} = \frac{BE}{DE}$, which is equivalent to $\frac{10}{5} = \frac{x + 8}{8}$. To solve for x, we cross-multiply to get $80 = 5x + 40$, so that $5x = 40$ and $x = 8$.

QUADRILATERALS, POLYGONS, AND CIRCLES

Quadrilaterals are figures in the plane with four sides, each of which is a line segment. You should be familiar with all of the following quadrilaterals for the HiSET® exam:

Quadrilateral	Defining Characteristics	Illustration
Parallelogram	Two pairs of parallel sides	$\overline{AB}$ parallel to $\overline{DC}$ $\overline{AD}$ parallel to $\overline{BC}$
Rectangle	Two pairs of parallel sides and a right angle	$\overline{AB}$ parallel to $\overline{DC}$ $\overline{AD}$ parallel to $\overline{BC}$
Rhombus	Two pairs of parallel sides and all four sides are congruent	$\overline{AB}$ parallel to $\overline{DC}$ $\overline{AD}$ parallel to $\overline{BC}$
Square	Two pairs of parallel sides, all four sides congruent, and a right angle	$\overline{AB}$ parallel to $\overline{DC}$ $\overline{AD}$ parallel to $\overline{BC}$

Quadrilateral	Defining Characteristics	Illustration
Trapezoid	Exactly one pair of parallel sides	$\overline{AD}$ parallel to $\overline{BC}$
Isosceles Trapezoid	Exactly one pair of parallel sides and one pair of opposite sides are congruent	$\overline{AD}$ parallel to $\overline{BC}$

Two quadrilaterals of the same type are congruent if their corresponding sides are all congruent, and they are called **similar** if the four ratios of their corresponding sides are equal.

7. Which of the following is NOT an accurate description of the following quadrilateral?

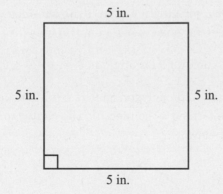

5 in.

5 in.   5 in.

5 in.

(A) Trapezoid
(B) Square
(C) Parallelogram
(D) Rectangle
(E) Rhombus

The answer is (A). A trapezoid has one pair of parallel sides, whereas the illustrated quadrilateral has two.

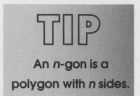

An *n*-gon is a polygon with *n* sides.

Polygons

More generally, a **polygon** is a figure in the plane that has *several* sides that are all line segments. The naming convention of a polygon is linked to its number of sides. For instance, a **pentagon** is a polygon with 5 sides, a **hexagon** is one with 6 sides, an **octagon** has 8 sides, etc.

There are two main types of angles of interest when looking at polygons: **interior angles** and **exterior angles**. These are pictured in the following polygon:

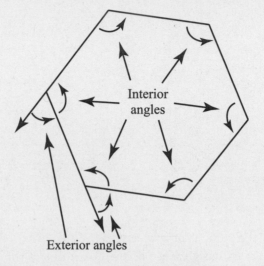

If a polygon is equilateral (meaning all sides are congruent) and equiangular (meaning all interior angles are congruent), then it is called **regular**. Such polygons are particularly nice because there is a formula for computing the measure of their interior and exterior angles. Specifically, for a regular *n*-gon, the measure of each exterior angle is $\dfrac{360°}{n}$ and the measure of each interior angle is $\dfrac{(n-2)180°}{n}$. Also, for regular *n*-gons, the **center** is the point inside the polygon that is equidistant from all vertices, and a **central angle** is an angle formed by connecting the center to two consecutive vertices of the polygon, as shown below:

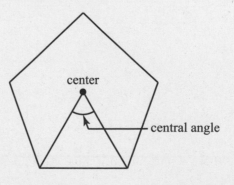

The measure of every central angle of a regular *n*-gon is also $\dfrac{360°}{n}$.

8. A regular polygon has a central angle with measure 10°. How many sides does the polygon have?

   (A) 10

   (B) 12

   (C) 18

   (D) 24

   (E) 36

The correct answer is (E). Since the polygon is regular, we know that a central angle has measure $\frac{360°}{n}$, where n is the number of sides. Equating this expression to 10° and solving for n, we see that $n = 36$.

Circles

The set of all points in the plane that are a given distance r from a fixed point P is a **circle.** The following is basic terminology involving circles you will need to know in order to understand and answer questions on the HiSET®.

Term	Definition	Illustration
Center	The point P equidistant from all points on the circle.	
Radius	The common distance r which points on the circle are from the center.	

Term	Definition	Illustration
Chord	A line segment joining two points on the circle.	
Diameter	A chord that passes through the center of the circle. (Its length is twice the radius.)	
Tangent	A line or line segment outside the circle that intersects it in only one point.	
Arc	A portion of the circle lying between two points.	

Term	Definition	Illustration
Central Angle	An angle formed between two radial segments.	
Sector	The region between two radial segments.	

SOLIDS

Just as triangles, quadrilaterals, and polygons can be classified according to their sides and angles, some three-dimensional solids can be classified according to their faces, edges, and vertices.

A **polyhedron** is a solid with faces made up of all congruent polygons. When you have such a solid, you can envision cutting it along various edges and lying it flat on the table to get a so-called **net diagram,** and then, in reverse, taking that net and reconnecting the edges to form the solid. The following are three common polyhedrons and their net diagrams:

Polyhedron	Illustration	Net Diagram
Cube		

Polyhedron	Illustration	Net Diagram
Tetrahedron	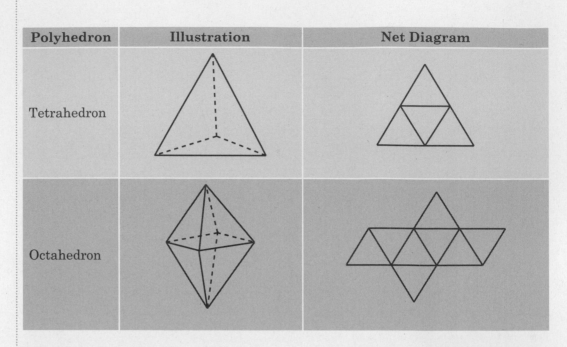	
Octahedron		

The following four categories of solids are characterized by the number and shape of their bases:

Solid	Characteristics	Illustration
Pyramid	One base that is a polygon. One point above the base (called the *apex*) to which all vertices of the base connect. All faces are triangles.	apex, triangular faces, polygonal base
Cone	One base that is a circle. One point above the base (called the *apex*) to which all points of the base connect.	apex, bases are closed regions

Solid	Characteristics	Illustration
Prism	Two congruent bases that are polygons. Vertices of one base connect to the corresponding vertices on the other base. All faces are parallelograms.	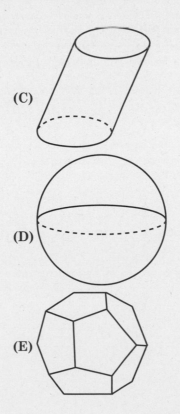 parallelogram faces → ← polygonal bases (congruent)
Cylinder	Two congruent bases that are circles. Points of one base connect to the corresponding points on the other base.	bases are closed regions (congruent)

9. Which of the following is a prism?

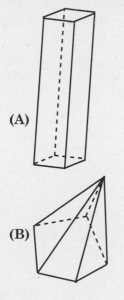

(A)

(B)

(C)

(D)

(E)

The correct answer is (A). You must compare each of the solids to the definition of a prism to determine which one possesses all of the characteristics.

Solids can also be formed by revolving regions in the plane 360 degrees about a line. Such solids are called **solids of revolution.** The following are some common examples:

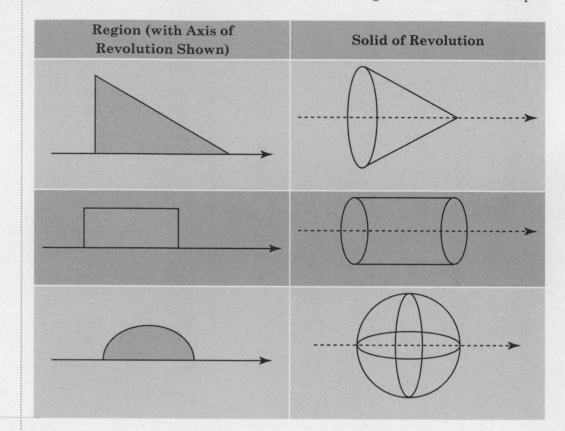

Region (with Axis of Revolution Shown)	Solid of Revolution

10. Which of the following regions can be revolved about the line shown to produce this solid?

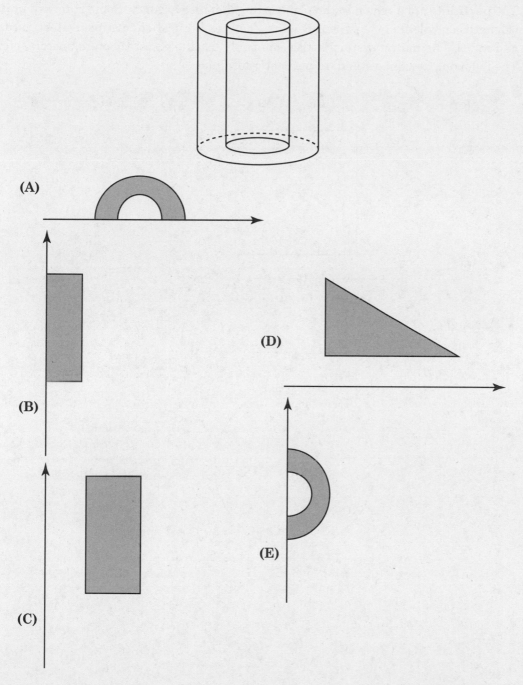

The correct answer is (C). It is helpful to produce the solid of revolution in each case. Since there is a hole bored through the middle of the given solid, there must be a gap between the region being revolved and the line about which it is being revolved. Also, since we want the solid to be cylindrical, we know the region must be a rectangle of some sort. The only choice satisfying both of these conditions is choice (C).

PERIMETER

The **perimeter** of a region in the plane is the "distance around." Some standard units of length you will likely see when answering perimeter questions are inches, feet, yards, and miles. The metric system is also commonly used (e.g., centimeters, meters, etc.) The following are some standard perimeter formulas:

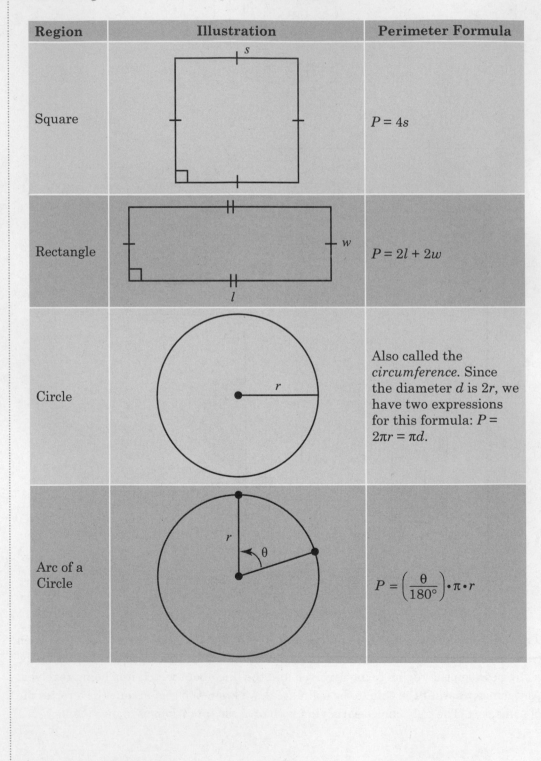

Region	Illustration	Perimeter Formula
Square		$P = 4s$
Rectangle		$P = 2l + 2w$
Circle		Also called the *circumference*. Since the diameter d is $2r$, we have two expressions for this formula: $P = 2\pi r = \pi d$.
Arc of a Circle		$P = \left(\dfrac{\theta}{180°}\right) \cdot \pi \cdot r$

Calculating of the perimeters of triangles, parallelograms, trapezoids, etc., unless given all of the measurements, usually requires that you measure the length of a diagonal (or hypotenuse of a triangle). This, in turn, requires the Pythagorean theorem. Let's look at a sample problem that involves this type of calculation.

11. A square plot of land enclosed by an open wooden fence that is 200 feet long around its perimeter is being constructed to store chopped wood for the winter season. What is the approximate length of the diagonal of this enclosure to the nearest foot?

   (A) 50 feet
   (B) 71 feet
   (C) 100 feet
   (D) 142 feet
   (E) 2,500 feet

The correct answer is (B). Since the enclosure is a square, each of its four sides has the same length. Since the perimeter is 200 feet, each side has length 50 feet. The diagonal of the enclosure can be viewed as the hypotenuse d of a right triangle whose legs both have length 50 feet. Using the Pythagorean theorem yields $50^2 + 50^2 = d^2$, which simplifies to $d^2 = 5,000$. So, $d = \sqrt{5,000} \approx 71$ feet.

Sometimes, figures are drawn in the coordinate plane. In such case, the lengths of any line segments that are vertical or horizontal are easily computed by simply subtracting the y- or x-coordinates, respectively, and taking the absolute value of the result.

For diagonal segments, the distance formula comes in handy:

The distance between two points $P(x_1, y_1)$ and $Q(x_2, y_2)$ is $\sqrt{\left(x_2 - x_1\right)^2 + \left(y_2 - y_1\right)^2}$.

12. Determine the perimeter, rounded to the nearest tenth, of the following polygonal region:

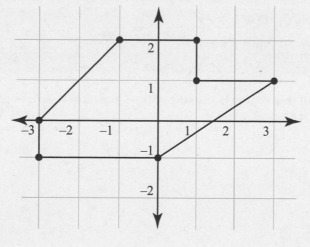

   (A) 9.0 units
   (B) 12.2 units
   (C) 15.4 units
   (D) 16.1 units
   (E) 18.3 units

ALERT!

Length cannot be negative! Don't forget to take the absolute value whenever calculating distance between two points.

The correct answer is (C). The idea is to divide the polygon into distinct line segments, as shown:

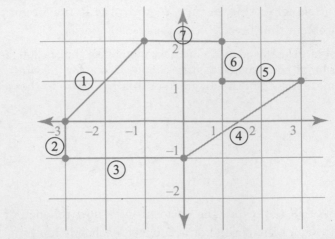

Now, find the length of each segment separately:

Length of **(1)**	Use distance formula with points $(-1,2)$ and $(-3,0)$: $\sqrt{(-1-(-3))^2 + (2-0)^2} = \sqrt{8}$
Length of **(2)**	$0 - (-1) = 1$
Length of **(3)**	$0 - (-3) = 3$
Length of **(4)**	Use distance formula with points $(0,-1)$ and $(3,1)$: $\sqrt{(0-3)^2 + (-1-1)^2} = \sqrt{13}$
Length of **(5)**	$3 - 1 = 2$
Length of **(6)**	$2 - 1 = 1$
Length of **(7)**	$1 - (-1) = 2$

So, the perimeter of this region is the sum of the lengths of these seven segments, which is $9 + \sqrt{8} + \sqrt{13} \approx 15.4$ units.

AREA

The **area** of a region in the plane is the number of *unit squares* needed to cover it. The standard units of measure used in area problems are square inches, square feet, square yards, etc.; the metric system is also commonly used (e.g., square centimeters, square meters). The following are some standard area formulas:

Region	Illustration	Area Formula
Square	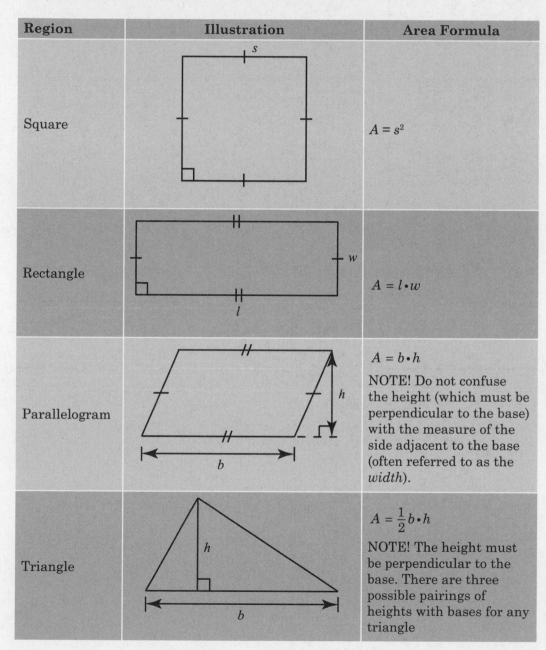	$A = s^2$
Rectangle		$A = l \cdot w$
Parallelogram		$A = b \cdot h$ NOTE! Do not confuse the height (which must be perpendicular to the base) with the measure of the side adjacent to the base (often referred to as the *width*).
Triangle		$A = \frac{1}{2} b \cdot h$ NOTE! The height must be perpendicular to the base. There are three possible pairings of heights with bases for any triangle

Region	Illustration	Area Formula
Trapezoid	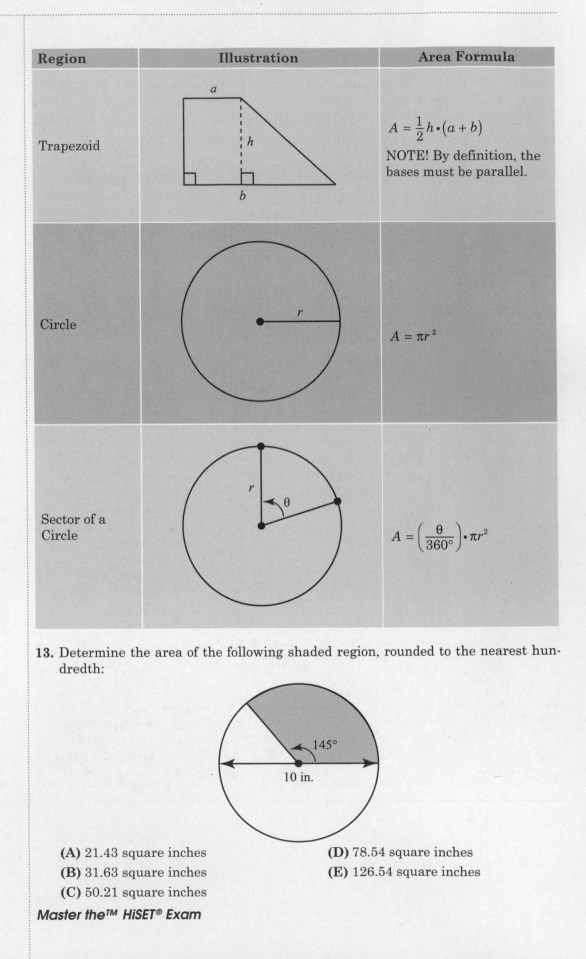	$A = \frac{1}{2} h \cdot (a + b)$ NOTE! By definition, the bases must be parallel.
Circle		$A = \pi r^2$
Sector of a Circle		$A = \left(\frac{\theta}{360°} \right) \cdot \pi r^2$

13. Determine the area of the following shaded region, rounded to the nearest hundredth:

145°

10 in.

(A) 21.43 square inches

(B) 31.63 square inches

(C) 50.21 square inches

(D) 78.54 square inches

(E) 126.54 square inches

The correct answer is (B). The shaded region is the sector of a circle. The diameter is 10 inches, so the radius of the circle is 5 inches. Using the above formula then yields

$$A = \left(\frac{145°}{360°}\right) \cdot \pi(5)^2 \approx 31.63 \text{ square inches.}$$

If you can chop up a region R into distinct, nonoverlapping pieces, as shown below, then you can find the area of R by adding the individual areas of the regions.

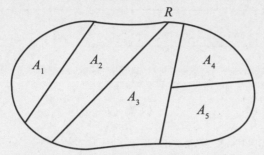

Sometimes, figures are drawn in the coordinate plane. Using the above property, we can chop them into distinct pieces for which there is a known area formula, and sum the areas of these pieces, as in the following sample problem.

14. Determine the area of the following polygonal region:

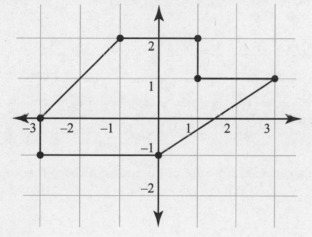

(A) 5 square units

(B) 7 square units

(C) 8 square units

(D) 11 square units

(E) 13 square units

The correct answer is (D). The idea is to divide the polygonal curve into distinct regions, as shown:

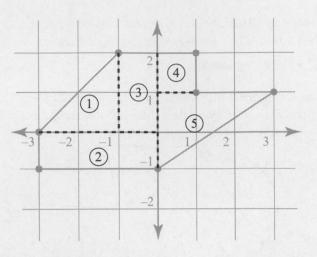

Now, find the areas of each region separately:

Area of **(1)**	Triangle with base 2 and height 2: $A = \frac{1}{2}(2)(2) = 2$
Area of **(2)**	Rectangle with length 3 and width 1: $A = 3 \cdot 1 = 3$
Area of **(3)**	Rectangle with length 2 and width 1: $A = 2 \cdot 1 = 2$
Area of **(4)**	Square with side 1: $A = 1^2 = 1$
Area of **(5)**	Triangle with base 2 and height 3: $A = \frac{1}{2}(3)(2) = 3$

So, the area of this region is the sum of the areas of these five regions, which is 11 square units.

SURFACE AREA

As we discussed earlier in this chapter, net diagrams can help you visualize how to form a polyhedron. Another use of net diagrams is to help develop formulas that can be used to determine the **surface area** of solids. In a net diagram, a solid is cut up and flattened out so it can be visualized as a group of recognizable figures with areas that can be easily computed. Since surface area is a measure of area, the standard units of measure are square inches, square feet, square yards, etc.; the metric system is also commonly used (e.g., square centimeters, square meters). The following are formulas for the surface area of some common three-dimensional figures:

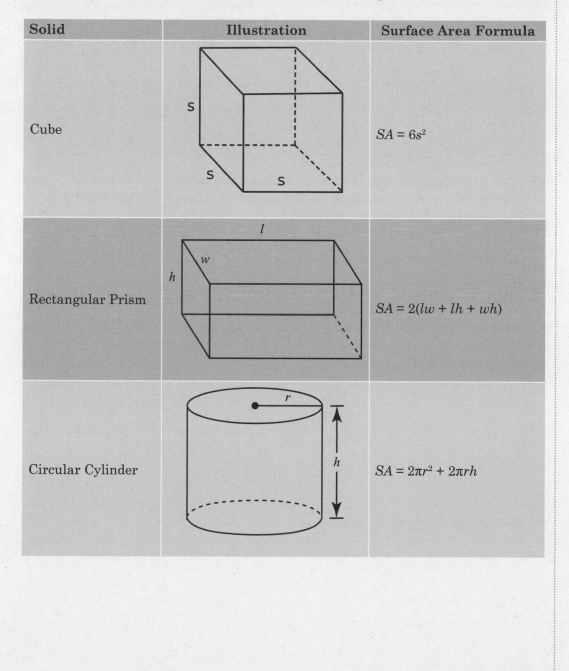

Solid	Illustration	Surface Area Formula
Cube		$SA = 6s^2$
Rectangular Prism		$SA = 2(lw + lh + wh)$
Circular Cylinder		$SA = 2\pi r^2 + 2\pi rh$

Solid	Illustration	Surface Area Formula
Circular Cone	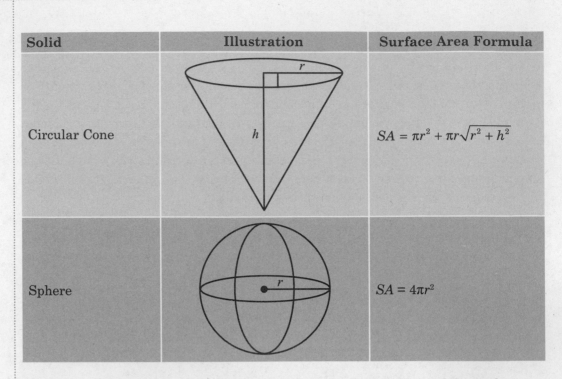	$SA = \pi r^2 + \pi r \sqrt{r^2 + h^2}$
Sphere		$SA = 4\pi r^2$

15. If the height of a circular cylinder equals four times the radius and the surface area is 360π square inches, which of the following is the diameter of the base?

(A) 6 inches

(B) 12 inches

(C) 18 inches

(D) 24 inches

(E) 36 inches

The correct answer is (B). Let r represent the radius of the base. Then, the height $h = 4r$. Using the surface area formula for a circular cylinder yields the following equation that we must solve for r:

$$360\pi = 2\pi r^2 + 2\pi r(4r)$$
$$360\pi = 2\pi r^2 + 8\pi r^2$$
$$360\pi = 10\pi r^2$$
$$36 = r^2$$
$$6 = r$$

So, the diameter must be 12 inches.

16. Dan wishes to apply sealant to the four walls and ceiling of the work shed. The ceiling has dimensions 8 feet by 12 feet and the height of the shed is 9 feet. If each can of sealant is used to seal 200 square feet of wall, how many cans must he purchase?

(A) 1

(B) 2

(C) 3

(D) 4

(E) 5

The correct answer is (C). First, we must determine the total surface area to be sealed. The shed is in the shape of a rectangular prism, whose surface area formula is given above. We must account for four walls and a ceiling, but NOT the floor. So, the surface area is

$$\underbrace{(8 \cdot 12)}_{\text{Ceiling}} + \underbrace{2(8 \cdot 9) + 2(12 \cdot 9)}_{\text{Walls}} = 456 \text{ square feet.}$$

Since each can coats 200 square feet, he must purchase 3 cans of sealant.

VOLUME

The **volume** of a solid in space is the number of *unit cubes* needed to fill it. The standard units of measure of volume are cubic inches, cubic feet, cubic yards, etc.; the metric system is also commonly used (e.g., cubic centimeters, cubic meters). The following are formulas for the volume of some common solids:

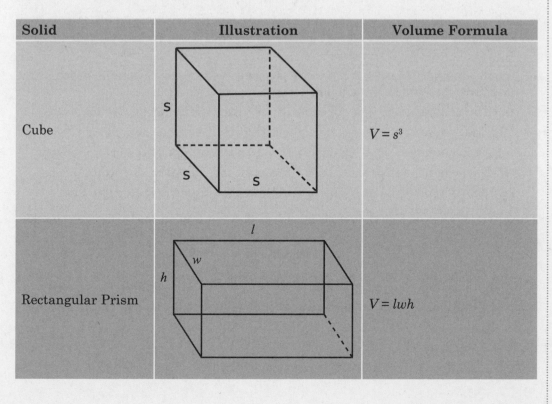

Solid	Illustration	Volume Formula
Cube		$V = s^3$
Rectangular Prism		$V = lwh$

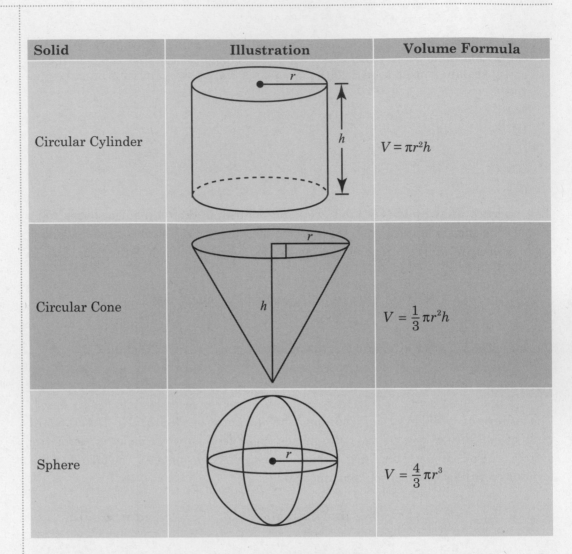

Solid	Illustration	Volume Formula
Circular Cylinder		$V = \pi r^2 h$
Circular Cone		$V = \frac{1}{3}\pi r^2 h$
Sphere		$V = \frac{4}{3}\pi r^3$

17. A cube has side length s. A new cube is formed whose sides are half as long as the original cube. Which of the following statements is true?

(A) The volume of the new cube is half the volume of the original cube.

(B) The volume of the new cube is twice the volume of the original cube.

(C) The volume of the new cube is one-fourth the volume of the original cube.

(D) The volume of the new cube is one-eighth the volume of the original cube.

(E) The volume of the new cube is one-third the volume of the original cube.

The correct answer is (D). We need to determine expressions for both cubes and then compare them. The volume of the original cube is $V_{\text{original}} = s^3$. The length of a side of the new cube is $\frac{1}{2}s$. So, the volume of the new cube is $V_{\text{new}} = \left(\frac{1}{2}s\right)^3 = \frac{1}{8}s^3$. Comparing the two formulas, we see that the volume of the new cube is one-eighth the volume of the original cube.

18. A cylindrical glass is full of water and is to be poured into a rectangular pan of height 3 inches. The base of the pan is 15 inches by 10 inches and the height of the cylinder is 15 inches. What must the radius of the cylinder be so that the water fills the pan, but does not spill?

(A) 5 inches

(B) $\frac{\pi}{5}$ inches

(C) $\frac{\sqrt{\pi}}{15}$ inches

(D) $\sqrt{2\pi}$ inches

(E) $\sqrt{\frac{30}{\pi}}$ inches

The correct answer is (E). First, we need to determine the volume of the rectangular pan. To do so, we simply multiply the three dimensions to get $3 \times 10 \times 15 = 450$ cubic inches. Next, let r denote the radius of the cylinder. Since we know its height is $h = 15$ inches, a formula for its volume is $\pi r^2(15)$. In order for the water to fill, but not spill over the edge of, the pan, the two volumes must be equal. This yields the equation $\pi r^2(15) = 450$. We solve for r as follows:

$$\pi r^2(15) = 450$$
$$\pi r^2 = 30$$
$$r^2 = \frac{30}{\pi}$$
$$r = \sqrt{\frac{30}{\pi}}$$

So, the radius must be $\sqrt{\frac{30}{\pi}}$ inches.

DENSITY

If you have ever attended a rock concert and felt like the audience was packed into the auditorium like a can of sardines, you experienced the effects of a high **density.** The exact opposite effect would be felt if you were to visit Antarctica, where the population is scarce. You can think of the above two examples as "number of people per *unit area*," and if you were measuring the number of fish in a portion of the ocean, you could think of density as "number of fish per *unit volume*." This idea also comes up when computing concentrations of chemicals in a solution (like pollution per unit volume of a lake). A good way of thinking about density is by using the following "verbal" formula:

$$\text{Density} = \frac{\text{Number of ``individuals''}}{\text{Total} = \text{``space''}}$$

Here, "individuals" could be people, fish, amount of chemical, etc., and "space" is typically amount of square footage or volume. Consider the following two sample problems.

19. Population biologists have approximated that there are 30 grizzly bears per square mile in a certain national forest. If the entire forest takes up 25 square miles, which of the following is the number of grizzly bears in the entire forest?

(A) 350

(B) 750

(C) 1,250

(D) 1,500

(E) 2,500

The correct answer is (B). This problem requires us to solve the formula

$$\text{Density} = \frac{\text{Number of "individuals"}}{\text{Total = "space"}}$$

for *Number of "individuals."* To do so, we cross-multiply to obtain (30)(25) = 750 grizzly bears in the entire forest.

20. The concentration of pollutant in a small pond is 0.25 ounces per cubic yard. If the total amount of pollution in the lake is 1,100 ounces, what is the volume of the pond?

(A) 350 cubic yards

(B) 1,200 cubic yards

(C) 2,500 cubic yards

(D) 3,200 cubic yards

(E) 4,400 cubic yards

The correct answer is (E). This problem requires us to solve the formula $\text{Density} = \frac{\text{Number of "individuals"}}{\text{Total = "space"}}$ for *Total "space,"* which is the number of cubic yards of water in the pond. We do so by dividing 1,100 ounces by 0.25 ounces per cubic yard. Doing so yields 4,400 cubic yards.

SUMMING IT UP

- When converting from a smaller unit of measure to a larger one, divide by the conversion factor; if you are converting from a larger unit of measure to a smaller one, multiply by the conversion factor. However, when more than one unit of measure is involved, it is convenient to use ratios to see the units cancel.

- An **acute angle** measures between 0 and 90 degrees; a **right angle** measures 90 degrees; an **obtuse angle** measures between 90 and 180 degrees. **Complementary** angles sum to 90 degrees, and **supplementary** angles sum to 180 degrees.

- **The Triangle Sum Rule:** the sum of the measures of the three angles in any triangle must be 180°; **the Triangle Inequality:** the sum of the lengths of any two sides of a triangle must be strictly larger than the length of the third side.

- The **Pythagorean theorem** says that $a^2 + b^2 = c^2$. (a and b are the legs of the triangle, and c is the hypotenuse, the side opposite the right angle.)

- Specifically, for a regular n-gon, the measure of each exterior angle is $\dfrac{360°}{n}$ and the measure of each interior angle is $\dfrac{(n-2)180°}{n}$. The measure of every central angle of a regular n-gon is $\dfrac{360°}{n}$.

- A **polyhedron** is a solid with faces made up of all congruent polygons. To find the surface area of a polyhedron, envision cutting it along various edges and lying it flat on the table to get a net diagram; then, compute the area of all net segments and add together.

- Calculating the perimeters of triangles, parallelograms, trapezoids, etc., usually requires that you measure the length of a diagonal (or hypotenuse of a triangle). You will need to use the Pythagorean theorem.

- The distance between two points $P(x_1, y_1)$ and $Q(x_2, y_2)$ on a coordinate plane is $\sqrt{(x_2 - x_1)^2 + (y_2 - y_1)^2}$.

- If you can chop up a region R into distinct, nonoverlapping pieces, then you can find the area of R by adding the individual areas of the regions.

- The volume of a solid in space is the number of **unit cubes** needed to fill it.

- $\text{Density} = \dfrac{\text{Number of "individuals"}}{\text{Total} = \text{"space"}}$

Data Analysis, Probability, and Statistics

chapter 11

OVERVIEW

- **Data collection, sampling, and making inferences**
- **Counting principles**
- **Probability**
- **Random variables**
- **Measures of central tendency and variability**
- **Visualizing data**
- **Linear relationships**
- **Summing It Up**

Statistics is the collection of procedures used for gathering data and analyzing information. Many word problems on the HiSET® Mathematics subtest require you to interpret both mathematical and visual representations of data. Then, you will often have to take that data to calculate values like probability and measures of central tendency. This chapter will define HiSET® terminology that covers probability and statistics, and you will find a review of the variety of problem types you will likely see on the exam.

DATA COLLECTION, SAMPLING, AND MAKING INFERENCES

Suppose you have a data set—for example, the number of text messages college students send daily, weights of cats at a pet store, and so on. Each measurement in the data set originates from a distinct source (in these cases a college student or a cat) called a **unit.** The complete collection of units about which information is sought is called the **population.**

Given a population, we often want to understand the responses of its members to some question. A **variable** is a characteristic of the population we are interested in: how many text messages were sent or the weight of the cats. The **data** are the observed values of a variable: x number of text messages for each person surveyed or y pounds for every cat weighed. There are two main types of variables: **qualitative** and **quantitative.** A qualitative variable is one whose values are categories (e.g., gender, hair color, demographic information). A quantitative variable is one whose values are numerical quantities (e.g., height, temperature, number of heads obtained in 3 flips of a coin).

TIP

It is rarely possible to collect data for every single unit in a population due to limited resources and/or the inability to actually collect an infinite number of scientific measurements. Therefore, a representative subset of the population of units, called a sample, is often observed to gather information for the variable of interest.

Some critical elements of sampling are:

- The sample should be reasonably large. For instance, if the population of your study is the entire U.S. population, you wouldn't want to choose your sample to consist of merely 5 people from Ohio.

- The sample should be devoid of **bias.** A study is said to be biased if it systematically favors certain outcomes. For instance, suppose that you were investigating a question in which females would likely respond differently than males and that your population is equally split between males and females. In such case, a sample consisting of 95% females could potentially yield biased results.

There are several ways to go about constructing a sample:

- **Random sampling**—Use a random number generator, or other randomized scheme, to choose the sample.

- **Systematic sampling**—Number each subject of the population and then select every kth number. You must make certain that the pattern you choose does not give rise to a bias. For example, if the list alternated as *Male, Female, Male, Female,* choosing even multiples would generate a list of all females, while odd multiples would generate a list of all males.

- **Stratified sampling**—Divide the population into groups according to some characteristic important to the study. Then, choose a sample from each group and combine them all into a single sample at the end. For example, suppose the college president wants to know about student reaction to the decision about constructing a new stadium. One could divide the student population into the four groups—for example, *Freshman, Sophomore, Junior, Senior*—and further subdivide each of these into *Male, Female.* Then, sample from each of the eight groups to ensure a more representative sample of the student population.

- **Cluster sampling**—Choose subjects according to groups representative of the population. For example, suppose a researcher wishes to investigate an issue that requires her to gather information from people who live in apartments. If there are ten apartment buildings (of approximately equal size) in the city, she might choose two buildings and interview everyone in each building.

- **Convenience sampling**—Choose subjects based on convenience, such as interviewing people at the local mall one afternoon.

1. As part of a survey, 160 college students were asked about how many ounces of tea they consumed daily. The participants were obtained at the most popular coffee and tea shop in town. Which of the following best describes a potential issue with interpreting the results of this survey?

    (A) Not every college student was surveyed.

    (B) Sample surveys tend to be unreliable.

    (C) Not every student drinks tea.

    (D) The sample is biased because it was taken at a coffee and tea shop.

    (E) There are no issues.

The correct answer is (D). Since the participants in the sample were all obtained at the coffee and tea shop, it is likely that they drink more tea than those who do *not* visit such a shop. So, the results would not necessarily generalize to *all* college students.

2. In a large school district, all teachers from two buildings are interviewed to determine whether they believe the students have less homework to do now than in previous years. What type of sampling is this an example of?

    (A) Convenience sampling

    (B) Stratified sampling

    (C) Cluster sampling

    (D) Systematic sampling

    (E) Qualitative sampling

The correct answer is (C). This is an example of cluster sampling because subjects are being chosen according to intact groups that are representative of the population.

COUNTING PRINCIPLES

Determining the *total* number of possible outcomes in an experiment, whether tossing a coin 5 times, rolling a die twice, or randomly selecting colored balls from a bin, is an important step to assessing likelihood, or chance, of getting each possible outcome. Answering this question type requires a systematic way of counting that includes two main concepts: **combinations** and **permutations.**

A *permutation* of a set of objects is an arrangement of those objects in which each object is used once and only once. For example, if you have objects labeled A, B, C, D, and E, some permutations of these objects are ABCDE and DECBA. Any unique ordering of the letters produces a different permutation. The number of ways to arrange n objects in such a manner is $n!$.

Sometimes, we want to only arrange *some* of the objects in a given set. That is, what if we had n letters but we only wanted to arrange k of them? This is a "permutation of n objects taken k at a time." The number of such arrangements is written as: $P(n,k) = \dfrac{n!}{(n-k)!}$. Let's look at an example.

TIP

To calculate these concepts, let's first define an important part of each formula. For any positive integer n, n! = n × (n − 1) × (n − 2) × ... × 3 × 2 × 1. For instance, 4! = 4 × 3 × 2 × 1.

ALERT!

In permutations, order matters.

3. In how many ways can 4 books from a collection of 7 be arranged on a shelf?
   (A) 120
   (B) 210
   (C) 720
   (D) 840
   (E) 5,040

The correct answer is (D). We wish to arrange 4 of the 7 books, so we must calculate $P(7, 4)$:

$$P(7,4) = \frac{7!}{(7-4)!} = \frac{7!}{3!} = \frac{7 \times 6 \times 5 \times 4 \times \cancel{3} \times \cancel{2} \times \cancel{1}}{\cancel{3} \times \cancel{2} \times \cancel{1}} = 7 \times 6 \times 5 \times 4 = 840$$

Sometimes, the order in which objects are arranged is *not* relevant, like when forming a committee of 4 people from a group of 10 people in which all committee members have the same influence, or when simply selecting 5 cards randomly from a standard deck of 52 cards. To determine the number of such selections, a *combination* is required.

The number of ways of selecting k objects from a group of n objects in which order does NOT matter is given by the formula $C(n,k) = \dfrac{n!}{k!(n-k)!}$ and is called "the number of combinations of n objects taken k at a time."

Let's take a look at a sample HiSET® question that covers this concept.

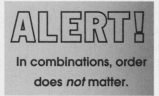

ALERT!

In combinations, order does *not* matter.

4. Max found 10 used books in a clearance bin that he likes equally well, but he only has enough money to purchase 3 of them. In how many different ways can he select 3 books to purchase?
   (A) 120
   (B) 500
   (C) 720
   (D) 604,800
   (E) 3,628,800

The correct answer is (A). Order does not matter here because he is simply purchasing a collection of unrelated books. (He is not, as in the previous example, ordering them in a certain way on a shelf.) So, we use the combinations formula with $n = 10$ and $k = 3$:

$$C(10,3) = \frac{10!}{3!(10-3)!} = \frac{10!}{3!7!} = \frac{10 \times 9 \times 8 \times \cancel{7}!}{(3 \times 2 \times 1) \times \cancel{7}!} = 120$$

PROBABILITY

A HiSET® question that asks you about any process involving uncertainty or chance (e.g., predicting the stock market or weather, guessing the percentage of votes a candidate will receive, or simply flipping a coin) tests your knowledge of probability.

An **outcome** is the result of a single trial of a probability experiment, and the collection of all outcomes is the **sample space,** which is written as a set. For instance, if you roll a typical six-sided die and record the number of the face on which it comes to rest, the outcomes are the labels on the faces, namely $S = \{1, 2, 3, 4, 5, 6\}$. An **event** is a subset of the sample space and is usually described using one or more conditions. For instance, the event that "the die lands on an even number" is the subset $E = \{2, 4, 6\}$. Suppose E and F represent events of some probability experiment. Some common events formed using them are as follows:

Event	Description in words
Complement of E	All outcomes NOT in E
E or F	All outcomes in E OR in F OR in both
E and F	All outcomes in common to E AND F

You are likely familiar with the notion of chance, such as the percent chance it will rain on a given day or likelihood that a professional basketball player will make a three-point shot. Using the terminology you will see on the HiSET®, the *probability* of an event A is denoted by $P(A)$ and is a number between 0 and 1, inclusive, that is a percent chance of event A occurring. But, how do we actually compute such a quantity? The answer can be rather complicated, but for most of the experiments you will encounter, each outcome in the sample space is *equally likely*. So, if the sample space contains N outcomes, then the probability of any *one* of them occurring is $\frac{1}{N}$. This can be extended to events in the sense that if A contains k elements, then

$$P(A) = \frac{\text{Number of outcomes in } A}{\text{Number of possible outcomes}} = \frac{k}{N}.$$

For instance, in the above dice experiment, since the event "the die lands on an even number" is the subset $E = \{2, 4, 6\}$, and all outcomes are equally likely, $P(E) = \frac{3}{6} = \frac{1}{2}$. So, there's a 50% chance of the die landing on an even number.

Sometimes, data from an experiment (like a survey) are in the form of **frequencies.** For instance, you ask a question of 120 people, all randomly chosen, and there is 1 of 5 responses possible. You tabulate the number of responses (that is, the *frequencies*) for each choice and divide that number by 120 (the total number of responses). This *relative frequency* can be used to make an educated guess about how *the entire population from which the respondents were chosen* would answer this question. Let's take a look at how this concept might be presented on the HiSET®.

5. Hospital records indicated that 157 maternity parents stayed in the hospital for the number of days shown in the following distribution:

Number of days stayed	Frequency
3	15
4	32
5	56
6	49
7	5

TIP

Two events are *mutually exclusive* if they do not share any outcomes.

Compute the probability that a maternity patient will stay at most 4 days.

(A) 0.20

(B) 0.25

(C) 0.30

(D) 0.50

(E) 0.75

The correct answer is (C). We use the relative frequency to determine the percentage of people of those who satisfy the condition. Then, we use that to assign the probability to the event for *general* maternity patients. "No more than four days" translates to "3 days or 4 days" in the present problem. The number of people who satisfy this is 15 + 32 = 47. So, the relative frequency is $\frac{47}{157} \approx 0.30$. So, the desired probability is 0.30.

Computing the probability of a **compound event,** like A or B, can be a bit tricky because there can be outcomes common to both A and B, and we don't want to count them twice! This is where the following *addition formula* is useful:

$$P(A \text{ or } B) = P(A) + P(B) - P(A \text{ and } B)$$

6. Suppose you select a card at random from a standard 52-card deck. What is the probability that the card you pull is a queen or a spade?

(A) $\frac{1}{4}$

(B) $\frac{1}{13}$

(C) $\frac{1}{52}$

(D) $\frac{4}{13}$

(E) $\frac{17}{52}$

The correct answer is (D). Let A be the event "card is a queen" and B be the event "card is a spade." Since there are 4 queens in a standard deck, $P(A) = \frac{4}{52} = \frac{1}{13}$, and since there are 13 spades in a standard deck, $P(B) = \frac{13}{52} = \frac{1}{4}$. Finally, there is ONE queen of spades. So, $P(A \text{ and } B) = \frac{1}{52}$. Using the addition formula then yields P(A or B) = P(A) + P(B) − P(A and B) = $\frac{1}{13} + \frac{1}{4} - \frac{1}{52} = \frac{16}{52} = \frac{4}{13}$.

RANDOM VARIABLES

Consider the experiment of rolling two fair dice and recording the values of Die 1 and Die 2 in an ordered pair. The sample space consists of 36 elements (including redundancies if we do not distinguish between Die 1 and Die 2), pictured below:

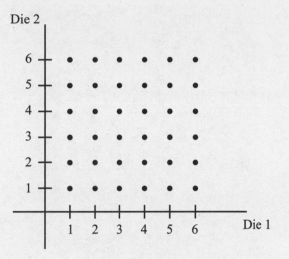

Suppose we are interested in how likely it is to get the various sums of the two dice when you roll the dice, but we are less interested in the actual outcomes that produce these sums. We could define a function that assigns the sum to each possible roll and then calculate the frequencies to answer our question. Such a function is called a **random variable** in probability lingo.

Let us define a random variable X to be the sum of the dots appearing on Die 1 and Die 2 when they've come to rest. The assignment of the values of X for the members of the sample space is as follows:

$$X(1, 1) = 2$$
$$X(1, 2) = X(2, 1) = 3$$
$$X(1, 3) = X(2, 2) = X(3, 1) = 4$$
$$X(1, 4) = X(2, 3) = X(3, 2) = X(4, 1) = 5$$
$$X(1, 5) = X(2, 4) = X(3, 3) = X(4, 2) = X(5, 1) = 6$$
$$X(1, 6) = X(2, 5) = X(3, 4) = X(4, 3) = X(5, 2) = X(6, 1) = 7$$
$$X(2, 6) = X(3, 5) = X(4, 4) = X(5, 3) = X(6, 2) = 8$$
$$X(3, 6) = X(4, 5) = X(5, 4) = X(6, 3) = 9$$
$$X(4, 6) = X(5, 5) = X(6, 4) = 10$$
$$X(5, 6) = X(6, 5) = 11$$
$$X(6, 6) = 12$$

Now, since the dice were both fair, all outcomes in the sample space are equally likely. As such, we are guided by classical probability and assign the probabilities to each value of X in a manner consistent with the relative frequency of the value. This is tabulated below—for simplicity, the fractions are not simplified:

Value x of X	Probability $P(X = x)$
2	$\frac{1}{36}$
3	$\frac{2}{36}$
4	$\frac{3}{36}$
5	$\frac{4}{36}$
6	$\frac{5}{36}$
7	$\frac{6}{36}$
8	$\frac{5}{36}$
9	$\frac{4}{36}$
10	$\frac{3}{36}$
11	$\frac{2}{36}$
12	$\frac{1}{36}$

This is an example of a **probability distribution.** We can pictorially represent it using a bar graph called a **probability histogram:**

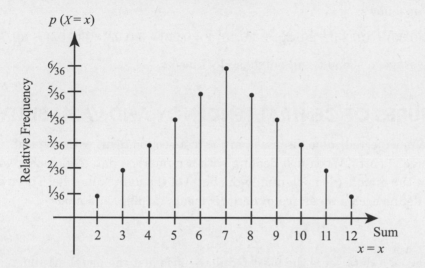

7. A survey of Wildfire.com shoppers reveals the following probability distribution of the number of books purchased per site visit:

x	0	1	2	3	4	5	6	7
$P(X = x)$	0.35	0.25	0.20	0.08	0.06	0.03	0.02	0.01

What is the probability that a shopper will buy between 3 and 5 books, inclusive?

(A) 0.06

(B) 0.09

(C) 0.11

(D) 0.14

(E) 0.17

The correct answer is (E). Using the given data, the event "between 3 and 5 books, inclusive" corresponds to buying 3, 4, or 5 books, all of which are mutually exclusive, written $3 \leq X \leq 5$. So, the probability of this event is $P(3 \leq X \leq 5) = P(X = 3) + P(X = 4) + P(X = 5) = 0.08 + 0.06 + 0.03 = 0.17$.

A weighted average of all possible values of a random variable X, computed using their probabilities, often provides insight on what to *expect* in the long run. It is called the *expected value*, denoted E(X), and is computed using the formula $E(X) = \sum x \cdot P(X = x)$. The value you get will likely NOT be an outcome produced by X, but rather it is viewed as a *typical value* of that random variable.

8. According to the Wildfire.com table from the previous question, what is the expected number of books that a shopper, on average, will purchase?

(A) 1.47

(B) 2.1

(C) 2.5

(D) 3

(E) 4.3

The correct answer is (A). Whenever asked for what happens "on average," you want to compute the expected value. Using the formula given, the expected value here is given as follows:

$$E(X) = 0(0.35) + 1(0.25) + 2(0.20) + 3(0.08) + 4(0.06) + 5(0.03) + 6(0.02) + 7(0.01) = 1.47$$

So, on average, a shopper will purchase 1.47 books.

MEASURES OF CENTRAL TENDENCY AND VARIABILITY

The idea of expected value discussed in the last section dealt with "typical" values or an average of sorts. When just dealing with a numerical data set, such a value tells us where the middle (and potentially the bulk) of the data values lie. There are three ways to define such a **measure of center:** mean, median, and mode.

Mean

The **mean** of a data set is the most familiar—it is just the usual arithmetic average of the data values. Just add them up and divide by the number of values you added.

If there are no "extreme values" in the data set, then this gives a good idea about the average value of the data set. But in a data set like {10, 10, 10, 10, 110}, in some sense the "average value" is 10 since 4 of the 5 values are 10, but the mean is actually 30—not a good descriptor of the center of this data set! For such a situation, we need a different way of computing "average" or center. Data sets for which the mean is an appropriate measure of center have **symmetric histograms,** meaning that the picture is more or less bell-shaped with peak at or near the mean, as shown below:

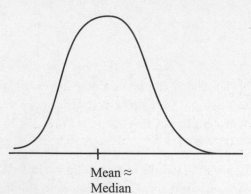

Mean ≈
Median

Median

The **median** is another way of computing the center of a data set that is immune to such effects of extreme values. To compute it, arrange the values in the data set in numerical order, from smallest to largest. If there is an odd number of data values, then the median is the data value smack dab in the middle of the set. For instance, if there are 21 data values arranged in numerical order, the median is the value in the 11th position (obtained by dividing 21 by 2 and adding 1 to the whole part). If, on the other hand, there is an even number of data values, then the median is the arithmetic

ALERT!

Even if zero is among the values you included in the sum, you MUST include that value in the total count by which you divide; otherwise, you have not accounted for its effect on the average.

average of the "middle two" values. For instance, if there are 20 data values arranged in numerical order, then median is the average of the values in the 10th and 11th positions.

By definition, literally half of the data values lie to the left of the median and half lie to its right. Data sets for which the median is an appropriate measure of center have **skewed histograms,** meaning that the picture representation has a peak to the left or right with a large tail to the other side; the median is positioned near the peak, but the mean is pulled toward the tail, as shown below:

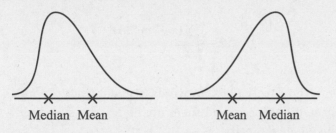

Mode

The mean and median are only defined for data sets of numerical values. If the data was *qualitative* in nature (e.g., favorite sport, ice cream flavor preference, etc.), then they cannot be used to talk about "average value." That's where the **mode** comes into play. The mode of a data set is the value(s) that occur most frequently. For instance, the mode of the data set {vanilla, vanilla, chocolate, vanilla, strawberry, butter pecan} is vanilla, while the modes of the data set {3, 5, 5, 3, 6, 7, 5, 3} are 3 and 5. If all values of a data set occur the same number of times, then we say there is no mode.

8. Every data value in a data set composed of at least eighteen values is 40, except for one that has a value of 5. Which statement best describes the median of this data set?

   (A) The median is greater than 40.

   (B) The median equals 40.

   (C) The median is less than 40.

   (D) The median may be greater than or less than 40, depending on the size of the data set.

   (E) This cannot be determined, irrespective of the size of the data set.

The correct answer is (B). If the values are placed in order, the first value will be 5 and then the remaining values will be 40. There would simply need to be three data values in the data set in order to ensure the median is 40. And so, since there are more than 18 total values, the middle value must be 40.

Measures of Variability

Measures of center provide half the story. They give us an idea of where the balance point of the data set is, but they do not give us any indication of how the data are *spread out.* For instance, the following two data sets both have a mean of 10, but they are VERY different:

$$\{10, 10, 10, 10, 10, 10\} \text{ and } \{5, 5, 5, 15, 15, 15\}$$

There are two commonly used **measures of variability:** standard deviation and interquartile range. Which one is used depends on which measure of center—mean or the median—is being used.

The **standard deviation,** s, is based on the mean, so it is generally used with data sets whose center is best described by the mean. It is a measure of the *typical distance* that data values are from the mean. The formula for the standard deviation for a data set containing n data values is as follows:

$$s = \sqrt{\frac{\sum (x - \text{mean})^2}{n - 1}}$$

Here, x represents the data values. In words, you subtract the mean from each data value, square those differences, add them up, divide the sum by $n - 1$, and take the square root of the whole quantity.

In the extreme case that $s = 0$, all data values would be identical (as in the data set $\{10, 10, 10, 10, 10\}$), and hence each one would equal the mean. Any value that is more than two standard deviations from the mean is called an **outlier,** or unusual value.

The **interquartile range (IQR)** is used with data sets whose center is best described by the median. It measures the spread of the middle 50% of the data set. In order to compute the IQR, we must determine the **quartiles,** or data values in the 25th, 50th, and 75th positions in the data set once it has been arranged in numerically increasing order.

- The 50th quartile is just the median, so that value is already known.

- To find the 25th quartile, divide the number of values in the data set by 4. The resulting number is the position of the 25th quartile. To get the value, locate the data value whose position is the *whole* portion of this quotient. If the decimal portion is between 0 and 0.35, use that as the position; if it is between 0.35 and 0.65, average that data value and the next one to get the quartile; and if the decimal portion is larger than 0.65, use the value in the next position as the quartile. The value you get is denoted Q_1, and 25% of the data set lies below it.

- The third quartile, denoted by Q_3, is computed in a similar manner; 75% of the data set lies below it.

The IQR is defined to be $Q_3 - Q_1$. This tells you that the middle 50% of the data set varies by about $Q_3 - Q_1$ *units*.

9. At the beginning of each practice, a coach times and records how long it takes each of his athletes to complete one mile around the track. The distribution is symmetric, with a mean of 414 seconds and a standard deviation of 55 seconds. Which of these statements is not true?

    (A) The middle 50% of mile run times must have a range of 102 seconds.

    (B) Most mile run times are between 359 seconds and 469 seconds.

    (C) The typical mile run time for an athlete varied by about 55 seconds from 414 seconds.

TIP

You will likely not need to compute standard deviation by hand, but you should know that the larger the s value, the more spread out the data.

(D) A mile run time slower than 538 seconds would be labeled as an outlier.

(E) The median is close to 414 seconds.

The correct answer is (A). The statement in choice (A) is an interpretation of the IQR which is not given. In fact, it cannot be computed given the information.

VISUALIZING DATA

A **dot plot** is a useful way to display data for small data sets. Dot plots are similar to bar graphs (and the histograms that we discussed earlier). You decide on a scale, and then put a dot above each value along the *x*-axis; multiple occurrences of values in a data set are represented by stacked dots above that value on the *x*-axis. Consider the following example:

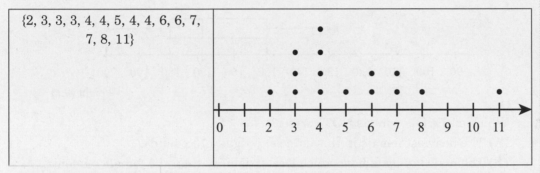

{2, 3, 3, 3, 4, 4, 5, 4, 4, 6, 6, 7, 7, 8, 11}

A **box plot** is a way to visualize a data set using five summary statistics: minimum value, first quartile, median, third quartile, and maximum value. The graph consists of two points corresponding to the smallest and largest values in the data set and three vertical line segments corresponding to the quartiles and median. A box is constructed with the quartiles as two parallel sides, and line segments are drawn from these two sides to the minimum and maximum values. Consider the following example:

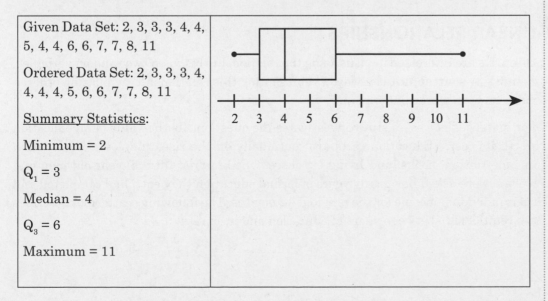

Given Data Set: 2, 3, 3, 3, 4, 4, 5, 4, 4, 6, 6, 7, 7, 8, 11

Ordered Data Set: 2, 3, 3, 3, 4, 4, 4, 4, 5, 6, 6, 7, 7, 8, 11

Summary Statistics:

Minimum = 2

$Q_1 = 3$

Median = 4

$Q_3 = 6$

Maximum = 11

> **TIP**
>
> From the dot plot, we can see that the bulk of the data lies to the left of 5 and that there is a potential outlier at 11.

Outliers can be detected using the IQR. Here, IQR = 7 − 3 = 4. A general rule of thumb is the following: *An outlier is a value in the data set that is less than $Q_1 − 1.5 \times IQR$ or larger than $Q_3 + 1.5 \times IQR$.*

For the above example, any value less than 3 − 1.5(4) = −3 or greater than 7 + 1.5(4) = 12 is an outlier; therefore, 11 is not an outlier.

Box plots are useful when trying to compare two data sets on the same variable, as in the following sample question:

10. The weights of the male and female students in a class are summarized in the following box plots:

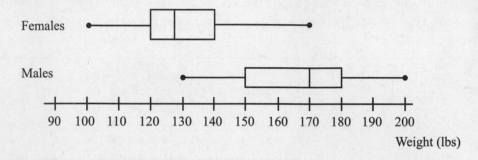

Which of the following is NOT correct?

(A) The heaviest female in this data set weighs 170 pounds.

(B) The male students have much less variability than the female students.

(C) About 25% of female students have weights more than 140 pounds.

(D) The median weight of male students is about 170 pounds.

(E) About 50% of the male students have weights between 150 and 180 pounds.

The correct answer is (B). The two box plots appear very similar, even though the actual quartile values for males are greater than those for the females.

LINEAR RELATIONSHIPS

Often, we are interested in visualizing the relationship between two random variables, X and Y. A **scatterplot** is a way of representing this relationship by plotting ordered pairs (x, y) on a coordinate plane.

For instance, let's say a study investigates the question, "Is the value of an education worth its cost?" Education costs are continually on the rise, and costs of education include tuition, books, and living expenses. One-hundred fifty 30-year-old men and women were asked how many years of formal education they each had completed and their individual income for the previous 12 months. The following scatterplot describes the relationship between years of education and income.

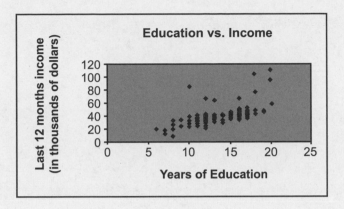

From this scatterplot, we can infer that the more years of education a person has, the higher their salary. This trend can be described even more precisely by fitting a "best fit line" to the scatterplot. We call the relationship between X and Y **linear** if the trend between X and Y is reasonably described by a line. If there is another curve (e.g., parabola, exponential curve, etc.) that more reasonably describes the relationship, we call it **nonlinear.**

Generally, the more tightly packed the points are in a scatterplot, the stronger the relationship. If the data points rise from left to right, we say the relationship is *positive,* while if they fall from left to right, we say the trend is *negative.* The table below shows some basic examples:

Relationship between X and Y	Typical Scatterplot
Strong positive linear relationship	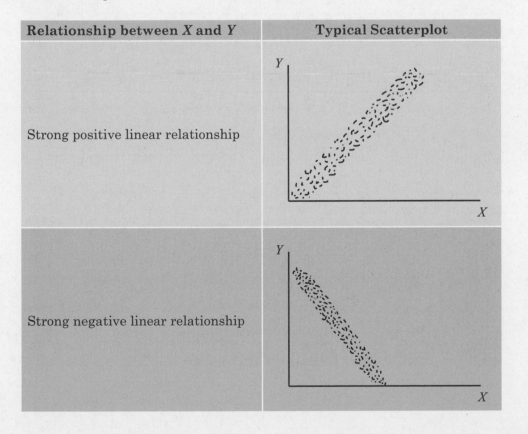
Strong negative linear relationship	

Relationship between X and Y	Typical Scatterplot
Weak-to-moderate positive linear relationship	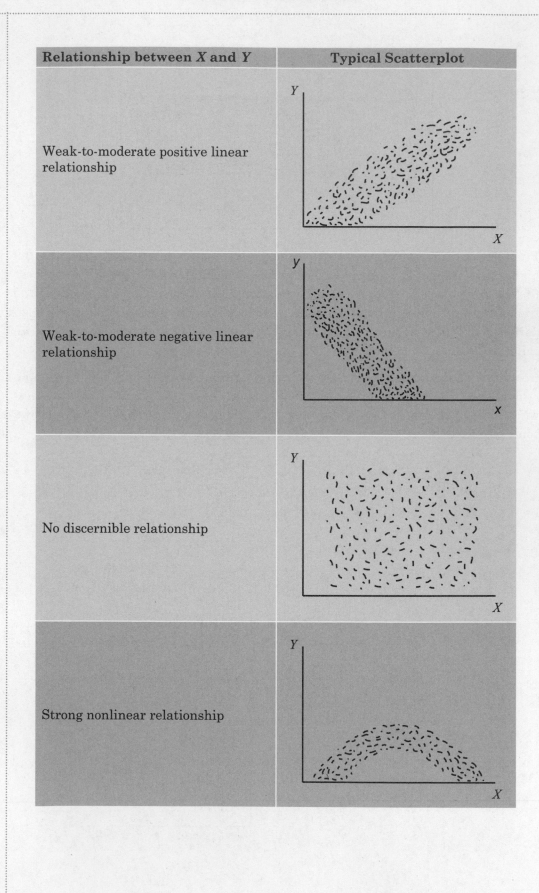
Weak-to-moderate negative linear relationship	
No discernible relationship	
Strong nonlinear relationship	

11. The question, "Do people with larger hands send text messages at a slower pace?" was studied by a college student in a statistics class. A numerical scale 1–8 was devised to describe "hand size," in which larger numbers correspond to larger hands. The following scatterplot is a visualization of the data she gathered:

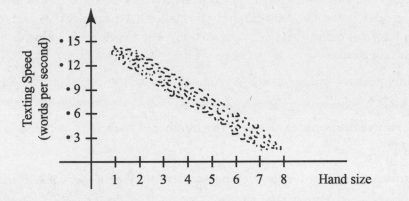

Which of the following best describes the relationship between hand size and texting speed?

(A) There is no relationship between these two variables.

(B) As texting speed increases, hand size increases.

(C) The larger one's hand size, in general, the slower they type text messages.

(D) The relationship between hand size and texting speed is positive.

(E) A nonlinear curve best fits the data depicted in the scatterplot.

The correct answer is (C). The relationship between hand size and texting speed is strong, negative, and linear. So, the larger the hand size, the slower the texting speed. This is quantified in choice (C).

SUMMING IT UP

- A **variable** is a characteristic of the population you want to observe, and **data** are the observed values of a variable. A **qualitative** variable's values are categories (e.g., gender, hair color, demographic information). A **quantitative** variable's values are numerical quantities (e.g., height, temperature, number of heads obtained in 3 flips of a coin).

- For any positive integer n, $n! = n \times (n-1) \times (n-2) \times \dots \times 3 \times 2 \times 1$. For example, $4! = 4 \times 3 \times 2 \times 1$.

- In **permutations,** order matters. The number of such arrangements is written as $P(n,k) = \dfrac{n!}{(n-k)!}$.

- In **combinations,** order does *not* matter. The number of ways of selecting k objects from a group of n objects is written as $C(n,k) = \dfrac{n!}{k!(n-k)!}$.

- If a sample space contains N outcomes, then the probability of any *one* of them occurring is $\dfrac{1}{N}$. This can be extended to events in the sense that if A contains k elements, then $P(A) = \dfrac{\text{Number of outcomes in } A}{\text{Number of possible outcomes}} = \dfrac{k}{N}$. To find the probability of a **compound event,** use $P(A \text{ or } B) = P(A) + P(B) - P(A \text{ and } B)$.

- The **mean** of a data set is the arithmetic average of the data values. To compute the **median,** arrange the values in the data set in numerical order, from smallest to largest. If there is an odd number of data values, then the median is the data value in the middle of the set. If there is an even number of data values, then the median is the arithmetic average of the middle two values. The **mode** of a data set is the value(s) that occurs most frequently.

- The formula for the standard deviation for a data set containing n data values is

$$s = \sqrt{\frac{\sum (x - \text{mean})^2}{n-1}}.$$

- In order to compute the IQR, determine the **quartiles,** or data values in the 25th, 50th, and 75th positions in the data set once it has been arranged in numerically increasing order. The IQR is $Q_3 - Q_1$.

- In a scatterplot, the relationship between X and Y is **linear** if the trend between X and Y can be described by a line. If there is another curve that more reasonably describes the relationship, the relationship is **nonlinear.**

Algebraic Concepts

chapter 12

OVERVIEW

- **Working with algebraic expressions**
- **Linear equations and inequalities**
- **Quadratic equations**
- **Functions**
- **Graphs and their properties**
- **Summing It Up**

Algebra is major branch of mathematics that includes everything from dealing with expressions involving variables and solving different types of equations, to graphing functions and setting up and solving systems of linear equations and inequalities. This chapter reviews the algebra foundations you need to know for the HiSET®.

WORKING WITH ALGEBRAIC EXPRESSIONS

What makes algebra different from just basic work with number systems is the use of variables. A **variable** is an unknown quantity represented by a letter, like x, y, or z; a **constant** is a real number whose value does not change. A **term** is a variable or a constant, or products of powers thereof, and an **algebraic expression** is an arithmetic combination of terms, like $5x - 3yz$ or $2xy^3 - 5xz + 3$. If two terms have the same "variable part" they are called *like terms*. For instance, $43a^5$ and $-6a^5$ are like terms because both have a base of a with an exponent of 5. Even though the terms have different coefficients, they are still like terms. If two terms have different variable parts, then the two terms are NOT like terms. For example, $7zy$ and $7xy$ are unlike because they have different variable parts; $3m^3$ and $4m^6$ are also unlike even though the bases are powers of the same variable.

Since variables represent real numbers, it makes sense that all of the rules (e.g., order of operations, exponent rules, etc.) and properties of arithmetic (e.g., commutative property, associative property, distributive property) should apply to algebraic expressions. To add (or subtract) like terms, we add (or subtract) the coefficients of the terms and keep the variable parts unchanged. For instance, $2x^4 + 4x^4 = 6x^4$. When multiplying or dividing terms, use the exponent rules just as when simplifying arithmetic expressions. This might require using the distributive property repeatedly. Remember the FOIL method when multiplying two binomials? This is actually the distributive property applied twice! For instance:

$$(x + y)(2x - 1) = \underbrace{x(2x) + x(-1)}_{\substack{\text{first application of} \\ \text{distributive property}}} + \underbrace{y(2x) + y(-1)}_{\substack{\text{second application of} \\ \text{distributive property}}} = 2x^2 - x + 2xy - y$$

This same process works for multiplying trinomials and polynomials with even more terms. You simply have more products to compute and more terms to combine. Let's look at another example.

1. Simplify the following algebraic expression:

$$5x^3y - \frac{2x^2y^3}{(xy)^2}$$

(A) $7x^3y$

(B) $3x^3y$

(C) $3x^6y^2$

(D) $5x^3y - 2x^4y^2$

(E) $3x^7y^3$

The correct answer is (B). We use the exponent rules to simplify the quotient in this expression, and then add like terms:

$$5x^3y - \frac{2x^5y^3}{(xy)^2} = 5x^3y - \frac{2x^5y^3}{x^2y^2}$$
$$= 5x^3y - 2x^3y$$
$$= 3x^3y$$

When evaluating algebraic expressions for specific values of the variables, simply substitute the values in and simplify the arithmetic expression.

2. Evaluate the expression $-s^2(s + 2t)^2 + 3st$ when $s = -1$ and $t = -2$.

(A) -44

(B) -19

(C) -4

(D) 16

(E) 31

The correct answer is (B). Substitute $s = -1$ and $t = -2$ into the expression and simplify using the order of operations, as follows:

$$-s^2(s + 2t)^2 + 3st = -(-1)^2\left(-1 + 2(-2)\right)^2 + 3(-1)(-2)$$
$$= -(1)(-5)^2 + 3(-1)(-2)$$
$$= -1(25) + 3(-1)(-2)$$
$$= -25 + 6$$
$$= -19$$

TIP

Powers must be the same for like variables to also be like terms!

LINEAR EQUATIONS AND INEQUALITIES

Linear equations are equations in which the unknown variable is raised to the first power, like $5x = 13$ and $4(x-1) = 3$. To solve linear equation, simplify various expressions by clearing fractions and using the order of operations, together with the distributive property of multiplication, to isolate the variable on one side of the equation. The basic rule to remember is balancing both sides of the equations. If you add or subtract a number from one side, you *must* do so to the other side; if you divide or multiply one side by a number, you *must* do it to the other side, as well. Here are two basic examples:

TIP
A linear equation has only *one* solution.

Equation	Description of Process
$3x = -9$ $\frac{1}{3}3x = \frac{1}{3} \cdot (-9)$ $x = -3$	The variable is already on one side by itself. Simply divide both sides by its coefficient, which is the same thing as multiplying both sides by the reciprocal of the coefficient.
$2x - 5 = 13$ $2x - 5 + 5 = 13 + 5$ $2x = 18$ $\frac{1}{2} \cdot 2x = \frac{1}{2} \cdot 18$ $x = 9$	This one involves one additional step. First, in order to isolate x on one side, you must add 5 to both sides. Once done, divide both sides by 2, the reciprocal of the coefficient of x.

Solving all linear equations basically boils down to solving equations in the same step-by-step manner as in the table. Let's take a look at an example that follows the same method, but has a few extra steps.

3. Solve the following equation:

$$5[2 - 3(1 - 2x)] = 3 - 2x$$

(A) $-\frac{1}{4}$

(B) $\frac{1}{14}$

(C) $\frac{1}{4}$

(D) 1

(E) 4

The correct answer is (C). The order of operations applies to solving linear equations—after all, the variable x represents a real number. We simplify the left side using distributivity multiple times. We then get the x terms on the left side and constants on the right, combine like terms and finally divide by the coefficient of x:

$$5\left[2 - 3(1 - 2x)\right] = 3 - 2x$$
$$5\left[2 - 3 + 6x\right] = 3 - 2x$$
$$5[-1 + 6x] = 3 - 2x$$
$$-5 + 30x = 3 - 2x$$
$$5 - 5 + 30x = 5 + 3 - 2x$$
$$30x = 8 - 2x$$
$$30x + 2x = 8 - 2x + 2x$$
$$32x = 8$$
$$\frac{1}{32} \cdot 32x = \frac{1}{32} \cdot 8$$
$$x = \frac{1}{4}$$

Sometimes, a linear equation will involve multiple letters and you will be asked to solve for one of them "in terms of" the others. The same exact procedure applies for this problem type, even though it might look strange. For instance, you can solve the equation $ax + by = c$ for y simply by subtracting ax from both sides and then dividing both sides by b:

$$ax + by = c$$
$$by = c - ax$$
$$y = \frac{c - ax}{b}$$

Linear Inequalities

The same basic strategy is also used to solve linear inequalities, with the one additional feature: the inequality sign is switched whenever both sides of the inequality are multiplied by a negative real number. Another distinguishing factor of linear inequalities in contrast to linear equations is that the **solution set** of an inequality (that is, set of real numbers that satisfies the inequality) contains an infinite number of values.

The solution set to a linear inequality is often pictured on a number line or represented using interval notation, as follows:

Linear Inequality	Interval Notation	Picture on Number Line
$x > a$	(a, ∞)	
$x \geq a$	$[a, \infty)$	

Linear Inequality	Interval Notation	Picture on Number Line
$x < a$	$(-\infty, a)$	
$x \leq a$	$(-\infty, a]$	
$a \leq x \leq b$	$[a, b]$	
$a < x < b$	(a, b)	
$-\infty < x < \infty$	$(-\infty, \infty)$	

Absolute Value

On the HiSET® Mathematics subtest, you might also see linear equations and inequalities involving absolute values. Solutions to these basic equations can be expressed using plain old linear equations and inequalities that do *not* include absolute values, as follows:

Absolute Value Equation/Inequality	Solution
$|x| = a$	$x = a$ or $x = -a$
$|x| \leq a$	$-a \leq x \leq a$
$|x| < a$	$-a < x < a$
$|x| \geq a$	$x \geq a$ or $x \leq -a$
$|x| > a$	$x > a$ or $x < -a$

Solving linear equations and inequalities is very important, but setting them up to solve an applied problem is equally important. Consider the following sample problem.

4. Suppose you spend $4000 on a one-time cost for photography equipment for a small business you are starting. For each photo shoot, you earn $400, but it costs $10 in electricity, $35 in materials, and 20% in taxes on the full amount a customer pays. Which of the following equations could be used to determine the number of photo shoots you need to conduct in order to *break even,* meaning that your income equals your expenses?

   (A) $4000 = 400x$

   (B) $125x = 400x$

   (C) $4000 + 125x = 400x$

   (D) $4,125 = 400x$

   (E) $4000 = 400x + 125x$

> **TIP**
>
> Absolute value inequalities arise in applications when quantifying an error that could involve a certain amount in either the positive or negative direction—for instance, weight readings produced by a scale are off by 0.5 pound either *way* (too much or too little).

The correct answer is (C). Let x represent the number of photo shoots conducted. We need to determine an expression for the cost of conducting x photo shoots and an expression for the income earned from conducting x photo shoots. For each photo shoot, you must pay $45 and 20% of $400, which is $80. So, each photo shoot costs $125, and, as such, x photo shoots cost $125x$. Your income from x photo shoots is $400x$. Finally, for *total cost*, we must include the initial $4000 used to purchase equipment. So, the cost is $4000 + 125x$ dollars. Equating this expression to the income, $400x$, yields the equation $4000 + 125x = 400x$. The solution to this equation would give the break-even point.

QUADRATIC EQUATIONS

Not all equations that must be solved are linear. Another common type of equation is a **quadratic equation,** which is of the form $ax^2 + bx + c = 0$, where a, b, and c are real numbers and $a \neq 0$.

There are several methods that can be used to solve quadratic equations: factoring, quadratic formula, and completing the square. In each technique, you must first write the equation in the form $ax^2 + bx + c = 0$, which might require moving terms to one side of the equation. Let's look in detail at each of these three methods:

TIP

A quadratic equation can have 0, 1, or 2 solutions.

Method	Process and Comments	Solving $2x^2 + 5x - 3 = 0$.
Factoring	If possible, factor the quadratic expression into a product of two factors. (NOTE: When you *are* able to factor the expression, it is possible that there is only *one* factor, but it is squared.) Once factored, set each factor equal to zero and solve for x.	$2x^2 + 5x - 3 = 0$ $(2x - 1)(x + 3) = 0$ $2x - 1 = 0 \text{ or } x + 3 = 0$ $x = -3, \frac{1}{2}$
Quadratic Formula	The solutions to $ax^2 + bx + c = 0$ are given by the formula: $$x = \frac{-b \pm \sqrt{b^2 - 4ac}}{2a}$$	Use $a = 2$, $b = 5$, and $c = -3$ in the formula: $$x = \frac{-b \pm \sqrt{b^2 - 4ac}}{2a}$$ $$= \frac{-5 \pm \sqrt{5^2 - 4(2)(-3)}}{2(2)}$$ $$= \frac{-5 \pm \sqrt{49}}{4}$$ $$= \frac{-5 \pm 7}{4} = -3, \frac{1}{2}$$

Method	Process and Comments	Solving $2x^2 + 5x - 3 = 0$.
Completing the Square	This process is actually used to derive the quadratic formula. So, it is rarely used to *solve* quadratic equations outright, but the technique is useful when graphing quadratic functions, which we will discuss later in this chapter. The goal of the method is to rewrite the equation $ax^2 + bx + c = 0$ in the form $a(x - h)^2 + k = 0$, From there, you would isolate the squared term, take the square root of both sides, and solve for x.	$2x^2 + 5x - 3 = 0$ $2\left(x^2 + \frac{5}{2}x\right) - 3 = 0$ $2\left(x^2 + \frac{5}{2}x + \left(\frac{1}{2} \times \frac{5}{2}\right)^2\right) - 3 - 2\left(\frac{1}{2} \times \frac{5}{2}\right)^2 = 0$ $2\left(x + \frac{5}{4}\right)^2 - \frac{49}{8} = 0$ $\left(x + \frac{5}{4}\right)^2 = \frac{49}{16}$ $x + \frac{5}{4} = \pm\sqrt{\frac{49}{16}} = \pm\frac{7}{4}$ $x = -\frac{5}{4} \pm \frac{7}{4} = -3, \frac{1}{2}$

5. Solve the equation $6x^2 + 11x - 10 = 0$

   (A) $\frac{2}{3} \pm \frac{5}{2}i$

   (B) $-\frac{2}{3}i$ and $\frac{5}{2}i$

   (C) $\frac{2}{3}i$ and $-\frac{5}{2}i$

   (D) $\frac{2}{3}$ and $-\frac{5}{2}$

   (E) $-\frac{2}{3}$ and $\frac{5}{2}$

The correct answer is (D). The factoring method works here, although if you did not see that, you can always use the quadratic formula:

$$6x^2 + 11x - 10 = 0$$
$$(3x - 2)(2x + 5) = 0$$
$$3x - 2 = 0 \text{ or } 2x + 5 = 0$$
$$x = \frac{2}{3}, -\frac{5}{2}$$

6. Which of the following quadratic equations has a repeated real solution?
   (A) $7x^2 + 23x = 0$
   (B) $x^2 - 7x - 10 = 0$
   (C) $4x^2 + 4x + 1 = 0$
   (D) $x^2 + 18x + 1 = 0$
   (E) $x^2 - 17 = 0$

The correct answer is (C). Factoring is a quick way to solve this problem. Observe that the quadratic expression in the equation $4x^2 + 4x + 1 = 0$ factors, enabling us to write it in the equivalent form $(2x + 1)^2 = 0$. The only x-value that satisfies this equation is $x = -\frac{1}{2}$, which is a repeated real solution.

FUNCTIONS

A "function f from X to Y" is a rule that assigns to each element x in X exactly one element y (denoted by $f(x)$) in Y. Functions are generally described using algebraic expressions or graphs and are denoted using letters, such as f or g. An expression of the form $y = f(x)$ is used to emphasize the input-output defining relationship of a function. Some examples of functions are $f(x) = 3x$, $g(x) = 2x^2 + 3x - 1$, and $h(x) = |x|$. In order to evaluate a function, like $f(x)$, at a specific x-value, all you must do is substitute that value in for x and simplify the resulting arithmetic expression. For instance, $g(3) = 2(3)^2 + 3(3) - 1 = 18 + 9 - 1 = 10$.

At this stage of mathematics, the functions we deal with are all **real-valued,** meaning that the input and output of the function are both real numbers. The **domain** of a function is the set of all possible x-values for which there corresponds an output, y. When an algebraic expression is used to define a function $y = f(x)$, the domain is thought about as the set of all values of x that can be substituted into the expression and yield a meaningful output. For example, the domain of the functions $f(x) = 3x$, $g(x) = 2x^2 + 1$, and $h(x) = |x|$ is the set of all real numbers because *any* real number that is substituted in for x in any of these expressions will yield a real number.

The **range** of a function is the set of all possible y-values attained at some x-value of the domain. Generally, this is more difficult to determine unless you have a graph.

> **TIP**
>
> The domain of $j(x) = \sqrt{x}$ is the set of all *non-negative* real numbers because you cannot take the square root of a negative number.

7. For $f(x) = \dfrac{2x}{2x - 1} - \dfrac{x}{x^2 + 1}$, compute $f(-1)$, if possible.

   (A) $-\dfrac{3}{5}$

   (B) $\dfrac{3}{5}$

   (C) $\dfrac{3}{4}$

   (D) $\dfrac{7}{6}$

   (E) Not defined, because -1 is not in the domain of f

The correct answer is (D). Everywhere you see an x, substitute -1 and then simplify the resulting arithmetic expression:

$$f(-1) = \frac{2(-1)}{2(-1)-1} - \frac{(-1)}{(-1)^2+1} = \frac{-2}{-3} - \frac{-1}{2} = \frac{2}{3} + \frac{1}{2} = \frac{7}{6}$$

Based on our experience adding, subtracting, multiplying, and dividing real numbers, we can define arithmetic operations using functions. Let f and g be functions. The sum function $(f + g)(x)$ is defined to be $f(x) + g(x)$. Likewise, the difference function $(f - g)$ (x) is defined to be $f(x) - g(x)$, and the product function $(f \cdot g)(x)$ is defined to be $f(x) \cdot g(x)$. The domains of each of these new functions contain only those x-values for which both $f(x)$ *and* $g(x)$ are defined. If either one is *not* defined at a particular x, then these arithmetic combinations are not defined at that value. The quotient function $\left(\dfrac{f}{g}\right)(x)$ is defined to be $\dfrac{f(x)}{g(x)}$. Its domain contains only those x-values for which both $f(x)$ and $g(x)$ are defined AND for which $g(x)$ is not equal to zero (otherwise, you would be dividing by zero). Arithmetic combinations of more than two functions can be formed in the same way.

8. What is the domain of the function $f(x) = \dfrac{x+1}{(x-2)(x-3)}$?

   (A) $(-\infty, 2)$

   (B) $(3, \infty)$

   (C) $(2, 3) \cup (3, \infty)$

   (D) $(-\infty, 2) \cup (2, 3) \cup (3, \infty)$

   (E) All real numbers

The correct answer is (D). This is a quotient of two functions, both of which have the set of all real numbers as its domain. However, since we cannot divide by zero, we must eliminate those x-values for which the denominator is zero, namely 2 and 3. Therefore, the domain is the set of all real numbers except 2 and 3, which is expressed as $(-\infty, 2) \cup (2, 3) \cup (3, \infty)$.

GRAPHS AND THEIR PROPERTIES

The graph of a function $y = f(x)$ is the set of all points $(x, f(x))$, where x is in the domain of $f(x)$. The most basic type of function is a **linear function**, defined by an equation of the form $f(x) = mx + b$, where m and b are real numbers. You study these functions in disguise when studying lines and linear equations. Recall that m indicates the slope of the line and b is its y-intercept (meaning that the graph of the line crosses the y-axis at the point $(0, b)$).

TIP

Slope measures steepness of the line or the change in *y*-value per unit change in *x*-value.

More conveniently, if you have a point (x_1, y_1) on the line and its slope m, then the **point-slope** equation is $y - y_1 = m(x - x_1)$. If you solve this equation for y and simplify, the form will be $f(x) = mx + b$. Consider the following sample question.

9. Suppose $f(x)$ is a linear function. If $f(2) = -1$ and $f(1) = -5$, find the equation for $f(x)$.
   (A) $f(x) = 2x + 5$
   (B) $f(x) = x - 5$
   (C) $f(x) = x + 5$
   (D) $f(x) = \frac{1}{2}x - 5$
   (E) $f(x) = 2x - 5$

The correct answer is (E). First, determine the slope:

$$\text{slope} = m = \frac{-1 - (-5)}{2 - 1} = 2$$

The notation $f(2) = -1$ means that the point $(2, -1)$ is on the graph of $y = f(x)$. So, using point-slope formula, the equation of the line passing through these two points is $y - (-1) = 2(x - 2)$. This is equivalent to $y = 2x - 5$. Since $y = f(x)$, the linear function is $f(x) = 2x - 5$.

When you have a graph of a function, you can determine if an x-value belongs to the domain of f by simply determining if an ordered pair with that x-value belongs to the graph of f.

The following are the graphs of some of the most common functions you will encounter:

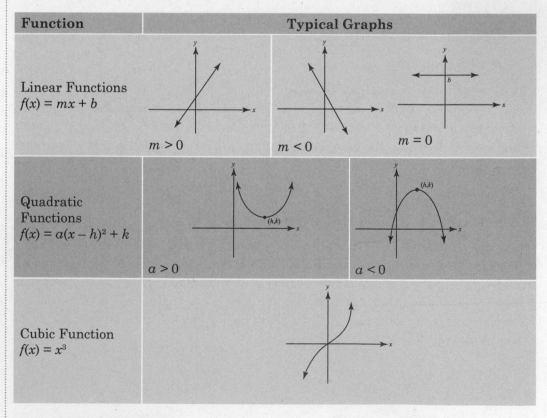

Function	Typical Graphs
Linear Functions $f(x) = mx + b$	$m > 0$ $m < 0$ $m = 0$
Quadratic Functions $f(x) = a(x - h)^2 + k$	$a > 0$ $a < 0$
Cubic Function $f(x) = x^3$	

Function	Typical Graphs
Square Root Function $f(x) = \sqrt{x}$	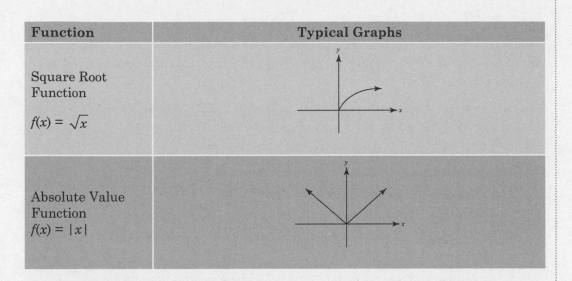
Absolute Value Function $f(x) = |x|$	

All of these functions can be moved about the coordinate plane using horizontal and vertical translations and reflections, defined as follows. Here, let h and k be positive real numbers:

New Function	Verbal Description of How to Graph This Function by Translation or Reflecting the Graph of $y = f(x)$
$F(x) = f(x) + k$	Translate the graph of $y = f(x)$ k units vertically upward.
$F(x) = f(x) - k$	Translate the graph of $y = f(x)$ k units vertically downward.
$F(x) = f(x - k)$	Translate the graph of $y = f(x)$ k units to the right.
$F(x) = f(x + k)$	Translate the graph of $y = f(x)$ k units to the left.
$F(x) = -f(x)$	Reflect the graph of $y = f(x)$ over the x-axis.

Of course, you can perform multiple translations and reflections to the same function to move it up or down, left or right, and flip or not flip. Consider the following sample question.

10. Which of the following functions is the result of translating the graph of $f(x) = x^2$ three units to the left and five units vertically down?

   (A) $g(x) = (x - 3)^2 + 5$
   (B) $g(x) = (x + 3)^2 + 5$
   (C) $g(x) = (x - 3)^2 - 5$
   (D) $g(x) = (x + 3)^2 - 5$
   (E) $g(x) = -(x + 3)^2 + 5$

The correct answer is (D). Translating $y = f(x)$ to the left three units amounts to replacing x by $x + 3$, and translating it vertically downward 5 units amounts to subtracting 5 from the entire squared term. The end result of doing both of these is the function $g(x) = (x + 3)^2 - 5$.

The following are some features of function graphs (of the general form $y = f(x)$) that are key to remember when faced with problems on the HiSET®:

1. The *maximum of f* is the largest y-value in the range of f.

2. The *minimum of f* is the smallest y-value in the range of f.

3. f is *increasing* on an interval if its graph rises from left to right as you progress through the interval from left to right.

4. f is *decreasing* if its graph falls from left to right as you progress through the interval from left to right.

5. An *x-intercept of f* is a point of the form $(x,0)$. These are found solving $f(x) = 0$.

6. A *y-intercept of f* is the point of the form $(0, f(0))$.

SUMMING IT UP

- A **variable** is an unknown quantity represented by a letter, like x, y, or z. If two terms have the same "variable part" (for example, x^5 and $4x^5$) they are called *like terms*, even if they have different coefficients. To add or subtract like terms, add or subtract the coefficients of the terms and keep the variable parts unchanged. When multiplying or dividing terms, use the exponent rules just as when simplifying arithmetic expressions.

- To solve linear equations, isolate the variable on one side of the equation. If you add or subtract a number from one side, you MUST do so to the other; if you divide or multiply one side by a number, you MUST do it to the other side as well. When solving linear inequalities, the inequality sign is switched whenever both sides of the inequality are multiplied by a negative real number.

- A **quadratic equation** is of the form $ax^2 + bx + c = 0$, where a, b, and c are real numbers and $a \neq 0$. There are several methods that can be used to solve quadratic equations: factoring, quadratic formula, and completing the square. The quadratic formula is $x = \dfrac{-b \pm \sqrt{b^2 - 4ac}}{2a}$

- The **domain** of a function is the set of all possible x-values for which there corresponds an output, y. The **range** of a function is the set of all possible y-values attained at some member of the domain.

- The sum function $(f + g)(x)$ is defined to be $f(x) + g(x)$. Likewise, the difference function $(f - g)(x)$ is defined to be $f(x) - g(x)$, and the product function $(f \cdot g)(x)$ is defined to be $f(x) \cdot g(x)$.

- The most basic type of function is a **linear function**, defined by an equation of the form $f(x) = mx + b$, where m and b are real numbers.

- The graph of a function $y = f(x)$ is the set of all points $(x, f(x))$, where x is in the domain of $f(x)$. To find the slope of a line when given two points, use the **point-slope** equation: $y - y_1 = m(x - x_1)$.

PART V

SCIENCE

Life Science

chapter 13

OVERVIEW

- Organisms
- Living environments
- Life cycles
- Interdependence of organisms
- Structure and function in living systems
- Summing It Up

The HiSET® Science subtest consists of multiple-choice questions that cover life science, physical science, and earth science. Most science questions will be based on a descriptive passage, diagram, table, or graph—you will need to answer several questions based on the given information. The test might present the results of an experiment, for example, or a diagram charting a physical process. Using your background knowledge of science, you can often find all the information you need for the correct answer right in the question! Careful reading and analytical thinking will be as important as your science knowledge.

The following chapters offer a brief review of the major science topics covered on the HiSET® exam. Each section provides a quick review of some key topics, followed by sample HiSET® practice questions. Use the sample questions to gauge your comfort level with each topic, and then review the concepts where you need a refresher.

Let's start with a review of life science, the study of living things. Broadly speaking, it includes the fields of biology and ecology, including evolution. Questions might cover the structure of an organism's body or examine the relationship between organisms or between an organism and the environment. Life science questions are the single largest portion of the test, usually making up about 49% of the questions. Let's get started!

ORGANISMS

In life science, an **organism** is any living thing—everything from a tiny, microscopic bacterium to a gigantic blue whale. All animals and plants are organisms. Organisms are the foundation of all life science, which encompasses the study of all living things and living systems.

All organisms are made up of **cells,** defined as the smallest structural unit of an organism (think of a brick in a wall), enclosed by a **cell membrane,** which allows products and waste made by the cell to exit and required nutrients to enter. Organisms with just one cell are called **unicellular** (e.g., bacteria) and those made of multiple cells are called **multicellular** (e.g., elephant).

Major Types of Organisms

There are three major types of organisms, categorized depending on how they obtain the energy they need to survive. All of these categories exist both on land and in water:

- **Producers:** A **producer** (also called an **autotroph**) is any organism that can make its own food using nutrients and an energy source found in its environment. Examples of producers are green plants, as well as certain bacteria, algae, and plankton. The most common way for a producer to make its own food is through **photosynthesis.** In photosynthesis, producers use energy from the sun to turn carbon dioxide from the air into sugar that they use to build their bodies.

- **Consumers:** A **consumer (**also called a **heterotroph**) is any organism that gets energy by consuming other organisms. Some examples of consumers are beetles, mosquitoes, snakes, deer, vultures, fish, or lions. Consumers can obtain energy by consuming plants or other consumers, even dead animals. Consumers that eat dead animals are known as scavengers.

- **Decomposers:** A **decomposer** is any organism that breaks down dead plants, animals, or any other waste material. Some examples of decomposers are bacteria, earthworms, and mushrooms. Decomposers are similar to consumers in that they cannot make their own food—they are heterotrophs—but they obtain energy by breaking down dead plants and animals into simple materials rather than eating them.

Classification

Besides producers, consumers, and decomposers, scientists also classify organisms into groups based on their relationships to one another. The basic groups include animals (Animalia), Plants (Plantae), fungi, and two different types of bacteria: Archaebacteria and Eubacteria. The smallest and most important category is **species**. All organisms on Earth belong to a species, the most specific group of similar organisms capable of interbreeding. Organisms within a species tend to reproduce sexually with other organisms within the species; for example, lions reproduce with other lions. However, hybrid organisms can occur when sexual reproduction takes place between organisms of different species; for instance, a liger results from a hybrid cross between a male lion and a female tigress, while a tigon results from a hybrid cross between a male tiger and female lioness.

Survival and Reproduction in the Environment

Every species of organism has special features and abilities called **adaptations** that help it live in its environment. Adaptations can be almost anything, depending on where an organism lives.

TIP

A cheetah's speed, a snail's shell, a shark's teeth, a snake's venom, a bee's sting, a dog's sense of smell— all of these are adaptations.

For example, flounder are fish that swim quite slowly. Therefore, in order to catch food or avoid danger, they have colors that make them look like mud in the bottom of the sea.

The ability to hide in an environment is called **camouflage.** Plants adapt, as well. For example, many plants that live in dense forests grow very quickly. A plant adapted to grow quickly can grow tall and reach the limited sunlight through a small gap in the other trees before other plants do.

Organisms can also adapt to a changing environment, but it takes time. Adaptations are the result of **evolution,** or changes in a population that occur over time and many generations. When there is variation between organisms, some of the variations are more successful than others, and those successful variations can be passed down to the next generation via a process called **natural selection.** When a new feature, or **trait,** helps an organism survive better than other members of its species, it will produce more offspring. Those offspring will have the same advantage that their parent had and will eventually have more offspring of their own, until the helpful trait—the adaptation—occurs in every member of that species.

Take the cheetah, the fastest animal on Earth, for an example. At some point in the past, a cheetah was born with the muscles to run extremely fast and used this ability to catch more gazelles. That cheetah had more kittens than other cheetahs since it had more to eat. Those kittens all had the same muscles and could also run fast, and *they* all caught more food and had more kittens. Fast cheetahs had an advantage over other cheetahs, and after many generations, fast cheetahs became more common until only fast cheetahs were able to reproduce at all. Now all cheetahs are fast!

For most organisms, reproduction, or producing a new generation of offspring, is the most important ability (more important than their own survival). There are two main strategies for reproduction: sexual and asexual. **Sexual reproduction** requires breeding between two individuals, and the offspring will have the combined genetic material of each parent. Virtually all animals, as well as many plants and fungi, reproduce sexually. **Asexual reproduction** is reproduction from only one parent, where the offspring is an identical copy of the parent. This type of reproduction occurs in organisms such as bacteria, simple fungi, and some plants.

Each strategy has its own advantages. Asexual reproduction is much faster, but there is less diversity in the population—if the environment changes, the entire population can be at risk. Sexual reproduction is slower, but a greater variety of offspring increases the chance that some will be able to adjust to any changes in the environment.

Let's look at some sample questions that explore organisms.

1. Scientists exploring a cave discover a completely new species of mouse living there. The mouse is perfectly adapted to life in the cave. Which of the following traits does NOT increase the mouse's fitness inside the totally dark cave?

   (A) Exceptionally keen internal heating

   (B) An excellent sense of smell

   (C) Long whiskers that help them sense vibrations in the air

   (D) Moss-colored fur

The correct answer is (D). The question wants you to think about which traits benefit an organism in a particular environment. In a very dark environment, camouflage does not benefit an organism very much, since it can't be seen anyway.

2. A biologist places an unknown organism in a tank with access to air, water, and food, but no light. After one week, the organism had grown two inches. After two weeks, the organism died. The food remained unchanged. What is the most likely explanation for what happened?

    (A) The organism is an autotroph and underwent photosynthesis, but died from lack of light.

    (B) The organism is an autotroph that works off a mechanism other than photosynthesis, and died when its source materials ran out.

    (C) The organism is heterotrophic, but died from lack of food.

    (D) The organism is a decomposer.

The correct answer is (B). The question requires you to know the three major categories of organisms and to understand that photosynthesis requires air and sunlight to function. Without sunlight the organism cannot be photosynthetic (it would not have grown at all), but if the food is untouched, then it must be an autotroph that does not use photosynthesis.

LIVING ENVIRONMENTS

As you have now reviewed, organisms are adapted to live and thrive in a variety of different environments, from high mountain peaks to the deepest ocean depths. The structure and functioning of environments, not just individual organisms, is a common topic on the HiSET®.

The Structure of Living Environments

Environments are defined by everything in them, from the individual organism level all the way up to the entire planet, including the ocean. The main units are:

Organism → Species → Population → Ecosystem

- **Population:** The next level of organization above species, population refers to all the individuals of the *same species* in the same place. Example: All the grizzly bears in Yellowstone National Park.

- **Community:** A community is all the different interacting populations in a given area. Example: The carnivore community in Yellowstone—so not only grizzly bears, but also hawks, wolves, and rattlesnakes.

- **Ecosystem:** An ecosystem is all the living and nonliving components of the environment together. You may also see the living components of an ecosystem called **"biotic"** and the nonliving components called **"abiotic."** An ecosystem contains all the different communities in an area, as well as their environment—rocks, caves, snow, etc. Example: The ecosystem is all of Yellowstone, including the wildlife, the forests, the meadows, mountains, rivers, and everything else.

The three other important concepts you should understand are **habitat, niche,** and **biome:**

- **Habitat:** A habitat is the particular type of environment where a species naturally lives. For example, chimpanzees live in African rain forests; the rain forest is their habitat.

- **Niche:** Related to habitat is niche, which is defined as all of the biotic and abiotic features a species needs to survive in its environment. Think of it as the particular role or job of a species in its environment. For example, consider all the insects in a rotting log. Some eat the decayed wood, others lay their eggs in it, and some feed on the smaller insects—each of these is a niche in that one environment.

- **Biome:** Biomes are the general environment types of Earth, categorized by the general type of vegetation found and the rainfall received. Some examples of biomes are: tundra, taiga, temperate deciduous forest, temperate rain forest, tropical rain forest, savanna, temperate grassland, shrubland, and desert.

Ecosystem Function

Now that you have reviewed the structure of ecosystems, we can look at how they are arranged. In every ecosystem, the biotic and abiotic components interact very closely, as organisms need the abiotic components—such as air, sunlight, water, or nutrients—in order to survive.

Biogeochemical Cycles

Biogeochemical cycles refer to the ways in which important components of the environment cycle back and forth between the living and nonliving parts of an ecosystem. There are many biogeochemical cycles, including water, carbon, nitrogen, oxygen, rock, and numerous minerals such as phosphorus.

Let's take a closer look at the **carbon cycle.** Photosynthesis by plants or other primary producers is central to the carbon cycle. Photosynthesis pulls carbon dioxide (CO_2) out of the atmosphere and uses sunlight for energy to turn that carbon dioxide into oxygen and carbon. The oxygen is released back into the atmosphere, and the carbon becomes the starch that makes up the body of the plant. That carbon either stays in the plant or is eaten by an animal and stays in the body of the animal.

During **respiration,** some carbon is breathed back out as waste CO_2 in exchange for oxygen that most cells need. The rest stays in a plant's or animal's body until it dies. After death, some of the carbon is either released back to the atmosphere through decomposition or stored deep in the Earth as **fossil fuels,** such as coal or oil. The total amount of carbon in the system, whether in the form of fossil fuels, CO_2, or in an organism's body, does not change.

Human Impacts on the Living Environment

Ecosystems are not controlled, pristine environments. Human activities can disrupt ecosystem function in all kinds of ways. **Pollution,** or the addition of industrial products

TIP

The key to every cycle is that the actual amount being cycled does not change, only its place in the system.

or by-products in the environment, can taint ecosystems by making resources such as air or water unusable. **Habitat destruction,** such as deforestation (the removal of forests) can destroy habitats or niches where species can live. Human activity is especially disruptive of nutrient cycles. Burning fossil fuels, implicated in **climate change,** or the warming and alteration of Earth's climate, is really just an acceleration of the carbon cycle.

Let's look at some review questions that cover information about different living environments.

3. Shawna wants to test the theory that sand and rocks are important parts of a snake's niche that it uses in order to warm itself in the sun. She creates two large cages, one with a large rock in it and one full of sand and puts a snake in each. She measures each snake's body temperature before sunrise and after sunrise. In the second measurement, both snakes were warm, but the body temperature of the snake in the sandy enclosure is two degrees warmer than the snake in the rocky enclosure. What is the best conclusion she can make about the results?

   (A) Only rocks are important to snakes.

   (B) Only sand is important to snakes.

   (C) Both sand and rock are equally important to snakes, but sand is slightly better than rocks.

   (D) Both sand and rock are equally important to snakes.

The correct answer is (C). The question needs you to have some idea what a niche is, but mostly to carefully pay attention to the outcome of the experiment. Since both sand and rocks warmed the snakes, then both are useful. However, the slightly higher temperature achieved in the sandy enclosure makes choice (C) the best response.

4. The following diagram shows the phosphorus cycle.

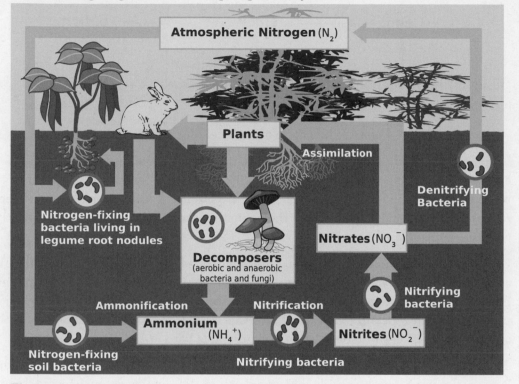

The main commercial use of nitrogen is fertilizer, which is made from nitrogen gas through industrial fixation. The major impact of this activity on the nitrogen cycle is to transfer

(A) nitrogen from the soil to the atmosphere.

(B) phosphorus from the atmosphere into soil.

(C) nitrogen from the rock to the soil.

(D) nitrogen from the soil into rocks.

The correct answer is (B). The question wants to make sure you understand the basics of biogeochemical cycles, but all the information you need is in the diagram. If the phosphate is fixed from nitrogen gas and added to plants, it has to move from the atmosphere into the soil.

LIFE CYCLES

We have now reviewed organisms, their environments, and the connections between them. Now it's time to take a closer look at the lives of individual organisms. For most organisms, life is divided into stages. Taken together, all of these different stages between the beginning of an organism's life and its death are called the **life cycle.**

Unicellular organisms, such as bacteria, have a very simple life cycle, reproducing through a process called **mitosis** and then maturing without any intermediate steps. Through mitosis, the cell splits, and each offspring cell has exactly the same amount of genetic material as the parent.

Most multicellular organisms' life cycles follow a different basic pattern.

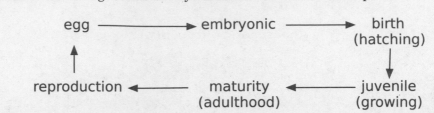

Figure 1: Life cycle of multicellular organisms.

Egg: In a multicellular life cycle, the egg is the very first stage of development. An egg specifically refers to a reproductive cell produced by females (the sperm is the reproductive cell produced by males). Eggs are produced when special cells undergo **meiosis.** Through meiosis, cells split their genetic material in half instead of replicating genetic material.

Embryonic: In sexual reproduction, an egg must be fertilized. Its genetic material is combined with that of another parent, at which point the cells begin to multiply into more cells. At this stage, the organism is an **embryo,** growing until the point when its independent life officially starts. In plants, this occurs inside the seed. In animals, this occurs inside the egg or uterus before the animal is born or hatched.

Juvenile: After birth or hatching (sprouting in plants), an organism continues to grow, but it is not yet an adult—this is the juvenile stage. In some cases, such as in humans, juveniles are just smaller versions of adults. In other cases, as in the figure below, the juvenile stage is different in appearance and habits from the adult. As also seen in Figure 2, there can be multiple stages of juvenile before adulthood, as an organism uses different habitats or niches at different stages. Many organisms—including insects, amphibians, and fish—undergo physical changes during the juvenile stage. When there is a major change from one life stage to another, it is called **metamorphosis.**

Adult: As an adult, an organism does not change anymore, although in some cases—as in many fish—it might continue to grow larger. At this stage, the organism is reproductively mature and therefore ready to reproduce. In sexually reproducing organisms, specialized cells will now undergo meiosis. The cycle begins again.

> **TIP**
>
> A caterpillar changing into a butterfly or a tadpole changing into a frog are examples of metamorphosis.

> **TIP**
>
> Ordinary cells reproduce through *mitosis*, not meiosis.

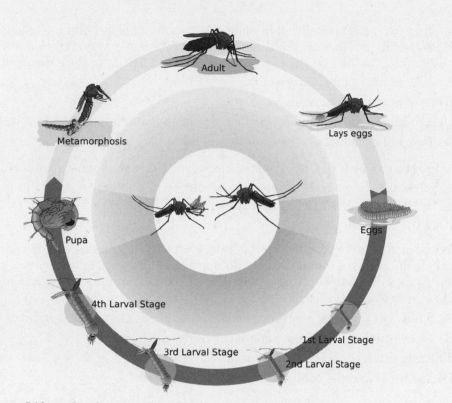

Figure 2: Life cycle of a mosquito. Notice that the larval phase exists in water only.

Plant Life Cycle

Plants have a slightly different lifestyle and do not undergo metamorphosis—seedlings will grow into adult plants without any further changes. The basic path of a flowering plant life cycle is as shown.

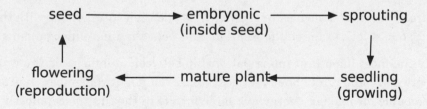

Figure 3: Life cycle of a flowering plant.

The specifics of plant life cycles depend very much on the plant type. For example, a conifer tree, such as a pine tree, has cones instead of flowers. Simpler plants, like ferns and mosses, have different life cycles that include an aquatic stage.

Now that you've reviewed the basics of life cycles, you're ready to practice.

5. You find two insects fossilized in amber, but you are not sure if they belong to different species or if they are the same species at different stages. Which new fossil(s) would prove that the two fossils you already found belong to the same species?

(A) A fossil of the larval stage of the insect

(B) A fossil of the adult stage of the insect

(C) A fossil of one of the insects in the process of metamorphosis into the other

(D) Two additional fossils from additional life stages

The correct answer is (C). The question needs you to use your general understanding of life cycles to decide which information would prove the existence of different life stages. Only a fossil demonstrating metamorphosis would show that both fossils are definitely the same species.

6. Many organisms rely on different habitats, even other organisms, at different stages of their life cycles. A common parasitic worm lives as an egg in water, as a juvenile in a snail, and as an adult in a bird. What hypothetical life cycle would allow for all of these stages to occur?

(A) Snails eat the eggs; birds eat the snails; adult worms lay eggs in birds

(B) The worm lays eggs in the snail; the birds eat the eggs

(C) Birds drink the water and then eat the snails

(D) The birds and the snails both drink the water

The correct answer is (A). The question needs you to think carefully about a hypothetical lifestyle and fit the different life stages to the different scenarios listed. It is not necessary to remember life stages in detail. Only choice (A) fits the scenario described, since it is the only case where birds and the adult life stage of the worm overlap.

INTERDEPENDENCE OF ORGANISMS

We've already reviewed the nature of organisms and their interactions with their environment, so now let's examine the relationships *between* different organisms.

Probably the most important interrelationship between organisms is the way energy moves between them throughout the ecosystem. You might remember that producers are responsible for making energy available for life in the first place, mostly through photosynthesis. Without producers, energy would exist only in the form of sunlight and would be unavailable to consumers or decomposers. That's why producers are also called **primary producers**—they provide the energy base for all life on Earth.

Energy is then transferred to consumers when the body of a producer is consumed or eaten. Consumers that feed directly on producers are called **primary consumers.** An example might be ants or grasshoppers.

Energy does not stop with primary consumers. Primary consumers can be consumed by **secondary consumers**—any consumer that feeds on primary consumers. Some examples are skunks or crayfish. But the energy flow does not stop there! It can keep going as long as there are consumers who can eat smaller consumers. A consumer that eats secondary consumers is called a **tertiary consumer.** The consumers at the absolute top are called **apex predators.**

You can see that the basic movement of energy from producer through the different levels of consumer is really a list of feeding relationships. Plant A is eaten by animal B is eaten by animal C is eaten by Animal D, and so on. This simple relationship where each organism is food for the next is called a **food chain.** Each level in the food chain (for example, secondary consumers) is called a **trophic level.**

In every food chain, organisms may be defined based not just on their position in the chain, but also on their specific diet. Every chain has predators and prey. A **predator** is any consumer that eats other consumers, and **prey** is any consumer at risk of being consumed. There are also **herbivores,** which only eat producers (such as plants); **carnivores,** which only eat other consumers; and **omnivores,** which eat almost everything: plants, animals, fungi, and more. Omnivores feed at multiple levels in a food chain.

Each organism at a trophic level shares the same function in the food chain.

Carnivores are also known as meat eaters.

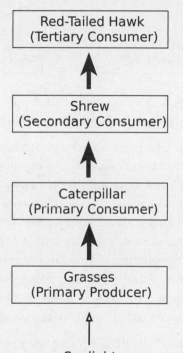

Figure 4: A basic food chain. Arrows indicate the direction of energy flow from prey to predator.

Of course, energy flow through an ecosystem is not so simple as to flow in a straight line from one producer on up to a single apex predator. Almost every ecosystem has multiple producers, and almost every consumer eats more than one type of food. Real ecosystems are made of several different food chains, starting from multiple producers, and they all overlap since consumers in one food chain can feed in others. All of the food chains in an ecosystem together are known as a **food web.** Look at a simple forest food web in Figure 5. Food for thought: which are the omnivores? Where would a mosquito fit in?

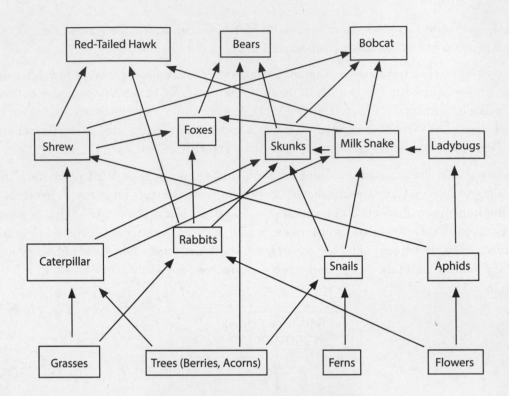

Figure 5: A simple forest food web.
This is only a sampling of relationships in this ecosystem.

Now that you're aware of energy flow in an ecosystem through food webs, don't assume that the only relationships between organisms are feeding relationships. **Competition,** where two different species seek the same limited resource, is a very important relationship between organisms in an ecosystem. Look at Figure 5—any two or more species that eat the same prey are in competition for that prey. Organisms can compete for any resource: shelter, habitat, and food, to name only a few. Relationships between organisms can even be mutually beneficial—this kind of relationship is called **mutualism.** An example of mutualism is the snapping shrimp, which live in large colonies inside tropical sponges. The sponges provide shelter for the shrimp colony, and in return the shrimp will drive off predators that attempt to feed on the sponge.

The number of relationships in an ecosystem can also be important. The food web shown in Figure 5 is just a tiny version of a real forest food web, which would be much larger and more complicated, with many more species and many more relationships between them. This is **biodiversity.** The simple definition of biodiversity is the number of different species in an area, but it is often taken to include genetic diversity and habitat diversity, as well.

Biodiversity is very important to ecosystems, as more diverse ecosystems tend to be more resistant to changes or disturbances within the ecosystem. When there are more species and more relationships, disruption to a few of those species will not disrupt the entire ecosystem, whereas when there are only a few species, the loss of one might make a big difference. Diverse species keep an ecosystem functioning by pollinating plants, dispersing seeds, removing waste, keeping populations in check, and much more.

The loss of biodiversity is one of the greatest impacts human activity has upon the environment. Species may be lost through habitat destruction before they are even discovered, with unknown impacts on the ecosystem as a whole.

7. Biodiversity tends to increase as area increases, since larger areas can support higher numbers of organisms and more diversity. The relationship of the number of species to area is called a species-area curve. The graph below shows a species-area curve for the number of bird species in a warm temperate forest. Based on this curve, *approximately* how many bird species should be present in 150 km²?

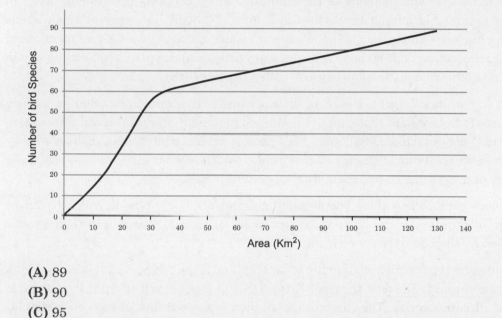

(A) 89

(B) 90

(C) 95

(D) 100

The correct answer is (D). To find the correct estimate, it is necessary to understand the chart and be able to predict what the future slope of the curve might look like. In this case, for most of the graph after it flattens out, about 10 more bird species are present for every additional 20 km². Therefore, the best estimate is choice (D).

8. In the food chain shown in Figure 4, what would be the most likely result if the caterpillar population declined steeply?

(A) The grasses would decrease.

(B) The grasses would increase.

(C) The shrews would increase.

(D) Energy flow in the system would increase.

The correct answer is (B). The question requires you to recognize that if one trophic level declines, the level below will increase in numbers and the level above will decline. In this case, a decline in caterpillars means fewer caterpillars to eat the grass, so more grass would grow as a result.

STRUCTURE AND FUNCTION IN LIVING SYSTEMS

Now that we have reviewed organisms and the relationships among organisms, their environment, and their neighbor organisms, let's take a closer look at how organisms are structured and how they maintain themselves.

Cells, DNA, and Proteins

At the beginning of this chapter, we learned that the basic building block of all organisms is the cell. However, cells themselves have internal components of their own that all perform a different essential function. These structures are called **organelles.** Probably the most important organelle is the **nucleus,** which contains the genetic material bound by a membrane and directs the functioning of the cell. Not every organism's cells have a nucleus—in bacteria, genetic material is not enclosed by a defined membrane. Organisms whose cells do have a nucleus are called **eukaryotic,** while those whose cells do not have a distinct nucleus are called **prokaryotic.**

Plant and animal cells have most of their organelles in common, but there are a few features found in plant cells that are not found in animal cells. **Chloroplasts,** organelles that contain chlorophyll, are where photosynthesis occurs. Plant cells also have a rigid **cell wall** outside their cell membrane, which is what gives plants, especially woody plants such as trees, their stiff, unyielding structure.

Now let's explore how these complex cell systems are built. Whether prokaryotic or eukaryotic, all organisms carry the instructions for their functioning in their genetic material, called deoxyribonucleic acid (**DNA**).

DNA directs the function of all living organisms and is the cell part that is passed from one generation to the next (**heritability**). DNA in a cell is organized into structures called **chromosomes.** The chromosome is then organized into **genes,** or particular units of DNA that carry specific instructions.

DNA directs the functioning of cells (and by extension, organisms) by directing the cell to produce chains of **amino acids.** When several chains of amino acids fold together, the resulting molecule is called a **protein,** and the proteins a cell creates carry out the functions of cells and of all life. Basically, any action that occurs in the course of an organism's life is simply the manufacture and distribution of particular proteins. Proteins make skin, brains, leaves, fish tails, snake venom—almost everything. Proteins are produced by a body to heal wounds or to increase the heart rate. One important group of proteins is **enzymes,** which speed up chemical reactions. Enzymes are important for all manner of body functions, such as digesting food.

Cells that all work together for a common function will produce related proteins. For example, skin cells will all produce the proteins required to maintain skin. These cells are then organized into **tissues,** and when multiple tissues work together, it is called an **organ,** e.g., the liver. When multiple organs work together to carry out related life functions, it is called **an organ system** (see Table 1).

TIP

The DNA in an organism is the same in every cell except the sex cells.

TIP

Not every gene is used at once, and some sections of the DNA are never used at all.

Table 1. Major Human Organ Systems

Name	Main Organs	Function
Cardiovascular	Heart, blood vessels	Circulate blood
Respiratory	Lungs, trachea, bronchi	Oxygen supply
Nervous	Brain, spinal cord, nerves	Sensory input, control all bodily functions
Digestive	Stomach, intestines, liver, esophagus, pancreas	Extract nutrients and excrete waste from food
Urinary	Kidneys, bladder	Filter waste from blood
Endocrine	Hypothalamus, thyroid, most glands	Control major organs through chemical signals
Reproductive (M and F)	Testes, ovaries, uterus	Reproduction
Skin	Skin, underlying tissues	Protective barrier
Blood	Marrow, blood cells	Transportation throughout body
Musculoskeletal	Muscles, bones, connective tissue	Structure and movement

Homeostasis

All the organ systems of a body are constantly active, working in concert to maintain life and respond to disturbance or injury. This process of maintaining internal stability in the face of changes outside the body is called **homeostasis.** Both plants and animals maintain homeostasis. The best example is temperature—humans maintain a steady body temperature of approximately 98° Fahrenheit, no matter what the temperature is outside. Homeostasis is typically maintained by **hormones,** which are chemicals produced by glands that carry signals to different organs through the blood. In the temperature example, as summer turns to fall, the nervous system relays the information to the brain that it's cooling down, stimulating the thyroid to produce thyroid hormones, increasing metabolism and raising heat production. (Hormones are the final control, but multiple systems are involved.) Homeostasis is typically controlled through **negative feedback,** when a condition is decreased in response to overstimulation. Sweating is an example of negative feedback—it is induced to reduce temperatures in response to excessive heat.

Let's try a few review questions that cover these topics.

9. Positive feedback is the opposite of negative feedback. It means a condition is stimulated to increase instead of decrease. Which of the following is an example of positive feedback?

   (A) Childbirth: The hormone oxytocin speeds birth contractions, which stimulates more production of oxytocin.

   (B) Blood pressure: When the body senses an increase in blood pressure, the brain signals a slowdown in the heart rate to decrease pressure.

   (C) Hunger: Metabolism slows in response to hunger, allowing the body to function longer without food.

   (D) A plant in a drought slows photosynthesis by closing the stoma (openings in leaves that allow in carbon dioxide), slowing water loss.

The correct answer is (A). The question requires a brief understanding of positive and negative feedback loops, but the question really explains what is needed. Only choice (A) is an example where a condition (contractions) is increased in response to a signal, instead of decreased.

10. A student wants to examine the functions of different organelles in an animal cell. She examines slides of cells, where each slide shows a cell with different organelles removed. In the cell missing the organelle called the Golgi apparatus, proteins produced by the cell are built up inside the cytoplasm (material that fills the inside of a cell). What is the most likely function of the Golgi apparatus?

   (A) Transportation of materials throughout the cell

   (B) Preparation of the proteins for excretion across the cell membrane

   (C) Providing energy to fuel the cell's metabolism

   (D) Protecting the genetic information and control mechanisms of the cell

The correct answer is (B). The question only requires a careful reading and a logical interpretation of the results of the experiment. If proteins do not leave a cell that has no Golgi apparatus, then this organelle must be involved in protein excretion.

SUMMING IT UP

- An **organism** is any living thing—all animals and plants are organisms. All organisms are made up of one or more **cells.** There are three major types of organisms: **producers** (which make food using nutrients and an energy source found in their environment)**, consumers** (which get energy by consuming other organisms), and **decomposers** (which break down dead plants, animals, or any other waste material).

- Every species of organism has special features and abilities called **adaptations** that help it live in its environment. When there is variation between organisms, some traits are more successful than others. Successful variations are passed down to the next generation via **natural selection.** When a **trait** helps an organism survive better than other members of its species, it will produce more offspring.

- The main units of environments are: Organism Species Population Ecosystem. An ecosystem is all the living (**biotic**) and nonliving (**abiotic**) components of the environment together. These components interact very closely, as organisms need the abiotic components—such as air, sunlight, water, or nutrients—in order to survive.

- In the carbon cycle—as in any cycle—the total amount of carbon in the system, whether in the form of fossil fuels, CO_2, or in an organism's body, does not change.

- The different stages between the beginning of an organism's life and its death are called the **life cycle.** Most multicellular organisms undergo **meiosis**—splitting their genetic material in half. Reproductive cells are then fertilized, become embryos, become juvenile, become adult, and then reproduce anew to start the cycle again.

- **Primary producers** provide the energy base for all life on Earth. Consumers that feed directly on producers are called **primary consumers.** Then, primary consumers can be consumed by **secondary consumers.** The chain keeps going as long as there are consumers who can eat smaller consumers. The relationship where each organism is food for the next is called a **food chain.**

- **Biodiversity** refers to the number of different species in an area, along with its genetic and habitat diversity. More diverse ecosystems tend to be more resistant to disturbances within the ecosystem. When there are more species and more relationships, disruption to a few of those species will not disrupt the entire ecosystem.

- Cells are made up of **organelles.** The most important organelle is the **nucleus,** which contains a cell's **DNA.** DNA leads to the production of amino acids, which leads to the production of **proteins.** Proteins carry out the functions of cells and of all life.

- Homeostasis is this process of maintaining internal stability within a body. Homeostasis is maintained by **hormones,** which are chemicals produced by glands that carry signals to different organs through the blood.

Physical Science

OVERVIEW

- Observable properties of matter
- Position and motion of objects
- Light
- Heat
- Electricity
- Magnetism
- Summing It Up

Physical science is the study of nonliving things. It's a big topic, covering the basic structure, form, function, and movement of all materials and energy. Physical science questions will make up approximately 28 percent of the HiSET® Science subtest.

OBSERVABLE PROPERTIES OF MATTER

Matter is anything that takes up space and has mass. Bricks, frogs, trains, a block of wood, a cotton ball—all are matter, a very general term that refers to everything that is not energy. (**Energy,** such as light or heat, is a *transferable* property, so it can move from one object to another.)

All matter has certain inherent characteristics pertaining to its structure or form; these are its observable properties. **Physical properties** relate only to one material, such as color, odor, magnetism, etc.

Types of Matter

One common term is **substance,** a type of matter that has uniform (all the same) properties. If a substance can be separated into different parts, it is called a **mixture.** A common type of mixture is a **solution,** where one material is completely incorporated into another, often a solid into a liquid (think of salt water). The **solubility** of a substance is the amount of that substance that can be dissolved completely in a unit of another substance and form a solution. For example, the solubility of salt in water is 35.7 g salt/100 mL of water.

A more fundamental type of matter is an **element.** An element is a pure substance that *cannot* be broken down into simpler component substances. Elements are made of only one type of **atom.** A **compound** is a substance made of more than one element.

chapter 14

TIP

For example, hydrogen, H, is an element. Water, H$_2$O, is made of both hydrogen (H) and Oxygen (O), so water is a compound.

TIP

Neither matter nor energy may be created or destroyed.

The Atom

An **atom** is the smallest unit of matter. Atoms are often referred to as the building blocks of matter. Every atom consists of a few basic parts:

Nucleus: At the center of every atom is the nucleus—a dense, positively charged region that contains **protons** and **neutrons.**

Protons: Protons are positively charged particles inside the nucleus of an atom. The number of protons in the nucleus determines an element's **atomic number.**

Neutrons: Neutrons are neutrally charged particles inside the nucleus of every atom, each about the same mass as a proton.

Electrons: Electrons are negatively charged particles that orbit the nucleus of an atom. The number of electrons in an atom determines how the atom reacts with other atoms.

NUCLEUS
PROTON
NEUTRON
ELECTRON

Figure 1: Simple diagram of an atom.

Any structure made up of multiple atoms is a **molecule.** Substances and mixtures are all composed of multiple molecules.

Physical Properties

Now that we have reviewed the basic types of matter, we can turn to the physical properties of matter, such as odor, color, solubility, electrical conductance, and so on. There are a few key properties you should know for the HiSET®:

Mass: Mass is a very basic property—it is the amount of matter in an object. Since atoms are the basic unit of matter, mass can be seen as the number of atoms in an object. Mass is always measured in kilograms. Related to mass is **weight,** or the force gravity exerts on an object.

Density: Weight and mass are influenced by the size of an object, so a more inherent property of a substance is **density,** which is not related to its size. Density is a measure of how compact an object is, or mass per a standard unit of size. For example, the density of lead is approximately 11 grams per cubic centimeter (cm^3), while cork weighs only 0.24 grams/cm^3.

Phase

Matter can exist in multiple different states. For example, water at room temperature is a liquid; when chilled, it freezes into a solid (ice); when heated enough, it boils and turns into steam, a gas. These different states of matter are called **phases.** When matter changes from one state to another, as when water freezes, it is called a **phase change.** The three main phases are **solid, liquid,** and **gas.** (There is a fourth phase, called **plasma.**) In general, solids are denser than liquids, and liquids have greater density than gas, but there are exceptions, such as water ice. The solid form of water is less dense than liquid! Most substances can be in any phase, but extreme temperatures can be required to induce a phase change. Materials also have **specific heat,** the energy required to raise a specified mass of a material by 1°C.

Connected to temperature is **volume,** or the amount of space matter occupies. For example, a square rock that is 3 centimeters high by 3 centimeters wide by 3 centimeters deep has a volume of 3 cm³. Liquids and gases, however, have no fixed shape, and so they will have the same volume as the space or container they are in. Related to volume is **pressure,** which is *force exerted per unit area*—for example pounds per square inch, or PSI.

Now that we've reviewed the basic observable properties of matter, let's see what HiSET® questions that cover matter will look like on the exam.

1. Hardness is an observable property that is determined by how difficult it is to scratch or damage a substance. A student wants to determine the hardness of aluminum. He scratches a piece of aluminum with a wooden dowel and uses a steel nail to scratch a piece of steel. When there is no mark on the aluminum, he concludes that aluminum is harder than steel. What is the problem with this conclusion?

   (A) Since wood is softer than a nail, aluminum must be softer than steel.

   (B) Since steel is harder than wood, steel must be harder than aluminum.

   (C) Unless the two metals are scratched with the same object, the hardness cannot be properly compared.

   (D) He should have tried to bend the metals to determine the hardness.

The correct answer is (C). The question provides all the information about hardness that is required, so the question is really about the experiment itself. Scratching the two metals with different substances is not an accurate test; they must be scratched with the same material to measure the respective hardness of each.

2. A one-gallon kettle is completely filled with water, sealed, and heated. As the water passes its boiling point, the kettle bends and then explodes. Why?

   (A) The volume of the water increased when it boiled, destroying the kettle.

   (B) The temperature of the kettle increased, inducing a phase change in the kettle.

   (C) The pressure on the kettle decreased, causing the kettle to expand and burst.

   (D) The density of the water increased, bursting the kettle.

> **TIP**
>
> Note that temperature, pressure, and volume are all related. Increasing temperature usually leads to an increase in volume, which then increases the pressure of a gas or a liquid on its container.

The correct answer is (A). The question requires a basic knowledge of the relationship between temperature, volume, and pressure. As temperature increases, so does volume. Therefore, the answer must be choice (A).

POSITION AND MOTION OF OBJECTS

Now that we've reviewed the basics of matter, let's review how, and under what circumstances, objects move. There are two main types of motion—**linear** (in a straight line) and **circular.** The two types behave in similar ways, but there are a few terms unique to circular motion that we will review in this section.

Energy, Force, and Work

We cannot review motion without reviewing the two main types of energy. **Kinetic energy** is the energy of motion—there cannot be motion at all without energy. **Potential energy** is energy waiting to turn *into* kinetic energy. Potential energy is based on an object's position, not its motion. For example, think of a shopping cart at the top of a hill—before it rolls down the hill, it has potential energy. Once it starts rolling, that potential energy becomes kinetic energy.

Also crucial to understanding the motion of objects is **force,** or anything that causes change in an object's motion. In the shopping cart example, the gravity that causes the cart to roll downhill is a force influencing the cart's direction (downward).

Lastly, there is work. **Work** is when a force is exerted on an object and successfully moves the object. Think of the shopping cart as it rolls downhill. If a person waits halfway down the hill and shoves the cart sideways as it rolls past, she will change the direction of the cart. She is doing work to the cart. That is different from force, since in this case the force is her shoving of the cart, not the cart's actual change of direction. Force results in work.

Factors That Influence Motion

Now that we have covered the basics of motion, let's review the factors that can influence it. One example is **speed,** which is the distance covered by an object in a set time. Don't confuse speed with **velocity,** which is an object's speed *and* its direction. Velocity is a **vector,** which is anything that has both a magnitude and a direction. **Acceleration** is the rate at which velocity (not speed) changes over time, so it is also a vector. Acceleration, speed, and velocity will all be influenced by force. Think about it—the harder you shove the cart as it passes, the more it will change the direction and the faster it will do so.

Momentum is related to mass and velocity; the more mass and velocity an object has, the more momentum it has. An object with a lot of momentum, say a runaway truck, takes a lot of force to stop it. A related term is **inertia,** which is the resistance to change in motion. Objects in motion try to keep moving at their same velocity, thanks to inertia.

TIP

Momentum is any object with mass in motion. So if an object in motion has mass, then it also has momentum.

Other forces tend to counteract motion rather than enabling it to continue. **Wind resistance,** or **drag,** is the force of air acting against an object. As an object passes through air, the air drags against it, counteracting its motion.

Similarly, **friction** is the force that results when one object passes over (or through) another object. The rubbing of the two objects creates resistance, which slows the object's motion. An example is runners on a sled. Without runners, the entire belly of the sled drags in the snow and creates a lot more friction, preventing the sled from moving as quickly.

Circular Motion

We've been discussing linear motion so far, but all of the terms we've discussed also apply to objects moving in a circular or curved motion. There are a few unique forces that apply only to circular motion. **Centrifugal force** is the force that pulls outwards on an object moving on a curve, encouraging it to go straight. You can feel centrifugal force when you drive around a long turn. (What would happen if you let go of the wheel?) The opposite of centrifugal is **centripetal force,** which is a force that pulls an object inward toward the center of a circular path. There is also **torque,** or rotational force, which causes an object to rotate around an axis.

Mechanical Advantage, Balance, and Machines

We've now reviewed all the influences on objects in motion. Humans understand those influences and have found ways to minimize the effort involved in moving objects. For this we use **mechanical advantage**, which is the extra force provided by a mechanism. More mechanical advantage equals less work! Mechanical advantage often makes use of an object's **center of balance,** or the point on an object where all forces are equal. An object held at its center of balance may remain balanced indefinitely. Most spoons, for example, may be balanced on a finger at a point near the head. When dangled from above, the center of balance is the point where an object will be level while hanging.

Mechanical advantage is often accomplished through a **simple machine,** or a device that changes either the magnitude or direction of a force. Two or more simple machines working together make a **complex machine.** A classic example of a simple machine is a **lever,** or a rigid rod or plank that pivots at a particular point, called a **fulcrum.** Mechanical advantage provided by a lever is called **leverage.** Levers, the simplest way to move a heavier load (they offer mechanical advantage), can be classified into first, second, or third degree based on where the fulcrum is located relative to the load being lifted (see Figure 2). In a **first-degree lever,** the fulcrum sits between the load and the force being used to move it—think of a seesaw. The closer the fulcrum is to the load, and the longer the other end, the less force is required to lift the load. In a **second-degree** lever, the force is on one end of the lever, the load is in the middle, and the fulcrum is at the other end, as in a wheelbarrow—the wheel is the fulcrum. Finally, there are **third-degree levers**, where the load is on one end, the fulcrum on the other, and the force is in the middle—think of a forearm, with the load in your hand and your elbow as fulcrum. The bicep muscle (above the elbow) provides the force. Only

TIP

Aircraft are sleek and streamlined in order to counter wind resistance, allowing planes to move through air with less counteracting force.

first- and second-degree levers provide any mechanical advantage. In a third-degree lever such as your forearm, your bicep must be sufficiently strong to lift the weight in your hand, or it will not rise.

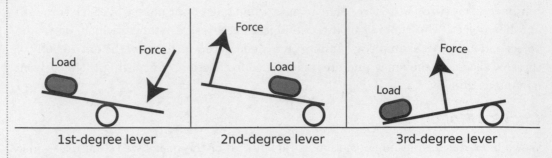

Figure 2: Types of levers.

3. A child weighing 75 pounds wants to lift a 100-pound weight with the first-degree lever shown in the image. At which place on the lever, indicated by a letter, should the child sit in order to best lift the weight?

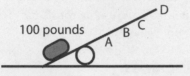

(A) Point A
(B) Point B
(C) Point C
(D) Point D

The correct answer is (D). Remember that in a first-degree lever, the longer the distance opposite the fulcrum from the weight, the more mechanical advantage the lever provides. Since the child is lighter than the load, in order to achieve maximum force from the lever she needs to sit as far away from the fulcrum as possible, which is indicated by point D.

4. A coiled spring is tightly wound inside a can. When the lid of the can is removed, the spring will uncoil and leap out of the can with great force. What is the status of the spring when it is still inside the can?

(A) The spring is loaded with potential energy.

(B) The spring is loaded with kinetic energy.

(C) The spring is loaded with momentum.

(D) The spring is loaded with torque.

The correct answer is (A). The question requires you to remember the basic states of energy of motion. Before the lid is released, the energy of the spring has not yet been realized—it is energy waiting to happen, which is potential energy.

LIGHT

Now it is time to review some of the different forms of energy, starting with light. The term **light** typically means "**visible light,**" which is electromagnetic radiation that is visible to the eye. (There are also forms of light that are not visible to the eye, which we will discuss later in the chapter.) Light is what makes sight possible. On Earth, the main source of light is the sun, which is the source of photosynthesis and responsible for most of the life on Earth.

Properties of Light

Light is a form of energy that has some confusing properties. The nature of light is that it can exist as either a particle or a wave. A light particle is called a **photon,** or the smallest unit of light. However, many aspects of light cannot be explained by photons, so light also exists as an electromagnetic **wave.** A wave of light can be explained as a continuous stream of light, not broken up into particles—think of light as a continuous rope. Light also has **intensity,** which is the rate at which a light wave delivers energy to a fixed area. For example, the light of a hot summer sun at noon will have higher intensity than on a cloudy fall evening.

Light cannot penetrate many objects, and many times the light bounces off an object, returning in the direction that it came from. Think of the sunlight gleaming off a mirror—when the light bounces away from an object like this, it is called **reflection.** Light can pass through transparent materials, like windows. In many cases, like a window, the light wave passes right through. In other cases, light waves bend; this is called **refraction.** Water can refract light, for example. Think about looking at an object underwater—it appears slightly offset from its actual position. **Lenses,** or curved pieces of glass or other transparent material, can also bend light. **Convex** lenses are curved outward and bend light inward; **concave** lenses are curved inward and reflect light outward.

The Electromagnetic Spectrum

Let's move on to the features that give different types of light their particular characteristics. If you could look at light from the side, it would look like an evenly spaced series of rolling hills. Since light is a wave, it behaves like a wave and oscillates up and down (see Figure 3). Like the ocean waves, light waves are a repeating pattern of highs and lows. The distance between each peak is called the **wavelength,** depicted by the Greek letter lambda (λ). The number of oscillations (peaks) in a given period of time is called the **frequency.**

TIP

To envision light, it might also be helpful to think of ocean waves continuously rolling in to shore.

TIP

Magnifying lenses such as in a telescope or microscope are convex.

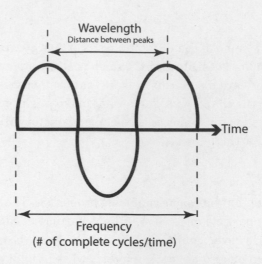

Figure 3: Frequency and wavelength of light.

The wavelength and frequency of a light wave give light unique characteristics. For example, blue light has a different frequency and wavelength than red light. Every wavelength of electromagnetic radiation, from very low to very high, is referred to as the **electromagnetic (EM) spectrum.** Humans can see light only in a narrow range in the middle of the EM spectrum, from around 390 nm to 700 nm; this is called the **visible spectrum.** Ultraviolet light is found at frequencies slightly lower than the visible spectrum; infrared occurs at frequencies above the visible range. We do not perceive each color separately—we see all light at once as white light.

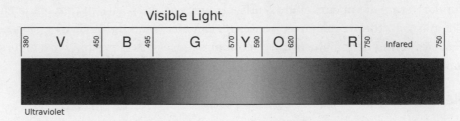

Figure 4: The visible spectrum.

Light Speed

The speed of light is 299,792,458 meters per second. Nothing can go faster than light. In most cases, light appears instantaneous to us, but at large enough distances, the fact that light has a speed limit becomes noticeable. For example, when communicating with the Mars Rovers, NASA has a lag of several minutes from when a command is sent to when the computer on the Rover receives it.

Let's try some practice questions that cover concepts related to the properties of light.

5. When visible light is shined through a prism, many different colors of light are visible on the other side of the prism. What is the most likely explanation?

    (A) The prism has refracted the light as a whole.

    (B) The prism has refracted each wavelength of visible light separately.

(C) The prism has reflected the light.

(D) The prism has converted the light wave into a particle.

The correct answer is (B). The question requires you to understand that visible light contains an entire spectrum of colors.

6. One property of light is brightness, or the strength of light. Brightness is not related to the color of light. Refer back to Figure 3, which shows a general light wave. Which aspect of the wave represents the intensity?

   (A) The height of each oscillation (hill)

   (B) The wavelength

   (C) The number of oscillations over time

   (D) The frequency

The correct answer is (A). This question may be answered through the process of elimination and the knowledge that wavelength and frequency determine the color of light. If color is determined by the number of oscillations and the distance between them, then the strength of each oscillation must represent brightness.

HEAT

Let's move on to another familiar type of energy—heat. Think back to your review of atoms earlier in the chapter, where we discussed that all molecules are made up of atoms, and all matter is made of molecules. When atoms and molecules vibrate or move, the energy associated with that movement is **thermal energy.** As the molecules move more and more, there is more and more thermal energy, with more energy in the object composed of those molecules. When something cools down, the molecules' motion slows down. **Heat,** or **heat transfer,** is the transfer of thermal energy from a hot object to a cooler one. Think about what you feel when you open your car door in the hot sun. The hot car has more thermal energy than your hand, so you feel the transfer from the car in the form of heat. In other words, the car feels hot, because the car has more thermal energy than you do, and the car is giving you some of this energy. When you open your car on a freezing winter day, you are transferring thermal energy to the cold door handle, and so it feels cold to you.

Fire is the most common visible form of heat. In **combustion,** when an object catches fire, fuel and oxygen have a rapid reaction that leads to light and heat being produced. Fire is that light and heat. Heat should not be confused with **temperature,** which for us is the measurement of thermal energy on a particular scale (e.g., Fahrenheit or Celsius). As temperature increases, thermal energy increases. Temperature can be measured with an instrument such as thermometer; heat itself cannot. Now that we have some background on the concept of heat, let's look at some of its properties.

Methods of Heat Transfer

Heat can move between and among objects or substances in three ways: conduction, convection, and radiation. Remember that thermal energy is the motion and collision

TIP

Heat and thermal energy are closely related, but heat is how thermal energy is moved around and is really responsible for how we feel and experience thermal energy.

of molecules, and that heat moves from warmer to cooler objects. In **conduction,** the molecules of a hot object are in motion and collide directly with the molecules of the second object, making the second object hotter. An example is a spoon becoming hot in a cup of hot tea.

Convection is a type of heat transfer that mostly occurs within a sample of liquid or gas. Thermal energy moves upward. As the molecules move around, they move farther apart, decreasing in density. (This is why heat rises.) In convection, those hotter, less dense molecules of liquid move upward and the cooler, denser molecules move downward until eventually all the molecules in the sample are the same temperature. When they reach the point where the temperature is even throughout, the sample is said to be in **thermal equilibrium.**

Radiation is heat transfer in the form of electromagnetic waves. Radiation does not require any intermediate material or particles. For example, the sun warms the Earth; heat comes directly from the sun to Earth with nothing in between.

All forms of heat transfer can be reduced or blocked with **insulation,** or separating an object from its heat source through a material or barrier that does not conduct heat. An oven mitt is a great example of insulation.

Let's try some review questions.

7. A calorie is a unit of energy, referring to the energy required to raise the temperature of 1 gram of water by 1°C. As the calories increase, which statement best describes what is happening to the water?

   (A) The water is undergoing combustion.

   (B) Conduction of the water is increasing.

   (C) Convection of the water is decreasing.

   (D) The thermal energy of the water is increasing.

The correct answer is (D). This question requires some knowledge of the very basic concepts of heat. In this case, remember that thermal energy is what increases as the temperature rises, so the answer must be choice (D).

8. The following figure shows a graph of the vapor pressure of water as temperature increases. Which statement best describes the relationship of pressure to temperature?

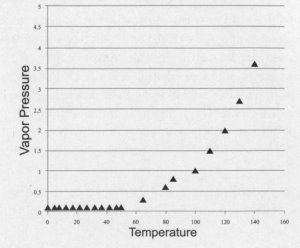

(A) Pressure steadily increases as temperature increases.

(B) Temperature steadily increases as pressure increases.

(C) Pressure increases very slowly at first, then rapidly.

(D) Pressure steadily decreases as temperature decreases.

The correct answer is (C). It is not necessary to fully understand the relationship between temperature and pressure to answer this question. It is enough to look at the graph and remember that the two are related to one another. In this case, the response of pressure to temperature is never steady, so only choice (C) can be the correct answer.

ELECTRICITY

We have now reviewed several of the key concepts of physical science: matter, movement, light, and heat. Let's turn our attention to a force that makes many of the conveniences of modern life possible—it powers our lights, televisions, and offices. Let's review electricity.

Electricity is a very general term that refers to all the phenomena associated with **electric charge.** Electric charge is a property of particles that defines how they will interact with other particles. Opposites attract, so a positive charge will be attracted to a negative charge and will repel another positive charge. Negative charges repel other negative charges. Think back to the beginning of this chapter—electrons are the negatively charged particles that orbit the center of an atom. A negative charge simply means that a particle has too many electrons. Objects that carry an electric charge generate a field in all directions, which affects the behavior of charged particles within its range. This field is called an **electromagnetic field (**the electrical component of the field is called an **electric field).**

The electricity we commonly refer to (the kind that powers our televisions) is **electric current,** which refers to the flow of charged particles, typically electrons, and the rate of that flow over a fixed point (measured in **amperes,** or amps). The energy transmitted by the flow of electrons is called **electrical energy.**

Just like heat, some materials are better at allowing electrons to move through them than others—a material that allows the movement of electrons is called a **conductor.** Copper, for example, is an excellent conductor and is used to transport electricity in many modern devices. The fewer electrons a conductor loses in transit, the better it is at conducting (meaning its conductance is high). The opposite is **resistance,** which is the impediment of electric currents. Water, for example, has almost no resistance, but a nonmetal substance, such as plastic, has much more. A material with very high resistance that completely or almost completely blocks the transmission of electric current is an **insulator.**

Terminology of Electricity

There are two main types of electrical current: **direct current** (DC) and **alternating current** (AC). The two terms refer to the direction of movement. In direct current, the electrons always move in one direction in a constant flow. Alternating current changes direction, alternating between one direction and then the opposite. Both types of current flow through a **circuit,** which is a complete path of electrical energy from start to finish, including the source where the current was first generated. A battery-powered flashlight contains a circuit from the battery to the bulb connected by a conductor, typically a wire.

There are several other terms relating to current you should recognize. One of them, amperes (amps), was already mentioned—amps are the unit of measurement for the strength of an electric current. Another term is **voltage.** Voltage refers to the amount of electrical energy available in a circuit. If a river were an electric current, the volume of water flowing through the river would be measured in amps. The voltage would be the total amount of water available, say the width of the river (compared to how fast it is flowing, which would be the current).

There are also a few important electrical components in a circuit, such as **resistors,** which introduce resistance to an electric circuit and lower the voltage on the far side of the resistor. **Transistors** are devices that can amplify (strengthen) a current, or switch a current between two circuits. **Capacitors** are devices used in circuits to store or block electrical energy temporarily. The result is to switch between AC and DC current, since a capacitor can block one type, say a DC current, but let the AC current through. At the end of a circuit is the **load,** which is the object being powered—a light bulb, for example.

We've now completed our brief review of electricity, so let's try some practice questions!

9. A conveyor belt is carrying buckets of sand from a gravel pit to a dump truck. In this scenario, which component would be most similar to the load?

   (A) The dump truck

   (B) The conveyor belt

   (C) The size of each bucket

   (D) The number of buckets per minute

The correct answer is (A). The question requires an understanding of the basic terminology of a circuit. The load in a circuit is what is being powered, for example a light bulb, so the closest equivalent in the conveyor belt case is the truck. The entire system is doing the work of filling the truck, so the truck is the load.

10. Rubber sheathing is typically used to cover wires in household electric circuits to increase efficiency and prevent accidents. Which statement best contains the reason this material is used?

   (A) Rubber sheathing makes an excellent transistor.

   (B) Rubber sheathing makes an excellent capacitor.

   (C) Rubber sheathing has very high resistance, limiting current from escaping the wire.

   (D) Rubber sheathing has its own electromagnetic field.

The correct answer is (C). In order to answer this question, it is necessary to make the educated guess that a loss of current from the wire will reduce efficiency. Only choice (C) contains the description of resistance and the function of rubber insulation.

> **TIP**
>
> In the United States, most of the power grid is powered by AC. DC is used to charge batteries in many electronics.

MAGNETISM

Magnetism refers to the phenomena associated with magnetic fields. **Magnetic fields** are created by electric currents passing through particular materials—not all materials are capable of producing magnetic fields. Materials that can produce a magnetic field when exposed to an electric charge are called **magnetic materials,** or **ferromagnetic.**

An object that can produce and maintain a magnetic field—that is, become magnetized— is called a **magnet.** Magnets are typically made of iron, nickel, cobalt, some soft and reactive metals called rare-earth magnets, and a naturally occurring mineral called lodestone. Magnetic fields produce **magnetic force,** which is the force that acts on other magnetic materials, particularly steel and iron. The strength of a magnet is dependent only on the strength of its magnetic field, not the size of the magnet.

Polarity

Each end of a magnet—wherever the end may be, as a magnet does not need to be a straight line— is called a **pole.** One pole will be negative and one will be positive; the negative pole will only attract the positive pole of another magnet and will repel another negative pole. The positive pole will do the opposite, only attracting a negative pole and repelling another positive pole.

Magnetic fields are oriented in particular lines of force, leaving one pole and rejoining the opposite pole along an elliptical path (see Figure 5). When pieces of a ferromagnetic material, such as iron filings, for example, are sprinkled over a magnet, they will orient themselves along these lines. The number of lines is proportional to the strength of the magnet.

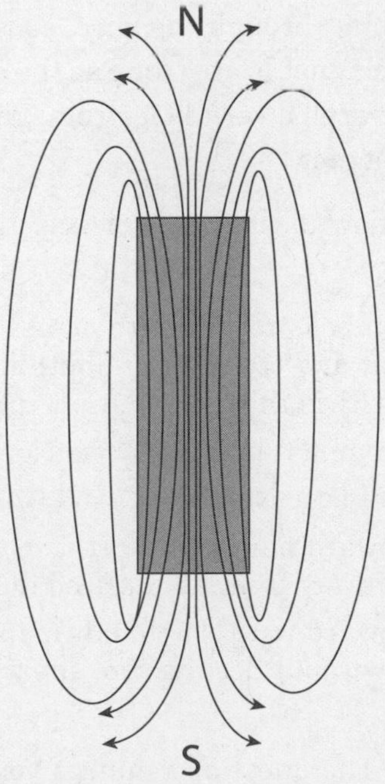

Figure 5: Magnetic field lines of a bar magnet. One pole of the magnet is positive (+), the other is negative (–). Poles of a magnet are named north (N) and south (S).

> **TIP**
>
> Magnetism and electricity are closely related (recall the electromagnetic field that surrounds objects that carry a charge).

The largest magnetic field is the field generated by the Earth's core, with one magnetic pole in the north and another in the south. The Earth's northern magnetic pole is the place where the Earth's magnetic field is oriented directly upwards at a 90° angle. At the southern magnetic pole, the Earth's magnetic field points directly downward at a 90° angle. Technically, the poles on a magnet are called north and south, as well. The north end, if allowed to move freely, will point toward Earth's north magnetic field, a fact which is useful in navigation. A **compass** is a really just a small magnet that is suspended in a fluid and allowed to freely move, pointing toward the magnetic north pole at all times.

Types of Magnets

Now that we've reviewed the basics of magnetism, let's take a look at the types of magnets. Magnets can occur naturally or be constructed by giving a charge to a ferromagnetic material. Naturally occurring magnets are called **natural magnets.**

A magnet that can permanently maintain a magnetic field, such as a refrigerator magnet, is called a **permanent magnet.** Permanent magnets can temporarily transfer a magnetic field to a ferromagnetic object through contact. For example, try rubbing a magnet against a steel nail for a few minutes. For a short while, the nail will be able to attract other magnetic materials, such as iron filings or another nail. The nail has become a temporary magnet. After a time, it will stop generating a magnetic field and will no longer exert a magnetic force.

Another type of magnet is an **electromagnet,** a magnet created by running an electric current through a coil of wire. Often, the coil is wrapped around a bar of ferromagnetic material, which enhances an electromagnetic field. The electromagnet is only a magnet as long as the current is passing through the wire, so these types of magnets can be turned on and off. The electromagnet is as strong as the current running through it, so a strong current can create a very powerful electromagnet. A tighter coil allows more current to flow through the magnet.

We've now completed our review of physical science. Let's finish with some sample questions covering magnetism.

11. An explorer is using a compass to navigate across a wilderness. The difference between the magnetic lines and true North-South lines is called declination, and on Earth it is about 10°. Why is this information vital to the explorer?

   (A) It does not matter; a compass points to true North.

   (B) It does not matter; magnetic North and true North are identical.

   (C) The compass points toward magnetic North, so without declination, the explorer will walk 10° away from her desired direction.

   (D) The compass points toward true North, but maps are oriented according to magnetic north, so without declination, she will walk 10° away from her desired direction.

The correct answer is (C). The question requires you to remember that magnetic North and geographic North are not the same. Remembering that compasses are magnets and that compasses point toward the magnetic poles, the answer must be choice (C).

TIP

The magnetic poles are not the same as the northernmost and southernmost spots on the Earth; those are the geographic poles.

12. A scrap-yard owner is building a strong electromagnet that she can use to lift heavy pieces of metal. She has the use of a 100-watt generator. Which ingredients should she buy in order to build the strongest possible magnet?

(A) 10 feet of copper wire

(B) 10 feet of copper wire and a bar of nickel

(C) 100 feet of copper wire

(D) 100 feet of copper wire and a bar of nickel

The correct answer is (D). The answer requires a basic knowledge of electromagnets—specifically that more current, especially when wrapped around a ferromagnetic material, makes a stronger magnet. All the answers have the same power supply, so the answer must be choice (D), since it contains a section of ferromagnetic material and a longer wire that can be used to make a longer coil.

SUMMING IT UP

- **Matter** takes up space and has mass. A fundamental type of matter is an **element,** a pure substance that *cannot* be broken down into simpler component substances. Elements are made up of **atoms,** the smallest units of matter.

- Physical properties of matter include odor, color, **mass** (the amount of matter in an object, measured in kilograms), **weight** (the force gravity exerts on an object), and **density** (mass per a standard unit of size).

- **Kinetic energy** is the energy of motion; **potential energy** is energy waiting to turn *into* kinetic energy. Potential energy is based on an object's position. **Force** is anything that causes change in an object's motion, while **work** is when a force is exerted on an object and successfully moves the object.

- **Speed** is the distance covered by an object in a set time, while **velocity** is an object's speed *and* its direction. **Momentum** is related to mass and velocity; the more mass and velocity an object has, the more momentum it has.

- **Mechanical advantage,** the extra force provided by a mechanism, often makes use of an object's **center of balance,** or the point on an object where all forces are equal. Mechanical advantage provided by a lever is called **leverage.**

- **Light,** which is electromagnetic radiation that is visible to the eye, makes sight possible. It can exist as a particle or as a wave. Wavelengths of electromagnetic radiation have a place on the **electromagnetic (EM) spectrum.** Humans can see light only in a narrow range in the middle of the EM spectrum, called the **visible spectrum.** We see all light at once as white light.

- **Thermal energy** is energy associated with the movement and vibration of atoms and molecules. **Heat** is the transfer of thermal energy from a hot object to a cooler one. Heat should not be confused with **temperature,** which is the measurement of thermal energy. Heat can move between and among objects or substances in three ways: conduction, convection, and radiation.

- **Electric charge** defines how particles will interact with other particles. A positive charge will attract a negative charge and will repel another positive charge. Negative charges repel other negative charges. A material that allows the movement of electrons is called a **conductor. Amps** measure the strength of an electric current, and **voltage** is the amount of electrical energy available in a circuit.

- **Magnetic fields** are created by electric currents passing through materials that are **ferromagnetic.** Magnets are typically made of iron, nickel, cobalt, some soft and reactive metals called rare-earth magnets, and a naturally occurring mineral called lodestone. **Magnetic force** is the force that acts on other magnetic materials, particularly steel and iron.

- In a magnet, one pole will be negative and one will be positive; the negative pole will attract the positive pole of another magnet and will repel another negative pole. The positive pole will do the opposite, only attracting a negative pole and repelling another positive pole. The largest magnetic field is the field generated by the Earth's core, with one magnetic pole in the north and another in the south.

Earth Science

OVERVIEW

- The Earth's materials
- Geologic structures and time
- Earth's movements in the solar system
- Summing It Up

Earth science, the study of the planet Earth and its place in the solar system and the galaxy, is a broad topic that might include the Earth's structure, history, geologic features such as volcanoes, and even the oceans, atmosphere, and climate. Earth science questions make up about 23 percent of the HiSET® Science subtest.

THE EARTH'S MATERIALS

Let's begin our review of Earth science with a look at Earth's materials. A good place to start is a quick review of the Earth itself.

The Earth

The Earth is around 12,000 km (8,000 miles) in diameter and is made of layers. The innermost layer is the **core.** The core's inner portion is solid, with a molten liquid core surrounding the solid part. Above the inner core is the **mantle,** which makes up most of the Earth's interior. The uppermost layer of the mantle is harder and rockier than the deeper, partially liquid layers. Above the mantle is the outermost layer, the **crust,** which is lighter. The crust and the hard outer layer of the mantle together form the **lithosphere.**

Above the crust is the **atmosphere,** or the gasses that surround the Earth and make life possible. The atmosphere is also divided into layers (see Figure 1), the lowest of which is the **troposphere,** where most oxygen is found. Related to atmosphere is the **climate,** which is the variations in atmospheric conditions, such as temperature, over long periods of time. **Weather,** by contrast, refers to conditions in a local area on any given day. Long-term change in the climate caused by human activities, such as burning fossil fuels, is called **anthropogenic climate change.**

Oceans are also considered part of Earth science. Oceans are salt water, since they contain dissolved salt carried there by water runoff from land. Salt water is much more common on Earth than fresh water.

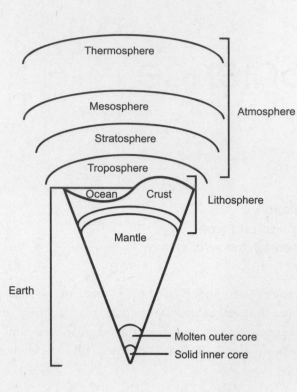

chapter 15

Figure 1: The Earth system.

Rocks and Minerals

The strong forces within the lithosphere and the mantle are responsible for the formation of most rocks. Even a few kilometers below the surface (and increasing with more depth), the temperature and pressure become extreme, enough to deform or even melt rocks. **Rocks** are solid and made of multiple grains of one or more minerals. A **mineral** is naturally occurring, solid, can be an element or a compound. Minerals are not derived from a living organism (they are **inorganic**) and typically have a crystalline structure.

Types of Rock

Rock that is beneath the surface and still molten (in a liquid state) is called **magma.** When magma reaches the surface it becomes **lava,** which remains liquid at first but will cool and harden into solid rock at the surface. Rocks are classified based on how they are formed. There are three major types of rocks:

- **Igneous rock** is formed when molten rock (either magma or lava) turns solid, so igneous rocks occur where there is or once was volcanic activity. Common examples include granite, basalt, or obsidian, also known as volcanic glass. Magma that forces itself into other rock formations is called **intrusive;** when it is forced to the surface, as in a volcanic eruption, it is called **extrusive.** When igneous rock cools quickly, the grains tend to be very fine; when the cooling occurs slowly, larger grains and crystals tend to be present.

- **Sedimentary rocks** are formed when grains or smaller rocks break off and are moved—usually by wind, water, or ice—to a new location. The process where the rock surface is worn away into smaller pieces, which break off, is called **weathering.** These transported smaller grains are called **sediment.** Sediment grains can be any size. In the new location, the grains are cemented together over time, usually through the pressure of additional material settling on top. Sedimentary rock sometimes has a layered appearance, called **bedding,** reflecting how different sediments are laid down and turned into rock at different times. Some examples include sandstone and limestone. Sedimentary rocks can be **classic** (formed as explained above), **chemical** (formed by the precipitation of minerals out of existing rock by the action of water), or **biochemical** (formed by the shells of organisms). Classic sedimentary rocks are classified by the size of the grains; when the grains are a mixture of sizes it is called **conglomerate.**

- **Metamorphic rocks** are formed when a rock is transformed into a different type of rock by temperature and pressure. Given enough temperature and pressure, any rock can become metamorphic. An example is marble, which is made of a transformed sedimentary rock, limestone. Rocks can metamorphose when the land subsides and rocks are buried deeply, subjecting them to heat and pressure, or even when subjected to sudden heat like a lava flow. The same type of rock might turn into two different metamorphic rocks if subjected to different temperatures or pressures.

The Rock Cycle

As you'll see later in this chapter, the Earth is constantly remaking itself. In the process, the different types of rocks are constantly being transformed from one type into another. The constant formation and transformation of rocks is known as the **rock cycle,** and it can take many forms. For example, magma can be extruded, as in a volcano. Then, over time, pieces break off the igneous rocks formed when the magma cools to form sedimentary rock. The sedimentary rock is buried deeply, subjected to heat and pressure, and turns into metamorphic rock. The metamorphic rock might be subjected to weathering and form new sedimentary rocks, or maybe the metamorphic rock eventually melts completely, turning back into magma and maybe one day forming new igneous rock. The rock cycle can work in many different ways, but eventually all rocks change.

Let's try a few review questions.

1. After a volcanic eruption, lava flows down a mountain to the sea, where it cools. The water breaks the cooled lava into smaller pieces. Those pieces sink to the bottom of the sea where they mix with mud and eventually turn into rock. The new rock is buried and crushed until new minerals are formed inside, making it into new rock with new characteristics.

   The description above is an example of

   (A) the Earth cycle.

   (B) weathering.

   (C) bedding.

   (D) the rock cycle.

The correct answer is (D). Only the rock cycle, choice (D), includes all the elements mentioned in the question.

2. If you could bore a small tunnel from the surface down to the core of the Earth, which two main characteristics would change as the depth increased?
   (A) Temperature and pressure
   (B) Pressure and hardness
   (C) Temperature and hardness
   (D) Hardness and bedding

The correct answer is (A). The answer requires you to distinguish general characteristics of the Earth versus properties of specific minerals. Temperature and pressure always increase with depth, while hardness and bedding are specific ways to tell minerals and rocks apart. They are not related to depth.

GEOLOGIC STRUCTURES AND TIME

Having completed our review of Earth, its components, and their properties, we can turn our attention to larger forces and structures. Earth is a dynamic system that is always changing—as we learned in the last section, even rocks can change over time. Those changes, on a larger scale, result in the current appearance of our planet.

The Formation of Geologic Features

The most familiar features of Earth are the **continents,** the large expanses of land above the ocean. In most discussions, there are seven continents: North America, South America, Europe, Asia, Africa, Australia, and Antarctica. However, the division between Europe and Asia is political, not geological, so really there are six land masses. Between the continents are the huge bowl-shaped formations below sea level that hold the oceans; these are the **ocean basins.** A piece of land surrounded by water but much smaller than a continent is called an **island.**

A more unusual feature is a **crater.** Craters are formed by the impact of an extraterrestrial object, such as a meteorite. They are also associated with volcanoes.

Let's examine how the different types of land features are formed. The number one way that new land is formed or changed is through **volcanism,** or the action of volcanoes. Any opening where magma can reach the surface is called a **vent.** When the lava or ash from inside the vent builds up on the spot to form a mountain, it is called a volcano. Volcanoes starting underwater can add material and rise until they break the surface, resulting in a **volcanic island,** like Hawaii. Lava can also flow into the sea and cool, forming new land.

TIP

Not all islands are volcanic.

Another force that can create new features is water. **Glaciers** are vast sheets of ice that move slowly but do not melt, not even in the summer. Their huge weight moving across the land can carve valleys or other features and push large boulders of rock in front of them. Regular water can also shape the land. The action of currents and waves can alter the shape of the coastline, and the movement of rivers and floodwaters over time can carve plains or canyons, such as the Grand Canyon.

At a larger scale, features are determined by **plate tectonics,** the movement of plates. The lithosphere is divided up into roughly 20 pieces, each called a **plate,** which are constantly in motion. Until about 200 million years ago, all of the continents formed one giant landmass, a "supercontinent" called **Pangaea.** Movement of the plates caused the continents to move apart, which is called **continental drift.** Where the interior areas of the plates are relatively stable, geologic changes happen most often in the areas where two plates meet. These areas are called **plate boundaries.** Plate boundaries result in **faults,** or fractures, where one body of rock moves relative to another. The movement of land at faults can result in **earthquakes.**

There are three different types of plate boundaries:

1. In a **divergent boundary,** two plates are moving away from one another. The opening can allow magma from the mantle to rise to the surface, building up new seafloor and resulting in mid-ocean ridges (volcanic islands). On land, divergent boundaries create massive **rift valleys,** such as those found in East Africa.

2. In a **convergent boundary,** an oceanic plate meets a continental plate—but instead of spreading apart, the continents collide. The heavier oceanic plate is forced underneath the lighter continental crust in a process called **subduction.** Deep ocean **trenches** form at these boundaries. In many cases the continental crust is forced upwards. This process can sometimes form a mountain range—the Himalayas, which are still growing, are an example.

3. In a **transform boundary,** the plates are moving parallel to one another in different directions. There is no subduction or release of magma, but the forces of the two plates sliding past each other will fracture the crust. The earthquake-prone San Andreas Fault in California is a transform boundary.

Geologic Time

All of these changes occur over long periods of time, and the entire 4.5 billion-year-old history of the Earth is called geologic time. Geologic time is divided up into **eons** (the largest division), **eras, periods,** and finally **epochs.** Periods are distinguished by the fossils found in the rocks during that time and are divided by major geologic events. Dinosaurs, for example, lived in three major periods: the Triassic, the Jurassic, and the Cretaceous, which ended about 65 million years ago. Global conditions, like climate, change substantially from one period to the next.

We've completed our review of geologic features and time. Let's try some practice questions.

TIP

We are currently living in the Holocene epoch of the Quarternary Period, although the changes wrought by humans have been so profound that many scientists are advocating for a new name, the Anthropocene.

3. The following image shows a top-down view of a transform fault, where the arrows indicate the direction of movement of each plate. Which geological feature or event is most likely to occur at point A?

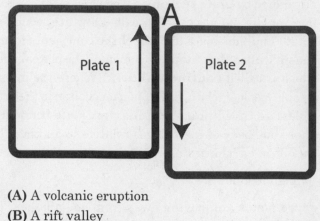

(A) A volcanic eruption

(B) A rift valley

(C) A trench

(D) An earthquake

The correct answer is (D). The question does require some knowledge of the main fault types, in particular that no subductions or eruptions occur at transform faults. No answer except choice (D) is associated with this kind of structure.

4. The Cretaceous-Tertiary Boundary (K-T boundary) is visible in certain rock formations as a thin layer of a metal called iridium. Iridium is very rare and mostly found in meteorites. The presence of iridium at the K-T boundary suggests that

(A) climate changes led to the end of the Cretaceous.

(B) a meteorite may have caused the changes that ended the Cretaceous.

(C) volcanic eruptions may have ended the Cretaceous.

(D) dinosaurs went extinct at the end of the Cretaceous.

The correct answer is (B). The question requires you to look past all information except the iridium. All of the answer choices are true, but only choice (B) actually relates to the presence of iridium at the K-T boundary.

EARTH'S MOVEMENTS IN THE SOLAR SYSTEM

The Earth is part of a larger system of objects orbiting the sun. Together these parts compose the **solar system,** a key topic covered on the HiSET®.

Earth's Orbit

All objects in the solar system move in a regular, curved pattern, called **orbit,** around the sun. The time it takes the Earth to circle the sun one complete time is 365 days, or one year. The orbit of the Earth and the other planets is **elliptical,** not circular (see following figure). The point in an orbit where a planet is furthest from the sun is called **aphelion;** the point where it is closest is called **perihelion.** The Earth itself is also tilted at a constant angle of 23.5°—this angle causes the Northern Hemisphere to point towards the sun at aphelion and away from the sun at perihelion. Since the areas where sunlight is hitting the Earth more directly are warmer, the Earth is actually further from the sun during the Northern Hemisphere summer. The opposite is true for the Southern Hemisphere.

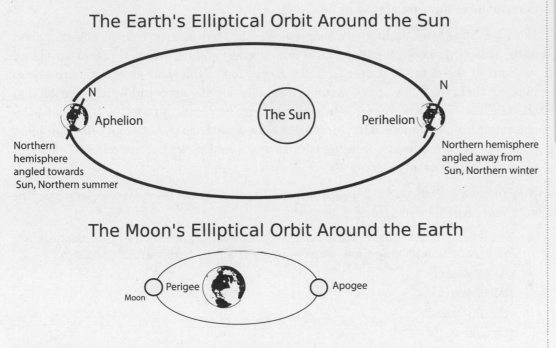

The Earth's Elliptical Orbit Around the Sun

The Moon's Elliptical Orbit Around the Earth

TIP

An orbit occurs any time a smaller body circles a larger body; it does not just refer to objects circling the sun.

The Earth not only orbits the sun, it also spins around on its axis. One spin takes 24 hours, or one day. As the Earth spins, different sides of the Earth face the sun at different times; this causes time zones, or areas where the hour is different across the Earth. The parts of Earth facing away from the sun experience night.

The Moon

A smaller object orbiting a larger one is called a **satellite.** One example is the moon, which circles the Earth in an elliptical orbit. The point where the moon is closest to the Earth is called **perigee,** and the point where the moon is furthest away is call **apogee.** The moon is large enough and close enough that its gravity exerts a direct force on the Earth. Tides, for example, are partially a result of the moon's influence. When the moon's position in its orbit is just right, the moon can come between the Earth and the sun, temporarily blocking the view of the sun in an event known as a **solar eclipse.** When the sun, moon, and Earth align so that the moon passes into Earth's shadow, we have a **lunar eclipse.**

Other Planets and Objects in the Solar System

Starting closest to the sun and moving outward, the planets are Mercury, Venus, Earth, Mars, Jupiter, Saturn, Uranus, Neptune, and a dwarf planet called Pluto. The farther a planet is from the sun, the longer it takes to complete one orbit. Mercury, the closest planet to the sun, only takes 88 days to orbit the sun.

Mercury, Venus, Earth, and Mars are known as the **inner planets,** while Jupiter, Saturn, Uranus, and Neptune are called the **outer planets.** The outer planets tend to be much larger and are composed primarily of gas, while the smaller inner planets are rockier. Of the inner planets, only Earth and Mars have moons, while all of the large outer planets have numerous moons.

Between Mars and Jupiter are numerous rocky, irregularly shaped objects called **asteroids.** These objects range in size from a grain of dust to nearly planet-sized and are part of the debris left over from the formation of the solar system. There are so many of them that they orbit the sun in a band called the **asteroid belt.** Occasionally, one of these objects hits the Earth's atmosphere, becoming a **meteor.** If it lands, the object is known as a **meteorite.** Most meteorites come from the asteroid belt. The oldest objects of all are **comets,** freezing chunks of ice and rock that are leftover material from the formation of stars.

Now that we've reviewed the basics of Earth's motion in the solar system, let's practice with more test-like questions.

5. The dwarf planet Pluto orbits the sun beyond even Neptune, the outermost planet. Which of the following time spans represents Pluto's orbit around the sun?
   (A) 12 years
   (B) 29 years
   (C) 165 years
   (D) 248 years

The correct answer is (D). To answer this question, it is not necessary to have memorized the actual orbit time. You only need to know that the farther an object is from the sun, the longer its orbit takes. According to the question, Pluto is the furthest object there is, so the longest orbit must be correct.

6. The tropics on Earth, between 23.5° North and 23.5° South latitude, never become cold, even in winter. What is the explanation for this situation? (Refer to the previous figure).
   (A) The tropics always face the sun.
   (B) The tilt of the Earth means the tropics never angle away from the sun.
   (C) The tropics are constantly at perihelion.
   (D) The tropics are constantly at aphelion.

The correct answer is (B). The figure shows the tilt of the Earth and its relationship to the seasons. A close look shows that the middle portion of the planet is always partially angled toward the sun, so these latitudes never fully experience winter, as stated in answer choice (B).

SUMMING IT UP

- The **core** is the Earth's innermost layer. Above the inner core is the **mantle,** which makes up most of the interior of Earth. Above the mantle is the outermost layer, the **crust.** Above the crust is the **atmosphere,** or the gasses that surround the Earth and make life possible. **Climate** is the variation in atmospheric conditions, such as temperature, over long periods of time, while **weather** refers to conditions in a local area on any given day.

- There are three major types of rocks: **igneous rocks** (formed when molten rock turns solid), **metamorphic rocks** (formed when a rock is transformed into a different type of rock by temperature and pressure), and **sedimentary rocks** (formed when smaller rocks break off, are moved naturally to a new location, and cement together over time).

- The number one way that new land is formed or changed is through **volcanism,** the action of volcanoes. Volcanoes starting underwater can add material and rise until they break the surface. **Glaciers** move across the land and can carve valleys or other features. The action of currents and waves can alter the shape of the coastline, and the movement of rivers and floodwaters over time can create plains or canyons.

- Larger features are determined by **plate tectonics,** the movement of plates. Geologic changes happen most often in the areas where two plates meet. These areas are called **plate boundaries.** There are three different types of plate boundaries: a **divergent boundary** (where two plates move away from one another), a **convergent boundary** (where an oceanic plate meets a continental plate and the continents collide), and a **transform boundary** (where the forces of the two plates sliding past each other will fracture the crust).

- Objects in the solar system move in a regular, curved pattern, called an orbit, around the sun. The orbit of the Earth and the other planets is **elliptical,** not circular. The Earth also spins on its axis, causing different sides of the Earth to face the sun at different times.

- The moon can come between the Earth and the sun, temporarily blocking the view of the sun in a **solar eclipse.** When the sun, moon, and Earth align, and the moon moves into the Earth's shadow, it is a **lunar eclipse.**

- **Asteroids,** which range in size from a grain of dust to nearly planet-sized, are part of the debris left over from the formation of the solar system.

PART VI

SOCIAL STUDIES

Important Eras in U.S. History

OVERVIEW

- Exploration to revolution and the new nation
- Expansion and reform (1801–1861)
- Civil War and Reconstruction (1850–1877)
- The development of the industrial United States (1870–1900)
- The emergence of modern America (1890–1930)
- The Great Depression and World War II (1929–1945)
- Post-War United States (1945–1970s)
- Contemporary United States (1968 to the Present)
- Summing It Up

History helps us define our identity. It can tell us who we are, where we come from, and how we are connected. How we interpret and understand history shapes the way we look at and understand current events and tells us why things are the way they are today. The HiSET® Social Studies subtest will test your understanding of history by presenting you with a series of historical documents, speeches, images, articles, cartoons, and more. The better knowledge base of history you have, the easier it will be for you to understand what you read on test day. This chapter gives you a basic overview of U.S. history, so you can face history questions on the HiSET® Social Studies exam with confidence.

EXPLORATION TO REVOLUTION AND THE NEW NATION

Europeans began leaving their continent in the 1500s to explore and colonize the Americas. These colonies often reflected the traditions of their European homelands, but they were also shaped by the geography of the new lands they settled and by the Native Americans who had been living there for centuries. Christopher Columbus's first voyage to the Americas in 1492 led to a period of European exploration and colonization. Europeans now looked to this new world for exploration, discovery, and potential wealth through new trade opportunities.

Native Americans and the Colonization of North America

The original Native Americans developed many cultures with distinct societies and languages in the thousands of years before the arrival of Europeans. The native peoples' knowledge of life and survival in North America was vital to the survival of European explorers and settlers. Although European colonists settling in North

America benefited from their ongoing interactions with the Native Americans, these encounters devastated the native peoples of the Americas. Native American cultures throughout the Americas were changed and destroyed by war, disease, and enslavement practices. As European colonists expanded their territories in North America, most Native Americans were pushed from their lands as the Europeans fought for control of the continent.

Founding the 13 Colonies

Increasing numbers of immigrants in the 1600s led to the creation of the 13 original English colonies. These colonies were grouped into three general geographic groups: the New England colonies (Massachusetts, Connecticut, Rhode Island, and New Hampshire), the middle colonies (New York, New Jersey, Pennsylvania, and Delaware), and the southern colonies (Maryland, Virginia, North Carolina, South Carolina, and Georgia). Differences in geography, availability of natural resources, and climate—along with patterns of settlement—caused the three regions to develop differently. All these factors resulted in significantly different economies and lifestyles.

The French and Indian War

Long rivals and wartime enemies, France and Great Britain had battled each other in Europe many times. As both countries tried to grow and strengthen their hold on North America, war erupted in 1754. The conflict between Britain and France in North America was called the **French and Indian War.** Conflicts would eventually ignite throughout the world wherever Britain and France had territorial shared interests.

American colonists and some Native American tribes fought alongside British soldiers against the French. France's mostly peaceful relationships with Native Americans brought them highly skillful fighting partners, when tribes started to side with the French. Adopting Native American guerilla war tactics, the French were initially successful at defeating the British. As the war progressed, however, British and American soldiers adapted to wilderness fighting and were able to counter French and Native American strategies.

TIP

The French and Indian War originally began over ownership of the upper Ohio River valley region.

Britain had great advantage in financial resources, and its ability to supply industrial resources, food supplies, and war equipment to its soldiers was too much for France to overcome. After nine years of fighting, England and France signed the **Treaty of Paris** in 1763. France gave nearly all of its North America territories to Britain. Britain also claimed Spanish-controlled Florida from Spain, because it had supported France in the war.

The American Revolution

Victory in the French and Indian War left the British government with overwhelming debt. In the 1760s, the English imposed several unpopular taxes on the American colonies to help pay off the debt. King George III of England also instituted several laws that the colonists thought severely restricted their freedoms. In December of 1773, Samuel Adams led a group of angry colonists disguised as Native Americans to dump British-owned tea into Boston Harbor to protest British control of the American economy. This event became known as the **Boston Tea Party.** As punishment, the British enacted the 1774 **Intolerable Acts,** which outlawed town meetings and closed Boston Harbor. Resistance intensified, and in April 1775, British soldiers exchanged shots with American colonists at the battles of Lexington and Concord, sparking the **American Revolution.**

Colonists had established the **Continental Congress** in 1774 to unite the colonies. In 1775, the Second Continental Congress appointed **George Washington** as commander of the Continental Army. The Continental Congress remained the government of the United States until the U.S. Constitution was ratified in 1789.

With the publication of Thomas Paine's pamphlet *Common Sense* in 1776, talk of independence gained strength. The Continental Congress appointed 5 members, including Thomas Jefferson, to write a **Declaration of Independence,** which was eventually issued on July 4, 1776.

Facing the most highly trained and equipped army in the world, Washington's Continental Army suffered defeat after defeat in the early years of the war. Finally, following the Army's first victory at Saratoga, France began providing aid to the Americans, which proved to be crucial to their successes.

In 1781, fighting moved south when British General Charles Cornwallis invaded Virginia. A French naval fleet surprised Cornwallis and drove off the British fleet meant to provide supplies to land forces. Washington, his troops, and French troops then marched to Virginia and surrounded Cornwallis's army. **The Treaty of Paris,** signed in 1783, brought the war to an end.

The New Nation

In November 1777, during the Revolutionary War, the Continental Congress adopted the **Articles of Confederation** as a way to unite the colonies under some type of central government. The Articles of Confederation became the first national constitution of the United States. However, with the war ended and the new nation facing massive war debts, the Articles proved to be too weak and ineffective—Congress could not even tax the states without their permission. Finally, leaders from all the states met in Philadelphia at the Constitutional Convention of 1787 to create the **United States Constitution.** The new Constitution set up a strong central government with specifically defined powers over the states. In 1789, George Washington became the first president elected under the U.S. Constitution.

The Louisiana Purchase

The treaty of 1783 set the boundaries of the United States from Canada to the north to Florida and the Gulf of Mexico to the south. The treaty also gave the United States western lands as far as the Mississippi River. In 1803, President Thomas Jefferson bought the Louisiana Territory from France. The Louisiana Territory took in more than 800,000 square miles west of the Mississippi River and gave the United States complete control of the great river.

War of 1812

War between England and France in 1812 soon brought the United States into conflict with England once again. In an attempt to cripple France's war efforts, England intercepted American ships trading with France. Once stopped, the British often captured the American sailors and forced them to serve on English ships, an act known as **impressment.** Many Americans also blamed the British in Canada for arming Native Americans and encouraging attacks on American settlements on the frontier. Eventually, the United States sided with France and went to war against England.

The War of 1812 lasted only 18 months and ended with a treaty that left boundaries the same and did not address the causes of the war. The war did have several important effects, however. The United States established its rights at sea and gained the respect of foreign nations. The war also sparked a new spirit of patriotism and helped create a sense of national unity.

EXPANSION AND REFORM (1801–1861)

After the War of 1812, the United States entered a period described as the "Era of Good Feelings." A strong sense of national pride swept the country, and Americans looked west to the vast expanse of open land.

Manifest Destiny

Many Americans believed in the concept of **Manifest Destiny**—the idea that the United States and its ideals were destined to eventually control the entire continent. Americans, according to Manifest Destiny, had the duty to bring democracy and progress to the Western Hemisphere. Beginning in the 1820s, Americans began moving in large numbers west across the Great Plains. By 1848, the United States had taken the Southwest from Mexico and divided Oregon with Great Britain. The country had, indeed, achieved its "destiny" to reach from sea to shining sea.

The United States was not alone in looking to the potential of western North America and Latin America. To protect these valued lands, President James Monroe issued a proclamation in 1823 stating that European nations must not interfere with any nations in the Western Hemisphere or try to acquire new territory there. This **"Monroe Doctrine"** has been a foundation of U.S. foreign policy ever since.

Reforms

In the early decades of the 1800s, a religious revival swept the United States, which created an environment for great social change in the country. Strengthened by a new sense of purpose and the belief in the power of individuals to improve society and themselves, many Americans engaged in reform movements.

One striking feature of the reform movement efforts was the influential presence of women. Women began demanding more political rights. Susan B. Anthony, Elizabeth Cady Stanton, and others organized the women's suffrage movement and issued the Declaration of Sentiments and Resolutions at the **Seneca Falls Convention** in 1848. This gathering of women reformers marked the beginning of an organized woman's movement.

Among the other significant reform efforts in the 1800s was the **temperance movement.** Supporters of temperance, or moderation in the consumption of alcohol, worked to spread information about the dangers of alcohol and in some cases ban the sale of alcohol altogether. The spirit of reform also prompted some people to try to improve the prison system and the conditions in which prisoners were held. A major theme of the prison reform movement was the belief in rehabilitating prisoners. Reformers also worked to create a system of public education open to all citizens. Others sought mandatory school attendance laws and more educational opportunities for females.

Perhaps the reform movement that had the greatest impact in the 1800s was the **abolitionist movement.** Supporters of this movement wanted to abolish, or end, slavery in the United States. The antislavery movement grew rapidly in the North, where industrialization had replaced much manual labor. The South remained tied to agriculture and to the labor-intensive growing and exporting of cotton. The economic and cultural differences between the North and South were heightened by the debate over slavery.

CIVIL WAR AND RECONSTRUCTION (1850–1877)

Attempts at compromise between the North and South over slavery failed to end the sectional differences. **Sectionalism** is the practice of regions of a country supporting their own self-interests instead of the nation's interests as a whole. As the country expanded and new states entered the union, the main debate centered on whether new states would be free or allow slavery.

Causes of the Civil War

By the middle of the nineteenth century, all Northern states had abolished slavery, and by the 1860 presidential election, the United States was divided into 18 free states and 15 slave states. As the North and the South became more and more different, their goals and desires also separated. The North's economic progress helped fan the fires of resentment, since the Southern economy had stalled. "States' rights," or the right of individual states to overrule federal law and make their own laws, including slavery laws, became a key argument of the South's opposition to the federal government.

The South Secedes and War Begins

In the lead-up to the 1860 presidential election, the slavery issue split the Democratic Party. The election evolved into a four-way race, with Republican **Abraham Lincoln** winning. Southerners were sure that Lincoln meant to take away their right to govern themselves, abolish slavery, and destroy the Southern economy. Southern leaders felt that the only way to protect themselves was to no longer be a part of the United States of America. Shortly after Lincoln's victory, South Carolina announced that it was **seceding,** or withdrawing, from the Union. By February 1861, Georgia, Florida, Alabama, Mississippi, Texas, and Louisiana had seceded as well. These states created a union called the **Confederate States of America.**

In April 1861, Confederate forces fired upon and eventually captured Fort Sumter, a federal base in Charleston harbor. Virginia, North Carolina, Tennessee, and Arkansas soon joined the Confederacy. Maryland, Delaware, Kentucky, and Missouri, which were all slave states, remained in the Union as the Border States.

As both sides prepared for war, the North's advantage became obvious. The population of the Union was more than 22 million, while the Confederacy numbered only around 9 million. The Union also held a large advantage in the number of factories necessary to produce war materials and in transportation networks, including more railroads.

The Civil War

Confederate forces under the command of **General Robert E. Lee** and others scored several key victories in the first two years of the war. Fighting on familiar terrain was a significant advantage for the Confederate armies. Southern generals proved to be remarkably adept at exploiting the Union's weaknesses to secure victories, often against much larger forces. Lincoln, on the other hand, could not find a Union general capable of taking the fight. Finally, in 1863, **Ulysses S. Grant** emerged as the fighter Lincoln needed.

In early July 1863, the Union scored two significant victories: forces defeated Lee's army at the three-day battle at Gettysburg, Pennsylvania, and, on the same day, a Union army under Grant accepted the surrender of Confederate forces defending the vital Mississippi river town of Vicksburg, Mississippi. With Vicksburg in Union hands, the North controlled the entire Mississippi River, cutting off crucial Confederate east-west supply lines.

Lincoln promoted Grant to general in chief of all Union forces in spring 1864. As Grant chased Lee in Virginia, Union General William T. Sherman captured and destroyed much of Atlanta. He then moved his army on a march through Georgia to the sea, destroying anything that might help the Confederate war effort. Unable to slip away from the pursuing Grant, and with supplies running out, Lee surrendered to Grant at Appomattox Courthouse on April 9, 1865.

Reconstruction

The majority of fighting during the Civil War took place on Southern soil, causing massive destruction. The period after the war during which the nation rebuilt the South and attempted to reunite the country was called **Reconstruction.**

President Lincoln's assassination in spring 1865 set the stage for twelve long years of conflict and uncertainty for Southern states and the nation as a whole. Ratification of the Thirteenth Amendment ended slavery forever, and the Fourteenth Amendment

TIP

The American Civil War was the first modern war. The Union and Confederacy built huge armies supplied with mass-produced weapons, and railroads. The telegraph ensured rapid movement of supplies, troops, communication, and news.

granted freed slaves full rights of citizenship. By 1870, all former Confederate states had met the requirements to be readmitted to the Union, including accepting the Fourteenth Amendment and writing a new state constitution.

As Reconstruction came to an end in the late 1870s, Southern whites reclaimed control of many state governments. With this new power, they chipped away at the gains made by African Americans after the Civil War. Restrictive regulations known as **Jim Crow Laws** that denied African Americans equal opportunities and rights were put in place. African American voting rights were limited and "separate but equal" education and employment policies would restrict African Americans' civil rights for the next eighty years.

Now let's take a look how the HiSET® exam will test you on your ability to understand and synthesize social studies information.

Directions: Use the following information to answer the two questions that follow.

In the presidential election of 1876, Republicans chose not to nominate President Ulysses S. Grant for a third term in office. Grant's two terms were damaged by political scandals that hurt and distracted the nation's Reconstruction efforts in the South. Republicans instead nominated Rutherford B. Hayes as their candidate. The left cartoon shows President Grant riding a carpetbag on the back of the "Solid South" and propped up by Union troops. On the right is Rutherford B. Hayes using a plow labeled "Let 'Em Alone Policy" to bury rifles and carpetbags.

The "Strong" Government 1869–1877/The "Weak" Government 1877–1881

Artist: James Albert Wales

1. On the basis of the details in the cartoons, which of the following conclusions is the most reasonable?
   (A) The artist has a higher opinion of Rutherford B. Hayes.
   (B) The artist shows no preference for either politician.
   (C) The artist has a higher opinion of Ulysses S. Grant.
   (D) The artist's work shows a lack of respect for both politicians.

The correct answer is (A). The artist clearly has a higher opinion of Hayes. Details such as the thriving economy in the background and an energetic and productive Hayes plowing a field that contains rifles and carpetbags show why the artist approves of Hayes.

2. Which statement best reflects the artist's view about President Grant's handling of Reconstruction efforts in the South?

   (A) Grant has led the South back to economic growth.

   (B) Grant has burdened the South and ruined its economies.

   (C) Grant's efforts have won the full support of the Southern people.

   (D) Grant's use of military troops in the South has helped the Reconstruction efforts.

The correct answer is (B). Details in the cartoon depicting Grant show a destroyed economy in the background. The woman, who represents the South, is straining under the weight of Grant and his overfilled carpetbag. Grant's Reconstruction policies have crippled and burdened the South.

THE DEVELOPMENT OF THE INDUSTRIAL UNITED STATES (1870–1900)

In the years following the destruction and uncertainty of the Civil War and Reconstruction, the United States began a dramatic transformation from a rural nation to an industrial, urban country.

The Industrial Revolution in the United States

Although the **Industrial Revolution**—the change from making goods by hand to making goods with power-driven machines—had begun in England in the late 1700s, it did not begin in earnest in the United States until after the Civil War. The United States grew into an industrial power very rapidly. Many factors fostered this industrialization, including abundant supplies of raw materials and natural resources, cheap labor, and new inventions and technology. Among the significant technological advances made in this era are the emergence of railroads and agricultural machinery. More powerful and efficient farming equipment helped American farmers produce more crops than ever before. Railroads could deliver their products to American coastal ports where they were shipped to Europe and other markets. Advancements in refrigeration technology also allowed meat and dairy products to be shipped to distant markets. In the late 1800s, inventions such as the telephone and the light bulb spurred economic development and dramatically changed the way people lived.

The Rise of Corporations

Shrewd and visionary Americans harnessed the plentiful resources and large number of potential workers to build large, successful corporations, often amassing fortunes. Their factories and operations employed millions of Americans. These large corporations could produce more goods more efficiently and at lower costs for consumers. These factors spurred the growth of big business.

Labor Unions Emerge

Not all Americans prospered with these changes. Factory conditions were often unsafe—children worked for long hours for low wages, and many workers were forced to live in slum areas of large urban centers. Workers formed labor unions in the late 1800s to try to improve their wages and working conditions and limit work hours. One of the only bargaining powers unions had was the threat of a work strike. However, many strikes in this era led to violence, which hurt the image of unions and slowed their growth.

Social and Economic Changes

Much of the wealth from the nation's new industries went to the owners of very large companies. Most Americans, including its political leaders, believed that the wealthy would reinvest their profits to continue the cycle of economic growth to benefit all Americans in the long run. As inequality among Americans grew at the end of the 1800s, many people demanded reforms in government and economic conditions. New political parties emerged, such as the People's Party, which supported concepts like "the little man" against "big business."

Native American Policies

As white American settlers moved into Native American lands on the Great Plains and other regions, armed conflicts erupted. Clashes continued as the government tried to force Native Americans onto reservations and encouraged them to assimilate into American society. Greatly outnumbered, Native Americans unsuccessfully tried to stop the advancing American settlers. Full citizenship was not granted to Native Americans until 1924, when Congress passed the **Citizenship Act.**

THE EMERGENCE OF MODERN AMERICA (1890–1930)

Between 1890 and 1920, the United States underwent two significant developments. First, the country started its rise to become a global superpower. Second, reformers concerned about the negative effects of industrialization on society began changing the scope and reach of government to solve problems.

Expansion and Imperialism

International economic and military competition convinced American leaders that the United States had to become a world power. To do so, the country increased its trade and military presence in East Asia and Latin America. The construction of a powerful modern navy, the annexing of Hawaii, and the forcing of Japan to open its markets to the West all played crucial roles in building an American empire.

The event that best reflected America's new world-power status was the **Spanish-American War.** Within weeks, American forces defeated the Spanish in Cuba, while the U.S. Pacific fleet destroyed the Spanish fleet in the Philippines. The peace treaty forced Spain to give up Puerto Rico and the Pacific island of Guam to the United States.

TIP

The Spanish-American War was the shortest war in U.S. history.

Spain sold the Philippines, which it had ruled for more than 350 years, to the United States.

The Progressive Movement

Industrialization dramatically changed American society. Americans and immigrants flooded into urban areas and cities became very crowded. Many employees had to work in unsafe conditions, and the old political system was unable to effectively deal with these issues. These conditions helped create the **Progressive Movement.** Progressives campaigned for both political and social reforms to make government more efficient and more responsive to citizens. Other reformers focused on social welfare problems such as child labor, unsafe working conditions, and alcohol abuse. Many progressives joined the women's rights movement, eventually leading to the ratification of the Nineteenth Amendment in 1920, which granted women the right to vote.

World War I

Tensions among European nations were building in 1914. European leaders had been forming military alliances that teamed up some nations against others. These alliances encouraged militarism—the aggressive buildup of armed forces to intimidate and threaten other nations. Under these alliances, nations signed treaties that promised mutual support in case any of them was attacked. In June 1914, the assassination of **Archduke Franz Ferdinand,** an heir to the Austro-Hungarian throne, sparked conflict and triggered the alliances. World War I had begun.

One side was made up of England, France, and Russia **(the Allied Powers).** Opposing the Allied powers was the alliance formed by Germany, Austria-Hungary, and Turkey **(the Central Powers).** President Woodrow Wilson kept the United States out of Europe's war for three years.

Technological advancements in weaponry caused both sides to lose millions of men during World War I. More powerful and accurate artillery guns caused great destruction. Poisonous gas was used for the first time in warfare, and both sides used airplanes, tanks, and submarines with great effect. The continued targeting and sinking of American vessels by German submarines, or **U-boats,** finally brought the United States into the war in April 1917.

When American troops arrived in Europe, the war had evolved into a bloody stalemate. Despite bitter fighting, battle lines had changed little during the years of fighting. Both sides had dug trenches from the French coast to the border of Switzerland. More than two million American troops would eventually reach European soil, and their presence boosted the morale of Allied forces. With the addition of American troops on the battlefield, the Allies forced the Germans to finally retreat. Germany surrendered on November 11, 1918.

THE GREAT DEPRESSION AND WORLD WAR II (1929–1945)

The 1920s saw widespread use of new technology like automobiles, airplanes, radios, and electric appliances, which helped create a booming economy. American consumers spent more of their money, and stock prices continued to climb. But Americans were caught off guard in October 1929. Risky speculation in the stock market, questionable lending practices by banks, overproduction of goods, and uneven income distribution eventually undermined the U.S. economy, leading to an economic depression.

The Great Depression

The Great Depression caused high unemployment, business failures, and farm fore-closures. President Hoover tried to fix the economy by providing loans to banks and corporations and by starting public works projects. However, he was strongly opposed to giving direct federal aid to the homeless and jobless. This aid, he thought, should come from local governments. By early 1932, local governments were running out of money and were unable to provide the resources necessary to handle the growing crisis.

As presidential candidate in 1932, Democrat **Franklin D. Roosevelt** promised a "new deal" for struggling Americans. Roosevelt won the election and immediately began to put **New Deal** programs to work. Within the first 100 days in office, Roosevelt and Congress passed 15 major acts of legislation. The New Deal provided federal aid to small business owners and farmers. Even though he faced political and legal challenges to his New Deal programs, Roosevelt pushed through a second round of legislation in 1935. As the 1940s arrived, the worst years of the Great Depression were over.

Directions: Use the following information to answer the practice question.

When Franklin Delano Roosevelt became president in 1933, the United States was in the midst of the worst economic crisis in its history. Roosevelt and his advisors believed that action was needed immediately. In this passage from President Franklin D. Roosevelt's first inaugural address, he outlines his plan for resolving the crisis.

"Our greatest primary task is to put people to work. This is no unsolvable problem if we face it wisely and courageously. It can be accomplished in part by direct recruiting by the Government itself, treating the task as we would treat the emergency of a war, but at the same time, through this employment, accomplishing greatly needed projects to stimulate and reorganize the use of our natural resources."

... Finally, in our progress toward a resumption of work we require two safeguards against a return of the evils of the old order: there must be a strict supervision of all banking and credits and investments, so that there will be an end to speculation with other people's money; and there must be provision for an adequate but sound currency."

—President Franklin Delano Roosevelt,
First Inaugural Address
(March 4, 1933)

3. According to the passage, which of the following statements would best reflect Franklin Roosevelt's view of the role of government in American society?

    (A) Government's main responsibility should be matters of war.

    (B) Government should have broad powers to ensure the welfare of American citizens.

    (C) Government should have complete control over the nation's banking and financial industries.

    (D) Government should maintain a "hands-off" approach in all economic matters.

The correct answer is (B). This question requires you to understand how Roosevelt planned to fight the Great Depression and establish practices to prevent future economic crises. Roosevelt thought that if the government stepped up and handled the economic crisis as it would a war, the effects would be lessened. Roosevelt advocated government hiring of Americans to put them to work and also the government having a greater role in managing and regulating the nation's national resources and banking system.

World War II

In the largest conflict of the twentieth century, **World War II,** two powerful alliances—the **Allies** and the **Axis**—fought to control much of the developed world. The Allies and the Axis powers followed vastly different political ideologies. The Allies, led by the United Kingdom and France, were two of the largest democracies. The Allies would later be joined by the communist Soviet Union and the democratic United States. Fighting the Allies was the Axis alliance, led by the fascist nations of Germany and Italy. Japan was also a member of the Axis powers.

World War II began in 1939, when Nazi Germany's leader, Adolf Hitler, ordered the invasion of Poland. England and France both declared war on Germany in 1939 as part of an alliance agreement. In Asia, Japan invaded China and prepared to take over Southeast Asia. Germany went on to conquer most of Europe. In 1940, France surrendered, leaving England alone in the fight against the Axis powers in Europe. Japanese forces captured and controlled large territories in East Asia and islands in the Pacific Ocean.

Significant events in the early years of WWII:

- Great Britain, led by Winston Churchill, stood firm against the threat of German invasion during the Battle of Britain in 1940, despite the bombing of London and other major cities.

- Despite having signed an anti-aggression agreement with Soviet leader Joseph Stalin, Hitler invaded the Soviet Union in June 1941, bringing the Soviet Union into the war on the Allies' side.

- In December 1941, Japan attacked the U.S. naval base at Pearl Harbor, Hawaii. The United States declared war on Japan; Germany and Italy then declared war on the United States.

- American naval forces defeated the Japanese at the Battle of Midway in June 1942, putting Japan on the defensive.

- Soviet forces scored a major victory over the Germans at Stalingrad in February 1943; German forces retreated and never fully recovered.

- American and British forces invaded and defeated the Axis armies in North Africa in 1943.

- The Allies began the retaking of Europe, first through Sicily and Italy in 1943.

With the Axis forces on the defensive in Europe, the long-awaited major Allied invasion of the continent came on June 6, 1944—the **D-Day Invasion** at Normandy, France. Allied armies fought their way east to Germany over the next year, while Soviet forces moved west, squeezing the German armies. Germany surrendered in May of 1945.

With the war in Europe over, the Allies turned their full attention to the war against Japan. The Allies "hopped" across the Pacific starting in 1943, capturing territories closer and closer to mainland Japan. Even with defeat in sight, Japan showed no signs of surrender. In August 1945, the United States dropped atomic bombs on the Japanese cities of Hiroshima and Nagasaki. The massive destruction caused by these new weapons convinced the Japanese to surrender.

Directions: Use the following information to answer the practice question.

August 1945 marked the end of World War II, the second massive conflict of the twentieth century. This passage considers the actions the Allied powers took to establish order in the defeated countries and to rebuild lasting relationships.

> In the aftermath of World War I, some Allied leaders wanted to punish Germany for the suffering they had inflicted on the rest of Europe. The Treaty of Versailles, which negotiated the end of the war, imposed harsh punishments on Germany. The economic and political chaos created by the treaty led to the rise of Adolf Hitler and the Nazis, and consequently, World War II.
>
> Following WWII, the United States implemented the Marshall Plan. The plan provided economic assistance to all of Western Europe, including former enemies Germany, Italy, and Austria. The Marshall Plan helped to rebuild European economies. It also stimulated the U.S. economy by establishing markets for American goods. The Soviet Union, however, was very suspicious of the economic revival of Western Europe, especially West Germany.

4. According to the passage, which of the following statements best describes the major goal of the Marshall Plan?
   (A) The Marshall Plan was created to establish the United States as the dominant military power in Europe.
   (B) The Marshall Plan aimed to weaken the Soviet Union's influence in Europe.

(C) The primary goal of the Marshall Plan was to expand American economic markets.

(D) The Marshall Plan's emphasis on economic aid was aimed at preventing economic and political turmoil that might lead to future crises.

The correct answer is (D). This question requires you to make interconnections between the past events and the situations following World Wars I and II. The harsh punishments imposed on Germany after World War I created great turmoil. To make sure the Allies did not make the same mistake, the Marshall Plan provided generous economic and humanitarian aid to rebuild the countries destroyed during the war.

POST-WAR UNITED STATES (1945–1970s)

After World War II ended, the United States and the Soviet Union were the world's two most powerful countries. Growing tensions between the United States and the Soviet Union led to a constant threat of nuclear war. The tensions between the countries were based on their conflicting ideologies: the Soviet Union's communism and the United States' democratic government. These and many more disputes between the United States and the Soviet Union developed into the **Cold War.**

The Korean War

President Harry Truman worked to contain communism by supporting countries that were threatened by Soviet aggression. The communist threat spread to Asia in 1949, when Chinese revolutionaries took control and adopted a communist government. A year later, armies from communist North Korea invaded South Korea. Attempts to keep South Korea free from communism led the United States to military intervention, resulting in the **Korean War** (1950–1953). United States forces and armies from the United Nations fought for three years to prevent the communists from taking control, eventually leading to a stalemate and a cease fire.

The Vietnam War

American military forces also were sent to halt the spread of communism in Southeast Asia. During the 1950s, President Eisenhower sent money and advisers to South Vietnam to help stop North Vietnamese communists from taking control. Presidents Kennedy and Johnson continued the aid throughout the 1960s. By 1968, the United States had more than 500,000 troops fighting in Vietnam. Tens of thousands of American soldiers were killed fighting, and yet the United States could not defeat the communists. The war dragged on with little progress, leading many Americans to question the nation's involvement. The war divided the nation as protests erupted in city streets and on college campuses. President Richard M. Nixon finally pulled American troops from Vietnam in 1973, and in 1975, South Vietnam fell to the communists.

Post-War Prosperity and Domestic Policies

After World War II, the United States experienced years of steady economic growth. American consumer spending increased, driving prices and wages up. America entered a period of post-war abundance, with expanding suburbs, growing families, and more white-collar jobs.

Struggles for Racial and Gender Equality

The civil rights movement gained momentum rapidly after World War II. African Americans and other civil rights supporters challenged segregation in the United States. In 1954, the Supreme Court overturned the "separate but equal" doctrine that had become the cornerstone of segregation. In the 1960s, President Johnson pushed for more civil rights legislation. Congress passed the **Civil Rights Act of 1964,** which outlawed discrimination against African Americans, women, and other minorities in the workforce. The **Voting Rights Act of 1965** strengthened protections for southern African Americans to exercise their voting rights.

The women's movement was reenergized in the 1960s. Many women had become increasingly dissatisfied with society's perception of them and their place in society. Many women joined organizations that worked to improve or increase their roles in society.

Directions: Use the following information to answer the practice question.

Television forced mass communication industries to reevaluate their industries. The motion picture industry suffered declining attendance, as young and old Americans were drawn to television. In radio, the comedies, dramas, and soap operas that were popular before the war were no longer relevant to America's youth. Radio stations reacted by broadcasting music, news, and sports programs. The popularity of car radios helped the radio industry rebound.

Then, in the early 1950s, a new form of music emerged: rock 'n' roll. Characterized by loud, steady, heavy beats, rock 'n' roll was perfect for dancing. Young songwriters wrote tunes about cars, romance, and other topics popular with teens.

Young people, especially teens, in every generation, across most cultures try to separate themselves from their parents and older generations. The booming post-war economy provided many teens with disposable income that they spent on entertainment, music in particular. This led to a new youth culture that was distinct from other segments of society. Mostly unpopular with parents and older Americans, rock 'n' roll provided the source of separation that teens were looking for. This divide between the cultural preferences of children and their parents became known as the generation gap.

5. According to the passage, which of the following was primarily responsible for the emergence of a generation gap in the 1950s?

   (A) Television.

   (B) Car culture

   (C) Rock 'n' roll music

   (D) Radio

The correct answer is (C). Although television, radio, and the rise of the car culture were important factors, the emergence of rock 'n' roll was the driving force in creating the generation gap. The popularity of rock 'n' roll that teens throughout the United States shared united them and set them apart.

CONTEMPORARY UNITED STATES (1968 TO THE PRESENT)

After winning the 1968 election, President Richard Nixon began working to ease Cold War tensions with China and the Soviet Union. He visited China in 1972 and agreed to establish better relations with the communist country. The friendly relations he began with the Chinese have grown since, with China becoming a major trade partner of the United States today.

With the election of Ronald Reagan in 1980, the United States entered an era of more conservative approaches to solve the nation's problems. Reagan cut taxes, deregulated several industries, and appointed conservative judges. He also began a massive military buildup that greatly increased the country's deficit and stepped up aid to foreign groups fighting the spread of communism.

The Soviet Union collapsed in 1991, ending the Cold War and leaving the United States as the world's lone superpower. The United States, however, was thrown into a large military operation in the Middle East in 1990, when Iraq invaded oil-rich Kuwait. A multinational coalition of U.S. and UN forces drove the Iraqis out.

The 1990s

A computer and technology boom swept the country in the 1990s. The rise of the Internet revolutionized the workplace and the way people communicate. The economic growth in the 1990s was the longest sustained period of growth in American history.

The 1990s also saw a rise in the number of terrorist attacks, both in the United States and around the world. Terrorists bombed part of the World Trade Center in New York City in 1993. American militants bombed a federal building in Oklahoma City in 1995. Abroad, American embassies in the African countries of Kenya and Tanzania were attacked in 1998.

September 11, 2001

On September 11, 2001, terrorists associated with the organization Al-Qaeda hijacked four American commercial airliners. Two jets slammed into the towers of the World Trade Center in New York City; another was flown into the Pentagon in Washington, DC. Passengers aboard the fourth jet diverted the hijacking but perished when the plane crashed in Pennsylvania. Around 3,000 people died in the attacks. The United States soon launched a "War on Terror," which involved halting terrorists' access to funding and an invasion of Afghanistan, where Al-Qaeda's leader, **Osama bin Laden,** was based. In 2003, an American-led coalition force attacked Iraq and toppled the regime of Saddam Hussein. American leaders had been concerned that Iraq might have been producing weapons of mass destruction that could be used against the United States and its allies. Although the invasions of Afghanistan and Iraq removed oppressive and brutal regimes, establishing stable, effective governments has proven difficult, as both Iraq and Afghanistan remain politically uncertain.

Financial Collapse

On January 20, 2009, Barack Obama became the first African American President. Immediately upon assuming the presidency, Obama was thrown into a global crisis. During the autumn of 2008, Americans faced an economic crisis centered on the financial industry. The crisis stemmed in part from "subprime" home mortgage loans that banks had made to less-qualified and potentially risky borrowers. In September 2008, the stock market plunged, pushing the nation into the worst economic crisis since the Great Depression. The effects of the "Great Recession," as the crisis has been called, persisted for several years, as unemployment remained high, housing prices stalled, and economic crises in Europe prevented growth.

SUMMING IT UP

- Christopher Columbus's arrival in the Americas in 1492 led to a period of European exploration and colonization. The native peoples' knowledge of life and survival in North America was vital to settlers when they arrived in the 1500s. Upon colonization, Native American cultures throughout the Americas were changed and destroyed by war, disease, and enslavement practices.

- **The French and Indian War** began in 1754 over ownership of the region of the upper Ohio River valley. After nine years of fighting, England and France signed the **Treaty of Paris** in 1763. France gave nearly all its North America territories to Britain, and Britain claimed Florida from Spain, since Spain had supported France in the war.

- After England imposed taxes on the American colonies to pay off war debts, colonists took parts in the **Boston Tea Party** protest, leading to the **Intolerable Acts,** which outlawed town meetings and closed Boston Harbor. These actions helped spark the **American Revolution.** France provided aid to the Americans, which proved to be crucial to the successes of the Continental Army. **The Treaty of Paris,** signed in 1783, brought the war to an end and America's independence.

- During the war, the **Articles of Confederation**, the first national constitution of the United States, united the colonies under a central government. When the war ended, a stronger document was needed. **The United States Constitution** was created in Philadelphia at the Constitutional Convention of 1787. It set up a strong central government with specifically defined powers over the states.

- In 1812, in an attempt to cripple France's war efforts, England intercepted American ships trading with France. The United States sided with France and went to war against England in the **War of 1812.** At the war's end, the United States established its rights at sea and gained the respect of foreign nations.

- Beginning in the 1820, spurred by the concept of **Manifest Destiny**—the idea that the United States and its ideals would eventually control the continent—Americans began moving in large numbers west across the Great Plains. President James Monroe issued the **Monroe Doctrine** in 1823, which stated that European nations must not interfere with any nations in the Western Hemisphere or try to acquire new territory there.

- The economic and cultural differences between the North and South were heightened by the debate of slavery. **States' rights** became a key argument of the South's opposition to the federal government. Southern leaders felt the only way to protect themselves from Abraham Lincoln was to secede as the Confederate States of America. Confederate forces fought under the command of General Robert E. Lee; after some hardships, Union forces fought under Ulysses S. Grant. Lee surrendered to Grant at Appomattox Courthouse on April

9, 1865. The period after the war during which the nation rebuilt the South and attempted to reunite the country was called **Reconstruction.**

- The **Industrial Revolution**—the change from making goods by hand to making goods with machines—began after the Civil War. More powerful and efficient farming equipment helped American farmers produce more crops, and railroads could deliver their products to American coastal ports where they were shipped abroad. Inventions like the telephone and light bulb dramatically changed the way people lived. As a result, factories and operations employed millions of Americans and spurred the growth of big business. However, unsafe factory conditions caused workers to form labor unions, leading to violent strikes.

- In June 1914, the assassination of Archduke Franz Ferdinand sparked conflict and started **World War I.** Initially, one side was made up of England, France, and Russia (the Allied Powers); the opposing side included Germany, Austria-Hungary, and Turkey (the Central Powers). Poisonous gas was used for the first time in battle, and both sides used airplanes, tanks, and submarines. The continued targeting of American vessels by German U-boats finally brought the United States into the war in April 1917. The Allies forced the Germans to finally retreat and surrender on November 11, 1918.

- Risky speculation in the stock market, questionable lending practices by banks, overproduction of goods, and uneven income distribution led to the start of the **Great Depression** in 1929. President Herbert Hoover tried to fix the economy, but opposed giving direct federal aid to the homeless and jobless—local governments ran out of money, and the crisis grew. Soon, Franklin D. Roosevelt won the election and put **New Deal** programs to work, which provided federal aid to small business owners and farmers. The Depression ended by the 1940s.

- **World War II** began in 1939 when Adolf Hitler ordered the invasion of Poland, causing England and France to declare war on Germany. In Asia, Japan invaded China and prepared to take over Southeast Asia. The Allies (led by the United Kingdom and France and later joined by the Soviet Union and the United States) and the Axis powers (led by German and Italy, and including Japan) fought to control much of the developed world. In December 1941, Japan attacked the U.S. naval base at Pearl Harbor, Hawaii. The United States declared war on Japan, and Germany and Italy then declared war on the United States. The long-awaited major Allied invasion of Europe came on June 6, 1944—the D-Day Invasion at Normandy, France. Germany eventually surrendered in May of 1945. In August of that year, the United States dropped atomic bombs on the Japanese cities of Hiroshima and Nagasaki, causing the Japanese to surrender.

- Post-World War II brought about many more conflicts for the United States. The disputes between the United States and the Soviet Union after World War II developed into the **Cold War;** the Soviet Union collapsed in 1991, ending this struggle. When armies from communist North Korea invaded South Korea, attempts to keep South Korea free from communism led the United

States to military intervention, resulting in the **Korean War.** In the 1950s, President Eisenhower sent money and advisers to South Vietnam to help stop North Vietnam communists from taking control. By 1968, the United States had more than 500,000 troops fighting in the unsuccessful **Vietnam War.** This era also brought many internal struggles for the country, as African Americans and other civil rights supporters challenged segregation. Congress passed the **Civil Rights Act of 1964,** which outlawed discrimination against African Americans, women, and other minorities in the workforce. The **Voting Rights Act of 1965** strengthened protections for southern African Americans to exercise their voting rights.

- The 1990s saw a rise in terrorist attacks in the United States and around the world. Then, on September 11, 2001, terrorists associated with the organization Al-Qaeda hijacked and crashed four American commercial airliners, leading to the deaths of about 3,000 people. The United States launched a **"War on Terror."** In 2003, an American-led coalition force attacked Iraq and toppled the regime of Saddam Hussein—American leaders were concerned that Iraq might have been producing weapons of mass destruction that could be used against the United States and its allies.

- In 2008, the nation entered its worst economic crisis since the Great Depression. Its effects, brought about by risky lending practices by banks, persisted for several years.

Important Eras in World History

OVERVIEW

- Early civilizations and the emergence of pastoral people (4000–1000 BCE)
- Classical traditions, major religions, and giant empires (1000 BCE–300 CE)
- Expanding zones of exchange and encounter (300–1000 CE)
- Intensified hemispheric interactions (1000–1500 CE)
- The emergence of the first global age (1450–1770)
- Age of revolutions (1750–1914)
- A half-century of crisis and achievement (1900–1945)
- Since 1945: promises and paradoxes
- Summing It Up

The longest era in human history is the period historians call the Paleolithic era, or the "old stone age," which ranged from the beginning of human existence until around 12,000 years ago. The principal characteristic of the Paleolithic era was that human beings foraged for their food by hunting wild animals or gathering edible products from plants. Between 12,000 and 6000 years ago, humans learned to cultivate crops as a source of food, a discovery that ushered in the Neolithic Revolution, or the agricultural revolution. The shift from hunting and gathering to food production is one of the great breakthroughs in human history. People began living in larger, more organized permanent communities, creating the foundation of a much more complex way of life—civilization. This chapter gives you a basic overview of world history's major civilizations.

EARLY CIVILIZATIONS AND THE EMERGENCE OF PASTORAL PEOPLE (4000–1000 BCE)

A civilization is a complex culture in which large numbers of people share common elements. Among the most important elements of civilizations are large cities, organized government, religion, social structure, writing, and art.

Mesopotamia

One of the first civilizations arose in Mesopotamia between the Tigris and Euphrates rivers in what is now Iraq. The capital of this civilization was the city of Babylon. The Mesopotamians developed political, military, social, and religious institutions to effectively handle the basic problems of human existence and organization. They also devised systems of writing that enabled them to keep records and create literature, leading to the development of cultural traditions.

King Hammurabi, who ruled from around 1792–1750 BCE, developed the first recorded set of laws. Hammurabi recognized that a single, uniform code would help to unify the diverse groups within his empire. Two centuries after Hammurabi's reign, the Babylonian Empire fell to nomadic warriors.

Ancient Egypt

The Ancient Egyptian culture emerged along the banks of the Nile River in northern Africa. The Nile, the longest river in the world, was essential to the development of ancient Egypt. Every year, the river flooded the valley, enriching the soil with silt and minerals. Using this fertile black soil, the Egyptians could grow a variety of crops. In addition, Egyptian traders developed sophisticated trading networks with the people of Mesopotamia and the people of Nubia and Kush in the south.

The Egyptians believed their kings, called pharaohs, to be gods and that they ruled even after death. Since pharaohs were expected to reign forever, their tombs were very important. For the kings of the Old Kingdom, the resting place after death was a structure called a pyramid. The Old Kingdom was the great age of pyramid building in ancient Egypt. The largest tomb, called the Great Pyramid, was built in 2530 BCE. Its base covers an area of 13 acres. Like the Mesopotamians, the Egyptians developed their own system of writing called hieroglyphics.

Indus Valley

In India, another civilization emerged about 2500 BCE in the valley of the Indus River. The Indus River flows through the modern nation of Pakistan. Scholars have not yet deciphered the Indus system of writing, and consequently, knowledge of this civilization comes largely from archaeological digs. At its height, however, the civilization of the Indus Valley influenced an area much larger than either Mesopotamia or Egypt.

A strong agricultural economy made it possible for the people of the Indus Valley to build a complex society that included trade with cultures as far away as Mesopotamia. A key achievement of the Indus Valley people was their sophisticated and complex city planning. Cities in the Indus valley were laid out on a precise grid system. Cities featured a fortified area called a citadel, which contained the most important buildings.

China

Another important Asian civilization developed around 1700 BCE along the banks of the Hwang Ho River in northern China. Chinese history is marked by a succession of dynasties. Historians describe the pattern of rise, decline, and replacement of dynasties as the dynastic cycle. Two of the earliest and most influential Chinese dynasties were the **Shang** and the **Zhou.** Shang leaders were the first Chinese rulers to leave written records. The Chinese written language helped unify a large and diverse land. From

TIP

Key Mesopotamian contributions include the invention of the wheel, the sail, and the plow. Mesopotamians were the first people to use bronze and to conduct scientific investigations in the areas of astronomy, chemistry, and diseases.

TIP

Indus Valley civilization is sometimes called Harappan civilization.

earliest times, Chinese culture has placed the well-being of the group above that of the individual. Above all, people were driven by their duties to their families and their king or emperor.

The Zhou built roads and canals, stimulating trade and agriculture. The Zhou also introduced coined money, which also promoted trade. Zhou leaders introduced a new class of civil servants, or government administrative workers, to help run their cities. Among the technological advancements in the Zhou Dynasty was the use of iron—the Zhou developed blast furnaces that enabled them to make cast iron.

CLASSICAL TRADITIONS, MAJOR RELIGIONS, AND GIANT EMPIRES (1000 BCE–300 CE)

During the classical era, the Mediterranean region became much more tightly integrated as Greeks—and later the Romans—established sophisticated trading partnerships that promoted interaction throughout the area.

Ancient Greece

The ancient Greeks built city-states on the lands surrounding the Aegean Sea. About 500 BCE, the Greeks established a government known as a **democracy.** In a democracy, the people rule themselves. In Athens, the most influential Greek city-state, citizens participated directly in political decision-making. Each Greek city-state was like an independent country because each had its own government and laws. Many political systems today reflect the forms of government that the ancient Greeks created.

Greece's **Golden Age** lasted from 480 to 430 BCE. The artistic and literary legacies of this time continue to influence societies today. For example, many elements of Greek architecture are followed today, and the principles of modern drama were first practiced by Greek playwrights. The Greeks also made key discoveries in the sciences and mathematics.

Perhaps the Greeks' greatest contribution was in the field of philosophy. Socrates, Plato, and Aristotle were three influential Greek philosophers who lived in the city-state of Athens. Their ideas have guided the way people have thought about the meaning of life, the true nature of the world, and the proper role of citizens.

Constant wars weakened the city-states. In 338 BCE, Philip of Macedonia conquered Greece. Philip's son, Alexander the Great, would eventually conquer most of the lands between Greece in the west, Egypt in the south, and India in the east.

TIP

Euclid established some of the basic rules of geometry. Hippocrates played a key role in medical discoveries, including the writing of a code of ethics for doctors.

Directions: Refer to the following chart to answer the questions that follow.

Athenian Democracy	U.S. Democracy
Citizens: Males 18 years or older or sons of parents who are citizens of Athens	Citizens: born in United States or children of U.S. citizens or completed citizenship process
Laws proposed and voted on by an assembly of all legal citizens of Athens	Laws proposed, written, and voted on by representatives elected by U.S. citizens
Leader chosen by lottery	President elected by vote of U.S. citizens
Executive branch consisting of a council of 500 men	Executive branch made up of elected and appointed officials
Juries varied in size	Juries composed of 12 jurors

1. What does this chart suggest to you about the origins of U. S. democracy?
   (A) U.S. democracy is an exact copy of Athenian democracy.
   (B) U.S. democracy is completely different from Athenian democracy.
   (C) U.S. democracy is greatly influenced by Athenian democracy, but it has variations.
   (D) U.S. democracy only follows Athenian democracy in legal issues.

The correct answer is (C). U.S. democracy has been greatly influenced by Athenian democracy. Athenian democracy, however, was a direct democracy, in which all legal citizens actively participated in government. U.S democracy, on the other hand, is a representative democracy, or indirect democracy. American citizens elect officials who then vote on policy, legislate laws, and appoint other governmental officials.

2. What is the main difference between Athenian citizenship and citizenship in the United States?
   (A) Citizenship in Athens was restricted by gender.
   (B) Citizenship in Athens was based on jury service.
   (C) Citizenship in Athens was determined by a vote of the leadership council.
   (D) Citizenship in Athens was granted by a yearly lottery.

The correct answer is (A). In Athenian democracy, only males could become legal citizens. U.S. citizenship is open to both women and men.

Ancient Rome

Farmers first settled the region around the present-day city of Rome in about 750 BCE. A northern tribe called the **Etruscans** overran the farmers. In 509 BCE, Roman aristocrats drove the Etruscans and their king out of the city. The Romans then established a new form of government and called it a "republic." A republic is a form of government in which power rests with citizens who elect representatives to run their government.

Rome expanded its territories through conquest and trade. By 70 BCE, Rome's Mediterranean empire stretched from Anatolia (modern-day Turkey) in the east to Spain in the west. Roman leaders established a unified set of laws, created a skilled force of civil servants to administer government, and used their well-disciplined army to maintain peace and stability throughout the empire. Over time, however, governing Rome and all its territories proved problematic. Powerful Roman generals, such as **Julius Caesar,** often developed great influence. In 46 BCE, he marched his armies on Rome and defeated his Roman rivals. Caesar became dictator and governed as an absolute ruler. A long line of emperors followed Julius Caesar. Rome was most powerful from 27 BCE to 180 CE. For 207 years, peace reigned mostly throughout the empire. This period of peace and prosperity is known as the *Pax Romana*—"Roman peace."

Major Religions

The five largest religions in the world today—Christianity, Judaism, Islam, Hinduism, and Buddhism—all emerged in some of the world's earliest civilizations. Throughout the centuries, people have altered and shaped these religions into many variations.

Judaism

Palestine, the area along the eastern shores of the Mediterranean, was the ancient home of the Hebrews, later called the Jews. It is from the Hebrew tradition that Judaism, the religion of the Jews, evolved. Their history, legends, and moral laws have been major influences on Western culture, as well as being influential in the creation of Christianity and Islam. Unlike the other early religions of the time, Judaism taught that there was one God, rather than many gods.

Most of what is known about the early history of the Hebrews is contained in the first five books of the Hebrew Bible. These books are called the Torah and are considered the most sacred writings in the Jewish tradition. Today, approximately 1 percent of the world's population follows the teachings of Judaism.

Christianity

Christianity descended from Judaism. The central belief in Christianity maintains that Jesus of Nazareth is the promised messiah of the Hebrew Scriptures—the son of God. Christianity is one of the three monotheistic Abrahamic faiths, along with Islam and Judaism, which traces its history to the Hebrew Scriptures. Its sacred text is the Bible. Rome, as the center of western civilization at the time, eventually became the home of the Church. Christianity spread throughout Europe and eventually the rest of the world. Today, 33 percent of the world's population follow the teachings of Christianity.

Islam

Islam originated with the teachings of Muhammad in the seventh century CE. Those who follow the teachings of Islam are called Muslims. Muslims believe Muhammad is the final of all religious prophets and that the Quran, which is the Islamic scripture, was revealed to him by God, or Allah. Devout Muslims must follow the five pillars,

TIP

The Roman republic endured for more than 500 years as the dominant power in the Mediterranean region.

TIP

The belief in one god is called monotheism.

or tenets, of Islam, which are the testimony of faith (*shahada*), daily prayer (*salah*), giving alms (*zakah*), fasting during Ramadan (*sawm*), and the pilgrimage to Mecca (*hajj*). Muslims today make up approximately 24 percent of the world's population.

Hinduism

Hinduism is one of the world's oldest surviving religions, originating in India in the second and first millennium BCE. Hinduism is an extremely diverse set of beliefs and practices with no single founder or religious authority. Instead, it developed over several thousand years. Hindus may worship one or many deities. The most common gods are Vishnu, Shiva, and a mother goddess, Devi. The goal of religious life is to learn to act so as to finally achieve liberation (*moksha*) of one's soul, escaping the rebirth cycle. Today, 14 percent of the world's population follow the Hindu religion.

Buddhism

Buddhism began during the sixth century BCE in India, inspired by the teachings of Siddhartha Gautama, also known as Gautama Buddha, "the enlightened one." Buddhism focuses on the goal of spiritual enlightenment and an understanding of the Buddha's Four Noble Truths: existence is suffering; suffering has a cause; there is an end to suffering that is called nirvana; and there is an eightfold path to the end of suffering. Today, Buddhists account for about 6 percent of the world's population.

EXPANDING ZONES OF EXCHANGE AND ENCOUNTER (300–1000 CE)

Much of Europe, Eurasia, and northern Africa experienced disruption and change between 300 and 1000 CE. Populations, cities, and trade declined. The large empires collapsed and armies of pastoral nomads attacked settled peoples.

The Byzantine Empire

As the Roman Empire slowly declined, the Emperor **Constantine** anticipated its eventual collapse. In 330 CE, he rebuilt the old port city of Byzantium on the Bosporus (in modern-day Turkey) renamed it Constantinople, and made it the capital of the Roman Empire. In 476 CE, the western half of the Roman Empire fell. Constantine's eastern empire survived, however. The Byzantine Empire thrived in many ways. Emperor Justinian codified the old Roman law into a clearer and more systematic form. The Justinian Code decided legal questions that regulated whole areas of Byzantine life. Marriage, slavery, property, inheritance, women's rights, and crimes were just some of those areas. The Byzantine Empire also excelled in architecture and art. The church of Hagia Sophia, built in 537 CE in the shape of a Greek cross, is still used today. Byzantine scholars used Greek and Roman literature as textbooks when teaching. In this way, they preserved many of the great works of Greece and Rome that may otherwise have been lost.

The Muslim World

By the early 600s, **Muhammad,** the founder of Islam, had become not only a powerful and influential religious leader, but also a successful military leader. His forces captured just about all of the Arabian Peninsula. The Arabic language and Islam spread widely as Muslim control expanded into different lands. Muslims created a huge empire that included lands on three continents, and their influence produced a cultural blending that has continued into the modern world.

Muslims encouraged the development of an extensive trade and communication network through which people, goods, crops, and knowledge moved freely. In addition, Muslim scholars developed standards and techniques for research that are a part of the basic methods of today's research. Muslim contributions in the sciences include significant achievements in medicine, mathematics, and astronomy.

Change in East Asia

War and nomadic invasions led to population decline in much of northern China following the collapse of the Han Dynasty in 220 CE. By the mid-fifth century, the heartland of classical China was devastated by invading armies. China was again unified under the Sui dynasty (581–618 CE). The **Tang dynasty** in China developed into one of the greatest empires of the era. Tang leaders established successful diplomatic relationships, created economic prosperity, and promoted a highly diverse society that included merchants, clerics, and diplomats from throughout east and southwest Asia.

The Middle Ages

Historians call the 1000 years after the fall of the Roman Empire the **Middle Ages,** or the medieval period. It is called the Middle Ages because it spans the years between the ancient world and the modern world. The early Middle Ages are often referred to as the Dark Ages. Education, science, and trade, most especially in Europe, were diminished during this time. The most influential leader in this time was Charles the Great, or Charlemagne, whom Pope Leo III crowned as the Holy Roman Emperor in 800 BCE. Charlemagne ruled over most of Europe, an area that included the present-day countries of France, Switzerland, Belgium, and the Netherlands, as well as parts of Germany, Spain, and Italy.

The political turmoil and constant warfare that followed the death of Charlemagne led to the rise of feudalism—a military and political system based on land ownership and personal loyalty. In Europe during the Middle Ages, the majority of people were peasants. Most peasants were serfs, people who could not lawfully leave the place where they were born. Serfs, however, were not slaves—their lords could not sell or buy them. The feudal lords were dependent upon the labor supplied by peasants.

During the Middle Ages, the manor system was the most common economic arrangement. The manor system was based on a set of rights and obligations between a lord and his serfs. From the lord the serfs obtained their housing, farmland, and protection. In return, serfs were obligated to take care of the lord's lands and animals, as well as do other work to run the estate.

Directions: Refer to the following passage to answer the questions that follow.

> The structure of feudal society was like a pyramid. At the peak was the monarchy—the king or queen. Next came wealthy landowners, such as nobles and bishops, called vassals. Next were knights, who pledged to defend their lords' lands in exchange for land. At the base of the pyramid were landless peasants, or serfs, who toiled in the fields. Most peasants had little if no education and rarely traveled more than 30 miles from their homes. Serfs lived in crowded cottages, were taxed by their lords for all their supplies, and ate a very simple diet. Out of the bit of extra money they managed to save, they had to pay a church tax to the local priest. Like most Christians during the Middle Ages, most serfs believed that God determined a person's place in society.

3. Based on the information in the passage, which of the following would be the best explanation why serfs accepted their status in life?
   (A) Orders from the monarchy
   (B) Fear of military service
   (C) Lack of an education
   (D) Their religious beliefs

The correct answer is (D). During the Middle Ages, the Church played a very important role in the lives of serfs. They would have accepted their lot in life as part of the Church's teachings.

Societies and Civilizations in Africa

An important early African kingdom was **Aksum,** which reached its height between 325 and 360 CE. It was located south of the ancient kingdom of Kush on a rugged plateau on the Red Sea, in what is now Eritrea and Ethiopia. Because of its location and expansion, Aksum was an important trading center. Aksum also controlled miles of coastline and ports on the Red Sea. This gave the kingdom influence over sea trade on the Mediterranean Sea and Indian Ocean as well. Among the characteristics of Aksum was its diverse cultural heritage. Aksum was the only ancient African kingdom known to have developed a written language and the first sub-Saharan to mint its own coins.

Civilizations in Mesoamerica and Andean South America

The first civilizations in the Americas emerged in a region archaeologists and historians refer to as **Mesoamerica.** This area stretches south from present-day central Mexico to the northern parts of modern-day Honduras.

The Olmec

The Olmec flourished from 1200 BC to 400 BC. They lived along the Gulf Coast of Mexico, in the modern-day Mexican states of Veracruz and Tabasco. The oldest Olmec site, San Lorenzo, dates back to around 1150 BCE. Scholars think the Olmec were a prosperous people who developed and controlled a large trading network throughout Mesoamerica. This trade network created wealth and spread Olmec influence to other parts of Mesoamerica.

The Zapotec

By 500 BCE, the Zapotec people were developing an advanced society in what is now the southern Mexican state of Oaxaca. This civilization developed early forms of hieroglyphic writing and a calendar system. The Zapotec built complex cities and are considered the first city builders in the Americas. The first true urban center in the Americas was the Zapotec city of Monte Albán. By 200 BCE, around 15,000 people lived in Monte Albán, eventually reaching a population of 25,000. In the center of Monte Albán was a giant plaza paved with stones. Surrounding the plaza were large stone pyramids, palaces, and temples. The layout and design of Monte Albán influenced the development of future urban centers in Mesoamerican civilizations.

The Chavín

The first significant and influential civilization in South America emerged in the Andes Mountains, in the northern highlands of present-day Peru. This culture is known as the Chavín. It flourished from around 900 to 200 BCE. The Chavín are named after a major ruin, Chavín de Huántar, located more than 10,000 feet above sea level. The ruins here contain plazas, pyramids, and massive earthen mounds. Because archaeologists have not discovered evidence of political or economic organization, many scholars think the Chavín were primarily a religious civilization.

The Nazca and Moche

The Nazca and Moche built advanced societies that flourished for centuries in the Andes region of South America. The Nazca culture lived along the southern coast of Peru from around 200 BCE to 600 CE. The Nazca people are noted for developing extensive irrigation systems, including underground canals that allowed them to farm the extremely dry land.

The Moche culture lasted from about 100 to 700 CE. The Moche built complex irrigation systems to water a variety of crops, including corn, beans, potatoes, squash, and peanuts. Archaeological excavations have discovered jewelry made from gold, silver, and semiprecious stones, leading scholars to assume that the Moche civilization contained great wealth. The Moche are also known to have been accomplished ceramic artists. Moche pottery often includes scenes from everyday life, such as doctors working on patients, women weaving cloth, and musicians playing instruments.

INTENSIFIED HEMISPHERIC INTERACTIONS (1000–1500 CE)

Between 1000 and 1300, agriculture, trade, and finance made tremendous strides and sparked remarkable growth. Towns and cities grew larger as populations increased and states expanded their territories and explored and developed relationships with far-flung peoples.

Powerful Empires in Asia

From 500 to 1500 CE, the world's most powerful societies were non-European imperial states. China's Tang dynasty, the Byzantine Empire in the eastern Mediterranean region, and the Mongol empires controlled much of the known world. During the Tang and Song dynasties, from about 600 CE to 1300 CE, China grew in population, trade, wealth, new ideas, and artistic achievements. China's population nearly doubled, soaring to 100 million. China had become not only the most populous country in the world but also the most advanced.

A group of nomadic warriors called the **Mongols** united under Genghis Khan in about 1200. By 1221, Central Asia was under Mongol control. In all, the Mongols conquered territory from China to Poland in less than 50 years, creating the largest unified empire in history. The Mongols were not known for their cultural or scientific contributions. However, from the mid-1200s to the mid-1300s, the Mongols imposed stability and law and order across much of Eurasia. This period is sometimes called the Mongol Peace.

Sub-Saharan African Kingdoms

During this era, three powerful societies emerged and flourished in West Africa. These ancient African empires arose in the Sahel—the savanna region south of the Sahara Desert. These empires grew strong through the controlling of two of the most important trade items—gold and salt. The rulers of the kingdom of Ghana grew wealthy from taxing the goods that traders carried through their territory and by 800 CE had built an empire.

By 1235, the kingdom of **Mali** had emerged. Located south of Ghana, Mali's wealth, like that of Ghana's, was built on controlling the gold trade. Under its most famous ruler, Mansa Musa, Mali effectively held control over the gold and salt trade, expanding the empire to almost twice the size of Ghana.

The Songhai Empire emerged in the 1400s. The ruler **Sunni Ali** expanded the empire through his skill as a military commander and his aggressive leadership. Sunni Ali's forces went on to capture the important trade cities of Timbuktu and Djenné. In 1591, Moroccan invaders equipped with cannons invaded and defeated the Songhai.

The Crusades

In 1095, Pope Urban II issued a call for a "holy war," a **Crusade,** to conquer and control the Holy Land. Over the next 200 years, many Crusades were launched. The goal of these military actions was to recover Jerusalem and the Holy Land from the Muslim

Turks. Although successful initially, in the end the Crusades failed. The Holy Lands returned to Muslim control. The Crusades did, however, have some positive effects in that they stimulated trade between Europe and Southwest Asia.

Political, Economic, and Cultural Transformations

Agricultural innovations helped spark a great European revival. Farmers developed new methods of farming, including using horses instead of oxen and utilizing three crop fields rather than two. The result of these changes was an increase in population. People began having larger, healthier families that could better resist disease and live longer.

By the 1000s, trade routes spread across Europe from Northwest Europe to Italy in the south. Italian traders traveled the Mediterranean to ports such as Constantinople. Many also established trade networks with Muslim merchants on the North African coast. The Crusades also opened up trade opportunities with Asia. Throughout Europe, as trade increased, towns attracted more and more people. Many people moved to such towns to pursue the economic and social opportunities they offered. These opportunities helped in part to break down the old feudal system.

The Renaissance

The years 1300 to 1600 saw an explosion of creativity in Europe. Historians call this period the **Renaissance,** a term that means rebirth. In this situation, it was a rebirth of art and learning. Renaissance scholars promoted a return to the works and ideas of the Greeks and Romans. These studies led to humanism, a philosophy that emphasized human potential and achievements and a concern for real human issues in this world.

In 1452, Johannes Gutenberg invented the printing press and completely changed the way people learned. Books could now be produced in large numbers and made available to large populations. The works and ideas of influential thinkers and artists were spread far and wide. Artists such as Leonardo da Vinci, Michelangelo, and Raphael exemplified the Renaissance spirit by displaying a curiosity about the world and the belief in human potential. Dante, Erasmus, and Martin Luther were influential Renaissance writers. Scientists such as Copernicus and Galileo challenged traditional views of astronomy and proposed new ideas based on new scientific understandings.

The Age of Exploration

The Renaissance also sparked an "age of exploration" during which mariners from Portugal and Spain, and later other countries, set out to explore the world and discover new water routes to Asia in search of wealth and power. Explorers such as Bartolomeu Dias and Vasco da Gama sailed south from Europe and established a route to India. In search of a shorter and more direct route to Asia, Christopher Columbus traveled west across the Atlantic Ocean in 1492 and landed in the Americas. In 1497, John Cabot became the first European since the Vikings to set foot on the mainland of North America. These events set in motion a process that would bring together the peoples of Europe, Asia, Africa, and the Americas.

Expansion of States and Civilizations in the Americas

The first peoples of North America created complex societies that established long-distance trade networks and constructed magnificent buildings, as well as effective systems of government. There were hundreds of different patterns of North American Indian life. Some societies were small and did not travel extensively. Other cultures grew larger and established trade networks and cultural relationships with other groups in North America and Mesoamerica.

Mesoamerica and South American Societies

The three most prominent and influential cultures to emerge in Mesoamerica and South America before 1500 were the Maya, the Aztec, and the Inca. All three societies developed sophisticated ways of life. The **Mayan** civilization was among the original cultures of the New World. The rise of the Maya began about 250 CE and lasted until about 900 CE. Mayan culture is known for its spectacular art, impressive architecture, and complex mathematical and astronomical systems.

The **Aztec Empire** was the most powerful Mesoamerican kingdom. By the early 1500s, the Aztec empire was divided into 38 provinces with a total population of between 5 and 15 million people. The Aztecs gained their power through military conquest and tributes from conquered territories. By the time the Spanish arrived in 1519, the Aztec capital city of Tenochtitlan was an impressive urban center with an estimated population of about 200,000.

Another society, **the Inca,** were creating an equally powerful state in South America. From their capital in southern Peru, the Inca spread outward in all directions. They brought various societies living in the region under their control and established the largest empire in the Americas at that time.

THE EMERGENCE OF THE FIRST GLOBAL AGE (1450–1770)

The age of exploration expeditions opened the door to steady trade, permanent links between the world's various regions. Few events have altered the world as much as the Columbian Exchange, the global transfer of foods, plants, and animals during the colonization of the Americas. This global transfer of goods brought together the Eastern and Western hemispheres. European explorers returning from the Americas brought back items that Europeans, Asians, and Africans had never before seen, including corn, potatoes, tomatoes, cacao beans, squash, pineapples, and tobacco. The Columbian Exchange also had negative effects. As more Europeans arrived in the Americas, they brought infectious and contagious diseases with them for which the native peoples had no immunity. Measles, diphtheria, whooping cough, influenza, and, most horrifically, smallpox touched off deadly epidemics that sometimes destroyed entire societies.

Large Eurasian Empires

In 1526, under the leadership of Babur, the **Mughal Empire** brought Turks, Persians, and Indians together to establish a powerful empire. The Mughal Empire reached its height under Babur's grandson Akbar, who ruled from 1556 to 1605. Akbar extended the Mughal Empire and welcomed influences from the many cultures in the region. At Akbar's death in 1605, the empire extended from Afghanistan to the Bay of Bengal and southward to Gujarat and the northern Deccan.

Between 1300 and 1326, a popular and powerful Muslim leader named Osman established a small state in Anatolia, which is present-day Turkey. People in the West called him Othman, however, and named his followers Ottomans. Osman's successors greatly expanded the kingdom, making the **Ottoman Empire** one of the most powerful states in the world during the fifteenth and sixteenth centuries. The empire was at its greatest from 1520–1566, under the rule of Suleiman the Magnificent.

Rise of European Power

Because Europeans were developing regular travels between the world's key regions, they were exposed to greater opportunities. These opportunities eventually resulted in great wealth, power, and influence. The explorations to the Americas and Oceania after 1500 enabled the Europeans to become empire builders. The booming trade industry strengthened the status and power of the European merchant class and helped accelerate the growth of towns and large cities. Most of Europe's population, however, still lived in rural areas and remained poor.

AGE OF REVOLUTIONS (1750–1914)

As feudalism declined, stronger national kingdoms emerged under the control of absolute rulers. By the mid-eighteenth century, however, new ideas about human society and government were sweeping across Europe. This intellectual movement, known as the Enlightenment, helped spark new revolutionary ideas like democracy and individual rights.

The Enlightenment

The Renaissance helped create an environment in which scholars started to question ideas that had been accepted for hundreds of years. That same spirit of inquiry and curiosity that fueled the Renaissance led scientists to question traditional beliefs about the workings of the universe. The work of important scientists, such as Copernicus, Galileo, and Isaac Newton, helped ignite a Scientific Revolution that challenged how people viewed their place in the universe. The ideas and spirit of the Scientific Revolution paved the way for a new movement called the **Enlightenment,** or the **Age of Reason.** This movement reached its height in the mid-1700s. While the Scientific Revolution focused on the physical world, the Enlightenment attempted to explain the purpose of government and describe the best form of it.

The French Revolution

The ideas of the Enlightenment led to revolutions, first in the English colonies in America in 1776 and then in France in 1789. Revolutionaries in the colonies and France said that they were fighting to regain and preserve their natural rights, based on ideas developed by the English philosopher John Locke. In late eighteenth century, the people of France were still divided into three large social classes, or estates. The First Estate was the clergy of the Roman Catholic Church, the Second Estate was the nobility, and the Third Estate was everyone else—merchants, artisans, urban lower class workers, and peasants. Most French citizens belonged to the Third Estate. Political power and wealth, as well as land ownership, however, was controlled by the minority First and Second Estates. Enlightenment ideas about power and authority in government were spread throughout the Third Estate. On July 14, 1789, French citizens stormed and took control of the Bastille, a prison in Paris, and launched **the French Revolution.** The new revolutionary government of France made reforms but also used terror and violence to maintain its power.

In 1799, **Napoleon Bonaparte,** a successful and popular French general, toppled the government and seized power. Five years later, he crowned himself emperor. Napoleon reformed many aspects of society, including adopting a new uniform legal code that preserved many of the principles that the revolutionaries had fought for: equality of all citizens; the right of the individual to choose a profession; religious toleration; and the abolition of serfdom and all feudal obligations.

Directions: Refer to the following passage to answer the questions that follow.

The Enlightenment sparked a revolution in thinking that greatly changed Europeans' views of government and society. English philosopher John Locke promoted a positive view of human nature. He believed that people were capable of learning from experience to improve themselves and society. According to Locke, people had the natural ability to govern themselves and manage the welfare of society. His experiences of living through the political turmoil and horrors of the English Civil War of England in the 1600s led him to distrust and criticize monarchies. Locke thought that a government's right to rule came from the people, who were born with certain natural rights, including the right to life, liberty, and property. People established governments to protect these rights. A contract was created in which citizens agreed to obey the government's laws while the government protected their natural rights. If a ruler violated those rights, the people were justified in rebelling.

4. According to Locke, what is the source of a government's right to rule?
   (A) Wealthy property owners
   (B) The people
   (C) Contracts
   (D) An absolute monarch

The correct answer is (B). John Locke strongly believed that all people, common citizens included, had the capacity and potential to govern themselves and did not need a king or wealthy class to run a government. Consequently, Locke argued that the people of a nation are the source of a government's right to rule.

Nationalism

The ideals of the American and French Revolutions sparked a wave of nationalism. Citizens with the same language and culture wanted to have their own country. The people of Latin America rebelled against Spanish and Portuguese rule in the early nineteenth century. In Europe, Germany began to unify under Prussia, its largest state. Finally, in 1871, the nation of Germany was born with William of Prussia as its emperor. The Italians defeated Austrian forces and created the modern nation of Italy in 1870.

The Industrial Revolution

When James Watt developed a steam engine that could drive machinery in the 1780s, he helped launched the Industrial Revolution. Within decades, machines rapidly replaced hand labor as the principal means of producing goods. This period of dramatic factory growth is known as the **Industrial Revolution.** Factories were built to house large manufacturing machines, creating a new and modern class of labor—the factory worker. Industrialization also spurred urbanization, as large numbers of people moved from rural areas to cities to work in factories.

Imperialism

In the 1800s and early 1900s, the British Empire controlled colonies and protectorates in Asia, Africa, the Middle East, the Pacific region, and the Americas. Imperialism, the extension of a nation's power over other lands, swept through Europe as nations developed colonization policies in hopes of increasing their power and influence. France established protectorates and colonies in Southeast Asia, Africa, and South America. Portugal had colonies in Africa and China. Even the new nations of Germany and Italy joined the race by establishing colonies in Africa. These imperialist actions were successful because European countries were economically and militarily much stronger than the areas they conquered.

A HALF-CENTURY OF CRISIS AND ACHIEVEMENT (1900–1945)

World War I

Nationalism sparked intense competition between European nations. By the turn of the twentieth century, a fierce rivalry had developed among Europe's most powerful countries. Those nations were Germany, Austria-Hungary, Great Britain, Russia, Italy, and France. The growing rivalries led to the signing of several military alliances among the Great Powers. In June 1914, the assassination of **Archduke Franz Ferdinand,** an heir to the Austro-Hungarian throne, triggered the alliances, and **World War I** began. One side was made up of England, France, and Russia (the Allied Powers). Fighting the Allied powers was the alliance formed by Germany, Austria-Hungary, and Turkey (the Central Powers). The United States joined the Allies in 1917, after German submarines attacked American ships.

World War I lasted for four long and bloody years. World War I was, in many ways, a new kind of war. Armies used more powerful weapons and other technologies. It also ushered in the concept of war on a global scale.

The Rise of Communism

In March 1917, a revolt by Russian workers toppled the old Russian Government under Czar (Tsar) Nicholas II. Later that year, Bolshevik revolutionaries rose up and seized power. A new communist government with **Vladimir Lenin** as leader took control. From 1918 to 1920, a bloody civil war raged in Russia between Reds (communists) and Whites (their opponents). Around 15 million Russians died in the three-year struggle and the famine that followed. In the end, the communists prevailed and crushed all opposition. In 1922, Russia became the Union of Soviet Socialist Republics, most often simply called the **Soviet Union.**

TIP

World War I ended at 11 a.m. on the 11th day of the 11th month of 1918.

Directions: Use the following passage to answer the two questions that follow.

Rapid industrialization ignited great unrest among the Russian people in the late 1800s and early 1900s. The rise of factories created dangerous and miserable working conditions, very low wages, and even child labor. In addition, workers were not allowed to form unions. Workers had become increasingly unhappy with their low standard of living and lack of political power. The gap between rich and poor was huge and growing wider. Following a revolution in 1917 and a three-year civil war, the Bolsheviks controlled the government and ushered in the first communist government. The Bolsheviks believed that the industrial class of workers should form "a dictatorship of the proletariat," in which the workers would rule.

Within ten years, the Soviet Union under leader Joseph Stalin had built a command economy—a system in which the government made all economic decisions. Under this system, government leaders determined the country's economic needs and decided what to do. In addition, Stalin ruled a totalitarian regime. The government controlled every aspect of the workers' lives. Government leaders chose workers, determined where they would work, and even decided working hours. Employees even needed permission to move.

5. What is the most likely reason the Bolsheviks revolted?

   (A) Workers were angry that children were forced to work in factories.

   (B) Industrial workers were not permitted to have government jobs.

   (C) The industrial class of workers was oppressed by low standards of living and no political power.

   (D) Unions had been outlawed.

The correct answer is (C). The primary cause of the workers' revolution was the low standard of living that most workers endured. Without political power, they had no way to make changes to improve their lives. Consequently, they took up arms and revolted.

6. The information in the passage supports which of the following conclusions?

   (A) Stalin's economic policies ushered in a new era of worker-citizen participation in government.

   (B) Stalin legalized trade unions, which led to economic prosperity.

   (C) Totalitarian regimes are best equipped to protect the rights of workers.

   (D) Communist economic policies eventually became oppressive and did not grant workers increased political power.

The correct answer is (D). The Bolsheviks, and later Stalin, severely limited the common citizens' ability to participate in politics and make decisions that affected them. Totalitarian regimes are oppressive and restrict the rights of citizens. Consequently, in some ways, the lives of common citizens did not get much better under Stalin and the communists. Much in their lives was out of their control, and they lacked the political power to change the system.

Search for Peace and Stability

Following World War I, the Allies tried to craft a lasting peace to prevent another global war. They created the League of Nations, an organization that would preserve peace by pledging to respect and protect each other's territory and political independence. Despite President Woodrow Wilson's support, the U.S. Congress refused to join the **League of Nations.** Without the United States, the League of Nations' effectiveness was weakened.

Severe economic crises in the 1920s and 1930s created political instability. Soon, authoritarian political leaders used widespread fear of disorder to gain power. Once in power, they violently suppressed all opposition. Several countries, including Japan, Germany, and Italy, adopted aggressive, militaristic policies.

World War II

Several dictators emerged out of the chaos of World War I. Many Germans were bitter over the harsh penalties imposed on Germany by the terms of the Treaty of Versailles. In 1933, the German people voted **Adolf Hitler** chancellor, or prime minister, of Germany. Within a short time, he gained total control over the country. Hitler's Nazi Party improved the economy by creating large-scale building programs. The Nazis also began passing laws depriving Jews of most of their rights. Violence against Jews grew stronger, signaling the start of the process of eliminating the Jews from German life.

Germany and then Italy, which was under the control of **Benito Mussolini** and his Fascist Party, built strong armies. Hitler took over German-speaking territories on Germany's border. Italy invaded Ethiopia in Africa. In 1938, the British and the French, wanting to avoid war at all costs, gave in to Hitler. After taking over Czechoslovakia in 1938, Hitler set his sights on Poland. Hitler and Soviet leader **Joseph Stalin** had signed a secret nonaggression pact, pledging not to attack each other. Freed from his worry about a war with the Soviet Union, Hitler attacked Poland on September 1, 1939. Two days later, Britain and France declared war on Germany, igniting **World War II.**

Hitler swept west and took control of France in June of 1940. Only the United Kingdom stood in the way of Hitler's goal of controlling all of Western Europe. After the ten-month Battle of Britain in the skies over England, Hitler rolled back the attacks on England.

In June 1941, Hitler broke the nonaggression pact with Stalin by attacking the Soviet Union. The German's blitzkrieg attack, or "lightning war," initially drove deep into Soviet territory. After almost two years of fierce fighting, Soviet forces and the oppressive Russian winters proved too formidable. By February 1943, German forces had been beaten back. By the spring, even Hitler knew that the Germans would not defeat the Soviet Union.

On December 7, 1941, Japanese warplanes attacked the U.S. naval base at **Pearl Harbor,** Hawaii. The United States declared war on Japan; consequently, Germany and Italy declared war on the United States. The United States was at war with the Axis powers on two fronts—Europe and Asia. The Allies struck quickly, attacking German armies in North Africa first and then defeating Germany's other ally, Italy. On June 6, 1944, a day known as **D-Day**, Allied troops invaded France, beginning the retaking of Europe from Germany.

Hitler committed suicide on April 30, 1945, two days after Italian resistance fighters killed Mussolini. On May 7, 1945, Germany surrendered. The war in Europe was over. The Allies soon learned about the concentration camps the Germans had built. More than six million Jews and millions of other groups of people whom the Nazis thought inferior were murdered in these death camps. In August 1945, Americans dropped atomic bombs on the Japanese cities of Hiroshima and Nagasaki. The blasts killed several hundred thousand people. Japan surrendered on August 14, 1945. World War II was over.

SINCE 1945: PROMISES AND PARADOXES

The Post-war World

After the war, instead of imposing harsh punishment on the defeated countries, the United States implemented the **Marshall Plan.** This plan provided economic assistance to help Germany, Italy, and other European nations rebuild their economies. Economic assistance was also provided to Japan.

In April 1945, as World War II was near its end, leaders from 50 countries met to establish the **United Nations (the UN).** They conceived the UN as replacement for the League of Nations, with the goal to establish a more effective organization to ensure peace.

The dropping of the atomic bombs in Japan marked the beginning of the Nuclear Age. In August 1949, the Soviet Union exploded its first atomic bomb, starting an arms race with the United States that lasted forty years. The tension created by the arms race is known as the **Cold War.** The United States and the Soviet Union, the world's two superpowers, battled for world supremacy and demanded that other nations take sides.

The Cold War had a profound impact on many countries throughout the world. The communist threat spread to Asia in 1949 when Chinese revolutionaries took control and adopted a communist government. A year later, armies from communist North Korea invaded South Korea. U.S. forces tried to prevent the communist takeover of South Korea and sent troops, leading to the **Korean War** (1950–1953). The war ended in a stalemate. As a result, there is still a communist North Korea and a non-communist South Korea. Germany was also divided into East Germany (run by communists) and West Germany (a democracy).

The Southeast Asian country of **Vietnam** split in 1954 when elections to reunite the country were not held. With economic and military aid from the United States, South Vietnam unsuccessfully fought to hold off the communist North Vietnamese throughout the 1960s. However, in 1975, Vietnam was reunited under communist rule.

The Modern World

Advances in technology after World War II led to increased global interaction and improved quality of life for many societies in the world. Because of medical and technological innovations, people are living longer than at any other time in history. Population growth, however, could become a major concern as food and resources get stretched.

Another concern is the environment. Most scientists think that human activity has negatively affected much of the land, water, and air, leading to a warming of the planet and climate change.

Since World War II, the world is increasingly becoming one global culture. Transportation and communications innovations have made the world a much smaller place in many ways. People around the world share many of the same cultural elements. Much of this is because of a growing global market. In 1957, six European nations formed the **European Common Market.** The goal was to reduce the barriers to trade and to boost economic growth. Eventually, the Common Market was replaced by the **European Union (EU).** The EU created a common currency, the Euro, and a common bank to help promote economic and political cooperation among its European members.

As some regions have become more closely integrated, others have been pulled apart by ethnic and religious conflicts. Yugoslavia, Rwanda, Somalia, Indonesia, and other nations have experienced episodes of ethnic cleansing—the killing of members of other ethnic groups. In addition, the growth of fundamentalism—a strict belief in the basic truths and practice of a particular faith—also has contributed to conflicts, including acts of terrorism, in various regions of the world. Some fundamentalist groups have even gained control of a government and imposed their ideas on an entire nation. In Afghanistan in 1997, the **Taliban** movement took control of the government and imposed its view of Muslim law on the land. In 2014, the fundamentalist group ISIL (Islamic State of Iraq and the Levant) took control of a large region of land in Iraq and Syria and established a caliphate, an Islamic political-religious state.

The first African American President in United States history, President Barack Obama, promised change with a stimulus program for the economy, an end to the war in the Middle East, and creation of a Universal Health Care system as part of the Affordable Care Act labeled "Obamacare" by his opponents. Although President Obama would see Democrats face challenges from the growing Tea-Party movement, the continually struggling the economy, gun violence, and his healthcare program in the midterm elections of 2010, he would win a second term in 2012, and by the end of his time in office, the economy had improved and Osama Bin Laden had been killed by U.S. forces.

In 2016, political outsider and business mogul Donald Trump secured the Republican nomination using a Populist-like campaign and a message of "America First" and defeated former Secretary of State and first lady Hilary Clinton to become president of a drastically divided nation.

Despite some of the setbacks caused by global interdependence, the economic, political, and environmental issues facing people in the twenty-first century have continued to draw societies closer together. Humans throughout the world have recognized that they are dependent on each other in many ways and can be affected by the actions that take place far away.

SUMMING IT UP

- One of the first civilizations arose in **Mesopotamia,** in what is now Iraq. Mesopotamians developed political, military, social, and religious institutions and devised writing systems to keep records and create literature. **King Hammurabi,** who ruled from around 1792–1750 BCE, developed the first recorded set of laws to unify the diverse groups within his empire.

- The Old Kingdom was the great age of pyramid building in ancient Egypt. The largest tomb, called the Great Pyramid, was built in 2530 BCE. The Egyptians developed their own system of writing called hieroglyphics.

- A strong agricultural economy made it possible for the people of the **Indus Valley** to build a complex society that traded with cultures as far away as Mesopotamia. A key achievement of the Indus Valley people was their sophisticated and complex city planning, laid out on a precise grid system.

- Chinese history is marked by a succession of dynasties, including the influential Shang and Zhou. Shang leaders were the first Chinese rulers to leave written records. The Zhou built roads and canals and introduced coined money.

- In about 500 BCE, the Greeks established **democracy.** The artistic and literary legacies of Greece's Golden Age continue to influence societies today via architecture, drama, the sciences, and mathematics. The teachings of Socrates, Plato, and Aristotle have guided the way people have thought since their era. Alexander the Great eventually conquered most of the lands between Greece, Egypt, and India.

- In 509 BCE, after Roman aristocrats drove the Etruscans out of the city, the Romans established a new form of government called a republic, where power rests with citizens who elect representatives. Rome was most influential from 27 BCE to 180 CE—a period of peace and prosperity known as the *Pax Romana.*

- The five largest religions in the world today—Christianity, Judaism, Islam, Hinduism, and Buddhism—all emerged in some of the world's earliest civilizations.

- In 300 CE, Emperor Constantine of the Roman Empire rebuilt the port city of Byzantium, renamed it Constantinople, and made it the capital of the Roman Empire. In 476 CE, the western half of the Roman Empire fell, though the eastern half survived.

- By the early 600s, Muhammad, the founder of Islam, had become a powerful and influential religious leader and a successful military leader. Muslims created a huge empire that included lands on three continents and encouraged the development of an extensive trade and communication network.

- War and nomadic invasions led to population decline in much of northern China following the collapse of the Han Dynasty in 220 CE. China was again unified under the Sui dynasty (581–618 CE), and later, the Tang dynasty in China developed into one of the greatest empires of the era.

- The **Middle Age**s refer to the thousand or so years after the fall of the Roman Empire. Education, science, and trade were diminished during this time. The most influential leader was Charles the Great, or Charlemagne, the Holy Roman Emperor. His death gave rise to **feudalism.** The majority of people were peasants, or serfs, who could not lawfully leave their birthplace. The manor system was the most common economic arrangement, where serfs obtained housing, farmland, and protection from lords in exchange for taking care of the lord's estate.

- The important early African kingdom Aksum reached its height between 325 and 360 CE. Aksum, an important trading center, controlled miles of coastline and ports on the Red Sea, which gave it influence over sea trade on the Mediterranean Sea and Indian Ocean. Aksum was the only ancient African kingdom to develop a written language and the first sub-Saharan to mint its own coins.

- The first civilizations in the Americas emerged in a region referred to as **Mesoamerica,** which stretches south from present-day central Mexico to the northern parts of modern-day Honduras. **The Olmec** lived along the Gulf Coast of Mexico and developed and controlled a large trading network. **The Zapotec** people developed an advanced society in what is now the southern Mexican state of Oaxaca, creating early forms of hieroglyphic writing and a calendar system. They are considered the first city builders in the Americas. **The Chavín,** of the Andes Mountains, were the first significant and influential civilization in South America. The **Nazca** people, also of the Andes region, are noted for developing extensive irrigation systems, and the Moche people were accomplished ceramic artists.

- A group of nomadic warriors called the Mongols united under Genghis Khan in about 1200. By 1221, Central Asia was under Mongol control. In all, the Mongols conquered territory from China to Poland in less than 50 years, creating the largest unified empire in history.

- In 1095, Pope Urban II called for a "holy war," a Crusade, to conquer and control the Holy Land. The goal of the Crusades was to recover Jerusalem and the Holy Land from the Muslim Turks. Though the Crusades failed, and the Holy Lands returned to Muslim control, they opened up trade opportunities with Asia. Throughout Europe, as trade increased, towns attracted more and more people. The old feudal system began to break down.

- The period from 1300 to 1600 that brought an explosion of creativity in Europe is referred to as the **Renaissance.** In 1452, Johannes Gutenberg invented the printing press, leading to increased book production. Leonardo da Vinci, Michelangelo, Raphael, Copernicus, and Galileo challenged thought on arts and the sciences. The Renaissance also sparked an "age of exploration," during which explorers set out to discover new water routes to Asia in search of wealth and power. In search of a shorter and more direct route to Asia, Christopher Columbus traveled west across the Atlantic Ocean in 1492 and landed in the Americas.

- The most influential cultures to emerge in Mesoamerica and South America before 1500 were the Maya, the Aztec, and the Inca. From Peru, the Inca spread outward in all directions, establishing the largest empire in the Americas at that time.

- The **Columbian Exchange,** the global transfer of foods, plants, and animals during the colonization of the Americas, brought together the Eastern and Western hemispheres. Explorers returning from the Americas brought back items that Europeans, Asians, and Africans had never before seen. But as more Europeans arrived in the Americas, they brought infectious and contagious diseases with them for which the native peoples had no immunity.

- In 1526, under the leadership of Babur, Turks, Persians, and Indians joined together to establish the powerful Mughal Empire, which reached its height under Babur's grandson Akbar, who ruled from 1556 to 1605. Between 1300 and 1326, Muslim leader Osman established a small state in Anatolia, present-day Turkey—his followers were called Ottomans. The Ottoman Empire was one of the most powerful states in the world during the fifteenth and sixteenth centuries.

- By the mid-eighteenth century, the intellectual movement, known as the Enlightenment helped spark new revolutionary ideas, like democracy and individual rights. This movement, which attempted to explain the purpose of government and describe the best form of it, reached its height in the mid-1700s.

- In late eighteenth century, the people of France were still divided into three large social classes: the First Estate (the clergy of the Roman Catholic Church), the Second Estate (the nobility), and the Third Estate (merchants, artisans, urban lower class workers, and peasants). Enlightenment ideas about power spread throughout the Third Estate. In 1789, French citizens stormed and took control of the Bastille and launched the French Revolution. In 1799, Napoleon Bonaparte seized power.

- The Industrial Revolution began in the 1780s. Machines rapidly replaced hand labor as the principal means of producing goods, and factories were built to house large manufacturing machines, creating a new and modern class of labor—the factory worker. People moved from rural areas to cities to work in factories.

- In the 1800s and early 1900s, imperialism swept through Europe as nations developed colonization policies in hopes of increasing their power and influence. France established colonies in Southeast Asia, Africa, and South America; Portugal had colonies in Africa and China; and Germany and Italy established colonies in Africa.

- At the start of the twentieth century, rivalry had developed among Europe's most powerful countries. In June 1914, the assassination of Archduke Franz

Ferdinand triggered the start of World War I, which lasted until 1918. Afterwards, the Allied Powers created the League of Nations in hopes to protect each other's territory and political independence. The U.S. Congress refused to join the League of Nations; without the United States, the League of Nations' effectiveness was weakened.

- In March 1917, the Russian government under Czar (Tsar) Nicholas II was toppled. Bolshevik revolutionaries seized power, and a new communist government under Vladimir Lenin was formed. From 1918 to 1920, a civil war raged in Russia between Reds (communists) and Whites (their opponents). In 1922, Russia became the Union of Soviet Socialist Republics, or Soviet Union.

- In 1933, Adolf Hitler gained total control over Germany. Hitler's Nazi Party began passing laws depriving Jews of most of their rights. Hitler attacked Poland in 1939, and two days later, World War II started when Britain and France declared war on Germany. The United States entered the war when Japanese warplanes attacked the U.S. naval base at Pearl Harbor; Germany and Italy then declared war on the United States. On May 7, 1945, Germany surrendered, ending the war in Europe. Allies learned that more than 6 million Jews and millions of other groups of people had been murdered in concentration camps. In August 1945, Americans dropped atomic bombs on the Japanese cities of Hiroshima and Nagasaki. Japan surrendered on August 14, ending World War II. The United States implemented the **Marshall Plan** to provide economic assistance to help Germany, Italy, and other European nations (and Japan) rebuild their economies.

- In August 1949, the Soviet Union exploded its first atomic bomb, starting the Cold War, an arms race with the United States that lasted for 40 years. The communist threat spread when Chinese revolutionaries took control and adopted a communist government in 1949.

- In 1957, six European nations formed the European Common Market to reduce the barriers to trade and to boost economic growth—this was later replaced by the European Union (EU). But as some regions have become more integrated, others have been pulled apart by ethnic and religious conflicts. Yugoslavia, Rwanda, Somalia, Indonesia, and other nations have experienced episodes of ethnic cleansing. The growth of religious fundamentalism has also contributed to conflicts in various regions of the world. In Afghanistan in 1997, the Taliban movement took control of the government and imposed their view of Muslim law on the land. In 2014, the fundamentalist group ISIL (Islamic State of Iraq and the Levant) took control of a large region of land in Iraq and Syria and established a caliphate, an Islamic political-religious state.

- The first African American President in United States history, President Barack Obama, promised change with a stimulus program for the economy, an end to the war in the Middle East, and creation of a Universal Health Care system as part of the Affordable Care Act labeled "Obamacare" by his opponents

- In 2016, political outsider and business mogul Donald Trump secured the Republican nomination using a Populist-like campaign and a message of "America First" and defeated former Secretary of State and first lady Hilary Clinton to become president of a drastically divided nation.

Civics and Government

chapter 18

OVERVIEW

- **Power, authority, and government**
- **Characteristics of government systems**
- **Principles of American democracy**
- **The meaning of citizenship**
- **The role of citizens in a democracy**
- **Summing It Up**

An understanding of civic ideals and practices is critical to full participation in society, and is an essential component of education for citizenship. This chapter gives you a basic overview of the most-tested civics and government topics on the HiSET® Social Studies subtest. These concepts will not only come up in direct questions, but will also be woven into more general history and economics questions as well.

POWER, AUTHORITY, AND GOVERNMENT

Political behavior was a part of even the earliest human societies. Early people usually appointed leaders to decide group actions in times of crisis. As civilizations developed, governments were created. **Government** is the overall structure by which nations, states, and cities carry out their political, economic, and social agendas. The process of government leadership changed as societies developed. Early governments primarily benefited those who were in leadership positions. Often leaders wielded **absolute power,** claiming a divine right to rule that a god or deity bestowed on them. Because this power was god-given, the ruler was not accountable to the people. Other leaders with absolute power, such as dictators and warlords, often depended on brute force to terrorize to maintain their power. Their power was not legitimate in the eyes of those under their rule.

Around 500 BCE, the ancient Greek city-state of Athens created a **democracy.** In a democracy, the people rule themselves. Citizens participate directly in political decision-making. Government leaders in a democracy are granted authority, or power, that people accept as legitimate.

Governments today still bear responsibility for the welfare and safety of their people. Modern governments establish processes for choosing leaders and deciding how much authority the leaders will have. Every government also has a method for determining the goals of society, for making laws, and for enforcing those laws. Finally, each government must provide a system of justice. No society expects to be free of disputes.

It is the government's responsibility to see that disagreements among citizens are resolved in a fair and nonviolent way.

Directions: Use the following information to answer the two questions that follow.

In 1952, former Cuban president Fulgencio Batista saw an opportunity to return to government, running for the presidency. As Election Day approached, Batista was polling third. On March 10, 1952, he took control of the government in a military takeover. By 1953 Batista faced growing opposition. Batista then suspended constitutional guarantees and increasingly relied on strong-armed police tactics to frighten the population through open displays of brutality. Between 1954 and 1956, Batista made some political concessions, such as lifting press censorship and releasing political prisoners. The Cubans' anger and dissatisfaction with the Batista regime intensified, however, and Batista's police again responded by torturing and killing young men in the cities. The government was unable to suppress the growing revolutionary movement in the countryside. As the dictator of Cuba, Batista's unpopularity continued to grow. By the end of the decade, he was forced to flee, living in exile in Europe before dying in 1973.

1. Batista's rule of Cuba could most accurately be described as
   (A) a citizen-led government.
   (B) an example of divine right authority.
   (C) use of legitimate authority.
   (D) the illegitimate use of power.

The correct answer is (D). Batista illegally seized the government of Cuba and used power to terrorize and suppress the rights of Cuban citizens, without their consent.

2. Based on information in the passage, it could be concluded that Cuban citizens disliked Batista because he
   (A) lifted press censorship and released political prisoners.
   (B) suspended constitutional guarantees and used brutality to maintain power.
   (C) could not suppress the growing revolutionary movement in the countryside.
   (D) wanted to rewrite the Cuban constitution.

The correct answer is (B). Batista basically made it impossible for the Cuban people to participate in political and government activity. He stripped them of their constitutional guarantees and used brutal and deadly methods to suppress political dissent.

CHARACTERISTICS OF GOVERNMENT SYSTEMS

A system of government has always been necessary in nations and states. The government performs several major roles in a society, including maintaining order, providing security and public services, and guiding communities toward goals by making public policies. The form of government each society follows depends on a number of factors, including the size of the state and the traditions of its citizens. There have been many kinds of governments throughout history that have shaped the types of governments that exist today.

Democracy

An old and influential government system is a **democracy.** In a democracy, citizens participate in choosing government leaders and in the decisions these leaders make. There are two types of democracies: a true democracy and a representative democracy. In a true democracy, also called a direct democracy or pure democracy, citizens participate in making all governmental decisions. The ancient Greek city-state of Athens—where democracy began—was an example of a direct democracy. A direct democracy government is not practical for most countries today because of their large populations and geographic areas. In a representative democracy, citizens elect representatives to make decisions for them. The United States is an example of a representative democracy.

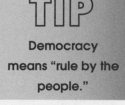

TIP

Democracy means "rule by the people."

Authoritarian Systems

An authoritarian government is a system in which citizens have no participation. Power is concentrated in the hands of a leader or a small group that does not answer to the people. Authoritarian leaders often use their powers arbitrarily and without regard to laws. These leaders usually cannot be replaced by citizens through free elections.

A **monarchy** is an authoritarian system that is older than democracy. A king or queen is usually the leader of a monarchy, and the right to rule in a monarchy is hereditary, or passed down through the family of the ruler.

There are two basic types of monarchies: absolute monarchy and a constitutional monarchy. In an **absolute monarchy,** the monarch has no or very few legal limitations in political matters. In a **constitutional monarchy,** such as Great Britain, the monarch's power is limited by a constitution and written laws. In these systems, the monarch performs a ceremonial role based on tradition but does not hold law-making powers.

TIP

Monarchy was the most common form of government until the nineteenth century.

Another form of authoritarian government is a **dictatorship.** Dictators, like absolute monarchs, exercise complete control over the government. Unlike monarchs, who usually acquire their power through heredity, dictators usually take power by force. To stay in power, most dictators rely on powerful police and military forces. Dictators often restrict or ban elections and limit freedoms of speech, assembly, and the press.

A **totalitarian system** is characterized by strong central rule that attempts to control all aspects of individual life, usually through force and repression. Many dictators impose totalitarian rule on their people. Like dictators, totalitarian leaders also limit individual freedoms. In addition, traditional social institutions and organizations are suppressed. Totalitarian leaders usually control the media to create propaganda to broadcast and promote an ideology.

Oligarchy

An **oligarchy** is a government system in which all power resides with a few people or with a dominant class or group within a society. Leaders of an oligarchy are not elected and often lead for corrupt or selfish reasons and use tactics or methods much in the style of a dictator. Power within the small group of leaders can shift, but it almost always returns to another member or group within the power structure.

PRINCIPLES OF AMERICAN DEMOCRACY

The framers of the U.S. Constitution relied on seven key principles to create a functioning representative government.

1. **Popular sovereignty:** Sovereignty, or "authority of the people," is reinforced with the opening line of the U.S. Constitution, "We the People." The framers identified the powers and rules by which American citizens would be ruled. The power granted to the government can only come from the consent of the people.

2. **Republicanism:** The United States is a republic, a form of indirect, or representative, democracy. Citizens who vote are sovereign and have the ultimate authority in a republican system of government. They elect representatives and give them the responsibility to make laws and run the government.

3. **Limited government:** The framers feared that a very strong federal government would eventually abuse its power. To prevent this, they identified specific powers in the Constitution that the government could use, limiting its authority. Articles I, II, and III of the Constitution describe the powers of the federal government and its limits. The Bill of Rights also describes government limits and guarantees citizens certain rights.

4. **Federalism:** Even though the framers created a strong federal government, they did not make the states powerless. The Constitution grants some powers to the federal government and some powers to the states. This principle of shared power is called federalism. There are three types of government powers defined in the Constitution: 1) Powers that belong exclusively to the federal government are called **enumerated powers.** Enumerated powers include the authority to declare war, regulate interstate and foreign trade, print and coin money, maintain armed forces, and create federal courts. 2) **Reserved powers** are those that are retained by the states, including authority to establish schools, regulate marriage and divorce laws, and regulate commerce within the state. 3) **Concurrent powers** are those that are shared by the federal and state governments. These powers include the right to raise taxes, borrow money, provide for public welfare, and regulate elections.

5. **Separation of powers:** According to the Constitution, each level of government is divided into three branches, each with separated duties. The three branches are the legislative branch, the executive branch, and the judicial branch. Separating the branches of government and giving them specific powers and duties prevents any single branch from gaining too much authority.

TIP

Reserved powers are not listed in the Constitution. Rather, the Tenth Amendment states that all powers not granted to the federal government are reserved to the states.

6. **Checks and balances:** The framers built a system of checks and balances that enabled each branch of government to check, or limit, the power of the other two branches. This too was a preventative measure against any one branch becoming too powerful.

7. **Individual rights:** In 1791, ten amendments were added to the Constitution. These amendments protect certain basic rights, including freedom of speech, religion, and the right to a trial by jury. The first ten amendments are known as the **Bill of Rights.** Seventeen more amendments have been added to the Constitution, giving additional rights to Americans and making changes to government processes.

The Three Branches of Government

The U.S. Constitution divides the government into three branches, each with its own responsibilities and duties. The legislative branch makes the laws, the executive branch enforces the laws, and the judicial branch interprets the laws.

Legislative Branch

Congress is the legislative, or lawmaking, branch of the government. The framers of the Constitution created a two-part, or bicameral, body to provide equal representation in one chamber but also allow for more populous states to have a greater voice in the other chamber.

- **House of Representatives:** The House is made up of 435 lawmakers. Each state is represented in the House, with the number of representatives determined by the state's population. Each state is guaranteed at least one member in the House, and each representative represents a district within his or her home state. House members serve two-year terms, with all 435 seats up for election every two years. The leader of the House is the Speaker of the House. The House has the ability to impeach officials and initiate finance and budget bills.

- **The Senate:** The Senate has 100 members, two from each state. Senators are elected to six-year terms that are staggered. The Senate has the power to consent to treaties before their ratification and to give consent or confirm appointments of Cabinet secretaries, federal judges, federal executive officials, military officers, ambassadors, and other federal uniformed officers.

The Executive Branch

It is the responsibility of the executive branch to enforce the country's laws. The head of the executive branch is the President. Presidential elections are held every four years. The President performs three key duties. As **chief executive,** the president is responsible for carrying out the nation's laws. As **chief diplomat,** the president directs foreign policy, appoints ambassadors, and negotiates treaties with other nations. As **Commander in Chief** of the U.S. military, the president has the authority to direct military forces in times of emergency. The president is the highest-ranking commander of all U.S. armed forces.

The executive branch relies on executive offices, departments, and independent agencies to help carry out its responsibilities. Department heads have the title of secretary and are members of the president's **cabinet,** which helps the president set policies and make decisions. Working closely with the president is the vice president, who would assume the role of president should the current president not be capable of carrying out the duties of the office.

The Judicial Branch

The judicial branch is the third branch of government. The **U.S. Supreme Court** is the head of the judicial branch, which also includes "lower courts" throughout the country. These are federal district courts and federal courts of appeals. The Supreme Court's main responsibility is to hear appealed cases from lower courts. The head of the judicial branch is the Chief Justice of the Supreme Court. All justices of the Supreme Court are nominated by the president, approved by the Senate, and given lifetime appointments.

Directions: Use this information to answer the two questions that follow.

> U.S. Presidents can enact initiatives without congressional approval. Presidents have been issuing executive orders since 1789, even though the Constitution does not explicitly give them the authority to do so. An executive order has the full effect of law and is directed to federal agencies that are charged with carrying out the order. Congress cannot directly vote to override an executive order in the way it can a veto. Rather, Congress must pass a new bill canceling or changing the order in a manner it sees fit. However, the president will usually veto that bill. The Supreme Court can negate an Executive Order by ruling it unconstitutional if a case is brought before it.

3. Which foundational American democratic principle might a Senator argue is being violated by the president issuing an Executive Order?

   (A) Individual rights

   (B) Federalism

   (C) Limited government

   (D) Separation of powers

The correct answer is (D). Article I Section 1 of the Constitution says that all legislative powers are granted to Congress. Because an Executive Order has the full effect of the law, some members of Congress might argue that the president is exercising rights not granted to the office in the Constitution and is therefore violating the principle of separation of powers.

4. Which of the following is a conclusion based on the information in the passage?

   (A) Only Congress has the power to reverse or cancel a presidential executive order.

   (B) The judicial branch is the branch of government that determines the constitutionality of legislation.

   (C) Executive orders are the only laws that can never be reversed or canceled.

   (D) Presidents must consult Congress before issuing an executive order.

The correct answer is (B). Article III of the Constitution outlines the role of the judicial branch as the branch to hear and rule on constitutional issues.

THE MEANING OF CITIZENSHIP

A citizen is a person who owes loyalty to a state, nation, or government and in return is entitled to protection from it. The concept of citizenship dates back more than 2,500 years to ancient Greece and Rome. Then, only male property owners could vote and take part in government. In most countries today, people are citizens of the countries in which they live. Gender, wealth, and property ownership are no longer requirements for citizenship.

Being a citizen means much more than just living in a country. For example, Americans who live in foreign countries are still citizens of the United States. Their U.S. citizenship connects them to all other Americans. Citizens of a country often share a common history, common customs, and common beliefs. Americans also share specific values about their right to freedom, liberty, and equality. Other American values include opportunity, justice, democracy, unity, respect, and tolerance. Another way in which Americans are united is in a common civic and political heritage based on the country's important founding documents. These key documents include the Declaration of Independence, the U.S. Constitution of 1787, and the Bill of Rights of 1791. American ideals of individual rights to "life, liberty, and the pursuit of happiness" are in these founding documents.

Directions: Read the passage and answer the question that follows.

President John F. Kennedy established the Peace Corps by executive order on March 1, 1961. Initially, the Peace Corps program was an outgrowth of the Cold War. Kennedy pointed out that the Soviet Union "had hundreds of men and women, scientists, physicists, teachers, engineers, doctors, and nurses . . . prepared to spend their lives abroad in the service of world communism." The United States had no such program, and Kennedy wanted to involve Americans more actively around the world.

5. Based on information in the passage, the spreading of which of the following American political values was the initial inspiration for creating the Peace Corps?

   (A) Democracy

   (B) The pursuit of happiness

   (C) Opportunity

   (D) Justice

The correct answer is (A). Kennedy was alarmed that the Soviet Union was sending young workers throughout the world to spread communism. Kennedy's plan was to send young Americans around the world as ambassadors of democracy, peace, and development.

Directions: Read the information and answer the question that follows.

The Tenth Amendment to the U.S. Constitution states:

The powers not delegated to the United States by the Constitution, nor prohibited by it to the States, are reserved to the States respectively, or to the people.

6. Which of the following statements best summarizes the key purpose for the Tenth Amendment?
   (A) To provide a means for people to override the Constitution
   (B) To create a power struggle between the people and their state governments
   (C) To prevent the federal government from becoming too powerful
   (D) To make the states more powerful than the federal government

The correct answer is (C). The Tenth Amendment protects the states and the people from the federal government. It is a "check" on the "necessary and proper" power of the federal government, which is provided for in Article 1, Section 8 of the Constitution.

THE ROLE OF CITIZENS IN A DEMOCRACY

For a democratic government to be effective, citizens must fulfill their civic duties and responsibilities. Living in a system of self-government ultimately means that all citizens are in part responsible for how their society is governed and for the actions the government takes on their behalf. The American ideal of citizenship has always emphasized each citizen's responsibility to participate and work to make his or her community a safe and productive place in which to live.

Individual Rights

The rights of Americans fall into three broad categories: the right to be protected from unfair actions of the government, the right to receive equal treatment under the law, and the right to retain certain basic freedoms. Parts of the Constitution and the Bill of Rights protect all Americans from unfair treatment by the government or the law. Among these rights are the right to a lawyer when accused of a crime and the right to trial by jury when charged with a crime.

All Americans, regardless of race, religion, or political beliefs, have the right to be treated the same under the law. The Fifth Amendment states that no person shall be deprived of life, liberty, or property without due process of law.

The basic freedoms are described in the First Amendment: freedom of speech, freedom of religion, freedom of the press, freedom of assembly, and the right to petition. In a democracy, power rests in the hands of the people. Therefore, citizens in a democratic society must be able to exchange ideas freely. The First Amendment allows citizens

TIP

Due process means that the government must follow procedures established by law and guaranteed by the Constitution.

to criticize the government in speech or in the press without fear of punishment. In addition, the Ninth Amendment states that the rights of Americans are not limited to those in the Constitution. This has allowed Americans to assert other basic rights over the years that have been upheld in court or assured by amending the Constitution.

Individual Duties and Responsibilities

U.S. citizenship brings with it certain duties and responsibilities. Fulfilling both duties and responsibilities helps ensure good government and protects the people's rights.

Individual Duties

National, state, and local laws require Americans to perform certain duties. Failure to perform them could lead to fines or imprisonment. Some countries require much from their citizens. For example, citizens of some countries must serve in the armed forces for a period of time. Much less is required of American citizens than in many other countries. The U.S. government does require its citizens to perform the following duties:

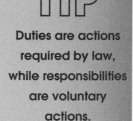

TIP

Duties are actions required by law, while responsibilities are voluntary actions.

- **Obey Laws:** This is one of a citizen's most important civic duties. Communities may have problems maintaining order or protecting the health, safety, and property of its residents if citizens do not obey the law.

- **Pay Taxes:** Americans also have a duty to pay taxes. Taxes provide most of the money the government needs to function. Taxes are used to pay government employees, defend the nation, build roads and bridges, and assist people in need. Local communities rely on taxes to hire and pay police and firefighters and fund local public schools.

- **Register for the Draft:** Under the law, men aged 18 to 25 are required to register with the government in case the nation needs to draft them, or call on them for military service. Since the end of the Vietnam War, there has been no draft, and America's military has been made up of volunteers.

- **Serve on Juries:** The Constitution guarantees all Americans the right to a trial by jury. Every adult citizen must be prepared to serve on a jury. People involved in court cases depend on their fellow citizens to to reach a fair verdict. Another duty is to serve as witness at a trial if called to do so.

- **Attend School:** All young people have access to free public schools and, in most states, are required to attend school until the age of 16.

Individual Responsibilities

Because the responsibilities of American citizens are not written laws, they are not as clear as duties. Nonetheless, civic responsibilities are just as important because they help maintain the quality of government and society.

In order for Americans to enjoy their rights, they have a responsibility to respect the rights of others. Tolerance is respecting and accepting others, regardless of their beliefs, practices, or differences, which is essential in a democracy. Responsible citizens show concern for others as well as for themselves. They are willing to give time, effort, and money to improve their communities. Responsible citizens of a community are actively concerned with protecting and promoting the health and welfare of everyone. This creates an environment in which every citizen actively works to contribute to the common good.

Perhaps the most important responsibility is to vote. All citizens 18 years of age and older have the right to vote. By voting, citizens have the chance to shape the future of their communities, states, and nation. Responsible voters study the candidates and issues carefully before making their ballot decisions. When voters elect people to represent them in government, they exercise their right of self-government. Thoughtful citizens also regularly check to see what their elected leaders are doing. If an official's performance does not meet expectations, voters have the opportunity to choose someone else in the next election.

Responsible citizenship requires citizens to be well-informed. Thomas Jefferson once wrote, "Wherever the people are well informed they can be trusted with their own government." Americans have a responsibility to know what the government is doing so that they can voice their opinions on matters about which they feel strongly. All citizens must keep in mind that government decisions affect their lives.

Directions: Read the information and answer the questions that follow.

The Sixth Amendment to the U.S. Constitution states:

In all criminal prosecutions, the accused shall enjoy the right to a speedy and public trial by an impartial jury of the state and district wherein the crime shall have been committed, which district shall have been previously ascertained by law, and to be informed of the nature and cause of the accusation; to be confronted with the witnesses against him; to have compulsory process for obtaining witnesses in his favor; and to have the assistance of counsel for his defense.

---

7. Which situation below would be prohibited by the Sixth Amendment?
   (A) A person's home is searched by police who have not obtained a warrant.
   (B) The accused is denied bail.
   (C) The accused cannot afford an attorney and is denied one.
   (D) A judge refuses to allow more than 10 witnesses to testify.

The correct answer is (C). Of the possible answers, only the right to have assistance of counsel is mentioned in the Sixth Amendment.

8. Which of the following titles would best represent the theme of this timeline?

1810	Last religious prerequisite for voting is eliminated
1850	Property ownership and tax requirements eliminated by 1850
1870	Fifteenth Amendment ratified, giving former male slaves the right to vote
1920	Nineteenth Amendment ratified, guaranteeing women the right to vote
1924	Indian Citizenship Act grants all Native Americans the right to vote in federal elections
1971	Twenty-sixth Amendment ratified, setting the minimum voting age at 18

(A) Effects of Voting Legislation on Minorities

(B) The Expansion of Voting Rights in the United States

(C) Key Voting Restrictions in the United States

(D) Gender and U.S. Voting Laws

The correct answer is (B). Each item on the timeline describes legislation that expanded voting rights in the United States.

SUMMING IT UP

- **Government** is the overall structure by which nations, states, and cities carry out their political, economic, and social agendas. Early governments primarily benefited those who were in leadership positions. Then, around 500 BCE, the ancient Greek city-state of Athens created a **democracy.** Modern governments establish processes for choosing leaders and deciding how much authority the leaders will have. Governments see that disagreements among citizens are resolved in a fair and nonviolent way.

- In a **democracy,** citizens choose government leaders and, indirectly, the decisions these leaders make. In a true democracy, citizens participate in making all governmental decisions. In a representative democracy (such as the United States), citizens elect representatives to make decisions for them. A **monarchy** is an authoritarian system where a king or queen rules and gains this position through heredity. In a **dictatorship,** the leader exercises complete control over the government—unlike monarchs, they take and maintain power by force. A **totalitarian system** controls all aspects of individual life through force and repression. An **oligarchy** is a government system in which all power resides with a few people or a dominant class or group within the society.

- The framers of the U.S. Constitution created a government based on seven key principles: **popular sovereignty** ("authority of the people"), **republicanism** (representative democracy, where citizens elect representatives and give them the responsibility), **limited government** (Articles I, II, III of the Constitution describe the powers of the federal government and its limits), **federalism** (the granting of some powers to the federal government and some powers to the states), **separation of powers** (dividing each level of government into three branches: the legislative branch, the executive branch, and the judicial branch), **checks and balances** (where each branch of government can limit the power of the other two branches), and **individual rights** (amendments that protect basic rights like freedom of speech, religion, and the right to a trial by jury).

- The government has three branches: the **legislative branch** (comprised of the House of Representatives and Senate), which makes the laws; the **executive branch** (headed by the President and including the Cabinet), which enforces the laws; and the **judicial branch** (headed by the U.S. Supreme Court), which interprets the laws.

- The rights of American citizens fall into three broad categories: the right to be protected from unfair actions of the government, the right to receive equal treatment under the law, and the right to retain certain basic freedoms. U.S. citizenship also brings with it certain duties and responsibilities. The U.S. government requires its citizens to obey laws, pay taxes, register for the draft, serve on juries, and attend school. Responsible citizens vote, respect others, and work to improve the welfare of their communities.

Economics

chapter 19

OVERVIEW

- Scarcity, needs, and wants
- The impact of technology on economics
- The interdependent nature of economics
- How government affects economies
- Variations of government effects over time
- Summing It Up

The study of economics is the study of the way society uses limited resources to meet its material needs through the production, distribution, and consumption of goods. Economists develop economic principles and models on two levels: microeconomics and macroeconomics. Microeconomics is the part of economics that deals with decision-making by individual customers, workers, households, and businesses. Macroeconomics examines either the economy as whole or its basic subdivisions, such as government, households, and business sectors. Economics questions on the HiSET® Social Studies subtest will test your comprehension by presenting you with a series of passages, graphs, political cartoons, and more.

SCARCITY, NEEDS, AND WANTS

A key issue in economics is the problem of scarcity. Scarcity means that people's wants are unlimited while the resources to fulfill those wants are limited. A person is dealing with the problem of scarcity, for example, if he or she wants to purchase a new television and a new couch but only has enough money to pay for just one of these items. Because of scarcity, individuals, families, businesses, and governments must make choices that enable them to satisfy some of their unlimited wants with limited resources. Much of economics examines how people make choices to satisfy their needs and wants with their limited resources. **Needs** are the basic things people must have to survive, such as food, shelter, and clothing. **Wants** are things that are not necessary for survival but make life more comfortable, such as a vacation or a new video game.

The Principle of Supply and Demand

The primary force and one of the basic principles of economics is that of **supply and demand.** Economists say that prices are determined by the relationship between supply and demand. Supply is the quantity of a good or service that a producer is willing to sell at a certain price. The law of supply says that if the price of a product is high, the producers will be willing to sell more of it to increase the amount of money they will make. If the price is low, they will want to sell less of it. Demand is the degree to which people want a product and are willing and able to pay for it. The law of demand states that if the price of a product is high, consumers will demand less of it. If the price is low, they will demand more of it. These factors working together make up the principle of supply and demand.

Directions: Use the given information to answer the questions that follow.

> Because of scarcity, any time a choice is made to fulfill wants and needs, there are alternatives that are *not* chosen. More precisely, there is always one *next best* alternative that is not chosen. In economics, the value of the next best alternative is called opportunity cost.
>
> For example, the Jackson family of Detroit just inherited $2,000 and must decide what to do with the money. Mr. and Mrs. Jackson are anticipating a $500 dollar rent increase for their apartment that will begin three months before Mrs. Jackson's yearly salary raise takes effect. Their three kids have also been expressing a desire to go on a family trip to Florida or to a weekend stay at a local theme park.

1. Based on the information about the Jackson family, what is the need that they must think about when determining how to spend the extra $2,000?

   (A) The time between Mrs. Jackson's yearly raise in salary and the rent increase

   (B) The cost of the trip to Florida

   (C) The cost of the weekend at the theme park

   (D) The $500 rent increase

The correct answer is (D). Only the rent increase is a *need* that Jackson family must fulfill.

2. Mrs. Jackson's salary raise was pushed ahead three months. The Jacksons decide to spend the $2,000 on an extended weekend trip to the local theme park. What is the opportunity cost of the trip to the theme park?

   (A) The price of admission to the theme park

   (B) Travel time lost driving to the theme park

   (C) The family trip to Florida

   (D) Two months of reduced rent payments

The correct answer is (C). Because the Jacksons decided to go the theme park instead of Florida, the opportunity cost was the trip to Florida, the next best alternative.

> In a free market economy, the price of a product is determined at the point where the quantity that consumers want to buy is equal to the quantity that producers want to sell. This is called the market price, or equilibrium. Equilibrium occurs when the supply of a product or service equals the demand for it. When the price of a product is more than the equilibrium point, demand decreases and there is an oversupply of the product on the market.

3. Which of the following statements accurately reflects the result of the price of a product falling below the equilibrium point?

   (A) The demand for the product will tend to decrease.

   (B) There will be an undersupply of the product.

   (C) The equilibrium point rises.

   (D) There will be an oversupply of the product.

The correct answer is (B). When the price falls below the equilibrium point, demand for the product increases because consumers are eager to spend less money to purchase the product. Consequently, the supply of the product will decrease, leading to undersupply.

THE IMPACT OF TECHNOLOGY ON ECONOMICS

Technological change is part of the economic process. Competition and the search to find better and more efficient ways to produce and provide goods and services lead businesses to take advantage of new technologies. In this way, technology plays a significant role in fueling economic growth.

According to classical economic theory, the accumulation of physical **capital**—tools, vehicles, and assembly lines, for example—is responsible for increasing worker productivity. **Productivity** is the amount of output per unit of input and is often used as a measure of an economy's health. When productivity is growing, living standards tend to rise. When productivity is stagnating, the economy generally stagnates as well.

The impact of technology has been felt for centuries. The woolen mills of the early Industrial Revolution put small cottage industries operating handlooms out of business. In the late eighteenth- and early nineteenth-century United States, much of what Americans needed and wanted was produced on a small scale. In small-scale production, all the factors of production—land, labor, and capital—were used, but the human labor involved was much greater than it is today. Consequently, productivity was lower. Technological advances used in today's economy enable goods to be mass-produced. Machines and more efficient energy sources require fewer workers to produce many more goods and services than in the past. This all leads to increased productivity. Technological innovation makes it possible to do more with less.

Technological innovation comes with a price, however. While new technology creates new jobs, it often destroys other jobs at the same time. Workers who lose their jobs are usually the first to feel the impact of technological innovation. Often, those who are displaced by technological advances may find it difficult to become reemployed because many new jobs require advanced skills or highly specific knowledge they do not possess.

Directions: Use the following information to answer the two questions that follow.

> Semiconductor and computer makers achieved remarkable productivity gains in the late 1990s, providing better and more capable computers to businesses and consumers at ever-lower prices. That manufacturing performance was so exceptional that it boosted the growth of national productivity significantly. According to many economic analysts, advances in computer technology caused a large part of that acceleration in potential total productivity growth. These advances also reduced the cost of business investment in computer and other related equipment, which contributed to economic growth, as measured by Gross Domestic Product. Gross Domestic Product, or GDP, represents the total market value of all goods and services during a given year.

4. According to the passage, which of the following was primarily responsible for the significant increase in productivity in the late 1990s?
   (A) The rapid growth of the country's GDP
   (B) The emergence of personal computers used in private homes
   (C) Advances in computer technology
   (D) The rise in costs of investing in computer equipment

The correct answer is (C). The significant innovations in computer technology and manufacturing made computers and other equipment less expensive and more widely used. This produced a ripple effect that had substantial impact throughout the economy.

5. Which of the following titles would best represent the theme of this passage?
   (A) Effects of GDP Growth in the Late 1990s
   (B) Tracking the Use of Personal Computers in the 1990s
   (C) Effects of Computer Technology on National Productivity
   (D) Effects of Peripheral Equipment on Computer Manufacturing

The correct answer is (C). The passage describes how innovations in computer technology, including manufacturing, all had positive effects on productivity in the United States.

THE INTERDEPENDENT NATURE OF ECONOMICS

The United States' economy and most modern-day economies around the world have a remarkable degree of economic interdependence. People must rely on others to provide most of the goods and services they consume. As a result, economic events in one part of the world can have a large effect in other parts. Economic interdependence is a characteristic of a society or economy with a high degree of division of labor and specialization, where people depend on other people to produce most of the goods and services required to provide needs and wants. Division of labor, a way of organizing work so that each individual worker completes a separate part of the work, is one important factor that helps boost productivity.

The more individuals and nations specialize and trade, the more dependent they become on each other to supply their basic needs. For example, very few people have the resources and abilities to grow all their own food. They must rely on farmers. Farmers, in turn, rely on other producers to provide seed, fertilizers, and farm machinery. This complicated web of interdependence that develops from trade among individuals, businesses, and national economies helps create strong incentives for cooperation and mutually beneficial relationships.

Consumers and producers are interconnected through a continuous circular flow of buying and selling. The key feature of the circular flow is the market, a location or other mechanism that allows buyers and sellers to exchange specific products. Markets may be local, national, or global—and they can even exist in cyberspace. An important fundamental of the circular flow model is that one person's spending is another person's revenue. The hard-earned income that a person spends to purchase products ends up as income for those who produce or sell those products. These people then spend this revenue to purchase other products, which then becomes income for other producers, and the cycle continues.

The circular flow diagram below shows the high degree of economic interdependence in our economy. In the diagram, the factors of production and the products made from them flow in one direction. The money consumers spend on goods and services flows in the opposite direction.

> **TIP**
>
> In most cases, a worker who performs a few tasks many times a day is likely to be more proficient than a worker who performs hundreds of different tasks in the same period.

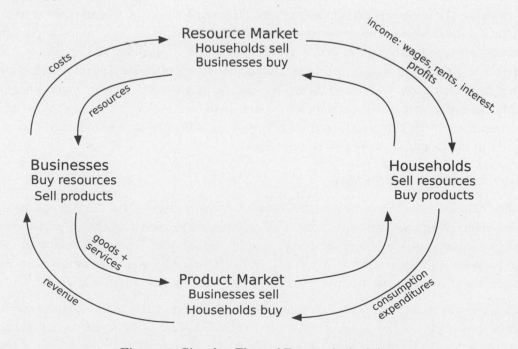

Figure 1: Circular Flow of Economic Activity.

6. Which of the following would be determined in the product market?
   (A) The price of a new mobile phone
   (B) The price of equipment used in a manufacturing plant
   (C) The price of office building real estate
   (D) The salary of a corporate CEO

The correct answer is (A). Manufacturing equipment, real estate, and salaries are factors that are determined in the resource market. The price of a product, such as a mobile phone, would be determined in the product market.

7. In this circular flow diagram,
   (A) households are on the selling side of the product market.
   (B) resources flow counterclockwise.
   (C) goods and services flow clockwise.
   (D) money flows counterclockwise.

The correct answer is (B). In this diagram, resources flow counterclockwise from households to businesses through the resource market and products flow from businesses to households through the product market.

HOW GOVERNMENT AFFECTS ECONOMIES

The three basic economic systems in the world today are capitalism, communism, and socialism.

The U.S. economic system is largely capitalistic. Another name for **capitalism** is free enterprise. Free enterprise is based on a principle known as the free market system. A free market system relies on several key factors, including self-interest, profits, competition, and the right to own private property. In capitalism, the private sector makes most of the economic decisions. The private sector includes all those businesses that individuals own and run by themselves. In **communism,** the government controls almost all economic activity in some way. **Socialism** blends elements of capitalism and communism, with the private sector holding some influence over economic decisions but still not as much as the government does.

The American Economy

Although the United States is primarily a free market economy, the federal government serves important economic functions. The government has considerable impact on the U.S. economy, since it determines taxes, employs several million people, and borrows and spends a great amount of money. In addition, both the executive and legislative branches of government are involved in creating the U.S. government budget.

The federal government is also responsible for maintaining and regulating the conditions that allow the free market system to work most efficiently. Departments within the government establish laws and provide courts to maintain property rights and enforce legal and fair business standards. One way the government regulates private enterprise is by seeking, either directly or indirectly, to control prices. Traditionally, the government has sought to prevent monopolies, such as electric utilities, from raising prices beyond the level that would ensure them reasonable profits. It is also the government's responsibility to maintain a stable currency and operate the U.S. Mint, which makes coins and paper money.

The U.S. Constitution states that one of the primary jobs of Congress is to promote the general welfare of the nation. To accomplish this, Congress grants departments within the government the power to provide functions that the free market system does not or cannot provide. For example, the government collects taxes to redistribute some money to people who don't earn enough to meet their needs.

The government also exercises control over private companies to achieve social goals, such as protecting the public's health and safety or maintaining a clean and healthy environment. For example, the U.S. Food and Drug Administration (FDA) bans harmful drugs, and the Occupational Safety and Health Administration (OSHA) helps to protect workers from hazards they may encounter in their jobs. The Environmental Protection Agency (EPA) is tasked with limiting water and air pollution throughout the United States. All these functions impact the economy.

The Federal Reserve System

The Federal Reserve System is the United States' central banking system. The Federal Reserve, or the Fed, manages the total amount of money available for lending and borrowing in the private banking system and partially controls interest rates. The Federal Reserve serves as the central mechanism for government intervention in the economy. The Fed is basically a bank for banks. It holds a certain percentage of the banks' deposits and provides loans to banks.

Economic Instability: Inflation and Recession

The U.S. government fights economic instability on two main fronts: fiscal (budget) policy and monetary (money) policy. The government's fiscal policies decide how it will tax the people and how it will spend the money it collects. Its monetary policies dictate how much money will flow through the economy.

Inflation occurs when total demand and spending are greater than total production. To control inflation, the government may enact fiscal policies that reduce its spending. Reducing the government's demand for goods and services reduces total demand, which tends to reduce inflation. The government can achieve the same result by increasing taxes without increasing government spending. Higher taxes will mean that individuals and businesses will have less money to spend. This will lower total demand and will tend to reduce inflation. During periods of inflation, the Federal Reserve can implement monetary policies that reduce the amount of money flowing through the economy. Money then increases in value because it is scarcer, and the rise in prices slows down.

A **recession** is a period of general economic decline, typically defined as a decline in GDP for two or more consecutive quarters. A recession is usually accompanied by a

TIP

The government also manages much of the nation's infrastructure, such as the interstate highway system and airports, which indirectly support economic activity.

drop in the stock market, an increase in unemployment, and a decline in the housing market. To fight recession, the government will reverse its fiscal policy. Instead of trying to reduce spending, the government will try to encourage it. The government can increase its own spending with the aim of boosting production, increasing jobs, and raising incomes. The government can also reduce taxes, leaving individuals and businesses with more money to spend and invest. During a recession, the Federal Reserve expands the money supply. This encourages producers to make more goods, giving the economy a needed boost.

The federal government has two main ways to manipulate the economy. The first is fiscal policy, in which the government increases or decreases taxes and government spending to influence the economy. The second is monetary policy, in which the Federal Reserve increases or decreases the supply of money to stimulate or slow the economy.

8. Which of the following describes the main similarity between monetary and fiscal policy?

   (A) Both affect the amount of money circulating in the economy.

   (B) Both are budgetary tools of local and state governments.

   (C) Both involve raising taxes.

   (D) Both involve reducing taxes.

The correct answer is (A). Both monetary and fiscal policies are tools the government uses to control the money supply circulating in the economy. Increasing the money supply by lowering taxes or lowering interest rates boosts the economy, and decreasing the money supply slows the economy.

9. Which of the following policies might the Federal Reserve implement to slow rapid economic growth and to decrease the risk of inflation?

   (A) Buy back government securities from bond holders.

   (B) Lower the discount interest rates it charges banks to borrow money from the Federal Reserve.

   (C) Lower income tax rates on all citizens.

   (D) Sell government bonds and Treasury bills to investors.

The correct answer is (D). All the policies except selling government bonds and Treasury bills are enacted to stimulate the economy. When the Federal Reserve sells government bonds and Treasury bills, it decreases the money supply by removing cash from the economy in exchange for bonds.

VARIATIONS OF GOVERNMENT EFFECTS OVER TIME

The role of the U.S. federal government in the economy has been a central debate among economists and politicians for more than 200 years. Many economists argue for a strict interpretation of the Constitution that argues for a limited or no role of the federal government in the economy, while others argue for an increased role of the federal government.

For much of the early years in United States history, many Americans embraced the idea of **laissez-faire,** a French phrase that means "let people do as they choose." Supporters of laissez-faire believe the government should not interfere in the economy other than to protect private property rights and maintain peace. They argue that if the government regulates the economy, it increases costs and eventually hurts the economy and society more than it helps. Laissez-faire relies on supply and demand, rather than the government, to regulate wages and prices. Supporters believe a free market with competing companies leads to greater efficiency and creates more wealth for everyone. Laissez-faire advocates also support low taxes and limited government debt to ensure that private citizens, not the government, will make most of the decisions about how the nation's wealth is spent.

Although the country generally followed laissez-faire policies, the federal government did introduce policies that led to more governmental reach into the economy. By the end of the Civil War in 1865, tariff rates had tripled. **Tariffs** are taxes placed on imported goods. This made it more expensive for Americans to purchase these goods and led to decreased foreign trade because foreign countries responded by increasing tariffs on American exports. The government also provided large loans and subsidies to promote western expansion that greatly impacted large industries.

In the early years of the 1900s the federal government also implemented polices aimed at reigning in the power of large business organizations, or trusts. Much of this was an attempt to prevent these large organizations from monopolizing crucial industries. President Theodore Roosevelt's actions earned him the nickname "Trustbuster." Roosevelt and other American leaders also focused on regulating big business by creating the Department of Commerce and Labor in 1903.

American attitudes about regulation changed significantly in the twentieth century. In the 1970s, policy makers grew increasingly concerned that economic regulation protected inefficient companies at the expense of consumers. This led to a succession of laws easing regulation. Leaders across the political spectrum generally favored economic deregulation during the 1970s, 1980s, and 1990s. During the presidency of Ronald Reagan in the 1980s, the government also relaxed rules to protect workers, consumers, and the environment, arguing that regulation interfered with free enterprise, increased the costs of doing business, and consequently contributed to inflation.

Directions: Use the following information to answer the two questions that follow.

The political cartoon below was published in 1888 in *Judge* magazine, a political satire publication. The original caption read "Goods Will Be So Much Cheaper—Democratic argument. But what will become of all the American Industries?" The cartoon shows a man labeled "Mills" opening a "protection" gate so that a waterfall of "European pauper manufacturers" floods American industries and mills. Several of the buildings are labeled "American Factory."

10. Which of the following statements might best reflect the artist's view about the cause of the flood of European goods and the destruction of American factories?

   (A) American big-business monopolies

   (B) Inefficient American factories

   (C) Government laissez-faire economic policies

   (D) Strict government regulation of American industries

The correct answer is (C). Because the gate is labeled "Protection," the implication is that any protection that American factories had was no longer helping. The primary protection was provided by government policies. Laissez-faire policies support as little governmental involvement as possible.

11. Which of the following policies might have prevented the flood of European products?

    (A) Allowing more non-European products in to prevent European monopolies on imports

    (B) Tariffs placed on European manufactured goods

    (C) Tightening regulation on American factories to make them more productive

    (D) Cutting all American exports to European countries

The correct answer is (B). Tariffs can help to protect smaller American industries from foreign competition that can crowd out American businesses.

SUMMING IT UP

- Economics questions on the HiSET® Social Studies subtest will test your comprehension by giving you a series of passages, graphs, political cartoons, and more.

- Economics examines how people make choices to satisfy their **needs** (the basic things people must have to survive, such as food, shelter, and clothing) and **wants** (things that are not necessary for survival but make life more comfortable) with their limited resources. Prices of goods and services are determined by the relationship between **supply** (the quantity of a good or service that a producer is willing to sell at a certain price) and **demand** (the degree to which people want a product and are willing and able to pay for it).

- **Productivity** is the amount of output per unit of input and is often used as a measure of an economy's health. Technological advances in society enable goods to be mass-produced, requiring fewer workers to produce more goods and services, which leads to increased productivity. On the downside, new technology destroys some jobs at the gain of this technological innovation.

- Economic interdependence is when people must rely on others to provide most of the goods and services they consume—this means economic events in one part of the world can have a large effect in other parts. The more individuals and nations specialize and trade, the more dependent they become on each other to supply their needs and wants. This causes a circular flow, where one person's or nation's spending is another person's or nation's revenue.

- The federal government has considerable impact on the U.S. economy. Among many other functions, it determines taxes, employs several million people, borrows and spends money, and works to create the U.S. government budget. Government departments also establish laws that maintain property rights and enforce legal and fair business standards. **The Federal Reserve System** manages the total amount of money available for lending and borrowing in the private banking system.

- **Inflation** occurs when total demand and spending are greater than total production. To control inflation, the government may enact fiscal policies that reduce its spending. A **recession** is a period of general economic decline, typically defined as a decline in GDP for two or more consecutive quarters. To fight recession, the government will encourage spending. During a recession, the Federal Reserve expands the money supply, encouraging producers to make more goods.

- Early on in United States history, many Americans supported the concept of **laissez-faire,** a French phrase that means "let people do as they choose." They argued that government should not interfere in the economy, because interference would increase costs and eventually hurt society. In the early twentieth century, the federal government implemented polices aimed at reigning in the power of large business organizations (trusts) to prevent these large organizations from monopolizing crucial industries. In the 1980s, the government relaxed rules to protect workers, consumers, and the environment, arguing that regulation interfered with free enterprise and contributed to inflation.

Geography

OVERVIEW

- **Physical geography**
- **Human geography**
- **Economic, political, and social factors affecting geography**
- **Summing It Up**

Geography is the study of the physical features on Earth and the ways in which people have adapted to these features. Geographers are scientists who study the physical and cultural geographic features on Earth. Only about 10 percent of questions on the HiSET® Social Studies subtest will cover geography. Let's take a quick look at the topic so you'll have a basic familiarity of it going into test day.

PHYSICAL GEOGRAPHY

Physical geographic features include land, water, mountains, plains, and plateaus. Human architecture and human-caused changes to geographic features are considered cultural geographic features.

Seven large landmasses, called continents, make up most of Earth's land surface. The continents are Africa, Antarctica, Asia, Australia, Europe, North America, and South America. Differences in elevation help define the different kinds of landforms found on these continents, such as plains, plateaus, hills, and mountains. Wind and water are constantly reshaping these landforms, however, through the process of **erosion.** Water is one of the most important and abundant substances found on Earth's surface, covering three-fourths of the planet's surface.

Geographers often categorize areas on Earth as **regions.** A region has one or more significant characteristics that make it unique from other nearby areas. A region can be made up of part of a country, the entire country, or a group of countries. The characteristics that distinguish a region may be physical characteristics or cultural characteristics.

chapter 20

Directions: Use the following information to answer the two questions that follow.

Two of the most important tools geographers use in their work are globes and maps. A globe is a sphere that is a model of the Earth. Because both the Earth and a globe are round, a globe is the most accurate way to examine Earth's surfaces. Some information geographers are interested in, however, is not effectively shown on a globe. Consequently, maps are often the most effective tools to study geography. There are many different types of maps that convey a wide variety of information. Political maps show political borders or boundaries between countries, states, and counties. Population maps show the population density or how many people live in a region or area. Topographical maps show physical geographic features like valleys, rivers, mountains, hills, or prairies. A contour map illustrates the elevation of physical features.

1. Which of the following would be the best use of a globe?
   (A) To study the street layout of London, England
   (B) To find all the major cities in each county in the state of Texas
   (C) To use as an elevation guide while hiking in the mountains of Peru
   (D) To get an accurate visual picture of the nearest landmasses to the North and South Poles

The correct answer is (D). Because a flat map cannot accurately illustrate a round surface and distances, a globe is the most accurate representation of the Earth's surface, especially around the poles.

2. Which of the following maps would be most useful in locating and identifying the major rivers in Africa?
   (A) A political map
   (B) A contour map
   (C) A population map
   (D) A topographical map

The correct answer is (D). A topographical map shows and identifies political boundaries, city populations, capital cities, bodies of water, and much more.

HUMAN GEOGRAPHY

Human geography is the study of where humans live and why. Human geographers also study the interactions of humans with their environment and draw on some basic elements of physical geography. Climate and landforms have always had significant influence on where people choose to settle. Over the course of human history, people have tended to settle in favorable physical environments. For example, the majority of settlements and cities have always been built along seacoasts and rivers. These locations offer good transportation routes and water for drinking and growing crops.

Generally, people on all continents tend to live crowded together in cities and on fertile farmland or in areas that contain natural resources needed to survive or prosper.

Population distributions are also greatly affected by how urban and rural areas are developed. Before the 1900s, the vast majority of people around the world made their living by farming and lived in rural, or agricultural, regions. As manufacturing and industry have grown, more and more people have moved to cities or large urban areas. When urban areas become crowded, people often move away, shifting the population into the nearby countryside, leading to suburban development. Suburban growth, including housing and commercial development, often takes up land once used for agricultural purposes.

TIP

In wealthy countries, more people live in urban areas, or areas in and around cities, than in rural areas.

Directions: Use the following map, which shows the population growth of each state, to answer the two questions that follow.

3. Based on the map, which of the following statements is accurate?

   (A) West Virginia saw growth at the same rate as Illinois.

   (B) The southwest states of New Mexico and Arizona outpaced the northeast states of New York and Pennsylvania.

   (C) States west of Minnesota and Iowa and east of Oregon and Washington saw only minimal population growth.

   (D) Georgia experienced the same increase as Nevada.

The correct answer is (C). Only statement (C) can be concluded from the information on the map.

4. Which of the following is a conclusion that can be drawn from the map?

   (A) All states on the East Coast saw huge population increases.

   (B) Mississippi actually lost population.

   (C) Texas and California saw the most significant population increases.

   (D) North and South Dakota did not see any population increases.

The correct answer is (C). Both California and Texas saw the highest population increases. None of the other statements can be determined by the map. None of the other statements can be determined by the map.

ECONOMIC, POLITICAL, AND SOCIAL FACTORS AFFECTING GEOGRAPHY

People tend to move where there are resources, jobs, and other favorable conditions. These conditions constantly change, however, because of politics, economic development, climate, and social and cultural factors.

Economic Factors

The movement and growth of population groups play a major role in defining and changing geographic regions. As human populations have grown, they have dramatically altered the natural environments. For example, if not properly managed, large commercial agriculture practices can deplete or degrade water supplies and the soil used to grow crops. As agriculture developed and became necessary for human survival, people cleared large areas of natural forests. Natural grasslands in many regions have also been destroyed to make room for fields of wheat, corn, and other crops. The drive to meet growing food requirements continues today, as large areas of critically important forests have been slashed, including the Amazon rainforest, which helps supply a large portion of oxygen to the Earth and ingredients used in many of the world's medicines. Very large areas of land are turning into deserts because of the removal of trees and shrubs that are crucial to holding fertile topsoil in place. In addition, concentrated areas of manufacturing and urbanization increase air and water pollution. Consequently, food and water supplies can become endangered.

Political Factors

Political conflicts can also change the cultural character of a region. Disputes over boundaries and wars between nations have led to significant local population shifts. For example, the Jewish Holocaust during World War II led to the loss of millions of European Jews through deportation and death camps. After World War II, the state of Israel was established, attracting many Jews to the Middle East. Continuing conflicts within the Middle East and other disputed regions have led to further population shifts of different groups of people in the affected areas.

Social Factors

As more natural environments have been impacted by human development, calls for conservation have become louder. Conservation is the careful use of natural resources such as soil, plant and animal life, water, air, and mineral reserves. Natural resources are either renewable or nonrenewable. Renewable resources can be sustained through replacement. For example, trees that have been cut down can be replaced by planting new trees. Solar and wind energy are renewable because the supply of sunlight and wind never runs out. Nonrenewable resources are those that people use but cannot replace. Oil, natural gas, and minerals like iron, copper, and coal are examples of non-renewable resources. People who promote the sustainable use of resources are called conservationists. In addition to protecting natural resources for economic reasons, carefully using natural resources helps sustain the ecosystems on Earth that help keep the planet healthy. Healthy ecosystems contribute to providing crucial resources such as water, air, and plant and animal life.

> **Directions:** Use the following information to answer the two questions that follow.

Although they cover only about 6 percent of the Earth's land surface, rainforests are home to more than 50 percent of global biodiversity. Rainforests take in huge amounts of carbon dioxide and release oxygen through photosynthesis, which has also given them the nickname "lungs of the planet." They also store very large amounts of carbon, and so cutting and burning their biomass contributes to global climate change. All major tropical forests, including those in the Americas, Africa, Southeast Asia, and Indonesia, are disappearing. People living in these regions are clearing the forests to make way for livestock and crop production to help sustain and increase food supplies. Tropical deforestation does help feed local populations. However, it can also have significant negative effects, such as the extinction of plants and animals.

5. Based on the information in the passage, which of the following is the most serious threat to the world's rainforests?
   (A) Increasing urban sprawl
   (B) Increases in livestock production
   (C) Climate change
   (D) Human adaption of the Earth's features

The correct answer is (D). Human adaption, such as cutting down and clearing large areas of rainforest, is the most serious threat to the rain forests.

6. Which of the following consequences of rainforest deforestation would have the greatest impact around the world?
   (A) Reduced quantities of carbon in the world's oceans
   (B) More carbon dioxide in the atmosphere
   (C) Too much biodiversity
   (D) Dangerous levels of oxygen in the atmosphere

The correct answer is (B). The methods of deforestation increase the amount of carbon dioxide released into the atmosphere because of the huge amount of carbon in rainforests. Carbon is released in the form of carbon dioxide—a major greenhouse gas and contributor to climate change.

SUMMING IT UP

- The seven **continents** that make up most of Earth's land surface are Africa, Antarctica, Asia, Australia, Europe, North America, and South America. Water, one of the most important and abundant substances found on Earth's surface, covers three-fourths of the planet.

- Human geography explores where humans live and why. For example, the majority of settlements and cities have always been built along seacoasts and rivers, locations near transportation routes and water for drinking and growing crops. Before the twentieth century, the majority of people around the world made their living by farming and lived in rural regions. As manufacturing and industry have grown, more people have moved to cities or large urban areas. Overcrowding in urban areas then leads to suburban development.

- The geography of both large and small areas is affected by outside factors brought about by climate and people through economic development and changing politics. Social and cultural factors also alter geography, either for the better (increased awareness of renewable energy sources like solar and wind energy) or for the worse (use of nonrenewable resources like oil and natural gas and minerals like iron, copper, and coal).

PART VII
TWO PRACTICE TESTS

PRACTICE TEST 1

PRACTICE TEST 2

ANSWER SHEET PRACTICE TEST 1

Language Arts—Reading

1. Ⓐ Ⓑ Ⓒ Ⓓ	11. Ⓐ Ⓑ Ⓒ Ⓓ	21. Ⓐ Ⓑ Ⓒ Ⓓ	31. Ⓐ Ⓑ Ⓒ Ⓓ
2. Ⓐ Ⓑ Ⓒ Ⓓ	12. Ⓐ Ⓑ Ⓒ Ⓓ	22. Ⓐ Ⓑ Ⓒ Ⓓ	32. Ⓐ Ⓑ Ⓒ Ⓓ
3. Ⓐ Ⓑ Ⓒ Ⓓ	13. Ⓐ Ⓑ Ⓒ Ⓓ	23. Ⓐ Ⓑ Ⓒ Ⓓ	33. Ⓐ Ⓑ Ⓒ Ⓓ
4. Ⓐ Ⓑ Ⓒ Ⓓ	14. Ⓐ Ⓑ Ⓒ Ⓓ	24. Ⓐ Ⓑ Ⓒ Ⓓ	34. Ⓐ Ⓑ Ⓒ Ⓓ
5. Ⓐ Ⓑ Ⓒ Ⓓ	15. Ⓐ Ⓑ Ⓒ Ⓓ	25. Ⓐ Ⓑ Ⓒ Ⓓ	35. Ⓐ Ⓑ Ⓒ Ⓓ
6. Ⓐ Ⓑ Ⓒ Ⓓ	16. Ⓐ Ⓑ Ⓒ Ⓓ	26. Ⓐ Ⓑ Ⓒ Ⓓ	36. Ⓐ Ⓑ Ⓒ Ⓓ
7. Ⓐ Ⓑ Ⓒ Ⓓ	17. Ⓐ Ⓑ Ⓒ Ⓓ	27. Ⓐ Ⓑ Ⓒ Ⓓ	37. Ⓐ Ⓑ Ⓒ Ⓓ
8. Ⓐ Ⓑ Ⓒ Ⓓ	18. Ⓐ Ⓑ Ⓒ Ⓓ	28. Ⓐ Ⓑ Ⓒ Ⓓ	38. Ⓐ Ⓑ Ⓒ Ⓓ
9. Ⓐ Ⓑ Ⓒ Ⓓ	19. Ⓐ Ⓑ Ⓒ Ⓓ	29. Ⓐ Ⓑ Ⓒ Ⓓ	39. Ⓐ Ⓑ Ⓒ Ⓓ
10. Ⓐ Ⓑ Ⓒ Ⓓ	20. Ⓐ Ⓑ Ⓒ Ⓓ	30. Ⓐ Ⓑ Ⓒ Ⓓ	40. Ⓐ Ⓑ Ⓒ Ⓓ

Language Arts—Writing

Part 1

1. Ⓐ Ⓑ Ⓒ Ⓓ	11. Ⓐ Ⓑ Ⓒ Ⓓ	21. Ⓐ Ⓑ Ⓒ Ⓓ	31. Ⓐ Ⓑ Ⓒ Ⓓ	41. Ⓐ Ⓑ Ⓒ Ⓓ
2. Ⓐ Ⓑ Ⓒ Ⓓ	12. Ⓐ Ⓑ Ⓒ Ⓓ	22. Ⓐ Ⓑ Ⓒ Ⓓ	32. Ⓐ Ⓑ Ⓒ Ⓓ	42. Ⓐ Ⓑ Ⓒ Ⓓ
3. Ⓐ Ⓑ Ⓒ Ⓓ	13. Ⓐ Ⓑ Ⓒ Ⓓ	23. Ⓐ Ⓑ Ⓒ Ⓓ	33. Ⓐ Ⓑ Ⓒ Ⓓ	43. Ⓐ Ⓑ Ⓒ Ⓓ
4. Ⓐ Ⓑ Ⓒ Ⓓ	14. Ⓐ Ⓑ Ⓒ Ⓓ	24. Ⓐ Ⓑ Ⓒ Ⓓ	34. Ⓐ Ⓑ Ⓒ Ⓓ	44. Ⓐ Ⓑ Ⓒ Ⓓ
5. Ⓐ Ⓑ Ⓒ Ⓓ	15. Ⓐ Ⓑ Ⓒ Ⓓ	25. Ⓐ Ⓑ Ⓒ Ⓓ	35. Ⓐ Ⓑ Ⓒ Ⓓ	45. Ⓐ Ⓑ Ⓒ Ⓓ
6. Ⓐ Ⓑ Ⓒ Ⓓ	16. Ⓐ Ⓑ Ⓒ Ⓓ	26. Ⓐ Ⓑ Ⓒ Ⓓ	36. Ⓐ Ⓑ Ⓒ Ⓓ	46. Ⓐ Ⓑ Ⓒ Ⓓ
7. Ⓐ Ⓑ Ⓒ Ⓓ	17. Ⓐ Ⓑ Ⓒ Ⓓ	27. Ⓐ Ⓑ Ⓒ Ⓓ	37. Ⓐ Ⓑ Ⓒ Ⓓ	47. Ⓐ Ⓑ Ⓒ Ⓓ
8. Ⓐ Ⓑ Ⓒ Ⓓ	18. Ⓐ Ⓑ Ⓒ Ⓓ	28. Ⓐ Ⓑ Ⓒ Ⓓ	38. Ⓐ Ⓑ Ⓒ Ⓓ	48. Ⓐ Ⓑ Ⓒ Ⓓ
9. Ⓐ Ⓑ Ⓒ Ⓓ	19. Ⓐ Ⓑ Ⓒ Ⓓ	29. Ⓐ Ⓑ Ⓒ Ⓓ	39. Ⓐ Ⓑ Ⓒ Ⓓ	49. Ⓐ Ⓑ Ⓒ Ⓓ
10. Ⓐ Ⓑ Ⓒ Ⓓ	20. Ⓐ Ⓑ Ⓒ Ⓓ	30. Ⓐ Ⓑ Ⓒ Ⓓ	40. Ⓐ Ⓑ Ⓒ Ⓓ	50. Ⓐ Ⓑ Ⓒ Ⓓ

answer sheet

Part 2

_____

_____

_____

_____

_____

_____

_____

_____

_____

_____

_____

_____

_____

_____

_____

_____

_____

_____

_____

_____

_____

_____

_____

answer sheet

Mathematics

1. Ⓐ Ⓑ Ⓒ Ⓓ Ⓔ 11. Ⓐ Ⓑ Ⓒ Ⓓ Ⓔ 21. Ⓐ Ⓑ Ⓒ Ⓓ Ⓔ 31. Ⓐ Ⓑ Ⓒ Ⓓ Ⓔ 41. Ⓐ Ⓑ Ⓒ Ⓓ Ⓔ

2. Ⓐ Ⓑ Ⓒ Ⓓ Ⓔ 12. Ⓐ Ⓑ Ⓒ Ⓓ Ⓔ 22. Ⓐ Ⓑ Ⓒ Ⓓ Ⓔ 32. Ⓐ Ⓑ Ⓒ Ⓓ Ⓔ 42. Ⓐ Ⓑ Ⓒ Ⓓ Ⓔ

3. Ⓐ Ⓑ Ⓒ Ⓓ Ⓔ 13. Ⓐ Ⓑ Ⓒ Ⓓ Ⓔ 23. Ⓐ Ⓑ Ⓒ Ⓓ Ⓔ 33. Ⓐ Ⓑ Ⓒ Ⓓ Ⓔ 43. Ⓐ Ⓑ Ⓒ Ⓓ Ⓔ

4. Ⓐ Ⓑ Ⓒ Ⓓ Ⓔ 14. Ⓐ Ⓑ Ⓒ Ⓓ Ⓔ 24. Ⓐ Ⓑ Ⓒ Ⓓ Ⓔ 34. Ⓐ Ⓑ Ⓒ Ⓓ Ⓔ 44. Ⓐ Ⓑ Ⓒ Ⓓ Ⓔ

5. Ⓐ Ⓑ Ⓒ Ⓓ Ⓔ 15. Ⓐ Ⓑ Ⓒ Ⓓ Ⓔ 25. Ⓐ Ⓑ Ⓒ Ⓓ Ⓔ 35. Ⓐ Ⓑ Ⓒ Ⓓ Ⓔ 45. Ⓐ Ⓑ Ⓒ Ⓓ Ⓔ

6. Ⓐ Ⓑ Ⓒ Ⓓ Ⓔ 16. Ⓐ Ⓑ Ⓒ Ⓓ Ⓔ 26. Ⓐ Ⓑ Ⓒ Ⓓ Ⓔ 36. Ⓐ Ⓑ Ⓒ Ⓓ Ⓔ 46. Ⓐ Ⓑ Ⓒ Ⓓ Ⓔ

7. Ⓐ Ⓑ Ⓒ Ⓓ Ⓔ 17. Ⓐ Ⓑ Ⓒ Ⓓ Ⓔ 27. Ⓐ Ⓑ Ⓒ Ⓓ Ⓔ 37. Ⓐ Ⓑ Ⓒ Ⓓ Ⓔ 47. Ⓐ Ⓑ Ⓒ Ⓓ Ⓔ

8. Ⓐ Ⓑ Ⓒ Ⓓ Ⓔ 18. Ⓐ Ⓑ Ⓒ Ⓓ Ⓔ 28. Ⓐ Ⓑ Ⓒ Ⓓ Ⓔ 38. Ⓐ Ⓑ Ⓒ Ⓓ Ⓔ 48. Ⓐ Ⓑ Ⓒ Ⓓ Ⓔ

9. Ⓐ Ⓑ Ⓒ Ⓓ Ⓔ 19. Ⓐ Ⓑ Ⓒ Ⓓ Ⓔ 29. Ⓐ Ⓑ Ⓒ Ⓓ Ⓔ 39. Ⓐ Ⓑ Ⓒ Ⓓ Ⓔ 49. Ⓐ Ⓑ Ⓒ Ⓓ Ⓔ

10. Ⓐ Ⓑ Ⓒ Ⓓ Ⓔ 20. Ⓐ Ⓑ Ⓒ Ⓓ Ⓔ 30. Ⓐ Ⓑ Ⓒ Ⓓ Ⓔ 40. Ⓐ Ⓑ Ⓒ Ⓓ Ⓔ 50. Ⓐ Ⓑ Ⓒ Ⓓ Ⓔ

Science

1. Ⓐ Ⓑ Ⓒ Ⓓ 11. Ⓐ Ⓑ Ⓒ Ⓓ 21. Ⓐ Ⓑ Ⓒ Ⓓ 31. Ⓐ Ⓑ Ⓒ Ⓓ 41. Ⓐ Ⓑ Ⓒ Ⓓ

2. Ⓐ Ⓑ Ⓒ Ⓓ 12. Ⓐ Ⓑ Ⓒ Ⓓ 22. Ⓐ Ⓑ Ⓒ Ⓓ 32. Ⓐ Ⓑ Ⓒ Ⓓ 42. Ⓐ Ⓑ Ⓒ Ⓓ

3. Ⓐ Ⓑ Ⓒ Ⓓ 13. Ⓐ Ⓑ Ⓒ Ⓓ 23. Ⓐ Ⓑ Ⓒ Ⓓ 33. Ⓐ Ⓑ Ⓒ Ⓓ 43. Ⓐ Ⓑ Ⓒ Ⓓ

4. Ⓐ Ⓑ Ⓒ Ⓓ 14. Ⓐ Ⓑ Ⓒ Ⓓ 24. Ⓐ Ⓑ Ⓒ Ⓓ 34. Ⓐ Ⓑ Ⓒ Ⓓ 44. Ⓐ Ⓑ Ⓒ Ⓓ

5. Ⓐ Ⓑ Ⓒ Ⓓ 15. Ⓐ Ⓑ Ⓒ Ⓓ 25. Ⓐ Ⓑ Ⓒ Ⓓ 35. Ⓐ Ⓑ Ⓒ Ⓓ 45. Ⓐ Ⓑ Ⓒ Ⓓ

6. Ⓐ Ⓑ Ⓒ Ⓓ 16. Ⓐ Ⓑ Ⓒ Ⓓ 26. Ⓐ Ⓑ Ⓒ Ⓓ 36. Ⓐ Ⓑ Ⓒ Ⓓ 46. Ⓐ Ⓑ Ⓒ Ⓓ

7. Ⓐ Ⓑ Ⓒ Ⓓ 17. Ⓐ Ⓑ Ⓒ Ⓓ 27. Ⓐ Ⓑ Ⓒ Ⓓ 37. Ⓐ Ⓑ Ⓒ Ⓓ 47. Ⓐ Ⓑ Ⓒ Ⓓ

8. Ⓐ Ⓑ Ⓒ Ⓓ 18. Ⓐ Ⓑ Ⓒ Ⓓ 28. Ⓐ Ⓑ Ⓒ Ⓓ 38. Ⓐ Ⓑ Ⓒ Ⓓ 48. Ⓐ Ⓑ Ⓒ Ⓓ

9. Ⓐ Ⓑ Ⓒ Ⓓ 19. Ⓐ Ⓑ Ⓒ Ⓓ 29. Ⓐ Ⓑ Ⓒ Ⓓ 39. Ⓐ Ⓑ Ⓒ Ⓓ 49. Ⓐ Ⓑ Ⓒ Ⓓ

10. Ⓐ Ⓑ Ⓒ Ⓓ 20. Ⓐ Ⓑ Ⓒ Ⓓ 30. Ⓐ Ⓑ Ⓒ Ⓓ 40. Ⓐ Ⓑ Ⓒ Ⓓ 50. Ⓐ Ⓑ Ⓒ Ⓓ

Social Studies

1. (A) (B) (C) (D)　　11. (A) (B) (C) (D)　　21. (A) (B) (C) (D)　　31. (A) (B) (C) (D)　　41. (A) (B) (C) (D)
2. (A) (B) (C) (D)　　12. (A) (B) (C) (D)　　22. (A) (B) (C) (D)　　32. (A) (B) (C) (D)　　42. (A) (B) (C) (D)
3. (A) (B) (C) (D)　　13. (A) (B) (C) (D)　　23. (A) (B) (C) (D)　　33. (A) (B) (C) (D)　　43. (A) (B) (C) (D)
4. (A) (B) (C) (D)　　14. (A) (B) (C) (D)　　24. (A) (B) (C) (D)　　34. (A) (B) (C) (D)　　44. (A) (B) (C) (D)
5. (A) (B) (C) (D)　　15. (A) (B) (C) (D)　　25. (A) (B) (C) (D)　　35. (A) (B) (C) (D)　　45. (A) (B) (C) (D)
6. (A) (B) (C) (D)　　16. (A) (B) (C) (D)　　26. (A) (B) (C) (D)　　36. (A) (B) (C) (D)　　46. (A) (B) (C) (D)
7. (A) (B) (C) (D)　　17. (A) (B) (C) (D)　　27. (A) (B) (C) (D)　　37. (A) (B) (C) (D)　　47. (A) (B) (C) (D)
8. (A) (B) (C) (D)　　18. (A) (B) (C) (D)　　28. (A) (B) (C) (D)　　38. (A) (B) (C) (D)　　48. (A) (B) (C) (D)
9. (A) (B) (C) (D)　　19. (A) (B) (C) (D)　　29. (A) (B) (C) (D)　　39. (A) (B) (C) (D)　　49. (A) (B) (C) (D)
10. (A) (B) (C) (D)　　20. (A) (B) (C) (D)　　30. (A) (B) (C) (D)　　40. (A) (B) (C) (D)　　50. (A) (B) (C) (D)

answer sheet

Practice Test 1

The following is a practice test that mimics the official HiSET® exam. For the best preparation, follow the allotted time for each subtest.

For each question, choose the best answer and mark your choice on the answer sheet. Work as quickly as you can; do not spend too much time on a question that you can't answer. Skip it and return to it later, if you have time. If you decide to skip a question, make sure to also skip a row on the answer sheet. This will ensure that you are marking the correct space on the answer sheet for all questions.

Mark all your answers on the answer sheet. Mark only one answer to each question. If you decide to change your answer, completely erase your mark. If more than one answer is marked, the question will not be counted.

Remember, don't leave a question unanswered. Your score is derived from the number of questions you answer correctly. You will not receive a penalty for a wrong answer. It just won't contribute to your score.

LANGUAGE ARTS—READING

40 Questions • 65 Minutes

QUESTIONS 1 THROUGH 6 ARE BASED ON THE FOLLOWING PASSAGE.

Throughout history, lasting and positive change often comes in the wake of unimaginable tragedy. The Triangle Shirtwaist Factory fire, a
5 horrific disaster that occurred in 1911 and led to the death of 146 garment factory workers, helped usher in sweeping and essential landmark reforms regarding labor
10 laws, permissible working conditions, and employee rights in the United States.

The 10-story building that housed the Triangle Shirtwaist
15 Factory was located in New York City, in Greenwich Village. This garment-producing company, which manufactured women's blouses (known colloquially in the
20 era as shirtwaists), occupied the top three floors of the building. The factory, on average, employed approximately 500 employees, who toiled long hours in substandard
25 conditions for meager wages—a work environment that would not be legally permissible today. The vast majority of employees were young immigrant women (many
30 of whom would now be considered underage and in violation of child labor laws) who labored for nine hour days, six to seven days a week, in hot and uncomfortable
35 conditions. Employees cut, sewed, and assembled blouses all day, often with no breaks allowed, for around $10 a week—wages that would be well below minimum
40 wage in today's dollars.

On March 25, 1911, just after 4:00 pm while shirtwaist manufacturing was moving full steam ahead as on any other day, a
45 wooden bin full of hundreds of pounds of textile scraps suddenly caught fire (the fire department later concluded that this was the likely result of either a match or
50 cigarette that was carelessly tossed away, or an errant spark from a nearby sewing machine). Because of the amount of fabric and wood in the surrounding area, the flames
55 quickly spread. An inadequate coordinated fire safety and exit strategy, a lack of audible fire alarms on at least one of the three factory floors, and some of the exits
60 being either locked due to carelessness or blocked by fire led to a highly chaotic scene as the flames spread and choking black smoke filled the dank, poorly ventilated
65 rooms. According to some reports, a number of stairwell exits were locked intentionally to help keep employees working and to control their exit to monitor for theft at the
70 end of long work shifts. Although some workers were able to flee in the ensuing bedlam, 123 women and 23 men were killed in this tragic event, either due to fire or
75 smoke inhalation, or as the result of jumping from the roof or from windows in an attempt to escape.

As a result of this tragedy— which many historians have
80 claimed was entirely avoidable—a call for improved employee conditions and legislative reform to protect the rights of workers grew. The Committee for Public
85 Safety, the Factory Investigating Commission, and the American Society of Safety Engineers were formed in New York City to root out and eradicate similarly haz-
90 ardous working conditions, and

to lobby for widespread reform and improvements. The strength, power, and voice of the International Ladies' Garment Workers
95 Union grew dramatically in the wake of this tragedy, in an effort to fight for improved working conditions for its members. Necessary reforms that followed the Triangle
100 Shirtwaist Factory fire include dozens of new laws that mandated improved employee work hours, wages, and working conditions, as well as a number of new laws
105 pertaining to fire safety.

Today, the Asch building that housed the Triangle Shirtwaist Factory is now a part of New York University, and stands as a his-
110 torical landmark and a sobering yet inspiring reminder of both our nation's past and its evolution regarding labor laws and employee rights.

1. This passage is mainly about
   (A) the author's opinions regarding employee safety and rights.
   (B) the Triangle Shirtwaist Factory fire and ensuing labor reforms.
   (C) the history of the Triangle Shirtwaist Factory.
   (D) the evolution of the International Ladies' Garment Workers Union.

2. The tone of this passage can best be described as
   (A) informative.
   (B) critical.
   (C) enthusiastic.
   (D) doubtful.

3. What does "errant" (line 51) mean?
   (A) Burning
   (B) Roaming
   (C) Extra
   (D) Stray

4. The author of this passage most likely believes that reforms that followed the Triangle Shirtwaist Factory fire were
   (A) not important.
   (B) long overdue.
   (C) helpful, but too expensive.
   (D) came too soon.

5. Based on details in the passage, which of the following can be concluded about the time in which it was written?
   (A) Not much had changed since the time of the Triangle Shirtwaist Factory fire.
   (B) Labor laws are more favorable than in the era that the Triangle Shirtwaist Factory operated.
   (C) Labor laws have gotten worse since the Triangle Shirtwaist Factory fire.
   (D) The author would rather live in the era when the Triangle Shirtwaist Factory operated.

6. Which of the following is *not* mentioned as a positive reform resulting from the Triangle Shirtwaist Factory tragedy?
   (A) Improved employee work hours
   (B) Better workplace fire safety regulations
   (C) Greater health insurance benefits for all employees
   (D) Fairer employee wages

QUESTIONS 7 THROUGH 12 ARE BASED ON THE FOLLOWING PASSAGE.

People develop their literary tastes as they read more. This excerpt from a work of non-fiction attempts to clarify some misconceptions about developing one's literary tastes.

At the beginning a misconception must be removed from the path. Many people, if not most, look on literary taste as an elegant accom-
5 plishment, by acquiring which they will complete themselves, and make themselves finally fit as members of a correct society. They are secretly ashamed of their igno-
10 rance of literature, in the same way as they would be ashamed of their ignorance of etiquette at a high entertainment, or of their inability to ride a horse if suddenly called
15 upon to do so. There are certain things that a man ought to know, or to know about, and literature is one of them: such is their idea. They have learnt to dress themselves
20 with propriety, and to behave with propriety on all occasions; they are fairly "up" in the questions of the day; by industry and enterprise they are succeeding in their voca-
25 tions; it behooves them, then, not to forget that an acquaintance with literature is an indispensable part of a self-respecting man's personal baggage. Painting doesn't matter;
30 music doesn't matter very much. But "everyone is supposed to know" about literature. Then, literature is such a charming distraction! Literary taste thus serves two
35 purposes: as a certificate of correct culture and as a private pastime. A young professor of mathematics, immense at mathematics and games, dangerous at chess, capable
40 of Haydn on the violin, once said to me, after listening to some chat on books, "Yes, I must take up literature." As though saying: "I was rather forgetting literature.
45 However, I've polished off all these other things. I'll have a try at literature now."

This attitude, or any attitude which resembles it, is wrong. To
50 him who really comprehends what literature is, and what the function of literature is, this attitude is simply ludicrous. It is also fatal to the formation of literary taste.
55 People who regard literary taste simply as an accomplishment, and literature simply as a distraction, will never truly succeed either in acquiring the accomplishment
60 or in using it half-acquired as a distraction; though the one is the most perfect of distractions, and though the others unsurpassed by any other accomplishment in
65 elegance or in power to impress the universal snobbery of civilized mankind. Literature, instead of being an accessory, is the fundamental sine qua non of complete
70 living.

Excerpt from *Literary Taste: How to Form It* by Arnold Bennett.

7. Read the following sentence from lines 15–18:

There are certain things that a man ought to know, or to know about, and literature is one of them: such is their idea.

In which sentence from the passage does the author essentially restate this information?

(A) But "everyone is supposed to know" about literature.

(B) Then, literature is such a charming distraction!

(C) However, I've polished off all these other things.

(D) This attitude, or any attitude which resembles it, is wrong.

8. Which of the following is an observation in this passage?

   (A) At the beginning a misconception must be removed from the path.

   (B) Many people, if not most, look on literary taste as an elegant accomplishment, by acquiring which they will complete themselves, and make themselves finally fit as members of a correct society.

   (C) A young professor of mathematics, immense at mathematics and games, dangerous at chess, capable of Haydn on the violin, once said to me, after listening to some chat on books, "Yes, I must take up literature."

   (D) Literature, instead of being an accessory, is the fundamental *sine qua non* of complete living.

9. When the author uses the term "snobbery" in line 66, he

   (A) explains how some people enjoy literature.

   (B) describes the motivation behind his essay.

   (C) argues that pretentiousness is the enemy of art.

   (D) criticizes those who do not share his opinion.

10. The author of this passage believes that literature

   (A) is an essential component of life.

   (B) is indicative of one's education.

   (C) should not be debated as much as it is.

   (D) is highly influential on painting and music.

11. Read the following opinion:

   Too often academia is pushed as a career stepping-stone. Instead of emphasizing the personal enrichment that comes with a refined understanding of literature, history, culture, art, and all the other intellectual gift boxes waiting to be unwrapped at the university level, students are programmed to merely "get through" subjects that do not directly relate to their career paths.

   Both Arnold Bennett and the writer of this opinion

   (A) express disdain for the business world.

   (B) believe in the value of personal enrichment.

   (C) think that higher education is over-emphasized.

   (D) value literature above all other art forms.

12. Based on details in paragraph 1, which of the following can be concluded about the time in which this passage was written?

   (A) Reading was considered to be a special skill.

   (B) Horse riding was a very common way to travel.

   (C) The Industrial Revolution had begun recently.

   (D) Chess was more popular than it is today.

QUESTIONS 13 THROUGH 18 ARE BASED ON THE FOLLOWING PASSAGE.

A man wakes one morning to discover he has turned into a giant insect. This excerpt from a work of fiction finds the man struggling to understand his condition.

One morning, when Gregor Samsa woke from troubled dreams, he found himself transformed in his bed into a horrible vermin. He lay
5 on his armour-like back, and if he lifted his head a little he could see his brown belly, slightly domed and divided by arches into stiff sections. The bedding was hardly
10 able to cover it and seemed ready to slide off any moment. His many legs, pitifully thin compared with the size of the rest of him, waved about helplessly as he looked.
15 "What's happened to me?" he thought. It wasn't a dream. His room, a proper human room although a little too small, lay peacefully between its four familiar
20 walls. A collection of textile samples lay spread out on the table – Samsa was a traveling salesman – and above it there hung a picture that he had recently cut out of an illus-
25 trated magazine and housed in a nice, gilded frame. It showed a lady fitted out with a fur hat and fur boa who sat upright, raising a heavy fur muff that covered the whole of
30 her lower arm towards the viewer.
Gregor then turned to look out the window at the dull weather. Drops of rain could be heard hitting the pane, which made him feel
35 quite sad. "How about if I sleep a little bit longer and forget all this nonsense", he thought, but that was something he was unable to do because he was used to sleeping on
40 his right, and in his present state couldn't get into that position. However hard he threw himself onto his right, he always rolled back to where he was. He must

45 have tried it a hundred times, shut his eyes so that he wouldn't have to look at the floundering legs, and only stopped when he began to feel a mild, dull pain there that he had
50 never felt before.
"Oh, God", he thought, "what a strenuous career it is that I've chosen! Traveling day in and day out. Doing business like this takes
55 much more effort than doing your own business at home, and on top of that there's the curse of traveling, worries about making train connections, bad and irregular
60 food, contact with different people all the time so that you can never get to know anyone or become friendly with them."
He felt a slight itch up on his
65 belly; pushed himself slowly up on his back towards the headboard so that he could lift his head better; found where the itch was, and saw that it was covered with lots of
70 little white spots which he didn't know what to make of; and when he tried to feel the place with one of his legs he drew it quickly back because as soon as he touched it he
75 was overcome by a cold shudder.
He slid back into his former position. "Getting up early all the time", he thought, "it makes you stupid. You've got to get enough
80 sleep. Other traveling salesmen live a life of luxury. For instance, whenever I go back to the guest house during the morning to copy out the contract, these gentlemen
85 are always still sitting there eating their breakfasts. I ought to just try that with my boss; I'd get kicked out on the spot. But who knows, maybe that would be the best thing
90 for me."

Excerpt from *Metamorphosis* by Frank Kafka.

13. The author most likely intends Gregor's condition to
   (A) indicate that Gregor is dreaming.
   (B) symbolize Gregor's monstrousness.
   (C) indicate Gregor's exhaustion.
   (D) symbolize Gregor's career.

14. Based on details in paragraph 6, the reader can infer that Gregor is
   (A) spiteful.
   (B) envious.
   (C) vicious.
   (D) fearful.

15. What does "floundering" (line 47) mean?
   (A) Gliding
   (B) Striding
   (C) Jutting
   (D) Thrashing

16. In what way is Gregor different from the salesmen he describes in paragraph 4?
   (A) Gregor is very ambitious.
   (B) Gregor does not work hard.
   (C) Gregor is unable to relax.
   (D) Gregor does not care about his job.

17. Based on this passage, the reader can conclude that Gregor
   (A) had been a giant insect since he was born.
   (B) hopes the other salesmen turn into insects.
   (C) knows the woman in the magazine picture.
   (D) reacts to his condition in an unexpected way.

18. Which of the following best describes the tone of this passage?
   (A) Somber
   (B) Comic
   (C) Frightened
   (D) Excited

QUESTIONS 19 THROUGH 23 ARE BASED ON THE FOLLOWING PASSAGE.

Two years before becoming a member of the House of Representatives, James Madison wrote a famous essay addressed to the people of the State of New York arguing that division into factions was a serious problem facing the United States. In this excerpt for his essay, Madison explains his definition of factions and how he proposes to prevent them.

By a faction, I understand a number of citizens, whether amounting to a majority or a minority of the whole, who are united and actuated by
5 some common impulse of passion, or of interest, adversed to the rights of other citizens, or to the permanent and aggregate interests of the community.

10   There are two methods of curing the mischiefs of faction: the one, by removing its causes; the other, by controlling its effects.

There are again two methods
15 of removing the causes of faction: the one, by destroying the liberty which is essential to its existence; the other, by giving to every citizen the same opinions, the same pas-
20 sions, and the same interests.

It could never be more truly said than of the first remedy, that it was worse than the disease. Liberty is to faction what air is
25 to fire, an aliment without which it instantly expires. But it could not be less folly to abolish liberty, which is essential to political life, because it nourishes faction, than
30 it would be to wish the annihilation

of air, which is essential to animal life, because it imparts to fire its destructive agency.

35 The second expedient is as impracticable as the first would be unwise. As long as the reason of man continues fallible, and he is at liberty to exercise it, different opinions will be formed. As
40 long as the connection subsists between his reason and his self-love, his opinions and his passions will have a reciprocal influence on each other; and the former will
45 be objects to which the latter will attach themselves. The diversity in the faculties of men, from which the rights of property originate, is not less an insuperable obstacle to
50 a uniformity of interests. The protection of these faculties is the first object of government. From the protection of different and unequal faculties of acquiring property,
55 the possession of different degrees and kinds of property immediately results; and from the influence of these on the sentiments and views of the respective proprictors,
60 ensues a division of the society into different interests and parties.

The latent causes of faction are thus sown in the nature of man; and we see them everywhere
65 brought into different degrees of activity, according to the different circumstances of civil society. A zeal for different opinions concerning religion, concerning
70 government, and many other points, as well of speculation as of practice; an attachment to different leaders ambitiously contending for pre-eminence and power; or
75 to persons of other descriptions whose fortunes have been interesting to the human passions, have, in turn, divided mankind into parties, inflamed them with
80 mutual animosity, and rendered them much more disposed to vex and oppress each other than to co-operate for their common good. So strong is this propensity
85 of mankind to fall into mutual animosities, that where no substantial occasion presents itself, the most frivolous and fanciful distinctions have been sufficient
90 to kindle their unfriendly passions and excite their most violent conflicts. But the most common and durable source of factions has been the various and unequal dis-
95 tribution of property. Those who hold and those who are without property have ever formed distinct interests in society. Those who are creditors, and those who are
100 debtors, fall under a like discrimination. A landed interest, a manufacturing interest, a mercantile interest, a moneyed interest, with many lesser interests, grow up of
105 necessity in civilized nations, and divide them into different classes, actuated by different sentiments and views. The regulation of these various and interfering interests
110 forms the principal task of modern legislation, and involves the spirit of party and faction in the necessary and ordinary operations of the government.

Excerpt from *Federalist 10*, by James Madison.

19. Which of the following is an assumption in this passage?

(A) But it could not be less folly to abolish liberty, which is essential to political life, because it nourishes faction, than it would be to wish the annihilation of air, which is essential to animal life, because it imparts to fire its destructive agency.

(B) As long as the reason of man continues fallible, and he is at liberty to exercise it, different opinions will be formed.

(C) Those who hold and those who are without property have ever formed distinct interests in society.

(D) A landed interest, a manufacturing interest, a mercantile interest, a moneyed interest, with many lesser interests, grow up of necessity in civilized nations, and divide them into different classes, actuated by different sentiments and views.

20. The author's use of words such as "destroying," "essential," and "passions" in paragraph 3 help establish a tone that is

(A) dispirited.

(B) heated.

(C) incensed.

(D) tragic.

21. Read the following sentence from paragraph 5:

From the protection of different and unequal faculties of acquiring property, the possession of different degrees and kinds of property immediately results; and from the influence of these on the sentiments and views of the respective proprietors, ensues a division of the society into different interests and parties.

In which sentence does the author essentially restate this information?

(A) The latent causes of faction are thus sown in the nature of man; and we see them everywhere brought into different degrees of activity, according to the different circumstances of civil society.

(B) So strong is this propensity of mankind to fall into mutual animosities, that where no substantial occasion presents itself, the most frivolous and fanciful distinctions have been sufficient to kindle their unfriendly passions and excite their most violent conflicts.

(C) But the most common and durable source of factions has been the various and unequal distribution of property.

(D) The regulation of these various and interfering interests forms the principal task of modern legislation, and involves the spirit of party and faction in the necessary and ordinary operations of the government.

22. Information in this passage would be most useful for

(A) encouraging people to split into unique and productive factions.

(B) figuring out how to dissuade people from splitting into factions.

(C) abolishing the existence of factions once and for all.

(D) countering arguments that factions are destructive forces.

23. Read the following sentence from paragraph 4:

It could never be more truly said than of the first remedy, that it was worse than the disease.

This means

(A) a remedy should never make a problem worse.

(B) problems get worse before they get better.

(C) factions are worse than any illness.

(D) the solution is worse than the problem.

QUESTIONS 24 THROUGH 29 ARE BASED ON THE FOLLOWING PASSAGE.

A lighthouse stands over the edge of the sea. In this poem, Henry Wadsworth Longfellow describes the lighthouse.

The rocky ledge runs far into the sea,
And on its outer point, some miles away,
The lighthouse lifts its massive masonry,
A pillar of fire by night, of cloud by day.

5 Even at this distance I can see the tides,
heaving, break unheard along its base,
A speechless wrath, that rises and subsides
in the white tip and tremor of the face.

And as the evening darkens, lo! how bright,
10 Through the deep purple of the twilight air,
Beams forth the sudden radiance of its light,
With strange, unearthly splendor in the glare!

No one alone: from each projecting cape
And perilous reef along the ocean's verge,
15 Starts into life a dim, gigantic shape,
Holding its lantern o'er the restless surge.

Like the great giant Christopher it stands
Upon the brink of the tempestuous wave,
Wading far out among the rocks and sands,
20 The night-o'ertaken mariner to save.

And the great ships sail outward and return
Bending and bowing o'er the billowy swells,
And ever joyful, as they see it burn
They wave their silent welcome and farewells.

practice test 1

25 They come forth from the darkness, and their sails
Gleam for a moment only in the blaze,
And eager faces, as the light unveils
Gaze at the tower, and vanish while they gaze.

The mariner remembers when a child,
30 on his first voyage, he saw it fade and sink;
And when, returning from adventures wild,
He saw it rise again o'er ocean's brink.

Steadfast, serene, immovable, the same
Year after year, through all the silent night
35 Burns on forevermore that quenchless flame,
Shines on that inextinguishable light!

It sees the ocean to its bosom clasp
The rocks and sea-sand with the kiss of peace;
It sees the wild winds lift it in their grasp,
40 And hold it up, and shake it like a fleece.

The startled waves leap over it; the storm
Smites it with all the scourges of the rain,
And steadily against its solid form
Press the great shoulders of the hurricane.

45 The sea-bird wheeling round it, with the din
Of wings and winds and solitary cries,
Blinded and maddened by the light within,
Dashes himself against the glare, and dies.

A new Prometheus, chained upon the rock,
50 Still grasping in his hand the fire of Jove,
It does not hear the cry, nor heed the shock,
But hails the mariner with words of love.

"Sail on!" it says, "sail on, ye stately ships!
And with your floating bridge the ocean span;
55 Be mine to guard this light from all eclipse,
Be yours to bring man nearer unto man!"

"The Lighthouse," by
Henry Wadsworth Longfellow

24. Which of the following states the primary purpose of this poem?

(A) To express concern for the dangers mariners face.

(B) To praise those who protect the imperiled.

(C) To celebrate the various qualities of a lighthouse.

(D) To compare a lighthouse's qualities to those of a person.

25. The final stanza might be used to support which of the following interpretations of the poem?

(A) The lighthouse represents the connection between people.

(B) The lighthouse symbolizes a bridge over the ocean.

(C) The lighthouse is the personification of love.

(D) The lighthouse signifies a living character.

26. Based on details in the poem, which of the following can be concluded about the lighthouse?

(A) It brings nothing but joy to nature.

(B) It has the ability to protect all creatures.

(C) Its effects are not always positive.

(D) Its light is capable of being extinguished.

27. The word "smites" (line 42) most nearly means

(A) unveils.

(B) attacks.

(C) returns.

(D) protects.

28. The phrase "words of love" (line 52) refers to

(A) Prometheus's passion.

(B) the sailor's gratefulness.

(C) Jove's intensity.

(D) the lighthouse's light.

29. According to the poem, how is the lighthouse like Christopher?

(A) It is tempestuous.

(B) It wades among rocks.

(C) It rescues mariners.

(D) It stands immobile.

QUESTIONS 30 THROUGH 34 ARE BASED ON THE FOLLOWING PASSAGES.

The passages in this pair are excerpts from novels. In Passage 1, a Time Traveler shows his invention to others. In Passage 2, the captain of a submarine shows off his craft.

Passage 1 by H.G. Wells

The thing the Time Traveller held in his hand was a glittering metallic framework, scarcely larger than a small clock, and
5 very delicately made. There was ivory in it, and some transparent crystalline substance. And now I must be explicit, for this that follows—unless his explanation is
10 to be accepted—is an absolutely unaccountable thing. He took one of the small octagonal tables that were scattered about the room, and set it in front of the fire, with
15 two legs on the hearthrug. On this table he placed the mechanism. Then he drew up a chair, and sat down. The only other object on the table was a small shaded lamp, the
20 bright light of which fell upon the model. There were also perhaps a dozen candles about, two in brass candlesticks upon the mantel and several in sconces, so that the room
25 was brilliantly illuminated. I sat in a low arm-chair nearest the fire, and I drew this forward so as to be almost between the Time Traveller and the fireplace. Filby sat behind
30 him, looking over his shoulder. The Medical Man and the Provincial Mayor watched him in profile from the right, the Psychologist from the left. The Very Young Man
35 stood behind the Psychologist. We were all on the alert. It appears incredible to me that any kind of trick, however subtly conceived and however adroitly done, could
40 have been played upon us under these conditions.

The Time Traveller looked at us, and then at the mechanism. 'Well?' said the Psychologist.
45 'This little affair,' said the Time Traveller, resting his elbows upon the table and pressing his hands together above the apparatus, 'is only a model. It is my plan for a
50 machine to travel through time.

You will notice that it looks singularly askew, and that there is an odd twinkling appearance about this bar, as though it was in some
55 way unreal.' He pointed to the part with his finger. 'Also, here is one little white lever, and here is another.'

The Medical Man got up out of
60 his chair and peered into the thing. 'It's beautifully made,' he said.

It took two years to make,' retorted the Time Traveller. Then, when we had all imitated the
65 action of the Medical Man, he said: 'Now I want you clearly to understand that this lever, being pressed over, sends the machine gliding into the future, and this other
70 reverses the motion. This saddle represents the seat of a time traveller. Presently I am going to press the lever, and off the machine will go. It will vanish, pass into future
75 Time, and disappear. Have a good look at the thing. Look at the table too, and satisfy yourselves there is no trickery. I don't want to waste this model, and then be told I'm a
80 quack.'

Passage 2 by Jules Verne

Clearly we could do nothing but submit, and afterwards Captain Nemo showed me his wondrous craft... It was indeed a thing of
5 marvels; for, besides the dining-room, it contained a large library of twelve thousand volumes, a drawing-room measuring thirty feet by eighteen, and fifteen high.
10 The walls of this apartment were adorned with masterpieces of the great painters, and beautiful marbles and bronzes. A large piano-organ stood in one corner,
15 and there were glass cases containing the rarest marine curiosities which a naturalist could wish to see. A collection of enormous pearls in a cabinet must have been
20 worth millions, and Captain Nemo

told me he had rifled every sea to find them.

The room assigned to me was fitted up with every luxury, yet
25 the captain's own apartment was as simply furnished as a monastic cell, but in it were contained all the ingenious instruments that controlled the movements of the
30 Nautilus, as his submarine was named. The electricity was manufactured by a process of extracting chloride of sodium from the sea-water, but the fresh air necessary
35 for the life of the crew could only be obtained by rising to the surface. The engine-room was sixty-five feet long, and in it was the machinery for producing electricity as well as
40 that for applying the power to the propeller.

The Nautilus, Captain Nemo explained, was capable of a speed of fifty miles an hour, and could be
45 made to sink or rise with precision by flooding or emptying a reservoir. In a box, raised somewhat above the hull and fitted with glass ten inches thick, the steersman had
50 his place, and a powerful electric reflector behind him illumined the sea for half a mile in front.

The submarine also carried a small torpedo-like boat, fitted in
55 a groove along the top, so that it could be entered from the Nautilus by opening a panel, and, after that was closed, the boat could be detached from the submarine, and
60 would then bob upwards to the surface like a cork. The importance of this and its bearing on my story will appear in due time.

It was on a desert island that
65 Captain Nemo had carried out the building of the Nautilus, and from many different places he had secured the various parts of the hull and machinery, in order to
70 maintain secrecy.

Deeply interested as I was in every detail of this extraordinary

vessel, and excited beyond measure at the wonders which awaited me
75 in exploring the world beneath the waves, I had still the feeling of a prisoner who dared scarcely hope that liberty might some day be obtained. But when the metal
80 plates which covered the windows of the saloon were rolled back as we sailed under the water, and on each hand I could see a thronging army of many-coloured aquatic creatures
85 swimming around us, attracted by our light, I was in an ecstasy of wonder and delight.

30. According to the first paragraph (lines 1–41) of Passage 1, the model of the time travelling apparatus contains

    (A) glitter.
    (B) crystal.
    (C) ivory.
    (D) wax.

31. It can be reasonably inferred from the passage that the Time Traveller in Passage 1 is

    (A) worried his time travelling apparatus will not work.
    (B) not concerned about what people think of him.
    (C) trying to make fools of his colleagues.
    (D) proud of his time travelling apparatus.

32. It can be inferred that Captain Nemo in Passage 2

    (A) values extravagance.
    (B) has specific goals.
    (C) avoids people.
    (D) values function over comfort.

33. Passage 2 suggests that the narrator feels

    (A) completely honored to have access to the Nautilus.
    (B) both amazed and uneasy in the Nautilus.
    (C) like a co-owner of the Nautilus.
    (D) terrified being underwater in the Nautilus.

34. Both the Time Traveller and Captain Nemo

    (A) invite people into their machines.
    (B) build dangerous weapons.
    (C) build unusual machines.
    (D) explore the oceans.

QUESTIONS 35 THROUGH 40 ARE BASED ON THE FOLLOWING PASSAGE.

Mr. March is away from home. In this excerpt from a work of fiction, Mrs. March reads a letter from her husband to her daughters.

They all drew to the fire, mother in the big chair with Beth at her feet, Meg and Amy perched on either arm of the chair, and Jo leaning
5   on the back, where no one would see any sign of emotion if the letter should happen to be touching. Very few letters were written in those hard times that were not touching,
10   especially those which fathers sent home. In this one little was said of the hardships endured, the dangers faced, or the homesickness conquered; it was a cheerful,
15   hopeful letter, full of lively descriptions of camp life, marches, and military news; and only at the end did the writer's heart overflow with fatherly love and longing for the
20   little girls at home.

"Give them all my dear love and a kiss. Tell them I think of them by day, pray for them by night, and find my best comfort in
25   their affection at all times. A year seems very long to wait before I see them, but remind them that while we wait we may all work, so that these hard days need
30   not be wasted. I know they will remember all I said to them, that they will be loving children to you, will do their duty faithfully, fight their bosom enemies bravely, and
35   conquer themselves so beautifully that when I come back to them I may be fonder and prouder than ever of my little women."

Everybody sniffed when they
40   came to that part; Jo wasn't ashamed of the great tear that dropped off the end of her nose, and Amy never minded the rumpling of her curls as she hid her face on her

45   mother's shoulder and sobbed out, "I am a selfish girl! But I'll truly try to be better, so he mayn't be disappointed in me by and by."

"We all will!" cried Meg. "I think
50   too much of my looks and hate to work, but won't any more if I can help it."

"I'll try and be what he loves to call me, 'a little woman' and not
55   be rough and wild; but do my duty here instead of wanting to be somewhere else," said Jo, thinking that keeping her temper at home was a much harder task than facing a
60   rebel or two down South.

Beth said nothing, but wiped away her tears with the blue army sock and began to knit with all her might, losing no time in doing the
65   duty that lay nearest her, while she resolved in her quiet little soul to be all that father hoped to find her when the year brought round the happy coming home.

Excerpt from *Little Women* by Louisa May Alcott.

35. This passage is mainly about

(A) the contents of and reaction to a letter.

(B) the emotions expressed by young girls.

(C) the intense homesickness of a father.

(D) the love of a mother for her children.

36. Based on this passage, the reader can infer that

(A) the March girls never got to know their father well.

(B) Mr. March prefers to be away from home.

(C) Mrs. March is not ashamed of expressing emotions.

(D) the March family has a very close bond.

37. Based on the passage, the reader can conclude that it is set

(A) during the summer.

(B) during wartime.

(C) in Great Britain.

(D) in the future.

38. Based on the passage, the reader can tell that Beth is

(A) less comfortable expressing herself than her sisters are.

(B) the most skilled and talented of the March sisters.

(C) not concerned about disappointing her father.

(D) far more mature than her sisters are.

39. Which of the following best describes the mood of this passage?

(A) Serene

(B) Jubilant

(C) Sentimental

(D) Anxious

40. What will the reader most likely learn next?

(A) What Mr. March is doing away from home.

(B) Where Meg and Amy decide to work.

(C) Which girl is the first to disappoint Mr. March.

(D) How well the March girls heed their father.

practice test 1

LANGUAGE ARTS—WRITING

Part 1

50 Questions • 120 Minutes

Directions: Read the following draft article. Then proceed to the expanded version and answer the questions, which offer options for improvement for each underlined part. Select the answer choice for each that best improves the written passage.

Para. 1 Are you looking to buy new headphones. If so, you may be surprised at the number of choices available today. There are headphones to fit every type of need, use, and budget. With some careful planning, you can find the perfect set of headphones for you. Also, with really cool headphones, you can impress people wearing them!

Para. 2 In-ear headphones, or ear buds, are designed to fit inside or close to the ear canal. It is smaller and more portable than larger over-the-ear headphones. There are many different types of headphones in this category, including ones for athletic activities, ones with outside noise cancellation capabilities, and ones with built-in microphones for making phone calls. They're also available in a variety of materials, including metal and plastic, and the comfort varies as well, depending on if they includes foam, rubber or plastic cushions for your ears.

Para. 3 Over-the-ear headphones are larger, and sit over the ears. Those who find in-ear headphones uncomfortable or too intrusive typically choose this type of headphones. Coming in a variety of shapes, colors, and materials, including noise cancellation and microphones, they offer many of the same options as in-ear headphones. They even have wireless models available now.

Para. 4 Which headphones are right for you? We never listen to music. The best strategy for getting the perfect pair is to do a little research. Many stores that sell headphones have display models that you can try on and test for yourself. We recommend that you try on several pairs before making a decision regarding which pair to buy. Take your time and choose the pair that best fits your budget, lifestyle, taste, and comfort level.

Para. 1 <u>Are you looking to buy new</u>
<u>**1**</u>

<u>headphones.</u> If so, you may be
1

surprised at the number of choices

available today. There are headphones

to fit every type of need, use, and

budget. With some careful planning, you

can find the perfect set of headphones

for you. Also, with really cool

headphones, <u>you can impress people</u>
2

<u>wearing them!</u>
2

Para. 2 In-ear headphones, or ear buds,

are designed to fit inside or close to the

ear canal. <u>It is</u> smaller and more
3

portable than larger over-the-ear

headphones. There are many different

types of headphones in this category,

including ones for athletic activities,

ones with outside noise cancellation

capabilities, and ones with built-in

microphones for making phone calls.

They're also available in a variety of

materials, including metal and plastic,

1. **(A)** (No change)
   (B) Are you looking to buy new headphones!
   (C) Are you looking to buy new headphones?
   (D) Are you, looking to buy, new headphones.

2. **(A)** (No change)
   (B) you can impress people while you wear them!
   (C) you can impress people who are wearing them!
   (D) you can't impress people wearing them!

3. **(A)** (No change)
   (B) It are
   (C) She is
   (D) They are

and the comfort varies as well,

<u>depending on if they includes foam,</u>
4

rubber, or plastic cushions for your ears.

Para. 3 Over-the-ear headphones are

larger, and sit over the ears. <u>Those who</u>
5

<u>find in-ear headphones uncomfortable</u>
5

<u>or too intrusive typically choose this</u>
5

<u>type of headphones.</u> <u>Coming in a</u>
5   **6**

<u>variety of shapes, colors, and materials,</u>
6

<u>including noise cancellation and</u>
6

<u>microphones, they offer many of the</u>
6

<u>same options as in-ear headphones.</u>
6

They even have wireless models

available now.

4. **(A)** (No change)
   (B) depending on if they including foam
   (C) depending on if they include foam
   (D) depending on if it included foam

5. **(A)** (No change)
   (B) Those who find in-ear headphones uncomfortable or too intrusive typically has chosen these types of headphones.
   (C) Those who are finding in-ear headphones uncomfortable or too intrusive typically choose this type of headphones.
   (D) Those who found in-ear headphones uncomfortable or too intrusive typically have been chosen by this type of headphones.

6. **(A)** (No change)
   (B) They offer many of the same noise cancellation and microphones, and also come in a variety of shapes, colors, and materials, just like in-ear headphone options.
   (C) They offer many of the same options as in-ear headphones, including noise cancellation and microphones, and also come in a variety of shapes, colors, and materials.
   (D) There are many in-ear headphones in a variety of shapes, colors, and materials, and also offer the same noise cancellation and microphones.

Para. 4 Which headphones are right for you? The best strategy for getting the <u>more perfect pair</u> is to do a little
7

research. Many stores that sell headphones have display models that you can try on and test for yourself. We recommend that you try on several pairs before making a decision regarding which pair to buy. Take your time and choose the pair that best fits <u>her</u> budget, lifestyle, taste, and comfort
8

level.

7. **(A)** (No change)
    (B) most perfectest
    (C) perfect
    (D) perfecter

8. **(A)** (No change)
    (B) your
    (C) his
    (D) their

Directions: Read the following draft workplace memo. Then proceed to the expanded version and answer the questions, which offer options for improvement for each underlined portion.

To: All ACME Warehouse Employees

From: ACME Company Management Team

RE: KEEPING THE EMPLOYEE BREAK ROOM CLEAN

All ACME team members:

Para. 1 The purpose of the employee break room is for all acme warehouse employees to have a safe, clean, and comfortable place to relax, enjoy lunch, and store their unrecognizable belongings during their work shifts. However, it has recently come to our attention that the cleanliness of the break room has become an issue. In light of this, we are reminding all employees of the following guidelines regarding the proper use of the break room.

Para. 2 The break room should only be used by employees on days they are scheduled to working. Employees who are off for the day, should not be in the break room, or whose shifts have ended more than an hour ago. Any employee found in the break room who should not be there will be written up accordingly.

Para. 3 Regarding eating in the employee break room: Employees should feel free to enjoy her lunches as always. However, some employees have been leaving their trash and uneaten food lying around on the tables, which is not permitted. Uneaten food should be placed in a cabinet or in the refrigerator. All paper and plastic trash should be sorted for recycling. All trash should be placed in the appropriate receptacle. We all want to avoid having insects or rodents in the break room!

Para. 4 Regarding storing your personal belongings in the break room: Employees should feel free to use the lockers to store their personal belongings while on shift. However, items should not be stored overnight or when an employee is not scheduled to work. Any items stored overnight or while off shift will be removed from the lockers and must be retrieved from the manager's office.

Para. 5 Thank you for taking the time to review these guidelines. Welcome to ACME Warehouse! Remember, the break room is designed for the enjoyment and use of all ACME Warehouse employees, and these rules are designed to help us keep it a welcome place for everyone.

To: All ACME Warehouse Employees
From: ACME Company Management Team

RE: KEEPING THE EMPLOYEE BREAK ROOM CLEAN
All ACME team members:

Para. 1 The purpose of the employee break room is for all <u>acme warehouse</u>
9
employees to have a safe, clean, and comfortable place to relax, enjoy lunch, and store their personal belongings during their work shifts. However, it has recently come to our attention that the cleanliness of the break room has become an <u>issue</u>.
10
 In light of this, we are reminding all employees of the following guidelines regarding the proper use of the break room.

Para. 2 The break room should only be used by employees on days they are

9. **(A)** (No change)
   (B) Acme Warehouse
   (C) ACME Warehouse
   (D) ACME warehouse

10. **(A)** (No change)
    (B) issue?
    (C) issue!
    (D) issue,

scheduled <u>to working</u>. <u>Employees who</u>
         11   **12**

<u>are off for the day, should not be in the</u>
                12

<u>break room, or whose shifts have ended</u>
                12

<u>more than an hour ago.</u> Any employee
        12

found in the break room who should not

be there will be written up accordingly.

Para. 3 Regarding eating in the

employee break room: Employees should

feel free to enjoy <u>her</u> lunches as always.
                13

However, some employees have been

leaving their trash and uneaten food

lying around on the tables, which is not

permitted. Uneaten food should be

placed in a cabinet or in the

refrigerator. <u>All paper and plastic trash</u>
                      14

<u>should be sorted for recycling. All trash</u>
                14

<u>should be placed in the appropriate</u>
                14

<u>receptacle can.</u> We all want to avoid
        14

having insects or rodents in the break

room!

11. **(A)** (No change)
    (B) to works
    (C) to worked
    (D) to work

12. **(A)** (No change)
    (B) Employees, should not be in the break room, who are off for the day, or whose shifts have ended more than an hour ago.
    (C) Employees who are off for the day, or whose shifts have ended more than an hour ago, should not be in the break room.
    (D) An hour ago, employees should not be in the break room who are off for the day, or whose shifts have ended.

13. **(A)** (No change)
    (B) his
    (C) its
    (D) their

14. What is the most appropriate way to effectively combine these two sentences?
    (A) (No change)
    (B) All paper and plastic trash should be sorted for recycling, or else it should be placed in the appropriate receptacle can.
    (C) Only paper and plastic should be thrown into the trash, so it can be recycled.
    (D) All trash should be placed in the appropriate receptacle, and all paper and plastic should be sorted for recycling.

Para. 4 Regarding storing your personal belongings in the break room: Employees should feel free to use the lockers to store their personal belongings while on shift. <u>However,</u>
15

items should not be stored overnight or when an employee is not schedule to work. Any items stored overnight or while off shift will be removed from the lockers and must be retrieved from the manager's office.

Para. ***5*** Thank you for taking the time to review these guidelines. Remember, the break room is designed for the enjoyment and use of all ACME Warehouse employees, and these rules are designed to help us keep it an <u>uncomfortable</u> place for everyone.
16

15. **(A)** (No change)
    (B) However!
    (C) However;
    (D) How ever,

16. Which of the following choices is the best?
    (A) (No change)
    (B) spacious
    (C) confusing
    (D) welcome

Directions: Read the following draft article. Then proceed to the expanded version and answer the questions, which offer options for improvement for each underlined portion.

Moss Hollow County Government Election Results

Para. 1 March 01, 2015—the results of the Moss Hollow elections that took place last Tuesday have been tabulated and the results are in. All three elections were close, especially the race for town treasurer, with only a handful of votes separating the winner and the loser. The winners in each race will take office one month from today, and it will be interesting to see how they shape local politics moving forward.

Para. 2 "I'm thrilled at having the opportunity to serve the people for another term," said Thompkins during his reelection victory party. In the election for county legislator, incumbent Jesse thompkins faced fierce competition from rival Linda Denville, the former Saltsburg Assistant District Attorney who ran a tough campaign, promising to fight for political reform if elected. Despite Denville proving to be a formidable opponent, the incumbent won reelection to a third term, with 58% of the votes.

Para. 3 The race for county comptroller was also close. The current comptroller, Nickie Finkins, announced last december that this term, her fourth, would be her last, as she has accepted a private sector consulting position. The race was between Darren Jenkins, a democrat who will be working in local politics for the past decade, and Cynthia Gopnicki, a lifelong republican, Moss Hollow resident, and private practice attorney. Gopnicki won a very tight race, with 53% of the votes, and is looking forward to taking office.

Para. 4 Elections don't get much closer than the race for town treasurer this election cycle. Juan Vevrallo narrowly squeaking past his rival for the position, Dan Hammersmith, by just 14 votes, the closest election in Moss Hollow on record. Vevrallo vowed to serve the people of Moss Hollow to the least of his ability, and has reported that his primary goal as treasurer would be to work towards a more efficient use of county funds for education.

Moss Hollow County Government Election Results

Para. 1 March 01, 2015—the results of the Moss Hollow elections that took place last Tuesday have been tabulated and the results are in. All three elections <u>were close</u>, <u>especially</u> the race for town
  17   **18**
treasurer, with only a handful of votes separating the winner and the loser. The winners in each race <u>have taken</u>
                    19
office one month from today, and it will be interesting to see how they shape local politics moving forward.

Para. 2

In the election for county legislator, incumbent Jesse <u>thompkins</u> faced fierce
                  20
competition from rival Linda Denville, the former Saltsburg Assistant District Attorney who ran a tough campaign, promising to fight for political reform if

17. **(A)** (No change)
    (B) was close
    (C) are close
    (D) is close

18. **(A)** (No change)
    (B) subsequently
    (C) unfortunately
    (D) however

19. **(A)** (No change)
    (B) recently took
    (C) may took
    (D) will take

20. **(A)** (No change)
    (B) Thompkins
    (C) thomkins
    (D) Tompkins

elected. Despite Denville proving to be a formidable opponent, the incumbent won reelection to a third term, with 58% of the votes.

"I'm thrilled at having the opportunity to serve the people for another term," said Thompkins during his reelection victory party.

Para. 3 The race for county comptroller was also close. The current comptroller, Nickie Finkins, announced last

<u>december</u> that this term, her fourth,
21

would be her last, as she has accepted a private sector consulting position. The race was between Darren Jenkins, a democrat who <u>will be working</u> in local
22

politics for the past decade, and Cynthia Gopnicki, a lifelong republican, Moss Hollow resident, and private practice attorney. Gopnicki won a very tight race, with 53% of the votes, and is looking forward to taking office.

21. **(A)** (No change)
    (B) december
    (C) December,
    (D) December

22. **(A)** (No change)
    (B) could soon be working
    (C) should be working
    (D) has been working

Para. 4 Elections don't get much closer than the race for town treasurer this election cycle. Juan Vevrallo narrowly <u>squeaking</u> past his rival for the position,
23

Dan Hammersmith, by just 14 votes, the closest election in Moss Hollow on record. Vevrallo vowed to serve the people of Moss Hollow to the <u>least</u> of his
24

ability, and has reported that his primary goal as treasurer would be to work towards a more efficient use of county funds for education.

23. **(A)** (No change)
(B) squawk
(C) squeak
(D) squeaked

24. **(A)** (No change)
(B) worst
(C) best
(D) most

Directions: Read the following draft blog entry. Then proceed to the expanded version and answer the questions, which offer options for improvement for each underlined portion.

Review of the Meadowbrook Annual Autumn Harvest Festival

Para. 1 Each year, the residents of Meadowbrook; look forward to the annual Autumn Harvest Festival, and for good reason. The festival, which is a joint effort of the Meadowbrook town council and the Meadowbrook Rotarians, is always a fun seasonal highlight, with great food, activities, and entertainment for the whole family. This year's festival was no exception. Tomorrow, the Meadowbrook town council will vote on the new highway expansion proposal.

Para. 2 There were plenty of rides and acitivities, including a starship rollercoaster, bumper cars, spinning teacups, and a beautiful old wooden carousel. Pony rides were available for the kid, and there was a big brass band and dance floor for her to enjoy. Clowns and jugglers walked the fairgrounds and helped keep people entertained while waiting in lines, which I thought was a great idea.

Para. 3 As always, the food choices at the festival were plentiful, with options for every type of palate. There were roast turkeys and hams, a large variety of salads, tacos, and even spaghetti, as well as more typical fare such as burgers, nachos, pizza, and snack foods like popcorn and ice cream. Many of the local restaurants, so people can try their different creations, set up booths at the festival. This year, there was even a food raffle—the lucky winner receiving a $75 gift card to spend at any of the participating Meadowbrook restaurants.

Para. 4 Each year, the highlight of the Meadowbrook Autumn Harvest Festival is the pie contest. The best pie makers in town gather, equipped with their best recipes, and compete for the coveted blue ribbon and $500 prize. This year's competition was fierce, and came down to two perennial favorites—Mr. Johansen's blueberry crumble pie and Mrs. Richtenberg's sour apple crisp pie. Mr. Johansen narrowly edged out the competition to claim the ribbon, ending Mrs. Richtenberg's four-year reign as top muffin maker in Meadowbrook. Everyone seemed to have a great time!

Review of the Meadowbrook Annual Autumn Harvest Festival

Para. 1 Each year, the residents of

Meadowbrook; look forward to the
            25

annual Autumn Harvest Festival, and

for good reason. The festival, which is a

joint effort of the Meadowbrook town

council and the Meadowbrook

Rotarians, is always a fun seasonal

highlight, with great food, activities,

and entertainment for the whole family.

This year's festival was no exception.

Tomorrow, the Meadowbrook town
              26

council will vote on the new highway
              26

expansion proposal.
       26

Para. 2 There were plenty of rides

and acitivities, including a starship
       27

rollercoaster, bumper cars, spinning

teacups, and a beautiful old wooden

carousel. Pony rides were available for
                    28

the kid, and there was a big brass band
              28

and dance floor for her to enjoy. Clowns
              28

25. **(A)** (No change)
    (B) Meadowbrook,
    (C) Meadowbrook
    (D) Meadowbrook:

26. Which of the following choices is the best choice for this sentence?
    (A) (No change)
    (B) Move the sentence to the beginning of the paragraph (Paragraph 1).
    (C) Move the sentence to the end of the last paragraph (Paragraph 4).
    (D) Omit the sentence.

27. **(A)** (No change)
    (B) activitese
    (C) activiteis
    (D) activities

28. **(A)** (No change)
    (B) Pony rides were available for the kids, and there was a big brass band and dance floor for everyone to enjoy.
    (C) Pony rides were available for the kids, and there was a big brass band and dance floor for her to enjoy.
    (D) Pony rides were available for the kid, and there was a big brass band and dance floor for everyone to enjoy.

and jugglers walked the fairgrounds and helped keep people entertained while waiting in lines, which I thought was a great idea.

Para. 3 As always, the food choices at the festival were plentiful, with options for every type of palate. There were roast turkeys and hams, a large variety of salads, tacos, and even spaghetti, as well as more typical fare such as burgers, nachos, pizza, and snack foods like popcorn and ice cream. <u>Many of the</u> **29** <u>local restaurants, so people can try their</u> **29** <u>different creations, set up booths at the</u> **29** <u>festival.</u> This year, there was even a **29** food raffle—the lucky winner <u>receive</u> **30** a $75 gift card to spend at any of the participating Meadowbrook restaurants.

Para. 4 Each year, the highlight of the Meadowbrook Autumn Harvest Festival is the pie contest. The best pie makers in town gather, equipped with their best recipes, and compete for the

29. **(A)** (No change)
 (B) Many of the local restaurants set up booths at the festival, so people could try their different creations.
 (C) People, set up booths at the festival, so many of the local restaurants could try their different creations.
 (D) There are many different local restaurant creations, so people set up booths at the festival.

30. **(A)** (No change)
 (B) receivable
 (C) has been receiving
 (D) received

coveted blue ribbon and $500 prize. This year's competition was fierce, and came down to two perennial favorites—Mr. Johansen's blueberry crumble pie and Mrs. Richtenberg's sour apple crisp pie. Mr. Johansen narrowly edged out the competition to claim the ribbon, ending Mrs. Richtenberg's four-year reign as <u>top muffin maker</u> in Meadowbrook.
31

Everyone <u>seemed to have</u> a great time!
32

31. **(A)** (No change)
    (B) best muffin maker
    (C) best pie maker
    (D) worst pic maker

32. **(A)** (No change)
    (B) seem to have
    (C) seemed to has
    (D) seeming to have

practice test 1

Para. 1 A hot topic among educators, administrators, policymakers, and parents concerns whether or not students in high school should be required to complete a mandatory number of hours of community service in order to successfully meet the requirements of graduation. Whether or not this bold plan will come into fruition will ultimitely depend on which side makes the more compelling argument.

Para. 2 Those who reject the notion to require the completion of a mandatory number of community service hours claim that students who actively volunteer in support of their communities become better adults—more mature, responsible, and civic-minded individuals who are eager to make the world a better place. He often notes that today's students are more self-centered and irresponsible than ever before, and performing community service is the perfect way to reverse this disturbing trend.

Para. 3 Those against the idea of mandatory community service argue that the lives of students are busy enough already. Between classes extracurricular activities, social pursuits, and often, paid employment, there was already enough items on the plates of today's students—some say more than ever before—and adding additional pressure and demands would have a negative effect.

Para. 4 There are strong opinions on both sides of the issue, and many people feel that there is merit to both sides of the debate, which makes coming to a decision a challenging proposition. Thus far, only one thing is certain— debate on both sides will continue for quite a while before a decision regarding the issue is made. Without a doubt, a pilot program involving a select number of students who'd be willing to take part is a logical next step?

Para. 1 A hot topic among educators, administrators, policymakers, and parents concerns whether or not students in high school should be required to complete a mandatory number of hours of community service in order to successfully meet the requirements of graduation. Whether or not this bold plan will come into fruition will <u>ultimitely</u> depend on which side
33

makes the more compelling argument.

Para. 2 <u>Those who reject</u> the notion to
34

require the completion of a mandatory number of community service hours claim that students who actively volunteer in support of their communities become better adults— more mature, responsible, and civic-minded individuals who are eager to make the world a better place. <u>He often</u>
35

<u>notes</u> that today's students are more
35

33. **(A)** (No change)
    (B) ultamately
    (C) ultimately
    (D) altimately

34. **(A)** (No change)
    (B) Those who support
    (C) Those who dislike
    (D) Those who hate

35. **(A)** (No change)
    (B) He often note
    (C) She often notes
    (D) They often note

self-centered and irresponsible than
ever before, and performing community
service is the perfect way to reverse this
disturbing trend.

Para. 3 Those against the idea of
mandatory community service argue
that the lives of students are busy
enough already. <u>Between classes</u>
                     36

<u>extracurricular activities,</u> social
              36

pursuits, and often, paid employment,
<u>there was</u> already enough items on the
   37

plates of today's students—some say
more than ever before—and adding
additional pressure and demands would
have a negative effect.

36. **(A)** (No change)
    (B) Between classes extracurricular
        activities
    (C) Between classes, extracurricular
        activities,
    (D) Between classes extracurricular,
        activities

37. **(A)** (No change)
    (B) there are
    (C) there will be
    (D) there were

Para. 4 There are strong opinions on both sides of the issue, and many people feel that there is merit to both sides of the debate, which makes coming to a decision a challenging proposition. Thus far, only one thing is certain—debate on both sides will continue for quite a while before a decision regarding the issue is made. <u>Without a doubt,</u> a pilot program
38
involving a select number of students who'd be willing to take part is a logical next step?

38. **(A)** (No change)
    (B) Regrettably,
    (C) Unquestionably
    (D) Perhaps

Directions: Read the following draft article entry. Then proceed to the expanded version and answer the questions, which offer options for improvement for each underlined portion.

Para. 1 People all over the world enjoy a good cup of coffee, and there are several ways to enjoy it, at any time of the day. You can spend the money for a good cup of coffee at a coffee house, but if you're not near a coffee house or want to enjoy a satisfying cup of coffee at home, you can learn to sell coffee yourself.

Para. 2 The first step in brewing coffee is making sure you have all the proper equipment. There are many different tools for brewing coffee, including single serve brewers, French presses, and fully programmable countertop coffeemakers, which can vary wildly in price and quality. Choose the tool that best fits my needs and budget, and be sure to carefully read the instructions—you may need to buy additional items such as paper coffee filters.

Para. 3 Just as important as the brewer you decide to purchase are the coffee beans. The key to a great cup of coffee is selecting the beans that best suit your taste. Including flavor notes ranging from chocolate to cinnamon and vanilla and many more, from light to medium and dark roasts, there are beans to meet every palate that are grown all over the world. You can really amaze people making delicious flavored coffee! Coffee beans taste best when they're fresh, so make sure to buy just the right amount.

Para. 4 Also important is getting the right grind for your beans. You can buy and grind your beans at home with a coffee grinder, or have them ground where you purchase them. Getting the right size grind for your beans—from fine to coarse or in between—depends on the brewing method and equipment you're using, so choose carefully. All of this might seem like a lot of work, but with a little time, pateince, and effort, you'll soon be making great coffee at home whenever you're in the mood for a cup.

Para. 1 People all over the world enjoy a good cup of coffee, and there are several ways to enjoy it, at any time of the day. You can spend the money for a good cup of coffee at a coffee house, but if you're not near a coffee house or want to enjoy a satisfying cup of coffee at home, you can learn to <u>sell</u> coffee yourself.
39

Para. 2 The first step in brewing coffee is making sure you have all the proper equipment. There are many different tools for brewing coffee, including single serve brewers, French presses, and fully programmable countertop coffeemakers, which can vary wildly in price and quality. Choose the tool that best fits <u>my</u> needs and
40
budget, and be sure to carefully read the instructions—you may need to buy additional items such as paper coffee filters.

Para. 3 Just as important as the brewer you decide to purchase are the coffee beans. The key to a great cup of coffee is

39. **(A)** (No change)
    (B) buy
    (C) make
    (D) freeze

40. **(A)** (No change)
    (B) her
    (C) your
    (D) their

selecting the beans that best suit your

taste. <u>Including flavor notes ranging</u>
 41

<u>from chocolate to cinnamon and vanilla</u>
 41

<u>and many more, from light to medium</u>
 41

<u>and dark roasts, there are beans to meet</u>
 41

<u>every palate that are grown all over the</u>
 41

<u>world.</u> You can really amaze people
 41

<u>making delicious flavored coffee!</u> Coffee
 42

beans taste best when they're fresh, so

make sure to buy just the right amount.
Para. 4 Also important is getting

the right grind for your beans.

<u>You can buy and grind your beans</u>
 43

<u>at home with a coffee grinder,</u>
 43

or have them ground where you

purchase them. Getting the right size

grind for your beans—from fine to

coarse or in between—depends on the

brewing method and equipment you're

using, so choose carefully. All of this

41. (A) (No change)
 (B) There are beans to meet every palate that are grown all over the world, from light to medium and dark roasts, with flavor notes ranging from chocolate to cinnamon and vanilla and many more.
 (C) From light to medium and dark roasts and flavor notes from all over the world, ranging from chocolate to cinnamon and vanilla and many more, there are beans to meet every palate.
 (D) All over the world there are beans, from chocolate to cinnamon and vanilla and many more, including light to medium and dark roasts for every palate.

42. (A) (No change)
 (B) who are making delicious flavored coffee
 (C) that make delicious flavored coffee
 (D) by making delicious flavored coffee

43. (A) (No change)
 (B) You can buy a coffee grinder and grind your beans at home,
 (C) Beans can buy a grinder and make your coffee at home,
 (D) You can buy a home, coffee beans, and a grinder,

might seem like a lot of work, but with a little time, <u>pateince</u>, and effort,
44

you'll soon be making great coffee at home whenever you're in the mood for a cup.

44. **(A)** (No change)
    (B) paishence
    (C) patiense
    (D) patience

Directions: Read the following draft article entry. Then proceed to the expanded version and answer the questions, which offer options for improvement for each underlined portion.

Para. 1 Did you ever wonder what causes a tornado? Tornadoes are among the most awe-inspiring and potentially destructive weather events. These destructive funnels of spinning air have been known to reach speeds of hundreds of miles per hour and devastate the miles of ground that it typically travels across—obliterating anything in their paths, including homes, cars, buildings, and everything in between. But where do they come from?

Para. 2 Alterations in wind speed and direction creates a funnel effect of rotating air from a thunderstorm cloud to the ground, leading to the characteristic tornado that we all recognize. Although tornado length, speed, and duration of tornadoes can vary wildly, the average tornado is between 200–300 feet across, travels less than 100 mph, and travels for just a few miles before scattering. Tornadoes occur when warm, moist air mixes with cool, dry air, usually during a thunderstorm, to form an unstable atmospheric event.

Para. 3 Tornadoes come in a variety of shapes, sizes, and even colors, depending on the weather conditions that lead to their creation. The only continent never to have witnessed a tornado is Antarctica. Tornado intensity is ranked on a scale from F0 (weak; light damage) to F5 (strong; intense damage). Tornado winds are the fastest winds on Earth. Did you know that the fastest tornado winds ever recorded were just over 300 mph! Tornadoes are destructive forces of nature, spinning at unbelievable speeds, races across the land, and destroying everything in their paths.

Para. 4 With hundreds of tornadoes occurring each year in the United States alone, it's important to be aware of tornado safety strategies. Signs of a pending tornado include loud, ongoing noise, heavy rain, and shifting winds with a rotating cloud base. If you suspect a tornado is incoming, avoid windows and get as low to the ground as possible. Seek shelter in an unknown, enclosed area and, if possible, cover yourself with a blanket, mattress, or other soft, heavily padded material for protection against falling objects. Staying safe during dangerous weather should always be your top priority.

Para. 1 Did you ever wonder what causes a tornado? Tornadoes are among the most awe-inspiring and potentially destructive weather events. These destructive funnels of spinning air <u>have been known</u> to reach speeds of
45
hundreds of miles per hour and devastate the miles of ground that <u>it typically travels</u> across—obliterating
46
anything in their paths, including homes, cars, buildings, and everything in between. But where do they come from?

Para. 2 Alterations in wind speed and direction creates a funnel effect of rotating air from a thunderstorm cloud to the ground, leading to the characteristic tornado that we all recognize. Although tornado length, speed, and duration of tornadoes can vary wildly, the average tornado is between 200–300 feet across, travels

45. (A) (No change)
   (B) will be known
   (C) used to be known
   (D) soon to be knowing

46. (A) (No change)
   (B) it typically travel
   (C) they typically travel
   (D) he typically travels

less than 100 mph, and travels for just a

few miles before scattering. Tornadoes
                                   47

occur when warm, moist air mixes with
                   47

cool, dry air, usually during a
              47

thunderstorm, to form an unstable
                47

atmospheric event.
        47

Para. 3 Tornadoes come in a variety of
                        48

shapes, sizes, and even colors,
                48

depending on the weather conditions
                48

that lead to their creation. The only
              48

continent never to have witnessed a

tornado is Antarctica. Tornado intensity

is ranked on a scale from F0 (weak;

light damage) to F5 (strong; intense

damage). Tornado winds are the fastest

winds on Earth. Did you know that the

47. Which of the following choices is the best choice for this sentence?
   (A) (No change)
   (B) Move to the beginning of the paragraph (Paragraph 2).
   (C) Omit the sentence
   (D) Move to the end of the last paragraph (Paragraph 4).

48. Which of the following sentences would best fit at the beginning of this paragraph (Paragraph 3), to transition from the previous paragraph (Paragraph 2)?
   (A) Have you ever been in a tornado?
   (B) Tornadoes are even more dangerous than hurricanes.
   (C) This is why people are afraid of tornadoes.
   (D) The following are some interesting tornado facts.

fastest tornado winds ever recorded were just over 300 mph! <u>Tornadoes are</u>
49

<u>destructive forces of nature, spinning at</u>
49

<u>unbelievable speeds, races across the</u>
49

<u>land, and destroying everything in their</u>
49

<u>paths.</u>
49

Para. 4 With hundreds of tornadoes occurring each year in the United States alone, it's important to be aware of tornado safety strategies. Signs of a pending tornado include loud, ongoing noise, heavy rain, and shifting winds with a rotating cloud base. If you suspect a tornado is incoming, avoid windows and get as low to the ground as possible. Seek shelter in <u>an unknown,</u>
50

enclosed area and, if possible, cover yourself with a blanket, mattress, or other soft, heavily padded material for protection against falling objects. Staying safe during dangerous weather should always be your top priority.

49. **(A)** (No change)
   (B) Tornadoes are destructive forces of nature, spins at unbelievable speeds, races across the land, and destroys everything in their paths.
   (C) Tornadoes are destructive forces of nature, spinning at unbelievable speeds, racing across the land, and destroying everything in their paths.
   (D) Tornadoes are destructive forces of nature, spun at unbelievable speeds, raced across the land, and destroyed everything in their paths.

50. **(A)** (No change)
   (B) a perilous
   (C) a safe
   (D) a new

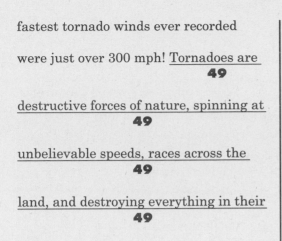

Part 2

1 Essay • 45 Minutes

Directions: This is a test of your writing skills. Your response will be scored based on:

- Development of a central position through explanation of supporting reasons and examples from passages and personal experience

- Language use, including varied word choice, varied sentence constructions, and appropriate voice

- Clarity and correctness of writing conventions

- Clear organization of ideas, including an introduction and conclusion, logical paragraphs, and effective transitions

Below you will find two passages in which the authors put forth differing perspectives on an issue of importance. Read both passages carefully, noting the strengths and weaknesses of each discussion. Then, you will write an essay in which you explain your own opinion on the issue.

A sociology teacher had students perform research on the issue of college education costs and present their findings to the other students. The following two excerpts were required reading for the project.

The Economics of Higher Education (a report prepared by the Department of Treasury along with the Department of Education)

There is substantial evidence that education raises earnings. Individuals with a bachelor's degree earn more and are less likely to be unemployed than those with only a high school diploma. In 2011, the median weekly earnings for bachelor's degree holders were 65 percent higher than earnings of high school graduates ($1,053 compared to $638). Those with a high school diploma were nearly twice as likely to be unemployed as those with a college or advanced degree. In aggregate, the additional earnings from two or four years of college (relative to only high school) were $2.4 trillion, or 16 percent of the $15 trillion in total Gross Domestic Product.

While the financial benefits of earning a college degree are well established, higher education may also bring non-financial benefits to graduates as well as benefits to the economy at large. College graduates report being in better health, have lower mortality rates and higher civic engagement, and are less likely to draw on the social safety net. Research universities also devote significant resources to knowledge creation and innovation, which benefits not just the university and its students, but also the general public.

Education also enhances intergenerational mobility, the ability of children to move up and down the economic ladder independent of their parents' economic status. Further, an individual's level of educational attainment is highly correlated with parental income. While students across the entire income distribution are now more likely to go to college now than a generation ago, these gains are significantly larger for children from high-income families.

Five Ways to Offset Education Costs

College can be very expensive. To help students and their parents, the IRS offers the following five ways to offset education costs.

1. The American Opportunity Credit: This credit can help parents and students pay part of the cost of the first four years of college. The American Recovery and Reinvestment Act modifies the existing Hope Credit, making it available to a broader range of taxpayers. Eligible taxpayers may qualify for the maximum annual credit of $2,500 per student. Generally, 40 percent of the credit is refundable, which means that you may be able to receive up to $1,000, even if you owe no taxes.

2. The Hope Credit: The credit can help students and parents pay part of the cost of the first two years of college.

3. The Lifetime Learning Credit: This credit can help pay for undergraduate, graduate and professional degree courses—Including courses to improve job skills—regardless of the number of years in the program. Eligible taxpayers may qualify for up to $2,000 to $4,000 if a student in a Midwestern disaster area – per tax return.

4. Enhanced benefits for 529 college savings plans: Certain computer technology purchases are now added to the list of college expenses that can be paid for by a qualified tuition program, commonly referred to as a 529 plan. The law expands the definition of qualified higher education expenses to include expenses for computer technology and equipment or Internet access and related services.

5. Tuition and fees deduction: Students and their parents may be able to deduct qualified college tuition and related expenses of up to $4,000. This deduction is an adjustment to income, which means the deduction will reduce the amount of your income subject to tax. The Tuition and Fees Deduction may be beneficial to you if you do not qualify for the American opportunity, Hope, or lifetime learning credits.

Write an essay in which you explain your own position on the following question: Do college education costs need to be addressed and reformed?

Be sure to use evidence from the passages and specific reasons and examples from your own experience and knowledge to support your position. Your essay should, at minimum, acknowledge opposing or alternate ideas.

MATHEMATICS

50 Questions • 90 Minutes

Formula Sheet

Perimeter/Circumference

RECTANGLE
Perimeter = 2(length) + 2(width)

CIRCLE
Circumference = 2π(radius)

Area

CIRCLE
Area = π(radius)²

TRIANGLE
Area = $\frac{1}{2}$ (base)(height)

PARALLELOGRAM
Area = (base)(height)

TRAPEZOID
Area = $\frac{1}{2}$ (base$_1$ + base$_2$)(height)

Volume

PRISM/CYLINDER

Volume = (area of the base)(height)

PYRAMID/CONE

Volume = $\frac{1}{3}$ (area of the base)(height)

SPHERE
Volume = $\frac{4}{3}$ π(radius)³

Length

1 foot = 12 inches
1 yard = 3 feet
1 mile = 5,280 feet
1 meter = 1,000 millimeters
1 meter = 100 centimeters
1 kilometer = 1,000 meteres
1 mile ≈ 1.6 kilometers
1 inch = 2.54 centimeters
1 foot ≈ 0.3 meter

Capacity/Volume

1 cup = 8 fluid ounces
1 pint = 2 cups
1 quart = 2 pints
1 gallon = 4 quarts
1 gallon = 231 cubic inches
1 liter = 1,000 milliliters
1 liter ≈ 0.264 gallon

Weight

1 pound = 16 ounces
1 ton = 2,000 pounds
1 gram = 1,000 milligrams
1 kilogram = 1,000 grams
1 kilogram = 2.2 pounds
1 ounce = 28.3 grams

---

1. Violet spends $1,500 on a one-time cost for materials necessary to start her deck power-washing business. For each deck she power washes, she earns $150, but it costs $10 in gas for each job, as well as $35 for a part-time helper. What number of decks must Violet power wash before she breaks even?

   (A) 10
   (B) 14
   (C) 15
   (D) 25
   (E) 30

2. Solve for I_2: $\frac{1}{I_1} + \frac{1}{I_2} = V$

   (A) $I_2 = \frac{1}{V} - I_1$

   (B) $I_2 = \frac{I_1}{VI_1 - 1}$

   (C) $I_2 = V - \frac{1}{I_1}$

   (D) $I_2 = \frac{I_1}{V - 1}$

   (E) $I_2 = \frac{VI_1 - 1}{I_1}$

3. Temperature readings of a barn are taken hourly throughout the day during early spring and recorded in a chart.

Time	Temperature (in degrees)
12 a.m.	45
1 a.m.	46
2 a.m.	43
3 a.m.	46
4 a.m.	45
5 a.m.	47
6 a.m.	47
7 a.m.	48
8 a.m.	49
9 a.m.	52
10 a.m.	53
11 a.m.	55
12 p.m.	58
1 p.m.	61
2 p.m.	62
3 p.m.	62
4 p.m.	60
5 p.m.	57
6 p.m.	56
7 p.m.	53
8 p.m.	51
9 p.m.	49
10 p.m.	48
11 p.m.	45

If 12 a.m. corresponds to $t = 0$, which of the following would best describe this distribution of temperatures?

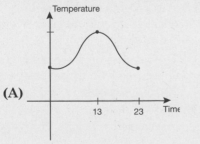

(A)

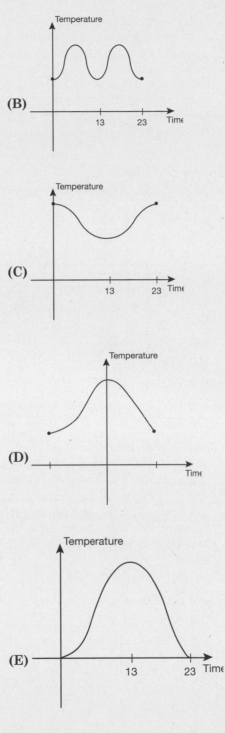

(B)

(C)

(D)

(E)

4. The solutions to the equation $x^2 + 3x = 4$ are m and n, such that $m > n$. What is the value of m?

(A) -4

(B) -1

(C) 1

(D) 2

(E) 4

5. Fifty random university staff members are asked to provide the number of social media friends they currently have. Their number is rounded to the nearest multiple of 40, and those with more than 280 contacts are grouped into a single category. The data are depicted by the following distribution.

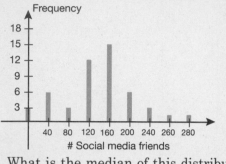

What is the median of this distribution?

(A) 120

(B) 154

(C) 160

(D) 180

(E) 200

6. In a lab, an experimental calculation of the specific heat of aluminum was found to be 0.174 cal/g°C. Based on the calibration of the equipment, it is known that the maximum percent error in the readings is 20%. Which of the following readings is NOT possible?

(A) 0.102 cal/g°C

(B) 0.1392 cal/g°C

(C) 0.1983 cal/g°C

(D) 0.2010 cal/g°C

(E) 0.2088 cal/g°C

7. On any given weekday, Jordan rides his bike 2.5 miles from home to school, then 0.25 miles from school to the baseball field for practice, and finally 2.25 miles from the baseball field to home. If 1.75 inches are equal to 1 mile on a town map, how far does Jordan ride his bike in terms of the map's scale?

(A) 1.75 inches

(B) 4.375 inches

(C) 4.8125 inches

(D) 6.75 inches

(E) 8.75 inches

8. A rectangular prism has a length of 6 inches, a width of 2 inches, a height of 4 inches, and volume V_1 cubic inches. A second prism has the same length and width, but a height that is 5 inches larger than the height of the first prism. Its volume is V_2 cubic inches. What is $V_2 - V_1$?

(A) 48

(B) 60

(C) 108

(D) 192

(E) 240

9. Consider the line $y = -\frac{5}{7}x + 3$. Which of the following is a correct interpretation of the quantity $-\frac{5}{7}$?

(A) The graph of the line crosses the y-axis at $\left(1, -\frac{5}{7}\right)$.

(B) The y-value on the graph increases by 5 units for every 7 units increase in x.

(C) The y-value on the graph decreases by 7 units for every 5 units increase in x.

(D) The y-value on the graph decreases by 5 units for every 7 units increase in x.

(E) The y-value on the graph increases by 7 units for every 5 units increase in x.

10. On average, there are 21 clementines in a 3-pound bag purchased at the local organic market. Customers have reported that the actual number in a bag can vary by as much as 4. If n represents the number of clementines, which of the following inequalities describes the range of the number of clementines in a 3-pound bag?

(A) $|n - 21| \le 4$

(B) $|n + 21| > 4$

(C) $|n - 21| \ge 4$

(D) $21 - n \le 4$

(E) $|n - 4| \le 21$

11. Diego has saved $4,500 earned by working as a camp counselor for the past four summers. He intends to use this money for weekly expenses while at college during his first year. He would like to devote $50 for coffees and lunches, $30 for gas needed for commuting back and forth between campuses, and $70 for miscellaneous activities. He must keep at least $1,000 in the account to prevent the bank from imposing maintenance fees. Which of the following inequalities can be used to determine the number of weeks, x, he can continue to withdraw from the account?

(A) $150 + 4,500x \ge 1,000$

(B) $-150x + 4,500 \ge 1,000$

(C) $4,500 \le 1,000 + 150x$

(D) $150x + 4,500 \ge 1,000$

(E) $50x + 4,500 \le 1,000$

12. Madeline wishes to produce a right circular cylinder with height 10 inches and base radius 2 inches by rotating a region in an xy-plane around the y-axis. Rotating which of the following regions about the y-axis will yield this result?

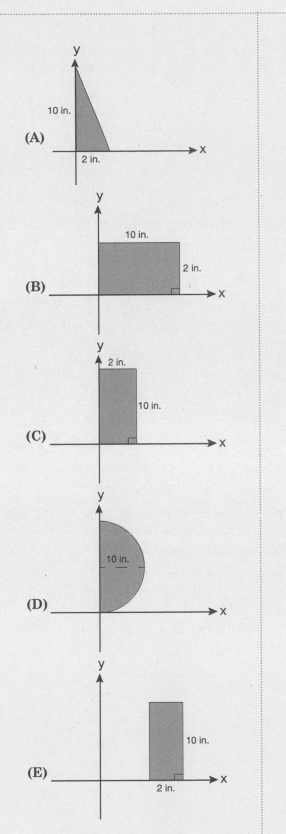

13. Conservationists have approximated that there are 2,400 trees per square mile in a certain national forest. If the entire forest covers 6.5 square miles, which of the following is the approximate number of trees in the entire forest?

    (A) 400
    (B) 1,200
    (C) 2,400
    (D) 7,500
    (E) 15,600

USE THE FOLLOWING DIAGRAM TO ANSWER QUESTIONS 14 THROUGH 16.

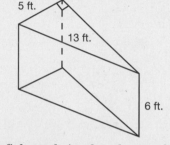

14. A fish tank in the shape of a right triangular prism, as shown, has been built to fit nicely into a corner of a pet store. What is the volume of the tank in cubic feet?

    (A) 30 cubic feet
    (B) 78 cubic feet
    (C) 195 cubic feet
    (D) 180 cubic feet
    (E) 390 cubic feet

15. The store manager has received so many compliments on the fish tank that he wants to put another one in the opposite corner. The building is not perfectly symmetric, so that corner is a bit wider. He needs to construct the second tank with the same depth of 6 feet, but with a slightly larger base. In fact, the bases of the two tanks must be similar triangles with a 2:3 ratio. What must be the base and height of the new tank?

    (A) base = 10 feet, height = 26 feet
    (B) base = 15 feet, height = 39 feet
    (C) base = 9 feet, height = 17 feet
    (D) base = 7.5 feet, height = 18 feet
    (E) base = 6 feet, height = 15 feet

16. The fish tank holds approximately 1,343 gallons of water when completely full. The store manager infuses 0.17459 ounces of mineral solution in the tank daily to help keep the fish healthy. Which of the following is the best approximation to the concentration of mineral solution in the tank in ounces per cubic foot? (Note: 1 cubic foot = 7.463 gallons)

    (A) 1.34×10^{-1} oz/ft.^{3}
    (B) 1.34×10^{-4} oz/ft.^{3}
    (C) 9.70×10^{-4} oz/ft.^{3}
    (D) 9.70×10^{-1} oz/ft.^{3}
    (E) 3.55×10^{-3} oz/ft.^{3}

17. Two friends in different age brackets decide to participate in a marathon. The younger one is given a 0.5 mile head start and jogs at a pace of 4 miles per hour for t hours. The older participant jogs at a pace of 5 miles per hour for t hours. Which of the following is an accurate description of the distance d (in miles) between the two joggers at any time t (in hours)?

    (A) $d = 0.5 + 4t$
    (B) $d = 4t - 5t$
    (C) $d = 0.5 + 9t$
    (D) $d = 0.5 - t$
    (E) $d = 5t$

18. The mean of the data set
$\{1, 4, x, 4, 2, x + 3, 10, 6\}$ is $\dfrac{23}{4}$.
What is the value of x?

(A) 8

(B) $\dfrac{19}{2}$

(C) $\dfrac{87}{8}$

(D) 46

(E) $\dfrac{207}{4}$

19. A frozen yogurt shop decides to offer a weekend special in the hope of attracting new customers. The owners decide to increase the radius of the base of their waffle cones by 50%, but decrease the height by 50%. Which of the following statements accurately describes the comparison of the volumes of these two waffle cones? (The volume of a cone with height h and base radius r is $\dfrac{1}{3}\pi r^2 h$.)

(A) The new waffle cone holds 50% more yogurt than the original one.

(B) The new waffle cone holds 75% more yogurt than the original one.

(C) The new waffle cone holds 25% less yogurt than the original one.

(D) The new waffle cone holds 12.5% more yogurt than the original one.

(E) The two waffle cones hold the same amount of yogurt.

20. Suppose the following set of numbers is the sample space for an experiment:

$\{1, 3, 5, 7, 9, 20, 23, 26, 29, 35, 49, 50, 101, 200\}$

A number is selected at random. Which of the following sets represents the event "the number selected is odd or prime"?

(A) $\{1, 3, 5, 7, 23, 29, 101\}$

(B) $\{1, 3, 5, 7, 9, 23, 29, 35, 49, 101\}$

(C) $\{20, 26, 50, 200\}$

(D) $\{1, 3, 5, 7\}$

(E) $\{20, 50, 200\}$

21. Which of the following is an illustration that the quotient of two irrational numbers need not be irrational?

(A) $\dfrac{\sqrt{3}}{\sqrt{2}}$

(B) $\dfrac{1}{\pi}$

(C) $\dfrac{\sqrt{8}}{\sqrt{4}}$

(D) $\dfrac{2\sqrt{\pi}}{\sqrt{25\pi}}$

(E) $\dfrac{3\sqrt{3}}{\sqrt{9}}$

22. Data suggest the more scratches a bowling ball has on its surface, the slower it generally rolls down the lane, though there are some exceptions. Which of the following scatterplots provides a visual illustration of the relationship between *number of scratches* and rolling speed?

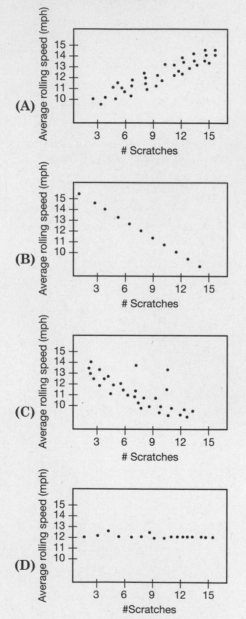

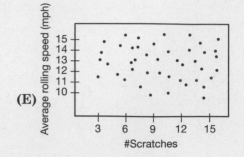

23. Teams from the fourth, sixth, and eighth grades compete in a one-mile race. The average time it takes a sixth-grader to complete one mile is 9 minutes 30 seconds, while it takes a typical eighth-grader 8 minutes 10 seconds to complete one mile. In order to make the race fair, fourth-grade participants are granted a head start equivalent to 40% of the difference between the average sixth- and eighth-grade times. Which of the following is the head start they are granted?

(A) 20 seconds

(B) 32 seconds

(C) 40 seconds

(D) 65 seconds

(E) 80 seconds

24. The manager of a department with 30 members would like to select a single employee to represent the department at the company open house. To do this, she randomly selects a letter from the alphabet and then chooses the first employee in an employee roster (alphabetized by first name) whose first name begins with that letter. Which statement below is true?

(A) The selection is unfair because she did a random selection of letters instead of numbers.

(B) The selection is fair because each letter has an equal chance of being selected.

(C) The selection is fair because employees with an uncommon first name will not be singled out.

(D) The selection is unfair because there may not be an equal number of employees for each letter.

(E) This would be fair for a department with 100 or more members, but not for one with 30.

25. Which of the following is equivalent to $3\left(27^{\frac{1}{3}} - 16^{\frac{1}{2}}\right) + 2$?

(A) -3

(B) -1

(C) 5

(D) 7

(E) 21

26. To enter a contest, a person completes an index card with their name and phone number and then places it into a large bin. To select winners for three different prizes from the 250 entries, contest organizers randomly select 3 cards, one at a time and without replacement. How many different first, second, and third place winners are possible?

(A) 250^3

(B) 3×250

(C) $250 + 249 + 248$

(D) $250 \times 249 \times 248$

(E) $C(250,3)$

27. Observe the graph of a polynomial of degree 5.

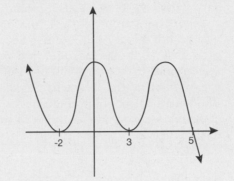

Which of the following CANNOT be a factor of this polynomial?

(A) $(x + 2)$

(B) $(x - 3)^2$

(C) x

(D) $(x - 5)$

(E) $(x + 2)^2$

28. Which of the following has numerical value greater than π?

(A) $(0.8)^2\pi$

(B) 0.95π

(C) $\frac{2}{3}\pi$

(D) $(1.1)^2\pi$

(E) $\sqrt{\pi}$

29. Luisa travels to Germany for a six-week workshop and takes a phone card worth $200. She uses it to make calls within Europe and internationally to her home in Missouri. Local calls cost $0.20 per minute, and international calls cost $0.50 per minute. Which of the following regions illustrates all possible combinations of minutes devoted to local and international calls?

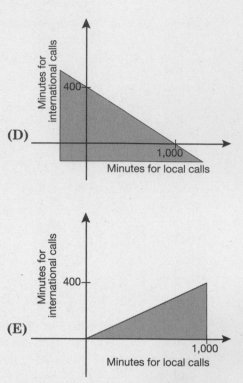

(D)

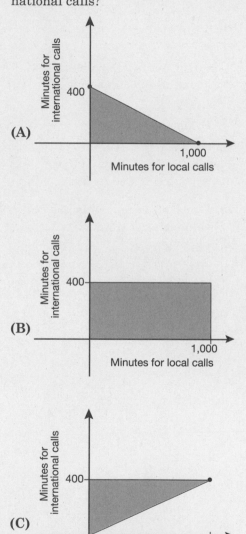

(A)

(B)

(C)

(E)

30. Which of the following expressions is NOT equivalent to $(w - z)(2w + 4z)$?

(A) $(w - z)(4z + 2w)$

(B) $(2w + 4z)(w - z)$

(C) $w(2w + 4z) - z(2w + 4z)$

(D) $-2(z - w)(w + 2z)$

(E) $2w^2 - 4z^2$

31. The length of a rectangular family room is 10 feet more than twice the width of the room. The area of the room is 300 square feet. What is the length of the room?

(A) 5 feet

(B) 10 feet

(C) 15 feet

(D) 20 feet

(E) 30 feet

32. Which of the following is the graph of the parabola $y = -(x + 3)^2 - 2$?

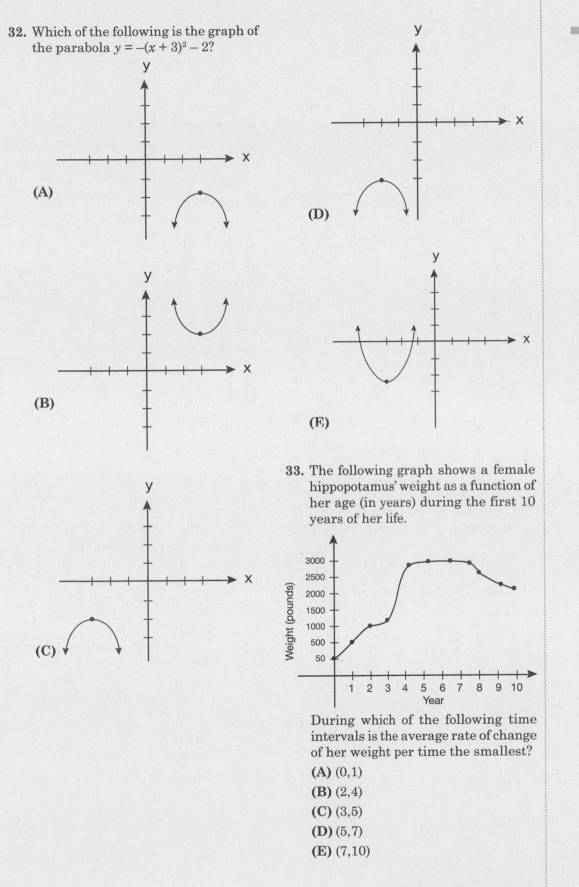

(A)

(B)

(C)

(D)

(E)

33. The following graph shows a female hippopotamus' weight as a function of her age (in years) during the first 10 years of her life.

During which of the following time intervals is the average rate of change of her weight per time the smallest?

(A) $(0, 1)$

(B) $(2, 4)$

(C) $(3, 5)$

(D) $(5, 7)$

(E) $(7, 10)$

34. Which of the following is equivalent to $2\left(\dfrac{3}{2} - 4x^2\right) - 3\left(-1 + \dfrac{1}{3}x - 3x^2\right)$?

    (A) $6 - x + x^2$

    (B) $5 + \dfrac{1}{3}x - 7x^2$

    (C) $-1 + x - 17x^2$

    (D) $6 + x^2$

    (E) $x^2 - \dfrac{1}{3}x + 2$

35. Which of the following is equivalent to $\left(\sqrt{27} - \sqrt{3}\right)\left(\sqrt{3} - \sqrt{9}\right)$?

    (A) $\sqrt{81} - \sqrt{27}$

    (B) $6\left(1 - \sqrt{3}\right)$

    (C) $3\sqrt{3} - 6$

    (D) $\sqrt{27} - 3$

    (E) $6 - \sqrt{3}$

36. There are three lanes at a car wash, labeled A, B, and C. Lane A is equipped with new equipment and handles twice as many cars per hour as Lane B. Lane C is the oldest of the three lanes and is prone to periodic breakdowns—it handles no more than one-half the cars that Lane B handles. If we let A, B, and C represent the number of cars that Lanes A, B, and C, respectively, can wash per hour, which of the following is true?

    (A) $4C \leq A$

    (B) $4C \geq 2B$

    (C) $A + B + C < 10$

    (D) $B + C \geq A$

    (E) $4C > B$

37. A room measures 15 feet by 20 feet, and the ceiling is 10 feet high. A gallon of paint is needed to apply one coat of paint to 350 square feet of wall space. Two coats of paint must be applied to complete the job. If Robert has one 5-gallon barrel of paint, what percentage of the job can he complete?

    (A) 17.5%

    (B) 50%

    (C) 75%

    (D) 87.5%

    (E) 100%

38. Which of the following would be a correct first step in solving the equation $\dfrac{3}{5}x - 3 = -\dfrac{3}{10}x + 1$?

    (A) $3x - 15 = -3x + 10$

    (B) $\dfrac{3}{5}x = -\dfrac{3}{10}x - 2$

    (C) $6x - 30 = -3x + 10$

    (D) $\dfrac{3}{5}x - \dfrac{3}{10}x = 1 - 3$

    (E) $6x - 3 = -3x + 1$

39. Epidemiologists are trying to determine how widespread the influenza virus is in a certain city. They use sampling to make their conclusion. Which of the following approaches is valid?

    (A) Their agency dispatches 15 different teams who then disperse through different regions of the city and choose 50 people at random to test for influenza infection. They then tally the number of the 750 people who are infected, compute the percentage, and use *this* as an estimate of the entire city's population that are infected with influenza.

    (B) Choose 2 people at random from the city, assess if they have the influenza virus. From this information, conclude that the entire city is infected, half the population is infected, or none is infected.

(C) A team is dispatched and they test every tenant of a high-rise apartment building. From this information, they compute the percentage of those infected and use *this* as an estimate of the entire city's population that are infected with influenza.

(D) All three are valid approaches.

(E) None of the approaches is valid.

40. Carole invested a total of $40,000 in two stocks. Stock A paid 5% simple interest for the year, and Stock B paid 7% simple interest for the year. The total interest from the two funds for the year was $3,500. If a represents the total invested in Stock A and b represents the total invested in Stock B, which of the following systems can be used to determine how much was invested in each stock?

(A) $\begin{cases} a + b = 40,000 \\ 0.05a + 0.07b = 3,500 \end{cases}$

(B) $\begin{cases} a + b = 3,500 \\ 0.05a + 0.07b = 40,000 \end{cases}$

(C) $\begin{cases} a + b = 40,000 \\ 5a + 7b = 3,500 \end{cases}$

(D) $\begin{cases} a + b = 40,000 \\ 0.5a + 0.7b = 3,500 \end{cases}$

(E) $\begin{cases} a + b = 3,500 \\ 5a + 7b = 40,000 \end{cases}$

41. A triangle A is pictured in the figure. A new triangle B is formed by increasing the base b by 25% and decreasing the height h by 40%. What percent of the area of triangle A is the area of triangle B? (Note that the area of a triangle with height H and base B is $\frac{1}{2}BH$.)

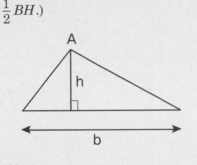

(A) 75%

(B) 60%

(C) 125%

(D) $\frac{3}{4}$%

(E) $32\frac{1}{2}$%

42. Devon purchased two 30-foot ropes, eight clamps, three chalk bags, and one backpack in preparation for his rock-climbing trip. If the cost of one 30-foot rope is r dollars, the cost of a clamp is c dollars, the cost of a chalk bag is b dollars, and the cost of one backpack is p dollars, which of the following represents the total cost C of all of the equipment?

(A) $C = r \cdot c \cdot b \cdot p$

(B) $C = r + c + b + p$

(C) $C = (2r)(8c)(3b)p$

(D) $C = 14(r + c + b + p)$

(E) $C = 2r + 8c + 3b + p$

43. On average, the bolts produced by a certain machine weigh 4 ounces. There is very little variation in this weight from bolt to bolt because of the precision of the machine. Which of the following distributions best describes this scenario?

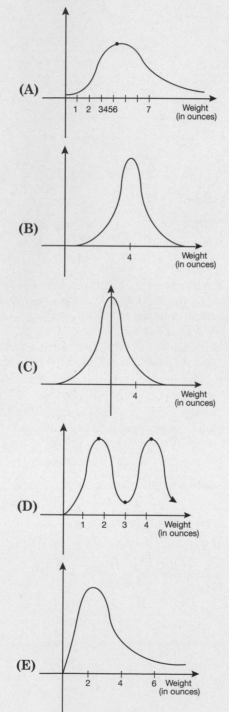

44. A child takes an ice cream sandwich out of a freezer that is kept at 25°F, goes outside where it is 85°F, places it on an unshaded lawn chair, and leaves it there for 30 minutes. Then, he comes back and quickly takes it back into the house and leaves it in the freezer for 30 minutes. Which of the following graphs best represents what happens to the temperature of the ice cream sandwich during this hour?

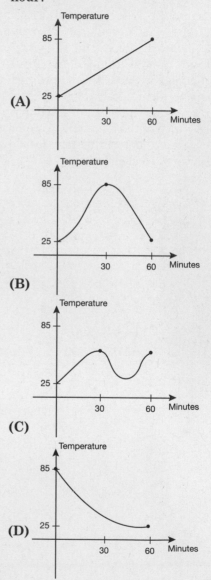

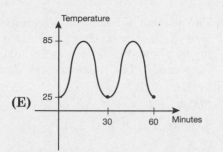

(E)

45. The volume of a certain right circular cylinder with height h and base radius r is given by $V = \pi r^2 h$. If we wish to create another right circular cylinder with 3 times the volume of this one, which of the following modifications would yield this desired result?

(A) Double the radius and keep the height the same.

(B) Triple the radius and keep the height the same.

(C) Triple the height and keep the radius the same.

(D) Double both the radius and the height.

(E) Triple both the radius and the height.

46. An amateur bowler can roll the ball at the ideal speed of 21 miles per hour. Which of the following numerical expressions is the speed of her roll in feet per minute?

(A) $\dfrac{21 \times 60 \times 60}{5,280}$ feet per minute

(B) $\dfrac{21 \times 5,280}{60 \times 60}$ feet per minute

(C) $\dfrac{21}{60 \times 60}$ feet per minute

(D) $\dfrac{21}{60}$ feet per minute

(E) $\dfrac{21 \times 5,280}{60}$ feet per minute

47. The number of gallons of gasoline per minute needed to operate a snowblower depends on the depth of the snow (measured in inches) being removed. The following table describes this relationship:

Depth of Snow (in inches)	Number of gallons of gasoline needed per minute
1.0	0.005
1.5	0.010
2.0	0.015
2.5	0.020

What is the number of gallons of gasoline needed per minute to operate a snowblower when the depth of the snow is 6 inches?

(A) 0.04

(B) 0.06

(C) 0.03

(D) 0.4

(E) 0.6

48. What is the y-intercept of the line sketched below?

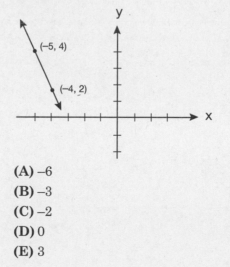

(A) −6

(B) −3

(C) −2

(D) 0

(E) 3

49. The sum of three integers is 104. The middle-valued integer in the list of three integers is five less than twice the smallest of the three integers, and the largest of the three integers is four times the smallest one. Which of the following equations can be used to determine the value of the smallest integer?

(A) $3z = 104$

(B) $z + 4z = 2z - 5$

(C) $z + (2z - 5) + 4z = 104$

(D) $z + (5z - 2) + (z + 4) = 104$

(E) $z + 2(z - 5) + 4z = 104$

50. The number of bags that 25 randomly chosen passengers check while traveling by plane through a popular airline is recorded. The numbers are shown here:

0, 0, 2, 1, 0, 1, 1, 1, >2, 0

1, 1, >2, 1, 1, 0, 0, 0, 2, 1

0, 2, >2, 1, 1

Based on this sample, what is the probability that a passenger checks no more than one bag?

(A) 0.32

(B) 0.76

(C) 0.44

(D) 0.12

(E) 0.24

SCIENCE

50 Questions • 80 Minutes

QUESTIONS 1 THROUGH 5 ARE BASED ON THE FOLLOWING INFORMATION.

Phytoplankton are a type of single-celled plankton that use photosynthesis to help them grow, like plants. To study the effect of sunlight on phytoplankton growth, researchers measured the amount of phytoplankton at different depths in the ocean. They also measured the amount of sunlight at different depths. The results are shown here.

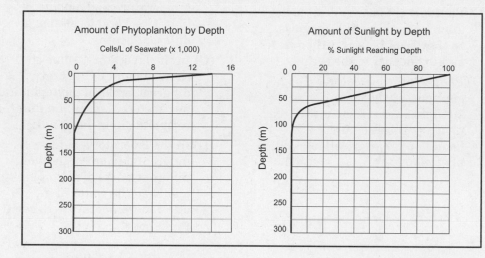

1. Which of the following best states the hypothesis being tested in this study?

   (A) Phytoplankton grow best at the surface of the ocean.

   (B) The amount of light that reaches phytoplankton affects their growth.

   (C) The amount of light that phytoplankton receive must be constant.

   (D) Phytoplankton grow best in the deepest part of the ocean.

2. Based on the results of the study, which of the following best states the relationship between phytoplankton growth and sunlight?

   (A) As sunlight increases, phytoplankton growth decreases.

   (B) As sunlight decreases, phytoplankton growth increases.

   (C) As sunlight increases, phytoplankton growth increases.

   (D) There does not appear to be a relationship between phytoplankton growth and sunlight.

3. Based on the two graphs, if the graph of sunlight by depth showed 80% light penetration at 80 meters, what would be the approximate shape of the line depicting phytoplankton growth by depth through 100 meters?

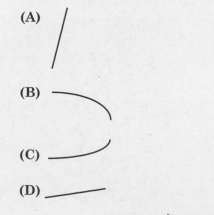

4. What is the best explanation for the results of this study?

(A) Sunlight increases water temperature, so the more sunlight there is, the warmer the water is, leading to more growth of phytoplankton.

(B) Phytoplankton concentrate sunlight in an area, so the more phytoplankton there are, the more sunlight there is.

(C) Phytoplankton are microscopic animals with small body mass, so they tend to float rather than sinking deeper in the ocean.

(D) Photosynthesis requires sunlight, so the more sunlight there is, the more photosynthesis occurs, leading to more growth of phytoplankton.

5. The graph of ocean temperature at different depths is similar to that for sunlight. What is the best way for researchers to test if it is sunlight or temperature that is affecting the growth of phytoplankton?

(A) In the ocean, measure the amount of light, amount of phytoplankton, and water temperature at different depths.

(B) In the ocean, measure the water temperature and amount of light at several locations, at different depths.

(C) In the laboratory, shine the same amount of light on different tanks of phytoplankton but keep the water at a different temperature in each tank.

(D) In the laboratory, shine a different amount of light on different tanks of phytoplankton and keep the water at a different temperature in each tank.

QUESTIONS 6 THROUGH 10 ARE BASED ON THE FOLLOWING INFORMATION.

Lactase is the enzyme that breaks down the sugar lactose, which is a sugar commonly found in milk. The effects of temperature and pH on lactase activity were studied in the following two experiments.

Experiment 1

Six test tubes were each filled with a solution containing 5.0 mg of lactose. The same amount of lactase enzyme was added to each tube. The tubes were placed into six different water baths and allowed to sit for 30 minutes. At the end of that time, the amount of lactose left in each tube was measured. The results are given in the table.

Temperature of Water Bath (°C)	Amount of Lactose Remaining After 30 Minutes (mg)
0	4.8
5	4.5
25	2.8
37	2.5
60	4.0
100	5.0

Experiment 2

Six test tubes were each filled with a solution containing 5.0 mg of lactose. The same amount of lactase enzyme was added to each tube, and 5.0 mL of buffer solution of a specific pH were also added to each tube. The tubes were all placed into a 37°C water bath for 30 minutes. At the end of that time, the amount of lactose left in each tube was measured. The results are given in the table.

pH of Buffer Solution Added	Amount of Lactose Remaining After 30 Minutes (mg)
2	4.8
4	4.5
6	2.5
8	3.3
10	4.5
12	5.0

6. When lactase activity increases, the amount of lactose broken down also increases, decreasing the amount of lactose remaining. What is the best conclusion that can be made from Experiment 1?

   (A) Lactase activity continuously increases as temperature increases.

   (B) Lactase activity increases with temperature until it peaks at 37°C and decreases above that temperature.

   (C) Lactase activity continuously decreases as temperature decreases.

   (D) Lactase activity peaks at 0°C and decreases with temperature until it reaches a low at 37°C, and then increases with temperature until it peaks again at 100°C.

7. What is the pH value in Experiment 2 that promotes the highest lactase activity?

   (A) 2
   (B) 6
   (C) 8
   (D) 12

8. Which of the following graphs best illustrates the relationship between lactase activity and pH shown in Experiment 2?

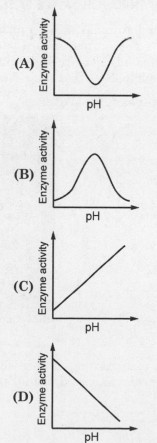

9. Considering that human lactase was used in both experiments, what is the best explanation for the optimum temperature and pH for lactase activity found in these experiments?

(A) The optimum temperature and pH for lactase activity found in these experiments are closest to those found in the human body.

(B) The optimum temperature and pH for lactase activity found in these experiments are closest to those found in cow's milk.

(C) The optimum temperature and pH for lactase activity found in these experiments are closest to those found at room temperature.

(D) The optimum temperature and pH for lactase activity found in

these experiments are closest to those found in the laboratory.

10. Lactase, like all enzymes, is a protein. What is the best explanation for the pH and temperature found in Experiments 1 and 2 at which lactase activity is lowest?

(A) Lactase activity is lowest at pH and temperatures that do not contain enough energy to activate it.

(B) Lactase activity is lowest at pH and temperatures that freeze the enzyme.

(C) Lactase activity is lowest at pH and temperatures that encourage binding of lactose.

(D) Lactase activity is lowest at pH and temperatures that cause it to denature or break down.

QUESTIONS 11 THROUGH 14 ARE BASED ON THE FOLLOWING INFORMATION.

The graph featured is called a phase diagram. It shows the phases of water at different temperatures and pressures. In the shaded areas, water exists at the phase indicated. Along the solid lines, water can exist as both phases on either side of the line. Note that the x- and y-axes are not drawn to scale.

Phase Diagram for Water

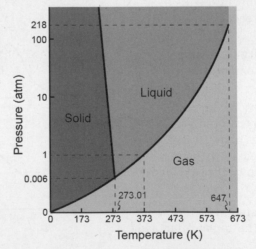

11. At which temperature and pressure can water exist as a solid, liquid, and gas?

(A) 0 atm, 273.01 K

(B) 1 atm, 373 K

(C) 0.006 atm, 273.01 K

(D) 218 atm, 647 K

12. In what phase(s) can water exist at 1 atm and 298 K?

(A) Solid

(B) Liquid

(C) Gas

(D) Liquid and gas

13. What general trend can be deduced from the phase diagram?

   (A) As temperature and pressure increase, liquid water turns into a solid.

   (B) As temperature and pressure decrease, liquid water turns into a gas.

   (C) As temperature and pressure increase, solid water turns into a liquid or gas.

   (D) As temperature and pressure decrease, solid water turns into a liquid or gas.

14. If you have a sample of liquid water at 1 atm and 300 K, which of the processes below will transform the liquid to a gas?

   (A) Increasing temperature while keeping pressure the same

   (B) Decreasing temperature while keeping pressure the same

   (C) Increasing pressure while keeping temperature the same

   (D) Decreasing temperature and increasing pressure

QUESTIONS 15 THROUGH 19 ARE BASED ON THE FOLLOWING INFORMATION.

A researcher investigated competition for food between two different species of crabs. Blue crabs and green crabs were put into a tank alone, with another crab of the same species, or with a crab of the other species. A piece of food was dropped into the tank and the amount of time it took for any crab to first find the food was measured. The same food was used in each test. The results are shown in the table.

Test Number	Crab(s) in Tank	Average Amount of Time for Any Crab to First Find Food (Seconds)
1	1 blue crab only	495
2	2 blue crabs	450
3	1 green crab only	90
4	2 green crabs	80
5	1 blue crab and 1 green crab	If blue crab found food first: 550 If green crab found food first: 160

15. Which of the following is the best statement of the hypothesis being tested in this experiment?

   (A) Blue crabs eat different food than green crabs.

   (B) Water temperature affects how quickly a crab can find food.

   (C) Green crabs will fight for food only if it is a preferred food item.

   (D) The presence of another crab will affect how quickly a crab can find food.

16. Which of the following conclusions is supported by the results of this experiment?

   (A) Crabs take the longest time to find food when they are placed in a tank with a crab of a different species.

   (B) Crabs take the least amount of time to find food when they are alone in a tank.

   (C) The presence of other crabs does not affect the amount of time it takes a crab to find food.

   (D) Only the presence of a different species of crab affects the amount of time it takes to find food.

17. Although this experiment is studying competition between crabs, why were tests 1 and 3 performed in which there was just one crab in the tank?

    (A) They were performed when there were not enough crabs to put together in one tank.

    (B) They are looking at the effect of water temperature on crab feeding times.

    (C) They are controls to see the normal behavior of crabs when they are alone.

    (D) They are looking at the effect of the type of food on crab feeding times.

18. If the green crab were replaced with a lobster, which test would be most likely to show a different result?

    (A) Test 1

    (B) Test 2

    (C) Tests 3 and 5

    (D) Tests 3, 4, and 5

19. Which of the following would be the most reasonable application of the results of this experiment to crab behavior in the wild?

    (A) In the wild, green crabs may be more successful than blue crabs because they can find food more quickly.

    (B) In the wild, blue crabs may be more successful than green crabs because they can find food more quickly.

    (C) In the wild, green crabs and blue crabs can live in the same environment without affecting the other species.

    (D) In the wild, blue crabs and green crabs do not compete with each other for food.

QUESTIONS 20 THROUGH 23 ARE BASED ON THE FOLLOWING INFORMATION.

To investigate how particles are transported by moving water, researchers dropped painted rocks of different shapes and sizes into a fast-moving stream with a rocky bottom and measured how far they had traveled after two months. The results are shown in the table.

Rock Shape	Average Distance Traveled by Rocks (m)		
	Small Rocks (<1,000 g)	Medium Rocks (1,000–1,999 g)	Large Rocks (>2,000 g)
Spheres	21.4	51.0	36.0
Blades	25.4	5.1	2.0
Rods	43.6	7.7	10.3
Discs	40.0	4.2	2.5

20. Which of the following characteristics of the study is least relevant to the outcome of the study?

    (A) The shape of the rock

    (B) The type of rock (quartz, etc.) used

    (C) The temperature of the water in the stream

    (D) The speed of the current in the stream

21. If a blade with a mass of 1,400 g were dropped into this stream, how far would it most likely travel after two months?

    (A) 5 m

    (B) 10 m

    (C) 25 m

    (D) 40 m

22. Reading down a single column in the table allows the researchers to compare the transport of particles of

    (A) the same size but different shapes.

    (B) the same size and same shape.

    (C) different sizes and different shapes.

    (D) different sizes but the same shape.

23. The researchers hypothesize that small spheres travel less far than medium and large spheres because they get stuck more easily in the rocky bottom of the stream. What is the best way to test this hypothesis?

    (A) Drop more small spheres into the same rocky-bottomed stream and measure how far they travel after two months.

    (B) Drop small rocks with new shapes, such as cubes and stars, into the same rocky-bottomed stream and measure how far they travel after two months.

    (C) Drop small, medium, and large spheres into a stream with no rocks on the bottom and measure how far they travel after two months.

    (D) Drop small spheres, rods, blades, and discs into a stream with no rocks on the bottom and measure how far they travel after two months.

QUESTIONS 24 THROUGH 28 ARE BASED ON THE FOLLOWING INFORMATION.

In fruit flies, red eyes are caused by a dominant gene, R. White eyes are caused by a recessive gene, r. A fruit fly gets one copy of the eye color gene from each parent, so a fruit fly can have a RR, Rr, or rr gene makeup, or genotype. Dominant genes cover up the characteristics of the recessive gene, so both RR and Rr flies have red eyes. Only rr flies have white eyes. To determine the genotype of a fruit fly with red eyes, it is mated with a fruit fly with white eyes. The genotype of the red-eyed fly is unknown. The possible outcomes of this mating are shown here.

If the red-eyed fly is RR: 100% of the offspring will be Rr.	If the red-eyed fly is Rr: 50% of the offspring will be Rr, 50% will be rr.

The offspring from several matings were counted and the results are shown in the table.

Mating Number	Number of Red-Eyed Offspring	Number of White-Eyed Offspring
1	26	27
2	31	30
3	29	30

24. Which of the following is the main question that this experiment is trying to answer?

(A) What is the genotype of the white-eyed fly?

(B) How many offspring do fruit flies have in each mating?

(C) What type of offspring do red- and white-eyed fruit flies have when they mate?

(D) Is the gene makeup of the red-eyed fly Rr or RR?

25. Based on the results of the matings, what is the genotype of the red-eyed fruit fly parent?

(A) RR

(B) Rr

(C) rr

(D) It cannot be determined from the results of this experiment.

26. If a fourth mating is carried out between the red-eyed parent and the white-eyed parent and there are 35 white-eyed offspring, about how many red-eyed offspring would be expected?

(A) 0

(B) 12

(C) 35

(D) 70

27. Which of the following is best described as an observation about this experiment?

(A) Red-eyed fruit flies prefer mating with other red-eyed fruit flies.

(B) Fruit flies pass on their genes to their offspring.

(C) In each mating, about half of the offspring had red eyes and the other half had white eyes.

(D) The number of each type of offspring will be the same if the red-eyed parent is mated to a different white-eyed fly.

28. If one of these red-eyed offspring is then mated to a white-eyed fly, what is the expected outcome of this mating?

(A) 100% of the offspring will be Rr.

(B) 50% of the offspring will be Rr, 50% will be rr.

(C) 50% of the offspring will be RR, 50% will be rr.

(D) 100% of the offspring will be rr.

QUESTIONS 29 THROUGH 32 ARE BASED ON THE FOLLOWING INFORMATION.

The Athabasca Glacier in the Canadian Rocky Mountains has been retreating, or shrinking, for almost 200 years. The glacier was at its largest in 1843, and the farthest distance it reached is called its maximum extent. This table shows the distance the glacier has retreated from its maximum extent and the average global temperature in various years.

Year	Distance Retreated from Maximum Extent (m)	Average Global Temperature (°C)
1906	208	13.6
1938	659	14.0
1948	905	13.8
1959	1,142	13.9
1979	1,327	14.2
1992	1,394	14.3
1999	1,510	14.4

29. How many meters did the Athabasca Glacier retreat between 1906 and 1999?

(A) 851 m

(B) 1,186 m

(C) 1,302 m

(D) 1,510 m

30. The average rate at which the glacier retreats in any time period can be calculated by dividing the distance retreated during the time period by the number of years that have passed. During which of the periods below did the glacier retreat the fastest?

(A) 1843 to 1906: distance retreated = 208 m in 63 years

(B) 1906 to 1938: distance retreated = 451 m in 32 years

(C) 1938 to 1948: distance retreated = 246 m in 10 years

(D) 1992 to 1999: distance retreated = 116 m in 7 years

31. Which of the following hypotheses about the Athabasca Glacier can be tested using the information provided in the table?

(A) The rate of glacier retreat is fastest when the least snow falls on the glacier.

(B) The rate of glacier retreat is fastest when the rate of temperature increase is fastest.

(C) The rate of glacier retreat is fastest when the most sediment is blown onto the glacier.

(D) The rate of glacier retreat is fastest when the most human use of glacier ice occurs.

32. Which of the following is a valid conclusion that can be made from the information provided in the table?

(A) Snowfall decreases substantially when the temperature increases above 14.0°C.

(B) The structure of the Canadian Rocky Mountains has changed in the past 200 years, causing the glacier to retreat from its maximum extent.

(C) A temperature decrease of only 0.2°C is enough to cause the Athabasca Glacier to stop shrinking.

(D) A temperature increase of only 0.3°C is enough to cause the Athabasca Glacier to retreat more than a kilometer from its maximum extent.

QUESTIONS 33 THROUGH 36 ARE BASED ON THE FOLLOWING INFORMATION.

Researchers are studying two rock formations, the Staghorn Formation and the Coyote Formation, which are 100 miles apart. The researchers hypothesize that the two formations are about the same age. They know that rock layers are the same age if they contain the same kinds of fossils. They also know from the principle of superposition that rock layers are deposited one at a time, with the oldest on the bottom and youngest on top. Drawings of the two formations are shown in the figure.

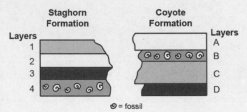

33. Which of the following is the most reasonable assumption that can be made about the rock layers?

(A) In the Staghorn Formation, Layer 3 is older than Layer 4 because it is on top of Layer 4.

(B) In the Coyote Formation, Layer B is older than Layer A because it is below Layer A.

(C) Layer 3 in the Staghorn Formation is the same age as Layer D in the Coyote Formation because they are the same color.

(D) Layer 1 in the Staghorn Formation and Layer A in the Coyote Formation are the same age because they are both the top layers in their formations.

34. Which layer is the youngest layer in the Coyote Formation?

(A) Layer A

(B) Layer B

(C) Layer C

(D) Layer D

35. Which layers are the same age?

(A) Layer 3 in the Staghorn Formation and Layer D in the Coyote Formation

(B) Layer 2 in the Staghorn Formation and Layer C in the Coyote Formation

(C) Layer 4 in the Staghorn Formation and Layer B in the Coyote Formation

(D) Layer 1 in the Staghorn Formation and Layer A in the Coyote Formation

36. By measuring the decay of radioactive elements present in both layers, the researchers determine that Layer 2 in the Staghorn Formation and Layer A in the Coyote Formation are also the same age. Based on this information, which of the following is a valid conclusion?

    (A) Layer 2 in the Staghorn Formation is younger than Layer C in the Coyote Formation.

    (B) Layer 4 in the Staghorn Formation is younger than Layer B in the Coyote Formation.

    (C) Layer 3 in the Staghorn Formation is younger than Layer C in the Coyote Formation.

    (D) Layer 1 in the Staghorn Formation is older than Layer A in the Coyote Formation.

QUESTIONS 37 THROUGH 40 ARE BASED ON THE FOLLOWING INFORMATION.

Nitric oxide gas (NO) reacts with nitrogen trioxide gas (NO_3) to form nitrogen dioxide gas (NO_2). Different concentrations of NO and NO_3 were mixed together at the same temperature to determine the effect of concentration on their rate of reaction. The results from different tests are shown in the table.

Test Number	Concentration of NO (M)	Concentration of NO_3 (M)	Initial Rate of Reaction (M/s)
1	0.001	0.001	1.57×10^4
2	0.001	0.002	3.14×10^4
3	0.003	0.001	4.71×10^4

37. By looking at the results of tests 1 and 2, a researcher can determine the effect of

    (A) changing the concentration of NO on rate.

    (B) changing the concentration of NO_3 on rate.

    (C) changing the reactants of the reaction on rate.

    (D) changing the products of the reaction on rate.

38. What happens to the rate of the reaction when the concentration of NO is tripled?

    (A) The rate doubles.

    (B) The rate is cut in half.

    (C) The rate stays the same.

    (D) The rate triples.

39. What happens to the rate of the reaction when the concentration of NO_3 is doubled?

    (A) The rate doubles.

    (B) The rate is cut in half.

    (C) The rate stays the same.

    (D) The rate triples.

40. Which of the following statements best describes the relationship of the concentration of NO and NO_3 to the rate of their reaction?

    (A) Rate stays the same no matter how the concentration of NO and NO_3 changes.

    (B) Rate decreases by the same amount that the concentration of NO and NO_3 increases.

    (C) Rate increases by the same amount that the concentration of NO and NO_3 increases.

    (D) Rate increases twice as fast as the concentration of NO and NO_3 increases.

41. When comparing a penguin, flamingo, and bat, what would be most useful in determining which two animals are most closely related?

    (A) The body parts of the animals

    (B) The habitats that the animals live in

    (C) The kind of food that the animals eat

    (D) The number of offspring that the animals have

42. Jorge suspects that he may be allergic to dairy products, seafood, or wheat. What would be the best way for Jorge to figure out which food he is allergic to?

    (A) Stop eating all three foods for several days.

    (B) Eat each food for a few days without eating the other two.

    (C) Decrease the amount of all three foods for several days.

    (D) Eat only dairy and seafood for a few days.

43. Objects appear to be a certain color because they reflect the wavelength of light that corresponds to that color, while absorbing the other wavelengths of light. How does a red stop sign interact with light?

    (A) The stop sign absorbs all wavelengths of light.

    (B) The stop sign absorbs wavelengths of red light.

    (C) The stop sign reflects wavelengths of red light.

    (D) The stop sign reflects wavelengths of green light.

44. A child on the playground is worried that the slide will be too hot to slide on. She takes several steps to decide which slide to use.

    Step 1: She notices that the slide is facing the direct sun

    Step 2: She thinks that the sun heats up the metal slide

    Step 3: She thinks that a slide in the shade might be cooler

    Step 4: She carefully places her hand first on the slide in the sun and the slide in the shade and finds that the sunny slide is too hot to touch.

    Which step constitutes data?

    (A) Step 1

    (B) Step 2

    (C) Step 3

    (D) Step 4

45. The carbon in a plant enters another stage of the carbon cycle when the plant

    (A) absorbs water through its roots.

    (B) is buried deep in the earth and turns into coal.

    (C) releases oxygen from its leaves.

    (D) is eaten by an animal.

46. A researcher wants to study if rain or insects have a larger effect on breaking down leaves that fall on the forest floor. What is the best way for the researcher to study the effect of rain alone on the leaves?

    (A) Cover a leafy section of the forest floor with a plastic dome that blocks both rain and insects.

    (B) Observe an uncovered leafy section of the forest floor.

    (C) Cover a leafy section of the forest floor with a mesh dome that blocks insects but not rain.

    (D) Cover a bare section of the forest floor with a mesh dome that blocks insects but not rain.

47. Two salt solutions of different concentrations are separated by a membrane that only allows water to pass through it, as shown in the figure. The solutions are left uncovered and untouched for several hours, and after this time, one of the solutions has increased in volume and the other has decreased in volume. Which of the following is the best explanation for what has occurred?

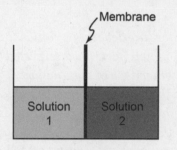

Original Setup

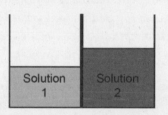

Several Hours Later

   (A) Water has evaporated from the solution that has decreased in volume.
   (B) Water has moved through the membrane from one solution to the other.
   (C) Salt has moved through the membrane from one solution to the other.
   (D) Water has been added to the solution that has increased in volume.

48. Bacteria produce new offspring every few minutes to every few hours. Why does this allow them to evolve quickly?
   (A) New traits can be passed on to the next generation very quickly.

   (B) New traits occur more often through mutation in bacteria.
   (C) New traits have a bigger effect on bacteria because they are simple organisms.
   (D) New traits can be passed between bacteria of the same generation very quickly.

49. Which of the following is the best evidence that the continents once fitted together in one large supercontinent?
   (A) Similar animals on different continents
   (B) Seafloor spreading
   (C) Rocks in eastern South America that match rocks in western Africa
   (D) Coastline shapes that look as if they might once have fit together

50. Two organisms are in symbiosis when they interact with each other in a way that benefits both. Which of the following is the best example of symbiosis?
   (A) Flea sucks blood from a dog, which causes the dog to develop itchy bumps where the flea bites.
   (B) Clownfish eats small animals that may harm an anemone, while the anemone protects the clownfish from animals that may eat it.
   (C) Lion kills a zebra, and vultures eat the scraps that are left over when the lion is finished eating.
   (D) Barnacles attach to a whale and are carried around to different food sources by the whale, while the whale is unharmed.

SOCIAL STUDIES

50 Questions • 70 Minutes

QUESTIONS 1 THROUGH 6 ARE BASED ON THE INFORMATION SHOWN.

The Senate debate on H.R. 7152, the Civil Rights Bill of 1964, saw the majority leader filing a routine motion to place the House-passed bill directly on the Senate calendar without the normal referral to the Judiciary Committee. The following comes from a letter by Clarence Mitchell chronicling the response on March 12, 1964.

"At this time (Thursday, March 12) southern senators are debating a motion to take up the Civil Rights Bill. This is a delaying tactic on their part. It was expected that civil rights opponents would use this and every other type of obstruction. It was also expected that the opponents would continue their opposition to the motion to take up for about two weeks. As this is written, there is some hope that the anti-civil rights forces will shorten their opposition to the motion to take up. This could mean that there will be a vote on this motion next week. *At that point, Senator Wayne Morse (D. -Ore.) is expected to make a motion to send the bill to Senator Eastland's Judiciary Committee for a ten-day period. Senator Morse says he wants to do this because "We owe it to the courts, we owe it to the Senate and we owe it to the American people to send this bill to the committee and get a committee report out of the Judiciary Committee."*

1. The tactic being described is known in the legislature as
   (A) cloture.
   (B) a pocket veto.
   (C) a hold.
   (D) logrolling.

2. Which of the following tactics would the southern senators most likely use to further delay the vote on the bill once it has been debated on the floor?
   (A) Filibustering
   (B) Senatorial courtesy
   (C) Obtaining a discharge petition
   (D) Obtaining a rider

3. The Civil Rights Bill described was passed in 1964 and attempted to further strengthen the rights created by which of the following amendments?
   (A) The First Amendment—freedom of speech, religion, and the press
   (B) The Fifth Amendment—due process of the law
   (C) The Fourteenth Amendment—guarantee of citizenship, due process, and equal protection
   (D) The Nineteenth Amendment—giving all citizens the vote, regardless of gender

4. The need for the Civil Rights Bill was created because of unfair practices made legal in the ruling of
   (A) Dred Scott v. Sandford.
   (B) Plessy v. Ferguson.
   (C) Roe v. Wade.
   (D) Gibbons v. Ogden.

5. Why would the southern senators look to delay the bill?

   (A) They were afraid the bill would not pass.

   (B) They were afraid the bill would pass.

   (C) They were waiting for the president to veto the bill.

   (D) They were writing their own bill that would give more rights.

6. During this period of history, and according to the excerpt, which political party would most likely be in support of the Civil Rights Bill?

   (A) Republicans

   (B) Democrats

   (C) Whigs

   (D) Tea

QUESTIONS 7 THROUGH 11 ARE BASED ON THE FOLLOWING INFORMATION.

The U.S. Constitution outlines the requirements for becoming a U.S. Senator, a U.S. House Representative, or U.S. President as shown.

Senator (Article I, Section 3)	House Representative (Article I, Section 2)	President (Article II, Section 1)
• at least 30 years of age • a U.S. citizen for at least nine years at time of election to Senate • a resident of the state one is elected to represent in the Senate	• at least 25 years of age • a U.S. citizen for at least seven years prior to election to the House • a resident of the state one is elected to represent in the House	• at least 35 years of age • a native born U.S. citizen • must live in the U.S. for at least 14 years

7. According to the chart, which of the following positions would a candidate be able to run for earliest in his or her career?

   (A) Senator

   (B) House representative

   (C) President

   (D) Any of the above

8. Based on the information, a 35-year-old candidate who has been a citizen of the United States for eight years could run for which of the following offices?

   (A) Senator

   (B) House representative

   (C) President

   (D) Any of the above

9. It can be concluded that the most restrictive requirement for all of the positions in the U.S. government would be

   (A) age.

   (B) citizenship.

   (C) residency.

   (D) religion.

10. Ronald Reagan was born in 1911 in Illinois and moved to Hollywood, CA, in 1937, where he lived until 1980. In 1980, for which of the following offices could he run?

    (A) Senator of Illinois

    (B) House Representative of Illinois

    (C) President of the United States

    (D) All of the above

11. According to the chart, which of the following offices could Alexander Hamilton, born in the 1750s in the West Indies and residing in New York until 1803, not run for in 1800?

(A) Senator of New York

(B) House of Representative of New York

(C) President of the United States

(D) Any of the above

QUESTIONS 12 THROUGH 19 REFER TO THE MAP SHOWN.

The 2000 election was one of the most controversial in history, taking over two weeks after election night to decide a definitive winner.

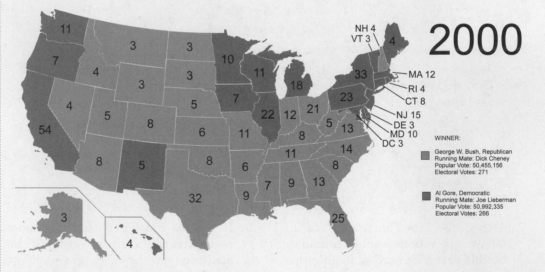

12. Which of the following is most important in determining a Presidential winner, according to the information shown on the map?

(A) Running mate

(B) Popular vote

(C) Electoral vote

(D) Geographic positioning

13. How would issues with an election in a "contingent election" be settled?

(A) Popular vote

(B) In the Senate

(C) In the House of Representatives

(D) By the Speaker of the House

14. It can be inferred by the results of the map that more people live where?

(A) On the coasts

(B) In the Midwest

(C) In the South

(D) In the Northwest

15. Which piece of information given via the map is least important in helping to determine a winner?

(A) Popular vote

(B) Electoral vote

(C) Color code

(D) Running mate

16. The colors used in the map are meant to represent which of the following for the candidates?

    (A) Age
    (B) Popular vote
    (C) Running mate
    (D) Political party

17. Both George W. Bush and Al Gore would need to fulfill all of the following criteria to run for President except

    (A) be at least 35 years of age.
    (B) be a natural born citizen of the United States.
    (C) reside in the states in which they were elected.
    (D) live in the United States for at least 14 years.

18. Which of the following terms became synonymous with the election of 2000?

    (A) Abandoned ballot
    (B) Hanging chad
    (C) Filibuster
    (D) Tabulator

19. Often, candidates will focus their attention on some states more than others. Which of the following states would a candidate most likely ignore in favor of the other three?

    (A) Ohio
    (B) Florida
    (C) Maryland and the District of Columbia
    (D) Pennsylvania

QUESTIONS 20 THROUGH 23 REFER TO THE INFORMATION FROM THE UNITED STATES CENSUS BUREAU COMPLIED IN 2010, COMPARING TOP INDUSTRIES AND THE WORKFORCE.

Job/Industry	1940	Job/Industry	2010
Manufacturing	23.4%	Education, healthcare, and social assistance	23.2%
Agriculture	18.5%	Retail trade	11.7%
Retail trade	14.0%	Management or administration services	10.6%
Personal service	8.9%	Manufacturing	10.4%
Professional services	7.4%	Construction	6.2%

20. Based on the information provided, the economy of the United States has become more dependent on which of the following to fund its workforce?

    (A) Home building
    (B) Private manufacturing
    (C) Service
    (D) Agriculture

21. Demand for manufacturing most likely would have declined due to which of the following factors?

    (A) Domestic competition
    (B) Outsourcing
    (C) Cheaper cost of production in the United States
    (D) Decrease in domestic workforce

22. Which of the following would have also seen an increase in number in 2010, to assist in the changing workforce?

(A) College degrees

(B) Small businesses

(C) Farms

(D) Retail space

23. According to the graph, it can be inferred that which of the following industries had the greatest decline in workforce from the period 1940–2010?

(A) Manufacturing

(B) Agriculture

(C) Retail trade

(D) Education

QUESTIONS 24 THROUGH 25 REFER TO THE FOLLOWING SCENARIO.

The advertising department of a famous soft drink company is designing a new campaign. The print advertisements, which will be featured in magazines and newspapers and on billboards starting in the late fall, will feature a picture of Santa Claus, surrounded by holiday lights, enjoying a bottle of their most popular soft drink. The text of the advertisement will read: "A Delicious Bottle of Holiday Cheer!"

24. This ad is attempting to sell its product by emphasizing

(A) taste.

(B) value.

(C) consumer popularity.

(D) an iconic figure.

25. The product being sold in the advertisement would best be classified as which of the following?

(A) Commodity

(B) Capital

(C) Collateral

(D) Durable

QUESTIONS 26 THROUGH 28 REFER TO THE FOLLOWING INFORMATION.

Denise is watching a television show that takes place in 1980. A character in the show buys a coat for $100, and Denise wants to find out how much the coat would be worth in the present year.

She finds a feature on the Bureau of Labor Statistics's Website called a CPI Inflation Calculator, which tells her the following information: $100.00 in 1980 has the same buying power as $284.86 in 2015.

26. Which of the following best describes the information found on the Website?

(A) Rise in the general price level

(B) Decrease in the worth of the dollar

(C) Increase in the deflation of prices

(D) Decrease in the cost of living

27. Which of the following would account for the information provided from the Website?

(A) Demand-pull inflation

(B) Cost-push inflation

(C) Demand-push deflation

(D) Cost-pull inflation

28. What does CPI stand for?

(A) Cost Product Index

(B) Gross Domestic Product

(C) Consumer Price Index

(D) Consumption Price Inflation

QUESTIONS 29 THROUGH 33 REFER TO THE CARTOON SHOWN

29. This cartoon is an example of
    (A) a product advertisement.
    (B) a campaign poster.
    (C) a piece of political satire.
    (D) a medical pamphlet.

30. The passage of the Pure Food and Drug Act in 1906 was in response to which of the following pieces of writing?
    (A) *The History of Standard Oil* by Ida Tarbell
    (B) *The Jungle* by Upton Sinclair
    (C) *How the Other Half Lives* by Jacob Riis
    (D) Letters by Sarah and Angelina Grimké

31. During what time period in United States history is this cartoon referencing?
    (A) The Progressive Era
    (B) World War II
    (C) Abolitionist Era
    (D) The Postwar Boom

32. What did the Pure Food and Drug Act of 1906 legislate?
    (A) Government oversight of food and drug production and labeling
    (B) Regulation of food and drug consumer costs
    (C) Socialization of healthcare and food stamps
    (D) Distribution of food and drug surpluses by government entities

33. What is the main idea of this cartoon?
    (A) Americans should trust their government to regulate the creation of safe medicine.
    (B) The United States should send more people to medical school.
    (C) Americans are being sold dangerous food and drugs from unethical industries.
    (D) The United States is a leading producer of safe food and drugs.

QUESTIONS 34 THROUGH 41 REFER TO THE POSTER SHOWN.

OUR CARELESSNESS
Their Secret Weapon

PREVENT FOREST FIRES

U. S. DEPT. OF AGRICULTURE
FOREST SERVICE

STATE
FOREST SERVICE

34. This type of poster is an example of which of the following?

(A) Satire

(B) Propaganda

(C) Realism

(D) Fundraising

35. What would have been the goal of the poster above?

(A) To win the hearts and minds of the American people

(B) To alert the people of America to a secret attack on their natural resources

(C) To show Americans what the enemy looks like

(D) To get more people involved in growing trees and farming agriculture

36. The theme of the poster shown would be which of the following?

(A) Recruitment

(B) Conservation

(C) Anti-immigration

(D) Fundraising

37. The United States would emerge from the period referenced in the poster as which of the following?

(A) Physically destroyed

(B) Financially destroyed

(C) A world superpower

(D) Politically divided

38. Which of the following countries are referenced in the poster?

(A) Germany and Italy

(B) Germany and Japan

(C) Germany and China

(D) Italy and Korea

39. This poster would have been created during which major event in history?

(A) World War I

(B) World War II

(C) The Cold War

(D) After 9/11

40. What was the name given to the powers referenced in the poster during this period?

(A) Allied powers

(B) Central powers

(C) Axis powers

(D) Nazi powers

41. Which of the following emotions is the poster above trying to evoke in its viewers?

(A) Sadness

(B) Anger

(C) Remorse

(D) Fear

QUESTIONS 42 THROUGH 47 REFER TO THESE DOCUMENTS, REGARDING THE SECESSION OF SOUTH CAROLINA IN 1860.

Document 1

"...*Thus the constituted compact has been deliberately broken and disregarded by the non-slaveholding States, and the consequence follows that South Carolina is released from her obligation...*

...*We, therefore, the People of South Carolina, by our delegates in Convention assembled, appealing to the Supreme Judge of the world for the rectitude of our intentions, have solemnly declared that the Union heretofore existing between this State and other States of North America, is dissolved, and that the State of South Carolina has resumed her position among the nations of the world, as a separate and independent State; with full power to levy war, conclude peace, contract alliances, establish commerce, and to do all other acts and things which independent States may of right do.*"

Source: Declaration of Immediate Causes Which Induce and Justify the Secession of South Carolina from the Federal Union. 1860. From Docsteach.org

Document 2

"...*I hold that, in contemplation of universal law, and of the Constitution, the Union of these States is perpetual. Perpetuity is implied, if not expressed, in the fundamental law of all National Governments. It is safe to assert that no Government proper ever had a provision in its organic law for its own termination. Continue to execute all the express provisions of our National Constitution, and the Union will endure forever-it being impossible to destroy it except by some action not provided for in the instrument itself...*

...*It follows, from these views, that no State, upon its own mere motion, can lawfully get out of the Union; that resolves and ordinances to that effect are legally void; and that acts of violence, within any State or States, against the authority of the United States, are insurrectionary or revolutionary, according to circumstances.*"

Source: Inaugural Address. 1860. Pamphlet of [President Abraham] Lincoln Speeches. 1912. From Docsteach.org

42. These two documents led to which of the following events in United States history?

(A) The American Revolution

(B) The Mexican War

(C) The Civil War

(D) World War I

43. The author of the first document believes in which type of theory in regard to secession?

(A) Contract

(B) Compact

(C) Natural law

(D) Constitutional

44. The author of the second document believes what in regard to secession?

(A) It is legal.

(B) It is not legal.

(C) It is too late.

(D) It should be discussed further.

45. The largest difference between the two passages revolves around which of the following?

(A) Slavery

(B) Economic stability

(C) Whether it is legal to secede

(D) Election of President Lincoln

46. Which of the following would most likely support the writer of the first passage?

(A) A Yankee

(B) A republican

(C) An abolitionist

(D) A Confederate

47. The author of the first passage would most likely look to which of the following documents for support of his cause?

(A) The Magna Carta

(B) Luther's 95 theses

(C) Churchill's "Iron Curtain" speech

(D) The Virginia and Kentucky Resolutions

QUESTIONS 48 THROUGH 50 RELATE TO THE MAP SHOWN, REGARDING TRANSPORTATION IN CHINA.

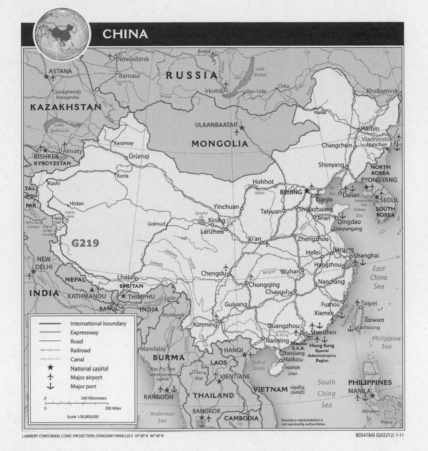

48. Which of the following points can be found on mainland China?

   (A) Taiwan
   (B) Thimphu
   (C) Khabarvosk
   (D) Shanghai

49. The statement "Beijing is north of Zhengzhou" would be classified as giving Beijing's

   (A) absolute location.
   (B) relative location.
   (C) physical geography.
   (D) spatial perspective.

50. Which of the following best explains why more airports and ports are found near the Eastern region of China than the Western?

   (A) Environmental determinism
   (B) Cultural landscape
   (C) Overpopulation
   (D) Commodification

ANSWER KEY AND EXPLANATIONS

Language Arts—Reading

1. B	9. D	17. D	25. A	33. B
2. A	10. A	18. A	26. C	34. C
3. D	11. B	19. A	27. B	35. A
4. B	12. B	20. B	28. D	36. D
5. B	13. D	21. C	29. C	37. B
6. C	14. B	22. B	30. C	38. A
7. A	15. D	23. D	31. D	39. C
8. B	16. C	24. C	32. A	40. D

1. **The correct answer is (B).** The primary purpose of this passage is to inform readers of the Triangle Shirtwaist Factory fire, and the sweeping labor reforms that resulted.

2. **The correct answer is (A).** The passage refrains from taking a strong emotional stance on the issues; instead, it adopts an informational tone, providing historical facts about a particular event, and its aftermath.

3. **The correct answer is (D).** Using the context clues in this sentence, we can determine that the spark from the sewing machine that may have wound up in the fabric bin was a *stray*, and did not belong there. The other choices don't make sense here, given the context.

4. **The correct answer is (B).** The references to the changes as "lasting and positive," and the reforms as "essential" and "necessary" indicate that the author of this passage most likely believes that reforms that followed the Triangle Shirtwaist Factory fire were long overdue.

5. **The correct answer is (B).** The takeaway message of the passage is that labor laws evolved to reflect positive and lasting change, as well as improved working conditions and employee rights on a wide scale, when compared to the era that the Triangle Shirtwaist Factory operated.

6. **The correct answer is (C).** The only item among the answer choices that is not specifically mentioned as a positive reform resulting from the Triangle Shirtwaist Factory tragedy is greater health insurance benefits for all employees.

7. **The correct answer is (A).** This sentence essentially restates the idea that all people in society are expected to have knowledge of literature.

8. **The correct answer is (B).** The author spends much of the passage expressing opinions, but this is a relatively reasonable observation to make after examining how people regard literature.

9. **The correct answer is (D).** The author uses the word *snobbery,* a negative term to describe arrogant and pretentious behavior, to describe those who would be impressed by one's knowledge of literature when the author believes literature serves a more meaningful purpose.

10. **The correct answer is (A).** The author believes that literature is an essential component of a rich and complete life and not merely a way to show off how knowledgeable one is.

11. **The correct answer is (B).** Arnold Bennett believes personal enrichment is the greatest value of reading and the author of this brief passage believes that personal enrichment is an underappreciated aspect of higher education.

12. **The correct answer is (B).** In paragraph 1, the author uses the "inability to ride a horse" as an example of something of which a person would be secretly ashamed, and this would only be a secret shame at a time when most people could ride horses.

13. **The correct answer is (D).** Gregor has been transformed into an inhuman insect, and he describes his career in dehumanizing terms, explaining that even though he meets a lot of people every day he "can never get to know anyone or become friendly with them."

14. **The correct answer is (B).** In paragraph 6, Gregor indicates that he is envious of the other salesmen he believes have easier lives than his.

15. **The correct answer is (D).** Only choice (D) is an accurate synonym of *floundering*. The word "thrashing" makes the most sense if used in place of *floundering* in paragraph 3.

16. **The correct answer is (C).** In paragraph 4, Gregor describes the stresses of his job that keep him from relaxing and he describes other salesmen who seem to be comparatively relaxed and carefree.

17. **The correct answer is (D).** One expects a man who has transformed into a giant insect to be concerned with his monstrous condition and not his everyday problems, but Gregor seems more concerned about his job than the fact that he is a giant insect.

18. **The correct answer is (A).** Gregor's unhappiness about his monstrous condition and his stressful job contribute to the somber tone, as do word choices such as "hopelessly," "pitifully," and "dull."

19. **The correct answer is (A).** The writer can only assume that abolishing liberty is as great a folly as annihilating air, since that is not possible.

20. **The correct answer is (B).** Only choice (B) identifies how these words affect the passage's tone. These are strong words that help establish the passage's heated tone.

21. **The correct answer is (C).** Only choice (C) contains restated information. Both sentences blame inequalities in property distribution for factions.

22. **The correct answer is (B).** Choice (B) is the most reasonable example of how information in this passage can be applied practically. One must understand the causes of a problem before solving it, and this passage explains the causes of factions.

23. **The correct answer is (D).** The author is figuratively referring to the problem of factions as a "disease" and the solution of destroying liberty as a "remedy."

24. **The correct answer is (C).** The poet celebrates the lighthouse for protecting and bringing joy to mariners, as well as for the aesthetic qualities of its structure and the "splendor" of its light.

25. **The correct answer is (A).** Only choice (A) is a reasonable analysis of the final stanza. The final line of the poem, "Be yours to bring man nearer unto man!" could be used to support this interpretation.

26. **The correct answer is (C).** The twelfth stanza describes a sea bird blinded, maddened, and ultimately killed by the lighthouse's intense light.

27. **The correct answer is (B).** Only choice (B) is an accurate synonym for

"smites." The word "attacks" makes the most sense if used in place of "smites" in the eleventh stanza.

28. **The correct answer is (D).** The poet uses the nonliteral image of the lighthouse hailing "the mariner with words of love" to describe how the lighthouse welcomes the mariner with its protecting light.

29. **The correct answer is (C).** In the fifth stanza, the poet compares the lighthouse to the giant Christopher, who wades into the sea to rescue mariners.

30. **The correct answer is (C).** This is a detail question, and the only substance in the apparatus the narrator identifies specifically is ivory, choice (C).

31. **The correct answer is (D).** Considering how the Time Traveller has gathered his colleagues together to examine the model of his time travelling apparatus, how he keeps pointing out its details, and how he boasts about how long it took him to make, it is clear he is proud of it.

32. **The correct answer is (A).** Captain Nemo filled his submarine with extravagances such as fine art, a huge organ, enormous pearls, and large, opulent rooms. He clearly values extravagance.

33. **The correct answer is (B).** While the narrator marvels at all the wonderments inside the Nautilus, he also says he feels like "a prisoner who dared scarcely hope that liberty might some day be obtained." Choice B sums up those conflicting feelings well.

34. **The correct answer is (C).** Passage 1 specifies that the Time Traveller built his time machine and Passage 2 specifies that Captain Nemo built his luxurious submarine, both of which are very unusual machines.

35. **The correct answer is (A).** This passage is mainly about the contents of Mr. March's letter and the ways his daughters react to them.

36. **The correct answer is (D).** Only choice (D) makes a reasonable inference based on information in the passage. The close bond of the March family is evident in the intense emotions expressed in Mr. March's letter and by his daughters when they listen to their mother reading it.

37. **The correct answer is (B).** References to the military, marching, rebels, and a blue army sock indicate that Mr. March is in the army and the passage is set during wartime.

38. **The correct answer is (A).** While her sisters weep openly when they hear their father's letter, Beth remains quiet and wipes away her tears.

39. **The correct answer is (C).** Only this choice identifies the mood of this passage. The great deal of emotion expressed in this passage helps to create a sentimental mood.

40. **The correct answer is (D).** Only this choice makes a logical prediction about what the reader will likely learn next. Mr. March ends his letter by requesting that his daughters work hard, and they then react to his request, so the reader will likely find out how well each daughter heeds his request.

Language Arts—Writing

Part 1

1. C	11. D	21. D	31. C	41. B
2. B	12. C	22. D	32. A	42. D
3. D	13. D	23. D	33. C	43. B
4. C	14. D	24. C	34. B	44. D
5. A	15. A	25. C	35. D	45. A
6. C	16. D	26. D	36. C	46. C
7. C	17. A	27. D	37. B	47. B
8. B	18. A	28. B	38. D	48. D
9. C	19. D	29. B	39. C	49. C
10. A	20. B	30. D	40. C	50. C

1. **The correct answer is (C).** This passage begins with a question and requires the appropriate end punctuation—a question mark.

2. **The correct answer is (B).** The construction of this sentence in the passage is confusing—it implies that the people you can potentially impress are wearing the headphones. It should be made clear that the phrase *wearing them* refers to *you*, the subject of the sentence.

3. **The correct answer is (D).** This sentence opens with a pronoun, which refers to *headphones* from the prior sentence. *Headphones* is a plural noun, so this sentence requires a plural pronoun and the matching verb form of *to be*—they are.

4. **The correct answer is (C).** A plural verb form is required to match *they* in the sentence. *They include* is the appropriate plural grammatical structure.

5. **The correct answer is (A).** This sentence demonstrates correct grammatical construction, with the appropriate tense and verb forms.

6. **The correct answer is (C).** This choice most clearly and effectively organizes the information in this sentence for the reader, briefly outlining the features available for over-the-ear headphones and their similarities to in-ear headphones.

7. **The correct answer is (C).** You are being asked to make an appropriate word choice here. Only choice C reflects an appropriate choice of words that is free from errors—*perfectest* and *perfecter* are not words, and *more perfect* does not make sense, as it is not possible to be *more* perfect than "perfect."

8. **The correct answer is (B).** The passage is addressing the reader directly, and requires the pronoun *your* in order to be grammatically correct. The *your* that appears earlier in the sentence is a strong context clue that you can effectively employ when answering this question.

9. **The correct answer is (C).** Proper nouns should always be capitalized appropriately. Context clues are always helpful when determining the correct spelling and capitalization of words, including company names.

The first line of the workplace memo indicates that ACME Warehouse is the correct spelling of the company name.

10. **The correct answer is (A).** This is a declarative sentence and should end with a period, as written. The other types of punctuation among the answer choices are inappropriate for this sentence.

11. **The correct answer is (D).** The correct verb form of *work* is required here. The present participle *working* is incorrect; *to work* is the appropriate form.

12. **The correct answer is (C).** Correct sentence structure and flow is required in order to effectively and clearly convey the ideas here. Choice (C) is the only version that contains a logical structure and order.

13. **The correct answer is (D).** The correct pronoun to refer to the warehouse employees is needed here. *Their* is the correct plural pronoun.

14. **The correct answer is (D).** This choice logically and appropriately combines all of the ideas conveyed in the original two sentences.

15. **The correct answer is (A).** This sentence correctly uses and punctuates *however* to transition from the ideas mentioned in the previous sentence.

16. **The correct answer is (D).** Based on the context clues provided, the goal of the memo is to try and make the break room as enjoyable and comfortable a space as possible. The word choice that best fits this notion is *welcome*.

17. **The correct answer is (A).** The appropriate verb tense is required here. The elections have already taken place, so the past tense is needed. *Were close* is correct in this sentence.

18. **The correct answer is (A).** *Especially* is the correct adverb for this sentence, which serves to highlight the closeness of the race for town treasurer. According to the passage, there were "only a handful of votes separating the winner and the loser."

19. **The correct answer is (D).** This question is asking you to make a decision regarding appropriate verb tense. We are told that the action in this sentence will occur "one month from today"—this should signal you that the future tense is needed, so *will take* is correct.

20. **The correct answer is (B).** Names are proper nouns and should always be capitalized.

21. **The correct answer is (D).** Months of the year are proper nouns and require capitalization. In this sentence, *December* should be capitalized, and no additional punctuation is required.

22. **The correct answer is (D).** The correct verb form is needed here. This sentence refers to Jenkins' past and ongoing work in local politics, so *has been working* is the correct form.

23. **The correct answer is (D).** The election is over, so the past verb tense is needed here. The past tense of this verb is *squeaked*.

24. **The correct answer is (C).** In order to make the most appropriate word choice for this sentence, you need to understand the context in which it will be used. Vevrallo is commenting on his plans following his election win. The most logical sentiment would be for him to vow to serve to the *best* of his ability.

25. **The correct answer is (C).** No punctuation is required at this part of the sentence.

26. **The correct answer is (D).** This blog entry is a review of the Meadowbrook Annual Autumn Harvest Festival. This sentence mentions an upcoming

highway expansion proposal vote by the town council and does not belong in this passage. It should be omitted.

27. **The correct answer is (D).** This is the proper spelling of the word *activities*.

28. **The correct answer is (B).** It makes the most sense that the pony rides were available for all of the children who came to the fair, so *kids* should be used in this sentence. It's also a logical conclusion that the brass band and dance floor were meant for all who attended the fair to enjoy, so *everyone* is the right pronoun choice.

29. **The correct answer is (B).** The construction of this sentence as it appears in the passage is awkward and confusing. This choice provides a more logical and effective flow of ideas, making it clear that the restaurants are running booths at the festival so attendees can try their food offerings.

30. **The correct answer is (D).** The correct verb tense of *to receive* in this sentence is the past tense, *received*.

31. **The correct answer is (C).** It is essential to remember the facts provided in the passage to make decisions regarding appropriate word choice and usage. The contest mentioned in the passage is a pie contest, and the fact that Mrs. Richtenberg lost makes it clear that her reign as the best pie maker was over.

32. **The correct answer is (A).** The correct verb construction in this sentence is *seemed to have*.

33. **The correct answer is (C).** This is the correct spelling of the word *ultimately*.

34. **The correct answer is (B).** Understanding context is essential for making the appropriate word choices. This sentence provides evidence that supports the idea of mandatory community service, that it creates "bet-

ter adults" who are "more mature, responsible, and civic-minded." These are clearly the thoughts of *those who support* this idea.

35. **The correct answer is (D).** The correct pronoun to refer to the supporters (plural) is *they*.

36. **The correct answer is (C).** This choice provides the appropriate grammatical separation of items, which are the various things that today's students have that occupy their busy schedules. Each should be separated by a comma.

37. **The correct answer is (B).** *There are*, which refers to the various *items* on the plates of today's students, is the correct plural present form required.

38. **The correct answer is (D).** This passage highlights both sides of an unsettled debate regarding a hot topic issue. It's clear that the author's position is that the issue is far from settled and that the best way to move forward is far from certain. Therefore, the use of the word *perhaps*, indicating that this is just one possible suggestion for moving forward, is the correct choice.

39. **The correct answer is (C).** This paragraph focuses on the notion that you can learn to "enjoy a satisfying cup of coffee at home." The most logical idea to follow is that the reader can do so by learning to *make* it.

40. **The correct answer is (C).** This passage is directly speaking to you, the reader. The correct pronoun to use in this instance is *your*.

41. **The correct answer is (B).** This choice presents the most clear, logical, and effective flow of ideas for this sentence.

42. **The correct answer is (D).** The construction of this sentence in the passage makes it unclear who's making the coffee—you or the people you

could potentially amaze. This choice makes it clear that you can amaze people if you make delicious coffee.

43. **The correct answer is (B).** As written in the passage, one might think you can buy your coffee beans at home. This is not true, and the confusion needs to be made clear—this choice makes it clear that you can grind your purchased beans at home with a grinder.

44. **The correct answer is (D).** This is the correct spelling of the word *patience*.

45. **The correct answer is (A).** This is the correct verb tense required in this sentence.

46. **The correct answer is (C).** The correct pronoun and verb forms are required to make this sentence grammatically correct. *Tornadoes* is a plural noun, and as such the plural pronoun *they* is required along with the appropriate verb form, *travel*.

47. **The correct answer is (B).** This sentence describes the beginning stages of tornado formation and should appear earlier in this paragraph, which focuses on how a tornado is formed.

48. **The correct answer is (D).** Paragraph 3 covers a variety of tornado facts, so this choice is the most appropriate way to introduce the main idea of this paragraph.

49. **The correct answer is (C).** The verbs in this sentence all need to be in the same tense in order for the sentence to be grammatically correct and have parallel structure: *spinning*, *racing*, and *destroying*.

50. **The correct answer is (C).** Use the context clues in this paragraph and sentence in order to make the most appropriate word choice. This paragraph offers advice on what to do if you find yourself in the path of a dangerous tornado. It makes logical sense that you should seek *a safe* shelter from the tornado in order to protect yourself.

answers   practice test 1

PART 2

SAMPLE SCORE 6 ESSAY

Earning a college degree is an important and admirable achievement, but should it come at the expense of my future financial well-being? I don't think so. Should a high achieving student, who worked hard in every grade—from kindergarten through high school—and gets accepted into the college of her dreams, but who doesn't have the means to pay for it, be forced to bear the weight of a gigantic tuition bill in order to make her academic dreams come true? Parents tell their kids to work hard in school, to study hard, and to earn good grades in order to achieve their goals. But if they follow those lessons and get into the college of their dreams, but don't come from a family that can easily afford the cost, has their hard work and achievement just earned them a big, expensive problem? The bottom line is that the current cost structure of college is an issue screaming for attention—and reform. The costs are simply too much, it's already much more than many families can handle, and something has to change.

Take a look at the countless benefits a college graduate has in "The Economics of Higher Education": higher earnings and hireability statistics, better health, lower mortality rates... the benefits are countless. Why should these only be available to the wealthy? How is this fair? If we want our society to be able to continue to thrive, we need to make the cost of getting an education manageable.

My older sister was a great student for as long as I can remember. She applied to her dream college and got accepted. My entire family was thrilled for her, but that excitement was quickly met by a rush of fear and anxiety when it was time to think about how to pay for it. My sister decided to pay for college with student loans, which at the time seemed like a manageable idea.

Fast forward 10 years: my sister is a high school English teacher, a mother of two great kids, and has barely been able to chip away at her student loans. Her family is now living in the basement of our parent's house, as she and her husband do what they can to pay off their student loan debts. And they are just one family among many who are struggling to cope as they shoulder the expensive burden of a college education.

I know it's not easy to change the entire educational system at the college level in order to make it more affordable to students, but just because it might be difficult does not mean it shouldn't be done. At the very least, we should explore the options for reducing the cost of college for everyone. The report from irs.gov is a good start, but with a few thousand dollars here and there, it barely seems to put a dent in what a college education costs. Perhaps change means changing the student loan industry, so students aren't saddled with large interest payments on top of their loan amounts. Perhaps colleges and universities nationwide need to explore ways to operate more efficiently on lower budgets, and pass on the savings to students. These are just some of the areas that could be looked at in an effort to make college more affordable.

I'm aware of the arguments on the other side. I know that there are tools in place for paying for college, like scholarships, grants, and paid employment opportunities. But often this is not nearly enough and not available for every student. I know that some individuals argue that there are schools to match every budget, including 2-year and 4-year schools, and public and private universities. But we live in a competitive society, one in which where people go to college can affect their opportunities after they graduate. Shouldn't the best students who have achieved the best grades have the opportunity to go to the best colleges and not get crushed—or worse deterred altogether—by the cost?

I'm not naïve enough to think that this problem will be solved overnight. But let's all admit that, at the very least, it's a troubling issue worth exploring to keep the American dream of a college education from becoming a nightmare.

SAMPLE SCORE 6 ESSAY EXPLANATION

Let's analyze this Score 6 essay in each of the core content categories measured on this part of the HiSET® exam.

Development of a Central Position or Claim

This exemplary essay offers a complete and well thought out central position regarding the issue of college cost and reform (*The bottom line is that the current cost structure of college is an issue screaming for attention—and reform. The costs are simply too much, it's already much more than many families can handle, and something has to change*). It also incorporates information from both passages. It would receive a score of 6 on the HiSET®—it makes a confident claim, develops it through supporting paragraphs with relevant evidence, addresses an opposing point-of-view, and even offers possible solutions for reform.

Organization of Ideas

This essay features an excellent organization that allows the author to effectively express his or her ideas and central claim regarding the issue of college costs. The essay opens with a strong introduction that clearly lays out the writer's central position:

"Parents tell their kids to work hard in school, to study hard, and to earn good grades in order to achieve their goals. But if they follow those lessons and get into the college of their dreams, but don't come from a family that can easily afford the cost, has their hard work and achievement just earned them a big, expensive problem?" After the initial introduction, the writer then goes on to back up his or her stance with examples throughout the body of the essay (i.e., facts about the unfair benefits those who are rich enough to afford college can enjoy in paragraph 2 and the real-life story of her sister in paragraph 3).

The writer includes a paragraph detailing opposing viewpoints—*"I'm aware of the arguments on the other side..."*—and addresses them with an impassioned rebuttal. The writer also begins and ends paragraphs with strong sentences that aid in the transition from one thought to another. A strong and engaging conclusion ties the essay together.

Language Facility

This Score 6 essay uses a variety of engaging sentence structures and vocabulary to keep the text interesting—asking and answering questions is a compelling tactic the writer uses throughout. The essay is interesting and informative, and completely answers the given prompt.

Writing Conventions

This essay also uses clear and concise language with minimal spelling and grammatical errors, and makes excellent use of reference sources.

SAMPLE SCORE 1 ESSAY

Why should I pay for school? Ive went to school for....12 years? 13 with kintergarden. All free, no money, none at all. People pay for collage to feel fancey. Their so fancy. With their fancey collage degree and they can say they paid like a million $ for school and get a big fancey job. Its SO DUMB. Get a job and learn a skill, college is for the birds. Why spend govt money on collage that is usless, anyway?

SAMPLE SCORE 1 ESSAY EXPLANATION

Let's analyze this Score 1 essay in each of the core content categories measured on this part of the HiSET® exam.

Development of a Central Position or Claim

An essay that receives a score of 1, like this one, does not respond coherently and effectively to the HiSET® essay prompt and task. While this essay does take somewhat of a murky stance against the high cost of higher education, the central claim is very poorly developed, and supporting ideas and relevant evidence are nonexistent. There is also only a passing mention to the provided sources (*"Why spend govt money on collage that is usless, anyway?"*) without any additional analysis.

Organization of Ideas

This essay does not reflect proper essay organization. It is just one meandering paragraph with no discernible, introduction, body, or conclusion—and no clear transition between ideas. The end result is a confusing jumble of loose ideas.

Language Facility

This written response reflects a poor grasp of language facility. Word choice is not sophisticated or compelling, and there are errors in word choice throughout. The structure and tone of this Score 1 essay is confusing and inappropriate. Furthermore, the language and voice are far too casual (*"Its SO DUMB"* is out of place in a formal essay).

Writing Conventions

This essay is full of spelling and grammar errors throughout (the lack of an apostrophe in *"Ive,"* the misspelling of *"fancey,"* and using *"their"* instead of *"they're"* are only a few examples, plus the rampant use of sentence fragments like, *"Their so fancy."*), which severely impact both the comprehension and effectiveness of this written response

Mathematics

1. C	11. B	21. D	31. E	41. A
2. B	12. C	22. C	32. C	42. E
3. A	13. E	23. B	33. E	43. B
4. C	14. D	24. D	34. A	44. B
5. C	15. D	25. B	35. B	45. C
6. A	16. C	26. D	36. A	46. E
7. E	17. D	27. C	37. D	47. B
8. B	18. A	28. D	38. C	48. A
9. D	19. D	29. A	39. A	49. C
10. A	20. B	30. E	40. A	50. B

1. **The correct answer is (C).** The key to solving this problem is expressing profit in terms of the number of decks power-washed. The $1,500 spent on materials yields *negative profit* and so, we express it as −1,500 in the profit expression. Next, since Violet earns $150 per deck and it costs ($10 + $35) = $45 per deck, her net profit per deck is $150 − $45 = $105. This is constant, and so the profit gained from power-washing x decks is $105x$. So, the profit for x decks is given by $P = 105x - 1,500$.

Next, to determine when Violet will break even, set the profit expression equal to zero and solve for x:

$$105x - 1,500 = 0$$
$$105x = 1,500$$
$$x = \frac{1,500}{105} \approx 14.29$$

So, you must round up and conclude that she will break even after power-washing 15 decks.

2. **The correct answer is (B).** This problem requires you to solve an equation for a variable in terms of other variables. But the same rules apply. First, we isolate the term involving I_2. Then, we cross–multiply both sides by I_2 and divide by its coefficient. Doing so yields:

$$\frac{1}{I_1} + \frac{1}{I_2} = V$$
$$\frac{1}{I_2} = V - \frac{1}{I_1}$$
$$1 = \left(V - \frac{1}{I_1}\right)I_2$$
$$\frac{1}{V - \frac{1}{I_1}} = I_2$$

Next, we simplify the left side by getting a common denominator in the bottom. Once you do this, flip the fraction over, since it occurs in the denominator:

$$\frac{1}{V - \frac{1}{I_1}} = \frac{1}{\frac{VI_1}{I_1} - \frac{1}{I_1}} = \frac{1}{\frac{VI_1 - 1}{I_1}} = \frac{I_1}{VI_1 - 1}$$

Thus, $I_2 = \frac{I_1}{VI_1 - 1}$.

3. **The correct answer is (A).** The temperatures rise steadily toward 1 p.m. (which corresponds to $t = 13$) and then fall steadily to about the same temperatures as time heads toward 11 p.m. So, there is one peak around $t = 13$, and the distribution should be symmetric around that line. Also, the temperatures at $t = 0$ and $t = 23$ should be above the t–axis. The dis-

tribution shown in choice (A) has all of these attributes.

4. **The correct answer is (C).** To answer this question, you must find the two solutions to the equation. Subtracting 4 from both sides and factoring results in the equation $(x + 4)(x - 1) = 0$, which has solutions $x = -4$ and $x = 1$. Since 1 is larger than -4, then you know $m = 1$.

5. **The correct answer is (C).** The median of a distribution is a real number for which 50% of the data lie to its left and 50% of the data lie to its right. The way this is computed for a data set of 50 values is to average the 25th and 26th data point of the *ordered* data set. Using the distribution, we start from the left and add the sizes of the bars until we locate the multiple of 40 that corresponds to the 25th and 26th data points. Both of these are 160, so the median is 160.

6. **The correct answer is (A).** This problem involves determining the range of possible values that can be obtained based on the maximum percent error. To get this range, compute 20% of 0.174 to get $0.20(0.174) = 0.0348$. Now, add and subtract it from 0.174 to get the range 0.1392 to 0.2088. Any number between these two, inclusive, is a possible reading. The only number *not* in this range is the one in choice (A).

7. **The correct answer is (E).** You must determine Jordan's total number of miles traveled, and then convert that to inches using the given scale factor. All told, Jordan rides his bike for 5 miles. Multiplying by 1.75 inches then gives 8.75 inches.

8. **The correct answer is (B).** The volume of any rectangular prism is the product of its length, width, and height. Therefore, the volume of the first prism is $V_1 = 6 \times 2 \times 4 = 48$ cubic inches. The second prism has a length of 6 inches, a width of 2 inches, and a

height of $4 + 5 = 9$ inches. So $V_2 = 6 \times 2 \times 9 = 108$ cubic inches. The difference is then $V2 - V1 = 108 - 48 = 60$.

9. **The correct answer is (D).** The slope of a line is equal to the change in y divided by the change in x. If the slope is negative, then the graph of the line falls from left to right, so that the y-values are decreasing as the x-values increase. For the given line, the slope is $-\frac{5}{7}$. We interpret this as meaning that the y-value on the graph decreases by 5 units for every 7 units increase in x.

10. **The correct answer is (A).** You need to remember that absolute value allows you to measure distance on both sides of a fixed quantity. Here, the fixed quantity is 21 clementines. We are told the number can vary by 4, which means there could be 1, 2, 3, or 4 clementines more than 21 in the bag; or there could be 1, 2, 3, or 4 fewer than 21 clementines in the bag; or there could be 21 in the bag. The inequality means "go left and right of 21 by 4," which perfectly describes this scenario.

11. **The correct answer is (B).** Let x represent the number of weeks that Diego can make withdrawals from the account. Since he withdraws $150 per week (combined), the total he withdraws in x weeks is $150x$. So, after x weeks, there is $4{,}500 - 150x$ dollars left in the account. This amount must be greater than or equal to 1,000 dollars in order to avoid fees. So, the inequality used to model this situation is $-150x + 4{,}500 \geq 1{,}000$.

12. **The correct answer is (C).** This problem requires you to visualize the solids you get by rotating specific regions around a specified line. The region in choice (C), when rotated around the y-axis, produces a cylinder with height 10 inches whose base (and

cross-sections parallel to the base) is a circle with radius 2 inches.

13. **The correct answer is (E).** This problem requires you to use the fact that density equals population per square mile. Given this number, multiply the density times the total number of square miles to get the size of the entire population: $(2,400)(6.5) = 15,600$ trees in the entire forest.

14. **The correct answer is (D).** The volume of a prism is computed by multiplying the area of the base times the height. Here, the base is a right triangle for which we are given the base and hypotenuse. So, we must first use the Pythagorean theorem to compute the height h: $5^2 + h^2 = 13^2$, so that $h^2 = 144$ and $h = 12$ ft. Now, the area of the base is $\frac{1}{2}(5 \text{ ft.})(12 \text{ ft.}) = 30 \text{ ft.}^2$. Finally, we multiply this by the height, 6 feet, to conclude that the volume is 180 cubic feet.

15. **The correct answer is (D).** This problem requires you to use similar triangles. Let b and h represent the base and height of the new, larger tank. We must first use the Pythagorean theorem to compute the height x of the smaller tank's base: $5^2 + x^2 = 13^2$, so that $x^2 = 144$ and $x = 12$ ft. Now, we set up two ratios to compute b and h:

$$\frac{5}{b} = \frac{2}{3} \Rightarrow 15 = 2b \Rightarrow b = 7.5$$

$$\frac{12}{h} = \frac{2}{3} \Rightarrow 36 = 2h \Rightarrow h = 18$$

So, for the second tank, base = 7.5 feet and height = 18 feet.

16. **The correct answer is (C).** First, divide 0.17459 by the number of gallons the tank holds to get the concentration in *ounces per gallon*: $0.17459 \div 1,343 = 0.00013$ ounces per gallon. Next, since we are given the conversion factor for cubic feet to gallons, multiply 0.00013 times 7.463 gallons to get 0.00097019 ounces per cubic

foot. Express this in scientific notation as approximately 9.70×10^{-4}.

17. **The correct answer is (D).** This problem requires that you recall *distance equals rate times time*. The distance the younger jogger has traveled at time t is the head start plus the rate at which he jogs *times* the time he has been jogging. Translating this into symbols yields the expression $0.5 + 4t$. Likewise, the distance the older jogger has traveled at time t is the rate at which he jogs *times* the time he has been jogging. In symbols, this is $5t$. To get their relative distance, subtract the two expressions: $d = 0.5 + 4t - 5t = 0.5 - t$.

18. **The correct answer is (A).** Use the given values to set up an equation. To find an average, add all of the values and divide by the number of values:

$$\frac{1 + 4 + x + 4 + 2 + (x+3) + 10 + 6}{8} = \frac{23}{4}$$

Multiply both sides by 8 and then solve the resulting equation:

$$8 \times \left(\frac{1 + 4 + x + 4 + 2 + (x+3) + 10 + 6}{8} \right)$$
$$= 8 \times \left(\frac{23}{4} \right)$$
$$1 + 4 + x + 4 + 2 + x + 3 + 10 + 6 = 2(23)$$
$$30 + 2x = 46$$
$$2x = 16$$
$$x = 8$$

19. **The correct answer is (D).** This problem requires you to compare two volumes of similar solids. Let r and h represent the base radius and height, respectively, of the original waffle cone. Its base radius increases by 50%, meaning that it is $r + 0.50r = 1.5r$, and the height decreases by 50%, meaning that it is $h - 0.5h = 0.5h$. We must next compute the volumes of both waffle cones and compare. The volume of the original waffle cone is $V_{original} = \frac{1}{3}\pi r^2 h$, and

the volume of the new waffle cone is

$$V_{new} = \frac{1}{3}\pi(1.5r)^2(0.5h)$$

$$= 1.125\left(\frac{1}{3}\pi r^2 h\right)$$

$$= 1.125 V_{original}$$

Therefore, the new cone holds 12.5% more than the original one.

20. **The correct answer is (B).** An event is a subset of the sample space. The elements in this event must be odd, prime, or both. All prime numbers are necessarily odd. So, we need only to identify the odd members of the sample space. The elements satisfying these conditions are: 1, 3, 5, 7, 9, 23, 29, 35, 49, 101.

21. **The correct answer is (D).** You need to determine which of these fractions is actually a rational number, which is a quotient of integers. The only one that simplifies to a rational number is $\frac{2\sqrt{\pi}}{\sqrt{25\pi}}$ because $\frac{2\sqrt{\pi}}{\sqrt{25\pi}} = \frac{2\sqrt{\pi}}{5\sqrt{\pi}} = \frac{2}{5}$.

None of the other choices can be simplified in such a way that the radicals or π are removed from the fraction.

22. **The correct answer is (C).** The trend being described is the speed decreases as the number of scratches on the ball increases, with some exceptions. In terms of a scatterplot, the data points should fall from left to right. They shouldn't be too tightly packed near a line, yet the trend should be discernible. There should be a few data points that stray away from the general trend. These characteristics are embodied by the scatterplot in choice (C).

23. **The correct answer is (B).** You must subtract the two given average times and then take 40% of that difference. Subtracting the times yields (9 minutes 30 seconds) – (8 minutes 10 seconds) = (1 minute 20 seconds). This is equal to 80 seconds. Forty

percent of this quantity is 0.40(80) = 32 seconds.

24. **The correct answer is (D).** A fair selection would result in each employee having an equal chance of being selected. However, if 2 employees have first names starting with the letter T, while 13 have first names starting with the letter M, then the employees do not have an equal chance of being selected.

25. **The correct answer is (B).** Recall that an exponent of $\frac{1}{2}$ is the same as the square root and an exponent of $\frac{1}{3}$ is the same as the cube root. So: $27^{\frac{1}{3}} = 3$ and $16^{\frac{1}{2}} = 4$. Now apply the order of operations to simplify the numerical expression:

$$3\left(27^{\frac{1}{3}} - 16^{\frac{1}{2}}\right) + 2 = 3(3-4) + 2 = 3(-1) + 2 = -3 + 2 = -1$$

26. **The correct answer is (D).** The three prizes are different and each person can only win one prize, as indicated by the information that the cards are selected one at a time, without replacement. This means that there are 250 possible winners for the first card being drawn, 249 for the next, and 248 for the last. Since all three cards are being drawn (this is not "or"), we multiply to find the total number of possibilities: 250 × 249 × 248. You could also think of this as a permutation: $P(250, 3)$.

27. **The correct answer is (C).** The x-intercepts of the graph (that is, the zeros of the graph) are –2, 3, and 5. Since the graph is tangent to the x-axis at –2 and 3, the multiplicity of each of these zeros is even. Likewise, since it crosses through the x-axis at 5, the multiplicity of this zero is odd. So, choices (A), (B), (D), and (E) are all plausible. If x were a factor of this

polynomial, its graph would have had to cross the x-axis at 0, but it does not. Therefore, choice (C) is the correct answer.

28. **The correct answer is (D).** Note that all quantities involve π. The answer is the choice that is the product of π and a number greater than 1. Since $(1.1)^2 = 1.21$, $(1.1)^2\pi = 1.21\pi$, which is greater than π.

29. **The correct answer is (A).** First, let us identify x as the *number of minutes for local calls* and y as the *number of minutes for international calls*. We determine the intercepts with the y-axis and x-axis—these are the number of minutes you could possibly spend on international and local calls, respectively, if you made only these types of calls. These values are (0, 400) and (1,000, 0), as shown. Next, connect those two points with a line. Any point on this line (with integer coordinates) is a possible combination that actually uses up the entire card. Also, any point in the first quadrant beneath this line is also a possible combination and would result in there being money left on the card. The region sketched in choice (A) possesses all of these characteristics.

30. **The correct answer is (E).** This problem involves using the various properties of arithmetic (commutativity, associativity, and distributivity). The expression in choice (E) is not equivalent to the one given because when foiling these two binomials, the middle terms $-2wz$ and $4wz$ are omitted.

31. **The correct answer is (E).** Let w represent the width of the room. Then, the length is $2w + 10$. The area of a rectangular room is length times width. Using this fact yields the following equation:

$$w(2w + 10) = 300$$

Solving this equation for w yields:

$$w(2w + 10) = 300$$
$$2w^2 + 10w = 300$$
$$2w^2 + 10w - 300 = 0$$
$$(2w + 30)(w - 10) = 0$$
$$w = \cancel{-15}, 10$$

So, the width of the room is 10 feet. Thus, the length is 30 feet.

32. **The correct answer is (C).** The vertex of the given parabola is $(-3, -2)$, and it opens downward because the coefficient of the squared term is negative. The only graph possessing these characteristics is shown in choice (C).

33. **The correct answer is (E).** The average rate of change of a graph on an interval (a,b) is the difference in y-values at a and b divided by $b - a$. This can also be viewed as the slope of the line segment connecting the points at a and b on the curve. Using this interpretation, we are looking for the interval for which the slope of this segment is the smallest. The only interval on which the slope is negative is $(7,10)$. So, this must be the smallest.

34. The correct answer is (A). To compute $2\left(\frac{3}{2} - 4x^2\right) - 3\left(-1 + \frac{1}{3}x - 3x^2\right)$, first distribute 2 through each term of the first binomial and distribute the −3 through each term of the second binomial. Then, add like terms:

$$2\left(\frac{3}{2} - 4x^2\right) - 3\left(-1 + \frac{1}{3}x - 3x^2\right) = 2\left(\frac{3}{2}\right) - 2\left(4x^2\right) - 3(-1) - 3\left(\frac{1}{3}x\right) + 3\left(3x^2\right)$$

$$= 3 - 8x^2 + 3 - x + 9x^2$$

$$= 6 - x + x^2$$

35. The correct answer is (B). For this problem, you must simplify the radicals that can be simplified (namely the first one in the first binomial and the second one in the second binomial), and then foil the resulting binomials. When doing so, use the fact that $\sqrt{3} \cdot \sqrt{3} = 3$:

$$\left(\sqrt{27} - \sqrt{3}\right)\left(\sqrt{3} - \sqrt{9}\right) = \left(3\sqrt{3} - \sqrt{3}\right)\left(\sqrt{3} - 3\right) = \left(3\sqrt{3}\right)\left(\sqrt{3}\right) - \left(3\sqrt{3}\right)(3)$$

$$= 9 - 9\sqrt{3} - 3 + 3\sqrt{3}$$

$$= 6 - 6\sqrt{3}$$

$$= 6\left(1 - \sqrt{3}\right)$$

36. The correct answer is (A). We must set up equations or inequalities that express the relationships between A, B, and C. There are two conditions described in the problem. First, "Lane A handles twice as many cars as Lane B" can be represented as the equation $A = 2B$. Second, "Lane C handles no more than one-half the cars that Lane B handles" can be represented as the inequality "$C \leq \frac{1}{2}B$."

Next, recall that you can multiply both sides of an inequality by a positive number and keep the same sign. So, we can multiply the inequality $C \leq \frac{1}{2}B$ by 4 to get an equivalent inequality $4C \leq 2B$. Finally, since $A = 2B$, substituting this into the previous inequality gives $4C \leq A$.

37. The correct answer is (D). Two of the walls have dimensions 15 feet by 10 feet; the combined area of these two walls is 2×150 feet$^2 = 300$ feet^2. The other two walls have dimensions 20 feet by 10 feet; the combined area of these two walls is 2×200 feet$^2 = 400$ feet^2. The ceiling has dimensions 15 feet by 20 feet, and so its area is 300 feet^2. Therefore, the total square footage that must be painted is 300 + 400 + 300 = 1,000 square feet. This must be doubled in order to apply two coats, making the total square footage 2,000 square feet. Since 1 gallon of paint will cover 350 square feet, the 5-gallon barrel will cover 1,750 feet^2. Finally, we divide 1,750 by 2,000 to get 0.875. Converting to a percent, we conclude that that 87.5% of the job can be completed.

38. **The correct answer is (C).** There are various correct first steps that can be taken when solving a linear equation such as this. Clearing the fractions by multiplying both sides by the least common denominator of all fractions occurring in the equation is a common approach. Doing so for this equation means you multiply both sides by 10:

$$10 \cdot \left(\frac{3}{5}x - 3 \right) = 10 \cdot \left(-\frac{3}{10}x + 1 \right)$$
$$6x - 30 = -3x + 10$$

39. **The correct answer is (A).** This problem requires you to assess if a sampling procedure captures enough information about an entire city's population in a non-biased manner. The procedure described in choice (A) uses a reasonable number of distinct people from different parts of the city to make a reasonable assessment of the percentage of the entire city's population that is infected with influenza.

40. **The correct answer is (A).** We must interpret symbolically the two conditions relating the investments in Stock A and B. First, we are told that the amount invested in Stocks A and B combined is 40,000. This gives the equation $a + b = 40,000$. Next, 5% interest on the amount invested in Stock A is represented as $0.05a$. Similarly, the 7% interest on the amount invested in Stock B is represented as $0.07b$. The sum of these two terms is $3,500. This results in the equation $0.05a + 0.07b = 3,500$. Both equations must hold simultaneously. This is given by the system in choice (A).

41. **The correct answer is (A).** This problem requires you to compute the areas of two triangles and compare the two numbers using percentages.

The area of triangle A is $\frac{1}{2}bh$. In order to compute the area of B, we need its base and height. Since the base of B is 25% larger than the base

of A, its length must be $b + 0.25b = 1.25b$. Similarly, since the height of A is 40% smaller than the height of A, its height must be $h - 0.40h = 0.60h$. Therefore,

$$\begin{aligned} \text{Area of B} &= \frac{1}{2}(1.25b)(0.60h) \\ &= \left(1.25 \times 0.60 \right) \times \left(\frac{1}{2}bh \right) \\ &= 0.75\left(\frac{1}{2}bh \right) \\ &= 0.75 \times \left(\text{Area of A} \right) \end{aligned}$$

So, the area of B is 75% of the area of A.

42. **The correct answer is (E).** First, you must determine the cost of each type of item, which is computed by multiplying the cost of one of them by the number of them being purchased. Then, add all of these individual costs together to get the total cost C. For instance, since a single 30-foot rope costs r dollars, two such ropes cost $2r$ dollars. Similarly, the cost for eight clamps, three chalk bags, and one backpack are $8c$, $3b$, and p dollars, respectively. Adding these costs together gives the total cost $C = 2r + 8c + 3b + p$.

43. **The correct answer is (B).** The distribution that describes this scenario should peak at 4 ounces and should dip down on either side very quickly (because of the very little variation in weight).

44. **The correct answer is (B).** The temperature of the ice cream sandwich starts out the same as the temperature of the freezer, which is 25°F. Then, while it rests on the chair in the hot summer sun, the temperature quickly rises and gets close to the temperature outside, which is 85°F. It peaks there because when it is put back into the freezer, its temperature quickly goes down toward 25°F. This is best described by the graph in B.

45. The correct answer is (C). We need to identify the radius and height of the new cylinder and substitute them into the volume formula. The combination listed that yields the volume of this new cylinder as $3\pi r^2 h$ is the correct answer. Of those listed, the combination in choice (C) is correct. Indeed, the height would be $3h$ and the radius remains r. So, the volume would be $V_{\text{new}} = \pi r^2 (3h) = 3\pi r^2 h$.

46. The correct answer is (E). This question requires you to appropriately convert miles to feet and hours to minutes. There are 60 minutes in an hour and there are 5,280 feet in a mile. Using these two facts enables us to convert from *miles per hour* to *feet per minute* as follows:

$$\frac{21 \text{ miles}}{1 \text{ hour}} = \frac{21 \text{ miles}}{1 \text{ hour}}$$
$$\times \frac{1 \text{ hour}}{60 \text{ minutes}} \times \frac{5,280 \text{ feet}}{1 \text{ mile}}$$
$$= \frac{21 \times 5,280}{60} \text{ feet per minute}$$

47. The correct answer is (B). For every half an inch, the fraction of a gallon of gas needed (per minute) increases by 0.005 gallons. As such, the number of gallons needed can be viewed as a function of the depth of snow (in inches). In particular, the slope of this function $\frac{0.005}{0.5} = \frac{1}{100}$. Also, if there is no snow, it uses 0 gallons of gasoline. So, the equation of this line is $G = \frac{1}{100}d$, where G is the number of gallons per minute needed and d represents the depth of the snow (in inches).

Now, substitute $d = 6$ to get $\frac{6}{100} = 0.06$ gallons of gasoline per minute needed for this depth of snow.

48. The correct answer is (A). We must determine the equation of the line first. To do so, we need the slope and a point on the line. We are given two points on the line, namely (–5, 4) and (–4, 2). Using them, we compute the slope as $m = \frac{4 - 2}{-5 - (-4)} = -2$. Now, using the point–slope formula for the equation of the line, $y - y_1 = m(x - x_1)$, with $m = -2$ and $(x_1, y_1) = (-4, 2)$, we see that the equation of the line is $y - 2 = -2(x + 4)$, which simplifies to $y - 2 = -2x - 8$, or equivalently, $y = -2x - 6$. Now, to get the y-intercept, substitute $x = 0$ into this equation to get $y = -6$.

49. The correct answer is (C). Let z be the smallest of the integers. Then, the largest one is $4z$, and the middle integer is $2z - 5$. The sum of all three integers is 104. We can represent this symbolically as the equation $z + (2z - 5) + 4z = 104$.

50. The correct answer is (B). This problem requires you to construct a frequency table and identify the event described in context of the data values. Here, the frequency distribution is:

Number of bags checked	Frequency
0	8
1	11
2	3
>2	3

The event described consists of 0 bags checked OR 1 bag checked. Nineteen of 25 passengers sampled checked this number of bags. Therefore, the probability is $\frac{19}{25} = 0.76$.

Science

1. B	11. C	21. A	31. B	41. A
2. C	12. B	22. A	32. D	42. B
3. A	13. C	23. C	33. B	43. C
4. D	14. A	24. D	34. A	44. D
5. C	15. D	25. B	35. C	45. D
6. B	16. A	26. C	36. A	46. C
7. B	17. C	27. C	37. B	47. B
8. B	18. D	28. B	38. D	48. A
9. A	19. A	29. C	39. A	49. C
10. D	20. C	30. C	40. C	50. B

1. **The correct answer is (B).** This question asks you to identify the question that is being asked in the study. The amount of phytoplankton and sunlight are both measured in this study, so the researchers are testing if light affects the growth of phytoplankton.

2. **The correct answer is (C).** This question asks you to figure out the relationship between phytoplankton growth and sunlight, or how one factor changes when the other one changes. If you look at the graphs for sunlight and phytoplankton growth at different depths, you'll see that they are very similar. So as one factor changes, the other changes in the same way. Therefore, as sunlight increases, phytoplankton growth also increases.

3. **The correct answer is (A).** This question requires you to apply your understanding of the relationship between phytoplankton and light to a hypothetical situation. According to the graphs, at 80% light phytoplankton is very close to its maximum when it has 100% light. According to the question, the 80% light extends all the way down to 80 meters, which is almost 100 meters, and there should be very little decrease in the amount of phytoplankton.

4. **The correct answer is (D).** This question requires you to explain why phytoplankton would have the greatest growth at shallower depths. The answer must relate to sunlight because that is the only data we have for this experiment. The question stem mentions that phytoplankton use photosynthesis to help them grow, and the amount of sunlight affects the amount of photosynthesis that occurs.

5. **The correct answer is (C).** This question asks you to design an experiment in which the effect of only one variable is tested. Both temperature and light have to be included in the experiment, but only one of these variables should change. Choice (C) is the experiment in which only one variable, temperature, is changing.

6. **The correct answer is (B).** This question requires you to identify the relationship between temperature and lactase activity. As stated in the question stem, lactase activity is high when there is less lactose remaining. Therefore, according to the results of Experiment 1, lactase activity is highest (it peaks) at 37°C. Lactase activity increases with temperatures

up to 37°C and then decreases with temperatures above 37°C.

7. **The correct answer is (B).** This question asks you to read the data from Experiment 2 to find the highest lactase activity. Lactase activity is highest when the amount of lactose remaining is the least, which occurs at a pH of 6.

8. **The correct answer is (B).** This question requires you to recognize the shape of the graph when enzyme activity is plotted against pH. Remember that it is enzyme activity that is being graphed, not amount of the lactose remaining, so you will not be directly graphing the information in the table. As explained in Question 6, lactase activity increases with temperatures up to 37°C and then decreases with temperatures above 37°C, so the graph should look like choice B, a curve that goes up and then down.

9. **The correct answer is (A).** This question asks you to explain why human lactase performs best at a certain pH and temperature. Enzymes are biological molecules that evolved to perform functions in different organisms. Thus, it would make sense that they evolved to perform best in the conditions that they would experience most. Human lactase should then perform best in the pH and temperature found in the human body.

10. **The correct answer is (D).** This question asks you the opposite of the previous question: it asks you to explain why lactase performs worst at certain pH and temperatures. All proteins, including enzymes, will denature or break down at certain pH and temperatures, causing them to stop working.

11. **The correct answer is (C).** This question asks you to find the spot on the graph where water can exist as all three phases: solid, liquid, and

gas. The question stem tells you that water can exist as two phases on the solid lines, so it should be able to exist as all three phases where the lines meet. This point occurs at 0.006 atm and 273.01 K and is called the triple point.

12. **The correct answer is (B).** This question asks you to read the phase diagram at 1 atm and 298 K. This point on the phase diagram is within the shaded area for liquid water, so water exists only as a liquid at this temperature and pressure.

13. **The correct answer is (C).** This question asks you to read the phase diagram and decide what processes occur when one phase of water turns into another. If you pick a spot in the area shaded for solids on the phase diagram and move to the right (increasing temperature), it will turn into a liquid or gas, depending on how far to the right you go. If you also move up the diagram (increasing pressure) while moving to the right, it will still turn into a liquid or gas.

14. **The correct answer is (A).** This question asks you to find a point on the phase diagram and then figure out how to turn the liquid water at that point to a gas. The shaded area for gas is to the right of the shaded area for liquid, so increasing temperature while keeping the pressure the same will turn a liquid to a gas.

15. **The correct answer is (D).** This question asks you to determine the idea being tested by this experiment. Different combinations of crabs are put into a tank with the same food and the amount of time it takes them to find the food is measured. Therefore, the hypothesis being tested is whether the presence of another crab will affect how quickly a crab finds food.

16. **The correct answer is (A).** This question requires you to read the data

from the experiment. From the table, both green and blue crabs took the longest to find food when they were put into a tank with another species of crab. Green crabs took about twice as long to find food when they were in a tank with a blue crab, while blue crabs took 55 to 100 seconds longer to find food if they were in a tank with a green crab.

17. **The correct answer is (C).** This question is testing your understanding of the concept of a control in an experiment. Controls show normal behavior or conditions that the experimental conditions can be compared to. The tests in which the crabs are alone are controls to show the normal behavior of crabs when they are not competing for food.

18. **The correct answer is (D).** This question requires you to examine the experimental procedure and consider how a change in the procedure might impact the results. Tests 1 and 2—choices (A) and (B)—use only blue crabs and would not be affected if a lobster were substituted for a green crab. In experiments 3 through 5 (Choice (D), there is no way to be 100% certain without trying it, but it is unlikely that the results would be exactly the same using a completely different species. Choice (C) is incorrect since the results of every single test using the lobster might be impacted.

19. **The correct answer is (A).** This question requires you to think about how the results of this experiment can be applied to crab behavior in the real world. The results of the experiment show that green crabs are always much faster than blue crabs in finding food. They then may be more successful because they can find food more quickly.

20. **The correct answer is (C).** This question requires you to examine the experimental variables and de-termine which of those variables is most likely to affect the results. The temperature of the water can affect buoyancy of lighter objects, but not something as heavy as rock. The shape of the rock is going to be highly relevant and seems to be one of the main variables in the study. The type of rock is relevant since different rock types have different densities and that might affect their movement through the stream. The speed of the current will affect how far any object in the stream might travel.

21. **The correct answer is (A).** This question asks you to use the results of the experiment to figure how far a rock of a certain size and shape will travel. A rock with a mass of 1,400 g would be a medium-sized rock. A medium-sized blade travels 5.1 m on average, so it would most likely travel 5 m.

22. **The correct answer is (A).** This question asks you to determine what the columns in the table represent. The headers of the columns are for rock size, so if you read down one column, you will be looking at rocks of the same size. As you move from one row to another down one column, you will be able to compare the transport of rocks of the same size but different shapes.

23. **The correct answer is (C).** This question asks you to design an experiment that will remove the effects of the rocky stream bottom when comparing the transport of spheres of all sizes. The easiest way to do this is to get rid of the rocky stream bottom. All three sizes of spheres should be dropped into a stream with no rocks on the bottom to compare how far they travel.

24. **The correct answer is (D).** This question requires you to determine what problem the experiment is trying to solve. The question stem says that the genotype of the red-eyed fly

is unknown and that the red-eyed fly is mated with the white-eyed fly to determine its genotype. From the question stem, we know that red-eyed flies have either RR or Rr as their genotype. Thus, the question the experiment is trying to answer is if the gene makeup of the red-eyed fly is Rr or RR.

25. **The correct answer is (B).** This question asks you to figure out the genotype of the red-eyed fruit fly based on the number and type of offspring produced in the matings. In all three matings, about half of the offspring had red eyes and the other half had white eyes. From the information in the question stem, this happens only when the red-eyed parent is Rr. If the parent were RR, then all of the offspring would have red eyes.

26. **The correct answer is (C).** This question asks you to predict the number of red-eyed offspring in a fourth mating between the same parents. Knowing that the red-eyed parent is Rr, you would predict that half of the offspring of any mating would have red eyes. Therefore, if 35 of the offspring have white eyes in a fourth mating, then about the same number (35) would have red eyes.

27. **The correct answer is (C).** This question asks you to find the statement that is something that can be directly seen in the experiment. The number of offspring in each mating is the only choice that can be directly observed in this experiment.

28. **The correct answer is (B).** This question asks you to predict the results if a red-eyed offspring from the experiment is mated to a white-eyed fly. Knowing that the parent is Rr, you can see from the information given in the question stem that all the red-eyed offspring are also Rr. Therefore, if another Rr fly is mated to a rr white-eyed fly, then the results will be the same as the original mat-

ings: 50% of the offspring will be Rr and the other 50% will be rr.

29. **The correct answer is (C).** This question asks you to calculate the total distance the glacier retreated between 1906 and 1999. To find this distance, you subtract the distance the glacier had retreated from the maximum extent in 1906 from that distance in 1999. 1,510 m − 208 m = 1,302 m.

30. **The correct answer is (C).** This question asks you to calculate the rate at which the glacier retreated during different time periods and choose the time period during which the rate is greatest, which is when the glacier retreated the fastest. To save time, you don't have to calculate each rate exactly, but estimate the rates from the numbers given. From 1843 to 1906, the rate of retreat is about 200 m/ 60 yr., or a little over 3 m/yr. From 1906 to 1938, the rate is about 450 m / 30 yr., or about 15 m/yr. From 1938 to 1948, the rate is 246 m / 10 yr. = 24.6 m/yr. From 1992 to 1999, a period of 7 years, the rate is about 120 m / 7 yr., or about 17 m/yr. Therefore, the glacier retreated the fastest from 1938 to 1948.

31. **The correct answer is (B).** This question requires you to look at the data given and determine what hypothesis can be tested. You're given only the distance that the glacier has retreated in different years and the average global temperature, so the only hypotheses that can be tested are ones that involve only glacier retreat and temperature. Choice B is the only answer that involves only these two variables.

32. **The correct answer is (D).** This question asks you to draw a conclusion from the data given. The only data given are for glacier retreat and temperature, so any conclusion will have to relate to glacier retreat, temperature, or both. Choice D is

the only conclusion supported by the data given. A temperature increase of only 0.3°C, from 13.6°C in 1906 to 13.9°C in 1959, was enough to cause the glacier to retreat 1,142 m from its maximum extent, a distance of more than a kilometer (1 km = 1,000 m).

33. The correct answer is (B). This question requires you to apply the basic principles of dating different rock layers that are explained in the question stem. The question stem tells you that rock layers are the same age if they have the same fossils. The stem also tells you that the oldest rock layers are at the bottom and the youngest are on top. Therefore, Layer B in the Coyote Formation is older than Layer A because it is below Layer A.

34. The correct answer is (A). This question requires you to apply the basic principles of dating different rock layers that are explained in the question stem. The stem tells you that the oldest rock layers are at the bottom and the youngest are on top. Therefore, the youngest layer in the Coyote Formation is Layer A.

35. The correct answer is (C). This question requires you to apply the basic principles of dating different rock layers that are explained in the question stem. The question stem tells you that rock layers are the same age if they have the same fossils. The only two layers that have the same fossils are Layer 4 in the Staghorn Formation and Layer B in the Coyote Formation, so they are the same age.

36. The correct answer is (A). This question requires you to apply the basic principles of dating different rock layers that are explained in the question stem, but now you are extending the principles across two different formations. The question stem tells you Layer 2 in the Staghorn Formation and Layer A in the Coyote Formation are the same age. The stem also tells you that the old-

est rock layers are at the bottom and the youngest are on top. This means that everything below Layer 2 is older than Layer 2 AND Layer A because Layer 2 and Layer A are the same age. Similarly, everything above Layer 2 is younger than Layer 2 AND Layer A, and everything below Layer A is older than Layer A AND Layer 2. Therefore, choice A is the only correct answer; Layer C is older than Layer 2, or in other words, Layer 2 is younger than Layer C.

37. The correct answer is (B). This question requires you to look at the variables that are changing in tests 1 and 2 and figure out what is being tested. In tests 1 and 2, the concentration of NO is the same, but the concentration of NO_3 and the rate of reaction both change. Therefore, the results of tests 1 and 2 show a researcher the effect of changing the concentration of NO_3 on rate.

38. The correct answer is (D). This question requires you to look for the tests in which the concentration of NO is tripled but that of NO_3 stays the same, and then see how rate is affected. In test 3, the concentration of NO is tripled from that in test 1, but NO_3 is unchanged. The reaction rate in test 3 is three times the rate in test 1. Thus, when the concentration of NO is tripled, rate triples as well.

39. The correct answer is (A). This question requires you to look for the tests in which the concentration of NO_3 is doubled but that of NO stays the same, and then see how rate is affected. In test 2, the concentration of NO_3 is doubled from that in test 1, but NO is unchanged. The reaction rate in test 2 is two times the rate in test 1. Thus, when the concentration of NO_3 is doubled, rate doubles as well.

40. The correct answer is (C). This question asks you to explain the general effect of changing reactant concentration on reaction rate. From the previous two questions, you found that reaction rate triples when the concentration of NO triples and that reaction rate doubles when the concentration of NO_3 doubles. Therefore, the rate changes by the same amount that the concentration of NO and NO_3 changes.

41. **The correct answer is (A).** This question tests if you understand what will best show if two animals share a common ancestor. If two animals are closely related, they will have a common ancestor and inherit some of the same characteristics (body parts and behavior) from that common ancestor. So the body parts of the animals will be most useful in determining which animals are most closely related.

42. **The correct answer is (B).** This question asks you to design an experiment that will test each possible food allergy one at a time. The only way to do this is to eat only one of the foods at a time without eating the other two.

43. **The correct answer is (C).** This question requires you to understand that objects reflect the wavelength of light of the color that they appear, and they absorb all other wavelengths of light. Thus, a red stop sign reflects wavelengths of red light and absorbs all other wavelengths of light.

44. **The correct answer is (D).** This question requires you to distinguish between an observation, and assumption, a hypothesis, and data. Recognize that data is information systematically collected, and does not have to be collected in a lab or by scientists. In the child's case, Step 1 is an observation, Step 2 is an assumption, and Step 3 is a hypothesis. But when she carefully touches each slide, she is gathering data about how sunlight affects the slide.

45. **The correct answer is (D).** This question requires you to recognize that for carbon to enter another stage in the carbon cycle, it has to move into another carbon source without getting trapped there. Choice (D) is the only answer choice in which carbon—not some other substance—moves into another carbon source (an animal) without being trapped. After the carbon of the plant is eaten by an animal, it is free to move into another part of the carbon cycle.

46. **The correct answer is (C).** This question asks you to design an experiment in which only the effect of rain on leaf breakdown is tested. Leaves must be present and the only variable affecting the leaves should be rain. Choice (C) is the only one that fulfills both of these conditions.

47. **The correct answer is (B).** This question requires you to remember what happens when solutions with different concentrations are separated by a membrane that permits the flow of water (a semipermeable membrane). Water will flow from the solution with the lower salt concentration to the one with the higher salt concentration, resulting in one side losing volume and the other side gaining volume.

48. **The correct answer is (A).** This question requires you to understand that evolution occurs when traits are passed on to the next generation and become widespread when the organisms with those traits produce more offspring than organisms without those traits. Because bacteria reproduce so quickly, they can pass new traits to the next generation very quickly, allowing them to evolve more quickly.

answers practice test 1

49. **The correct answer is (C).** This question requires you to use your knowledge of Earth's history and processes to evaluate different types of evidence. Rocks on one continent that match rocks on another continent are the best possible evidence of the choices, as it indicates that the rocks were once connected. A close match is not likely to occur any other way.

50. **The correct answer is (B).** This question requires you to find a relationship in which both organisms benefit, which is the definition of symbiosis given in the question stem. In the clownfish-anemone relationship, both the clownfish and the anemone benefit.

Social Studies

1. C	11. C	21. B	31. A	41. D
2. A	12. C	22. A	32. A	42. C
3. C	13. C	23. B	33. C	43. B
4. B	14. A	24. D	34. B	44. B
5. B	15. D	25. A	35. A	45. C
6. B	16. D	26. A	36. B	46. D
7. B	17. C	27. B	37. C	47. D
8. B	18. B	28. C	38. B	48. D
9. B	19. C	29. C	39. B	49. B
10. C	20. C	30. B	40. C	50. A

1. **The correct answer is (C).** A hold is a procedural practice where a senator temporarily blocks the consideration of a bill or nomination.

2. **The correct answer is (A).** The southern senators actually performed a filibuster in which they refused to relinquish the Senate floor to delay proceedings and prevent a vote on the controversial issue.

3. **The correct answer is (C).** The Fourteenth Amendment guaranteed privileges and immunities of citizenship, due process, and equal protection under the law. The Civil Rights Bill of 1964 went further to guarantee equal protection under the law and prevent discrimination based on race, religion, sex, or national origin in an attempt to strike back at individual states that attempted to violate the Fourteenth Amendment.

4. **The correct answer is (B).** *Plessy v. Ferguson* made "separate but equal" legal and allowed for Jim Crow laws to continue, specifically in the South. These practices were considered unfair and in direct violation of the Fourteenth Amendment.

5. **The correct answer is (B).** President Johnson and the Democrats who created the bill controlled much of Congress during this period, and there was much support for increased civil rights.

6. **The correct answer is (B).** African Americans strongly favored Democrats during this period, and Democratic leaders like President Johnson were key figures in the civil rights movement.

7. **The correct answer is (B).** The position as House representative has the lowest age and citizenship requirements.

8. **The correct answer is (B).** The candidate does not meet the citizenship requirement to become a senator or president.

9. **The correct answer is (B).** Citizenship requirements are more difficult to obtain than residency or age for a person; furthermore, you cannot become president if you were not a natural born citizen, making it the most difficult requirement to fulfill.

10. **The correct answer is (C).** In 1980, Reagan met all the age requirements for each position. But since he was no longer a resident of Illinois, he could not run for Senate or House Represen-

tative. That year, he did, in fact, run for President.

11. **The correct answer is (C).** Hamilton was not born in the United States, thus he could not run for President. He retained citizenship for a long enough period to run for other offices.

12. **The correct answer is (C).** The vote of the Electoral College is what elects a president, proven by the fact that George W. Bush had fewer popular votes but was elected president.

13. **The correct answer is (C).** The Twelfth Amendment deals with election of the President and Vice-President. In the case of an Electoral College deadlock or if no candidate receives the majority of votes, a "contingent election" is held. The election of the President goes to the House of Representatives. Each state delegation casts one vote for one of the top three contenders to determine a winner.

14. **The correct answer is (A).** Although only 20 states are colored blue, Gore still received just as many votes as Bush, who won 10 more states. The majority of the blue states can be found on the East and West coasts.

15. **The correct answer is (D).** The election results as shown by the map cannot be determined by knowing the candidates' running mates and does not reflect their inclusion.

16. **The correct answer is (D).** The colors correspond with political parties; red is commonly used for Republican and blue for Democrat.

17. **The correct answer is (C).** Because the president is elected for the country, it does not matter in which state he resides.

18. **The correct answer is (B).** A *chad* is the small fragment of paper that results when a hole is punched in a larger piece of paper. Incorrectly or incompletely punched holes on the ballots in Florida resulted in those ballots not being counted by the voting machines. The term *hanging chad* was used to describe the cause of the voting controversy in Florida during the election.

19. **The correct answer is (C).** Ohio, Florida, and Pennsylvania are considered "swing states"—ones that can move an election in favor of one candidate. Maryland and Washington, DC, do not hold as many votes or the ability to win an election for a candidate.

20. **The correct answer is (C).** The largest sector of the workforce in 2010 was employed in service sector jobs such as those found in education, heathcare, or social assistance.

21. **The correct answer is (B).** Outsourcing and international competition, allowing for cheaper products and consumer pricing, has led to the decline of domestic manufacturing.

22. **The correct answer is (A).** The demand for workers with college degrees would have increased dramatically based upon the type of industries that dominated the workforce in 2010. Skilled workers were being replaced with degree industries such as education, healthcare, and management.

23. **The correct answer is (B).** Agriculture is no longer part of the information provided, leading to the conclusion that it has dropped more than any other industry.

24. **The correct answer is (D).** The focus of the campaign is centered on the holiday of Christmas and Santa Claus.

25. **The correct answer is (A).** A soft drink is a marketable product that is produced to satisfy a need.

26. **The correct answer is (A).** The information describes inflation, which is defined as the rise in the general price level.

27. **The correct answer is (B).** Cost-push inflation is the result of an increase in the price of production that includes rapid wage increases or an increase in raw material prices.

28. **The correct answer is (C).** CPI is the Department of Labor's indicator for the Consumer Price Index. It is released each month.

29. **The correct answer is (C).** Political cartoons are an example of political satire, as they mock hot-button issues and scandals of the time. The meatpacking industry was a target of many satirists during the Progressive Era because of corrupt bosses, unsafe working conditions, and unsanitary and dishonest products for consumers.

30. **The correct answer is (B).** As a result of Sinclair's *The Jungle,* The Meat Inspection Act and the Pure Food and Drug Act were passed. His exposé kept the American public abreast of the unsanitary conditions of the meatpacking industry. Additionally, Sinclair exposed the dangerous working conditions for laborers.

31. **The correct answer is (A).** This cartoon targets the food and drug industry during the Progressive Era, as the conditions in factories were grossly unsanitary for consumers and unsafe for the laborers. Moreover, there was no truth in labeling to protect consumers—companies did not have to list ingredients in their products. During the Progressive Era, drug companies were notorious for putting out "miracle products" that simply did not work, so the government increased its role to oversee production of food and drugs.

32. **The correct answer is (A).** During the Progressive Era, many pieces of legislation were passed, including the Pure Food and Drug Act, which expanded the role of the federal government in overseeing the conditions under which food and drugs were produced and the labels placed on these consumer goods.

33. **The correct answer is (C).** The cartoon uses satire to expose the wrongdoing of the food and drug industry as unsanitary and dishonest. Prior to the Progressive Era, there was no oversight protecting the American consumer. The Progressive Era used science and government reform to improve and increase production, in addition to enacting measures to protect consumer and labor safety.

34. **The correct answer is (B).** The poster was designed to evoke emotion or fear in an attempt to create more support for a cause.

35. **The correct answer is (A).** Propaganda posters during World War II were meant to evoke emotion in people and get them to support the war effort.

36. **The correct answer is (B).** The poster is clearly aimed at protecting and preserving the environment and is distributed by the Department of Agriculture and Forest Service.

37. **The correct answer is (C).** The United States emerged from World War II physically undamaged (aside from Pearl Harbor), financially strong, and as one of two leading countries (along with the U.S.S.R.) in the world.

38. **The correct answer is (B).** The poster was designed during World War II when the United States was at war with the Axis powers of Germany and Japan. (Italy, also an Axis power, is not referenced in the poster.)

39. **The correct answer is (B).** The poster was created during the 1940s, which was the height of World War II.

40. **The correct answer is (C).** During World War II, Germany, Japan, and Italy comprised the Axis powers.

answers practice test 1

41. **The correct answer is (D).** The poster is trying to make people afraid of what will happen if they don't take action.

42. **The correct answer is (C).** Secession of South Carolina and other southern states would start a four-year war in America that split the country in two.

43. **The correct answer is (B).** South Carolina argued that compact theory justified its secession, as the states came together or "compacted" to form the union.

44. **The correct answer is (B).** Lincoln believed in contract theory, meaning all people signed an agreement with the Constitution, not the states, and thus the states cannot secede.

45. **The correct answer is (C).** The argument centers on the idea of secession and if a state has the actual right to secede from the Union.

46. **The correct answer is (D).** The Southern states that seceded from the Union were known as the Confederate States of America.

47. **The correct answer is (D).** The Virginia and Kentucky Resolutions stated that states had the right to nullify federal law.

48. **The correct answer is (D).** Shanghai, while written in the East China Sea, actually has its point located on mainland China.

49. **The correct answer is (B).** The relative location is the location in relation to somewhere else.

50. **The correct answer is (A).** The idea that human behavior is controlled by the physical environment best explains why more airports and ports are found near the Eastern region, which is also closest to the major waterway and seas of China.

ANSWER SHEET PRACTICE TEST 2

Language Arts—Reading

1. Ⓐ Ⓑ Ⓒ Ⓓ   11. Ⓐ Ⓑ Ⓒ Ⓓ   21. Ⓐ Ⓑ Ⓒ Ⓓ   31. Ⓐ Ⓑ Ⓒ Ⓓ
2. Ⓐ Ⓑ Ⓒ Ⓓ   12. Ⓐ Ⓑ Ⓒ Ⓓ   22. Ⓐ Ⓑ Ⓒ Ⓓ   32. Ⓐ Ⓑ Ⓒ Ⓓ
3. Ⓐ Ⓑ Ⓒ Ⓓ   13. Ⓐ Ⓑ Ⓒ Ⓓ   23. Ⓐ Ⓑ Ⓒ Ⓓ   33. Ⓐ Ⓑ Ⓒ Ⓓ
4. Ⓐ Ⓑ Ⓒ Ⓓ   14. Ⓐ Ⓑ Ⓒ Ⓓ   24. Ⓐ Ⓑ Ⓒ Ⓓ   34. Ⓐ Ⓑ Ⓒ Ⓓ
5. Ⓐ Ⓑ Ⓒ Ⓓ   15. Ⓐ Ⓑ Ⓒ Ⓓ   25. Ⓐ Ⓑ Ⓒ Ⓓ   35. Ⓐ Ⓑ Ⓒ Ⓓ
6. Ⓐ Ⓑ Ⓒ Ⓓ   16. Ⓐ Ⓑ Ⓒ Ⓓ   26. Ⓐ Ⓑ Ⓒ Ⓓ   36. Ⓐ Ⓑ Ⓒ Ⓓ
7. Ⓐ Ⓑ Ⓒ Ⓓ   17. Ⓐ Ⓑ Ⓒ Ⓓ   27. Ⓐ Ⓑ Ⓒ Ⓓ   37. Ⓐ Ⓑ Ⓒ Ⓓ
8. Ⓐ Ⓑ Ⓒ Ⓓ   18. Ⓐ Ⓑ Ⓒ Ⓓ   28. Ⓐ Ⓑ Ⓒ Ⓓ   38. Ⓐ Ⓑ Ⓒ Ⓓ
9. Ⓐ Ⓑ Ⓒ Ⓓ   19. Ⓐ Ⓑ Ⓒ Ⓓ   29. Ⓐ Ⓑ Ⓒ Ⓓ   39. Ⓐ Ⓑ Ⓒ Ⓓ
10. Ⓐ Ⓑ Ⓒ Ⓓ   20. Ⓐ Ⓑ Ⓒ Ⓓ   30. Ⓐ Ⓑ Ⓒ Ⓓ   40. Ⓐ Ⓑ Ⓒ Ⓓ

Language Arts—Writing

Part 1

1. Ⓐ Ⓑ Ⓒ Ⓓ   11. Ⓐ Ⓑ Ⓒ Ⓓ   21. Ⓐ Ⓑ Ⓒ Ⓓ   31. Ⓐ Ⓑ Ⓒ Ⓓ   41. Ⓐ Ⓑ Ⓒ Ⓓ
2. Ⓐ Ⓑ Ⓒ Ⓓ   12. Ⓐ Ⓑ Ⓒ Ⓓ   22. Ⓐ Ⓑ Ⓒ Ⓓ   32. Ⓐ Ⓑ Ⓒ Ⓓ   42. Ⓐ Ⓑ Ⓒ Ⓓ
3. Ⓐ Ⓑ Ⓒ Ⓓ   13. Ⓐ Ⓑ Ⓒ Ⓓ   23. Ⓐ Ⓑ Ⓒ Ⓓ   33. Ⓐ Ⓑ Ⓒ Ⓓ   43. Ⓐ Ⓑ Ⓒ Ⓓ
4. Ⓐ Ⓑ Ⓒ Ⓓ   14. Ⓐ Ⓑ Ⓒ Ⓓ   24. Ⓐ Ⓑ Ⓒ Ⓓ   34. Ⓐ Ⓑ Ⓒ Ⓓ   44. Ⓐ Ⓑ Ⓒ Ⓓ
5. Ⓐ Ⓑ Ⓒ Ⓓ   15. Ⓐ Ⓑ Ⓒ Ⓓ   25. Ⓐ Ⓑ Ⓒ Ⓓ   35. Ⓐ Ⓑ Ⓒ Ⓓ   45. Ⓐ Ⓑ Ⓒ Ⓓ
6. Ⓐ Ⓑ Ⓒ Ⓓ   16. Ⓐ Ⓑ Ⓒ Ⓓ   26. Ⓐ Ⓑ Ⓒ Ⓓ   36. Ⓐ Ⓑ Ⓒ Ⓓ   46. Ⓐ Ⓑ Ⓒ Ⓓ
7. Ⓐ Ⓑ Ⓒ Ⓓ   17. Ⓐ Ⓑ Ⓒ Ⓓ   27. Ⓐ Ⓑ Ⓒ Ⓓ   37. Ⓐ Ⓑ Ⓒ Ⓓ   47. Ⓐ Ⓑ Ⓒ Ⓓ
8. Ⓐ Ⓑ Ⓒ Ⓓ   18. Ⓐ Ⓑ Ⓒ Ⓓ   28. Ⓐ Ⓑ Ⓒ Ⓓ   38. Ⓐ Ⓑ Ⓒ Ⓓ   48. Ⓐ Ⓑ Ⓒ Ⓓ
9. Ⓐ Ⓑ Ⓒ Ⓓ   19. Ⓐ Ⓑ Ⓒ Ⓓ   29. Ⓐ Ⓑ Ⓒ Ⓓ   39. Ⓐ Ⓑ Ⓒ Ⓓ   49. Ⓐ Ⓑ Ⓒ Ⓓ
10. Ⓐ Ⓑ Ⓒ Ⓓ   20. Ⓐ Ⓑ Ⓒ Ⓓ   30. Ⓐ Ⓑ Ⓒ Ⓓ   40. Ⓐ Ⓑ Ⓒ Ⓓ   50. Ⓐ Ⓑ Ⓒ Ⓓ

answer sheet

Part 2

_____

_____

_____

_____

_____

_____

_____

_____

_____

_____

_____

_____

_____

_____

_____

_____

_____

_____

_____

_____

_____

answer sheet

_____

_____

_____

_____

_____

_____

_____

_____

_____

_____

_____

_____

_____

_____

_____

_____

_____

_____

_____

_____

_____

_____

_____

Mathematics

1. Ⓐ Ⓑ Ⓒ Ⓓ Ⓔ   11. Ⓐ Ⓑ Ⓒ Ⓓ Ⓔ   21. Ⓐ Ⓑ Ⓒ Ⓓ Ⓔ   31. Ⓐ Ⓑ Ⓒ Ⓓ Ⓔ   41. Ⓐ Ⓑ Ⓒ Ⓓ Ⓔ
2. Ⓐ Ⓑ Ⓒ Ⓓ Ⓔ   12. Ⓐ Ⓑ Ⓒ Ⓓ Ⓔ   22. Ⓐ Ⓑ Ⓒ Ⓓ Ⓔ   32. Ⓐ Ⓑ Ⓒ Ⓓ Ⓔ   42. Ⓐ Ⓑ Ⓒ Ⓓ Ⓔ
3. Ⓐ Ⓑ Ⓒ Ⓓ Ⓔ   13. Ⓐ Ⓑ Ⓒ Ⓓ Ⓔ   23. Ⓐ Ⓑ Ⓒ Ⓓ Ⓔ   33. Ⓐ Ⓑ Ⓒ Ⓓ Ⓔ   43. Ⓐ Ⓑ Ⓒ Ⓓ Ⓔ
4. Ⓐ Ⓑ Ⓒ Ⓓ Ⓔ   14. Ⓐ Ⓑ Ⓒ Ⓓ Ⓔ   24. Ⓐ Ⓑ Ⓒ Ⓓ Ⓔ   34. Ⓐ Ⓑ Ⓒ Ⓓ Ⓔ   44. Ⓐ Ⓑ Ⓒ Ⓓ Ⓔ
5. Ⓐ Ⓑ Ⓒ Ⓓ Ⓔ   15. Ⓐ Ⓑ Ⓒ Ⓓ Ⓔ   25. Ⓐ Ⓑ Ⓒ Ⓓ Ⓔ   35. Ⓐ Ⓑ Ⓒ Ⓓ Ⓔ   45. Ⓐ Ⓑ Ⓒ Ⓓ Ⓔ
6. Ⓐ Ⓑ Ⓒ Ⓓ Ⓔ   16. Ⓐ Ⓑ Ⓒ Ⓓ Ⓔ   26. Ⓐ Ⓑ Ⓒ Ⓓ Ⓔ   36. Ⓐ Ⓑ Ⓒ Ⓓ Ⓔ   46. Ⓐ Ⓑ Ⓒ Ⓓ Ⓔ
7. Ⓐ Ⓑ Ⓒ Ⓓ Ⓔ   17. Ⓐ Ⓑ Ⓒ Ⓓ Ⓔ   27. Ⓐ Ⓑ Ⓒ Ⓓ Ⓔ   37. Ⓐ Ⓑ Ⓒ Ⓓ Ⓔ   47. Ⓐ Ⓑ Ⓒ Ⓓ Ⓔ
8. Ⓐ Ⓑ Ⓒ Ⓓ Ⓔ   18. Ⓐ Ⓑ Ⓒ Ⓓ Ⓔ   28. Ⓐ Ⓑ Ⓒ Ⓓ Ⓔ   38. Ⓐ Ⓑ Ⓒ Ⓓ Ⓔ   48. Ⓐ Ⓑ Ⓒ Ⓓ Ⓔ
9. Ⓐ Ⓑ Ⓒ Ⓓ Ⓔ   19. Ⓐ Ⓑ Ⓒ Ⓓ Ⓔ   29. Ⓐ Ⓑ Ⓒ Ⓓ Ⓔ   39. Ⓐ Ⓑ Ⓒ Ⓓ Ⓔ   49. Ⓐ Ⓑ Ⓒ Ⓓ Ⓔ
10. Ⓐ Ⓑ Ⓒ Ⓓ Ⓔ   20. Ⓐ Ⓑ Ⓒ Ⓓ Ⓔ   30. Ⓐ Ⓑ Ⓒ Ⓓ Ⓔ   40. Ⓐ Ⓑ Ⓒ Ⓓ Ⓔ   50. Ⓐ Ⓑ Ⓒ Ⓓ Ⓔ

Science

1. Ⓐ Ⓑ Ⓒ Ⓓ   11. Ⓐ Ⓑ Ⓒ Ⓓ   21. Ⓐ Ⓑ Ⓒ Ⓓ   31. Ⓐ Ⓑ Ⓒ Ⓓ   41. Ⓐ Ⓑ Ⓒ Ⓓ
2. Ⓐ Ⓑ Ⓒ Ⓓ   12. Ⓐ Ⓑ Ⓒ Ⓓ   22. Ⓐ Ⓑ Ⓒ Ⓓ   32. Ⓐ Ⓑ Ⓒ Ⓓ   42. Ⓐ Ⓑ Ⓒ Ⓓ
3. Ⓐ Ⓑ Ⓒ Ⓓ   13. Ⓐ Ⓑ Ⓒ Ⓓ   23. Ⓐ Ⓑ Ⓒ Ⓓ   33. Ⓐ Ⓑ Ⓒ Ⓓ   43. Ⓐ Ⓑ Ⓒ Ⓓ
4. Ⓐ Ⓑ Ⓒ Ⓓ   14. Ⓐ Ⓑ Ⓒ Ⓓ   24. Ⓐ Ⓑ Ⓒ Ⓓ   34. Ⓐ Ⓑ Ⓒ Ⓓ   44. Ⓐ Ⓑ Ⓒ Ⓓ
5. Ⓐ Ⓑ Ⓒ Ⓓ   15. Ⓐ Ⓑ Ⓒ Ⓓ   25. Ⓐ Ⓑ Ⓒ Ⓓ   35. Ⓐ Ⓑ Ⓒ Ⓓ   45. Ⓐ Ⓑ Ⓒ Ⓓ
6. Ⓐ Ⓑ Ⓒ Ⓓ   16. Ⓐ Ⓑ Ⓒ Ⓓ   26. Ⓐ Ⓑ Ⓒ Ⓓ   36. Ⓐ Ⓑ Ⓒ Ⓓ   46. Ⓐ Ⓑ Ⓒ Ⓓ
7. Ⓐ Ⓑ Ⓒ Ⓓ   17. Ⓐ Ⓑ Ⓒ Ⓓ   27. Ⓐ Ⓑ Ⓒ Ⓓ   37. Ⓐ Ⓑ Ⓒ Ⓓ   47. Ⓐ Ⓑ Ⓒ Ⓓ
8. Ⓐ Ⓑ Ⓒ Ⓓ   18. Ⓐ Ⓑ Ⓒ Ⓓ   28. Ⓐ Ⓑ Ⓒ Ⓓ   38. Ⓐ Ⓑ Ⓒ Ⓓ   48. Ⓐ Ⓑ Ⓒ Ⓓ
9. Ⓐ Ⓑ Ⓒ Ⓓ   19. Ⓐ Ⓑ Ⓒ Ⓓ   29. Ⓐ Ⓑ Ⓒ Ⓓ   39. Ⓐ Ⓑ Ⓒ Ⓓ   49. Ⓐ Ⓑ Ⓒ Ⓓ
10. Ⓐ Ⓑ Ⓒ Ⓓ   20. Ⓐ Ⓑ Ⓒ Ⓓ   30. Ⓐ Ⓑ Ⓒ Ⓓ   40. Ⓐ Ⓑ Ⓒ Ⓓ   50. Ⓐ Ⓑ Ⓒ Ⓓ

Social Studies

1. Ⓐ Ⓑ Ⓒ Ⓓ   11. Ⓐ Ⓑ Ⓒ Ⓓ   21. Ⓐ Ⓑ Ⓒ Ⓓ   31. Ⓐ Ⓑ Ⓒ Ⓓ   41. Ⓐ Ⓑ Ⓒ Ⓓ

2. Ⓐ Ⓑ Ⓒ Ⓓ   12. Ⓐ Ⓑ Ⓒ Ⓓ   22. Ⓐ Ⓑ Ⓒ Ⓓ   32. Ⓐ Ⓑ Ⓒ Ⓓ   42. Ⓐ Ⓑ Ⓒ Ⓓ

3. Ⓐ Ⓑ Ⓒ Ⓓ   13. Ⓐ Ⓑ Ⓒ Ⓓ   23. Ⓐ Ⓑ Ⓒ Ⓓ   33. Ⓐ Ⓑ Ⓒ Ⓓ   43. Ⓐ Ⓑ Ⓒ Ⓓ

4. Ⓐ Ⓑ Ⓒ Ⓓ   14. Ⓐ Ⓑ Ⓒ Ⓓ   24. Ⓐ Ⓑ Ⓒ Ⓓ   34. Ⓐ Ⓑ Ⓒ Ⓓ   44. Ⓐ Ⓑ Ⓒ Ⓓ

5. Ⓐ Ⓑ Ⓒ Ⓓ   15. Ⓐ Ⓑ Ⓒ Ⓓ   25. Ⓐ Ⓑ Ⓒ Ⓓ   35. Ⓐ Ⓑ Ⓒ Ⓓ   45. Ⓐ Ⓑ Ⓒ Ⓓ

6. Ⓐ Ⓑ Ⓒ Ⓓ   16. Ⓐ Ⓑ Ⓒ Ⓓ   26. Ⓐ Ⓑ Ⓒ Ⓓ   36. Ⓐ Ⓑ Ⓒ Ⓓ   46. Ⓐ Ⓑ Ⓒ Ⓓ

7. Ⓐ Ⓑ Ⓒ Ⓓ   17. Ⓐ Ⓑ Ⓒ Ⓓ   27. Ⓐ Ⓑ Ⓒ Ⓓ   37. Ⓐ Ⓑ Ⓒ Ⓓ   47. Ⓐ Ⓑ Ⓒ Ⓓ

8. Ⓐ Ⓑ Ⓒ Ⓓ   18. Ⓐ Ⓑ Ⓒ Ⓓ   28. Ⓐ Ⓑ Ⓒ Ⓓ   38. Ⓐ Ⓑ Ⓒ Ⓓ   48. Ⓐ Ⓑ Ⓒ Ⓓ

9. Ⓐ Ⓑ Ⓒ Ⓓ   19. Ⓐ Ⓑ Ⓒ Ⓓ   29. Ⓐ Ⓑ Ⓒ Ⓓ   39. Ⓐ Ⓑ Ⓒ Ⓓ   49. Ⓐ Ⓑ Ⓒ Ⓓ

10. Ⓐ Ⓑ Ⓒ Ⓓ   20. Ⓐ Ⓑ Ⓒ Ⓓ   30. Ⓐ Ⓑ Ⓒ Ⓓ   40. Ⓐ Ⓑ Ⓒ Ⓓ   50. Ⓐ Ⓑ Ⓒ Ⓓ

answer sheet

Practice Test 2

The following is a practice test that mimics the official HiSET® exam. For the best preparation, follow the allotted time for each subtest.

For each question, choose the best answer and mark your choice on the answer sheet. Work as quickly as you can; do not spend too much time on a question that you can't answer. Skip it and return to it later, if you have time. If you decide to skip a question, make sure to also skip a row on the answer sheet. This will ensure that you are marking the correct space on the answer sheet for all questions.

Mark all your answers on the answer sheet. Mark only one answer to each question. If you decide to change your answer, completely erase your mark. If more than one answer is marked, the question will not be counted.

Remember, don't leave a question unanswered. Your score is derived from the number of questions you answer correctly. You will not receive a penalty for a wrong answer. It just won't contribute to your score.

LANGUAGE ARTS—READING

40 Questions • 65 Minutes

QUESTIONS 1 THROUGH 5 ARE BASED ON THE FOLLOWING PASSAGES.

The passages in this pair are excerpts from novels. In Passage 1, Rip van Winkle arrives in a village he doesn't recognize. In Passage 2, the narrator wakes up to find himself in a strange country.

Passage 1 by Washington Irving

The appearance of Rip, with his long, grizzled beard, his rusty fowling piece, his uncouth dress, and an army of women and children
5 at his heels, soon attracted the attention of the tavern politicians. They crowded round him, eyeing him from head to foot with great curiosity. The orator bustled up
10 to him, and, drawing him partly aside, inquired "On which side he voted?" Rip stared in vacant stupidity. Another short but busy little fellow pulled him by the arm,
15 and, rising on tiptoe, inquired in his ear, "Whether he was Federal or Democrat?" Rip was equally at a loss to comprehend the question; when a knowing, self-important old
20 gentleman, in a sharp cocked hat, made his way through the crowd, putting them to the right and left with his elbows as he passed, and planting himself before Van
25 Winkle, with one arm akimbo, the other resting on his cane, his keen eyes and sharp hat penetrating, as it were, into his very soul, demanded, in an austere tone,
30 "What brought him to the election with a gun on his shoulder, and a mob at his heels; and whether he meant to breed a riot in the village?"—"Alas! gentlemen," cried
35 Rip, somewhat dismayed, "I am a poor, quiet man, a native of the place, and a loyal subject of the king, God bless him!

Here a general shout burst from
40 the bystanders—"A tory! a tory! a spy! a refugee! hustle him! away with him!" It was with great difficulty that the self-important man in the cocked hat restored order;
45 and having assumed a tenfold austerity of brow, demanded again of the unknown culprit, what he came there for, and whom he was seeking! The poor man humbly
50 assured him that he meant no harm, but merely came there in search of some of his neighbors....
"Does nobody here know Rip Van Winkle?"
55 "Oh, Rip Van Winkle!" exclaimed two or three, "oh, to be sure! that's Rip Van Winkle yonder, leaning against the tree."
Rip looked, and beheld a precise
60 counterpart of himself, as he went up the mountain—apparently as lazy and certainly as ragged. The poor fellow was now completely confounded. He doubted his own
65 identity, and whether he was himself or another man. In the midst of his bewilderment, the man in the cocked hat demanded who he was, and what was his name.
70 "God knows," exclaimed he, at his wits' end; "I'm not myself—I'm somebody else—that's me yonder—no—that's somebody else got into my shoes—I was myself last night,
75 but I fell asleep on the mountain, and they've changed my gun, and everything's changed, and I'm changed, and I can't tell what's my name, or who I am!"
80 The bystanders began now to look at each other, nod, wink significantly, and tap their fingers against their foreheads. There was

a whisper, also, about securing
85 the gun, and keeping the old
fellow from doing mischief, at the
very suggestion of which the self-
important man in the cocked hat
retired with some precipitation.
90 At this critical moment a fresh,
comely woman pressed through
the throng to get a peep at the
gray-bearded man. She had a
chubby child in her arms, which,
95 frightened at his looks, began to
cry. "Hush, Rip," cried she, "hush,
you little fool; the old man won't
hurt you." The name of the child,
the air of the mother, the tone of
100 her voice, all awakened a train of
recollections in his mind. "What
is your name, my good woman?"
asked he.

"Judith Gardenier."

105 "And your father's name?"

"Ah, poor man, Rip Van Winkle
was his name, but it's twenty years
since he went away from home
with his gun, and never has been
110 heard of since—his dog came home
without him; but whether he shot
himself, or was carried away by the
Indians, nobody can tell. I was then
but a little girl."

Passage 2 by Mark Twain

Well, a man like that is a man that
is full of fight—that goes without
saying. With a couple of thousand
rough men under one, one has
5 plenty of that sort of amusement.
I had, anyway. At last I met my
match, and I got my dose. It was
during a misunderstanding conducted with crowbars with a fellow
10 we used to call Hercules. He laid
me out with a crusher alongside
the head that made everything
crack, and seemed to spring every
joint in my skull and made it
15 overlap its neighbor. Then the
world went out in darkness, and
I didn't feel anything more, and
didn't know anything at all —at
least for a while.

20   When I came to again, I was
sitting under an oak tree, on the
grass, with a whole beautiful
and broad country landscape all
to myself–nearly. Not entirely;
25 for there was a fellow on a horse,
looking down at me--a fellow fresh
out of a picture-book. He was in
old-time iron armor from head to
heel, with a helmet on his head the
30 shape of a nail-keg with slits in it;
and he had a shield, and a sword,
and a prodigious spear; and his
horse had armor on, too, and a steel
horn projecting from his forehead,
35 and gorgeous red and green silk
trappings that hung down all
around him like a bedquilt, nearly
to the ground.

"Fair sir, will ye just?" said this
40 fellow.

"Will I which?"

"Will ye try a passage of arms
for land or lady or for–"

"What are you giving me?" I
45 said. "Get along back to your circus,
or I'll report you."

Now what does this man do
but fall back a couple of hundred
yards and then come rushing at
50 me as hard as he could tear, with
his nail-keg bent down nearly to
his horse's neck and his long spear
pointed straight ahead. I saw he
meant business, so I was up the
55 tree when he arrived.

He allowed that I was his
property, the captive of his spear.
There was argument on his side-
-and the bulk of the advantage –so
60 I judged it best to humor him. We
fixed up an agreement whereby
I was to go with him and he was
not to hurt me. I came down, and
we started away, I walking by
65 the side of his horse. We marched
comfortably along, through glades
and over brooks which I could not
remember to have seen before–
which puzzled me and made me
70 wonder--and yet we did not come
to any circus or sign of a circus.

So I gave up the idea of a circus, and concluded he was from an asylum. But we never came to an
75 asylum—so I was up a stump, as you may say. I asked him how far we were from Hartford. He said he had never heard of the place; which I took to be a lie, but allowed it to
80 go at that. At the end of an hour we saw a far-away town sleeping in a valley by a winding river; and beyond it on a hill, a vast gray fortress, with towers and turrets,
85 the first I had ever seen out of a picture.

"Bridgeport?" said I, pointing.

"Camelot," said he.

1. It can be inferred from the second paragraph in Passage 1 that the by-standers are
   (A) very reasonable.
   (B) mistrustful of tories.
   (C) self important.
   (D) too humble.

2. The narrator of Passage 2 meets the man on the horse
   (A) after the narrator finds out he is in Camelot.
   (B) before the narrator wakes up under an oak tree.
   (C) after the narrator gets hit by a man called Hercules.
   (D) before the narrator hits a man called Hercules.

3. As it is used in line 64 of Passage 1, the word "confounded" most nearly means
   (A) funny.
   (B) confused.
   (C) tired.
   (D) mysterious.

4. The perspective of Rip Van Winkle in Passage 1 and the narrator of Passage 2 is that of a
   (A) child.
   (B) fighter.
   (C) leader.
   (D) lost man.

5. The people that both Rip Van Winkle and the narrator of passage 2 encounter can best be described as:
   (A) passionate.
   (B) hostile.
   (C) courageous.
   (D) cautious.

practice test 2

QUESTIONS 6 THROUGH 11 ARE BASED ON THE FOLLOWING PASSAGE.

As the Civil War ended, America became an increasingly industrialized nation. This excerpt compares American industry in 1919 to that transitional period at the end of the Civil War.

A comprehensive survey of the United States, at the end of the Civil War, would reveal a state of society which bears little resem-
5 blance to that of today. Almost all those commonplace fundamentals of existence, the things that contribute to our bodily comfort while they vex us with economic
10 and political problems, had not yet made their appearance. The America of Civil War days was a country without transcontinental railroads, without telephones,
15 without European cables, or wireless stations, or automobiles, or electric lights, or skyscrapers, or million-dollar hotels, or trolley cars, or a thousand other contriv-
20 ances that today supply the conveniences and comforts of what we call our American civilization. The cities of that period, with their unsewered and unpaved streets,
25 their dingy, flickering gaslights, their ambling horse-cars, and their hideous slums, seemed appropriate settings for the unformed social life and the rough-and-ready political
30 methods of American democracy. The railroads, with their fragile iron rails, their little wheezy locomotives, their wooden bridges, their unheated coaches, and their
35 kerosene lamps, fairly typified the prevailing frontier business and economic organization. But only by talking with the business leaders of that time could we have under-
40 stood the changes that have taken place in fifty years.
    For the most part we speak a business language which our fathers and grandfathers would
45 not have comprehended. The word "trust" had not become a part of their vocabulary; "restraint of trade" was a phrase which only the antiquarian lawyer could have
50 interpreted; "interlocking directorates," "holding companies," "subsidiaries," "underwriting syndicates," and "community of interest"—all this jargon of
55 modern business would have signified nothing to our immediate ancestors.
    Our nation of 1865 was a nation of farmers, city artisans, and
60 industrious, independent business men, and small-scale manufacturers. Millionaires, though they were not unknown, did not swarm all over the land. Luxury, though
65 it had made great progress in the latter years of the war, had not become the American standard of well-being. The industrial story of the United States in the last
70 fifty years is the story of the most amazing economic transformation that the world has ever known; a change which is fitly typified in the evolution of the independent
75 oil driller of western Pennsylvania into the Standard Oil Company, and of the ancient open-air forge on the banks of the Allegheny into the United States Steel Corporation.
80   The slow, unceasing ages had been accumulating a priceless inheritance for the American people. Nearly all of their natural resources, in 1865, were still lying
85 fallow, and even undiscovered in many instances. Americans had begun, it is true, to exploit their more obvious, external wealth, their forests and their land; the first
90 had made them one of the world's two greatest shipbuilding nations, while the second had furnished a

large part of the resources that had enabled the Federal Government 95 to fight what was, up to that time, the greatest war in history. But the extensive prairie plains whose settlement was to follow the railroad extensions of the sixties and the 100 seventies— Kansas, Nebraska, Iowa, Oklahoma, Minnesota, the Dakotas—had been only slightly penetrated. This region, with a rainfall not too abundant and not 105 too scanty, with a cultivable soil extending from eight inches to twenty feet under the ground, with hardly a rock in its whole extent, with scarcely a tree, except where 110 it bordered on the streams, has been pronounced by competent scientists the finest farming country to which man has ever set the plow.

Excerpt from *The Age of Big Business: A Chronicle of the Captains of Industry* by Burton J. Hendrick

6. The author of this passage seems to believe that

(A) America needs to stop abusing its natural resources.

(B) industrialization has made America a better place.

(C) industrialization has its positive and negative aspects.

(D) greater access to luxuries has made Americans lazy.

7. Information in this passage would be most useful for

(A) learning how to install a telephone line.

(B) getting a job at a major oil company.

(C) writing a story set in Civil War-era America.

(D) learning how to become a successful farmer.

8. Read the following paragraph.

Although life without the conveniences born in the post-Civil War era may be unthinkable now, there is a dear price we have paid for such amenities. The factories and machinery necessary to create our conveniences also pollute our air, soil, and water. The technology that has made our military more effective has also made war a business worth pursuing.

How does this paragraph differ from the main passage?

(A) This passage indicates the ill effects industrialization has had on the world.

(B) This passage explains ways industrialization has changed the world.

(C) This passage argues that the luxuries of industrialization were worth its ill effects.

(D) This passage insists that American life was better during the Civil War.

9. Based on details in this passage, people in the Civil War era were most likely

(A) unusually prosperous.

(B) ignorant of business.

(C) uniformly impoverished.

(D) often uncomfortable.

10. According to information in the passage, both the Civil War era and the post-Civil War era had

(A) underwriting syndicates.

(B) millionaires.

(C) trolley cars.

(D) sewers.

11. Based on information in this passage, the author MOST likely

(A) values both wealth and nature.

(B) does not care about pollution.

(C) worries about overpopulation.

(D) fears invasion from other nations.

QUESTIONS 12 THROUGH 17 ARE BASED ON THE FOLLOWING PASSAGE.

A mysterious stranger has come to Mrs. Hall's inn. In this excerpt from a work of fiction, Mrs. Hall attempts to communicate with the stranger.

The stranger came early in February one wintry day, through a biting wind and a driving snow, the last snowfall of the year, over the
5 down, walking as it seemed from Bramblehurst railway station and carrying a little black portmanteau in his thickly gloved hand. He was wrapped up from head to foot, and
10 the brim of his soft felt hat hid every inch of his face but the shiny tip of his nose; the snow had piled itself against his shoulders and chest, and added a white crest to
15 the burden he carried. He staggered into the Coach and Horses, more dead than alive as it seemed, and flung his portmanteau down. "A fire," he cried, "in the name of
20 human charity! A room and a fire!" He stamped and shook the snow from off himself in the bar, and followed Mrs. Hall into her guest parlour to strike his bargain. And
25 with that much introduction, that and a ready acquiescence to terms and a couple of sovereigns flung upon the table, he took up his quarters in the inn.
30 Mrs. Hall lit the fire and left him there while she went to prepare him a meal with her own hands. A guest to stop at Iping in the winter-time was an unheard-of
35 piece of luck, let alone a guest who was no "haggler," and she was resolved to show herself worthy of her good fortune. As soon as the bacon was well under way, and
40 Millie, her lymphatic aid, had been brisked up a bit by a few deftly chosen expressions of contempt, she carried the cloth, plates, and glasses into the parlour and began

45 to lay them with the utmost clat. Although the fire was burning up briskly, she was surprised to see that her visitor still wore his hat and coat, standing with his back to
50 her and staring out of the window at the falling snow in the yard. His gloved hands were clasped behind him, and he seemed to be lost in thought. She noticed that the
55 melted snow that still sprinkled his shoulders dripped upon her carpet. "Can I take your hat and coat, sir," she said, "and give them a good dry in the kitchen?"
60 "No," he said without turning. She was not sure she had heard him, and was about to repeat her question. He turned his head and looked
65 at her over his shoulder. "I prefer to keep them on," he said with emphasis, and she noticed that he wore big blue spectacles with side-lights and had a bushy side-
70 whisker over his coat-collar that completely hid his face. "Very well, sir," she said. "As you like. In a bit the room will be warmer."
75 He made no answer and had turned his face away from her again; and Mrs. Hall, feeling that her conversational advances were ill-timed, laid the rest of the table
80 things in a quick staccato and whisked out of the room. When she returned he was still standing there like a man of stone, his back hunched, his collar turned up, his
85 dripping hat-brim turned down, hiding his face and ears completely. She put down the eggs and bacon with considerable emphasis, and called rather than said to him,
90 "Your lunch is served, sir."

"Thank you," he said at the same time, and did not stir until she was closing the door.

Excerpt from *The Invisible Man* by H.G. Wells

12. What will the reader most likely learn as the story continues?

(A) How long the stranger plans to stay.

(B) Who Millie's other guests are.

(C) Where the stranger grew up.

(D) Why the man is wrapped up.

13. Based on information in this passage, the reader can conclude that

(A) the stranger wants to conceal his identity.

(B) Millie secretly despises the stranger.

(C) the stranger has committed a crime in his past.

(D) Millie wishes more of her guests were like the stranger.

14. The author uses words such as *quick staccato*, *clat*, and *hunched* to create a sense of

(A) tension.

(B) excitement.

(C) humor.

(D) drama.

15. What does "acquiescence" (line 26) mean?

(A) Argument

(B) Confusion

(C) Insinuation

(D) Agreement

16. Based on the information in the passage, why did Mrs. Hall consider her mysterious guest a stroke of "good fortune" (line 38)?

(A) The mysterious guest owed Mrs. Hall a great deal of money from an old debt.

(B) Mrs. Hall was waiting for the mysterious guest, and he arrived right on time.

(C) Mrs. Hall was lonely and really appreciated the company of a new guest.

(D) Mrs. Hall typically did not receive a lot of business during the winter at her inn.

17. Which of the following best describes the tone of the passage?

(A) Mystifying

(B) Humorous

(C) Romantic

(D) Informative

QUESTIONS 18 THROUGH 22 ARE BASED ON THE FOLLOWING PASSAGE.

Etiquette is the way one is expected to behave under particular circumstances. In this excerpt from a nonfiction work, the author expresses some of his thoughts about etiquette.

It is a matter of some slight surprise to me that in these days, full of improvement as they *have been* and certainly *are*, the science of
5 etiquette should be so little cultivated by the mass of the people. I have, therefore, in an idle moment, ventured to lay down the following suggestions for a proper bearing in
10 society, which may be found useful to the uninitiated.

The quality which a young man should most affect in intercourse with society is a decent modesty,
15 but he must avoid at the same time all bashfulness or timidity. His flights must not go too far, but so far as they go let them be marked by *perfect assurance* and coolness.
20 Familiarity of manner is the greatest vice of society, and when our *acquaintance* finds himself entitled to say, "Allow me, my dear fellow," or any such phrase, cut him
25 directly.

Never use the term genteel — it is only to be found in the mouths of those who have it nowhere else. Never enter your own house
30 without bowing to any one you may meet there, and on no account before strangers, grumble or find fault. A visit must always be returned; — an insult should never
35 be overlooked.

The style of your conversation should always be in keeping with the character of the visit. You must not talk about literature on a
40 visit of condolence, nor descant on political economy in a visit of ceremony. If you go to a house where there are children, you should take especial care to conciliate
45 their good will by a little manly *tête-à-tête*. Never ask a lady any question about anything whatever, unless it be the all-important one of "popping the question," which is
50 the star of the mind and heart from seventeen to thirty-two. Punning is now decidedly out of date. It is a silly and displeasing thing when it becomes a habit. Some one has
55 very appropriately styled it the wit of fools. Above all, never take your hat into a drawing-room.

Your first duty at the table is to attend to the wants of the lady
60 who sits next to you, the second to attend to your own. In performing the first, you should take care that the lady has all that she wishes, yet without appearing to direct your
65 attention too much to her plate, for nothing is more ill-bred than to watch a person eating. If the lady be something of a *gourmande*, and in over-zealous pursuit of the aroma
70 of the wind of a pigeon should raise an unmanageable portion to her mouth, you should cease all conversation with her and look steadfastly into the opposite part
75 of the room.

Excerpt from A Few Words on Etiquette," by Edgar Allan Poe

18. The author's main purpose in writing this article is to

(A) define the word *etiquette* for the reader.

(B) explain his thoughts on proper etiquette.

(C) prove that he has superior etiquette skills.

(D) show how proper etiquette improves one's life.

19. What evidence might someone use to support the opinion that this passage is very old-fashioned?

- **(A)** The writer's attitudes about women
- **(B)** The writer's emphasis on politeness
- **(C)** The writer's belief that etiquette is important
- **(D)** The writer's use of terms such as "coolness"

20. Which of the following is not an example of an etiquette suggestion made by Edgar Allen Poe in the passage?

- **(A)** Don't be timid or bashful when dealing with others.
- **(B)** A well-timed joke is a great addition to a conversation.
- **(C)** Always bow to others when entering your own house.
- **(D)** Never be too familiar with acquaintances.

21. Read the following paragraph.

While humor, itself, never goes out of style, forms of humor date in often embarrassing ways. Today, jokes about culture, gender, or race are generally taboo because they are often insensitive and offensive. The unenlightened days when such topics were considered fair game for humor are thankfully over.

Both the writer of this paragraph and Edgar Allan Poe agree that

- **(A)** jokes about gender are offensive.
- **(B)** comedy requires sensitivity.
- **(C)** one should never make jokes.
- **(D)** forms of humor go out of style.

22. Based on this passage, the reader can conclude that the writer is

- **(A)** very friendly.
- **(B)** kind and polite.
- **(C)** offended easily.
- **(D)** clever and witty.

QUESTIONS 23 THROUGH 28 ARE BASED ON THE FOLLOWING PASSAGE.

A man is faced with a choice. In this poem by Robert Frost, he must decide which road to travel.

> Two roads diverged in a yellow wood,
> And sorry I could not travel both
> And be one traveler, long I stood
> And looked down one as far as I could
> 5 To where it bent in the undergrowth.
>
> Then took the other, as just as fair,
> And having perhaps the better claim,
> Because it was grassy and wanted wear;
> Though as for that the passing there
> 10 Had worn them really about the same.
>
> And both that morning equally lay
> In leaves no step had trodden black.
> Oh, I kept the first for another day!
> Yet knowing how way leads on to way,
> 15 I doubted if I should ever come back.
>
> I shall be telling this with a sigh
> Somewhere ages and ages hence:
> Two roads diverged in a wood, and I—
> I took the one less traveled by,
> 20 And that has made all the difference.

>   "The Road Less Traveled," by
>   Robert Frost

23. Which of the following techniques does the poet use in the first stanza?

(A) Irony

(B) Oxymoron

(C) Pathos

(D) Repetition

24. This poem is mainly about

(A) taking a hike.

(B) making a choice.

(C) exploring a wood.

(D) finding something hidden.

25. What does "diverged" (line 1) mean?

(A) Separated

(B) Curled

(C) Joined

(D) Shined

26. If the paths in the poem symbolize career choices, then the wood might represent

(A) work.

(B) business.

(C) a city.

(D) life.

27. Based on details in the final stanza, the reader can conclude that the narrator

(A) is afraid he will forget the events in the poem.

(B) thinks he might regret his decision one day.

(C) wishes he never had to leave the wood.

(D) has a lot of trouble making up his mind.

28. This poem would have the greatest meaning to people who are

(A) planning a camping trip.

(B) nursing a sick friend back to health.

(C) choosing a school to attend.

(D) beginning their second year at a job.

QUESTIONS 29 THROUGH 33 ARE BASED ON THE FOLLOWING PASSAGE.

Helen Keller became deaf and blind when she was a little girl. In this excerpt from her autobiography, she describes the most important day in her life.

The most important day I remember in all my life is the one on which my teacher, Anne Mansfield Sullivan, came to me. I am filled with wonder
5   when I consider the immeasurable contrasts between the two lives which it connects. It was the third of March, 1887, three months before I was seven-years-old.
10   On the afternoon of that eventful day I stood on the porch—dumb, expectant. I guessed vaguely from my mother's signs and from the hurrying to and fro in the house
15   that something unusual was about to happen, so I went to the door and waited on the steps. The afternoon sun penetrated the mass of honeysuckle that covered the porch,
20   and fell on my upturned face. My fingers lingered almost unconsciously on the familiar leaves and blossoms which had just come forth to greet the sweet Southern spring.
25   I did not know what the future held of marvel or surprise for me. Anger and bitterness had preyed upon me continually for weeks, and a deep languor had succeeded this pas-
30   sionate struggle.

Have you ever been at sea in a dense fog when it seemed as if a tangible, white darkness shut you in, and the great ship, tense
35   and anxious, groped her way toward the shore with plummet and sounding line, and you waited with beating heart for something to happen? I was like that ship before
40   my education began, only I was without compass or sounding line and had no way of knowing how near the harbor was. "Light! Give me light!" was the wordless cry of

45   my soul, and the light of love shone on me in that very hour.

I felt approaching footsteps. I stretched out my hand, as I supposed, to my mother. Someone
50   took it, and I was caught up and held close in the arms of her who had come to reveal all things to me and, more than all things else, to love me.
55   The morning after my teacher came she led me into her room and gave me a doll. The little blind children at the Perkins Institution had sent it and Laura Bridgman
60   had dressed it; but I did not know this until afterward. When I had played with it a little while, Miss Sullivan slowly spelled into my hand the word "d-o-l-l." I was at
65   once interested in this finger play and tried to imitate it. When I finally succeeded in making the letters correctly I was flushed with childish pleasure and pride.

Excerpt from *The Story of My Life*, by Helen Keller

29. Which of the following sentences from the passage expresses an assumption?

(A) On the afternoon of that eventful day I stood on the porch—dumb, expectant.

(B) I did not know what the future held of marvel or surprise for me.

(C) I stretched out my hand, as I supposed, to my mother.

(D) I was at once interested in this finger play and tried to imitate it.

30. Based on details in paragraph 2, the reader can conclude that the author

(A) experienced the world through touch.

(B) was overcome with feelings of joy.

(C) felt that something bad might happen.

(D) was tired of waiting for her teacher.

31. Which of the following best describes the tone of paragraphs 1–3?

(A) Angry

(B) Meditative

(C) Mirthful

(D) Expectant

32. How is the author different after her teacher arrives?

(A) She is smarter.

(B) She is less curious.

(C) She is happier.

(D) She is more frustrated.

33. What did Helen Keller most likely mean when she referenced the "immeasurable contrasts" (lines 5–6) between herself and Anne Mansfield Sullivan?

(A) Helen Keller and Anne Mansfield Sullivan did not get along well when they initially met.

(B) Helen Keller and Anne Mansfield Sullivan were born and lived on opposite sides of the country.

(C) Helen Keller was a generous and kind person, whereas Anne Mansfield Sullivan was known to be cruel and selfish.

(D) Anne Mansfield Sullivan had full use of her physical senses and a life of experience, whereas Helen Keller had limited use of her physical senses and limited life experience.

QUESTIONS 34 THROUGH 40 ARE BASED ON THE FOLLOWING PASSAGE.

Scrivener is an antiquated term for a clerk. In this excerpt from a work of fiction, a lawyer calls his scrivener into his office to perform a task.

Now and then, in the haste of business, it had been my habit to assist in comparing some brief document myself, calling Turkey
5 or Nippers for this purpose. One object I had in placing Bartleby so handy to me behind the screen, was to avail myself of his services on such trivial occasions. It was
10 on the third day, I think, of his being with me, and before any necessity had arisen for having his own writing examined, that, being much hurried to complete a small
15 affair I had in hand, I abruptly called to Bartleby. In my haste and natural expectancy of instant compliance, I sat with my head bent over the original on my desk,
20 and my right hand sideways, and somewhat nervously extended with the copy, so that immediately upon emerging from his retreat, Bartleby might snatch it and proceed
25 to business without the least delay.

In this very attitude did I sit when I called to him, rapidly stating what it was I wanted him to do—namely, to examine a small
30 paper with me. Imagine my surprise, nay, my consternation, when without moving from his privacy, Bartleby in a singularly mild, firm voice, replied, "I would prefer not
35 to."

I sat awhile in perfect silence, rallying my stunned faculties. Immediately it occurred to me that my ears had deceived me, or
40 Bartleby had entirely misunderstood my meaning. I repeated my request in the clearest tone I could assume. But in quite as clear a one came the previous reply, "I would
45 prefer not to."

"Prefer not to," echoed I, rising in high excitement, and crossing the room with a stride. "What do you mean? Are you moon-struck? I

50 want you to help me compare this sheet here—take it," and I thrust it towards him.

"I would prefer not to," said he.

I looked at him steadfastly. His

55 face was leanly composed; his gray eye dimly calm. Not a wrinkle of agitation rippled him. Had there been the least uneasiness, anger, impatience or impertinence in his

60 manner; in other words, had there been any thing ordinarily human about him, doubtless I should have violently dismissed him from the premises. But as it was, I should

65 have as soon thought of turning my pale plaster-of-Paris bust of Cicero out of doors. I stood gazing at him awhile, as he went on with his own writing, and then reseated myself

70 at my desk. This is very strange, thought I. What had one best do? But my business hurried me. I concluded to forget the matter for the present, reserving it for my future

75 leisure. So calling Nippers from the other room, the paper was speedily examined.

Excerpt from *Bartleby the Scrivener,* by Herman Melville

34. Which of the following best describes the tone of this passage?

(A) Hostile

(B) Wry

(C) Romantic

(D) Playful

35. Which of the following literary devices does the author use in this passage?

(A) Extended metaphor

(B) Prologue

(C) First-person narrative

(D) Deus ex machina

36. Which of the following lines from paragraph 6 restates information from earlier in the passage?

(A) His face was leanly composed; his gray eye dimly calm.

(B) Not a wrinkle of agitation rippled him.

(C) This is very strange, thought I.

(D) What had one best do? But my business hurried me.

37. Based on the way he reacts to Bartleby, the narrator is most likely

(A) often rude and inconsiderate to his employees.

(B) not used to having his employees disobey him.

(C) more like his employees' father than their boss.

(D) tired of his job and hoping to change careers.

38. One theme of this passage is the

(A) beauty of simplicity.

(B) power of change.

(C) illusion of power.

(D) necessity of work.

39. Which of the following best describes Bartleby?

(A) Easily bullied

(B) Intimidating

(C) Self-assured

(D) Belligerent

40. Read the following sentence from lines 64–67.

"But as it was, I should have as soon thought of turning my pale plaster-of-Paris bust of Cicero out of doors."

This sentence means

(A) getting fired was unlikely to upset Bartleby.

(B) the narrator wanted to throw his bust in anger.

(C) Bartleby needed to go outside but would not.

(D) the narrator wanted Bartleby to take his bust away.

LANGUAGE ARTS—WRITING

Part 1

50 Questions • 120 Minutes

Directions: Read the following draft article. Then proceed to the expanded version and answer the questions, which offer options for improvement for each underlined part. Select the answer choice for each that best improves the written passage.

Para. 1 Composting is a great way to dispose of the organic waste in your home and provides numerous benefits to the environment. When done properly, compost is a nutrient-rich, natural fertilizer that can be used to nourish and fortify their lawn, garden, and houseplants. It is also a great way to handle recyclable materials, decreasing the amount of garbage your household throws away, and reduce the size of landfills.

Para. 2 There are numerous ways to compost, both inside your home and outdoors. The method you choose to utilize for composting should take into consideration the amount of space, time, and effort you want to devote to this worthwhile activity. When got started, don't forget that the Internet is a great source of information and advice for helping you determine what composting methods are right for you. I only use the Internet on the weekends.

Para. 3 Conventional composting requires a relatively small amount of effort and is a popular approach. The first step is to obtain a sturdy composting bin, which can be purchased (there are several wooden and plastic models available) or made from a garbage can or large wooden box—just be sure it includes holes to allow for proper aeration and has a lid or cover for protection. I prefer the bins created by the "compost king" company, which you can purchase online.

Para. 4 Your compost bin should be filled with disposable organic waste? Examples of viable organic waste for composting include vegetable and fruit peels, coffee grounds, eggshells, and various table scraps. Microorganisms also aid in breaking down the chemical components of your organic waste and converting them into compost. These include various types of bacteria and mold, as well as earthworms. The key to a successful and effective compost bin is a healthy ratio of carbon, nitrogen, oxygen, and water. Time and patience are also critical, but effective composting is well worth it. While composting, your friends and family will hopefully appreciate the effort.

Para. 1 Composting is a great way to dispose of the organic waste in your home and provides numerous benefits to the environment. When done properly, compost is a nutrient-rich, natural fertilizer that can be used to nourish and fortify <u>their</u> lawn, garden, and
2

houseplants. It is also a great way to handle recyclable materials, <u>decreasing</u>
3

the amount of garbage your household throws away, and reduce the size of landfills.

Para. 2 There are numerous ways to compost, both inside your home and outdoors. The method you choose to utilize for composting should take into consideration the amount of space, time, and effort you want to devote to this worthwhile activity. When <u>got</u> started,
4

don't forget that the Internet is a great source of information and advice for <u>(helping you determine)</u> what
5

composting methods are right for you.

1. Which of the following sentences would best fit at the beginning of the passage (Paragraph 1)?
   (A) Are you familiar with global warming?
   (B) I'm glad that you compost in your home!
   (C) Have you ever considered composting?
   (D) I've never composted in my life.

2. (A) (No change)
   (B) his
   (C) her
   (D) your

3. (A) (No change)
   (B) decrease
   (C) decreased
   (D) decreasers

4. (A) (No change)
   (B) getting
   (C) get
   (D) gotten

5. (A) (no change)
   (B) helping you determine
   (C) —helping you determine—
   (D , helping you determine,

Para. 3 Conventional composting requires a relatively small amount of effort and is a popular approach. The first step is to obtain a sturdy composting bin, which can be purchased (there are several wooden and plastic models available) or made from a garbage can or large wooden box—just be sure it includes holes to allow for proper aeration and has a lid or cover for protection. I prefer the bins created by the <u>"compost king"</u> company, which you
6

can purchase online.

Para. 4 <u>Your compost bin should be</u>
7

<u>filled with disposable organic waste?</u>
7

Examples of viable organic waste for composting include vegetable and fruit peels, coffee grounds, eggshells, and various table scraps. Microorganisms also aid in breaking down the chemical components of your organic waste and converting them into compost. These include various types of bacteria and

6. **(A)** (No change)
   (B) "compost king"
   (C) compost-king
   (D) Compost King

7. **(A)** (No change)
   (B) Your compost bin should be filled with disposable organic waste,
   (C) Your compost bin should be filled with disposable organic waste.
   (D) Your compost bin should be filled with disposable organic waste;

mold, as well as earthworms. The key to a successful and effective compost bin is a healthy ratio of carbon, nitrogen, oxygen, and water. Time and patience are also critical, but effective composting is well worth it. <u>While</u>
8

<u>composting, your friends and family</u>
8

<u>will hopefully appreciate the effort.</u>
8

8. **(A)** (No change)
   (B) If you compost, hopefully your friends and family will appreciate the effort.
   (C) While your friends and family are composting, hopefully they will appreciate your effort.
   (D) Your friends and family will compost, and hopefully you appreciate their effort.

practice test 2

Directions: Read the following draft informational piece. Then proceed to the expanded version and answer the questions, which offer options for improvement for each underlined portion.

Para. 1 There are many benefits to obtaining a U.S. passport. It is a viable form of name, address, and age of personal identification that can be used to substantiate you. It's also essential for international travel. If you've ever desired to see the world or have a job that requires international travel, consider following these simple steps to obtain your passport.

Para. 2 Eligibility requirements are determined by the U.S. Department of State, which is the federal executive department that is responsible for issuing passport books and distributed passport cards. All citizens of the United States and its territories (including Guam, Puerto Rico, the Northern Mariana Islands, and the U.S. Virgin Islands) are eligible to obtain a passport.

Para. 3 It's a simple process. Here's how to do it. Completion of an application is required to obtain a U.S. passport. The application form that you are required to complete is dependent on several factors, including your age and whether or not you have ever had a passport before. Currently, applications for a united states passport must be made in person, and can be obtained and completed in libraries and post offices.

Para. 4 Documentation required to obtain a passport includes an official birth certificate, valid state photo ID, and a passport photo that meets certain size and other requirements. In addition, there is a fee involved with obtaining a passport, which varies based on such factors as your age and whether you're applying for a first time or renewal passport. The first thing you should do after you have made the decision to obtain a passport is to determine whether or not you are eligible for one!

Para. 1 The first thing you should do after you have made the decision to obtain a passport is to determine whether or not you are eligible for one! There are many benefits to obtaining a U.S. passport. <u>It is a viable</u>
9

<u>form of name, address, and age of</u>
9

<u>personal identification that can be used</u>
9

<u>to substantiate you.</u> It's also essential
9

for international travel. Therefore, if you've ever desired to see the world or have a job that requires international travel, consider following these simple steps to <u>recover</u> your passport.
10

Para. 2 Eligibility requirements are determined by the U.S. Department of State, which is the federal executive department that is responsible for issuing passport books and <u>distributed</u>
11

passport cards. All citizens of the United States and its territories

9. **(A)** (No change)
   (B) Substantiate your name and age, and personal identification can be used to substantiate your address too.
   (C) It is a viable form of personal identification that can be used to substantiate your name, address, and age.
   (D) You don't need personal identification to substantiate your name, address, and age.

10. **(A** (no change)
    (B) lose
    (C) obtain
    (D) remember

11. **(A)** (No change)
    (B) distribute
    (C) distribution
    (D) distributing

(including Guam, Puerto Rico, the

Northern Mariana Islands, and the U.S.

Virgin Islands) are eligible to obtain a

passport.

Para. 3 <u>It's a simple process. Here's how to</u>
                                    12

<u>do it.</u> Completion of an application is
12

required to obtain a U.S. passport. The

application form that you are required

to complete <u>is</u> dependent on several
                13

factors, including your age and whether

or not you have ever had a passport

before. Currently, applications for a

<u>united states passport</u> must be made in
        14

person, and can be obtained and

completed in libraries and post offices.

Para. 4 Documentation required to

obtain a passport includes an official

birth certificate, valid state photo ID,

and a passport photo that meets certain

size and other <u>requirements?</u>
                    15

 In addition, there is a fee involved with

obtaining a passport, which varies

12. Which of the following is the most appropriate way to combine these short sentences into one logical sentence?
   (A) (No change)
   (B) It's a simple process, and here's how to do it.
   (C) It's a simple process, but here's how to do it.
   (D) It's a simple process, however here's how to do it.

13. (A) (No change)
   (B) are
   (C) was
   (D) were

14. (A) (No change)
   (B) united States passport
   (C) United states Passport
   (D) United States passport

15. (A) (No change)
   (B) requrements.
   (C) requrements!
   (D) requrements;

based on such factors as your age and whether you're applying for a first time or renewal passport.

Directions: Read the following draft memo. Then proceed to the expanded version and answer the questions, which offer options for improvement.

MEMORANDUM

From: Lafayette Village Condominium Tower Coop Board

To: Lafayette Village Condominium Tower residents

SUBJECT: New procedures for incoming/outgoing package deliveries

Para. 1 Welcome to Lafayette Village Condominium Tower! This memorandum outlines the new policies and procedures for sending and receiving packages for all residents of the Lafayette Village Condominium Tower complex. In light of increasing complaints from several Lafayette Village residents regarding missing or lost packages over the last several months, the Lafayette Village Condominium Tower Coop Board has voted to enact the following measures in an effort to decrease this alarming trend. Incoming packages will no longer be left at the doorsteps of residents.

Para. 2 Outgoing packages: All outgoing packages must be clearly marked with the sender's name and address, as well as the name and address of the package recipient. Cleanly and securely wrapped, residents must properly prepare packages for delivery. Outgoing packages must now be dropped off directly at the front desk for delivery. In addition, the new outgoing package logbook *must* be signed by the sender, including the date and time the package was dropped off. Outgoing packages that have not been recorded in the logbook will not be delivered.

Para. 3 Incoming packages: All incoming packages will be recorded into the new incoming package logbook by the front desk clerk on duty, prior to being delivered to the indicated Lafayette Village Condominium Tower resident. Upon delivery, the resident receiving the package must sign the logbook, confirming receipt of the package. Residents receiving a package directly at the front desk must also sign the logbook, confirming receipt.

Para. 4 Questions/Suggestions: As previously stated, the above-mentioned policy revisions have been voted on by the members of the Lafayette Village Condominium Tower Coop Board. These are the rules. They must be followed. If you have any questions or suggestions for her, please contact the Board Office at (555) 465-1873 or LafayetteVillageCondoBoard@email.com.

Thank you;

Lafayette Village Condominium Tower Coop Board

MEMORANDUM

From: Lafayette Village Condominium Tower Coop Board

To: Lafayette Village Condominium Tower residents

SUBJECT: New procedures for incoming/ outgoing package deliveries

Para. 1 This memorandum outlines the new policies and procedures for <u>sending and receive</u> packages for all
16
residents of the Lafayette Village Condominium Tower complex. In light of increasing complaints from several Lafayette Village residents regarding missing or lost packages over the last several months, the Lafayette Village Condominium Tower Coop Board has voted to enact the following measures in an effort to decrease this alarming trend. <u>Incoming packages will no longer</u>
17
<u>be left at the doorsteps of residents.</u>
17

16. **(A)** (no change)
    (B) send and receiving
    (C) send and receive
    (D) sending and receiving

17. Where is the best place for this sentence?
    (A) (No change)
    (B) Paragraph 2
    (C) Paragraph 3
    (D) Paragraph 4

Para. 2 Outgoing packages: All outgoing packages must be clearly marked with the sender's name and address, as well as the name and address of the package recipient. <u>Cleanly and securely</u>
18

<u>wrapped, residents must properly</u>
18

<u>prepare packages for delivery.</u> Outgoing
18

packages must now be dropped off directly at the front desk for delivery. In addition, the new outgoing package logbook *must* be signed by the sender, including the date and time the package was dropped off. Outgoing packages that have not been recorded in the logbook will not be delivered.

Para. 3 Incoming packages: All incoming packages will be recorded into the new incoming package logbook by the front desk clerk on duty, prior to being delivered to the indicated Lafayette Village Condominium Tower resident. Upon delivery, the resident

18. **(A)** (No change)
    (B) Residents must delivery properly and securely wrap packages to other residents.
    (C) Residents who want to receive properly and securely wrapped packages must request them for delivery.
    (D) Packages must be cleanly and securely wrapped by residents to properly prepare them for delivery.

receiving the package must sign the logbook, confirming receipt of the package. Residents receiving a package directly at the front desk must also sign the logbook, <u>confirming</u> receipt.
19

Para. 4 Questions/Suggestions: As previously stated, the above-mentioned policy revisions have been voted on by the members of the Lafayette Village Condominium Tower Coop Board. <u>These are the rules. They must be</u>
20

<u>followed.</u> If you have any questions or
20

suggestions for <u>her</u>, please contact the
21

Board Office at (555) 465-1873 or LafayetteVillageCondoBoard@email.com.

<u>Thank you;</u>
22

19. **(A)** (No change)
    (B) confirm
    (C) confirmed
    (D) confirmation

20. Which of the following is the most appropriate way to combine these short sentences into one logical sentence?
    (A) (No change)
    (B) These are the rules, but they must be followed.
    (C) These are the rules, and they must be followed.
    (D) These are the rules, who they must be followed.

21. **(A)** (No change)
    (B) them
    (C) it
    (D) his

22. **(A)** (No change)
    (B) Thank you:
    (C) Thank you.
    (D) Thank you,

Directions: Read the following draft article. Then proceed to the expanded version and answer the questions, which offer options for improvement.

Para. 1 Has history ever seen a more forward thinking innovator and genius than Nikola Tesla! Arising from humble beginnings in a nineteenth-century Croatian village, one of five children of a Serbian priest and his wife, Tesla is credited with contributing numerous ideas and advances in engineering, electricity, wireless communication and radio, and X-ray imaging, as well as hundreds of invention patents from around the world.

Para. 2 As a boy, he demonstrated tremendous skill and ability in mathematics. He eventually enrolled and excelled at an excellent and dubious Austrian University, though he never graduated. Tesla, throughout his life at telegraph and electrical companies, held employment positions, several of them, which helped influence what he chose to undertake, various experiments during his lifetime. His contributions to electrical power generation alone— particularly his work on alternating current (AC) electricity—have ensured his place in history.

Para. 3 Even at an early age, Tesla's genius was undeniable. Despite his achievements, Tesla was a volatile figure who had his share of struggles. His father never respected his academic accomplishments, instead wanting him to join the priesthood. Nikola's mental health was often in question; he fought a gambling addiction while in college and had suffered a nervous breakdown shortly after dropping out of school. He rarely slept and sacrificed close personal relationships during his life in pursuit of his intellectual passions. Furthermore, he often feuded with employers and colleagues over his ideas; his feud with Thomas Edison regarding whose system of current generation was superior is the stuff of legend.

Para. 4 Regardless of Tesla's numerous contributions to society, he died alone and penniless in a New York City hotel at the age of 86. Generations since his passing have acknowledged his remarkable genius, and Tesla's name has been honored in a variety of ways—on a museum as the name of an electric car company and as a unit of magnetic measure.

Para. 1 Has history ever seen a more forward thinking innovator and genius than Nikola Tesla! Arising from humble
23
beginnings in a nineteenth-century Croatian village, one of five children of a Serbian priest and his wife, Tesla is credited with contributing numerous ideas and advances in engineering, electricity, wireless communication and radio, and X-ray imaging, as well as hundreds of invention patents from around the world.

Para. 2 As a boy, Tesla demonstrated tremendous skill and ability in mathematics. He eventually enrolled
24
 and excelled at an excellent and prestigious Austrian University, but never graduated. Tesla, throughout
25

his life at telegraph and electrical
25

companies, held employment positions,
25

several of them, which helped influence
25

what he chose to undertake, various
25

experiments during his lifetime. His
25

23. **(A)** (No change)
(B) Tesla?
(C) Tesla.
(D) Tesla;

24. **(A)** (No change)
(B) They
(C) She
(D) It

25. **(A)** (No change)
(B) Undertaking his lifetime, several positions were held by Tesla, employment and various companies, telegraph and electrical, experimental and throughout his lifetime.
(C) Throughout his life, Tesla held several employment positions at telegraph and electrical companies, which helped influence the various experiments that he chose to undertake during his lifetime.
(D) Tesla held several telegraph and electrical companies, as well as helpful and influential jobs, which he undertook as various experiments during his lifetime.

contributions to electrical power generation alone—particularly his work on alternating current (AC) electricity—have ensured his place in history.

Para. 3 <u>Even at an early age, Tesla's</u> **26** <u>genius was undeniable.</u> **26** Despite his achievements, Tesla was a volatile figure who had his share of struggles. His father never respected his academic accomplishments, instead wanting him to join the priesthood. Nikola's mental health was often in question; he fought a gambling addiction while in college and had suffered a nervous breakdown shortly after <u>dropping</u> **27** out of school. He rarely slept and sacrificed close personal relationships during his life in pursuit of his intellectual passions. Furthermore, he often feuded with employers and colleagues over his ideas; his feud with Thomas Edison regarding whose system of current generation was superior is the stuff of legend.

26. Which of the following is the best choice for this sentence?
   (A) (No change)
   (B) Omit this sentence.
   (C) Place this sentence at the beginning of the second paragraph (Paragraph 2).
   (D) Place this sentence at the end of the last paragraph (Paragraph 4).

27. (A) (No change)
   (B) drop
   (C) dropper
   (D) dropped

Para. 4 Regardless of Tesla's numerous contributions to society, he died alone and penniless in a New York City hotel at the age of 86. Generations since his passing have <u>acknowledged</u> his
28

remarkable genius, and Tesla's name has been honored in a variety of ways— <u>on a museum as the name of an electric</u>
29

<u>car company and as a unit of magnetic</u>
29

<u>measure.</u>
29

28. **(A)** (No change)
    (B) aknoledged
    (C) acknoledged
    (D) aknowledged

29. **(A)** (No change)
    (B) on a museum as, the name of an electric, car company and as a unit, of magnetic measure.
    (C) on a museum as the name, of an electric car company, and as a unit of magnetic measure.
    (D) on a museum, as the name of an electric car company, and as a unit of magnetic measure.

practice test 2

Directions: Read the following restaurant review from a student's blog. Then proceed to the expanded version and answer the questions, which offer options for improvement.

Para. 1 Hazelton Heights has seen several new and promising restaurant openings in the last few years, which I've been really excited about. Some of them have been good—and some of them not so good—but trust me, if you only choose one new restaurant to go to this year, make it Rustica, a beautiful Italian trattoria that opened up 6 months ago, located just a few blocks north of the Palladia Mall. The Palladia Mall opened in 1986 and has been an important part of Hazelton Heights ever since.

Para. 2 I first heard about Rustica in October from a friend of mine in english class, who seems to have good taste. My family and I were coming home from a football game last week and were starving—let's just say that none of us are huge fans of greasy stadium food. I remembered what my friend told me about this new place, so I convinced my family to give it a try. And we're all glad we did!

Para. 3 We arrived at the restaurant and was warmly greeted by the friendly hostess. We were taken to a lovely table next to the old stone fireplace and had a chance to take in the ambiance of the room. It felt like we were in a charming rustic farmhouse, with large oak tables, brass fixtures and lanterns, and antique kitchen tools along the walls. The capable wait staff complemented the room, dressed in varying shades of gingham and equipped with fancy braided aprons.

Para. 4 While we read the menu, we were given a basket of warm, crusty rolls; olives; and a ramekin of oil for dipping. We decided to start off the meal with a Tuscan beef Carpaccio, which was perfectly sliced and seasoned, along with the mussels appetizer. The mussels were perfectly cooked and flavored with butter garlic and bacon. The only problem we had with them was dividing them evenly amongst my hungry family members. After our appetizers, we had some time to recap the football game until our entrees arrived—but they were more than worth the way. My dad had the farmhouse pork chop, a gorgeous cut of meat that was lightly crusted in toasted crushed pistachios and full of flavor. My mother had the capellini in a rich Bolognese sauce, and she couldn't have been more pleased. I had the veal, sautéed in butter and rosemary, and it was the perfect meal. Pleased with the meal, our waiter took a photo of our smiling faces. All I can say is that my entire family eagerly awaits our next meal here, and it gets my weakest recommendation!

Para. 1 Hazelton Heights has seen several new and promising restaurant openings in the last few years, which I've been really excited about. Some of them have been good—and some of them not so good—but trust me, if you only choose one new restaurant to go to this year, make it Rustica, a beautiful Italian trattoria that opened up 6 months ago, located just a few blocks north of the Palladia Mall.

<u>The Palladia Mall opened in 1986 and</u>
  30

<u>has been an important part</u>
  30

<u>of Hazelton Heights ever since.</u>
  30

Para. 2 I first heard about Rustica in October from a friend of mine in <u>english</u>
  31

<u>class</u>, who seems to have good taste. My
31

family and I were coming home from a football game last week and were starving—let's just say that none of us are huge fans of greasy stadium food. I remembered what my friend told me about this new place, so I convinced my

30. Which of the following is the best choice for this sentence?
   (A) (No change)
   (B) Omit this sentence.
   (C) Place this sentence at the end of the second paragraph (Paragraph 2).
   (D) Place this sentence at the beginning of the last paragraph (Paragraph 4).

31. **(A)** (No change)
   (B) English Class
   (C) English class
   (D) english Class

family to give it a try. And we're all glad we did!

Para. 3 We arrived at the restaurant and <u>was</u> warmly greeted by the friendly **32**

hostess. We were taken to a lovely table next to the old stone fireplace and had a chance to take in the ambiance of the room. It felt like we were in a charming rustic farmhouse, with large oak tables, brass fixtures and lanterns, and antique kitchen tools along the walls. The capable wait staff complemented the room, dressed in varying shades of gingham and <u>equipped</u> with fancy **33**

braided aprons.

Para. 4 While we read the menu, we were given a basket of warm, crusty rolls; olives; and a ramekin of oil for dipping. We decided to start off the meal with a Tuscan beef Carpaccio, which was perfectly sliced and seasoned, along with the mussels appetizer. The mussels were perfectly cooked and flavored with

<u>butter garlic and bacon</u>. The only **34**

32. **(A)** (No change)
    (B) were
    (C) is
    (D) will be

33. **(A)** (No change)
    (B) equip
    (C) equipping
    (D) equipper

34. **(A)** (No change)
    (B) butter garlic, and bacon
    (C) butter garlic, and bacon
    (D) butter, garlic, and bacon

problem we had with them was dividing them evenly amongst my hungry family members. After our appetizers, we had some time to recap the football game until our entrees arrived—but they were more than worth the way. My dad had the farmhouse pork chop, a gorgeous cut of meat that was lightly crusted in toasted crushed pistachios and full of flavor. My mother had the capellini in a rich Bolognese sauce, and she couldn't have been more pleased. I had the veal, sautéed in butter and rosemary, and it was the perfect meal.

<u>Pleased with the meal, our waiter took a</u>
35

<u>photo of our smiling faces.</u> All I can say
35

is that my entire family eagerly awaits our next meal here, and it gets my

<u>weakest recommendation!</u>
36

35. Which of the following is the most logical revision of this sentence?
   (A) (No change)
   (B) Our waiter pleased the meal with a photo of our smiling faces.
   (C) We were pleased with the meal, and our waiter took a photo of our smiling faces.
   (D) We took a photo of our meal, pleasing the waiter with our smiling faces.

36. (A) (No change)
   (B) strongest recommendation
   (C) harshest criticism
   (D) lowest criticism

Directions: Read the following draft of the meeting minutes for a recent town council meeting. Then proceed to the expanded version and answer the questions, which offer options for improvement.

MEETING MINUTES—JANUARY 24, 2015

CHESTNUT VALLEY TOWN COUNCIL MEETING

RE: Vote on construction of new downtown cultural center

Para. 1 This meeting of the Chestnut Valley Town Council, held at 4:00 p.m., was to discuss a recent proposal to construct a new culture and arts center (Chestnut Valley Preservation Society Culture and Arts Center) at 555 Pinewood Lane. All town council members was in attendance except for Mrs. Lucille Bowers, who was sick with the flu. Chestnut Valley awaited the council's vote. They couldn't wait for her. Mrs. Bowers agreed to abide by the majority decision of the other council members. The members reviewed the proposal, discussed the key points, and vote on whether or not to advance it to the next phase.

Para. 2 According to the proposal, if approved, construction on the Chestnut Valley Preservation Society Culture and Arts Center would conclude on March 1, 2015, and would be completed no later than March 1, 2016. The council members had the opportunity to review the blueprints that accompanied the proposal: The plan is for a three-story, 20,000 square foot commercial building to be built on the newly vacant lot, with the remaining lot space to be used for parking. The building will be fully handicap accessible and LEED certified by the U.S. Green Building Council. Funds for the construction and maintenance of the center will be provided by the Chestnut Valley Preservation Society, with matching funds provided by the town of Riverton.

Para. 3 The Town Council members reviewed the proposal timeline. The Chestnut Valley Town Council voted 23-1 in favor of moving this proposal to Phase 2 development and expressed their collective enthusiasm for this "much needed addition to the vibrancy and livelihood of Chestnut Valley's cultural scene." The one vote against advancing this proposal to Phase 2 development came from Mr. Lyle Starr, who expressed his desire to review additional proposals for use of 555 pinewood lane before making a decision.

MEETING MINUTES—
JANUARY 24, 2015

CHESTNUT VALLEY TOWN
COUNCIL MEETING

RE: Vote on construction of new
downtown cultural center

Para. 1 This meeting of the Chestnut

Valley Town Council, held at 4:00 p.m.,

was to discuss a recent proposal to

construct a new culture and arts center

(Chestnut Valley Preservation Society

Culture and Arts Center) at 555

Pinewood Lane. All town council

members <u>was</u> in attendance except for
37

Mrs. Lucille Bowers, who was sick with

the flu. <u>Chestnut Valley awaited the</u>
38

<u>council's vote. They couldn't wait for her.</u>
38

Mrs. Bowers agreed to abide by the

majority decision of the other council

members. The members reviewed the

proposal, discussed the key points, and

<u>vote</u> on whether or not to advance it to
39

the next phase.

37. **(A)** (No change)
    (B) were
    (C) is
    (D) weren't

38. Which of the following effectively combines the two independent clauses into a compound sentence?
    (A) (No change)
    (B) Chestnut Valley awaited the council's vote, although they couldn't wait for her.
    (C) Chestnut Valley awaited the council's vote, so they couldn't wait for her.
    (D) Chestnut Valley awaited the council's vote, because they couldn't wait for her.

39. **(A)** (No change)
    (B) voting
    (C) voters
    (D) voted

Para. 2 According to the proposal, if approved, construction on the Chestnut Valley Preservation Society Culture and Arts Center would <u>conclude</u> on March 1,
40

2015, and would be completed no later than March 1, 2016. The council members had the opportunity to review the blueprints that accompanied the proposal: The plan is for a three-story, 20,000 square foot commercial building to be built on the newly vacant lot, with the remaining lot space to be used for parking. The building will be fully handicap accessible and LEED certified by the U.S. Green Building Council. Funds for the construction and maintenance of the center will be provided by the Chestnut Valley Preservation Society, with matching funds provided by the town of Riverton.

Para. 3 <u>The Town Council members</u>
41

<u>reviewed the proposal timeline.</u> The
41

40. **(A)** (No change)
    (B) commence
    (C) terminate
    (D) extinguish

41. Which of the following is the best choice for this sentence?
    (A) (No change)
    (B) Move to the beginning of the first paragraph (Paragraph 1).
    (C) Move to the beginning of the second paragraph (Paragraph 2).
    (D) Move to the beginning of the last paragraph (Paragraph 3).

Chestnut Valley Town Council voted
23-1 in favor of moving this proposal to
Phase 2 development and expressed
their collective enthusiasm for this
"much needed addition to the vibrancy
and livelihood of Chestnut Valley's
cultural scene." The one vote against
advancing this proposal to Phase 2
development came from Mr. Lyle Starr,
who expressed <u>his</u> desire to review
42
additional proposals for use of <u>555</u>
43
<u>pinewood lane</u> before making a decision.
43

42. **(A)** (No change)
    (B) their
    (C) her
    (D) those

43. **(A)** (No change)
    (B) 555 Pinewood Lane
    (C) 555 pinewood Lane
    (D) five, five, five pinewood lane

Directions: Read the following draft article. Then proceed to the expanded version and answer the questions, which offer options for improvement.

Para. 1 Should people be fined for not recycling? This question has sparked a great deal of debate amongst politicians, policymakers, and citizens alike, many of whom have varying opinions regarding whether or not individuals should be punished—and what such a punishment should look like—for failing to properly recycle.

Para. 2 Many people feel that recycling was just too important to simply hope that people will do the right thing. Landfills are overflowing with nonbiodegradable materials, and the effects of our collectively wasteful lifestyles on the environment have become painfully clear in the last few decades. Proponents of giving fines for not recycling feel that we can't passively sit by as individuals continue to contribute to the problem. They argues that now is the time for each of us to make a positive change, and learning to recycle is a step in the right direction—hopefully a step that will lead to further environmentally conscious behavior. For these people, recycling is a simple process made up of steps that anyone who is responsible can manage: separate the recyclable materials, place them in the appropriate receptacles, and bring them to the recycling center.

Para. 3 The majority of those who are against imposing fines on individuals for not recycling aren't against the idea of recycling per se. Most of them truly feel that recycling is an important and beneficial thing—they just don't feel that a mandatory fine should be imposed on people for failing to do so. Proponents of this side of the debate feel that people are already forced to give too much of their earnings away—to taxes that are out of control, to rising prices of household goods, and to inflation. They feel that an effective information campaign that highlights the power and long-term benefits of recycling can be effective, and penalizing struggling people financially will have its own adverse effects. Recycling isn't always easy. While separating material for recycling, my dog often jumps excitedly through the trash.

Para. 4 Although it's hard to argue against the importance of recycling and the benefit it has on our environment, should there be a mandatory punishment for failing to do so, or should individuals be free to choose to be responsible members of society? If you agree that failing to recycle should include a fine, what should the fine structure look like? Should it increase for repeat offenders? Should it be based on an individuals income? Regardless of what side of the debate you're on, there are certainly lots of provocative questions that this issue raises.

Para. 1 <u>Should people be fined for not</u>
<u>44</u>

<u>recycling?</u> This question has sparked a
44

great deal of debate amongst politicians,

policymakers, and citizens alike, many

of whom have varying opinions

regarding whether or not individuals

should be punished—and what such a

punishment should look like—for failing

to properly recycle.

Para. 2 Many people feel that

recycling <u>was</u> just too important to
45

simply hope that people will do the right

thing. Landfills are overflowing with

nonbiodegradable materials, and the

effects of our collectively wasteful

lifestyles on the environment have

become painfully clear in the last few

decades. Proponents of giving fines for

not recycling feel that we can't passively

sit by as individuals continue to

contribute to the problem. They <u>argues</u>
46

that now is the time for each of us to

make a positive change, and learning to

recycle is a step in the right

44. **(A)** (No change)
  (B) Should people be fined for not recycling;
  (C) Should people be fined for not recycling.
  (D) Should people be fined for not recycling!

45. **(A)** (No change)
  (B) were
  (C) is
  (D) will be

46. **(A)** (No change)
  (B) argue
  (C) arguing
  (D) arguer

direction—hopefully a step that will lead to further environmentally conscious behavior. For these people, recycling is a simple process made up of steps that anyone who is responsible can manage: separate the recyclable materials, place them in the appropriate receptacles, and <u>take them</u> to the **47** recycling center.

47. **(A)** (No change)
(B) taking them
(C) taking it
(D) take it

Para. 3 The majority of those who are against imposing fines on individuals for not recycling aren't against the idea of recycling per se. Most of them truly feel that recycling is an important and beneficial thing—they just don't feel that a mandatory fine should be imposed on people for failing to do so. Proponents of this side of the debate feel that people are already forced to give too much of their earnings away—to taxes that are out of control, to rising prices of household goods, and to inflation. They feel that an effective information campaign that highlights the power and long-term benefits of recycling can be effective, and penalizing struggling people financially will have its own adverse effects. Recycling isn't always easy. <u>While</u>

48

<u>separating material for recycling, my</u>

48

<u>dog often jumps excitedly through the</u>

48

<u>trash.</u>

48

Para. 4 49 Although it's hard to argue against the importance of recycling and the benefit it has on our environment, should there be a mandatory punishment for failing to do so, or should individuals be free to choose to be responsible members of society? If you agree that failing to recycle should include a fine, what should the fine structure look like? Should it increase for repeat offenders? Should it be based on an <u>individuals income</u>? Regardless of

50

48. **(A)** (No change)
    (B) My dog often jumps excitedly through the trash, while separating material for recycling.
    (C) I'm separating material for recycling with my dog, often jumping excitedly through the trash.
    (D) While I'm separating material for recycling, my dog often jumps excitedly through the trash.

49. Which of the following sentences would best fit at the beginning of paragraph 4?
    (A) It's obvious that recycling should be universally mandatory.
    (B) It's clear that recycling is a wasted effort.
    (C) What's the right answer?
    (D) Maybe we should worry about recycling later?

50. **(A)** (No change)
    (B) individual income
    (C) individuals incomes
    (D) individual's income

Part 2

1 Essay • 45 Minutes

Directions: This is a test of your writing skills. Your response will be scored based on:

- Development of a central position through explanation of supporting reasons and examples from passages and personal experience

- Language use, including varied word choice, varied sentence constructions, and appropriate voice

- Clarity and correctness of writing conventions

- Clear organization of ideas, including an introduction and conclusion, logical paragraphs, and effective transitions

Below you will find two passages in which the authors put forth differing perspectives on an issue of importance. Read both passages carefully, noting the strengths and weaknesses of each discussion. Then, you will write an essay in which you explain your own opinion on the issue.

A driving course instructor had her students perform research on the issue of banning cell phone use while driving. The following two excerpts were required reading for the assignment.

One Text or Call Could Wreck It All
(the National Highway Traffic Safety Administration)

Did you know that "distracted driving" was the 2009 word of the year according to Webster's Dictionary? But unfortunately, this is no passing fad. Distracted driving has become a trend with deadly, real consequences.

- For anyone who thinks they can talk on their phone, text, apply make-up, or do any other distracting activity while driving, it's time for a crash course in reality from the National Highway Traffic Safety Administration (NHTSA):

- In 2012, 3,328 people were killed and approximately 421,000 were injured in motor vehicle crashes involving a distracted driver. (NHTSA)

- Drivers who use hand-held devices are four times as likely to be involved in a serious crash. (Insurance Institute for Highway Safety)

- Nine percent of fatal crashes in 2010 were reported as distraction-affected crashes. (NHTSA)

- In 2011, 11 percent of all drivers under the age of 20 involved in fatal crashes were reported as distracted at the time of the crash. This age group had the largest proportion of drivers who were distracted. (NHTSA)

While those numbers may sound like just statistics, they're anything but. They could be parents, children, neighbors and friends. There are too many sad tales of deaths and injuries that could have been prevented had drivers been paying attention to the road instead of someone or something else.

So, why do so many people participate in this dangerous behavior? With more technology now than ever, driver distractions have risen to unprecedented levels. We live in a world where people expect instant, real-time information 24 hours a day, and those desires don't stop just because they get behind the wheel. Drivers simply do not realize—or choose to ignore—the danger they create when they take their eyes off the road, their hands off the wheel, and their focus off driving.

People often say, "I can do two things at once. I've memorized where the numbers are on my phone, so I don't have to look." Or, "Sending or reading one text is pretty quick—that should be okay." They couldn't be more wrong.

For those who think they can do two things at once, think about this: According to a study by Carnegie Mellon, driving while using a cell phone reduces the amount of brain activity associated with driving by 37 percent. Can you really afford to lose that much brainpower? Driving is an activity that requires your full attention and focus in order to keep yourself and others safe.

No one is immune from the dangers of distracted driving. So please remember: One text or call could wreck it all.

Report by the Rural Transportation Safety and Security Center

Recent research shows Texting While Driving bans may be ineffective in reducing crashes. The Insurance Institute of Highway Safety cited a study conducted by the

Highway Loss Data Institute to measure crash data in states where Texting While Driving was banned compared to control states with similar characteristics but where no ban existed. The texting bans were not found to reduce crashes. In fact, crash rates increased in 3 of the 4 states where the bans were enacted, suggesting the bans may have actually increased crash risk.

In a previous study of states that enacted hand-held cell phone bans, trends in collision rates also did not vary.

Write an essay in which you explain your own position on the following question: Should cell phone use while driving be completely banned?

Be sure to use evidence from the passages and specific reasons and examples from your own experience and knowledge to support your position. Your essay should, at minimum, acknowledge opposing or alternate ideas.

practice test 2

Write an essay in which you explain your own position on the issue of banning cell phone usage while driving.

Be sure to use evidence from the passages and specific reasons and examples from your own experience and knowledge to support your position. Your essay should, at minimum, acknowledge opposing or alternate ideas.

MATHEMATICS

50 Questions • 90 Minutes

Formula Sheet

Perimeter/Circumference

RECTANGLE
Perimeter = 2(length) + 2(width)

CIRCLE
Circumference = 2π(radius)

Area

CIRCLE
Area = π(radius)^2

TRIANGLE
Area = $\frac{1}{2}$ (base)(height)

PARALLELOGRAM
Area = (base)(height)

TRAPEZOID
Area = $\frac{1}{2}$ (base$_1$ + base$_2$)(height)

Volume

PRISM/CYLINDER

Volume = (area of the base)(height)

PYRAMID/CONE

Volume = $\frac{1}{3}$ (area of the base)(height)

SPHERE
Volume = $\frac{4}{3}$ π(radius)^3

Length

1 foot = 12 inches
1 yard = 3 feet
1 mile = 5,280 feet
1 meter = 1,000 millimeters
1 meter = 100 centimeters
1 kilometer = 1,000 meteres
1 mile ≈ 1.6 kilometers
1 inch = 2.54 centimeters
1 foot ≈ 0.3 meter

Capacity/Volume

1 cup = 8 fluid ounces
1 pint = 2 cups
1 quart = 2 pints
1 gallon = 4 quarts
1 gallon = 231 cubic inches
1 liter = 1,000 milliliters
1 liter ≈ 0.264 gallon

Weight

1 pound = 16 ounces
1 ton = 2,000 pounds
1 gram = 1,000 milligrams
1 kilogram = 1,000 grams
1 kilogram = 2.2 pounds
1 ounce = 28.3 grams

1. On the weekends in the summer, Kyle rollerblades 5 miles from home to the skate park. Then, he rollerblades 1.75 miles to get to his friend's house. At the end of the day, he rollerblades 4.25 miles to get home. Kyle charts his progress on a map poster in his bedroom in which 1.25 inches corresponds to 0.5 miles. How far did Kyle rollerblade in terms of this smaller scale?

    (A) 6.875 inches
    (B) 11.0 inches
    (C) 13.75 inches
    (D) 20.25 inches
    (E) 27.5 inches

2. Plant biologists have approximated that there are 860 different species of plants per square mile in a certain portion of a rainforest. If the entire rainforest takes up 40 square miles, which of the following is the approximate number of species in the entire forest?

(A) 1,720

(B) 2,500

(C) 16,500

(D) 34,400

(E) 50,000

3. Suppose the following set of numbers is the sample space for an experiment:

{1, 3, 5, 7, 9, 20, 23, 26, 29, 35, 49, 50, 101, 200}

A number is selected at random. Which of the following sets represents the event "the number selected is even and larger than 40"?

(A) {49, 50, 101, 200}

(B) {1, 3, 5, 7, 9, 23, 29, 35, 49, 101}

(C) {20, 26, 50, 200}

(D) {49, 101}

(E) {50, 200}

4. In an enclosed greenhouse, temperature readings are taken hourly throughout the day and recorded as follows:

Time	Temperature (in Degrees)
12 a.m.	52
1 a.m.	54
2 a.m.	56
3 a.m.	58
4 a.m.	60
5 a.m.	62
6 a.m.	64
7 a.m.	62
8 a.m.	60
9 a.m.	58
10 a.m.	56
11 a.m.	54
12 p.m.	52
1 p.m.	54
2 p.m.	56
3 p.m.	58
4 p.m.	60
5 p.m.	62
6 p.m.	64
7 p.m.	62
8 p.m.	60
9 p.m.	58
10 p.m.	56
11 p.m.	54

If 12 a.m. corresponds to $t = 0$, which of the following would best describe this distribution of temperatures?

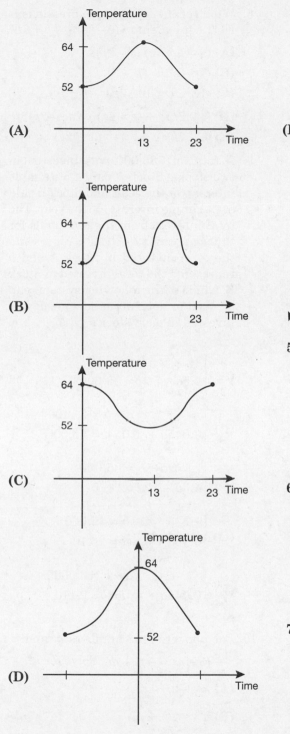

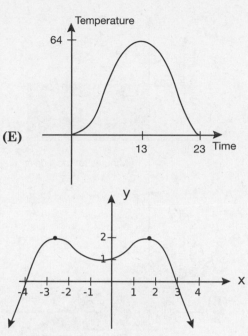

5. Which of the following is a factor of the polynomial graphed here?

(A) $(x + 3)$

(B) $(x + 4)$

(C) x

(D) $(x - 2)$

(E) $(x + 2)$

6. Which of the following quadratic equations has only ONE real solution?

(A) $4x^2 + 40x = 0$

(B) $x^2 - 3x - 9 = 0$

(C) $x^2 + 2x + 1 = 0$

(D) $x^2 + 12x + 3 = 0$

(E) $x^2 - 25 = 0$

7. Mackenzie travels to South America for a three-week vacation with a phone card worth $300. He uses it to make calls within South America and internationally to his home in Florida. Local calls cost $0.25 per minute, and international calls cost $0.60 per minute. Which of the following regions illustrates all possible combinations of minutes devoted to local and international calls?

practice test 2

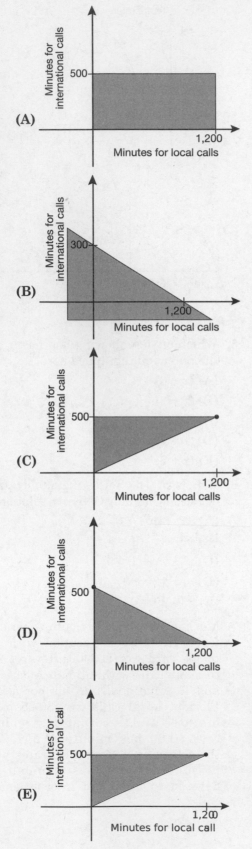

8. Which of the following expressions is NOT equivalent to $(e - 2f)(g - h + 3j)$?

   (A) $(g - h + 3j)(e - 2f)$

   (B) $(2f - e)(h - g - 3j)$

   (C) $e(g - h + 3j) - 2f(g - h + 3j)$

   (D) $(e - 2f)g + (e - 2f)h + (e - 2f)3j$

   (E) $(e - 2f)(g + 3j) - h(e - 2f)$

9. A total of $35,000 was invested in two stocks. Stock A paid 4.5% simple interest for the year, and Stock B paid 5.4% simple interest for the year. The total interest from the two funds for the year was $2,110. If a represents the total invested in Stock A and b represents the total invested in Stock B, which of the following systems can be used to determine how much was invested in each stock?

   (A) $\begin{cases} a + b = 2,110 \\ 4.5a + 5.4b = 35,000 \end{cases}$

   (B) $\begin{cases} a + b = 2,110 \\ 0.045a + 0.054b = 35,000 \end{cases}$

   (C) $\begin{cases} a + b = 35,000 \\ 4.5a + 5.4b = 2,110 \end{cases}$

   (D) $\begin{cases} a + b = 35,000 \\ 0.45a + 0.54b = 2,110 \end{cases}$

   (E) $\begin{cases} a + b = 35,000 \\ 0.045a + 0.054b = 2,110 \end{cases}$

10. For nonzero real numbers m and n, $\dfrac{3m}{n}(1 + n) = -\dfrac{2}{n} + m$. Solve for n.

    (A) $n = -2 + m$

    (B) $n = -2(1 + m)$

    (C) $n = \dfrac{-2(1 + m)}{3m}$

    (D) $n = \dfrac{-2 - 3m}{2m}$

    (E) $n = \dfrac{-2 - 3m}{1 - m}$

11. Which of the following is equivalent to $16^{\frac{3}{2}} - 27^{\frac{1}{3}}$?

    (A) 5
    (B) 9
    (C) 55
    (D) 61
    (E) 67

12. An amateur baseball pitcher can throw a fastball at the speed of 90 miles per hour. Which of the following numerical expressions is the speed of his pitch in feet per second?

    (A) $\dfrac{90 \times 5{,}280}{60}$ feet per second

    (B) $\dfrac{90 \times 5{,}280}{60 \times 60}$ feet per second

    (C) $\dfrac{90}{60 \times 60}$ feet per second

    (D) $\dfrac{90}{60}$ feet per second

    (E) $\dfrac{90 \times 60 \times 60}{5{,}280}$ feet per second

USE THE DIAGRAM SHOWN HERE TO ANSWER QUESTIONS 13–15.

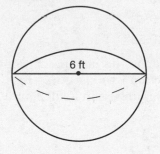

13. A spherical glass bowl sits in the front of a department store during the Halloween season. Initially, it is filled with water and then, with each day of October, more luminescent dye is added so that it glows all the brighter when black lights are turned on. What is the volume, in cubic feet, of the bowl?

    (A) 12π cubic feet
    (B) 27 cubic feet
    (C) 27π cubic feet
    (D) 36 cubic feet
    (E) 36π cubic feet

14. The store manager has received so many compliments on the bowl that he wants to assemble another one, this time in the shape of a right circular cylinder. The new container will sit at the other opening of the store. He wants the two containers to hold the same amount of water, and the height of the new container must be 4 feet in order to fit in the allotted space. What must the radius of the base of this new container be?

    (A) 3 feet
    (B) 3.5 feet
    (C) 4 feet
    (D) 4.5 feet
    (E) 5 feet

15. The spherical bowl and the right circular cylinder container each hold approximately 847 gallons of water when completely full. The store manager infuses 0.20 ounces of luminescent dye in each container daily to continually deepen the color. Which of the following is the best approximation to the concentration of dye in each container in ounces per cubic foot? (Note: 1 cubic foot = 7.463 gallons)

    (A) 1.79×10^{-4} oz./ft.^{3}
    (B) 1.79×10^{-3} oz./ft.^{3}
    (C) 1.79×10^{3} o.z/ft.^{3}
    (D) 1.79×10^{2} oz./ft.^{3}
    (E) 8.59×10^{-4} oz./ft.^{3}

16. Epidemiologists are trying to determine how widespread a superbug is in a county hospital. They use sampling to make their conclusion. Which of the following approaches is valid?

    (A) The scientists choose two rooms at random in the hospital and assess them carefully for infection. From this information, they conclude whether the hospital is clear of contamination, half infected, or entirely infected.

    (B) A team tests every room on a particular floor of a hospital. From this information, the scientists compute the percentage of the rooms infected with the superbug and use *this* as an estimate of the portion of the hospital infected by the superbug.

    (C) The scientists dispatch ten 10 different teams to each of the ten floors in the hospital and swab a surface at random in 20 different rooms on that floor. They analyze the samples and tally the number of the 200 samples that come back positive for contamination, compute the percentage, and use *this* as an estimate of the portion of the hospital infected by the superbug.

    (D) All three approaches valid.

    (E) None of the approaches is valid.

17. The number of times that 25 randomly chosen drivers fill their gas tanks per week is recorded. The numbers are shown here:

    1 1 2 2 3 2 1 1 3 1

    2 1 3 4 1 3 1 1 2 1

    1 3 1 2 1

    Based on this sample, what is the probability that a driver fills his or her tank no fewer than twice per week?

    (A) 0.04
    (B) 0.16
    (C) 0.24
    (D) 0.48
    (E) 0.52

18. What is the maximum value of the function $y = f(x) = -3(x - 6)^2 + 1$ for all real numbers in its domain x?

    (A) -6
    (B) -3
    (C) 1
    (D) 6
    (E) 18

19. The following graph shows the speed at which Tanya rides her bike during the half-hour trip it takes her to get to school.

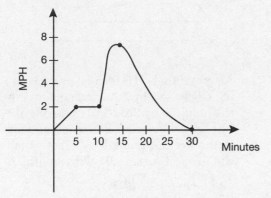

During which of the following time intervals is the average speed at which she pedals her bike negative?

(A) (0, 4)

(B) (9, 12)

(C) (5, 10)

(D) (15, 20)

(E) (3, 9)

20. Suppose you roll a four-sided tetrahedral die (with faces labeled A, B, C, D) four times and each time record the letter of the face on which the die comes to rest. You are interested in determining the probability that the die lands on the face labeled C at least twice. To compute this probability, you need the sample space. How many outcomes all told belong to the sample space?

(A) 4

(B) 8

(C) 16

(D) 64

(E) 256

21. Devon purchased two new paddles, three lifejackets, and one dry box in preparation for his canoeing trip. If the cost of one new paddle is p dollars, the cost of one lifejacket is l dollars, and the cost of a dry box is b dollars, which of the following represents the total cost C of all of the equipment?

(A) $C = l + b + p$

(B) $C = l \times b \times p$

(C) $C = 3l + b + 2p$

(D) $C = 6(l + b + p)$

(E) $C = (2p)(3l)b$

22. Consider the line $y = \frac{2}{5}x + 3$. Which of the following is a correct interpretation of the quantity $\frac{2}{5}$?

(A) The graph of the line crosses the y-axis at $\left(1, \frac{2}{5}\right)$.

(B) The y-value on the graph increases by 2 units for every 5 units increase in x.

(C) The y-value on the graph decreases by 2 units for every 5 units increase in x.

(D) The y-value on the graph decreases by 5 units for every 2 units increase in x.

(E) The y-value on the graph increases by 5 units for every 2 units increase in x.

23. An experimental calculation of the specific heat of tin was found in a lab to be $0.15 \frac{\text{cal}}{\text{g}°\text{C}}$. Based on the calibration of the equipment, it is known that maximum percent error in the readings is 10%. Which of the following readings is NOT possible?

(A) $0.139 \frac{\text{cal}}{\text{g}°\text{C}}$

(B) $0.1645 \frac{\text{cal}}{\text{g}°\text{C}}$

(C) $0.14 \frac{\text{cal}}{\text{g}°\text{C}}$

(D) $0.172 \frac{\text{cal}}{\text{g}°\text{C}}$

(E) $0.1352 \frac{\text{cal}}{\text{g}°\text{C}}$

24. Which of the following has numerical value *less than* $\sqrt{3}$?

(A) $\frac{8}{7}\sqrt{3}$

(B) $1.05\sqrt{3}$

(C) $(0.95)^2 \sqrt{3}$

(D) $(1.2)^2 \sqrt{3}$

(E) $\frac{\sqrt{3}}{0.1}$

25. Triangle A is pictured here:

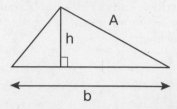

A new triangle B is formed by decreasing the base b by 30% and decreasing the height h by 20%. Fill in the blank: The area of triangle B is what percent of the area of triangle A? (Note that the area of a triangle with height h and base b is $\frac{1}{2}bh$.)

(A) 0.56%

(B) 0.70%

(C) 56%

(D) 70%

(E) 80%

26. The width of a recreation room is 3 feet less than twice the length of the room. The area of the room is 350 square feet. What is the width of the room?

(A) 14 feet

(B) 15 feet

(C) 20 feet

(D) 25 feet

(E) 30 feet

27. A volcano replica at a science museum is in the shape of a right circular cone. If the base has a diameter of 20 feet and the height is 12 feet, what is the volume of the volcano?

(A) 200π cubic feet

(B) $\frac{1,000}{3}\pi$ cubic feet

(C) 400π cubic feet

(D) 480 cubic feet

(E) $1,200\pi$ cubic feet

28. Two players roll a fair six-sided die 20 times and add the values of each roll. The player with the most points after these 20 rolls wins. Does each player have a fair chance of winning the game?

    (A) No, because the player who rolls the die first must end up with more points.

    (B) No, because one player may earn 5 points on a roll while another earns only 2, for instance.

    (C) No, because they did not roll the die enough times to ensure fairness.

    (D) Yes, because in the long run, each player will earn the same number of points, on average.

    (E) Yes, because the long run average number of points for each player is one.

29. On average, the gears produced by a certain machine weigh 3 ounces. There is very little variation in production from gear to gear because of the machine's precision. Which of the following distributions best describes this scenario?

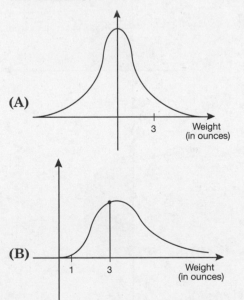

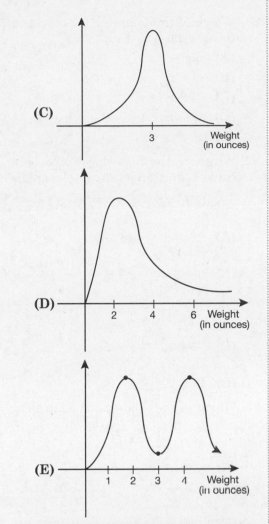

30. Miranda has saved $12,000 earned by working at an amusement park for the past three summers. She intends to use this money for monthly expenses while at college during her freshman year. She would like to devote $400 for rent, $100 for coffees and lunches, $300 for bills, and $125 for miscellaneous activities. She must keep at least $1,500 in the account to prevent the bank from imposing maintenance fees. Which of the following inequalities can be used to determine the number of months, m, she can continue to withdraw from the account?

    (A) $925 + 12,000m \geq 1,500$

    (B) $400m + 12,000 \leq 1,500$

    (C) $-925m + 12,000 \geq 1,500$

    (D) $925m + 12,000 \geq 1,500$

    (E) $12,000 \leq 1,500 + 925m$

31. Which of the following is equivalent to $x(2 - 3x) - 2(-1 - x - 3x^2)$?

   (A) $-9x^2 - 2$

   (B) $3x^2 + 4x + 2$

   (C) $-(3x^2 + 4x + 2)$

   (D) $2x^2 - 3x + 1$

   (E) $3x^2 - 4x + 2$

32. Which of the following would be a correct first step when solving the equation $-2x - \dfrac{1}{7} = -\dfrac{3}{14}x + 3$?

   (A) $-28x - 2 = -3x + 42$

   (B) $2x - \dfrac{1}{7} = \dfrac{3}{14}x + 3$

   (C) $-\dfrac{15}{7}x = \dfrac{39}{14}x$

   (D) $3 - \dfrac{1}{7} = -\dfrac{3}{14}x - 2x$

   (E) $-2x - 2 = -3x + 3$

33. Which of the following is equivalent to $\left(\sqrt{32} - 1\right)\left(\sqrt{8} - 1\right)$?

   (A) $6\sqrt{2} + 1$

   (B) $1 + 8\sqrt{2}$

   (C) $11\sqrt{2}$

   (D) 17

   (E) $17 - 6\sqrt{2}$

34. Which of the following is NOT a rational number?

   (A) $2\sqrt{16}$

   (B) $\dfrac{-1 + 5}{2 + 8}$

   (C) $\sqrt[3]{8} + 4$

   (D) $3\sqrt{2} - 4\sqrt{2}$

   (E) $6^8 + 4_2$

35. Madeline wants to produce a right circular cone with height 8 inches and base radius 6 inches by rotating a region in the xy-plane around the y-axis. Rotating which of the following regions about the y-axis will yield this result?

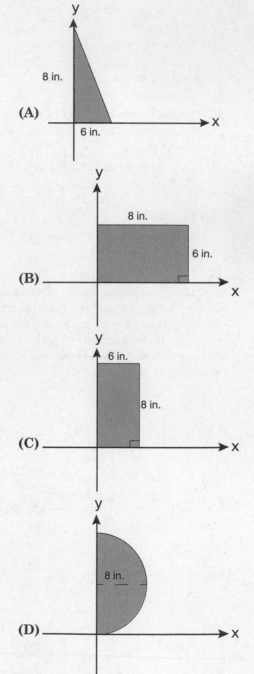

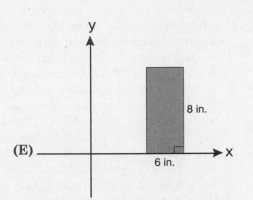

(E)

8 in.

6 in.

36. Studies suggest that the more minutes someone exercises daily, the lower his or her average pulse rate. The data suggest a very strong relationship. Which of the following scatterplots provides a visual illustration of the relationship between *minutes of daily exercise* and *average pulse rate*?

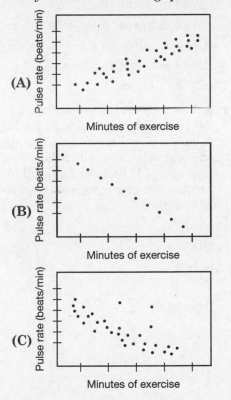

(A)

(B)

(C)

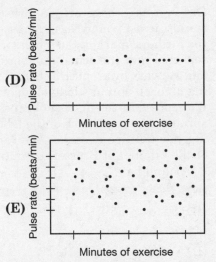

(D)

(E)

37. Suppose you spend $400 on a one-time cost for materials necessary to start a petsitting business. You earn $17 for each house visit, but each visit costs you $1.50 in gas. Determine the number of house visits you must complete before you break even.

(A) 20

(B) 26

(C) 28

(D) 32

(E) 40

38. Three checkout lines at a supermarket are labeled A, B, and C. Line A is operated by an experienced cashier who is able to handle three times as many customers per hour as the cashier in Line C. Line B is operated by a new cashier who can check out no more than one-third the customers processed in Line C. If we let A, B, and C represent the number of customers that Lines A, B, and C, respectively, can process per hour, which of the following is true?

(A) $3B > C$

(B) $9B \leq A$

(C) $A + B + C < 6$

(D) $2C \geq A$

(E) $3C < A$

39. On average, there are 55 Brussels sprouts in a 4-pound bag purchased at the farmers' market. Customers have reported that the actual number in a bag can vary by as much as 8 (depending on each sprout's individual size). If b represents the number of Brussels sprouts in a bag, which of the following inequalities describes the range of the number of Brussels sprouts in a 4-pound bag?

(A) $|b - 55| > 8$

(B) $|b - 8| \leq 55$

(C) $|b - 55| \leq 8$

(D) $b - 55 \leq 8$

(E) $|b + 55| > 8$

40. Jeffrey had 20 coins (dimes and quarters) totaling $2.45. Which of the following equations can be used to determine the number of each type of coin?

(A) $10x + 25(20 - x) = 2.45$

(B) $0.10x + 0.25(20 - x) = 2.45$

(C) $x + (20 - x) = 2.45$

(D) $0.10x + 0.25x = 20$

(E) $10x + 25(20 - x) = 20$

41. Two drivers compete in a road race. The driver with the older model car is given a two-mile head start and is able to maintain an average speed of 80 miles per hour for t hours. The driver of the newer model car is able to maintain an average speed of 90 miles per hour for t hours. Which of the following is an accurate description of the distance d (in miles) between the two drivers at any time t (in hours)?

(A) $d = 2 + 10t$

(B) $d = 80t - 90t$

(C) $d = 10 + 2t$

(D) $d = 10t$

(E) $d = 2 - 10t$

42. Members of the ninth, tenth, and eleventh grades are to complete an obstacle course as part of a fitness exam. Statistics show that the average time it takes a ninth-grader to complete the course is 15 minutes 20 seconds, while it takes a typical eleventh-grader 13 minutes 40 seconds to complete the course. Examiners have decided that the "average" time that it should take a tenth-grader to complete the course is the difference between the average time it takes a ninth-grader to complete the course and 55% of the difference between the average of the ninth- and eleventh-grade times. Which of the following is the average time it should take a tenth-grader to complete the course?

(A) 14 minutes 10 seconds

(B) 14 minutes 20 seconds

(C) 14 minutes 25 seconds

(D) 14 minutes 45 seconds

(E) 15 minutes

43. A dining room measures 20 feet by 15 feet, with a ceiling that is 10 feet high. A gallon of paint is needed to apply one coat of paint to 400 square feet of wall space. If Sean has one gallon of paint, what percentage of the job can he complete?

(A) 20%

(B) 40%

(C) 60%

(D) 80%

(E) 100%

44. An ice cream manufacturer decides to decrease the length and width of its rectangular-shaped ice cream bar by 25%, but increase its thickness by 20%. Which of the following statements accurately describes the comparison of the original ice cream bar's volume and its new volume?

(A) The volume of the new ice cream bar is about one-third less than the original one.

(B) The volume of the new ice cream bar is about one-half less than the original one.

(C) The volume of the new ice cream bar is about one-fourth more than the original one.

(D) The volume of the new ice cream bar is about one-half more than the original one.

(E) The volume of the new ice cream bar is about the same as the original one.

45. In a survey, the heads of 500 households were asked how people lived in their home, including themselves. The results of the survey are shown below.

Number of People in the Household	Number of Households
1	25
2	180
3	150
4	100
5	38
6	7

What is the median number of people living in the surveyed households?

(A) 2

(B) 2.5

(C) 3

(D) 3.5

(E) 6

46. A video game keeps track of the percentage of unlockable items players find for each level completed. A player's average for level 1 is 55%. The player runs through level 2 very quickly and does not search for unlockable items, so the percentage is 0%. The percentage for level 3 is 10 points lower than in level 4, and the percentage for level 4 is 10 points higher than in level 5. If the average percentage for all five levels is 61%, what was the player's percentage for level 4?

(A) 70

(B) 75

(C) 85

(D) 90

(E) 95

47. A child takes a grilled cheese sandwich right out of the frying pan at
150°F. He then walks outside, where
it is 20°F, to take a 20-minute walk
to a friend's house. By the time he arrives, the sandwich must be warmed
in the microwave. Which of the following graphs best represents what
happens to the temperature of the
grilled cheese sandwich during the
20-minute walk?

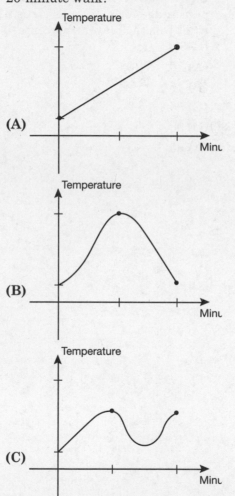

(A)

(B)

(C)

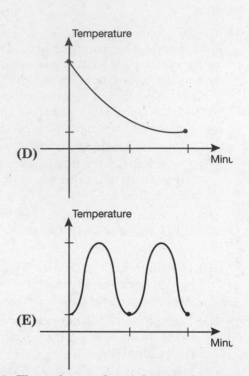

(D)

(E)

48. The volume of a right circular cone
with height h and base radius r is
given by $V = \frac{1}{3} \pi r^2 h$. If you wish to
create another right circular cone
with a volume that is one-fourth the
volume of the original cone, which
of the following modifications would
yield the desired result?

(A) Use half of the radius and keep
the height the same.

(B) Use one-third of the radius and
double the height.

(C) Use half of the height and keep
the radius the same.

(D) Use half of the height and half
of the radius.

(E) Use one-fourth of the radius and
keep the height the same.

49. The number of gallons of gasoline per minute needed to operate a lawnmower depends on the depth of the grass (measured in inches) being mowed. The following table describes this relationship.

Depth of Grass (in inches)	Gallons of Gasoline Needed per Minute
1	0.006
2	0.012
3	0.018
4	0.024

How many gallons of gasoline are needed per minute to operate a lawnmower when the depth of the grass is 5.5 inches?

(A) 0.021

(B) 0.028

(C) 0.030

(D) 0.033

(E) 0.036

50. A line passes through the points $(-1, 4)$ and $(3, 6)$ in the xy-coordinate plane. What is the x-intercept of this line?

(A) -9

(B) $-\dfrac{9}{4}$

(C) $\dfrac{1}{2}$

(D) $\dfrac{9}{2}$

(E) 2

practice test 2

SCIENCE

50 Questions • 80 Minutes

QUESTIONS 1 THROUGH 5 ARE BASED ON THE FOLLOWING INFORMATION.

Researchers are studying the evolution of fur color of a species of mouse that lives along the coast of Florida. The mice that live on beaches with light-colored sand tend to have light-colored fur, while mice that live on dark-colored inland fields tend to have dark-colored fur. The researchers conducted two different experiments to determine why these two different fur colors have evolved. In Experiment 1, they placed dark-colored and light-colored mice in a large laboratory cage with an owl. They used three different backgrounds on the floor of the cage for different tests. They then recorded the percentage of how often the owl captured mice of each color. The results of Experiment 1 are shown below.

Experiment 1

Background	Percentage of Animals Captured	
	Dark-colored Mice	Light-colored Mice
Dark-colored soil with few plants	33%	54%
Light-colored soil with few plants	55%	32%
Medium-colored soil with heavy plant cover	23%	12%

For Experiment 2, the researchers placed plastic models of dark- and light-colored mice at two locations in nature. They then looked for marks and scratches on the models that were made by attacks from other animals and calculated what percentage of the total number of attacks were made to each color of mouse. The results of Experiment 2 are shown below.

Experiment 2

Location	Percentage of Attacks Suffered	
	Dark-colored Mice	Light-colored Mice
Light-colored sandy beach	76%	24%
Dark-colored inland field	29%	71%

1. In Experiment 1, which background led to the greatest percentage of attacks against dark-colored mice?

   (A) Dark-colored soil with few plants

   (B) Light-colored soil with few plants

   (C) Medium-colored soil with heavy plant cover

   (D) Light-colored sandy beach

2. What is a possible reason that Experiment 2 was performed in addition to Experiment 1?

   (A) The researchers examined different colors of mice in Experiment 2.

   (B) Other animals did not attack the mice in the laboratory.

   (C) Experiments performed in the laboratory may not reflect what occurs in nature.

   (D) The researchers tested a larger number of backgrounds in Experiment 2.

3. What is the best explanation for why dark- and light-colored mice were captured at about the same amount of the time against medium-colored soil with heavy plant cover?

   (A) The increased number of plants gave both mice an equal chance of hiding.

   (B) Both mice were able to dig into the soil, giving them an equal chance of hiding.

   (C) Both mice were able to eat the plants, giving them more energy to escape the owl.

   (D) The owl preferred to eat the plants, giving the mice more chances to escape.

4. What is an observation that can be made in both experiments?

   (A) Light-colored mice suffer fewer attacks and are captured less often in dark-colored environments.

   (B) Dark-colored mice suffer fewer attacks and are captured less often in light-colored environments.

   (C) Light-colored mice suffer more attacks and are captured more often in light-colored environments.

   (D) Dark-colored mice suffer fewer attacks and are captured less often in dark-colored environments.

5. What is the best conclusion that can be drawn from both experiments?

   (A) These mice evolved fur color randomly, with some dark-colored mice doing better in light-colored environments.

   (B) These mice evolved fur color randomly, with mice of both colors doing equally well in all environments.

   (C) These mice evolved the fur color that is the opposite of the environment in which they live, to better find mates.

   (D) These mice evolved the fur color that would help them best avoid attack and capture by other animals.

QUESTIONS 6 THROUGH 9 ARE BASED ON THE FOLLOWING INFORMATION.

Researchers drilled into the sediments on the bottom of Anther Lake to determine local rainfall patterns over the past 150 years. Sediment is deposited on the bottom of the lake at the rate of about 1 cm/year. The researchers took samples of sediment every 10 cm for 150 cm below the sediment surface (the bottom of the lake). They analyzed each sample for its sand and clay content. Sediments with a higher percentage of sand were deposited in drier years, while sediments with a higher percentage of clay were deposited in wetter years. The results of their analysis are shown in the following graph.

Composition of Sediment Layers in Anther Lake

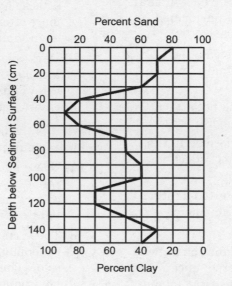

6. According to the graph, the sediment layer at which depth was deposited in the wettest year?

   (A) 0 cm
   (B) 50 cm
   (C) 110 cm
   (D) 140 cm

7. What is the best description of the relationship between percentage of sand in the sediment and depth?

   (A) There is a direct linear relationship between sand and depth.
   (B) There is an inverse linear relationship between sand and depth.
   (C) There is an exponential relationship between sand and depth.
   (D) There is no clear relationship between sand and depth.

8. Which of the following is an assumption that is made by the researchers?

   (A) Sand and clay are the only materials that make up the lake sediments.

   (B) Sediments with a higher percentage of clay were deposited in drier years.

   (C) Conditions at the lake were wetter 150 years ago than they are today.

   (D) Sediment samples were taken every 10 cm for 150 cm below the lake bottom.

9. Which of the following would be the best way for the researchers to confirm that sediment composition accurately shows the amount of rainfall in an area?

   (A) Analyze the sediments of a different lake 100 miles away.

   (B) Analyze sediments deeper than 150 cm below Anther Lake's bottom.

   (C) Determine the amounts of materials in the sediments besides sand and clay.

   (D) Look up the local rainfall records for the past 150 years.

QUESTIONS 10 THROUGH 14 ARE BASED ON THE FOLLOWING INFORMATION.

Several new species of bacteria have been collected from all over the world and from different environments. Researchers want to determine what carbon sources these new species of bacteria use. Bacteria can either get their carbon from outside sources (by consuming sugars, for example) or make it themselves. If they make it themselves, they use either sunlight or non-carbon substances to convert carbon dioxide (CO_2) into useful carbon compounds. The researchers place samples of each species of bacteria in solutions that contain all essential nutrients except for sugar and non-carbon energy sources. They then add either sugar, sunlight, or a non-carbon energy source to the experimental setup and observe if the bacteria grow. The results of their experiment are shown in the table.

Bacteria Species	Bacterial Growth Observed?		
	Sugar only added	Sunlight only added	Non-carbon energy source only added
A	No	Yes	No
B	Yes	No	No
C	Yes	No	No
D	No	No	Yes
E	Yes	No	No

10. Which species of bacteria gets its carbon by using non-carbon substances to convert CO_2 into useful carbon compounds?

    (A) Species A

    (B) Species B

    (C) Species C

    (D) Species D

11. Based on the results of this experiment, what is the most common source of carbon for bacteria?

    (A) Sunlight

    (B) Outside sources (sugars)

    (C) Non-carbon energy sources

    (D) Both sunlight and outside sources

12. What is another term for the process that Species A uses to get its carbon sources?

    (A) Respiration

    (B) Metamorphosis

    (C) Photosynthesis

    (D) Digestion

13. Species B is placed in a container and given access to sunlight as well as sugar, where an even higher rate of growth is observed. What does this new result indicate about species B?

    (A) Species B does not need sugar.

    (B) Species B must have sunlight.

    (C) Species B grows best with both sugar and sunlight.

    (D) Species B must have both sugar and sunlight.

14. What is the best explanation for why these species of bacteria evolved to require different sources of carbon?

    (A) Each bacteria species passed on mutations to their offspring.

    (B) They split apart from a single common ancestor during evolution.

    (C) Mutations became common in the different species of bacteria.

    (D) They adapted to use the resources available in their environments.

QUESTIONS 15 THROUGH 18 ARE BASED ON THE FOLLOWING INFORMATION.

The bicarbonate buffer system is a series of reactions that helps maintain acid–base balance in many organisms. The chemical equilibria that make up the bicarbonate buffer system are shown below:

$$CO_2(g) + H_2O\ (l) \rightleftarrows H_2CO_3(aq) \rightleftarrows H^+(aq) + HCO_3^-(aq)$$

A change in concentration of any of the reactants or products in the system above will cause the system to shift to bring it back to equilibrium. For example, if more reactants are added, then more products will be produced to bring the system back to equilibrium. Changes in one of the equilibrium reactions can affect the other. Thus, if the concentration of CO_2 changes, this will cause the concentration of H_2CO_3 to change, which will in turn change the concentrations of H^+ and HCO_3^-. The process of the system adjusting itself to return to equilibrium is called Le Chatelier's principle.

15. According to Le Chatelier's principle, what is the effect of adding more H^+ ions (more acid) to the system?

    (A) CO_2 will decrease.

    (B) H_2CO_3 will decrease.

    (C) HCO_3^- will increase.

    (D) H_2O will increase.

16. What is the effect of adding more HCO_3^- ions (more base) to the system?

    (A) H_2O will decrease.

    (B) H_2CO_3 will decrease.

    (C) CO_2 will increase.

    (D) H^+ will increase.

18. Humans are one of the species that uses the bicarbonate buffer system to maintain acid–base balance. A person exercises and exhales more CO_2 than usual. What will happen in the body to make up for this loss of CO_2?

(A) CO_2 and H_2O will decrease as they form more H_2CO_3, which will then break down to form more H^+ and HCO_3^-.

(B) H^+ and HCO_3^- will decrease as they form more H_2CO_3, which will then break down to form more CO_2.

(C) H^+ and HCO_3^- will increase as more H_2CO_3 breaks down.

(D) H_2CO_3 will decrease as it forms more H^+ and HCO_3^-.

QUESTIONS 19 THROUGH 23 ARE BASED ON THE FOLLOWING INFORMATION.

Incomplete dominance describes a system of inheritance in which the displayed traits (phenotypes) coded by dominant and recessive versions of a gene blend together in the offspring to create an intermediate trait. For example, if a homozygous dominant plant with red flowers (RR) is crossed with a homozygous recessive plant with white flowers (rr), and their heterozygous offspring (Rr) all have pink flowers, then the gene for flower color shows incomplete dominance. Contrast this with complete dominance, in which the phenotype coded by the dominant version of a gene totally covers up the phenotype coded by the recessive version of a gene. If the flower color gene from the previous example showed complete dominance instead, the offspring would all have red flowers.

Four crosses between homozygous dominant and homozygous recessive individuals are shown below. The phenotypes of the parents and heterozygous offspring are also shown.

Cross 1:
BB dark brown horse × bb cream-colored horse
↓
Bb tan horse

Cross 2:
RR red cow × rr white cow
↓
Rr red cow with white spots

Cross 3:
PP purple-kernel corn plant × pp yellow-kernel corn plant
↓
Pp purple-kernel corn plant

Cross 4:
HH straight-haired woman × hh curly-haired man
↓
Hh wavy-haired children

19. Which of these crosses result in offspring that display incomplete dominance?

(A) Cross 3 only

(B) Crosses 1 and 2

(C) Crosses 1 and 4

(D) Crosses 1, 2, and 4

20. Which of these crosses result in offspring that display complete dominance?

(A) Cross 2 only

(B) Cross 3 only

(C) Crosses 1 and 4

(D) Crosses 1, 2, and 4

21. One of these crosses results in offspring that display neither incomplete dominance nor complete dominance, but rather a condition called *codominance*. Based on the cross that results in codominance, what is the best way to describe codominance?

    (A) The phenotype of only the dominant version of a gene is present in heterozygous offspring.

    (B) The phenotypes of the dominant and recessive versions of a gene are *both* present in heterozygous offspring.

    (C) The phenotype of only the recessive version of a gene is present in the heterozygous offspring.

    (D) The phenotype of the dominant and recessive versions of a gene are blended, resulting in an intermediate phenotype in heterozygous offspring.

22. Two offspring of cross 3 (both purple kernel corn plants) are crossed together. The majority of the offspring of that cross will be

    (A) purple kernel corn plants.

    (B) yellow kernel corn plants.

    (C) purple and yellow kernels on one plant.

    (D) pale purple corn plants.

23. The crosses were performed to test the hypothesis that all crosses between homozygous dominant and homozygous recessive parents result in offspring that display either complete dominance or incomplete dominance. The appearance of offspring that display codominance has what effect on this hypothesis?

    (A) It proves it.

    (B) It supports but does not prove it.

    (C) It disproves it.

    (D) It makes it uncertain but does not disprove it.

QUESTIONS 24 THROUGH 27 ARE BASED ON THE FOLLOWING INFORMATION.

Carbon-14 is a radioactive form of carbon that decays slowly to a stable form of nitrogen (nitrogen-14). This graph shows the decay of carbon-14, or the percentage of an original amount of carbon-14 that remains after different amounts of time.

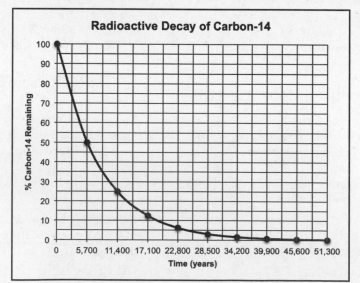

24. Approximately how many years will pass before only 2% of the original amount of carbon-14 is left?

   (A) 22,800 years

   (B) 28,500 years

   (C) 31,350 years

   (D) 39,900 years

25. *Half-life* is defined as the amount of time it takes for half of an original sample of a radioactive element to decay. According to the graph, what is the half-life of carbon-14?

   (A) 2,850 years

   (B) 5,700 years

   (C) 11,400 years

   (D) 25,650 years

26. Carbon-14 is often used to date carbon-containing artifacts from archaeological sites. By measuring the amount of carbon-14 left in an artifact, its age can be estimated. A wooden arrow shaft from a research site is found to have 35% of its original carbon-14 remaining. What is the approximate age of this arrow shaft?

   (A) 4,300 years

   (B) 5,700 years

   (C) 8,550 years

   (D) 11,400 years

27. The oldest objects that can be accurately dated using carbon-14 are about 50,000 years old. Examine the graph of the decay of carbon-14. What is the best explanation for why objects older than 50,000 years cannot be accurately dated using carbon-14?

   (A) After 50,000 years, carbon-14 stops decaying into nitrogen-14.

   (B) No carbon-containing objects that are older than 50,000 years have been found.

   (C) The rate at which carbon-14 decays slows down after 50,000 years.

   (D) After 50,000 years, there is so little carbon-14 left that it is difficult to measure.

QUESTIONS 28 THROUGH 31 ARE BASED ON THE FOLLOWING INFORMATION.

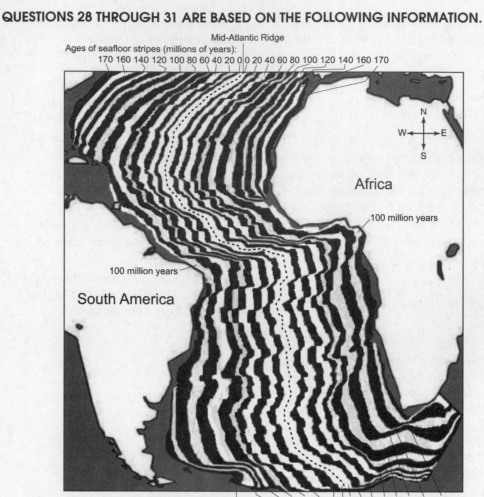

The map shows the ages of different parts of the Atlantic Ocean floor between South America and Africa, on either side of the Mid-Atlantic Ridge. The Mid-Atlantic Ridge is the boundary between the two major tectonic plates on which South America and Africa are located and is shown as a dashed line. At the Mid-Atlantic Ridge, these two plates are moving apart from each other, which allows magma to rise up from inside the earth and form new seafloor. The white stripes on the map have even-numbered ages (0, 20, 40 million years, etc.), while the black stripes have odd-numbered ages (10, 30, 50 million years, etc.). South America and Africa were once one continent, but have been moving apart from each other for millions of years. The Atlantic Ocean floor formed as South America and Africa were moving apart.

28. Which of the following is a hypothesis that can be tested using the information in this map?

    (A) North America is older than South America.

    (B) Older rocks are found at greater distances from the Mid-Atlantic Ridge.

    (C) There is a greater rate of subduction under the South American Plate.

    (D) The South American and North American Plates are also spreading apart.

29. What is the best evidence that the South American and African Plates are still moving apart today?

    (A) The seafloor at the Mid-Atlantic Ridge is 0 years old.

    (B) The seafloor next to the coasts of South America and Africa is about 140–180 million years old.

    (C) The seafloor next to the northwest coast of Africa is older than the seafloor next to the southwest coast of Africa.

    (D) The seafloor next to the northeast coast of South America is younger than the seafloor next to the southeast coast of South America.

30. Looking at the age of the seafloor stripes in the Atlantic Ocean, which of the following conclusions can be made?

    (A) The entire Atlantic Ocean floor formed at the same time because the age of the seafloor next to the continental coasts is the same throughout the entire ocean.

    (B) The southern coast of South America pulled away from Africa at an earlier time than the northern coast of South America because the seafloor next to the southern coast is older than the seafloor next to the northern coast.

    (C) The seafloor on the eastern side of the Mid-Atlantic Ridge formed before the seafloor on the western side of the Mid-Atlantic Ridge because the seafloor is not the same age on either side of the ridge.

    (D) The northern coast of Africa was the last to pull away from another tectonic plate because the seafloor next to the northern coast of Africa is the youngest in the Atlantic Ocean.

31. The youngest seafloor next to the east coast of South America and next to the west coast of Africa represents the final split between South America and Africa. Around what time did this final split occur?

    (A) 0 million years ago

    (B) 100 million years ago

    (C) 130 million years ago

    (D) 170 million years ago

QUESTIONS 32 THROUGH 35 ARE BASED ON THE FOLLOWING INFORMATION.

An automobile company tested the performance of its vehicles using professional drivers. The drivers drove vehicles of different masses at different speeds on different road surfaces and then turned on an automatic braking system. The distance it took for the vehicle to come to a complete stop was measured. The results are shown in the table.

Run	Vehicle	Mass (kg)	Speed (m/s)	Speed (mi/h)	Road surface	Stopping distance (m)
1	Car	1,500	10	22	Dry paved road	6.4
2	Car	1,500	30	67	Dry paved road	57.4
3	Car	1,500	10	22	Wet paved road	12.8
4	Car	1,500	30	67	Wet paved road	115
5	Truck	2,250	10	22	Dry paved road	6.4
6	Truck	2,250	30	67	Dry paved road	57.4
7	Truck	2,250	10	22	Wet paved road	12.8
8	Truck	2,250	30	67	Wet paved road	115

32. What is the hypothesis being tested in these runs?

(A) Vehicle stopping distance depends on the mass and speed of the vehicle as well as road surface.

(B) Road surface conditions are affected by vehicle mass and speed.

(C) The amount of time a vehicle takes to stop depends on its mass and speed only.

(D) Different tire and body materials can decrease the stopping distance of a vehicle on different road surfaces.

33. The difference in stopping distance between runs 1 and 3 is due to which of the following factors?

(A) Vehicle speed

(B) Vehicle mass

(C) Vehicle type

(D) Road surface

34. Which of the following pairs of runs tests only the effect of vehicle mass on stopping distance?

(A) Runs 4 and 5

(B) Runs 1 and 2

(C) Runs 5 and 6

(D) Runs 2 and 6

35. Based on the results of these runs, which of the following factors does NOT have an effect on vehicle stopping distance?

(A) Road surface

(B) Vehicle speed

(C) Vehicle mass

(D) Both vehicle mass and speed

QUESTIONS 36 THROUGH 40 ARE BASED ON THE FOLLOWING INFORMATION.

A researcher noticed that fish seemed to prefer living near underwater tree roots, especially those with a high number of organisms such as sponges, corals, and shellfish growing on them. The researcher performed two experiments to study this observation. In the first experiment, the researcher counted the number of fish and the number of root organisms along a 40 m straight line at several locations filled with underwater roots. The results are shown in the table.

Experiment 1

Location	Number of Fish	Number of Root Organisms
1	16	26
2	14	22
3	13	19
4	11	15
5	9	10
6	8	8

In the second experiment, the researcher counted the number of fish in a 20 m² area filled with underwater tree roots. The researcher then scrubbed the tree roots clean of all root organisms growing on them, waited 15 days for the area to settle, and then counted the number of fish in the same area again. The researcher also counted the number of fish in a control area, waited 15 days, and counted the fish again in the control area. The results are shown in the graph.

Experiment 2

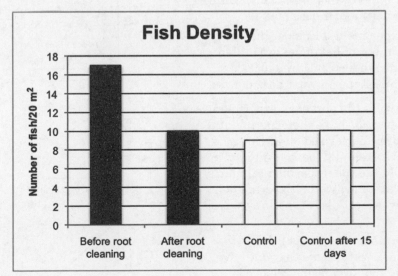

36. Which of the following is the hypothesis being tested in Experiment 1?

(A) Root organism growth is affected by the number of fish present.

(B) The number of root organisms affects the number of fish present.

(C) Fish are not attracted to underwater roots with no organisms growing on them.

(D) Fish are attacked less often by other fish in areas with many root organisms.

37. How is the hypothesis being tested in Experiment 2 different than the one tested in Experiment 1?

(A) Experiment 2 looks at the effect of removing all root organisms on the number of fish, while Experiment 1 does not.

(B) Experiment 2 looks at how changing numbers of root organisms changes the number of fish, while Experiment 1 does not.

(C) Experiment 2 looks at how the number of fish is affected by the number of root organisms, while Experiment 1 does not.

(D) Experiment 2 looks at the number of fish in an area filled with underwater tree roots, while Experiment 1 does not.

38. A control is the part of an experiment that does *not* have the experimental procedure performed on it. However, a control should be as similar as possible to the experimental parts in all other ways. In Experiment 2, what was most likely used as a control area?

(A) Another 20 m² area filled with underwater roots that *did* have the root organisms removed

(B) A 20 m² area filled with underwater roots that *did not* have the root organisms removed

(C) A 20 m² area filled with seagrass near an area with underwater roots

(D) A 40 m² area filled with underwater roots that *did not* have the root organisms removed

39. Which of the following questions CANNOT be answered by the results of these two experiments?

(A) Do fish prefer to live around underwater roots covered with more organisms?

(B) Do fish numbers increase as the number of root organisms increase?

(C) Do fish prefer to live in areas filled with underwater tree roots or in areas without roots?

(D) Do fish prefer to live around underwater roots covered with organisms or around roots with no organisms?

40. Which of the following graphs best shows the relationship between the number of fish and the number of root organisms?

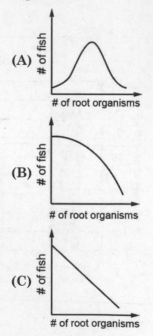

(A)

(B)

(C)

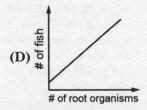

(D)

41. The type of volcanic eruption that occurs depends on the thickness (viscosity) of the lava and the amount of trapped gas in the lava. Thin, low-viscosity lava flows easily and over long distances. Thick, high-viscosity lava does not flow easily and tends to pile up before flowing very far. Lava with low amounts of gas flows quietly out of the ground, while lava with high amounts of gas erupts explosively. What is the best prediction for how lava with high viscosity and high gas will erupt?

(A) Quietly out of the ground over a long distance

(B) Quietly out of the ground over a short distance

(C) Explosively out of the ground over a long distance

(D) Explosively out of the ground over a short distance

42. The cardiovascular system moves blood from the heart to every part of the body and back again to the heart. Based on this information, which of the following tissues would most likely be part of the cardiovascular system?

(A) Hollow tube with flexible walls

(B) Solid gland that secretes hormones

(C) Solid organ that filters salts and wastes

(D) Hollow tube that contains digested food

43. Which of the following is an example of a chemical reaction?

(A) Ice melting into liquid water

(B) Sand mixing with mud in the bottom of a lake

(C) Meat turning brown as it cooks

(D) Crackers being broken into crumbs

44. Homeostasis is the normal, stable state of the body. Which of the following processes helps to maintain homeostasis?

(A) Body temperature rising on a hot day

(B) Sweating that cools off the body after exercise

(C) Losing fluids when ill through vomiting

(D) Heart rate speeding up when frightened

45. Michiko sees lightning flash in the distance, but she doesn't hear thunder until several seconds later. Why does she hear the thunder caused by the lightning after she sees the lightning?

(A) Thunder happens farther from her than lightning.

(B) Light waves travel faster than sound waves.

(C) Sound waves travel faster than light waves.

(D) Lightning happens closer to her than thunder.

46. In an ecosystem, a producer is an organism, such as a plant, that uses energy from an outside source, usually the sun, to make its own food. A consumer is an organism that eats other organisms or their remains. A predator is defined as an organism that attacks and eats another organism for food. Herbivores—organisms that eat plants—are generally not considered to be predators. Based on this information, which of the following statements is true?

(A) All consumers are predators.

(B) Herbivores are producers.

(C) All predators are consumers.

(D) Consumers only eat other consumers.

47. Which of the following best illustrates the transfer of kinetic energy (the energy of movement) from one object to another, without being converted to another type of energy?

(A) Sunlight being converted to electricity in a solar panel

(B) Heat energy being released as a log burns

(C) A rock held still over a puddle and then dropped

(D) A swinging foot kicking a ball down a field

48. In research studies, the independent variable is the factor that can be controlled by the researcher, while the dependent variable is the factor that is studied to see how it reacts to changes in the independent variable. The state health department is studying whether adding fluoride to drinking water helps prevent cavities in the state population. What is a dependent variable in this research study?

(A) Amount of fluoride added to drinking water

(B) Presence of fluoride in drinking water

(C) Number of cavities in the state population

(D) Number of dentists in the state population

49. A year on Earth is 356 days long because it takes the planet that many days to make a complete orbit around the sun. Earth is an average distance of 150 million km from the sun and travels a distance of about 940 million km during one orbit. Jupiter is an average distance of 778 million km from the sun and travels a distance of about 4,890 million km (about 5 billion km) during one orbit. Assuming that Jupiter orbits the sun at the same speed as Earth, about how long will it take Jupiter to complete one orbit around the sun?

(A) 1/5 earth year (356 days ÷ 5)

(B) 1/2 earth year (356 days ÷ 2)

(C) 2 earth years (356 days × 2)

(D) 5 earth years (356 days × 5)

50. Many processes that take place in the human body are a chain of reactions, or a cascade, in which one reaction has to happen before the next can happen. If a reaction early in the cascade does not occur, then all the steps that follow will not occur either. In the cascade below, each letter represents a different molecule. If reaction 2 does not occur, which of the following best describes the result?

$$A \xrightarrow{\text{reaction 1}} B \xrightarrow{\text{reaction 2}} C \xrightarrow{\text{reaction 3}} D \xrightarrow{\text{reaction 4}} E$$

(A) A and B will form, but C, D, and E will not form.

(B) A, B, and C will form, but D and E will not form.

(C) C will not form, but A, B, D, and E will form.

(D) B will not form, but A, C, D, and E will form.

SOCIAL STUDIES

50 Questions • 70 Minutes

QUESTIONS 1 THROUGH 4 REFER TO THE FOLLOWING CARTOON.

"TWO'S COMPANY, THREE'S A CROWD."
—Chapin in the St. Louis *Republic*.

1. Which constitutional amendment, ratified the year of this cartoon, gave women the right to vote?
   (A) The Fourteenth Amendment
   (B) The Eighteenth Amendment
   (C) The Nineteenth Amendment
   (D) The Twentieth Amendment

2. What is the main idea behind this cartoon?
   (A) Both political parties are in favor of women's suffrage.
   (B) Both political parties are possibly threatened by women's suffrage.
   (C) Neither political party is taking a stand on women's suffrage.
   (D) Both political parties want to elect a woman into national office.

3. The cartoonist most likely believes
   (A) women are not treated fairly in politics.
   (B) politicians are making room for women in government.
   (C) Republicans and Democrats will work together to help pass women's suffrage.
   (D) the next president elected will be a woman.

4. Which of the following events introduced and catapulted the women's suffrage movement to national attention?

(A) The Civil War

(B) The rise of imperialism

(C) The Seneca Falls Convention

(D) The Niagara Movement

QUESTIONS 5 THROUGH 8 ARE BASED ON THE FOLLOWING DOCUMENT.

Federalist #10

The Utility of the Union as a Safeguard Against Domestic Faction and Insurrection (continued)

***Daily Advertiser* Thursday, November 22, 1787 [James Madison]**

...By a faction, I understand a number of citizens, whether amounting to a majority or a minority of the whole, who are united and actuated by some common impulse of passion, or of interest, adversed to the rights of other citizens, or to the permanent and aggregate interests of the community.

There are two methods of curing the mischiefs of faction: the one, by removing its causes; the other, by controlling its effects.

There are again two methods of removing the causes of faction: the one, by destroying the liberty which is essential to its existence; the other, by giving to every citizen the same opinions, the same passions, and the same interests...

---

5. The term "faction" as used in the passage most clearly relates to which institution of the United States government?

(A) Terrorists

(B) Slaves

(C) Revolutionaries

(D) Political parties

6. All of the following would be considered a faction in today's government EXCEPT:

(A) Republicans

(B) Democrats

(C) The Tea Party

(D) The President of the United States

7. Which of the following is NOT a benefit of factions in the national government?

(A) They allow for uniformity in government.

(B) They represent the views of the people.

(C) They identify the concerns of the people.

(D) They unite people with similar views.

8. According to the passage, why would destroying a faction be a bad thing?

(A) It would take away the rights of the people.

(B) It would create debate over government decisions.

(C) Factions are anti-government in nature.

(D) Factions remove choice from the government.

QUESTIONS 9 THROUGH 13 ARE BASED ON THE FOLLOWING DOCUMENT.

Federalist #51

The Structure of the Government Must Furnish the Proper Checks and Balances Between the Different Departments

Independent Journal **Wednesday, February 6, 1788 [James Madison]**

...In order to lay a due foundation for that separate and distinct exercise of the different powers of government, which to a certain extent is admitted on all hands to be essential to the preservation of liberty, it is evident that each department should have a will of its own; and consequently should be so constituted that the members of each should have as little agency as possible in the appointment of the members of the others. Were this principle rigorously adhered to, it would require that all the appointments for the supreme executive, legislative, and judiciary magistracies should be drawn from the same fountain of authority, the people, through channels having no communication whatever with one another. Perhaps such a plan of constructing the several departments would be less difficult in practice than it may in contemplation appear. Some difficulties, however, and some additional expense would attend the execution of it...

---

9. From which of the following thinkers did Madison borrow his ideas of checks and balances?

   (A) Locke

   (B) Voltaire

   (C) Montesquieu

   (D) Jefferson

10. Which of the following is NOT a proper check on the powers of the national government?

    (A) Legislative over president

    (B) Executive over judicial

    (C) Judicial over legislative

    (D) Legislative over the Senate

11. Which of the following would be a tool used by the executive branch to check and balance another branch?

    (A) Veto

    (B) Executive order

    (C) Suspension of habeas corpus

    (D) State of the Union address

12. According to the passage, which of the following would be necessary for the system of checks and balances to work?

    (A) Creation of a monarchy

    (B) Creation of unicameral congress

    (C) Inclusion of the people in the process

    (D) Appointments of special magistrates to protect rights

13. What system of checks and balances is in place specifically for the legislative branch?

    (A) Having only one house to decide on propositions

    (B) Creating a bicameral legislature

    (C) Using the electoral college for election of the Senate

    (D) Being able to veto judicial decisions.

QUESTIONS 14 THROUGH 16 REFER TO THE DOCUMENT SHOWN HERE.

KEY JUDGMENTS
THE ECONOMY

The decade of the 1990s will be one of rigorous examination and future development will depend on how the economy adapts to the globalized economy, the degree of relaxation in traditional U.S. laissez-faire policy toward commerce, and the ability of the economy to maintain productivity (with concommitant productivity of the labor pool).

Changes affecting the U.S. economy will continue to occur at accelerated speed because, barring cataclysmic setback, economic conditions are closely linked with technological advancement.

A major factor in economic success will be the feasibility of continuous expansion of the world economy to the benefit of all, and the internal political feasibility of exposing U.S. enterprises and labor to the increasingly transnational system.

Continued automation of the goods producing sector is foreseen. A major factor will be the ability of producers to capture and hold fragmented and specialized markets. If there is hesitation then producers may be pushed toward basic products and away from high tech, ceding the latter to foreign competitors.

Quantity of labor, certain to decrease, will be secondary to quality of labor, much less certain. Further automation will expand job markets for workers with high technical training and for those with basic unspecialized skills; the ratio to be determined by demands posed by new technology. Workers in the middle levels may well be less in demand.

---

14. According to the document, which of the following is an example of a product that would continue to move the United States economy at an accelerated pace?

    (A) Sin taxes on things such as alcohol and cigarettes

    (B) The building of houses

    (C) The release of new products from manufacturers such as Apple and Microsoft

    (D) Increased government regulation of the economy

15. Which of the following could be blamed for a decrease in middle-level worker demand?

    (A) The economy

    (B) The government

    (C) Technology

    (D) Foreign policy

16. From where does the passage state most high-tech products will arrive?

    (A) Domestic businesses

    (B) International businesses

    (C) Government-backed corporations

    (D) Middle-class producers

QUESTIONS 17 THROUGH 20 REFER TO THE FOLLOWING PICTURE.

American Army Women Serving on All Fronts (1944)

Records of the Office of War Information, courtesy of National Archives

17. Considering its caption, which of the following best summarizes the picture?

   (A) Women effectively protested for equal representation in the job force.

   (B) Women were paid less money and thus hired more regularly in the job force to protect profits.

   (C) Women were needed in the workforce because men were off at war.

   (D) Women became more interested in engineering fields following the war.

18. How did men and most of society respond in the decade following the events of the picture?

   (A) They attempted to reintegrate women into the home, using tools such as advertising.

   (B) They created laws that protected women in the workforce.

   (C) They opened new schools and training facilities for women.

   (D) They passed laws that protected jobs of men.

19. What immediate result stemmed from the events and actions in the picture?

   (A) The United States experienced an extreme workforce shortage.

   (B) Women constantly used the strike as a tool to obtain equal pay.

   (C) New laws were created to protect workers from abuse and neglect.

   (D) The wartime production of the United States climbed to an all-time high.

20. Which of the following was the icon who represented women during this period?

   (A) Betty Boop

   (B) Rosie the Riveter

   (C) Minnie Mouse

   (D) Betty Friedan

QUESTIONS 21 THROUGH 23 REFER TO THE CHART SHOWN HERE.

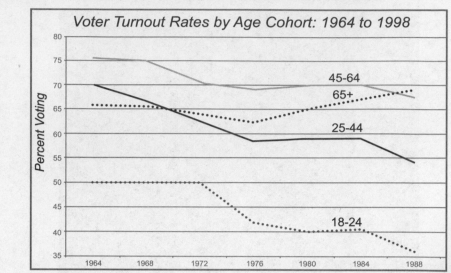

21. The chart shows data related to which right of American citizens?

    (A) Taxation

    (B) Education

    (C) Medicare

    (D) Suffrage

22. According to the chart, which of the following age groups has shown an upswing in turnout at the polls since 1984?

    (A) 18–24

    (B) 25–44

    (C) 45–64

    (D) 65+

23. Which of the following events best accounts for the higher level of voter turnout in the 1960s for most of the age groups?

    (A) The *Roe v. Wade* decision

    (B) The Vietnam War

    (C) Universal Healthcare

    (D) The Great Recession

QUESTIONS 24 THROUGH 26 REFER TO THE TEXT SHOWN HERE.

> There is to be a performance by the popular band The Economists this weekend at Jefferson High School. The auditorium only holds 1,000 people, but more than 2,000 students and parents have expressed a desire to attend the show.

24. Which of the following terms would best describe the situation regarding number of seats for the show?

    (A) Absolute advantage

    (B) Human capital

    (C) Scarcity

    (D) Quota

25. Which of the following options is the best way to allocate the tickets to those who want them the most?

(A) Add more seats to the auditorium.

(B) Hold a lottery.

(C) Charge a high price.

(D) Restrict the market that tickets are sold to.

26. The school decides to run a promotion for the tickets that states, "First come, first served," and allows patrons to line up outside the auditorium to buy tickets. Leaving your house to be first in line would be considered a response to which tactic?

(A) Change in supply

(B) Comparative advantage

(C) Capital resources

(D) Incentive

QUESTIONS 27 THROUGH 29 ARE BASED ON THE FOLLOWING DOCUMENT.

Regional and Interest Politics

It is reasonable to assume that politics on a subnational level will come to be more important in the next century. The complexity of the tasks that political bodies will confront might be more manageable if town, state, and regional governments, rather than the national government, deal with them. For this reason, new governing mechanisms are likely to be developed, or, at the very least, existing governing bodies will be improved, to deal with public issues in the coming decades.

In its effort to develop a more efficient and dynamic society, the American people will devise new bodies to govern the vast metropolitan areas that already cut across municipal, county, and state boundaries. Greater Los Angeles has an economy that in size exceeds that of many nations. The Baltimore-Washington area will be ever more closely interconnected in the next century. Greater New York will extend ever further outward from Manhattan. The vast urbanized region extending from Boston to Washington (BosWash) already contains one-sixth of the nation's population on 2.1 percent of its land, and by 2015 will contain an even larger share of this country's people, packed ever more densely together. A counter trend to this increasing concentration in certain areas, generally along the nation's coasts, will be an emptying out of other regions, most notably the rural areas of the midwest where many small towns are already in the process of disappearing.

Creating new mechanisms to govern these collections of human beings will take much political energy. Entrenched politicians will not want to cede power to larger, overarching entities. Inner-city politicians will not be eager to share power with suburban leaders, who, in turn, will not want to saddle their districts with the expensive problems of the core city. Governing entities will be developed to deal with the problems and goals of the larger regions. Business, social, and environmental concerns of these regions will be managed by new regional governing bodies that will have the power to overrule traditional political bodies.

27. According to the passage, which of the following will have the greatest influence on politics in the twenty-first century?

(A) The federal government

(B) Local and state governments

(C) The people

(D) Political parties

28. The passage implies that government and politics will become more _____ in the next decades.

(A) national

(B) patriotic

(C) divided

(D) regional

29. The system of government described in the last paragraph of the passage is most like one of

(A) checks and balances.

(B) unilateral power.

(C) chaos and confusion.

(D) a parliamentary system.

QUESTIONS 30 THROUGH 33 REFER TO THE FOLLOWING EXCERPT.

Good evening, my fellow citizens:

This Government, as promised, has maintained the closest surveillance of the Soviet military build-up on the island of Cuba. Within the past week, unmistakable evidence has established the fact that a series of offensive missile sites is now in preparation on that imprisoned island. The purpose of these bases can be none other than to provide a nuclear strike capability against the Western Hemisphere.

Cuban Missile Crisis Reading Copy, October 22, 1962

Courtesy of National Archives

30. The event described in the excerpt was part of a greater global conflict known as

(A) the Spanish American War.

(B) Imperialism.

(C) the Cold War.

(D) the War on Terror.

31. How did President Kennedy specifically respond to the event described in the excerpt?

(A) By declaring war on Cuba

(B) By declaring war on the Soviet Union

(C) By instituting a blockade

(D) By deploying a secret mission called the Bay of Pigs

32. The main difference of philosophy between the United States and the Soviet Union was regarding

(A) dictatorships.

(B) states' rights.

(C) Communism.

(D) racial equality.

33. Following the incident referred to in the excerpt, the next conflict between the United States and the Soviet Union took place in which country?

(A) Korea

(B) Vietnam

(C) Russia

(D) Iraq

QUESTIONS 34 THROUGH 36 REFER TO THE FOLLOWING DOCUMENT.

ADDRESS OF THE PRESIDENT

BROADCAST FROM THE OVAL OFFICE OF THE WHITE HOUSE, NATIONALLY, AND OVER A WORLD-WIDE HOOKUP

DECEMBER 9, 1941 – 10:00 p.m.

MY FELLOW AMERICANS:

The sudden criminal attacks perpetrated by the Japanese in the Pacific provide the climax of a decade of international immorality.

Powerful and resourceful gangsters have banded together to make war upon the whole human race. Their challenge has now been flung at the United States of America. The Japanese have treacherously violated the longstanding peace between us. Many American soldiers and sailors have been killed by enemy action. American ships have been sunk; American airplanes have been destroyed.

The Congress and the people of the United States have accepted that challenge.

Together with other free peoples, we are now fighting to maintain our right to live among our world neighbors in freedom, in common decency, without fear of assault.

Fireside Chat on the Declaration of War with Japan, December 1941

Courtesy of National Archives

34. Which of the following events led to the declaration issued in the document?
- **(A)** The Great Depression
- **(B)** The bombing of Hiroshima and Nagasaki
- **(C)** The attack on Pearl Harbor
- **(D)** The resumption of unrestricted submarine warfare

35. Which of the following would be considered a consequence of the actions taken by Japan?
- **(A)** The Korean War
- **(B)** Internment camps being created in the western part of the United States
- **(C)** Closing of the Open Door trade agreement
- **(D)** Creating an economic embargo on oils in the Pacific

36. Which of the following terms best describes the position of the United States with regard to world affairs prior to the events in this passage?
- **(A)** Isolationist
- **(B)** Interventionist
- **(C)** Economically stable and secure
- **(D)** Politically united

QUESTIONS 37 THROUGH 39 REFER TO THE FOLLOWING TABLE.

Economic Incentive	Who Offers This Incentive?	Purpose of the Incentive
Late fee on credit card	Credit card company	To prevent people from paying their card late
Buy one, get one free	Store or restaurant	To encourage customers to shop or eat there
$75 speeding ticket for driving too fast	Police	To encourage safe driving To discourage speeding

37. Which of the incentives above would be considered "positive"?
    (A) Late fee on credit card
    (B) Buy one, get one free
    (C) $75 speeding ticket
    (D) None of the above

38. Why would a company produce a negative incentive on a product?
    (A) To bring more customers into their business
    (B) To prevent abuse of their product or services
    (C) To profit from the neglect of its customers
    (D) Both B and C

39. Why would a driver intentionally drive over the speed limit if he or she were aware of the incentive attached to doing so?
    (A) The driver doesn't understand the incentive.
    (B) The driver doesn't care about the incentive.
    (C) The driver likes the incentive.
    (D) The driver wants to help the institution creating the incentive.

QUESTIONS 40 THROUGH 42 REFER TO THE FOLLOWING INFORMATION.

In his 1981 book, *The Nine Nations of North America*, author Joel Garreau states that the continent can be divided into nine "nations" with distinctive economic and cultural features. According to Garreau, these "nations" provide a more accurate way of understanding the true nature of North American society.

The Nine Nations of North America

- New England: Maine, New Hampshire, Vermont, Rhode Island, Massachusetts, and Connecticut and the Canadian Atlantic provinces of New Brunswick, Nova Scotia, Prince Edward Island, and Newfoundland and Labrador.

- The Foundry: Industrial areas of the northeastern United States and Great Lakes region stretching from New York City to Milwaukee, down to the suburbs of Washington, D.C. in Virginia, and including Chicago, Indianapolis, Pittsburgh, Cleveland, Toledo, Philadelphia, and Southern Ontario

- Dixie: The former Confederate States of America, centered on Atlanta, including Eastern Texas. Includes most of Virginia and West Virginia, Kentucky, portions of Missouri, southern Illinois, southern Indiana, and southeastern Oklahoma. The region also includes most of Florida, except for the southernmost part.

- The Breadbasket: Most of the Great Plains states and what are known as the "Prairie provinces": Iowa, Kansas, Minnesota, Nebraska, North Dakota, South Dakota, most of Oklahoma, parts of Missouri, western Wisconsin, eastern Colorado, eastern New Mexico, central Illinois, and north Texas.

- The Islands: South Florida, the Everglades and the Florida Keys, and the Carribean

- Mexamerica: The southern and Central Valley areas of California, southern Arizona, Texas along the Rio Grande, most of New Mexico, northern Mexico, and the Baja California peninsula

- Ecotopia: The Pacific Northwest coast and several Alaskan Pacific Coast Ranges, stretching from Alaska down through coastal British Columbia, Washington state, Oregon, and California north of Santa Barbara

- The Empty Quarter: Most of Alaska, Nevada, Utah, Wyoming, Idaho, Montana, and western Colorado; eastern portions of Oregon, California, Washington; Alberta and northern Canada, northern Arizona, parts of New Mexico

- Quebec

40. Which of the following professions is most likely to be held by someone living in the New England area?

    (A) Farmer

    (B) Merchant

    (C) Artisan

    (D) Rancher

41. Why would the region in the central United States be classified as the "bread basket"?

    (A) Its beneficial climate creates an increased agricultural output.

    (B) Its rich soil creates an increased agricultural output.

    (C) It's centrally located in the country.

    (D) Both A and B

42. Why would the general American population in the early colonial period be more likely to live near the East coast or New England and Foundry regions?

    (A) Their proximity to Great Britain

    (B) Their rich soil and beneficial climate for growing seasons

    (C) Their lack of forest area and ease of habitation

    (D) The tropical climate that produced larger crop totals during winter months

QUESTIONS 43 THROUGH 46 ARE BASED ON THE FOLLOWING DOCUMENT.

Bill of Rights of the United States of America (1791)

Amendment IX

The enumeration in the Constitution, of certain rights, shall not be construed to deny or disparage others retained by the people.

Amendment X

The powers not delegated to the United States by the Constitution, nor prohibited by it to the states, are reserved to the states respectively, or to the people.

---

43. Why was the Bill of Rights deemed necessary for some to ratify the United States Constitution?

    (A) To protect the rights of minorities

    (B) To have protections written down to prevent a situation similar to England's abuse of the colonists' rights from occurring

    (C) To be sure anti-Federalists had a say in the Constitution

    (D) To protect the voice of the party not in power

44. Authority not given directly to the federal government is given to which group?

    (A) The people themselves

    (B) The legislature

    (C) The president

    (D) The states

45. What does Amendment IX mean?

(A) Rights not expressed directly in the Constitution must still be upheld.

(B) The people can change the Constitution.

(C) The states hold all the powers not given to the federal government.

(D) People have freedom of speech, religion, and the press.

46. Which of the following examples attempted to use the Tenth Amendment to enact change?

(A) Gibbons v. Ogden

(B) The Emancipation Proclamation

(C) The Virginia and Kentucky Resolutions

(D) Filibuster

QUESTIONS 47 THROUGH 50 REFER TO THE FOLLOWING PICTURE.

Depression: "Runs on Banks": People Milling about Outside of Bank (1933)

Courtesy National Archives

47. The event shown in the picture was a result of which major event in U.S. history?

(A) The Great Depression

(B) The Cuban Missile Crisis

(C) The Vietnam War

(D) The Great Recession

48. Which of the following was created to protect against the fears created by the events leading to this picture?

(A) The SSA

(B) The CCC

(C) The HDIC

(D) The FDIC

49. Which of the following did NOT have an impact on creating the event shown in the picture?
    (A) Buying on credit
    (B) Too much government economic regulation
    (C) Overproduction
    (D) Unemployment

50. How did President Roosevelt attempt to fix the specific event referenced in the picture?
    (A) By bailing out the banks
    (B) By doing nothing and letting the economy recover on its own
    (C) By giving everyone a $5,000 stimulus check
    (D) By creating a bank holiday

ANSWER KEY AND EXPLANATIONS

English Language—Reading

1. B	9. D	17. A	25. A	33. D
2. C	10. B	18. B	26. D	34. B
3. B	11. A	19. A	27. B	35. C
4. D	12. D	20. B	28. C	36. B
5. B	13. A	21. D	29. C	37. B
6. B	14. A	22. C	30. A	38. C
7. C	15. D	23. D	31. D	39. C
8. A	16. D	24. B	32. C	40. A

1. **The correct answer is (B).** The bystanders accuse Rip Van Winkle of being a spy and demand he be taken away before even finding out who he is. This is not reasonable behavior.

2. **The correct answer is (C).** After getting hit by a man called Hercules, the narrator wakes up in a strange place and meets the man on the horse.

3. **The correct answer is (B).** At this point in the passage, Rip Van Winkle was "in the midst of his bewilderment" (lines 66–67) and even "doubted his own identity" (lines 64–65). The best way to describe his "confounded" state is *confused*.

4. **The correct answer is (D).** Both Rip Van Winkle and the narrator of Passage 2 are confused and seem to need guidance, which may make them seem child-like. However, neither character is an actual child, so choice D is a better answer.

5. **The correct answer is (B).** The people that Rip Van Winkle and the narrator of Passage 2 encounter express suspicion, hurl accusations, and engage in violent attacks. Such behavior is best described as hostile.

6. **The correct answer is (B).** Only choice (B) identifies the author's viewpoint. The author refers to America's lack of many conveniences before industrialization and praises its use of natural resources to farm, become a great shipbuilding nation, and fight wars.

7. **The correct answer is (C).** Only choice (C) identifies a practical application for information in the passage. All of the details about life in Civil War-era America would be good research for writing an authentic fictional story about that era.

8. **The correct answer is (A).** Only choice (A) identifies how this paragraph is different from the passage. While the main passage ignores the ill effects that industrialization has had on the world, this paragraph does not.

9. **The correct answer is (D).** Only choice (D) makes a reasonable inference based on details in the passage. Paragraph 1 describes various discomforts of the Civil War era.

10. **The correct answer is (B).** Only choice (B) makes an accurate comparison between the Civil War and post-Civil War eras. In paragraph 3, the author says that millionaires did exist in Civil War-era America, even if they were not as common as they became during industrialization.

11. **The correct answer is (A).** Only choice (A) makes a reasonable inference about the author. The author

spends much of the passage praising how industrialization has helped American business, but also praises modern farming techniques for enabling Americans to take full advantage of the fertile prairie plains.

12. **The correct answer is (D).** Only choice (D) makes an accurate prediction based on information in the passage. This passage establishes the man as a mysterious character, and part of that mystery is due to the fact that he is "wrapped up from head to foot." Mysteries such as these are usually solved.

13. **The correct answer is (A).** Only choice (A) draws a reasonable conclusion based on information in the passage. The stranger is "wrapped up from head to foot" and refuses to give his hat and coat to Millie.

14. **The correct answer is (A).** Only choice (A) analyzes how these words affect the passage's tone logically. These words suggest the hesitant movements, sudden noises, and tense postures common to a situation heavy with tension.

15. **The correct answer is (D).** Only choice (D) is an accurate synonym for *acquiescence*. The word *agreement* makes the most sense if used in place of *acquiescence*.

16. **The correct answer is (D).** Due to the inclement winter weather, Mrs. Hall typically did not receive a lot of business at her Inn during the cold season. According to the passage, a guest to stop at the inn in the winter-time was "an unheard-of piece of luck" (lines 34–35). The mysterious guest was a welcome bit of business for her.

17. **The correct answer is (A).** From the introduction of the "mysterious stranger" to his curious behavior and purpose for being at Mrs. Hall's secluded Inn at the dead of winter, the tone of the passage is cryptic and mystifying.

18. **The correct answer is (B).** Only choice (B) identifies the author's purpose in writing this passage. The author is mainly interested in explaining what he thinks constitutes proper etiquette.

19. **The correct answer is (A).** Only choice (A) identifies logical support for this analysis of the passage. The writer dates himself by suggesting that one should never ask women anything other than proposing marriage ("popping the question").

20. **The correct answer is (B).** All of the items mentioned among the answer choices are examples of etiquette suggestions made by Edgar Allen Poe in the passage except a well-timed joke being a great addition to a conversation

21. **The correct answer is (D).** Only choice (D) identifies a similarity between the two sources. The writer of this paragraph states that jokes about culture, gender, and race have gone out of style, and Edgar Allan Poe writes the same thing about puns in his passage.

22. **The correct answer is (C).** Only choice (C) draws a reasonable conclusion from information in the passage. Based on some of the inconsequential things he considers a breach of etiquette—such as using the word *genteel*, making puns, or asking women questions—the reader can conclude that the writer is offended easily.

23. **The correct answer is (D).** Only choice (D) correctly identifies a literary technique used in the first stanza. The poet uses repetition when beginning three of the five lines with the word *And*.

24. **The correct answer is (B).** Only choice (B) identifies what the main idea of the entire poem is: the poet choosing which path to travel.

25. **The correct answer is (A).** Only choice (A) is an accurate synonym of *diverged* as it is used in line 1 of the

poem. The word *separated* makes the most sense if used in place of *diverged* in line 1.

26. **The correct answer is (D).** Only choice (D) is a reasonable analysis. A career is an important part of life, and if the two paths in the poem symbolize career choices, then the wood in which they are would likely represent the chooser's life.

27. **The correct answer is (B).** Only choice (B) draws a reasonable conclusion based on information in the final stanza. The reader can draw this conclusion because the narrator says he will recall his decision "with a sigh" one day, and a sigh is a sound one often makes when expressing regret.

28. **The correct answer is (C).** Only choice (C) identifies a practical application for the poem. Someone who is in the process of making a major life decision, such as choosing which school to attend, would likely find the most inspiration from this poem.

29. **The correct answer is (C).** Only choice (C) is an assumption. In this line, Helen assumes her mother is approaching her, but it is actually her new teacher.

30. **The correct answer is (A).** Only choice (A) draws a reasonable conclusion. Because she could not see or hear, Helen Keller had to use her other senses to experience the world, and in paragraph 2 she describes how things such as sunlight, leaves, and blossoms felt to her.

31. **The correct answer is (D).** Only choice (D) describes the tone of the opening passages accurately. The author is waiting for her new teacher to arrive in paragraphs 1–3, and she writes of it in expectant tones.

32. **The correct answer is (C).** Only choice (C) contrasts the author before and after her teacher's arrival accurately. The author explains that she'd been feeling angry in the days before her teacher's arrival, but when she starts working with her teacher, she says she experiences "pleasure and pride," which are happier emotions.

33. **The correct answer is (D).** The only contrasts among the answer choices that are supported by the information provided in the passage are that Anne Mansfield Sullivan had full use of her physical senses and a life of experience, whereas Helen Keller had limited use of her physical senses and limited life experience. Helen spoke openly of her life before meeting her teacher, describing herself as a lost ship in a dark fog. Anne Mansfield Sullivan brought a world of light and experience to Helen's life when they began working together.

34. **The correct answer is (B).** Only choice (B) identifies the tone of this passage. *Wry* describes a twisted and ironic humor, and Bartleby's strange behavior and refusal to explain himself contributes to the passage's wry tone.

35. **The correct answer is (C).** Only choice (C) identifies a literary technique in the passage. A first-person narrative is when a character in the story is also the narrator, and Bartleby's boss narrates this story.

36. **The correct answer is (B).** Only choice (B) identifies a restatement of information. The author describes how composed and calm Bartleby is in the sentence before this one, and stating "Not a wrinkle of agitation rippled him" essentially repeats that information.

37. **The correct answer is (B).** Only choice (B) draws a reasonable conclusion about the narrator. The narrator is stunned when Bartleby refuses to do his job, which suggests he is unused to having his employees disobey him.

38. **The correct answer is (C).** Only choice (C) identifies a theme of this passage. Bartleby's boss thinks he has power over his employees, but this illusion is shattered when Bartleby refuses to do the task his boss asks him to do.

39. **The correct answer is (C).** Only choice (C) describes Bartleby. Bartleby is so self-assured that he refuses to do his job without losing his calm at all.

40. **The correct answer is (A).** Only choice (A) interprets this figurative sentence correctly. The author is comparing Bartleby to his plaster-of-Paris bust of Cicero because the man was as likely to be upset by getting fired from his job as a statue would be.

English Language—Writing

Part 1

1. C	11. D	21. B	31. C	41. C
2. D	12. B	22. D	32. B	42. A
3. B	13. A	23. B	33. A	43. B
4. B	14. D	24. A	34. D	44. A
5. B	15. B	25. C	35. C	45. C
6. D	16. D	26. C	36. B	46. B
7. C	17. C	27. A	37. B	47. A
8. B	18. D	28. A	38. C	48. D
9. C	19. A	29. D	39. D	49. C
10. C	20. C	30. B	40. B	50. D

1. **The correct answer is (C).** The opening of the passage should introduce the topic and grab the reader's attention. This choice poses an engaging question to get the reader to think about composting.

2. **The correct answer is (D).** The author of the passage is speaking directly to you, the reader. Therefore, the appropriate pronoun to use here is *your*.

3. **The correct answer is (B).** The verbs in this sentence should be in the same tense in order for the sentence to have appropriate parallel construction: *handle*, *decrease*, and *reduce*.

4. **The correct answer is (B).** The verb *got* is in past tense, but the action in the sentence hasn't started yet. The correct tense for this sentence is *getting*.

5. **The correct answer is (B).** The question is asking you to determine what correct punctuation is required within the sentence. The underlined portion of the sentence does not require any punctuation, so choice B is correct.

6. **The correct answer is (D).** The names of companies are usually capitalized.

7. **The correct answer is (C).** This is a complete sentence, and therefore it should end with a period.

8. **The correct answer is (B).** The way the original sentence is written, it is unclear who is composting, you or your friends and family. This choice makes the author's intent clear, that if you compost, hopefully your friends and family will appreciate the effort.

9. **The correct answer is (C).** This choice most clearly and effectively conveys the information in this sentence.

10. **The correct answer is (C).** This question is asking you to determine appropriate word choice, given the context of the sentence and passage. This passage is all about how to get your passport; therefore, the word that best fits here is *obtain*, which is a synonym for *get*.

11. **The correct answer is (D).** The verbs in this sentence need to be in the same tense in order for the sentence to be grammatically correct and

have parallel structure: *issuing* and *distributing*.

12. **The correct answer is (B).** To improve writing flow, short sentences like these two can often be combined into one sentence by adding an appropriate coordinating conjunction. Here, the addition of *and* can appropriately combine these two independent clauses into one sentence.

13. **The correct answer is (A).** The verb required here needs to agree with the subject, *the application form*, which is singular. The correct verb to use here is *is*.

14. **The correct answer is (D).** *United States* is the name of a country and a proper noun, so it should be capitalized.

15. **The correct answer is (B).** Here, we are being asked to determine appropriate end of sentence punctuation. This is a declarative sentence that simply requires a period at the end.

16. **The correct answer is (D).** This question is asking you to determine appropriate parallel verb structure and tense. Both of these verbs should be in the same parallel structure, and since this is an ongoing process that will likely exist from now into the foreseeable future, *sending and receiving* is the correct choice.

17. **The correct answer is (C).** This sentence provides information on incoming packages, so it makes logical sense that it be placed in the paragraph that focuses on incoming packages.

18. **The correct answer is (D).** This choice most clearly and logically presents the ideas in this sentence.

19. **The correct answer is (A).** *Confirming* is the appropriate present verb tense for this sentence.

20. **The correct answer is (C).** The appropriate coordinating conjunction, *and*, is needed here in order to effectively combine these two sentences.

21. **The correct answer is (B).** There are multiple members of the Lafayette Village Condominium Tower Coop Board, so a plural pronoun should be used here: *them*.

22. **The correct answer is (D).** In the closing of a letter or memo, a comma should be used right before the writer's signature.

23. **The correct answer is (B).** The opening sentence of the passage poses a question to engage the reader and needs to end in a question mark.

24. **The correct answer is (A).** This sentence is asking you to determine the appropriate pronoun to start this sentence. The first step to determine the correct pronoun is to determine the noun it is replacing. Here, the pronoun is being used to replace Nikola Tesla, so the appropriate pronoun to use here is the masculine *he*; therefore, the sentence is correct as written.

25. **The correct answer is (C).** This choice most logically and effectively conveys the information in the sentence.

26. **The correct answer is (C).** This paragraph begins by discussing Tesla's early academic accomplishments, which this sentence confirms. Therefore, the sentence would fit best as the opening to this paragraph.

27. **The correct answer is (A).** The sentence already contains the proper verb tense: *dropping*.

28. **The correct answer is (A).** This is the correct spelling of the word *acknowledged*.

29. **The correct answer is (D).** This version correctly adds commas to the sentence in order to clearly convey the information provided.

30. The correct answer is (B). Additional information about the Palladia Mall, beyond it being close to the location of the restaurant being reviewed, is unnecessary and out of place in this passage. It should be omitted.

31. The correct answer is (C). *English* is a proper noun and should always be capitalized.

32. The correct answer is (B). Proper subject/verb agreement is required; the plural subject *we* requires a plural verb, *were*. *We arrived at the restaurant and were warmly greeted by the friendly hostess.*

33. The correct answer is (A). Parallel verb tense is required in order for the sentence to be grammatically correct. The sentence as written contains appropriately parallel verbs.

34. The correct answer is (D). This version properly adds commas to the list of items in this sentence.

35. The correct answer is (C). This sentence is trying to convey the fact that the meal the family received pleased them and made them smile and that their waiter took a photo of them while they were smiling. This choice most clearly conveys that information.

36. The correct answer is (B). In order to make the most appropriate word choice for this sentence, you need to understand the context in which it will be used. It's clear from the information in the blog entry that the restaurant review was extremely positive. Therefore, it stands to reason that Rustica would receive the writer's *strongest recommendation*.

37. The correct answer is (B). The plural subject, *town council members*, requires a plural verb form, *were: All town council members were in attendance except for Mrs. Lucille Bowers, who was sick with the flu.*

38. The correct answer is (C). This choice effectively combines the two simple sentences into a compound sentence with the coordinating conjunction *so*.

39. The correct answer is (D). The verbs in this sentence must be in the same tense in order for the sentence to have appropriate parallel construction: *reviewed, discussed,* and *voted*.

40. The correct answer is (B). In the context of this sentence, it's clear that March 1, 2015, is when the construction would begin, or *commence*.

41. The correct answer is (C). The second paragraph opens with the proposed construction timeline for the Chestnut Valley Preservation Society Culture and Arts Center. This sentence would best fit at the beginning of this paragraph.

42. The correct answer is (A). A pronoun that matches the noun it refers to, *Mr. Lyle Starr*, is required here. *His* is the correct pronoun.

43. The correct answer is (B). Street names are proper nouns and should be capitalized.

44. The correct answer is (A). This is a question, and it should end in a question mark. It is correctly punctuated in the passage.

45. The correct answer is (C). The belief regarding the importance of recycling is ongoing, so the verb form *is* fits best in this sentence.

46. The correct answer is (B). In this sentence, the plural noun *they* requires a plural verb, *argue*.

47. The correct answer is (A). This sentence requires the appropriate parallel verb form (*separate, place, take*) and plural pronoun (*them*) in order to be grammatically correct. The sentence is correct as it appears in the passage.

48. The correct answer is (D). Is the dog separating material for recycling? This choice corrects the modifier placement and makes it clear who is doing the recycling.

49. The correct answer is (C). The tone of the passage makes it clear that the debate regarding mandatory recycling is unsettled, with strong opinions on both sides. This choice best captures this notion, that the question regarding mandatory recycling has not been definitively answered yet.

50. The correct answer is (D). Because we are referring to a possession of the individual, the noun *individual* needs to be in the possessive form: *individual's*.

PART 2

SAMPLE SCORE 6 ESSAY

Is a phone call more valuable than a life? Is a quick text to a friend or family member more important than the safety of our fellow citizens? I don't think so. I use my cell phone as much as everyone else does these days, and I understand that at any given moment a certain call or text may seem crucial, but it is simply not worth risking the well-being of citizens who drive on our roads. Cell phone use should be completely banned from use while driving— our lives are worth more than a phone call or text.

According to the information from NHSTA.gov, the available statistics regarding cell phone use while driving are alarming and clear—car accidents and risk increase, safety decreases, and innocent lives are put in jeopardy when people use their phones to call or text while driving. You can't argue with a statistic like the fact that, "Drivers who use hand-held devices are four times as likely to be involved in a serious crash" or "Driving while using a cell phone reduces the amount of brain activity associated with driving by 37 percent."

Aside from hard-and-fast facts, I have personally been affected by this issue. My aunt Helene was riding her bicycle last June, carefully obeying all the rules of the road, when she was struck from behind by a car. She was knocked off of her bike and suffered a fractured shoulder and three broken ribs. She was out of work for six weeks, needed help with caring for her kids and taking care of her home, and is still recovering. Thankfully, she was responsible enough to wear a helmet while riding her bicycle. If she wasn't wearing one, who knows what the outcome would have been? When the accident occurred, the driver of the car was texting her husband, reminding him to buy a gallon of milk on his way home. Was this gallon of milk more important than my aunt's life?

I've heard it said that the reason many people get into car accidents while using phones is that they're spending too much thought and effort trying to hide it, and if it were legal everywhere they could use their phones more effectively with less attention taken away from driving. The second excerpt from the Rural Transportation Safety and Security Center seems to suggest this hypothesis. Supporters also argue that phones have become a necessary and helpful driving tool, providing helpful mapping and trip navigation, so why not let them be used for calls and texts as well? Why not? Because one thing you can't argue with is statistics, which couldn't be clearer: all types of car accidents—from minor fender benders to catastrophic collisions—increase when people choose to call or text while driving.

Perhaps in the future, improved wireless and hands-free cell phone technology will truly make it safer to use our phones while driving, and this issue should be reopened for discussion. But for now, the risk is simply too high. I personally feel that my life, my aunt Helene's life, and the lives of everyone are worth more than a phone call or text. How valuable is the health and well-being of your friends, families, and loved ones to you?

SAMPLE SCORE 6 ESSAY EXPLANATION

Let's analyze this Score 6 essay in each of the core content categories measured on this part of the HiSET® exam.

Development of a Central Position or Claim

This essay does an excellent job at meeting the requirements of this content category—it takes a clear central position and develops this point of view over the course of the essay, while remaining focused on the core claim throughout the response. It also offers a wealth of compelling supportive ideas and credible evidence, and refers back to the source documents effectively. The end result is an essay that more than meets the task at hand.

Organization of Ideas

This written response demonstrates a strong understanding of effective idea organization and essay construction. The essay opens with an introduction that clearly lays out the writer's point of view (*... I understand that at any given moment a certain call or text may seem crucial, but it is simply not worth risking the well-being of citizens who drive on our roads."*). From here, the writer then goes on to back up the assertion with evidence in the body paragraphs (i.e., the availability of sobering statistics related to texting while driving, drawing in specific lines from the first passage). The author then segues into an effective personal story about a family member affected by the practice, to engage readers.

This essay also uses transitions well—instead of just diving into examples, the writer opens paragraphs with thoughts that clearly link the previous paragraph (i.e., *"Aside from hard-and-fast facts, I have personally been affected by this issue."*). Finally, the writer includes a paragraph detailing all the points a supporter of texting while driving might make and counters them, point-by-point (drawing in a fact from the second passage). A passionate, engaging conclusion ties the essay together and summarizes its main points.

Language Facility

The passion and conviction that the author feels about this subject rings true throughout this essay, resulting in an elegant and compelling written response on why texting while driving is a bad idea. This essay's tone is spot-on for its intended audience. It uses a variety of sentence structures and vocabulary to keep the text interesting and persuasive, along with a rich and varied choice of words throughout the piece. This essay will more than likely stick with its readers for a long time after reading it.

Writing Conventions

It's apparent that the author of this piece has a strong grasp of English-language mechanics. He or she uses clear and concise language throughout, with minimal spelling and grammatical errors. The author likely made the wise move of saving some time to proofread and polish his or her work while crafting this essay.

SAMPLE SCORE 1 ESSAY

Why should I pay for school? Ive went to school for....12 years? 13 with kintergarden. All free, no money, none at all. People pay for collage to feel fancey. Their so fancy. With their fancey collage degree and they can say they paid like a million $ for school and get a big fancey job. Its SO DUMB. Get a job and learn a skill, college is for the birds. Why spend govt money on collage that is usless, anyway?

SAMPLE SCORE 1 ESSAY EXPLANATION

Let's analyze this Score 1 essay in each of the core content categories measured on this part of the HiSET® exam.

Development of a Central Position or Claim

An essay that receives a score of 1, like this one, does not respond coherently and effectively to the HiSET® essay prompt and task. While this essay does take somewhat of a murky stance against the high cost of higher education, the central claim is very poorly developed, and supporting ideas and relevant evidence are nonexistent. There is also only a passing mention to the provided sources (*"Why spend govt money on collage that is usless, anyway?"*) without any additional analysis.

Organization of Ideas

This essay does not reflect proper essay organization. It is just one meandering paragraph with no discernible, introduction, body, or conclusion—and no clear transition between ideas. The end result is a confusing jumble of loose ideas.

Language Facility

This written response reflects a poor grasp of language facility. Word choice is not sophisticated or compelling, and there are errors in word choice throughout. The structure and tone of this Score 1 essay is confusing and inappropriate. Furthermore, the language and voice are far too casual (*"Its SO DUMB"* is out of place in a formal essay).

Writing Conventions

This essay is full of spelling and grammar errors throughout (the lack of an apostrophe in *"Ive,"* the misspelling of *"fancey,"* and using *"their"* instead of *"they're"* are only a few examples, plus the rampant use of sentence fragments like, *"Their so fancy."*), which severely impact both the comprehension and effectiveness of this written response.

Mathematics

1. E	11. D	21. C	31. B	41. E
2. D	12. B	22. B	32. A	42. C
3. E	13. E	23. D	33. E	43. B
4. B	14. A	24. C	34. D	44. A
5. B	15. B	25. C	35. A	45. C
6. C	16. C	26. D	36. B	46. D
7. D	17. D	27. C	37. B	47. D
8. D	18. C	28. D	38. B	48. A
9. E	19. D	29. C	39. C	49. D
10. D	20. E	30. C	40. B	50. A

1. **The correct answer is (E).** You must determine Kyle's total number of miles traveled, and then convert that to inches using the given scale factor. Altogether, Kyle rollerblades 11.0 miles. Let x represent the number of inches corresponding to this distance. We set up the following proportion:

$$\frac{11 \text{ miles}}{x \text{ inches}} = \frac{0.5 \text{ miles}}{1.25 \text{ inches}}$$

Cross-multiplying yields the equation $(11)(1.25) = 0.5x$, which is equivalent to $13.75 = 0.5x$. Solving for x then yields 27.5 inches.

2. **The correct answer is (D).** This problem requires you to use the fact that density equals number of species per square mile. Given this number, we multiply the density times the total number of square miles to get the total number of species in the entire forest: $(860)(40) = 34,400$ species in the entire rainforest.

3. **The correct answer is (E).** An event is a subset of the sample space. The elements in this event must be even and larger than 40. The elements satisfying these conditions are 50 and 200.

4. **The correct answer is (B).** The temperatures oscillate steadily from 52 to 64 degrees. The distribution shown in choice (B) exhibits this behavior.

5. **The correct answer is (B).** The x-intercepts of the graph (that is, the zeros of the graph) are −4 and 3. Therefore, the only linear factors are $(x + 4)$ and $(x − 3)$. All other factors must be quadratic.

6. **The correct answer is (C).** You could factor or use the quadratic formula for each choice individually, but to save time, you need only check the value of the discriminant. Remember, for a quadratic equation $ax^2 + bx + c = 0$, the discriminant is $b^2 − 4ac$. If this is equal to zero, then the equation has only one real solution. Observe that for choice (C), the discriminant is $2^2 − 4(1)(1) = 0$.

7. **The correct answer is (D).** First, identify x as the *number of minutes for local calls* and y as the *number of minutes for international calls*. Then, determine the intercepts with the y-axis and x-axis—these represent the number of minutes Mackenzie could spend on international and local calls, respectively, if he made only these types of calls. These values are (0, 500) and (1,200, 0), as shown.

Next, connect those two points with a line. Any point on this line (with integer coordinates) is a possible combination that actually uses up the entire card. Also, any point in the first quadrant beneath this line is also a possible combination, and would result in money remaining on the card. The region sketched in choice (D) possesses all of these characteristics.

8. **The correct answer is (D).** This problem involves using the various properties of arithmetic (commutativity, associativity, and distributivity). The expression in choice (D) is not equivalent to the one given because the middle term is missing a negative sign.

9. **The correct answer is (E).** We must interpret symbolically the two conditions relating the investments in Stocks A and B. First, we are told that the amount invested in Stocks A and B combined is $35,000. This gives the equation $a + b = 35,000$. Next, 4.5% interest on the amount invested in Stock A is represented as $0.045a$. Similarly, the 5.4% interest on the amount invested in Stock B is represented as $0.054b$. The sum of these two terms is $2,110. This results in the equation $0.045a + 0.054b = 2,110$. Both equations must hold simultaneously. This is given by the system in choice (E).

10. **The correct answer is (D).** To solve for n, clear fractions by multiplying both sides by n and then collect like terms. Make sure to remember to distribute in the second step:

$$n \times \left(\frac{3m}{n}(1+n) \right) = n \times \left(-\frac{2}{n} + m \right)$$
$$3m(1+n) = -2 + mn$$
$$3m + 3mn = -2 + mn$$
$$2mn = -2 - 3m$$
$$n = \frac{-2 - 3m}{2m}$$

11. **The correct answer is (D).** Simplify each of the two terms separately, and then subtract the two results.

Observe that $16^{\frac{3}{2}} = \left(\sqrt{16} \right)^3 = 4^3 = 64$

and $27^{\frac{1}{3}} = \left(3^3 \right)^{\frac{1}{3}} = 3$. Thus,

$16^{\frac{3}{2}} - 27^{\frac{1}{3}} = 64 - 3 = 61$.

12. The correct answer is (B). Convert miles to feet and hours to seconds. There are 60 minutes in an hour and 60 seconds in a minute, so there are 60×60 seconds in an hour. Also, there are 5,280 feet in a mile. Using these two facts enables us to convert from *miles per hour* to *feet per second* as follows:

$$\frac{90 \text{ miles}}{1 \text{ hour}} = \frac{90 \text{ miles}}{1 \text{ hour}} \times \frac{1 \text{ hour}}{60 \times 60 \text{ seconds}} \times \frac{5,280 \text{ feet}}{1 \text{ mile}} = \frac{90 \times 5,280}{60 \times 60} \text{ feet per second}$$

13. The correct answer is (E). The volume of a sphere is computed using the formula $V = \frac{4}{3}\pi r^3$, where r is the radius. Here, the diameter is 6 feet, so that its radius is 3 feet. Using the formula, we see that the volume is $\frac{4}{3}\pi(3)^3 = 36\pi$ cubic feet.

14. The correct answer is (A). Using the formula for the volume of a sphere, $V = \frac{4}{3}\pi r^3$, where r is the radius, you can determine that the desired volume of the new container is $V = 36\pi$ cubic feet. The volume formula for a right circular cylinder with height h and base radius r is $V = \pi r^2 h$. We are given that $h = 4$ feet. Substituting in this given information yields the following equation that must be solved for r: $36\pi = \pi r^2(4)$. Dividing both sides by 4π and then taking square roots shows that $r = 3$ feet.

15. The correct answer is (B). First, divide 0.20 by the number of gallons the container holds to get the concentration in *ounces per gallon*: $0.20/847 \approx 0.00024$ ounces per gallon. Next, since we are given the conversion factor for cubic feet to gallons, we multiply 0.00024 times 7.463 gallons to get 0.00179112 ounces per cubic foot. We can express this in scientific notation as approximately 1.79×10^{-3} ounces per cubic foot.

16. The correct answer is (C). This problem requires you to assess if a sampling procedure captures enough information about the portion of a hospital that is contaminated in a non-biased manner. The procedure described in choice (C) uses a reasonable number of distinct rooms from different parts of the hospital to make a reasonable assessment of the percentage of the entire hospital that is infected with the superbug.

17. The correct answer is (D). This problem requires you to construct a frequency table and identify the event described in context of the data values:

Times Tank Is Filled	Frequency
1	13
2	6
3	5
4	1

The event described consists of filling the tank 2, 3, or 4 times. Twelve of 25 drivers sampled filled the tank this many times. The probability is then $12/25 = 0.48$.

18. The correct answer is (C). The graph of this function is a parabola that opens downward. The maximum value is the y-value of the vertex. The function is given in the form $y = a(x - h)^2 + k$, where the vertex is (h,k). For $y = f(x) = -3(x - 6)^2 + 1$, the vertex is then $(6,1)$ and the y-value of this vertex is 1, which is the maximum value reached by the function.

19. The correct answer is (D). The average rate of change of a graph on an interval (a, b) is the difference in y-values at a and b divided by $b - a$. This can also be viewed as the slope of the line segment connecting the points at a and b on the curve. Using this interpretation, we are looking for the interval for which the slope of this segment is negative. The only interval of the five provided on which the slope is negative is (15, 20).

20. **The correct answer is (E).** A typical outcome of this experiment is an ordered arrangement of four objects, each of which is A, B, C, or D. For instance, ABDD is a typical element. To determine the number of outcomes, a tree diagram is helpful to visualize the outcomes. You can also use the multiplication rule since each of the four rolls is independent of the others. There are four different outcomes for each roll of the die and there are four rolls. So, there are $4 \times 4 \times 4 \times 4 = 4^4 = 256$ possible outcomes.

21. **The correct answer is (C).** First, determine the cost of each type of item, which is computed by multiplying the cost of one of them by the number of them being purchased. Then, add all of these individual costs together to get the total cost C. For instance, one new paddle costs p dollars, and two paddles cost $2p$ dollars. Similarly, the costs for 3 lifejackets and 1 dry box are $3l$ and b, respectively. Adding these costs together gives the total cost $C = 3l + b + 2p$.

22. **The correct answer is (B).** The slope of a line is equal to the change in y divided by the change in x. If the slope is positive, then the graph of the line rises from left to right, so that the y-values are increasing as the x-values increase. For the given line, the slope is $\frac{2}{5}$. We interpret this as meaning that the y-value on the graph increases by 2 units for every 5 units increase in x.

23. **The correct answer is (D).** This problem involves determining the range of possible values that can be obtained based on the maximum percent error. To get this range, compute 10% of 0.15 to get $0.10(0.15) = 0.015$. Then, add and subtract it from 0.15 to get the range 0.135 to 0.165. Any number between these two, inclusive, is a possible reading. The only number *not* in this range is choice (D).

24. **The correct answer is (C).** Note that all quantities involve $\sqrt{3}$. The answer is the choice that is the product of $\sqrt{3}$ and a number less than 1. Since $(0.95)^2 = 0.9025$, $(0.95)^2\sqrt{3} = 0.9025\sqrt{3}$, which is less than $\sqrt{3}$. So, choice (C) is the correct answer.

25. **The correct answer is (C).** This problem requires you to compute the areas of two triangles and compare the two numbers using percentages. The area of triangle A is $\frac{1}{2}bh$. In order to compute the area of B, we need its base and height. Since the base of B is 30% smaller than the base of A, its length must be $b - 0.30b = 0.70b$. Similarly, since the height of B is 20% smaller than the height of A, its height must be $h - 0.20h = 0.80h$. Therefore:

$$\text{Area of B} = \frac{1}{2}(0.70b)(0.80h) = (0.70 \times 0.80) \times \left(\frac{1}{2}bh\right) = 0.56\left(\frac{1}{2}bh\right) = 0.56 \times (\text{Area of A})$$

So, the area of B is 56% of the area of A.

26. **The correct answer is (D).** Let w represent the width of the room and l its length. Then, $w = 2l - 3$. The area of a rectangular room is length times width. Using this fact yields the following equation:

$$l \times (2l - 3) = 350$$

Solving this equation for l yields:

$$l \times (2l - 3) = 350$$
$$2l^2 - 3l = 350$$
$$2l^2 - 3l - 350 = 0$$
$$(2l + 25)(l - 14) = 0$$
$$l = \cancel{-12.5}, 14$$

So, the length of the room is 14 feet. Thus, the width is $2(14) - 3 = 25$ feet.

27. **The correct answer is (C).** The formula for the volume of a right circular cone with base radius r and height h is given by $V = \frac{1}{3}\pi r^2 h$. Since the diameter of the base is 20 feet, its radius is 10 feet. Substituting $r = 10$ and $h = 12$ into the volume formula then yields $V = \frac{1}{3}\pi(10)^2(12) = 400\pi$ cubic feet.

28. **The correct answer is (D).** For any individual roll, each player can expect, in the long run, to get $\frac{1}{6}(1) + \frac{1}{6}(2) + \frac{1}{6}(3) + \frac{1}{6}(4) + \frac{1}{6}(5) + \frac{1}{6}(6) = 3.5$ points. As such, over the long run, each player will average the same number of points so that neither has an edge over the other.

29. **The correct answer is (C).** The distribution describing this scenario should peak at 3 ounces and dip down on either side very quickly (because of the very little variation in weight). This is described by the distribution in choice (C).

30. **The correct answer is (C).** Let m represent the number of months Miranda can make withdrawals from the account. Since she withdraws $925 per month (combined), the total she withdraws in m months is $925m$. So, after m months, there are $12,000 - 925m$ dollars left in the account. This amount must be greater than or equal to 1,500 dollars in order to avoid fees. So, the inequality used to model this situation is $-925m + 12,000 \geq 1,500$.

31. **The correct answer is (B).** To compute $x(2 - 3x) - 2(-1 - x - 3x^2)$, first distribute x through each term of the first binomial and distribute the -2 through each term of the second trinomial. Then, add like terms:

$$x(2 - 3x) - 2(-1 - x - 3x^2) = 2x - 3x^2 + 2 + 2x + 6x^2 = 3x^2 + 4x + 2$$

32. **The correct answer is (A).** There are various correct first steps that can be taken when solving a linear equation. A common approach is clearing the fractions by multiplying both sides by the least common denominator of all fractions in the equation. Doing so for this equation means you multiply both sides by 14:

$$14 \times \left(-2x - \frac{1}{7} \right) = 14 \times \left(-\frac{3}{14}x + 3 \right)$$
$$-28x - 2 = -3x + 42$$

33. **The correct answer is (E).** For this problem, you must simplify the radicals that can be simplified and then foil the resulting binomials. When doing so, use the fact that $\sqrt{2} \cdot \sqrt{2} = 2$:

$$\left(\sqrt{32} - 1 \right)\left(\sqrt{8} - 1 \right) = \left(4\sqrt{2} - 1 \right)\left(2\sqrt{2} - 1 \right)$$
$$= \left(4\sqrt{2} \right)\left(2\sqrt{2} \right) - \left(4\sqrt{2} \right)(1) - (1)\left(2\sqrt{2} \right) + (-1)(-1)$$
$$= 16 - 4\sqrt{2} - 2\sqrt{2} + 1$$
$$= 17 - 6\sqrt{2}$$

34. **The correct answer is (D).** Rational numbers can always be written as fractions of integers. This includes all whole numbers, since they can always be written as a fraction with a denominator of 1. Checking each choice, choice (A) is really 2×4 = 8, choice (B) is just $\frac{4}{10}$, choice (C) is $2 + 4$, and choice (E) is two integers, since each base is to a positive whole number power. Only choice (D), $3\sqrt{2} - 4\sqrt{2} = -\sqrt{2}$, cannot be written as an integer.

35. **The correct answer is (A).** This problem requires you to visualize the solids you get by rotating specific regions around a specified line. The region in choice (A), when rotated around the y-axis produces a right circular cone with height 8 inches whose base is a circle with radius 6 inches.

36. **The correct answer is (B).** In the trend described, pulse rate decreases as the number of minutes of daily exercise increases, and the relationship should be strong. In terms of a scatterplot, the data points should fall from left to right. They should be tightly packed near a line. These characteristics are embodied by the scatterplot in choice (B).

37. **The correct answer is (B).** The key to solving this problem is expressing profit in terms of the number of house visits. The $400 spent on materials yields *negative profit*, so we express it as −400. Next, since you earn $17 per visit and it costs you $1.50 per visit, your net profit per visit is $15.50. This is constant, so the profit gained from x house visits is $15.5x$. Therefore, the profit for x house visits is given by $P = 15.5x - 400$.

Next, to determine when you will break even, set the profit expression equal to zero and solve for x:

$$15.5x - 400 = 0$$
$$15.5x = 400$$
$$x = \frac{400}{15.5} \approx 25.81$$

So, you must round up and conclude that you will break even after 26 house visits.

38. **The correct answer is (B).** Set up equations or inequalities that express the relationships among A, B, and C. There are two conditions described in the problem. First, "Line A handles three times as many customers as Line C" can be represented as the equation $A = 3C$. Second, "Line B handles no more than $\frac{1}{3}$ the customers that Line C handles" can be represented as the inequality "$B \leq \frac{1}{3}C$."

Next, recall that you can multiply both sides of an inequality by a positive number and keep the same sign. So, we can multiply the inequality $B \leq \frac{1}{3}C$ by 3 to get an equivalent inequality $3B \leq C$. Finally, since $A = 3C$, it follows that $C = \frac{1}{3}A$. Substituting this into the previous inequality gives $3B \leq \frac{1}{3}A$, which is equivalent to $9B \leq A$.

39. **The correct answer is (C).** Absolute value allows you to measure distance on both sides of a fixed quantity. Here, the fixed quantity is 55 Brussels sprouts. We are told the number can vary by 8, which means there could be 1, 2, 3, 4, 5, 6, 7, or 8 more than 55 Brussels sprouts in the bag, there could be 1, 2, 3, 4, 5, 6, 7, or 8 fewer than 55 Brussels sprouts in the bag, or there could be 55 in the bag. The inequality $|b - 55| \leq 8$ means "go left and right of 55 by 8", which perfectly describes this scenario.

40. **The correct answer is (B).** Let x represent the number of dimes. Then, there must be $20 - x$ quarters. Since the value of a dime is $0.10 and the value of a quarter is $0.25, multiplying the number of each type of coin by its value, adding those results together, and setting the sum equal to 2.45 will yield an equation that can be solved to tell you the number of dimes and quarters in Jeff's pocket: $0.10x + 0.25(20 - x) = 2.45$.

41. **The correct answer is (E).** This problem requires that you recall *distance equals rate times time*. The distance the driver of the older model car has traveled at time t is the head start plus the rate at which he drives *times* the time he has been driving. Translating this into symbols yields the expression $2 + 80t$. Likewise, the distance the driver of the new model car has traveled at time t is the rate at which he drives *times* the time he has been driving. In symbols, this is $90t$. To get their relative distance, subtract the two expressions: $d = 2 + 80t - 90t = 2 - 10t$.

42. **The correct answer is (C).** You must subtract the two given average times and then take 55 percent of that difference. Subtracting the times yields 1 minute 40 seconds, which equals 100 seconds. Fifty-five percent of this quantity is $0.55(100) = 55$ seconds. Subtracting this from the average 9th grade completion time yields 14 minutes 25 seconds.

43. **The correct answer is (B).** Two of the walls have dimensions 15 feet by 10 feet; the combined area of these two walls is 2×150 feet^2 = 300 feet^2. The other two walls have dimensions 20 feet by 10 feet; the combined area of these two walls is 2×200 feet^2 = 400 feet^2. The ceiling has dimensions 15 feet by 20 feet, so its area is 300 feet^2. Therefore, the total square footage that must be painted is $300 + 400 + 300 = 1,000$ square feet. Since 1 gallon of paint will cover 400 square feet, he can complete $\frac{400}{1,000} = \frac{2}{5} = 0.40$ of the job. Converting to a percent, we

conclude that 40% of the job can be completed.

44. **The correct answer is (A).** This problem requires you to compare two volumes of similar solids. Let l and w represent the length and width of the base of the original ice cream bar, and h its height (or thickness). The length of the new ice cream bar is $l - 0.25l = 0.75l$ and its width is $w - 0.25w = 0.75w$. The thickness of the new ice cream bar is $h + 0.20h = 1.20h$. Next, compute the volumes of both ice cream bars. The volume of the original ice cream bar is $V_{\text{original}} = lwh$ and the volume of the new ice cream bar is $V_{\text{new}} = (0.75l)(0.75w)(1.20h) = 0.675lwh = 0.675V_{\text{original}}$. Therefore, the volume of the new ice cream bar is 67.5% of the volume of the original one. So, its volume is about one-third less than the original one.

45. **The correct answer is (C).** In an ordered list of 500 numbers, the median is the average of the two middle numbers. You can think of an ordered list of 500 numbers as two lists of 250 numbers each. The median would then be the average of the 250th and the 251st numbers in the list. If the list of the answers for each household were written out, the first 25 would be 1s, and the next 180 would be 2s. That's 205 numbers so far. The next 150 would be 3s, which covers up through 355 values in the list. So the 250th and 251st numbers are both 3. The average of 3 and 3 is 3, so this is the median.

46. **The correct answer is (D).** We must set up an equation relating all the percentages of unlockable items found. Since the percentage for levels 3 and 4 are described in terms of the percentage for level 5, let x represent the percentage for the level 5. Then, $x + 10$ is the percentage for level 4 and $x + 10 - 10 = x$ is the percentage for level 3. We are given that the percentages for levels 1 and 2 are 55% and

0%, respectively. To average them, add the five percentages and divide the sum by 5, and set it equal to 61:

$$\frac{0 + 55 + x + (x + 10) + x}{5} = 61$$

Solving for x yields:

$$\frac{3x + 65}{5} = 61$$
$$3x + 65 = 305$$
$$3x = 240$$
$$x = 80$$

So, the percentage completion for level 4 is $80 + 10 = 90\%$.

47. **The correct answer is (D).** The temperature of the grilled cheese sandwich starts out the same as the temperature of the frying pan, which is 150°F. Then, during the walk to the friend's house, its temperature quickly decreases, getting closer to the temperature outside, which is 20°F. This is best described by the graph in choice (D).

48. **The correct answer is (A).** We need to identify the radius and height of the new cone and substitute them into the volume formula. The combination listed that yields the volume of this new cone as $\frac{1}{4}\left(\frac{1}{3}\pi r^2 h\right)$ is the correct answer. Of those listed, the combination in choice (A) is correct. Indeed, the height would remain h and the radius would be $\frac{1}{2}r$. Therefore, the volume would be

$$V_{\text{new}} = \frac{1}{3}\pi\left(\frac{1}{2}r\right)^2 h = \frac{1}{4}\left(\frac{1}{3}\pi r^2 h\right).$$

49. **The correct answer is (D).** For every inch, the fraction of a gallon of gas needed (per minute) increases by 0.006 gallons. As such, the number of gallons needed can be viewed as a function of the depth of grass (in inches). In particular, the slope of this function is $0.006/1 = 0.006$. Also, if there is no grass, it uses 0 gallons

of gasoline. So, the equation of this line is $G = \frac{6}{1,000}d = \frac{3}{500}d$, where G is the number of gallons per minute needed and d represents the depth of the grass (in inches).

Now, substitute $d = 5.5$ to get $G = \frac{3}{500}(5.5) = 0.033$ gallons of gasoline per minute is needed for this depth of grass.

50. **The correct answer is (A).** Find the equation of the line passing through the two points by first finding the slope and then using the point-slope formula. The slope is:

$$m = \frac{6-4}{3-(-1)} = \frac{2}{4} = \frac{1}{2}$$

The equation of the line is then:

$$y - y_1 = m(x - x_1)$$

$$y - 4 = \frac{1}{2}(x - (-1))$$

$$y - 4 = \frac{1}{2}(x + 1)$$

$$y - 4 = \frac{1}{2}x + \frac{1}{2}$$

$$y = \frac{1}{2}x + \frac{9}{2}$$

To find the x-intercept, let $y = 0$ and solve for x.

$$0 = \frac{1}{2}x + \frac{9}{2}$$

$$-\frac{9}{2} = \frac{1}{2}x$$

$$-9 = x$$

Science

1. B	11. B	21. B	31. B	41. D
2. C	12. C	22. A	32. A	42. A
3. A	13. C	23. C	33. D	43. C
4. D	14. D	24. C	34. D	44. B
5. D	15. D	25. B	35. C	45. B
6. B	16. C	26. C	36. B	46. C
7. D	17. A	27. D	37. A	47. D
8. A	18. B	28. B	38. B	48. C
9. D	19. C	29. A	39. C	49. D
10. D	20. B	30. B	40. D	50. A

1. **The correct answer is (B).** This question requires you to examine the results for Experiment 1 and find the background that led to the greatest percentage of attacks against dark-colored mice. Looking at the table of results for Experiment 1, dark-colored mice suffered the greatest percentage of attacks against light-colored soil with few plants. Don't confuse Experiment 1 with Experiment 2; while dark-colored mice did suffer a larger percentage of attacks against a light-colored sandy beach, this was in Experiment 2, not Experiment 1.

2. **The correct answer is (C).** This question asks you to explain why multiple experiments might be performed to test one research question. Experiment 1 was performed in a laboratory, which may not provide results that are the same as what is seen in nature. While lab studies can be extremely useful, it is always preferable to see how living things behave in their natural environment. Thus, Experiment 2 was performed to see how fur color affects mice in nature.

3. **The correct answer is (A).** This question asks you to explain the effects of medium-colored soil and heavy plant cover on Experiment 1. Plants are present in all of the tests performed in Experiment 1, so any difference in the results of this test would be due to the increased amount of plants. Similarly, soil was present in all three tests, so any difference in the results of this test would be due to the color of the soil. The only reasonable explanation is that the increased number of plants gave both mice an equal chance of hiding, resulting in their being captured by the owl at about the same rates.

4. **The correct answer is (D).** This question requires you to find a common observation from both experiments. From the results of both experiments, it is clear that mice are captured less often and suffer fewer attacks when they are in environments that are the same color as they are.

5. **The correct answer is (D).** This question requires you to understand that traits evolve to help animals survive and reproduce. You're told in the question stem that light-colored mice tend to live on light-colored beaches,

while dark-colored mice tend to live in dark-colored fields, which should be a hint that fur color did not evolve randomly. Based on the results of the experiments, mice appear to have evolved the fur color that would help them best avoid attack and capture by other animals—the fur color that would help them best survive.

6. **The correct answer is (B).** This question requires you to reason that if sediments with a higher percentage of clay are deposited in wetter years, then the sediment deposited in the wettest year must have the highest percentage of clay. The layer with the highest percentage of clay occurs at 50 cm below the sediment surface.

7. **The correct answer is (D).** This question requires you to examine the shape of the graph and draw conclusions about the relationship between the dependent and independent variables. In this case, the sand content varies according to moisture, not according to the depth of the sample, so the independent variable is actually moisture and not depth. As a result, sand content varies at depth according to outside forces unrelated to depth.

8. **The correct answer is (A).** This question asks you to correctly identify an assumption: something that is accepted as true without proof rather than directly observed or concluded from facts. The graph of sediment composition shows only two materials, sand and clay, and their percentages always add up to 100%. This means that the researchers assume sand and clay to be the only materials that make up the lake sediments.

9. **The correct answer is (D).** This question asks you to find supporting evidence for the rainfall patterns that can be deduced from sediment composition. The best way to determine rainfall patterns is to look up the actual rainfall records for the area.

10. **The correct answer is (D).** This question requires you to make the connection that bacteria will grow only if they are provided with the carbon source (or the method to make their carbon source) that they require. Species D is the only species that can grow when only a non-carbon energy source is provided, so it must get its carbon by using non-carbon substances to convert CO_2 into useful carbon compounds.

11. **The correct answer is (B).** This question requires you to make the connection that bacteria will grow only if they are provided with the carbon source (or the method to make their carbon source) that they require. Of the five species of bacteria studied, three grow when only sugar is provided, so this is the most common source of carbon for bacteria.

12. **The correct answer is (C).** This question requires you recall that photosynthesis is the process in which sunlight is used to convert CO_2 into useful carbon compounds. Species A will grow when only sunlight is provided, which means that it uses sunlight to convert CO_2 into useful carbon compounds. Thus, Species A uses photosynthesis to make its carbon sources.

13. **The correct answer is (C).** The question requires you to apply the results of the initial tests to a different situation. Growth improves when both sugar and sunlight are present, but that new information does not change the original results of the experiment.

14. **The correct answer is (D).** This question requires you to recall that evolution leads to organisms that fit their environments. The question passage tells you that the species of bacteria were collected from different environments all over the world, so it is most likely that they evolved to

best survive and reproduce using the resources available in their environments.

15. **The correct answer is (D).** This question requires you to apply the concept of Le Chatelier's principle, which states that a system in equilibrium will adjust itself to return to equilibrium if any changes are made to the system. Adding more H^+ ions to the system will push the reverse reaction in the final equilibrium to occur: $H^+ + HCO_3^- \rightarrow H_2CO_3$. The increased amount of H_2CO_3 will in turn cause H_2CO_3 to break down into more CO_2 and H_2O to reestablish the first equilibrium. Thus, adding more H^+ to the system will cause the amount of H_2O to increase.

16. **The correct answer is (C).** This question requires you to apply the concept of Le Chatelier's principle, which states that a system in equilibrium will adjust itself to return to equilibrium if any changes are made to the system. Adding more HCO_3^- to the system will push the reverse reaction in the final equilibrium to occur: $H^+ + HCO_3^- \rightarrow H_2CO_3$. The increased amount of H_2CO_3 will in turn cause H_2CO_3 to break down into more CO_2 and H_2O to reestablish the first equilibrium. This is the same effect as adding more acid to the system. Thus, adding more HCO_3^- to the system will cause the amount of CO_2 to increase.

17. **The correct answer is (A).** This question requires you to work backwards while applying the concept of Le Chatelier's principle. You are given a desired outcome, so you have to think about what changes need to be made to the system that will cause it to shift toward that outcome. To increase the amount of H_2CO_3 produced, we have to get the system to either combine more CO_2 and H_2O or combine more H^+ and HCO_3^-. This means that the amount of CO_2, H_2O, H^+, and/or HCO_3^- must be increased.

Thus, to increase the amount of H_2CO_3 produced, CO_2 must increase.

18. **The correct answer is (B).** This question requires you to apply the concept of Le Chatelier's principle, which states that a system in equilibrium will adjust itself to return to equilibrium if any changes are made to the system. Removing CO_2 from the system will push the system to replace the CO_2. The only answer that produces CO_2 is choice (B). H^+ and HCO_3^- will decrease as they form more H_2CO_3, which will then break down to form more CO_2.

19. **The correct answer is (C).** This question requires you to look for crosses whose offspring are blends of the parents, which is how incomplete dominance works. Crosses 1 and 4 have offspring that show incomplete dominance. In Cross 1, dark brown and cream-colored parents blend to make a tan offspring. In Cross 4, straight hair and curly hair blend to make wavy hair. In both crosses, the offspring has a phenotype that is in-between the phenotypes of the parents.

20. **The correct answer is (B).** This question requires you to look for crosses whose offspring have the same phenotype as the dominant parent, which is how complete dominance works. The only cross in which the offspring have the same phenotype as the dominant parent is Cross 3. The dominant purple-kernel corn plant crossed with a recessive yellow-kernel corn plant results in an offspring with purple kernels.

21. **The correct answer is (B).** This question requires you to look carefully at the offspring for the one that does not match the descriptions of incomplete dominance and complete dominance that were given in the question stem. Cross 2 has offspring that does not match the description of incomplete dominance (phenotype

is blend of parents) or complete dominance (same phenotype as dominant parent). If the offspring of Cross 2 displayed incomplete dominance, they would be pink (a blend of the red and white parents). If the offspring of Cross 2 displayed complete dominance, they would be red. Instead, the offspring in Cross 2 are white with red spots, which means they display the phenotype of both parents at the same time.

22. **The correct answer is (A).** The question requires you to apply your knowledge of types of dominance to a second generation. Cross 3 offspring are genotype (Pp), so the cross to analyze is Pp X Pp. The majority of the offspring will be Pp and PP. Since the original cross exhibited complete dominance in P, the same will be true in the offspring. Since most of the offspring have at least one copy of P, most will be the dominant purple kernel phenotype.

23. **The correct answer is (C).** This question asks you to consider how an observation affects a hypothesis. If the hypothesis is that all crosses between homozygous dominant and homozygous recessive parents result in offspring that display either complete dominance or incomplete dominance, then the appearance of a third type of offspring—those that display codominance—disproves the hypothesis. In other words, the appearance of offspring displaying codominance shows that the hypothesis is not correct.

24. **The correct answer is (C).** The question requires you to examine the graph and find a particular value of the independent variable (time) using the dependent variable (carbon 14 decay). The graph has an approximate x value of 2% directly in between 28,500 years and 34,200 years, or 31,350 years.

25. **The correct answer is (B).** This question requires you to make the connection that when half of an original sample of carbon-14 decays, 50% of the sample remains. Then read the graph of the radioactive decay of carbon-14 and find how many years it takes for 50% of the original sample to decay (leaving 50% of the original sample). Reading the graph, you should see there is 50% of an original amount of carbon-14 remaining after 5,700 years.

26. **The correct answer is (C).** This question requires you to read the graph of the radioactive decay of carbon-14 and find how many years must pass until 35% of an original sample of carbon-14 is left. As shown on the graph, after about 8,550 years, 35% of an original sample of carbon-14 remains. Therefore, the arrow shaft is about 8,550 years old.

27. **The correct answer is (D).** This question asks you to look at the decay graph of carbon-14 and figure out why objects older than 50,000 years cannot be accurately dated using carbon-14. From the previous question, you know that objects are dated by measuring the amount of carbon-14 left. If you look at the graph for objects that are 50,000 years or older, you see that the amount of carbon-14 remaining is close to zero. Thus, objects older than 50,000 years have so little carbon-14 left that it is difficult to measure. Therefore, it is difficult to use carbon-14 to date these objects.

28. **The correct answer is (B).** The question requires you to find a hypothesis that can be tested specifically using the information in the map. A close look at the map shows that older rocks are present where the continents are farther apart; this information can be used to test a hypothesis about rock age and distance between continents.

29. **The correct answer is (A).** This question requires you to recall that when tectonic plates move apart, magma rises up between them and forms new seafloor. This is stated in the question stem. New seafloor will be 0 years old because it just formed. Therefore, the best evidence that the South American and African Plates are still moving apart today is that the seafloor at the Mid-Atlantic Ridge is 0 years old. This means that the seafloor at the Mid-Atlantic Ridge is newly formed, which means that the plates on either side of the ridge are still moving apart, allowing magma to rise up and form new seafloor between them.

30. **The correct answer is (B).** This question requires you to look at the age of the seafloor stripes in the Atlantic Ocean and draw conclusions about their pattern. The age of the seafloor next to the coasts of South America and Africa are NOT the same throughout the entire ocean. The oldest stripes (170 millions years) are next to the northern coast of Africa, the next oldest stripes (130 million years) are next to the southern coasts of both continents, and the youngest stripes next to the continents (100 million years) are by the middle of Africa and the northern coast of South America. Thus, the seafloor next to the southern coast of South America formed at an earlier time than the seafloor next to the northern coast of South America, which means that the southern coast of South America moved away from Africa at an earlier time than the northern coast.

31. **The correct answer is (B).** This question requires you to find the youngest seafloor next to the east coast of South America and the west coast of Africa. Looking at the map, the oldest stripes (170 millions years) are next to the northern coast of Africa, the next oldest stripes (130 million years) are next to the southern coasts of both continents, and the youngest stripes next to the continents (100 million years) are by the middle of Africa and the northern coast of South America. Thus, the final split between South America and Africa occurred 100 million years ago.

32. **The correct answer is (A).** This question asks you to determine the hypothesis being tested in these runs. The automobile company is varying the mass and speed of the vehicle, as well as the road surface, and measuring the vehicle stopping distance. So the hypothesis being tested must relate these factors. The only answer that relates all of these factors is choice (A). Thus, the hypothesis being tested is that vehicle stopping distance depends on the mass and speed of the vehicle as well as road surface.

33. **The correct answer is (D).** This question requires you to understand that when looking at two experimental setups, the factor that is changing between the two setups is generally the one that is causing any changes in outcome. In runs 1 and 3, the vehicle type, mass, and speed are the same, but the road surface is different. Therefore, the road surface is most likely causing the difference in the stopping distance.

34. **The correct answer is (D).** This question requires you to understand that if a pair of runs is testing only the effect of vehicle mass on stopping distance, then only vehicle mass should be different in the two runs. With the choices given, only runs 2 and 6 differ only in vehicle mass (vehicle speed and road surface are the same in the two runs).

35. **The correct answer is (C).** This question requires you to look at the results of all the runs and choose the factor that does NOT seem to affect vehicle stopping distance. If you look

at the table of results, you should quickly see that the results for the car are the same for the truck at the same speeds and road surfaces, even though the mass of the car and truck are different. Therefore, vehicle mass does not seem to have an effect on stopping distance.

36. The correct answer is (B). This question requires you to determine the hypothesis being tested in Experiment 1. In Experiment 1, the number of fish and the number of root organisms are counted, so the hypothesis must relate to only these two factors. Choice B is the only one that relates these two factors, so the hypothesis being tested is that the number of root organisms affects the number of fish present. Since there are always root organisms present, the hypothesis that fish are not attracted to roots with no organisms, choice (C), cannot be tested in Experiment 1.

37. The correct answer is (A). This question asks you to find the difference between the hypotheses tested in the two experiments, which means you should look for differences in what is being observed in the two experiments. Both experiments look at how the number of root organisms affects the number of fish present, and both take place in locations filled with underwater roots. But in Experiment 2, the root organisms are completely removed in one part of the experiment, while in Experiment 1, root organisms are always present. Therefore, Experiment 2 looks at the effect of removing all root organisms on the number of fish, while Experiment 1 does not.

38. The correct answer is (B). This question requires you to understand the concept of a control and choose the setup that would work best as a control for Experiment 2. As the question stem states, a control should be as similar to the experimental

setup as possible, but without the experimental procedure performed on it. In Experiment 2, the experimental procedure is that all the root organisms are removed from the underwater roots. Therefore the control should NOT have the root organisms removed. However, all other factors should be the same, so the control should also be a 20 m² area filled with underwater roots.

39. The correct answer is (C). This question requires you to determine what conclusions can be drawn from the data provided by the two experiments. Between the two experiments, data have been gathered about the number of fish in areas filled with underwater roots and how the number of root organisms on the roots affects the number of fish. Observations have also been made about how completely removing the root organisms affects the number of fish. Therefore, the only question that CANNOT be answered is how the number of underwater tree roots affects the number of fish.

40. The correct answer is (D). This question requires you to analyze how fish numbers change with root organism numbers and select the model that best represents this relationship. While the table for Experiment 1 shows the number of fish and root organisms from highest to lowest, the actual relationship shown is that fish numbers increase as root organism numbers increase. The graph in choice (D) shows this relationship.

41. The correct answer is (D). This question requires you to predict the behavior of lava based on its viscosity and gas content. Lava with high viscosity will flow only a short distance, and lava with high amounts of gas will erupt explosively.

42. The correct answer is (A). This question requires you to consider the functional needs of tissues in the cardiovascular system. The cardiovascular system moves blood throughout the body, so it needs tissues that can hold blood. It would make sense that these tissues would be hollow. Since blood flow changes with the body's needs, it would also make sense that these tissues can adapt to these changes. Therefore, a hollow tube with flexible walls would most likely be part of the cardiovascular system. Indeed, all of our blood vessels can be described as hollow tubes with stretchy, flexible walls.

43. **The correct answer is (C).** This question requires you to understand the difference between chemical and physical reactions. Chemical reactions change the chemical nature of a substance. Physical reactions change only the appearance of a substance without changing its chemical nature. Meat turning brown as it cooks is the only one of the choices in which the chemical nature of the substance (meat) is changing.

44. **The correct answer is (B).** This question requires you to understand that homeostasis is the normal, stable (equilibrium) state in the body and that processes that maintain homeostasis try to bring the body back to that normal, stable state. The only process that brings the body back to the normal state is given in choice (B). When the body heats up during exercise, sweating cools the body back to its normal state.

45. **The correct answer is (B).** This question requires you to remember that lightning and thunder are associated with light and sound waves and also to recall the properties of light and sound waves. Lightning causes thunder by heating air to a very high temperature, which causes it to explode outward and make a loud, booming sound. The light waves given off by lightning travel to Michiko faster than the sound waves of thunder,

which is why she sees the lightning first and hears the thunder later.

46. **The correct answer is (C).** This question requires you to think carefully about the definitions of producers, consumers, predators, and herbivores. Consumers can be either predators or herbivores, which means that they can eat either producers or other consumers. Therefore, not all consumers are predators, but all predators are consumers.

47. **The correct answer is (D).** This question asks you to look for the example where kinetic energy is transferred without being turned into another type of energy. You should look for the choice that involves one object in motion moving another object. This occurs only in choice (D), where a swinging foot (object 1) kicks a ball (object 2) down a field.

48. **The correct answer is (C).** This question tests your understanding of the concept of dependent and independent variables. Independent variables are factors that the researchers can control, which in this case would be the presence and amount of fluoride in drinking water. Dependent variables are the factors being studied, which depend on the independent variables. The dependent variable would be the number of cavities in the state population.

49. **The correct answer is (D).** This question requires you to understand that the length of time to complete an orbit depends on the distance traveled during the orbit and the speed of the orbiting object. Jupiter's orbital distance is about five times longer than Earth's orbital distance (4,890 million km ÷ 940 million km ≈ 5,000 million km ÷ 1,000 million km ≈ 5). If Jupiter orbits the sun at the same speed as Earth, then it should take Jupiter about 5 times longer than Earth to orbit the sun, or about 5 Earth years. (In reality, Jupiter orbits the sun

answers practice test 2

more slowly than Earth and takes about 12 Earth years to complete one orbit.)

50. The correct answer is (A). This question requires you to understand that in a cascade, each reaction depends on the one that comes before it. Therefore, if a reaction stops occurring, the cascade stops dead, and all reactions after that will stop as well. So if reaction 2 does not occur, then reactions 3 and 4 also do not occur. Thus, A and B will form, but not C, D, or E.

Social Studies

1. C	11. A	21. D	31. C	41. D
2. B	12. C	22. D	32. C	42. A
3. A	13. B	23. B	33. B	43. B
4. C	14. C	24. C	34. C	44. D
5. D	15. C	25. C	35. B	45. A
6. D	16. B	26. D	36. A	46. C
7. A	17. C	27. B	37. B	47. A
8. A	18. A	28. D	38. D	48. D
9. C	19. D	29. A	39. B	49. B
10. D	20. B	30. C	40. B	50. D

1. **The correct answer is (C).** The Nineteenth Amendment gave women the right to vote in 1920 under President Woodrow Wilson. After many years of advocating for the vote coupled, with World War I and the participation of women on the home front, women's suffrage was inevitable.

2. **The correct answer is (B).** The author is depicting both Democrats and Republicans as uncomfortable with women's voting rights, as the cartoon is titled "Three's a Crowd." There were some representatives from both the Republicans and Democrats who did not believe in women's suffrage.

3. **The correct answer is (A).** The author most likely believes that both political parties feel a woman's vote is intrusive on the political system. Many men, prior to the Nineteenth Amendment and afterwards, did not believe women had a true understanding of American politics and that their place was in the home.

4. **The correct answer is (C).** The Seneca Falls Convention outlined 12 resolutions regarding women's rights and served as the foundation and national introduction to the women's suffrage movement in 1848. It was 72 years later that women's suffrage was passed.

5. **The correct answer is (D).** The term *faction* means a separation or group within a larger group. Political parties are an organization or faction of the political process attempting to take power from one another.

6. **The correct answer is (D).** The President is a member of a faction, but not an actual faction himself.

7. **The correct answer is (A).** Factions show different views and allow for policies to be debated and discussed instead of creating identical opinion or decisions.

8. **The correct answer is (A).** The passage states that liberty would be destroyed, and that liberty is essential to the government. Those liberties are seen in the rights of the people.

9. **The correct answer is (C).** Madison drew his ideas from the writings of Montesquieu's *The Spirit of Laws*, which advocated a system of checks on governments.

10. **The correct answer is (D).** The Senate is a part of the legislative branch, and thus cannot check itself.

11. **The correct answer is (A).** The president can veto a bill, which gives him the power to stop the bill.

12. **The correct answer is (C).** Madison states that the people must be the pool from which the departments of the government are pulled.

13. **The correct answer is (B).** The legislative branch is made up of two houses (the Senate and the House of Representatives). Each votes on bills and laws that both must pass before they go into effect.

14. **The correct answer is (C).** The passage connects technology with the continued growth of the economy, and companies such as Apple and Microsoft produce high-tech products.

15. **The correct answer is (C).** The passage states that future automation will dictate the demand for workers and could cause less need for middle-class workers who lack the skills necessary for positions. Technology also could lead to less-skilled workers obtaining positions.

16. **The correct answer is (B).** The passage states that the "latter," or high-tech products, will be left to foreign competitors.

17. **The correct answer is (C).** The workforce was depleted during WWII, which created opportunities for ethnic minorities and women to take the jobs left open by men at war.

18. **The correct answer is (A).** The decade following World War II (the 1950s) saw society attempting to force women back into the home to return to their domestic roles as mothers and homemakers.

19. **The correct answer is (D).** The economy of the United States exploded because of the total war production during WWII, including out-producing the Axis powers (two to one).

20. **The correct answer is (B).** Rosie the Riveter was a cultural icon that represented the workforce woman found in factories during WWII.

21. **The correct answer is (D).** *Suffrage* is defined as the right to vote, which is depicted in the chart displaying voter turnout.

22. **The correct answer is (D).** The only group that has increased its voting turnout is the age group 65 and older.

23. **The correct answer is (B).** The Vietnam War created a larger voter turnout. Many people held a vested interest in the direction of the country, whether because of fear of being drafted or the economic impacts of the ongoing war.

24. **The correct answer is (C).** Scarcity is the condition that results from the imbalance between relatively unlimited wants and the relatively limited resources available for satisfying those wants.

25. **The correct answer is (C).** By charging a higher price, those who want the tickets the most and are willing to pay the price will obtain them.

26. **The correct answer is (D).** An incentive is a factor that influences and motivates a decision.

27. **The correct answer is (B).** The passage states that local and state governments will need to be created to deal with regional problems that cannot be addressed properly by the national government.

28. **The correct answer is (D).** The passage discusses the issues of politics needing to be addressed more at state and local levels to better focus on issues specific to the areas involved.

29. **The correct answer is (A).** The passage is advocating for a balanced system of power where leaders are held accountable for reporting to

other entities and sharing duties and responsibilities within a region.

30. **The correct answer is (C).** The Cold War was a global conflict primarily between the United States and the Soviet Union from the years following WWII to the fall of the Berlin Wall.

31. **The correct answer is (C).** Kennedy took a middle-of-the-road approach in an attempt to prevent nuclear war by declaring a quarantine in the seas surrounding Cuba and threatening to strike if the Soviets tested the boundaries.

32. **The correct answer is (C).** The major difference between the U.S. and the U.S.S.R. during the Cold War revolved around the theories of capitalism and communism as both countries attempted to stabilize the economic landscape following the Great Depression and World War II.

33. **The correct answer is (B).** The United States and Soviet Union would both move to support separate sides in the civil war in Vietnam during the latter half of the 1960s.

34. **The correct answer is (C).** The Japanese attack on Pearl Harbor on December 7, 1941, led to a declaration of war against Japan by the United States.

35. **The correct answer is (B).** The United States government responded to the bombing on Pearl Harbor by creating internment camps for people of Japanese descent because of the fear that they might pose a threat.

36. **The correct answer is (A).** Following World War I and the Great Depression, most Americans—including many in the government—wished to stay away from foreign affairs and remained neutral during the early stages of World War II.

37. **The correct answer is (B).** The Buy one, get one free (BOGO) promotion brings more people into an establish-

ment because they believe they are getting a better deal.

38. **The correct answer is (D).** A company needs to protect its interests and also profit from its services; creating negative incentives allows a company to do both.

39. **The correct answer is (B).** A person who speeds either believes he or she will not get caught or is unafraid of any consequences.

40. **The correct answer is (B).** People living in New England are closest to the Atlantic Ocean and are more likely to be engaged in trade than any of the other professions listed.

41. **The correct answer is (D).** This region produces the largest supply of agricultural surplus because of its soil and climate.

42. **The correct answer is (A).** The ability to trade quickly with Great Britain via the Atlantic Ocean and the closeness to a major water source made habitation of the coastal area most desirable.

43. **The correct answer is (B).** Americans believed that certain rights, even if thought to be implied, needed to be written down and protected to prevent their abuse by a government.

44. **The correct answer is (D).** The Tenth Amendment gives all powers not given to the federal government to the states.

45. **The correct answer is (A).** The Ninth Amendment states that just because a right is not written in the Constitution does not mean it can be violated.

46. **The correct answer is (C).** The Virginia and Kentucky Resolutions attempted to nullify federal law in 1798 based on the principle of the Tenth Amendment.

47. **The correct answer is (A).** The Depression eventually led to a month-

long run on banks, as people no longer trusted the banking system to hold their money.

48. **The correct answer is (D).** The Federal Deposit Insurance Corporation (FDIC) is a government-backed agency that insures deposits into banks to protect people from losing their savings.

49. **The correct answer is (B).** There was a lack of government regulation, or laissez-faire, with regard to the economy of the United States in the 1920s and early 1930s that led to the Great Depression.

50. **The correct answer is (D).** Following his March 1933 inauguration, FDR closed all banks for four days and had them inspected before they could reopen to ensure confidence in the surviving banks.

NOTES

NOTES

NOTES

NOTES

NOTES

NOTES

NOTES